Saxony in German History

Social History, Popular Culture, and Politics in Germany
Geoff Eley, Series Editor

Saxony in German History: Culture, Society, and Politics, 1830–1933,
James Retallack, editor

*Little Tools of Knowledge: Historical Essays on Academic and Bureaucratic
Practices,* Peter Becker and William Clark, editors

*Public Spheres, Public Mores, and Democracy: Hamburg and Stockholm,
1870–1914,* Madeleine Hurd

*Making Security Social: Disability, Insurance, and the Birth of the Social
Entitlement State in Germany,* Greg Eghigian

*The German Problem Transformed: Institutions, Politics, and Foreign
Policy, 1945–1995,* Thomas Banchoff

*Building the East German Myth: Historical Mythology and Youth
Propaganda in the German Democratic Republic, 1945–1989,*
Alan L. Nothnagle

Mobility and Modernity: Migration in Germany, 1820–1989,
Steve Hochstadt

*Triumph of the Fatherland: German Unification and the Marginalization
of Women,* Brigitte Young

*Framed Visions: Popular Culture, Americanization, and the Contemporary
German and Austrian Imagination,* Gerd Gemünden

The Imperialist Imagination: German Colonialism and Its Legacy,
Sara Friedrichsmeyer, Sara Lennox, and Susanne Zantop, editors

*Contested City: Municipal Politics and the Rise of Nazism in Altona,
1917–1937,* Anthony McElligott

*Catholicism, Political Culture, and the Countryside: A Social History of the
Nazi Party in South Germany,* Oded Heilbronner

A User's Guide to German Cultural Studies, Scott Denham, Irene Kacandes,
and Jonathan Petropoulos, editors

*A Greener Vision of Home: Cultural Politics and Environmental Reform in
the German* Heimatschutz *Movement, 1904–1918,* William H. Rollins

*West Germany under Construction: Politics, Society, and Culture in
Germany in the Adenauer Era,* Robert G. Moeller, editor

*How German Is She? Postwar West German Reconstruction and the
Consuming Woman,* Erica Carter

(continued on last page)

Saxony in German History

Culture, Society, and Politics, 1830–1933

EDITED BY
JAMES RETALLACK

WITH A FOREWORD BY HARTMUT ZWAHR

Ann Arbor

THE UNIVERSITY OF MICHIGAN PRESS

Copyright © by the University of Michigan 2000
All rights reserved
Published in the United States of America by
The University of Michigan Press
Manufactured in the United States of America
♾ Printed on acid-free paper

2003   2002   2001   2000   4   3   2   1

A CIP catalog record for this book is available from the British Library.

Library of Congress Cataloging-in-Publication Data

Saxony in German history : culture, society, and politics,
    1830–1933 / edited by James Retallack ; with a foreword by
    Hartmut Zwahr.
        p.   cm. — (Social history, popular culture, and politics
    in Germany)
    Includes bibliographical references and index.
    ISBN 0-472-11104-3 (alk. paper)
    1. Saxony (Germany) — Social life and customs.   2. Saxony
(Germany) — Politics and government.   3. Jews — Germany — Saxony.
4. Saxony (Germany) — Intellectual life.   I. Retallack, James N.
II. Series.
DD801.S347 S39   2000
943′.21 — dc21   00-008714

This book is for

Helen,
Hanna,
and Stuart

Contents

Part 2. Emancipation, the Public Sphere, and the German Bourgeoisie

Part 3. Authoritarianism, Democracy, and the "Dangerous Classes"

Maps

Foreword

Hartmut Zwahr

This book is published in one of the oldest university towns in the United States, Ann Arbor, as part of a series about social history, popular culture, and politics in Germany. The editor of the volume, a Canadian teaching at the University of Toronto, has enlisted a social and economic historian from Leipzig to write the foreword. The authors of the work are mostly Germans — mainly west Germans, as it happens. This in itself is significant. It required the fall of the Berlin Wall and access to East German archives, which previously had been permitted only in special and isolated cases, to make up a deficit in the integration of Saxony into a comparative history of the German *Länder,* of Germany, and of Europe. Conversely, until the peaceful revolution of 1989–90, too few East German researchers studied modern Saxon history on the broad, solid front that historical social science facilitates. Yet among the authors in this volume, Americans, Canadians, and Britons have also turned their attention to Saxony and its history. This, too, demonstrates something special, something new: a truly international community of scholarship in an era when globalization increasingly pervades our lives. Thanks to the most modern means of communication, this scholarly community has overcome the obstacles to direct personal contact, continually increasing the intensity and speed with which ideas are exchanged.

The academic subject of this volume, Saxony's place in German history, carries its own specific weight and rationale: as confirmation of this, one only has to consider the signals for German, European, even world political change that emanated from the Saxon districts of Leipzig and Dresden in the autumn of 1989 — signals that marked the beginning of the revolution that led to Saxons' self-liberation and to German unification. These events also resulted in the reconstitution of Saxony as a Free State, almost four decades after the *Land* Saxony had been dissolved in 1952 when the German Democratic Republic regime staged a kind of coup d'état and replaced *Länder* with smaller administrative districts (*Bezirke*).

Viewed from overseas, Saxony is not much more than a dot on the world map. It appears slightly larger in a historical atlas of Europe. However, one reason "the local" and "the regional" operate so powerfully in modern history, and one reason they require such careful explanation, is that from such small units arise global consequences. Indeed, one should never forget that these units are themselves anchored in very complex "ways in the world," in larger societal units. One example of this relationship is provided by the Electorate (*Kurfürstentum*) of Saxony in the era of religious schism, when events in one of its cities, Wittenberg, signaled the beginning of Luther's Reformation.[1] To cite a further example, Saxony was so integrally enmeshed in the machinery of great-power rivalries during the Seven Years' War that it had an impact extending far beyond Europe's borders — even in the geographically distant "New World," where France lost eastern Canada to Britain. On the occasion of the Treaty of Hubertusburg, concluded near Leipzig on 15 February 1763, Saxony had to accept the bitter pill of defeat at the hands of a Prussian aggressor; thus it lost the cultural and political lustre it had enjoyed as a center of European affairs in the Augustan age.[2] From that time until 1866, a full century later, Saxony's relationship with Prussia was variable, as a result, first, of its rivalry with Frederickian Prussia and, second, of occupation by Prussia and Napoleon's military defeat. By 1806, after Saxony joined the Confederation of the Rhine, Napoleon had elevated Saxony to a kingdom, rewarding it with the ancient Brandenburg district of Cottbus. Subsequently it grew closer to the Habsburg Empire, Prussia's great nineteenth-century rival for hegemony in German-speaking Europe. Yet on balance, during this era Saxony belonged to the losers of history.[3] In 1815 at the Congress of Vienna, its territory was practically cut in half (to the advantage of Prussia). And in 1866 it shared the Austrians' bloody, decisive defeat in the Battle of Königgrätz. This latter occasion represented the final attempt of Saxony's aristocratic elite[4] to flex its diplomatic muscle independently and successfully; henceforth, the great political struggles "in" Germany and "for" Germany largely bypassed Saxony.

The contributions in this volume take up the theme of Saxony's loss of diplomatic influence by noting how Saxons' preferred areas of enterprise switched to the *cultural* and *economic* spheres after 1866. The authors examine how many different kinds of Saxon identity evolved:

---

1. See Helmar Junghans, *Wittenberg als Lutherstadt* (Berlin, 1979).

2. See Karl Czok, *August der Starke und Kursachsen* (Leipzig, 1987).

3. On this point see Theodor Flathe, *Geschichte des Kurstaates und Königreiches Sachsen,* vol. 3, *Neuere Geschichte Sachsens von 1806 bis 1866* (Gotha, 1873).

4. See Katrin Keller and Josef Matzerath, eds., *Geschichte des sächsischen Adels* (Weimar, 1997).

identities based on regional patriotism (*Landespatriotismus*), on German nationality, and—during the early phases of the Social Democratic movement—even on internationalist and pacifist principles. At least the *early* significance of Saxon Social Democracy was very substantially rooted in the anti-Prussian sentiment of anger deeply entrenched in all strata of the Saxon population. That anger was directed northward, but it elicited calls for Saxons themselves to renounce, abandon, or otherwise dissociate themselves politically from the rival whose unstoppable rise to great-power status had compelled Saxony's own assimilation in the federalism of Prusso-Germany.[5]

Saxony's splendor was henceforth based on its economy, its culture, the arts, and the inventive genius of its population. These strengths were exhibited, for example, in Saxony's leading per capita rank in German patent registrations, in the formation of state-level as well as national lobby groups, in the campaigns for electoral rights, and in the great attraction of Leipzig University. In the end, even the Lusatian Sorbs—that small west-Slavic ethnic remnant that had its Saxon center in Bautzen—became well known for their remarkable participation in the bourgeois epoch, which allowed them to prosper in Saxony despite various forms of state repression.[6]

All of this has shaped the Saxon people profoundly: it has motivated them, qualified them for larger endeavors, spurred them on, and contributed to what I have called elsewhere Saxon mass intelligence (*sächsische Massenintelligenz*).[7] Ever since 1798, when the first Saxon cotton spinning-mill was built, there has always been an undeniable urban, industrial component to this story. During the Great Depression, however, mass deprivation and political anxiety in Saxony also set free powerful destructive forces, to a great extent among the *Mittelstand,* farmers, and also workers. These factors set in train a series of events that helped Nazi tyranny gain a strong, early foothold in Saxony.[8] Yet one must not neglect

---

5. See Simone Lässig and Karl Heinrich Pohl, eds., *Sachsen im Kaiserreich: Politik, Wirtschaft und Gesellschaft im Umbruch* (Weimar, 1997).

6. On this point see Hartmut Zwahr, ed., *Meine Landsleute: Die Lausitz und die Sorben im Zeugnis deutscher Zeitgenossen: Von Spener und Lessing bis Pieck* (Bautzen, 1984, 1990).

7. See Hartmut Zwahr, "Die Revolution in der DDR," in *Revolution in Deutschland? 1789–1989,* ed. Manfred Hettling (Göttingen, 1991), 128; and Hartmut Zwahr, *Ende einer Selbstzerstörung: Leipzig und die Revolution in der DDR,* 2d ed. (Göttingen, 1993).

8. See Reiner Pommerin, ed., *Dresden unterm Hakenkreuz* (Weimar, 1998); the horrible reality of interaction with Jewish fellow citizens and neighbors is documented in Victor Klemperer's unique Dresden diaries: *Ich will Zeugnis ablegen bis zum letzten: Tagebücher,* 2 vols., 7th ed. (Berlin, 1996); an abridged version of vol. 1 is now available in English as *I Will Bear Witness: A Diary of the Nazi Years, 1933–1941,* trans. Martin Chalmers (New York, 1998).

the remarkable democratic spirit that is also encountered at every turn in modern Saxon history. This spirit, too, has been fed by a long and uninterrupted tradition. It profoundly impressed the young August Bebel when he arrived in Leipzig in May 1860. Bebel found that "a republican element was deemed self-evident among democratic aspirations," and that the "idea of democracy" was "widespread" among the population.[9] The revolutionary events of 1848–49,[10] preceded by those of 1830–31,[11] had established the bedrock for this attitude.

This foreword is aimed at putting the reader in the proper frame of mind. It cannot anticipate the historical explanations that will be presented in the volume, nor even bundle them for consumption. For in the final analysis, historical explanation does not submit easily to summarization: case studies and a specific focus are required in order to examine the repetitive structures that lie in events occurring uniquely in time and space. This book is an invitation to do just that. For the first time, and with a variety of thematic interconnections, it moves a German case study, Saxony, into the perspective of comparative history.

---

9. See August Bebel, "Aus dem Anfang der Arbeiterbewegung," in *Die Gründung der Deutschen Sozialdemokratie* (Leipzig, 1903), 8.

10. See Rolf Weber, *Die Revolution in Sachsen, 1848/49: Entwicklung und Analyse ihrer Triebkräfte* (Berlin, 1970).

11. See Michael Hammer, *Volksbewegung und Obrigkeiten: Revolution in Sachsen, 1830/31* (Weimar, 1997); and Hartmut Zwahr, *Revolutionen in Sachsen: Beiträge zur Sozial- und Kulturgeschichte* (Weimar, 1996).

Acknowledgments

Neither this book, nor the September 1998 conference in Toronto that allowed critical debate of its principal themes, would have been possible without the generous support of many people and institutions. It is a pleasure to thank them now.

I would like to express my gratitude, first, to the individual contributors, who with unfailing goodwill bowed to my appeals to deliver their very best effort, and in timely fashion. Second, I am grateful to the graduate students who helped me translate many of these texts: Erwin Fink and Nadine Roth (Toronto) and Miriam Rothgerber (York University). With insight and good humor, Erwin in particular was always available to meet with me for what became longer and longer discussions about such ambiguous terms as *Bildung, Teilkulturen, Vergesellschaftung, Gemeindebevollmächtigtenkollegium,* and *landsmannschaftliches Zusammengehörigkeitsgefühl.* The larger team of graduate students who helped host the Toronto conference comprised Ralph Czychun, Hilary Earl, Catherine Filejski, Erwin Fink, Marline Otte, Richard Steigmann-Gall, Geoff Wichert, and Rebecca Wittmann.

For their counsel and advice I am also grateful to Lynn Abrams, Celia Applegate, Richard Bessel, Roger Chickering, Brett Fairbairn, Martin Geyer, Thomas Goebel, Peter Hubrich, Larry Jones, Ulrich Köhn, Simone Lässig, Doina Popescu, Peter Steinbach, Mark Webber, and Bernd Weisbrod. Special thanks go to Susan Whitlock at the University of Michigan Press and to Geoff Eley, both of whom strongly supported this project from the outset. Their anonymous readers suggested many ways to improve this collection.

Generous funding was provided by the following colleagues at the University of Toronto: J. Robert S. Prichard, President; Adel Sedra, Vice-President and Provost; Heather Munroe-Blum, Vice-President, Research and International Relations; Marsha Chandler and Carl Amrhein, successively Deans of Arts and Science; Michael Marrus, Dean of Graduate Studies; A. P. (Gus) Dierick, former Chair of the Department of Germanic Languages and Literatures; Larry LeDuc and Scott Eddie, successively Academic Coordinators of the Joint Initiative in German and European Studies; and Craig Brown, Robert Accinelli, and Ron

Pruessen, successively Chairs of the Department of History. For other forms of support, including the research leaves that permitted me to recruit contributors and organize the 1998 conference, I am also grateful to the Connaught Committee at the University of Toronto; the Embassy of the Federal Republic of Germany, Ottawa (and in particular former Ambassador Hans-Günter Sulimma); the German Academic Exchange Service (especially its successive directors, Rolf Hoffmann and Britte Baron); the Goethe-Institut Toronto; the Alexander von Humboldt Foundation; the German Historical Institute, Washington, D.C.; the Social Sciences and Humanities Research Council of Canada; and the TransCoop Program of the German-American Academic Council Foundation.

For her help in proofreading the text and preparing the index, I am indebted to Andrea Geddes Poole.

The highest price of all has been paid by the members of my immediate family: Helen Graham, Hanna, and Stuart. During the period this book took shape, they suffered my absence, virtual or real, more often than I care to admit. I dedicate this book to them in gratitude for their constant encouragement, love, and ability to place things in perspective.

Abbreviations

GDR	Deutsche Demokratische Republik	German Democratic Republic (East Germany)
NL	*Nachlaß*	unpublished private papers
NSDAP	Nationalsozialistische Deutsche Arbeiterpartei	National Socialist German Workers' Party (Nazi Party)
SächsHStA	Sächsisches Hauptstaatsarchiv (Dresden)	Saxon Central State Archive (Dresden)
SPD	Sozialdemokratische Partei Deutschlands	German Social Democratic Party
SVP	Sächsische Volkspartei	Saxon People's Party

Note: The Saxon *Landtag* was officially known until 1918 as the Assembly of Estates (*Ständeversammlung*); the "I. Kammer" and the "II. Kammer" are referred to throughout the volume as the upper and lower house (or chamber), respectively.

Glossary

Alltagsgeschichte: history of everyday life, history of experience
Bildung: education, (self-)cultivation
Bund; Bundesstaat: confederation; federal state
bürgerlich: middle-class, bourgeois
Bürgertum: middle class, bourgeoisie
Erzgebirge: Ore Mountains
Gauleiter: district leader
Gemeinde: (Jewish) religious community
Großdeutschland: greater Germany, including German-speaking Austria
Habitus: (cultural) disposition, way of life
Heimat: home, homeland
Kleindeutschland: lesser Germany, dominated by Prussia, excluding Austria
Kulturkampf: struggle of civilizations (against the Catholic Church)
Land, pl. *Länder:* (federal) state(s)
Landesgeschichte: the history of territorial states
Landtag, pl. *Landtage:* state parliament(s)
Mittelstand: middle estate, lower-middle class
Paulskirche: St. Paul's Church, site of the 1848–49 Frankfurt Parliament
Regionalgeschichte: regional history
Ruhrgebiet: Ruhr district
Sonderweg: special path
symbolische Ortsbezogenheit: symbolic territoriality / sense of place / attachment to the locality
Zollverein: Customs Union

Introduction: Locating Saxony in the Landscape of German Regional History

James Retallack

I. Principal Themes

On 28 May 1916, an Australian woman stranded in Leipzig wrote that the local people had grown worried about their crops. "Saxony is an unlucky spot," wrote Caroline Ethel Cooper; "if it rains anywhere, it hails here, or if it is dry in Prussia, Saxony has a drought!"[1] Making such comparisons is certainly one way of locating Saxony in Germany's regional landscape. A different take on what made Saxony unique was offered half a century earlier by Wilhelm Liebknecht when he described a fellow traveler in the early Social Democratic movement. "For the first time in Germany," wrote Liebknecht, "I encountered in Christian Hadlich a type of man whom I subsequently met often in the Erzgebirge[2] and the Vogtland: from lively brown eyes shone understanding and kindheartedness; the body [was] weakened . . . by hunger and deprivation, [but] the face conveyed painful experience, deep reflection, and the profound consciousness of human misery."[3] A third way of differentiating Saxons from other Germans, as described in more than one essay in this collection, was simpler still: to insult, denounce, or shoot at Prussians whenever the opportunity arose.

Each of these three observations on the problem of locating Saxony

---

1. *Behind the Lines: One Woman's War, 1914–18: The Letters of Caroline Ethel Cooper,* edited and with an introduction by Decie Denholm (Sydney, 1982), 141.

2. This and other foreign terms encountered frequently in the volume are listed in the glossary.

3. Wilhelm Liebknecht, *Erinnerungen eines Soldaten der Revolution* (Berlin, 1976), 323–24, cited in Hartmut Zwahr, *Revolutionen in Sachsen: Beiträge zur Sozial- und Kulturgeschichte* (Weimar, 1996), 268.

in German history draws attention to a major theme of this book. Before proceeding to examine these themes, we might pause to locate Saxony within Germany in a more literal sense. The maps included in this volume provide a starting point. In the course of the histories narrated here, the Kingdom of Saxony (Königreich Sachsen) became a Free State (Freistaat Sachsen). Throughout this period the state measured roughly 15,000 square kilometers. In 1834 Saxony was home to approximately 1.6 million inhabitants. By 1871 that figure had risen to almost 2.6 million, making Saxony the third-largest federal state in the German Empire behind Prussia (with a population of 24.7 million) and Bavaria (pop. 4.9 million). In 1910, among a total German population of just under 65 million, Saxony numbered 4.8 million souls, very roughly equivalent to the population of today's Denmark, Finland, or Scotland. Even in the mid-nineteenth century, industrialization and urbanization were relatively far advanced: Saxony had by far the highest concentration of people of all German states (excluding the city-states), and one of the highest concentrations in Europe.[4] By 1910, only 27 percent of Saxons lived in communities of fewer than 2,000 inhabitants, compared to the German average of 40 percent. Correspondingly, almost three of every four Saxons lived in large cities (those with 20,000 or more inhabitants), whereas the German average was about one in two.

Of this volume's three central themes, the first concerns the way regions are discovered, constructed, forgotten, and remade in history. On the one hand this theme allows the authors to go beyond a metaphoric use of culture, so common these days in professional and public discourse, to speak of culture in the sense of symbolic representations that shaped and were shaped by social and political conditions. Discussing culture in a regional setting provides a means to gather together ideas about identities, mentalities, and loyalties without implying that there is something parochial about this exercise. Discussing culture in this way also allows the authors to explore how local, regional, and national cultures commingle, diverge, and influence each other. On the other hand, historians too often fail to note that a region's history is rooted, deeply rooted, in a matrix of direct spatial relationships, and that those relationships change over time. E. P. Thompson reminded us that "class" does not simply exist: class happens. But regions also "hap-

---

4. In 1871 the number of inhabitants per square kilometer in Saxony was 171; in 1910 that figure had risen to about 321. The corresponding averages for Germany were 75.9 and 120.0. In 1910 Saxony exceeded even the Rhineland's population density of 264. Figures have been rounded from data found in Thomas Klein, *Grundriß zur deutschen Verwaltungsgeschichte 1815–1945,* Reihe B, vol. 14, *Sachsen* (Marburg, 1982); and Gerd Hohorst, Jürgen Kocka, and Gerhard A. Ritter, *Sozialgeschichtliches Arbeitsbuch,* vol. 2, *Materialien zur Statistik des Kaiserreichs 1870–1914,* 2d ed. (Munich, 1978).

pen," though not always in a manner of their inhabitants' own choosing. Caroline Ethel Cooper's references to hail and drought invite us to take the "geography" in historical geography seriously — to take account, that is, of really existing physical boundaries and events that define regions, even as we also explore topographies of power, climates of opinion, and winds of change. To be sure, historians are increasingly aware that different historical environments allow regions to be remembered and imagined in particular ways. Yet mental maps and physical boundaries are most significant when they come together, for then they delimit particular ways of seeing and horizons of understanding. As Celia Applegate put it recently, historians need to consider "why people loved and hated the regional places in which they found themselves, why they worked to strengthen them, hastened to escape them, praised them, poured invective upon them, thought about them all the time, ignored them completely, and yet for all that dwelt many days of their lives within the 'networks of experience' that these regions sustained."[5]

The second theme is echoed in the observations of both Cooper and Liebknecht. It can be reduced to an interpretive couplet that is as provocative as it is untenable: the SID thesis — "Saxony is different" — and its obvious antithesis, SIS: "Saxony is the same."[6] To some observers, the history of Saxony is of special interest because it undermines the uniformity of German history. It disproves previous assumptions about what was going on at the "center," and yet it reveals dimensions of German history that no other region can. Thus Saxony may be particularly revealing because it has represented, at various points in its history, a worst-case scenario and the best of all possible worlds. Other observers, however, tend to ask whether Saxony is broadly representative, perhaps even typical, of developments that happened everywhere in Germany. Liebknecht's description adds a human dimension to these questions. It prompts the reader to ask whether there was in fact something uniquely "Saxon" about the bitter experiences etched into his colleague's face. Were these qualities encountered more frequently in the southwestern corner of Saxony than elsewhere? What sorts of analyses can be built on the tension between the diversity of Saxon society and whatever ideas of Saxonness or Germanness may have united it?

Third, what are we to make of Saxons' renowned antipathy to their Prussian neighbors? Such antipathy was always conditioned by the way

5. I wish here to express my gratitude to Celia Applegate, Roger Chickering, Jennifer Jenkins, Jacques Kornberg, Christoph Nonn, and Bernd Weisbrod for making their prepared commentaries on the Toronto conference papers available to me. My argument draws heavily upon their insights. In the interests of space, I have pared the following references to a bare minimum by simply naming the commentator in question.

6. Bernd Weisbrod.

The German Empire: Federal States and Provinces, 1871–1918, showing the
Geographic Districts and Major Cities of Saxony

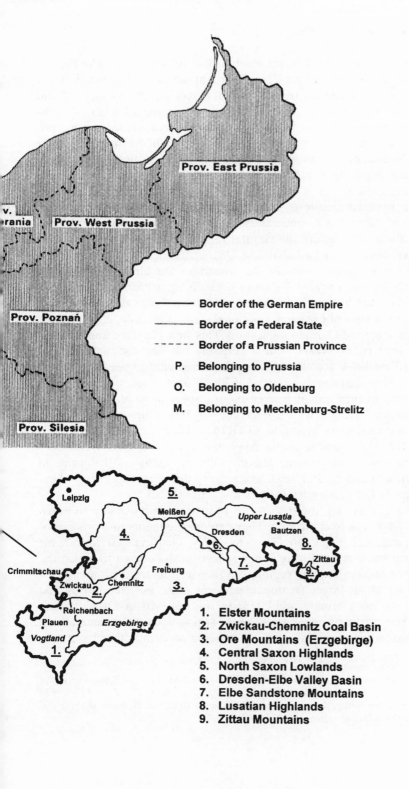

Prov. East Prussia

Prov. West Prussia

v. rania

Prov. Poznań

Prov. Silesia

Border of the German Empire
Border of a Federal State
Border of a Prussian Province
P.   Belonging to Prussia
O.   Belonging to Oldenburg
M.   Belonging to Mecklenburg-Strelitz

Leipzig

Meißen

Upper Lusatia

Dresden   Bautzen

Crimmitschau   Freiburg   Zittau

Zwickau   Chemnitz

Reichenbach

Plauen   Erzgebirge

Vogtland

1.   Elster Mountains
2.   Zwickau-Chemnitz Coal Basin
3.   Ore Mountains (Erzgebirge)
4.   Central Saxon Highlands
5.   North Saxon Lowlands
6.   Dresden-Elbe Valley Basin
7.   Elbe Sandstone Mountains
8.   Lusatian Highlands
9.   Zittau Mountains

Saxons appraised the future prospects of the federal ideal. Federalism in German history has always been a contentious issue; but rarely has it been explored in cultural terms. To what extent was the Saxons' *cultural* sense of belonging together — their *landsmannschaftliches Zusammengehörigkeitsgefühl* — congruent with their social, economic, and political integration into a national community? When they perceived that such congruency was growing, did they also believe that industrialization, democratization, and parliamentarization on a national scale were hastening the erosion of local and regional identities? Or is it possible that an optimistic outlook was enhanced by the persistence of such identities? Here it is not necessary to dress Saxons in white and Prussians in black to explore the cultural relevance of a sense of place, or what has been termed *symbolische Ortsbezogenheit*.[7] As the contributions to this volume demonstrate, historians are already thinking in conceptually innovative ways about overcoming a Prussocentric depiction of German history. Taken as a whole, these essays deviate substantially from a view of Bismarck's national state as the sole, inevitable, or actual outcome of German unification. This view has been under attack for at least twenty years,[8] but it certainly has not disappeared from standard textbook accounts. Moreover, if it is vital to see that a Prussianized Germany emerging from 1870–71 wasn't necessarily the way things had to turn out, it is even more important to recognize that a Prussianized Germany wasn't *in fact* the way things turned out either. In this sense too, more attention to German histories (in the plural) is called for. For example, Celia Applegate's and Siegfried Weichlein's contributions to this volume provide salutary reminders that pride in German unification after 1871 looked very different depending where you were in the *Kaiserreich* (and how you got there).

These, then, are the three areas of historical scholarship to which these essays seek to contribute. They explore the theory and practice of writing regional history in Germany today, charting new terrain for empirical work in the future. They reflect on the degree to which the history of one region, any region, can reconceptualize fundamental assumptions about larger (national) patterns. And they remind us that Prussia was not Germany and Germany was not Prussia. Overall, these essays suggest that greater attention to regional identities, mentalities, and ways of life enriches our understanding on many other fronts. By

---

7. Bernd Weisbrod.

8. For example, in James J. Sheehan, "What Is German History? Reflections on the Role of the *Nation* in German History and Historiography," *Journal of Modern History* 53 (1981): 1–23; see further the résumé provided in James Retallack, *Germany in the Age of Kaiser Wilhelm II* (Basingstoke and New York, 1996).

taking the long view of Saxon history, while placing this history in the context of several key themes of modern German historiography (examined further in section IV of this introduction), these essays argue that beliefs, idioms, and symbolic representations generated on the local and regional level really did matter — in their own right and for the nation as a whole. By engaging with what Applegate has termed the "placeness" of places, historians can uncover crucial constitutive elements in the mental and moral geography of all Germans.

II. A Saxon "Moment" in German Historiography

In answering the question: Why Saxony?, one runs the risk of claiming that one German history is more significant than all the other German histories. Still, is Saxony important in its own right, or isn't it? If the goal of recapturing elements of diversity and contingency in modern German history is patently a long-term project, Saxony is certainly not the only German region that deserves attention. The preceding section has argued that "region" itself, rather than the history of any one territory, provides the conceptual matrix onto which issues of power, identity, and solidarity can be projected. Hence the title of this volume suggests an undertaking not dissimilar to those attempted by such books as *The Holocaust in History, Faith in History,* and *Women in History.* Moreover, juxtaposing region and nation uncovers a complex, shifting, malleable relationship that has waited too long to be problematized and rethought by scholars. To prompt exactly this kind of reflection is the primary goal of this volume.

Nevertheless, Saxony provides a clear territorial focus and a firm foundation that scholars can use to draw comparisons outward. For practical reasons and at particular moments of history, some regions appear more suitable than others as a vehicle to permit reconsideration of larger problems. Such reasons include a growing body of scholarship in one particular area, which often produces empirical work of such density that a stock-taking is called for. In the last ten years Saxon historians have outpaced their colleagues in Germany's other new federal states in reconsidering the contours of their own regional history. Other reasons include the opening up of new archives and a growing intensification of debate among native and international scholars. Here too, Saxon historians and archivists are clearly in the vanguard. These considerations underscore the special timeliness of bringing scholarship on Saxony to the attention of an English-language audience. This introduction is not the place to explain *en détail* why Saxony has been the focus of so much scholarly writing in the 1990s; I have addressed these questions elsewhere.[9] A brief synopsis may nonetheless help explain why Saxon history currently provides such fertile ground for historical spadework on a number of fronts.

First, due to the repressive regime in the former German Democratic Republic and difficulties in gaining access to the archives in eastern Germany, Saxon history for many years remained terra incognita to most (though certainly not all) western scholars. Since German unification in 1990, outstanding work on Saxony has been pouring out of publishing houses at a remarkable rate, fueled by vibrant institutes of historical research at the universities of Leipzig, Dresden, and Chemnitz.[10] Yet very little of this scholarship is currently available in English. This volume brings these new findings to Anglo-American audiences for the first time, demonstrating their diversity and their depth. Thus one finds contributions from newly minted Ph.D.'s and from senior scholars in the field; essays derived from recent work in Saxony's local archives and "think-pieces" written from greater geographical and thematic distance; and differing perspectives offered by scholars in Canada, the United States, Great Britain, and both western and eastern Germany.

Second, many questions about political modernization in Germany have been explored for Prussian territory or the historically more accessible areas of Baden, Württemberg, Bavaria, and the Rhineland. As a consequence, Thomas Kühne has noted that this "western bias" may give rise to a "democratic bias."[11] This volume redirects scholarly attention toward persistent traditions of authoritarian rule in central Germany before 1933. Saxony does not fit neatly within the common east-west and north-south paradigms of German historiography. The oft-cited distinctions between French-influenced political cultures in southwestern Germany and Prussian authoritarian traditions in the north and east must be demonstrated, not just asserted, for the kingdom that straddled the Elbe

9. James Retallack, "Society and Politics in Saxony in the Nineteenth and Twentieth Centuries: Reflections on Recent Research," *Archiv für Sozialgeschichte* 38 (1998): 396–457; cf. idem, "Politische Kultur, Wahlkultur, Regionalgeschichte: Methodologische Überlegungen am Beispiel Sachsens und des Reiches," in *Modernisierung und Region im wilhelminischen Deutschland: Wahlen, Wahlrecht und Politische Kultur,* ed. Simone Lässig, Karl Heinrich Pohl, and James Retallack, 2d rev. ed. (Bielefeld, 1998), 15–38; and idem, "Politische Kultur in der Region," in *Politische Kultur in Ostmittel- und Südosteuropa,* ed. Werner Bramke and Thomas Adam (Leipzig, 1999), 15–46.

10. See the indispensable guide by Karsten Rudolph and Iris Weuster, *Bibliographie zur Geschichte der Demokratiebewegung in Mitteldeutschland (1789–1933)* (Weimar, 1997); further references are found in Retallack, "Society and Politics in Saxony."

11. Thomas Kühne, "Historische Wahlforschung in der Erweiterung," in *Modernisierung und Region,* ed. Lässig, Pohl, and Retallack, 39–67, here 47; see also Kühne's reflections on the marked gender bias still evident in recent electoral and political analyses of German history.

River. Just as the choice of Berlin rather than Bonn as the capital of a united Germany inevitably pulls the political center of gravity eastward, this volume seeks to demonstrate how the history of one eastern region might contribute to the task of reassessing Germany's larger past.

Third, as one of Germany's most industrialized regions even in the 1830s, Saxony became the seedbed of German socialism. For understandable reasons, research on pre-1933 Saxony has tended to focus on the Social Democratic Party (less so on trade unions and other elements of the labor movement). The essays by Thomas Adam, Brett Fairbairn, and Karsten Rudolph, among others, suggest that the history of Social Democracy will surely remain one starting point for future research on the Saxon party system. But for too long, the Saxon SPD has been studied in isolation. It was not until the very recent appearance of a volume on working-class women in nineteenth-century Saxony that a gendered perspective on Saxon industrialization was developed systematically, despite the early and important work on Saxon home weavers provided by Jean Quataert.[12] Historians have also been conspicuous in their failure to explore how Social Democrats, liberals, conservatives, and antisemites all competed for the allegiance of the disaffected *Mittelstand* in Saxony. A number of the essays in this volume therefore seek to embed the history of Saxon socialism in a broader picture of social, cultural, and political change.

Fourth, histories of bourgeois politics and histories of liberal politics provide good examples of how innovative studies of one region can help formulate new questions about other regions. New work on the Saxon *Bürgertum* has begun to bring its multiple, shifting political allegiances into focus. To be sure, many questions remain unanswered about how middle-class Saxons viewed their social, economic, cultural, and political status in Saxony and in the Reich. Yet a start has been made in exploring why Saxon burghers sometimes followed radical movements and why, at other times, they fought to assert their independence from extremists of both the Left and the Right. A number of essays in this volume push these investigations forward, sometimes with surprising results.

Fifth, inhabitants of today's Saxony are keenly interested in their own history. Not unlike other eastern Germans, they are still struggling to identify what is distinctive about a regional heritage that remains open to multiple readings. Efforts to resurrect a positive historical identity are

---

12. Susanne Schötz, ed., *Frauenalltag in Leipzig: Weibliche Lebenszusammenhänge im 19. und 20. Jahrhundert* (Weimar, 1997); Jean Quataert, "The Politics of Rural Industrialization: Class, Gender, and Collective Protest in the Saxon Oberlausitz of the Late Nineteenth Century," *Central European History* 20 (1987): 91–124.

themselves part of a historical debate in Germany that during the chancellorship of Helmut Kohl politicized the quest for national identity and threatened to reassert a meta-narrative of German exceptionalism. This tension within German historiography was recently described as the tension between a German past that was so "violently diverse" and its historical narrative, which has so far been "utterly homogenous."[13] By showcasing cutting-edge research, but also by providing broader reflection, this volume may speak to those Germans (and others) who know little about Saxony but who seek to understand how struggles for cultural identity and political pluralism in the past inform similar struggles in the present.

Pulling together the strands of this argument, what are the major findings of these essays, and what specific issues impart a sense of direction and novelty to recent Saxon research? Taking up the volume's first theme—the constructedness of regional identity—certainly the essays collected in Part 1 suggest that Saxons have been anything but unique in using the idea of "region" as a filter to discover, cultivate, or act upon collective identities and ways of seeing. Yet the essays in Parts 2 through 4 identify specific ways in which milieu behavior, political mentalities, and conceptions of the future did indeed evolve differently in Saxony. Saxons, for example, may initially have been as eager as Württembergers[14] or Pfälzer[15] to preserve their *Heimat* within the emerging German nation. By 1900, however, radical nationalism was more strongly entrenched in the mental maps of Saxon burghers than was any distinguishing sense of "Saxonness." Together with a pronounced fear of socialism (discussed further below), this mental orientation appears to have contributed to a relative hostility toward political reform, at least among Saxony's bourgeoisie. This hostility must not be exaggerated, as the essays by Karl Heinrich Pohl and Christoph Nonn suggest. Nevertheless, much of the recent literature on Saxony between 1900 and 1933 has stressed the underlying structural factors that consistently doomed efforts to break with an authoritarian past. The "left-wing republican project" that was tried in Saxony in the early 1920s is one among many unsuccessful attempts to overcome authoritarian traditions in the state.

With an eye to exploring these two issues—regional identity and the challenge of undertaking timely reform—historians have recently

---

13. Michael Geyer and Konrad H. Jarausch, "Great Men and Postmodern Ruptures: Overcoming the 'Belatedness' of German Historiography," *German Studies Review* 18 (1995): 253–73, here 267.

14. Alon Confino, *The Nation as a Local Metaphor: Württemberg, Imperial Germany, and National Memory, 1871–1918* (Chapel Hill, NC, 1997).

15. *Pfälzer* were inhabitants of the Bavarian Palatinate. See Celia Applegate, *A Nation of Provincials: The German Idea of Heimat* (Berkeley, CA, 1990).

focused on the role of suffrage reform and other "fairness issues" in conditioning Saxon political culture over the long term. More than one essay here considers the efforts of Saxon elites to disenfranchise or otherwise silence the political representatives of the "dangerous classes" at crucial turning points in German history. Karl Heinrich Pohl and Páll Björnsson consider municipal suffrage laws as a means to demonstrate how a conservative elite in Dresden and a liberal one in Leipzig each proved able to block the integration of outsiders into the political community.

What are we to make of the second theme: the opposition between the "Saxony is different" thesis and "Saxony is the same"? It is the *tension* between these alternatives, rather than any urge to opt for one thesis over the other, that currently drives Saxon historical writing. Historians will likely continue to direct their attention to the ways in which Saxony served as a "pioneer." And rightly so. Saxon history includes too many unprecedented political experiments to allow historians to ignore the singularity of events there. Brett Fairbairn notes in his contribution that Saxony seems to have led the way as Germany's first socialist state, its first antisocialist state, and its first postsocialist state. As Fairbairn notes, however, Saxony does not fit as comfortably into any of these roles as we once thought — just as it fits poorly into the classic paradigm of modernization theory. In fact, Saxon history frequently demonstrates the precariousness of regional innovation in the face of national trends. For example, Saxony abolished the death penalty in the mid-nineteenth century, only to be forced to accede to its reintroduction under the North German Confederation. Conversely, whereas the general trend among German states was to liberalize and widen the suffrage for *Landtag* elections, Saxony answered Kaiser Wilhelm II's call for a reactionary suffrage law in 1896 when it reverted from a relatively broad suffrage to a restrictive three-class one. Such examples reveal that democratization did not proceed in lockstep with other aspects of modernization but could actually be slowed down, stopped, or reversed.

Demonstrating the way in which this and related trends were accelerated, retarded, or redirected by regional factors is arguably where Saxon historians are contributing most to a rethinking of general explanations based on national patterns. A number of essays in this collection suggest how conflicting notions of regional identity, disputes over political sovereignty, and challenges arising from military defeat combined in Saxony to produce political blueprints whose novelty and variety force historians to see greater contingency within the national pattern. It should come as little surprise that the problems and promise of the age of mass politics should first have been recognized by contemporaries as particularly acute in the state where Social Democracy was farthest advanced and yet where entrenched elites proved to be particularly unaccommodating in the face of struggles for political emancipation.

Overall one finds more examples of the "worst-case scenario" than "the best of all possible worlds" in current writing on Saxony. Saxon statesmen generally score poor marks in reacting to political challenges with flexibility or generosity (although the conclusions presented here by Neemann and Krug point in the opposite direction). Moreover, if Saxon statesmen too seldom learned from past mistakes, a majority of Saxon burghers appear to have condoned the antiliberal, antidemocratic, and antisocialist policies undertaken by their leaders. Some readers may conclude from this that Saxons generally got the governments they deserved. Whatever assessment is reached, there seems ample evidence that Saxony was indeed a crucial testing ground (*Experimentierfeld*), and functioned as a special kind of mirror (*Brennspiegel*), for problems and conflicts found in less attenuated form elsewhere in Germany.

As to the volume's third major theme, a focus on Saxon history self-evidently undermines Prussocentric views of the German *Kaiserreich*. We have already noted that a sense of "Germanness" depended very much on where one lived in the empire. It was a function of whether one tended to see a good fit among local, regional, and national allegiances. And it was conditioned by one's conception of Germany's "national mission" both before and after 1871. Nevertheless, most attempts to postulate a "third" Saxon way, falling somewhere between Prussian reaction and southwest German liberalism, have proved dissatisfying. Although Saxon peculiarities continue to fuel arguments about the balance of progressive and reactionary forces in Germany as a whole, Saxony's "pioneering" role can be interpreted in very different ways. Christoph Nonn has written that social protest in Saxony, often based on the defense of consumer interests in the face of high meat prices, was already far advanced by 1906: "The recipe for success, used in the last years before World War One by Social Democrats in Prussia and the Reich to pit consumer protest against conservative political structures, was perfected first by Social Democrats in Saxony."[16] Conversely, Benjamin Lapp has argued that Saxony in 1923 lived up to its reputation as a pioneer in a very different way: it provided an "early example" of "the extent to which conservative bourgeois politicians were willing to sacrifice democratic institutions in the interests of a militant anti-Socialism."[17]

---

16. Christoph Nonn, "Arbeiter, Bürger, und 'Agrarier': Stadt-Land-Gegensatz und Klassenkonflikt im Wilhelminischen Deutschland am Beispiel des Königreichs Sachsen," in *Demokratie und Emanzipation zwischen Saale und Elbe: Beiträge zur Geschichte der sozialdemokratischen Arbeiterbewegung bis 1933*, ed. Helga Grebing, Hans Mommsen, and Karsten Rudolph (Essen, 1993), 101–13, here 106.

17. Benjamin Lapp, *Revolution from the Right: Politics, Class, and the Rise of Nazism in Saxony, 1919–1933* (Atlantic Highlands, NJ, 1997), 77.

The usefulness of non-Prussian perspectives is particularly evident as historians press ahead with their research on the Saxon *Bürgertum*. The essays collected here suggest that Saxony remains a useful laboratory in which to explore such concepts as *Bürgerlichkeit, Bürgerstolz,* and *Verbürgerlichung*. Yet such investigations, too, yield ambiguous conclusions. Historians recognize that the economic and cultural hegemony of the Saxon bourgeoisie on the eve of 1914 was virtually uncontested.[18] But in times of crisis, liberal burghers in Saxony were also conspicuously prone to relinquish their claim to political leadership to their longtime rivals in the conservative camp. Saxon burghers were particularly sensitive to the geopolitical dangers inherent in their state's position in Mitteleuropa. The convergence of east-west and north-south axes contributed to Saxons' ambivalent feelings on such issues as free trade, in- and out-migration, the place of ethnic minorities in society, and the perennial problem of Groß- or Kleindeutschland. Moreover, the preponderance of small producers and small workshops heightened the fear of many middle-class Saxons that they faced a special threat from organized labor. As it happens, recent research has suggested that the preponderance of small industrial units in Saxony was more typical of the German norm than we once thought.[19] Nonetheless, Benjamin Lapp, Claus-Christian Szejnmann, and Sean Dobson have argued — in each case with due consideration of local variations — that these components of bourgeois *Angst* underpinned "the poverty of civic discourse" among Saxon burghers.[20] This in turn allowed cynicism and self-interest to masquerade as ideology and undermine concern for the common good. More specifically, the perception that Grenzland Sachsen was situated precariously on the periphery of Germany, combined with real evidence of their susceptibility to economic dislocation and loss of social status, appears to have pushed Saxon burghers in the direction of radical nationalism. Nevertheless, because similar anxieties afflicted other Germans too, much more work is required before this hypothesis can be accepted as an explanation for why the Pan-German League and other radical nationalist groups experienced such success in recruiting members in Saxony.[21] Wherever readers come down on these and related questions,

18. The cultural orientations of Saxon burghers are highlighted in essays by Robert Beachy, Glenn Penny, and Marline Otte in *Saxon Signposts*, ed. James Retallack, published as a special issue of *German History* 17, no. 4 (1999).

19. Gary Herrigel, *Industrial Constructions: The Sources of German Industrial Power* (Cambridge, 1996). Herrigel draws frequently on Saxon circumstances to support his thesis, as does Frank B. Tipton Jr. in *Regional Variations in the Economic Development of Germany during the Nineteenth Century* (Middletown, CT, 1976).

20. Sean Raymond Dobson, "Authority and Revolution in Leipzig, 1910–1920" (Ph.D. diss., Columbia University, 1995; rev. MS 1998).

21. Gerald Kolditz, "Rolle und Wirksamkeit des Alldeutschen Verbandes in Dresden zwischen 1895 und 1918: Ein Beitrag zum bürgerlichen Vereinsleben der national-

it can hardly be disputed that the density of work now available on Saxony will continue to broaden the analytical terrain on which future questions about the German *Bürgertum* are posed.

If there is one area of debate among German historians where Saxony figures more prominently than any other, it is surely the alleged polarization between the socialist and nationalist "camps" (*Lager*). According to the prevailing view, because the Saxon population was overwhelmingly Lutheran, no Catholic camp existed in the state to mitigate extreme political conflict between these two opposing camps. In fact, however, much evidence suggests that the "unbridgeable" gulf between socialist and nationalist groups in Saxony was less clear-cut than previously imagined. Historians of Saxony have not met with unqualified success when they have attempted to explain such conflicts exclusively in terms of milieus, cleavages, or camps. Even Saxons who feared the "red menace" seem to have followed an uncertain, shifting political compass, and they often traversed the middle ground between these opposing camps. This middle ground has been variously identified as a "gray zone" between a lower-middle-class and a proletarian existence; as a "transitory zone" permitting migration between socialist and nonsocialist milieus; or as bountiful "hunting grounds" for SPD poachers seeking to recruit new followers.[22] The existence of such a zone has obvious importance to German circumstances in the 1920s, but in Saxony it existed even in the 1860s and 1870s. Hence it is less any consistent antisocialist mentality found among Saxony's Protestant middle classes than their shifting, ambivalent allegiances — considered over the *longue durée* and in the context of larger struggles for emancipation, democracy, and social fairness — that may help explain how other Germans lost their political anchor before 1933. Because *Mittelstandspolitik* and radical antisemitism in Saxony have yet to be the subject of sustained historical analysis, this issue certainly cannot be dismissed as *passé*.

In the final analysis it would be fruitless to deny that when basic questions about the course of modern German history are posed, Saxon historians often respond with tentative, even ambivalent, answers. In this sense they have done a better job establishing the legitimacy of the regional perspective itself than they have in achieving any consensus about how Saxon history forces us to reassess national paradigms. If some historians of Saxony are contributing decisively to the revision of a model that gave too much weight to Imperial Germany's imperviousness

---

istischen Kräfte in der wilhelminischen Ära des deutschen Kaiserreiches" (Ph.D. diss., Technical University Dresden, 1994); Barry Jackisch, " 'Make the Right-Wing Strong!': The Pan-German League, Radical Nationalism, and the German Right, 1918–1933" (Ph.D. diss. in progress, SUNY at Buffalo).

22. For references see Retallack, "Society and Politics in Saxony," 429.

to reform (both from above and from below), others currently stress the need for further research on the persistence of authoritarian habits of mind. If some have revealed the diversity of German blueprints for reform, thereby demonstrating the contingency of struggles for liberty and democracy, others are doubtful that reformist impulses in the *Kaiserreich* would have triumphed even without the interruption of the First World War. In short: one sees on the horizon no synthesis, no overarching explanation of where either Saxony or Germany was headed in the early twentieth century. For this reason alone, we should welcome signs that new approaches and new themes are being taken up by a younger generation of scholars.

III. "Doing" Regional History Today

This volume is not merely a collection of conference papers; it is a true collaborative effort. From the very beginning, the aim was to publish a coherent body of work to reflect the state of the art in one particular field of German regional history, and yet also to make available to nonspecialists methodological and theoretical reflections of a more general nature. Each of these essays was drafted in its present length and with the full scholarly apparatus prior to a conference held in Toronto in September 1998. Happily, because this volume went to press eight weeks after the conference, contributors were able to refine their arguments in the light of points raised by their peers. Whereas there is no opportunity to reflect the full diversity of views put forward during the conference or to publish the prepared commentaries on the papers, lest an already long book grow even longer, it is possible to identify a few key areas where some consensus emerged from the Toronto discussions. Isaiah Berlin might almost have been describing one such area of agreement when he warned against a "naïve craving for unity and symmetry at the expense of experience." Although Berlin made this observation in the context of the Germans' "hangover" after revolution and unification in 1989–90, elsewhere he advocated "allowing curiosity into the airless chamber of fixed certainty."[23] That curiosity was evident on the floor of the Toronto conference, as was a strong resistance to any "craving for symmetry." Nevertheless, such resistance has its positive and negative aspects.

On the positive side, scholars sustain this resistance by using a wide range of analytical tools to work their way through, around, and within regional histories. Only rarely do they still fall into the trap of identifying

---

23. Cited in a retrospective on Berlin's life published by William Thorsell in the *Globe and Mail* (Toronto), 15 Nov. 1997; see also Michael Ignatieff, *Isaiah Berlin: A Life* (Toronto, 1998).

too closely with their favorite *Ländl* or of believing that the region they study constitutes historical "reality" itself. Compared to the state of the art, say, thirty years ago, the practice of "doing" regional history today is much more methodologically self-conscious. Nevertheless, Celia Applegate has noted that there is "something both liberating *and* demoralizing about our current suspicion of allegedly overdeterministic explanations of change and its organizing categories." To be sure, the anti-explanatory mode currently prevalent among scholars seems to demand a certain degree of critical distancing both from our method of historical investigation (regional history) and from the object of study itself (the region). But this pose of ironic detachment can be overdone, in the manner of an awkward personal encounter: "let me introduce you to my spouse, but I'm not really committed to this relationship and it could well turn out to be something entirely different than a marriage and it's certainly in flux and under negotiation and filled with other possibilities and contingently related to all the other things going on in my life, and I wouldn't wish to suggest that there is some normative value adhering to this particular relationship. . . ."[24]

What might take the place of these normative values? At the risk of sampling too selectively from the plenary debates, four central issues seemed to attract the most attention in Toronto. The first concerned the lack of reflection with which historians still approach the concept of "region" itself. The second concerned the need for historians always to take into account change over time. The third concerned the way we gather together, and analyze together, the different sorts of mental maps that determine people's actions, including most conspicuously geographic maps, imaginative maps, and maps of experience. And the fourth concerned the use and abuse of "modernization" as a unifying concept to explore or explain historical change.

Taking up the first of these issues, certainly historians of Germany have too rarely reflected on the constructed nature of regions and regional identities. This deficit shows signs of shrinking, as the essays in Part 1 of this volume demonstrate. That is not to say, however, that historians should not be even more explicit about how they use "region" as a geographical limitation, as a framing device, for their own research. For example, the notion of "exceptionalism," identified earlier in this introduction, is too often dismissed as a remnant of an out-of-date style of regional history known as *Landesgeschichte*. Perhaps there are still too many good exceptionalists among us, each one imagining that his or her own unit of study — a single city, a province, a region — represents the paradigmatic case of this syndrome or that trend. Hamburg, the

---

24. Celia Applegate.

Rhineland, and Bavaria might be cited as examples here as readily as Saxony. Both in the past and in the study of the past, exceptionalism too often hardens into a myth that powerfully influences the way local and regional histories are conceptualized and narrated in the present. The relatively unreflective ways in which historians endorse the "production" of regions may become political projects of their own.[25] Whereas the methods of local and regional history are used to travel new paths, often we end up at the old destinations (including, significantly, restatements of modernization theory writ small).

Second, what are we to make of demands that regional historians devote more attention to change over time? Here too, the essays in this volume offer hints as to how this might be done. One can look at people on the move, as Helmut Walser Smith advocates, and consider migration as a factor reflecting the connections between identity and geography. One might consider how the "nuts and bolts" of regional consciousness — church or military institutions, dialects, networks of family connections, and myriad other cultural practices — are "set in motion" by challenges to the status quo. When did contemporaries reflect on their particular era as perpetuating or overcoming something special in their lives, and when did they focus on the arrival of something better in the future? Do historians accurately capture this sense of change over time when they write, for example, about a "postrevolutionary" epoch or a "pre-emancipatory" stage of development? Are we sufficiently aware of contemporaries' perceptions when we denote certain political movements as "rising," when we say others are in danger of "disappearing" from history, and when we find liberals trying to seize a "second chance"?

Such considerations can be couched in less abstract terms. For example, suffrage laws and railway maps, drawn and redrawn over the years, illustrate the way things have already evolved in the past; but they also capture potential sources of legitimacy or profit in the future. The main point is that a sense of place usually evolves in tandem with a sense of time. However, a sense of time is rarely included among the "modern" ways of seeing that regional historians consider. When do identities remain rooted, and when do they change at a recognizably accelerating pace? At what rate do spatial memories fade away? What is their relationship to the perceived "newness" of places and groups in which displaced persons find themselves? Ironically, such questions about change over time actually de-emphasize the priority historians have placed on the region-nation polarity as a process; they tend to reconceptualize it as a tension, one with many more layers and interpretations than we once imagined.

---

25. Jennifer Jenkins.

Historians, then, may be well advised to ask not "What is a region?" but what sets of practices define a sense of place? What identities adhere to "region," and what experiences constitute it? In considering these shifting practices, identities, and experiences, we risk losing track of the specificities of place — this is the third issue raised in the Toronto discussions. Many of the essays in this volume could be more explicit about the physical, social, and political boundaries within which their analyses are situated. Yet by discussing the importance of neighborhood boundaries, of states' territorial sovereignty, or of networks of transportation and communication, many contributions do take a first step toward the better integration of mental and physical topography — that is, toward a better understanding of the symbolic *and* the geographic "placeness" of place. That understanding in turn will help historians explore further what Applegate termed the "discernible patterns, identifiable limits, commonalities of experience — mental, physical, social, political — and even trends that at least felt inexorable at the time, even if they may not have been so."

Fourth, the methodological distancing noted earlier has contributed to a marked difference of opinion among scholars about the applicability of modernization as a central concept in the genre of regional history. The liabilities of modernization theory in its extreme form have always been particularly clear to local and regional historians — no less clear, in fact, than to practitioners of microhistory and *Alltagsgeschichte*.[26] For too long, regions were studied exclusively as the sites of resistance to modernity and nationalism, as the bastions of parochial outlooks and particularist navel-gazing. Too often one encountered the narcissism of small differences, and too often a strict polarity intruded where none actually existed in the past. But as Richard J. Evans has suggested, moving beyond the "generalizing social-science approach to the past" allows us to sidestep the teleologies that tend to wipe out "the cultural distance between the past and the present, losing the strangeness and individuality of the past in the process." Bringing the region back in restores one small part of that fascinating, frustrating strangeness of the past. Another part may be recaptured via Applegate's idea of the "mediated nation." The idea of mediation might be used by historians trying to understand how the filters of localism and regionalism conditioned ordinary Germans' perception of the nation. On the one hand, the nation

---

26. "The study of a small community, a single riot, a discrete event, a particular text, a historical family, a personal relationship, or an ordinary individual can often tell us more about the past than the wide-ranging teleologies of the 1960s and 1970s, from Marxism to modernization theory, ever managed to do." Richard J. Evans, *Rituals of Retribution: Capital Punishment in Germany, 1600–1987* (Oxford, 1996), ix, and for the passage below.

could not unproblematically be balanced, harmonized, or reconciled with the local except via the mediation of the region. On the other hand, mediation also suggests a way of linking everyday routines of politics (the micro) to larger plays of power (the macro).

Few essays in this volume deploy a concept of modernization that sees parochial remnants receding on all fronts in the face of modernity. To the contrary, many of them would agree with the practice of placing "modernization" always in quotation marks, to keep at bay what Roger Chickering described as "a floating, illusionary, elusive telos." Yet Chickering's own work on Freiburg during the First World War illustrates that local and regional history are the natural allies of total history, that is, a history encompassing as many aspects of the past as possible. Hence: Why not, as Brett Fairbairn and Thomas Mergel have advocated, retain the more convincing and heuristically useful *elements* of the modernization concept and dispense only with the prideful claim to explain how modernity — as a whole — "happened"? Why not, Christoph Nonn has asked, strive to avoid the pitfalls of middle-class, cultural, and national reductionism but nonetheless seek to write *histoire totale?* And why not continue to study such self-evidently important issues as class formation, political renewal, the uneven distribution of power, the overcoming of social inequality, and — of perennial importance — the failure of liberal democracy in Germany before 1945?

These are just a few of the keys that are generally included among what Geoff Eley has called the "connotative continuum of 'bourgeoisie = liberalism = democracy.' "[27] This is the continuum of classic modernization theory. Yet at the regional level — perhaps nowhere more obviously than at the regional level — this "implied causal chain" remains just that: implied, not proven. Modernization theory tended to render regions as a convenient black box. Everything that did not square with the straight path toward economic, social, and political modernity could be explained as coming out of that black box; or, rather, everything that did not fit could be explained away *into* it.[28] But we should never forget that mere interdependence among the social and cultural components of political democratization should not be taken as tending inevitably toward a "good fit." To choose to explore these issues is not to lock oneself into the iron cage of modernization theory or to accept rigid patterns of development from which no person or region or collectivity shall stray.[29] Rather, it is to suggest that questions of power and domination, patterns

---

27. Geoff Eley, "German History and the Contradictions of Modernity: The Bourgeoisie, the State, and the Mastery of Reform," in *Society, Culture, and the State in Germany, 1870–1930*, ed. idem (Ann Arbor, MI, 1996), 67–103, here 87.

28. Christoph Nonn.

29. Celia Applegate.

of social upheaval and economic development, and problems of social inequality were indeed important in German history. Concepts of structured change — like the concepts of political mobilization, participation, activization, pillarization, polarization, integration, and nationalization — must be used flexibly; they must be used contingently; but they can be used nevertheless.[30] Similarly, constructs of identity, if they are used as a heuristic tool, may be more or less useful; but the extent of their usefulness has to be proven.[31]

Arguably, one can discern in this volume more than a mere vestige of those polarities (modern, not-modern) that have always underpinned the modernization concept. One might consider the contending positions advocated by Wilhelm Heinrich Riehl and Gustav Freytag, where one thinker emphatically embraced precisely what the other condemned. Which city was more "modern," Dresden or Munich? Was Saxony more "progressive" than other states in the way it reformed its suffrage laws or tolerated consumer cooperatives? How might "modernization, National Liberal style" have served as a blueprint for the Reich? Did the Weimar Republic slip off the rails in Saxony first? Is there something peculiarly "localizing" about political violence (or memories of violence)?

Some readers may conclude that the trail-markers first laid down so long ago by the advocates of modernization theory are still pushing regional historians of Germany toward depicting a surprisingly familiar, well-trodden path. Yet the will to resist such pressure is surely growing. Historians are answering the call to put the telos of modernization at arm's length by explaining the erosion *and* persistence of traditional ways of seeing. In these essays the forces of modernity are sought at levels other than the national one. National aggregates, national averages, and the apparent homogeneity of long trends — what Charles Tilly playfully described as "big structures, large processes, [and] huge comparisons"[32] — yield pride of place to local and regional particularities, to discrete events, to sudden turning points, and to the actions of individuals whose role on the national stage was unexceptional.[33]

---

30. Celia Applegate.

31. Christoph Nonn formulated this idea in especially pointed form. All such constructs of identity have a "hard core beneath a soft and changing surface," he observed, adding: "That core may not be as hard as steel and unchangeable, but it is hard nevertheless."

32. Charles Tilly, *Big Structures, Large Processes, Huge Comparisons* (New York, 1984).

33. Cf. Peter Steinbach, "Deutungsmuster der historischen Modernisierungstheorie für die Analyse westeuropäischer Wahlen," in *Vergleichende europäische Wahlgeschichte,* ed. Otto Büsch and Peter Steinbach (Berlin, 1982), 158–246; and Thomas Mergel, "Geht es weiterhin voran? Die Modernisierungtheorie auf dem Weg zu einer Theorie der Mo-

In the process of such investigations, we find that contemporaries' attempts to hasten the arrival of "the modern" cannot neatly be placed in opposition to attempts to preserve tradition. Both projects jumble and jostle together, in effect decoupling the experience, consciousness, and identity of individuals and groups from a teleology of progress. On the one hand, this jostling makes it more difficult for historians to dress "national" modernizers alone as the protagonists of German history. It reminds us that those Germans whom David Blackbourn recently called the "martinets of modernity" were not assured of victory in their smaller homelands.[34] And it helps us avoid the trap of linear thinking: by discarding the notion of a special German path (*Sonderweg*) in the singular, we can more easily avoid both the Scylla of sentimentality and the Charybdis of censure. On the other hand, this approach yields a more "humanist" style of history, based on the idea of the individual as an active subject, and on the idea of history as fractured, contradictory, and open to multiple readings. In these ways it may, indeed, still prove possible to explore modernization's diverse forms, its reversible patterns, its constituent dilemmas, and its surface textures — if necessary, all without using the dreaded "m"-word.

In the end, the most any editor can hope is that his contributors will be judged as working hard at writing the kind of histories that are methodologically self-conscious, inventive, and demanding, but also respectful of the historical record. In seeking to bridge the rather unfruitful divides between empiricism and theory, between solid, careful history and the search for new avenues to insight, this collection tries to demonstrate that regional approaches can reveal the richness of Germany's multiple histories in new ways, as though one were observing them through telephoto and wide-angle lenses at the same time.

IV. Structure of the Volume

Why are the individual essays grouped as they are? Without attempting to render the collection all things to all people, the essays in Part 1 were pushed front and center in order to emphasize the rethinking of German regional history that this volume was meant to facilitate. Here the balance of two American and two German perspectives is not accidental. Subsequently, a rough chronological progression underlies the sequence of papers. No claim can be made that this volume provides a unified,

derne," in *Geschichte zwischen Kultur und Gesellschaft,* ed. idem and Thomas Welskopp (Munich, 1997), 203–32.

34. David Blackbourn, *Marpingen: Apparitions of the Virgin Mary in Bismarckian Germany* (Oxford, 1993), 14.

comprehensive history of Saxony between 1830 and 1933. Nevertheless, for English-language readers we have tried to open a window on the broad sweep of Saxon history for the first time. Lastly, individual papers were grouped around specific issues — ones that have achieved special resonance in Saxon history *and* in German historiography. As it happens, it did not take much effort to discover a multitude of such issues; the difficulty arose in choosing among them.

Both Hartmut Zwahr's foreword and section II of this introduction have alluded to certain criteria that one might use to embed Saxony within German history. The essays that follow suggest many more. A number of these derive from growing scholarly interest in political culture. There is some truth in Max Kaase's famous quip that the task of defining political culture is comparable to the attempt to nail a pudding against the wall.[35] Yet when we speak of political culture (or the culture of politics), we signal an interest in the social-psychological ambiance of a system of rule, the relationship between the state and its citizens, and countless other assumptions, usually unarticulated, that members of a given polity take for granted. Many of the contributors use "region" as a variable to explore exactly these kinds of relationships and assumptions. Here they follow the lead of Karl Rohe, who has shown the way in deploying the concept of *regional* political cultures flexibly: as a means to explore "politically relevant cultural peculiarities that have developed over time, whether on the level of 'worldviews' and mentalities, on the level of commonalities of thought, speech, sentiment, or behavior, [or] on the level of symbols and explicit ideologies."[36]

Culture is central to this volume in other ways. More than one essay considers the regional and national contours of the German reading public. Others examine liberal and monarchical attempts to exert hegemony over festival culture and public spaces. Still others explore Social Democratic cultural associations and sports clubs, or the cultural *Habitus* of Jews. In each of these cases, a discussion of culture is central to the task of examining the multiple layerings that make up individual and group identities. Culture, indeed, may provide the best key to explain why scholarly attention has recently shifted away from the kind of regional history that privileged structure and typology, toward one that increasingly emphasizes agency, perception, experience, mentalities, and language.

Part 1 provides four viewpoints on the methodologies and theories

---

35. See Eva Kolinsky and John Gaffney, introduction to *Political Culture in France and Germany*, ed. idem (London, 1991), 1–12, and for the following.

36. Karl Rohe, "Regionale (politische) Kultur: Ein sinnvolles Konzept für die Wahl- und Parteienforschung?" in *Parteien und regionale politische Traditionen in der Bundesrepublik Deutschland*, ed. Dieter Oberndörfer and Karl Schmitt (Berlin, 1991), 17–37, here 21.

that inform the writing of regional history today. In the opening essay, Celia Applegate demonstrates that the practice of regional history has offered an important handhold on the slippery face of German national identity, not only in the 1990s but also in the nineteenth century. No single map, no unitary vision of social change, emerges from her analysis. Even though Riehl and Freytag agree on many of the basic dynamics at work in the Germany evolving before their eyes, stark oppositions can be traced in these men's thinking. One pole was situated in the region and the locality, the other in the nation-state. Nevertheless, the valences attached to these polarities, though very different, mirrored each other to a remarkable degree. As the modernization debate itself demonstrates, those valences have proved to be as durable as they are controversial.

Another self-reflective map is proposed by Thomas Kühne in his wide-ranging effort to "imagine" and to "construct" regions in new ways. Like Applegate, Kühne is able to problematize the simple dualisms of modernization theory. Drawing on the work of Hermann Lübbe, he reminds us of a dominant motif in regional historiography: "The 'paths' of the *Heimat* movement and of regionalism do not lead away from modernity, but rather to its very core, for they are both intimately connected to that inherently negative dimension of modernity that corresponds to the concept of 'alienation.'" Yet Kühne also notes that to invoke "the region" is often in practice to criticize the concept of modernization without substituting something new in its place. To avoid stepping into the same trap, Kühne proposes various remedies. Highlighting the cognitive-emotional component in modern regional historiography, Kühne advocates greater attention to what German political scientists have previously discussed in the context of regional political cultures. Although a national identity may become a social and cultural "skin" that individuals, after a certain age, cannot easily shed, it is rarely a homogenous one. On the one hand, it is conditioned by a number of objective "thresholds" with which individuals confront the outside world. On the other hand, a larger political community is almost never homogenous but is fractured by subnational, ethnic, linguistic, regional, religious, or socioeconomic identities. The question then becomes one of determining, where possible, whether these cleavages reinforce or crosscut each other in certain individuals and groups.[37] To imagine that they reinforce each other exclusively, suggests Kühne, is to enter (and never escape) the "mythical world" of regional political cultures — to entrap oneself in a cultural and conceptual cage.

---

37. See Dirk Berg-Schlosser and Ralf Rytlewski, "Political Culture in Germany: A Paradigmatic Case," in *Political Culture in Germany,* ed. idem (Basingstoke, 1993), 3–12, here 6.

Helmut Walser Smith asks how we as historians might recapture the feel for the specificity and the variety of lives lived both "locally" and "on the move." His answer counsels us to abjure a spurious search for authenticity in local history if that search is meant only to serve larger, aggregating narratives. Smith is not overly concerned with the geographical scale that historians use, as long as they understand that neither its boundaries nor its internal structures are fixed and immutable. To the historian of Saxony, Smith offers no clear guideline as to which boundaries are relevant and how they change over time. But his aim is clearly not to do so. Instead, as he writes early on in his piece, the map he has in mind is "without a utopian moment." Subsequently he develops the argument that "approaches to local history . . . are not primarily about getting to the essence of local and regional identities"; rather, they are about destabilizing these identities.

In the last essay in Part 1, Thomas Mergel considers the spatial rootedness of collective identities. He, too, advocates more critical reflection about how milieus are mapped. Yet to a greater degree than the other contributions in Part 1, Mergel asks us to consider how three specific milieus — the Catholic milieu, the working-class milieu, and the middle-class milieu — each coalesced historically in ways that defy the "region-to-nation" progression discussed earlier. Explicitly dedicated to exploring the tension between regional socialization and the formation of national milieus, Mergel's essay successfully revives the issue of territoriality as a long-neglected component of the concept of sociomoral milieus. Decrying the fashionable practice of applying the label "milieu" even to units of analysis as small as friendship circles, Mergel reminds us that sociomoral milieus derive a large part of their legitimacy by politicizing certain loyalties. He then illustrates how the "mass" political movements of the late nineteenth century always relied on their ability to make national idioms and identities seem utterly familiar. (Germans have even devised a noun to describe this feeling of *Zuhause*.) In this way Mergel is also able to chart lines of inquiry that inform the essays in Part 4. In those latter contributions, the Nazis' success in winning the support of middle-class Protestant Germans is contrasted with their relative lack of success in destabilizing the working-class and Catholic milieus.

The essays in Part 2 demonstrate how the issue of emancipation still provides a useful vehicle for investigations that seek to transcend the traditional social, cultural, and political divides in Saxon and German historiography. Emancipation is seen to have engaged the attention of Germany's middle classes in many different ways, ranging from liberal parliamentarians' formal efforts to enhance the power of parliaments to a variety of public campaigns rooted in the idea of "self-help." Simone Lässig's broad chronological sweep encompasses almost a century in the history of Jewish emancipation. At the same time it provides a compelling example of how comparative historical analysis based on regional case studies can be pursued. In two other important ways Lässig sets the stage for the contributions that follow. On the one hand, she emphasizes key connections between the processes of Jewish emancipation and cultural embourgeoisement in nineteenth-century Germany. On the other hand, Lässig successfully calls into doubt the long-term success of German Jews, together with their liberal supporters, in overturning the legacy of suspicion and animosity inherited from previous centuries. The specifically German model of "conditional" emancipation "from above," which registered such notable success in Anhalt-Dessau, proved much more problematic in the Kingdom of Saxony, where state policies of conditional emancipation perpetuated the notion that Jews were persons of "lesser rights" (and hence of "lesser worth").[38] Whatever rights they received were up to the discretion of the state, and even those rights could be revoked. Although it does not fall within the scope of her study, the pioneering role of Saxony's antisemites from the 1870s onward already looms in the distance.

The contributions by Andreas Neemann and Christian Jansen provide another way of conceiving the expansion of the German public sphere at midcentury. One common denominator between these studies is that they bring the reader down to the level of individual personalities and concrete legislative issues, even while considering people and events in the larger context of German political development. The 1850s and 1860s have been a black hole in German historiography for so long that Jansen and Neemann barely scratch the surface of the important issues that merit consideration. Of these issues, the most important is the alleged "taming" of the bourgeoisie's will to power in the wake of 1848. As each of these authors demonstrates, even revolutionary failure did not prevent the emergence of entrenched ideas about the central role of political parties in the public's consciousness during the 1850s: after popular successes in political mobilization in 1848–49, there was simply no turning back.

In the essays by Páll Björnsson and Brett Fairbairn, the spatial rootedness of democratic ideas is examined from another angle. Björnsson successfully illustrates the extraordinary richness of associational life in Leipzig (which in turn complements the later analyses of Leipzig's socialist milieu provided by Thomas Adam and Marven Krug). Through a kind of historical triangulation, Björnsson juxtaposes social, cultural, and political conceptions of the "new man" in that city's thriving public sphere. Here Björnsson explores essentially the same political elite that Jansen has already introduced to the reader. Yet now the

---

38. Jacques Kornberg.

focus is transferred to the level of local politics in its concrete Leipzig setting. Moreover, Björnsson comes to rather different conclusions. Whereas Jansen sees a split that he describes in Weberian terms as one between the "ethic of responsibility" and the "ethic of ultimate ends," Björnsson warns against the prevailing tendency among students of German liberalism to see the liberal movement as an either-or proposition: as either a constitutional movement exclusively or a movement whose larger goal was to foster the cultural improvement and self-fulfillment of autonomous individuals.

It is not the task of an editor to arbitrate in such cases. But perhaps an observation by James J. Sheehan is relevant here: "[A] great deal of the political activity that goes on at the national level is designed to simplify issues, to clarify alignments, to reduce politics to a set of binary choices. . . . But . . . in the worlds of local politics, choices are frequently more fluid, alliances more uncertain, combinations more complex."[39] Sheehan's observation suggests why these analyses of the bourgeois public sphere in midcentury Germany accomplish two goals at the same time. They provide new archival evidence about how political communities of various sorts were articulated, organized, polarized, or simply forgotten.[40] Perhaps more interestingly, they also suggest patterns for making sense of midcentury contingencies that are useful for Saxon and non-Saxon historians alike—from the more well-known patterns of division and extremism to the less-explored options that permitted liberals to cooperate, to be pragmatic, and to live with political searching rather than political certainty.

Looking toward the essays collected in Part 3, Karsten Rudolph argues in a similar vein. He suggests that the "disappearance" of a political party—in this case the Saxon People's Party—has obscured not only established narratives, but potential ones as well. Those narratives, he argues, feed into political trajectories that do not necessarily point toward the Nazi seizure of power in 1933. Thomas Adam, too, shows that Leipzig's socialist milieu does not fit our assumptions about what such a milieu is supposed to be. How proletarian was the Social Democratic milieu, he asks? Not very, or at least not in the way that we are accustomed to seeing it. Hence, argues Adam, we should not be surprised that Leipzig's Social Democrats made their own kind of revolution in 1918. A common thread running through these contributions is the sustained effort to join questions about the changing nature of politics—the relationships between parties and parliaments, between popular discontent and its organized articulation, and between state and

---

39. Sheehan, "What Is German History?" 21–22.
40. Jennifer Jenkins.

society — with questions concerning regional and local identity. We discover that in both the public sphere and the region, political identities are fragile and easily torn. This may be particularly the case with respect to Saxon and German liberalism, but there is no reason that gendered conceptions of the "new man" or specifically bourgeois forms of civic activism — to take just two examples — need be limited to the analysis of liberalism alone.

Part 2 is rounded out by two very different essays that nonetheless both ask how local *ideas* of community are changed in the process of national integration and democratization. Siegfried Weichlein examines the progress of the national idea in Saxony by using a panoply of yardsticks (and, not surprisingly, ending up with multiple readings). Underlying Weichlein's analysis is an understanding that the local-regional-national equation too, not just the "regional-national" polarity, is best discussed as a tension, not as a linear chronological sequence. Working from Applegate's pathbreaking work on the German idea of *Heimat,* Weichlein echoes Wolfgang Hardtwig's insight that even the *Heimat* concept proved unsettling for nineteenth-century Germans in that "it undermined its own original integrative effort." Brett Fairbairn demonstrates that German cooperatives, "by virtue of their dual nature as democratic associations of people and as competitive enterprises," also presented contemporaries with choices that subtly revealed underlying dilemmas. Indeed, they continue to present challenges to historians today. As Fairbairn notes: "If there is a tendency among historians to regard 'local' as meaning 'traditional,' and 'national' (or 'international') as meaning 'modern,' then cooperatives squarely straddle these distinctions." The unfolding of Fairbairn's argument — which tackles a chronological period no less ambitious than Lässig's — soon reveals that on such issues as self-education, participation, and the articulation of a particular vision of community, the members of German cooperatives confronted many of the same questions that inform other essays in Part 2: the formation of middle-class identities, the struggle for emancipation, the reconciliation of liberal theory and practice, and the degree to which protests against the authoritarian state could be contained within the limits of the evolving public sphere.

As the thematic focus in Part 3 falls on the dynamics of political renewal, coalition-building, and the practice of civil liberties, the years from 1849 to 1879 are subjected to close scrutiny. This allows the contributors to provide complementary analyses of salient themes and issues. Karsten Rudolph reinterprets the trajectories of party politics in a way that does *not* force people's parties to perform the way modern historiographies would have them perform. My own contribution considers how conservative reformers conceived their "revolutions from above" as a means to relegitimize their own states within a specific federal context; it also suggests ways in which regional comparisons might be made internationally. Wolfgang Schröder considers how members of undemocratic parliaments can reform both their own rules and the structures of state administration.

Despite underscoring the ambiguous nature of the emerging antagonism between conservatives and socialists, these essays also direct attention to those who were so often caught in the middle — the liberals. Here the contributors see much more than just the hint of a new dawn of liberalism in the era of nation-building. This in itself is a marked inversion of accepted interpretations that until very recently have tended to see the demise of German liberalism, if not already in 1866, certainly by 1878–79. Looking to the backlog of reformist measures that were introduced in the essays by Jansen and Neemann, and yet looking forward to the disintegration of a political consensus among Protestant middle-class Germans after 1900 (examined in Part 4), these authors do not relegate cultural considerations to the sidelines. A number of the essays, for example, seek to discover how Saxons perceived their "frontiers of sovereignty" in these tumultuous decades. Others suggest how imagined political communities competed for hegemony over less-imagined ones. They do so by focusing on an era when the available models for democratic reform may have been in greater flux than at any point in German history before 1945.

All the essays in Part 3 examine the deep cleavage in Saxon political culture between socialist and nonsocialist groups in the state. Why did this antagonism take on such pernicious contours as early as the second half of the nineteenth century? No single answer emerges from these essays. Indeed, for the period before 1900 at least, these essays identify signs pointing toward a possible bridging of social conflicts (working class vs. middle class) and political conflicts (socialist vs. nonsocialist). In other words, a future calamity arising from extreme political polarization was not inevitable. It is hardly surprising that this negative consensus arises from studies that explore such diverse topics as milieu formation among members of Saxony's garden allotment movement, suffrage reform in Dresden's *Landtag,* and the exercise of civil liberties on the bustling streets of Leipzig.

And so we arrive at Part 4, where the essays provide a thematic progression of two sorts. It is not by chance that Benjamin Lapp's Weimar burghers are squeezed between two analyses of the "new" (post-1900) Saxon Left and two analyses of the even newer (post-1918) Saxon Right. Juxtaposing the essays by Karl Heinrich Pohl and Christoph Nonn, there is no question that the political trajectory of German liberalism between 1900 and 1918 remains contentious. Yet scholarly opinion has not hardened into opposing fronts. Pohl's contribution to this volume tends to reposition, rather than reaffirm, his conclusion (elaborated elsewhere) that municipal politics provided ample scope for the unfolding of German liberalism in the late imperial period. Dresden's underperforming liberals score poor marks in comparison with their counterparts in Munich. For the first time, however, Pohl has provided the larger context of Saxony's political culture that is necessary to judge the dismal showing of Dresden's liberal elites.

Wartime struggles to avoid economic and social collapse on the one hand and to preserve a measure of Saxon independence on the other are examined by Christoph Nonn. To good effect, Nonn carefully avoids the "might have beens, should have beens" of German history. Instead he proceeds like a detective, slowly uncovering the limited, hesitant steps taken by Saxony's National Liberal leaders in October 1918 to test the viability of a democratic parliamentary system. Into those already troubled waters Rudolf Heinze and his comrades dipped their toes with at least as much trepidation as did the Saxon statesmen who agreed to a sudden widening of the suffrage in 1868. This particular experiment in democracy was cut short by events in the second week of November 1918. Even so, it is impossible to overlook the degree to which both Pohl and Nonn emphasize the open-endedness, the real promise, of Saxon liberalism in the final years of the Second Reich.

The options still available to Saxon liberals in October 1918 stand in utter contrast to the situation after 1926, examined by Larry Eugene Jones and Claus-Christian Szejnmann. The bitter memories of socialist rule, cut short by the *Reichsexekution* against Saxony in 1923, imprinted Saxon identities with the same "friend-foe" dichotomy that had hamstrung prewar efforts to overcome division of Saxon political culture into two antagonistic camps. Whereas some contributors to this volume see that antagonism as having waned — at least in specific, limited ways — in the decades between the expiration of Bismarck's antisocialist laws in 1890 and the outbreak of revolution in November 1918, both Lapp and Szejnmann emphasize that the long-term roots of Saxony's highly polarized, conflict-ridden political culture of the 1920s must be sought in the nineteenth century (here Wolfgang Schröder would agree). There can be no doubt, however, that by the final half-decade of the Weimar experiment in democracy, the political situation in Saxony was unlikely to have a positive impact on the ability of German statesmen elsewhere to meet the challenges of economic, social, and political crisis. As Larry Eugene Jones demonstrates in his systematic analysis of political infighting both regionally and nationally, by 1930 the leaders of the Saxon Right had already embraced the political strategies that failed to keep either the Saxon Left or the Nazis at bay. Each essay in this section offers its own insights into the process whereby disarray on the Right turned into disintegration, and each successfully locates this story of fragmentation and collapse in the larger history of the bourgeois party system of the Weimar Republic.

Like Hartmut Zwahr's foreword, this introduction has attempted only to set the table for what follows. It has not tried to conceal the fact that each section of the menu is limited in its offerings. Certainly the bounty still available in Saxon archives promises more varied fare in the future. In the meantime we can proceed to the main course.

Part 1

WRITING LOCAL AND REGIONAL HISTORY TODAY

The Mediated Nation: Regions, Readers, and the German Past

Celia Applegate

I. Introduction

One of the more unheralded developments in the writing of modern European history over the past few decades has been the slow but steady increase in attention devoted to the civic and regional groupings that have constituted European historical experience below, beyond, and outside whatever we construe to be national experience. This attention has emerged from a number of sources: the waning of confidence in modernization paradigms of historical change, the near-hegemony of constructivist perspectives on the phenomena of collective identity (indeed, the very obsession with national identity itself), the experimentation with *Annales* and other microhistorical methods in more modern settings, and—not least—the seeming resurgence of regional groups within the context of European Community politics.[1] What this disparate body of work seems to be pushing toward, often unbeknownst to individual authors, is a reimagining of modern European history as the story of intertwining, shifting subnational entities. To quote Hans Mommsen out of context, this reimagining seems to take as its premise the proposition that "the nation is dead, long live the region."[2] To be sure, as Christopher Harvie has pointed out, such a history of Europe, "as it will come to be written," remains obscure. Nevertheless, as historians we are beginning to learn that we might profitably spend more time thinking about new ways to aggregate the often dispersed illuminations

---

1. For a more complete discussion, see Celia Applegate, "A Europe of Regions: Reflections on the Historiography of Sub-National Places in Modern Times," *American Historical Review* 104 (1999): 1157–82.

2. Hans Mommsen, "Die Nation ist tot. Es lebe die Region," in *Nation Deutschland?* ed. Guido Knopp, Siegfried Quant, and Herbert Scheffler (Munich, 1984), 35.

of local and regional research.[3] The task of "putting it all together" need not force us to revisit those generalizations about national histories that have masked the kinds of diversity and resistance we now value. Nor will we invariably arrive at radically new understandings of the past, such as are regularly promised in the process of paradigm shifting. Instead, we may gain some new insight into processes of aggregation themselves — for example, about how one construes many neighborhoods together as a nation.

The following observations seek to contribute to this agenda indirectly, by considering two nineteenth-century efforts to put together the pieces of central European political and cultural life into some explicable whole. The works to be considered are Gustav Freytag's *Bilder aus der deutschen Vergangenheit* (1859–67) and Wilhelm Heinrich Riehl's *Naturgeschichte des deutschen Volkes* (1851–69). Both were books of history and folklore written in the wake of the nation-building failures of 1848. Both were immensely popular from the moment they were published, appearing in successive editions well into the twentieth century. Both were essentially efforts at explaining the sense of a single entity made up of disparate and, at times, incomparable parts. Both were, in various ways, shaped by their authors' concerns about reconciling the realities of a dispersed cultural and political life with the drive to political and economic incorporation that characterized their own times. And both implicitly promoted a national consciousness, by means of which Germany might become something more than what Georg Hirth termed a "conglomeration of separate regions, communities, and individuals."[4] By focusing our attention on the extent to which Riehl and Freytag did and did not find space for regional and civic groupings in their attempts to make a recognizably German whole out of the material of history and folklife, we might gain some perspective on our own ongoing efforts at synthesis and generalization.[5]

The very different strategies pursued by the two writers reflect the range of possible imaginings of the nation that were attracting public interest in the decades before 1871. We have a choice here in how we explain their contribution to the national project. On the one hand, historians have emphasized the political and cultural content of nation-building: the struggles over *klein-* and *grossdeutsch* versions of political union; the search for symbols — hopefully *denkmalfähig* — of German-

---

3. Christopher Harvie, *The Rise of Regional Europe* (New York, 1994), x.

4. Hirth, cited in Karl Schleunes, *Schooling and Society: The Politics of Education in Prussia and Bavaria* (New York, 1989), 161.

5. There is a brilliant yet partial attempt to do just this — to analyze the forms of generalization and synthesis characteristic of the post-1848 generation — in the final chapter of Mack Walker's *German Home Towns* (Ithaca, NY, 1971), 418–25.

ness; the conflicts between Catholic and Protestant Germanys; the efforts to create canons of literary, artistic, and musical greatness; the writing of self-consciously national histories; and more. Certainly the works authored by Freytag and Riehl can easily be aligned with such efforts; they have a great deal to tell us about what kinds of character traits, values, and customs were being held up to the reading public as typically German. Comparing the two, we find both commonalities and contradictions. Thus we might well conclude that, even in an era said to be marked by gathering consensus in public culture about what constituted Germanness, any number of issues remained unresolved, not just the more predictable ones (Austrian/Prussian, Catholic/Protestant) on which historians have tended to focus.

On the other hand, a different strand of thinking about nationhood, which stretches from Karl Deutsch's work on social communication through Benedict Anderson's imagined communities (including that of his revisionists), places greater emphasis on the forms and means of national aggregation, just as it does on the importance of certain kinds of military recruitment, governmental diffusion, print capitalism, consumption, travel, and education. Riehl's and Freytag's works have a kind of double significance in such an interpretive context. The books themselves belong to a particular genre within print culture — popular nonfiction with a clear pedagogical purpose — that has not perhaps received the attention it deserves as a medium for giving shape to the imagined community of the nation. The "profound fictiveness" of the newspaper, which Anderson credited with creating "that remarkable confidence of community in anonymity which is the hallmark of modern nations," also characterized these quasi-factual reportages of life in the putative nation.[6] The wide distribution of both Riehl's *Naturgeschichte* and Freytag's *Bilder,* their steady circulation in lending libraries, and their frequent reprinting attest to their presence in the households of a far broader reading public than the educated elites who read the works of, for instance, Johann Gustav Droysen or even Heinrich von Treitschke. Indeed, their readership seems to have closely resembled that of the mass-circulation journal *Die Gartenlaube.* But beyond their role as literature qua popular literature, one must take into account the way in which both Riehl's and Freytag's writings maintained a commentary on those very cognitive issues that so preoccupy historians today, informing questions of how nationalizing perceptions arise, of how experiences and forces transform mental life, of how an emerging contemporary consciousness augments national belonging. Riehl's and Freytag's methodology, as we shall discover, powerfully literalized the processes of national consciousness-raising, to which their

---

6. Benedict Anderson, *Imagined Communities,* rev. ed. (New York, 1991), 33–35.

writings were devoted. Their works thus offer an intriguingly per-
formative commentary on their own times, insightful on its own terms and
culturally revealing in its limitations and nationalizing strategies.

II. Riehl, Freytag, and the Writing of German Histories

Before turning to the works themselves, we need briefly to take stock of
the marginality of both Riehl and Freytag to the historical profession of
their time—and by extension to the many histories of that era's well-
known passion for history writing. The reasons for this marginality were
professional and methodological. Even by still-emergent professional
standards, neither Riehl nor Freytag was a member of the guild. Freytag,
of course, was a journalist and a novelist. Just prior to publication of the
first volume of the *Bilder,* he had produced his astonishingly successful
paean to middle-class and German virtues, *Soll und Haben* (1855), which
gave him instant and lasting fame in middle-class, book-reading households.[7] As the major editorial writer for the *Grenzboten,* he was also well
known in liberal-nationalist circles. Indeed, in the early 1860s he became
quite friendly with Treitschke through regular encounters in the "Kitzing"
watering hole in Leipzig. Their friendship did not survive Treitschke's
growing infatuation with Bismarck, to whom Freytag remained impla-
cably hostile—surprisingly hostile, in fact, considering his willingness to
throw overboard so many of his liberal convictions into the wake of
Prussian triumphalism.[8] In any case, Freytag's friendship with Treitschke
had little impact on either author's decade-long effort at writing the history of Germany. Treitschke, to put it mildly, had nothing to learn from
Freytag's historical methods, and Freytag expressed his own ambitions in
the field of history writing in almost parodically modest terms: the *Bilder,*
he wrote in its opening dedication, sought only to serve as a "comfortable
houseguest" (*bequemer Hausfreund*).[9]

The case against Riehl's professionalism is somewhat less open-and-
shut. Through the political patronage of King Maximilian II, Riehl was
appointed professor at the University of Munich in 1859. But the

---

7. The enduring popularity and sales history of this "rather better than mediocre
book" are treated briefly in T. E. Carter, "Freytag's *Soll und Haben:* A Liberal National
Manifesto as a Bestseller," *German Life and Letters* 21 (July 1968): 320–29. Carter characterizes it as "a book for the intelligent schoolboy" and reports that one of its main sources
of distribution has been, and continues to be, as a confirmation present.

8. There are passing references to their friendship and its cooling-off in Andreas
Dorpalen, *Heinrich von Treitschke* (New Haven, CT, 1957), 72, 187–88; on Freytag's
resolute opposition to Bismarck, see Walter Bussmann, "Gustav Freytag: Maßstäbe seiner
Zeitkritik," *Archiv für Kulturgeschichte* 34 (1952): 272–78.

9. Gustav Freytag, *Bilder aus der deutschen Vergangenheit,* 10th ed. (Leipzig,
1876), 1:vi.

Naturgeschichte was mainly written earlier, and as David Diephouse has rightly observed, its "discursive mixture of scholarly pretense and popular style" emerged from the experiences of journalism and studenthood, not professorial professionalism.[10] Insofar as he was regarded as an academic at all, Riehl's contemporaries saw him as a folklorist and possibly also as a music critic and historian. An ambitious young historian like Karl Lamprecht, although interested in Riehl's way of parsing social life, nevertheless chose not to study under him in Munich.[11] The decision is revealing of something besides Lamprecht's search for more encompassing systems than Riehl's. It indicates Riehl's maverick status in the academic world: he was not even important enough to be controversial. To put it more bluntly, he was an academic lightweight.

Nevertheless, in the 1890s, at the end of or after their long lives, both Freytag and Riehl began to achieve a kind of partial recognition in the professional historical community, which itself tells us much about their earlier invisibility. The reasons they were interesting to the contentious historical community of the 1890s represented two sides of a single coin: they had contributed to the amorphous field of *Kulturgeschichte* (cultural history), and they had distanced themselves from the orthodoxies of political history during its golden age. Neither could be said to have been state-centered in his depictions of the past, and both explored the backroads and forgotten corners of both past and present in order to achieve their desired effect. For a partisan like Georg Steinhausen, energetic defender of *Kulturgeschichte* in whatever form it took, the unprofessionalism of Freytag and Riehl was what made them so inspiring. Steinhausen credited Freytag's *Bilder,* with its generous use of the memoirs and correspondence of ordinary people, for giving him the idea to write a history of letter-writing.[12] It also seems to have been Steinhausen who created the cliché of a nineteenth-century cultural-historical triumvirate, consisting of Freytag, Riehl, and Jakob Burckhardt — an oddly senseless group of disparate unequals that is most notable for its exclusion of Karl Lamprecht.[13] Whatever might ultimately be said about their contribution to

---

10. David J. Diephouse, introduction to W. H. Riehl, *The Natural History of the German People,* ed. and trans. David J. Diephouse (Lewiston, NY, 1990), 7.

11. Roger Chickering, *Karl Lamprecht: A German Academic Life (1856–1915)* (Atlantic Highlands, NJ, 1993), 39.

12. Georg Steinhausen, "Gustav Freytags Bedeutung für die Geschichtswissenschaft," *Zeitschrift für Kulturgeschichte* 3 (1896): 1–20.

13. For instances of this formulation, see Georg Steinhausen, "Freytag, Burckhardt, Riehl und ihre Auffassung der Kulturgeschichte," *Neue Jahrbücher für das klassische Altertum, Geschichte und deutsche Literatur und für Pädagogik* 1 (1898): 448–58; Georg von Below, *Die deutsche Geschichtsschreibung von der Befreiungskriegen bis zu unseren Tagen, Geschichte und Kulturgeschichte* (Leipzig, 1916), 61–71; Heinrich von Srbik, *Geist und Geschichte vom deutschen Humanismus bis zur Gegenwart,* 2 vols. (Mu-

the field of *Kulturgeschichte,* Freytag and Riehl did indeed pursue their historical vision independent of any school of academic research. This independence, combined with the popularity of their work (itself a cause of professional suspicion and marginalization), makes their efforts at creating a historical past for the nation particularly interesting. "Historians," wrote Eugen Weber, "were the clerisy of the nineteenth century because it fell to them to rewrite foundation myths; and history was the theology of the nineteenth century because it provided societies cast loose from the moorings of custom and habit with new anchorage in a rediscovered — or reinvented — past."[14] We already know a good deal about the foundation myths of the German nation as written by the Prusso-German school, with its unstinting admiration for the victors. We know far less, however, about the mythmaking and national invention practiced in places and by persons apart from the university mandarins: secondary school teachers, amateurs, archivists, antiquarians, and writers of historical fiction and popular history. Whatever else they may have been, Freytag and Riehl were the leaders of *that* pack of pedagogues, pedants, and earnest patriots.

III.   Unity and Diversity: Riehl's *Natural History of the German People*

Riehl's *Naturgeschichte* is probably better known today in the English-speaking world than anything written by Gustav Freytag. This is due in part to a recent translation of this multivolume work into English; but more significantly, it is also the consequence of a diffuse process of rediscovering Riehl's idiosyncratic insights through recent studies as diverse as Mack Walker's *German Home Towns* and Joan Campbell's *Joy in Work, German Work.*[15] Riehl's *Naturgeschichte* is not really a history at all. It is a conglomeration of descriptions, anecdotes, generalizations, and a motley assortment of observations both penetrating and exasperating. Riehl assembled these elements into what he hoped would add up to — in the uncharacteristically pompous phrase of his subtitle — the "foundation for a German sociopolitics."[16] He thought of his work as having direct appli-

nich, 1951), 1:139; and Walter Goetz, *Historiker in meiner Zeit* (Cologne, 1957), 256. This cliché found its way into English-language literature by way of G. P. Gooch, *History and Historians in the Nineteenth Century* (Boston, 1959), 523–24.

14.   Eugen Weber, *My France: Politics, Culture, Myth* (Cambridge, MA, 1991), 23.

15.   Walker, *German Home Towns,* 1–3, 422–25; Joan Campbell, *Joy in Work, German Work: The National Debate, 1800–1945* (Princeton, NJ, 1989), 32–49, 53–55.

16.   One could render the German phrase *Grundlage einer deutschen Sozialpolitik* somewhat less noxious by translating it as "basis of a German social policy." The first translation is the one favored by Mack Walker.

cability to the practices of government and politics. In the end, his wish to bring the lessons of his careful observations of German life in the locality to bear on the workings of provincial administration was fulfilled in only a small way, through his meddlings in the affairs of the Bavarian Palatinate.[17] But his original vision was grander than that. Playing off a distinction between state and society common to a number of German social theorists, he lamented the lack of attention to his own brand of "social statistics" among scientists of the state. A more sensible administration and a more effective politics would emerge, he believed, if the men of state and party were able to see value in something other than their artificial and universalizing constructs of law and constitution.[18]

In pursuit of that goal, Riehl's "natural history" is dedicated in all its parts to the depiction of diversity. For Riehl, diversity was not an abstract term or even an ideal—though at times it was that too—but a simple acknowledgment of reality, the reflection of that spirit of "tremendous realism" that he believed characterized his own age (29). Riehl never doubted that a German character existed, or that a German political unity could and should exist. But the hallmark of his representation of that quality of Germanness was to emphasize its essential, not its incidental, tendencies toward differentiation and separation. Even while the forces of change created "impulses toward unity" in all aspects of German life, Riehl saw "separatist instincts" surviving everywhere, though often in unacknowledged, even clandestine ways (36–38). This instinct was itself no simple thing, but constitutive of many different kinds of political tendencies and social phenomena in German life. In his most forceful statement of this insight, Riehl wrote that "the impulse towards diversity and separatism in national life is Germany's greatest calamity and at the same time its crowning glory." That impulse had produced, on the one hand, the "freshness and originality of our cultural heritage, the ant-like energy of our industrial life, the dogged yet flexible powers of rejuvenation that enable the German spirit, when it appears checked on one front, to strive ahead even more on ten others." On the other hand, he continued, at the same time "one finds discord and strife, fragmentation, the misery of an often unyielding particularism" (39).

As he worked his way through the material of geography, social

---

17. On his brief foray into Bavarian policy implementation in the Rhenish Palatinate, see Celia Applegate, *A Nation of Provincials: The German Idea of Heimat* (Berkeley, CA, 1990). For an account of his role in the creation of a new *Gesellschaftswissenschaft*, see Andrew Lees, *Revolution and Reflection: Intellectual Change in Germany during the 1850s* (The Hague, 1974), 56–65.

18. *Natural History*, ed. Diephouse, 29–31. Subsequent page references in the text will be to this English edition.

classes, and history, Riehl's constant theme was the existence of the vari-
eties and differences that themselves constituted the object in question.
For Riehl, as for nearly every other social thinker of his time, the German
burgher was at the center of his hopes and fears for the future. That
burgher provided a "striking manifestation of that simultaneous impulse
toward diversification and unification" (208). The "German peasant" as a
general category was as much "a mere ethnographic formula as 'Germany' remains a mere geographical formula": among *actual* peasants,
"the most persistent differences of region and landscape have embedded
themselves" (163). In many contexts, the main point Riehl was making
becomes rather banal, for to identify diversity as the essential characteristic of German geography is surely little more than a statement of the
obvious. And yet Riehl consistently escaped banality through the originality of his characterizations of that diversity. At a time when many of his
contemporaries construed the "dualism" of German character in terms of
the contrast between north German Protestant sobriety and south German Catholic frivolity (or some variation on this theme), Riehl proposed
a tripartite division of north, middle, and south. In this scheme, the north
and south were both "centralized lands" and came to have certain essential features in common, in contrast to the "individualized" country of the
central German plateau. The only true dualism he recognized was one
common to all Germany: reverting to his main theme, this was for Riehl
the "paradox of a land and people at once homogeneous and unified and
also polymorphic and disparate" (104).

Riehl's approach to understanding national unity was thus mi-
crosocial and microhistorical: "unity and uniformity," he wrote, "are two
different things." The larger point is that Riehl was always the enemy of
the latter, not the former (87). In his warnings about artificial and lifeless
social constructs and in his recommendations about a properly animated
Sozialpolitik, he gives us, in George Eliot's admiring phrase, "a species of
inquiry into the specific conditions under which a healthy national life
could hope to prosper."[19] And whereas Riehl was inconsistent about the
degree of political intervention that would be required to restore or maintain this kind of health in national life, he never wavered in his sense of
what national health and vitality looked like. Rather than debating which
of Germany's regional cultures "ranks higher or lower," he wrote, we
should "be happy that we are blessed with" so many types of culture side
by side. "After all," he pointed out, "it is the development of every
separate group within the nation, with all their diversity, that serves to
guarantee the vitality of the nation as a whole" (115). Or more forcefully

---

19. George Eliot, "The Natural History of German Life: Riehl," in *The Writings of
George Eliot,* 25 vols. (Boston, 1909), 21:241–42.

still: "the very nature of the German community precludes attempts at homogenization, whether social or political." Hence Riehl believed that whereas "every German patriot yearns for the consolidation" of the entire fatherland into "a single political and diplomatic unit," it would nevertheless be "an offense against the ethos of this German nation" if Germans tried to achieve social or cultural singularity as well: one must not "lump together in a single category all the various types of community, of civil and societal structures, to be found in its individual states and regions" (77).

For Riehl, the problem of aggregation — of putting this all together — was thus no problem at all. If Germany's politicians and leaders would simply accept that diversity was the essential characteristic of unity, then they could cease to fear diversity, cease to fret that there was no there there, or that Germany would turn out to be, in Georg Herwegh's phrase, "an empty shell." Directing his advice to "the conservative statesman" in particular, he noted that "in Germany, if anywhere, the strength of the nation is surely rooted in the great diversity of character traits that distinguish different regions and classes" (178). Riehl's whole sensibility cried out against schemes that attempted the artificial dissemination of some spurious national character. Thus we should not be surprised that it was Riehl who almost single-handedly invented the bogeyman of the radical schoolteacher as the agent of revolutionary contagion.[20] Yet he was no more sympathetic to the Prussianized schoolteacher spreading nationalist fantasies: "there is simply no such thing as a universal public education," he wrote; the task of the village schoolmaster should be to assist people "in realizing their own authentic character" (179). Admiring though he could be of Prussia's accomplishments in its own sphere of action, Riehl had no expectation that people's "authentic character" was identical to that of any number of other equally German alternatives.

How, then, was the German nation ever to know itself? Although Riehl never posed the question in quite these terms, his book served up myriad suggestions as to how Germans might, in effect, imagine the national community. Indeed, his tome is something of a primer in learning how to be German, and as one proceeds through its lessons, Riehl's method and his message increasingly overlap and intertwine. In an early section devoted to "trade secrets for the study of folklore," he introduced readers to the importance of travel, preferably by foot — a theme he reiterated throughout the book (42). Riehl himself never seems to have traveled anywhere outside of German-speaking central Europe, initially because of insufficient funds. Perhaps he shared the opinion of

---

20. Schleunes, *Schooling and Society*, 129.

John Mortimer's irascible father in *Journeys around My Father,* who declares that "nothing narrows the mind like foreign travel." In any case, he certainly believed that nothing improved the mind like extended walking tours in one's own native land, and he himself walked endlessly on the backroads that came to symbolize for him everything that was right about social life — functional enough to move people and goods from place to place, but not too fast, never too fast to miss all the in-between spaces and places (55–56).[21] No uncritical fan of railways, which he blamed for "here and there" eliminating "local peculiarities," he nevertheless recognized their more important contribution to "rendering such differences obvious and apparent to all" (153). In blandly social-scientific terms, one might identify this as the spread of social communication that comes in the wake of modernization and brings about nationalization (all of which was perfectly obvious to Riehl). But Riehl never lost sight of the cognitive dimension of such change, the impact on everyday ways of knowing and perceiving that it all entailed: "[I]n this day and age," he wrote, "when only a short journey separates the Berliner from Vienna and Munich, or the Rhinelander from the Baltic coast, or the coastal dweller from the heart of the interior, and people can see for themselves what basic differences distinguish them from their new neighbors, such bald categories as northern and southern Germany pale in significance." Indeed, he admonished, "if we are to become mature enough for national unification, we must first mature in our understanding and appreciation of differences in national character" (153). Nationalization, he thought in his more hopeful moments, did not have to result in uniformity.

One cannot help thinking that much of the popular appeal of Riehl's *Naturgeschichte* lay in its capacity to take the reader along on such a journey over the backroads, pausing — as his "trade secrets" suggest — to make direct inquiries of the "educated man," indirect inquiries of the less educated man, and to engage in rambling conversation with the local peasants (43). Riehl tells the reader how he does it, then he does it, then he urges the reader to do the same. "We immerse ourselves in small details," he wrote, "having all the while begun with the image of a totality to which we are striving to return." "We ramble about in open country so as to learn how to ramble about in the singularly dusty world of books" (45). We visit ruins, though not in a mood of romantic gushing (*Schwärmerei*); we go to folk festivals; we read novels

---

21. His marvelous sections on "fields and forests" and "roads and paths" in *Land und Leute,* one of the books of the *Naturgeschichte,* call to mind the work of Wolfgang Schivelbusch, *The Railway Journey* (Leamington Spa, 1986), and Simon Schama, *Landscape and History* (New York, 1995).

and newspapers and feuilletons; but above all we hike and hike and hike. The genius of Riehl's presentation is to suggest just how *ordinary* these "countless voyages of discovery into the German heartland" actually are, and how *accessible* they are to anyone at any time.

To be sure, Riehl's scathing account of life in "artificial" towns and cities, and his unkind analyses of the deracinated burghers and the proletarians (both poor and well-to-do) who inhabited them, would seem to exclude a rather large number of people from access to this "German heartland." Nevertheless, one should remember that his book was directed at precisely these sorts of people. Riehl knew the peasants would not be reading it, nor indeed would the *authentic* town dwellers, who, he observed, cared virtually nothing for life outside their own enclaves. No, the intended readership was always those people who Riehl felt were in danger of being lost to unreflective modernity. It was on them that he urged these journeys of discovery, for in the best German tradition they would be at the same time journeys of *self*-discovery. In this context, it would not be inappropriate to consider Riehl a patron saint of the guidebooks and weekend excursions that came to occupy such a central role in urban middle-class life by the end of the century. Cities, Riehl thought, were like encyclopedias: they gave the illusion of gathering everything together in one easy reference guide. But in a phrase that could be an epithet to Riehl's entire method, message, and conception of the national community, he warned his readers that "to see everything at once is to see nothing" (68).

IV. Erasing the Region: Freytag's *Pictures from the German Past*

With Gustav Freytag's *Bilder aus der deutschen Vergangenheit* we come to a work more conventionally historical in its goals and its methods. The relation of this work to the era of German unification and to Freytag's other activities as novelist and journalist is surely no mystery. Daniel Fulda has written that Freytag was "virtually the epitome of the genre-typical link between literature, scholarly historiography and, through his political activities, orientation towards the present."[22] Though that characterization overstates his ties to academic historians, it correctly depicts the links between the *Bilder* and Freytag's novels of bourgeois life: *Soll und Haben* on the one hand and, on the other, what we might call the fictional realization of the *Bilder,* the cycle of historical

---

22. Daniel Fulda, "Telling German History: Forms and Functions of the Historical Narrative against the Background of the National Unifications," in *1870/71–1989/90: German Unifications and the Change of Literatur Discourse,* ed. Walter Pape (Berlin, 1993), 199.

novels *Die Ahnen* (1873–81). Fulda's observation also captures the quality of Freytag's political engagement, which he forthrightly proclaimed as essential to his writing of the *Bilder:* "It is the right of the living to give meaning to all of the past according to the needs and the claims of their own times."[23] The specific meaning Freytag found in the past was the slow development and ultimately the full-blown emergence of the German middle classes. These middle classes were particularly interesting not in and of themselves but as the most perfect exemplars of the German spirit (*Volksseele*) and as the carriers of the movement toward freedom and enlightenment, both of which Freytag believed to be within reach of the German people in his own day. The *Bilder* thus directly reflected his liberal nationalism and his all-too-common conviction that liberal-nationalist hopes had been realized in the triumph of Hohenzollern Prussia.

Freytag has been called the popularizer of the *kleindeutsch* school of historians, someone who "on the whole" agreed with its view of present and past. But such a claim does not do justice to the originality and piquancy of Freytag's presentation.[24] For, prone though he was to making Rankean proclamations about the highest achievement of the folk spirit in the German state, et cetera and so on (e.g., 4:201), in Freytag's account of two thousand years of "German" history, the emotional weight lay entirely with individuals, and hardly at all with the state. The *Bilder* are in fact a series of portraits of individuals who had lived in central Europe and had left behind evidence of their lives — *Lebensäusserungen,* in Freytag's term — in the form of memoirs, letters, travel descriptions, confessions, poems, lays and songs, and other kinds of stories. Freytag had collected most of his sources from the *Monumenta Germaniae,* which he wove together with accounts of the political, social, and economic conditions in which they lived. His portraits are still vivid and convincing, though his narrative bridges are somewhat less so. Whereas each person served as a stand-in for the national soul — "in the soul of each person we find also a portrait in miniature of the collective personality of a people" (1:21) — Freytag gave them the fullest possible space to express themselves, allowing the national soul itself to remain for the most part implicit.

Nor were these people "great," in the Carlylean or any other sense. Although the usual cast of characters made their appearances in his

---

23. Freytag, *Bilder,* 4:489. All subsequent page references in the text will be to this edition, the tenth, published in Leipzig in 1876.

24. Fulda, "Telling German History," 202; see also von Below, *Deutsche Geschichtsschreibung,* 71. Below seems to have been still in the grip of his animus against Lamprecht when he not only corralled Freytag into the Rankean/Treitschkean enclosure but called the *Bilder* "the best German cultural history" that the nation possessed.

pages — Charlemagne, Luther, Frederick the Great — Freytag did not, literally, give them a voice, and he spent as much time enumerating their limitations as their achievements. As Walter Bussmann has shown, Freytag admired the work of Friedrich Wolf and Karl Lachmann on the sources of epic poetry in the total life of a people. Freytag was convinced of Wolf's thesis about a collective authorship to the Homerian epics and looked to draw parallel conclusions about German greatness.[25] The "no-single-author" theory, when applied to something as amorphous as a national spirit over an alleged two-thousand-year period of development, was certainly easy enough to prove; yet at the same time, it did push Freytag away from relying on a string of political leaders, generals, and kings to create his narrative. Early in his career, he wrote that it was "no sure sign of national strength, if a people brought forth many important personages." One should look, rather, to the development of "a great variety of characters."[26] This emphasis on ordinary people, together with his almost amateurish approach to the evidence, created further distance between Freytag and the *kleindeutsch* school of historians. He had not set out to tell the story of the rise of a mighty state, nor was he much interested in grubbing around in ministerial archives. And although he occasionally paused to praise a Prussian king, Walter Goetz was not incorrect in suggesting that Freytag's "cultural historical [*kulturgeschichtliche*] orientation" stood "equally distant from the *kleindeutsch* as from the *großdeutsch*" camp. Goetz also hit the mark when he observed that Freytag's "attachment to the nation consisted of a love of everything that the German people had endured and created in the course of their history."[27]

That said, we need to return to the question of how, in the absence of a consistent attention to state power, Freytag resolved the problem of making a whole out of his many stories. After all, two thousand years of vignettes, even if most came from the final three hundred of those years, present a considerable challenge to the writer seeking narrative continuity and coherence. In *Die Ahnen,* Freytag solved the problem by creating a series of fictive family relationships over the sprawl of history. But the *Bilder,* committed as it was to the genre of historical nonfiction, could make no such genealogical leaps. It relied instead on three themes of historical development: the emergence of a fully independent individual, the growth of public life and popular participation, and the eclipse

---

25. Bussmann, "Freytag," 261–87. There is also, of course, the obvious influence of Herder and Hegel. All that is spelled out in Ludwig Brauns, "Gustav Freytags Stellung in der Kulturgeschichtsschreibung nach seinen *Bildern aus der deutschen Vergangenheit*" (Ph.D. diss., University of Bonn, 1921).

26. Cited in Bussmann, "Freytag," 272.

27. Goetz, *Historiker,* 99.

of aristocracy and peasantry by the rising sun of the middle class. The pursuit of each of these themes involved Freytag in a systematic and (one can only assume) purposeful erasure of German regional and ethnic diversity. In startling contrast to Riehl's obsessive concern to draw attention to diversity—of places, of groups, of flora and fauna, of custom, of speech—Freytag simply had no comment on the matter. The differences that interested him all revolved around the individual personality: his national whole was a mass (Riehl would say undifferentiated and promiscuous mixture) of personalities, distinguished only according to their emotional, intellectual, spiritual, and political orientations. Thus the *Bilder* sought to depict "a number of paths of German character development" but admitted that it was unable to depict them all (4:3). To put it differently, Freytag's people all came from specific places—geographically he covered German territory from Lübeck to Konstanz, from Osnabrück to Breslau—but none of them were *of* the places from which they came. Indeed, as Lynne Tatlock has pointed out, regional dialect completely disappeared in Freytag's transcriptions of the memoirs, diaries, and letters that made up his portraiture: everyone spoke in High German.[28]

In these ways Freytag effectively erased "region," "place," and all intermediate social groupings and phenomena existing between an individual (or the public) on the one hand, and the state on the other. This strategy had its counterpart in Freytag's consistent denigration of any form of "narrowness," "narrow-mindedness" (*Kleinlichkeit*), or "corporatist distinctions" (*ständische Besonderheiten*) (4:8, 146). This attitude should not of course surprise us: it is simply a measure of the degree to which Freytag, as a liberal nationalist and in common with all European bourgeois elites since the Enlightenment, drew on a rich vocabulary that stigmatized the provincial, the particular, and the parochial. But as did Riehl's emphasis on diversity, it raises the question as to how one is to "know" the nation. Even if one assumed, as Freytag seemed to, that all middle-class Protestants carried the German spirit in them whether they knew it or not, he feared that a lingering "provincial spirit" often prevented people from becoming fully acquainted with the "great life of their nation" (4:3). The solution for Freytag was every bit as bound up with what he was doing in the *Bilder* and in his professional life generally as Riehl's solution was bound up with his practice as folklorist, journalist, and all-German hiker. Riehl had suggested that to know the nation was simply a matter of opening one's door and taking a

---

28. Lynne Tatlock, "Realist Historiography and the Historiography of Realism: Gustav Freytag's *Bilder aus der deutschen Vergangenheit,*" *German Quarterly* 63 (winter 1990): 62.

walk, or, for the city dweller, taking a train to somewhere. For Freytag, the key was books—his own included.

Freytag's unalloyed enthusiasm for the power of education and enlightenment and their capacity to lead Germans to their national "selves" seems an apt illustration of Riehl's comment that Germany was "a nation made up of dozens of clans, small towns, and social groupings, and at the same time, a nation of scholars" (38). Riehl feared scholars because of their tendency to encourage statesmen to bulldoze over social barriers and distinctions in the name of unity and good administration. But Freytag was just such a scholar—a scholar, moreover, who rejoiced in the capacity of books to create the nation or, as he might have put it himself, to develop that capacity for general thought that enabled people—that *had* in fact enabled him as a schoolboy in Silesia—to see beyond their narrow little worlds.[29] One of the key chapters of the *Bilder,* "And Then There Was Light" ("Es wird Licht"), began with a tribute to the printing press as something that created relationships among individuals and peoples. It then chronicled the spread of education—"the purpose of the book" (*der Zweck des Buches*)—throughout the burgher class.

Freytag's account of the origins and spread of Pietism amounted to a variation on this theme. Not education—to which, regrettably, the Pietists showed unjustified suspicion—but simple travel, communication, and the "meeting of like-minded people" encouraged a sense of nationhood. These "pious souls throughout all Germany" were responsible, thought Freytag, for reviving a commonality of mind after the horrifying period of fragmentation, suffering, and isolation during the Thirty Years' War. His representative individuals—Johanna Eleonora Petersen and Johann Wilhelm Petersen, as revealed through their autobiographical fragments—led lives of "traveling around and constant writing" (*Umherreisen und Schriftstellerei*) (4:59). For Freytag these were the two activities essential to bringing the national soul to maturity. One suspects that Benedict Anderson or Ernst Gellner, though they might put the case somewhat differently, would not disagree with Freytag here. For in stark contrast to Riehl's notion of travel, Freytag's was entirely concerned with what Mack Walker called "moving and doing," making connections with other people engaged in the same kinds of activities—that is, creating likenesses, not investigating difference. Freytag also waxed eloquent on the industriousness of the Pietists in establishing the truly "national institutions" of orphanages across the

---

29. For further evidence about how Freytag construed his childhood, see Gustav Freytag, *Erinnerungen aus meinem Leben* (Leipzig, 1887), 54–94. The power of education to lift one out of provincial stagnation was in fact the major theme of his memoirs. See also Adalbert von Hanstein, *Gustav Freytag: Gedächtnis-Rede* (Heidelberg, 1895), 5.

land (4:24). Freytag's curious enthusiasm for orphanages becomes clearer in the later chapter "And Then There Was Light." There Freytag credited the Pietist network of orphanages with providing a constant supply of young men available for teacher training. As teachers, they became the advance guard of the nation, spreading education through the cities and towns (4:122–23). One could not have invented a paradigm of "national man" better designed to illustrate the profound gulf separating Freytag from Riehl. On one side stands Freytag's orphaned schoolteacher-patriot, rootless offspring of an unplaced "national institution," fatherless, and thus dedicated only to the fatherland. On the other side stand Riehl's interlocutors — peasants and hometownsmen, for the most part — unmoved by orphans, unimpressed by schoolteachers, and determined to assert their own particularities against all trumped-up notions of the general good.

Freytag's understanding of the power of the word — especially its dual capacity to "draw things together" and to reveal the mystery of the national self with special clarity — informed more than just his accounts of historical personalities and developments. It extended to his practice of "realist historiography" in the *Bilder*.[30] Freytag fashioned his sketches and portraits with the novelist's sensibility, amending the original language of his texts to adhere to common usage in nineteenth-century Germany. Thus he rewrote archaic expressions, translated Latin, and suppressed dialect, all the while assuring his readers that the texts had been reproduced verbatim. Lynne Tatlock argues that these alterations, together with his introduction of the memoirs and letters with praise for the qualities their authors shared with "the narrators of nineteenth-century realism," created a gloss of authenticity over a practice of invention and revision of the past. The novelist-historian himself became the creator, not simply the chronicler, of a "German prose adequate to express German experience."[31]

Tatlock interprets this effort in the context of literary debates; hence she sees Freytag's *Bilder* mainly as an argument for the realist agenda in literature, part of an effort to win "prestige" for literary realism by associating it "with programs of cultural nationalism."[32] But these "programs of cultural nationalism" were themselves not self-evidently prestigious, nor for that matter were they faits accomplis. Freytag's *Bilder* did not so much constitute an effort to win prestige for literary realism as it sought to promote cultural nationalism itself, to disseminate this particular mythology about the past into as large a

---

30. The term is Lynne Tatlock's, whose analysis of the affinities between Freytag's novelistic and historical representations informs much of my discussion.

31. Tatlock, "Realist Historiography," 60–64.

32. Ibid., 68.

number of middle-class households as possible. And from that perspective, accessibility and believability—as Tatlock points out, both lodestars of realist fiction—were critically important. Freytag was clear about his intended audience: he called the *Bilder* his "modest illustrations of our political history," and he wrote that he had not loaded it down with footnotes because—to reiterate a point raised previously—the book "has no higher ambition than to serve as a comfortable houseguest" (1:vi). Treitschke remarked, approvingly if patronizingly, that the *Bilder* was "one of the few works of history which women can understand and read with pleasure."[33] Women of course were the great novel readers of the nineteenth century. Hence one could argue that Freytag's *Bilder,* with its novelistic form and its generous number of stories about women among the historical vignettes, had an implicit mission to the middle-class German woman. Such a claim would require further investigation and elaboration. But compared to Riehl's manly program of hiking and hobnobbing with strangers, a kind of gender inclusivity is certainly suggested by the *Bilder*'s promotion of genteel travel, language, reading, and storytelling as the means of access to the nation. Such inclusivity would surely have been distasteful to the patriarchal Riehl.

V. Conclusions

Drawing together the threads of this extended comparison, how might these two "conglomerations" of pieces of the German past instruct us in our own efforts to assimilate the findings of recent regional history? One ought to acknowledge right away that neither text and neither author had a particularly beneficent influence on the further development of German national culture. Riehl's social conservatism, his choleric attitude toward urbanization and the new working classes, and his hostility toward what a liberal like Freytag would call "social progress" made him a prime candidate for rediscovery and racialist exploitation in the 1920s and 1930s. Freytag's determined optimism about the inevitability of Prussian-led liberal reform, which he held against all odds, made him, too, an unlovely figure, complacent, self-deceived, and increasingly passive in public life. Most disturbing of all, both men contributed immeasurably to the cultural legitimation and spread of antisemitic stereotypes.[34] Every copy of *Soll und Haben* clutched in the hand of a teenage confirmant was another argument for the German Jew as an essentially

---

33. Ibid., 61.

34. The antisemitism of these writers, particularly Freytag, is the subject of much recent scholarship. See, for instance, George Mosse, *Germans and Jews: The Right, the Left, and the Search for a "Third Force" in Pre-Nazi Germany* (New York, 1970), 61–76.

foreign figure, capable of assimilation only at the cost of the total abandonment of his Jewishness. For Freytag especially, though less prominently in the *Bilder* than elsewhere in his work, the ability to deploy an
array of typical German individuals as constitutive of a national whole
relied on the propagation of "typical" non-Germans, whether Poles or
Jews, whose degenerate presence clarified what it was to be German.
Similarly, although Riehl was deeply committed to internalist definitions
of the German character and rarely relied on unflattering portraits of
other nationalities to highlight specifically German virtues, he too saved
a place of dishonor in his "wanderlogue" for that quintessentially internal stranger, the Jewish merchant.

These parallels notwithstanding, it still seems possible to make useful distinctions between the ways Riehl's and Freytag's models of national aggregation were (and were not) able to make sense of the process
that unfolded in the years following political unification. From this perspective, Riehl's assessment of the "separatist instincts in society" and
the capacity of intermediate social groups, whatever their principle of
conformity, to persist and to play a significant role in any common
political life surely has more to say about such phenomena as "re-
regionalization," religious revivals, and lower-middle-class volatility
than Freytag's simple model of the individual and the state. Had Riehl
cared to wander outside of his native land, he might have noticed that
these same phenomena of "self-generated divisions and distinctions,"
"separatist instincts," and diverse geographies and cultures were characteristic of the rest of Europe as well. For his part, Freytag in the *Bilder*
made himself the cheerleader of modernization, celebrating the gradual
decay of narrowness and predicting the triumph of individual freedom
and self-fulfillment in the context of a powerful national state. The
limitations of this worldview, which are so obvious to us in a historical
text like the *Bilder,* also dogged the proponents of modernization theory
in their effort to explain the transformation of European societies in the
era of nation-building. As we look for ways to account for the persistence of social segmentation by region, the development of specifically
regional political milieus, or the differentiated strategies of economic
organization transcending national boundaries, we could do worse than
to reread Riehl's *Naturgeschichte.* At the very least it would remind us of
one of those delicious ironies of modernity, that the instruments of
change (in this case, the book itself) can subvert their own purposes.
Indeed, the nation itself may exemplify the same irony more perfectly.
Its promise of an organic community—intact, ancient, and capable of
rescuing people from their own dislocation—turned out to be at the
same time the inner condition of modernity and, at least for a time, the
guarantor of its endurance.

Imagined Regions: The Construction of Traditional, Democratic, and Other Identities

Thomas Kühne

I. Regions in German History

Regional political culture, regional political traditions, regional disparities, regionalism — the terminology of space centering on the "region"
has been experiencing a boom in the historiography of the last two
decades. The integration of this academic trend into broader social usage is unmistakable. The stimulus of using "the region" as a cognitive
category in politics, administration, the economy, the media, science,
and culture began in the 1960s; but it continued more vigorously in the
1970s.

   The broad social resonance of the region has been explained more
than once as a compensatory phenomenon. Hermann Lübbe, for example, views it as a form of "political historicism." As a response to the
spread of "homogeneous structures" associated with the "acceleration of
civilizing change,"[1] emphasis on the region represents a reaction to actual or perceived tendencies toward centralization and uniformity. However, the "return of the regional"[2] is not simply backward-looking. The
"paths" of the *Heimat* movement and of regionalism do not lead away
from modernity, but rather to its very core, for they are both intimately
connected to that inherently negative dimension of modernity that corresponds to the concept of "alienation." In this context, alienation repre-

---

   1. Hermann Lübbe, "Politischer Historismus: Zur Philosophie des Regionalismus," *Politische Vierteljahresschrift* 20 (1979): 9. Corresponding to the conception of this
essay as a "think-piece," I have opted against providing extensive bibliographical references.
   2. Rolf Lindner, ed., *Die Wiederkehr des Regionalen: Über die Formen kultureller
Identität* (Frankfurt a. M., 1994).

sents a "spatial category, distinguishing between one's own sphere and that of the other, between proximity and distance."[3]

The renewed currency of the region as a historiographical category can also be understood as a countermovement. In particular, regional analysis has been directed against approaches emphasizing modernization theory, structuralist perspectives, and those narratives limited to the politics of "great men" and metropolitan institutions. In the 1960s and 1970s, German social history remained rooted in these categories, with which practitioners of historical social science believed they could explain the German *Sonderweg* and the long-term causes of the catastrophe of 1933. However, by the 1970s and increasingly in the 1980s, *Regionalgeschichte* took up the task of differentiating and challenging these overly crude interpretations. The impetus provided by regional history has thrived on the conscious juxtaposition of abstract political history from above with the authenticity of politics from below, which the historian clearly can analyze only on a small scale. Without doubt, this momentum has sustained extraordinarily rich research. Most conspicuously, regional historical studies have demonstrated that there is no such thing as *the* authoritarian German *Sonderweg,* nor even a Prusso-German *Sonderweg.* Instead, Germany encompassed numerous—regionally established—democratic "*Sonderwege,*" and many political traditions pointed not only toward 1933 but also toward 1949 or even 1989.

Nevertheless, this historiography has not proved itself immune to the tendency to idealize small lost worlds. This tendency accounts for some of the decidedly antimodern features of society's enthusiasm for "the region."[4] Frequently, deploying the concept of region serves as a magic formula, with which one can then attempt to explain all sorts of things. To be sure, it may shed new light on old questions concerning the relationship between "traditional," parochial, conservative trends on the one hand, and "modern," national, and progressive elements in German history on the other. Too often, however, to invoke "the region" is in practice to limit oneself to challenging the "myths of centralization"[5] or modernization, without substituting in their place something new. Despite isolated methodological forays by Peter Steinbach, Karl Rohe, and Alf Mintzel,[6] the expansion of regional historical research

---

3. Wolfgang Lipp, "Heimatbewegung, Regionalismus: Pfade aus der Moderne?" in *Kultur und Gesellschaft,* ed. Friedhelm Neidhardt, M. Rainer Lepsius, and Johannes Weiß (Opladen, 1986), 343–44.

4. Cf. Lipp, "Heimatbewegung," 334, 336, 338, 343.

5. Cf. Karl Schmitt, "Parteien und regionale politische Traditionen: Eine Einführung," in *Parteien und regionale politische Traditionen in der Bundesrepublik Deutschland,* ed. Dieter Oberndörfer and Karl Schmitt (Berlin, 1991), 9, passim.

6. See Thomas Kühne, "Wahlrecht—Wahlverhalten—Wahlkultur: Tradition und

and its substantial scientific yield stand in curious contrast to the markedly underdeveloped insistence on a theoretical framework. Even a precise conceptualization of the terms listed at the outset of this essay is entirely lacking in the literature.[7]

To date we have learned a great deal about regional differences in political attitudes and behavior, at least as far as these can be gathered from such indicators as election returns, the evolution of party systems, biographies of political deputies, or the willingness to strike. We now know that the grassroots politicization (*Fundamentalpolitisierung*) of German society—the great problem of German politics in the nineteenth and twentieth centuries—was a process that occurred in different places at widely varying speeds and in greatly differing forms. However, at present we know very little about the relative importance of the category of "region" in the political thinking, perceptions, and actions of individuals and groups. In the future, such topics might better be investigated by means of a regional analysis that is inspired by the aims and methods of cultural history. For no conception of the region, whether German or non-German, historical or contemporary, can manage without a "cognitive-emotional component." As Detlef Briesen and Jürgen Reulecke have written: "Whether a territory can be considered a region" will largely depend on "whether the people living there accept this space as a region and identify with it. Thus, essentially, the region is a mental construct."[8]

The current predicament of regional studies lies in the fact that they rarely reflect on the constructed quality of the region itself. Regions are artefacts. As such, they can be "produced" in fundamentally different ways, by researchers or by historical protagonists. The real problem stems from conflating these two processes. The way a historian conceives or defines a historical region—in order, say, to limit the scope of his or her investigation—is too often presented as historical reality itself.[9]

Innovation in der historischen Wahlforschung," *Archiv für Sozialgeschichte* 33 (1993): 481–547, esp. 512ff. and 532ff.

7. Cf. Detlef Briesen, "Region, Regionalismus, Regionalgeschichte—Versuch einer Annäherung aus der Perspektive der neueren und Zeitgeschichte," in *Region und Regionsbildung in Europa: Konzeptionen der Forschung und empirische Befunde,* ed. Gerhard Brunn (Baden-Baden, 1996), 151–62.

8. Detlef Briesen and Jürgen Reulecke, "Stand und Perspektiven einer neueren Regionalgeschichte," *Informationen zur Raumentwicklung* 11 (1993): i–iv, esp. ii. Cf. Hartmut Voit, "Regionale Identität im vereinigten Deutschland: Chancen und Probleme," in *Sachsen im Kaiserreich: Politik, Wirtschaft und Gesellschaft im Umbruch,* ed. Simone Lässig and Karl Heinrich Pohl (Weimar, 1996), 395–410, esp. 406–7.

9. For this and the following, see Hans Heinrich Blotevogel, Günter Heinritz, and Herbert Popp, " 'Regionalbewußtsein': Zum Stand der Diskussion um einen Stein des Anstoßes," *Geographische Zeitschrift* 77 (1989): 65–88; and Hans Heinrich Blotevogel,

II.   The Region as a Construct of Research

As a methodological artefact, the region is a construct used by scholars "to confer order upon reality."[10] The determination of what constitutes a region derives from the interest of researchers in geographically localized and isolated manifestations of one or more selected characteristics. "All those areas where a particular attribute shows a *similar* manifestation are spatially lumped together and interpreted in their entirety as a 'region.'"[11] A classic example of this form of regional study—that is, one based on the principle of similarity—is the cartographic branch of electoral sociology associated with André Siegfried.[12] The regions (or zones of political opinion) "produced" by electoral sociologists are homogeneous, in terms either of one specific factor or, often, of multiple, overlapping factors, such as voting patterns or social structure. This process of analysis, however, merely abstracts the territorial consciousness of the protagonists from such factors. For example, researchers prefer not to explain the homogeneity of regional voting patterns in "cultural" terms at all; rather, they refer to such "natural" factors as socio-structural or geographical circumstances. Apart from William Brustein,[13] one of the most fervent representatives of this approach in Germany is Heinrich Best. Best's "map of political interests" (*interessenpolitische Landkarte*) of early industrial Germany is based on the regional differentiation of petitions concerning trade policy submitted to the Paulskirche in 1848–49.[14]

An expressly national (or at least supraregional) scope of analysis is characteristic of this type of regional study. Regional deviations or *Sonderwege* become the focus of interest only insofar as they are elements that interfere with national development. In this context, a well-

"Auf dem Wege zu einer 'Theorie der Regionalität': Die Region als Forschungsobjekt der Geographie," in *Region,* ed. Brunn, 44–68. Peter Weichhart, *Raumbezogene Identität: Bausteine zu einer Theorie räumlich-sozialer Kognition und Identifikation* (Stuttgart, 1990), is indispensable.

10. Blotevogel, "Wege," 60, and more generally 58–60.

11. Peter Weichhart, "Die Region—Chimäre, Artefakt oder Strukturprinzip sozialer Systeme," in *Region,* ed. Brunn, 25–43, 29.

12. Cf. Kühne, "Wahlrecht," 499ff.

13. William Brustein, *The Social Origins of Political Regionalism: France, 1849–1981* (Berkeley, CA, 1988).

14. Heinrich Best, "Die regionale Differenzierung interessenpolitischer Orientierungen im frühindustriellen Deutschland—ihre Ursachen und ihre Auswirkungen auf politische Entscheidungsprozesse," in *Industrialisierung und Raum: Studien zur regionalen Differenzierung im Deutschland des 19. Jahrhunderts,* ed. Rainer Fremdling and Richard Tilly (Stuttgart, 1979), 251–77, cit. 259. Cf. Heinrich Best, "Politische Regionen in Deutschland: Historische (Dis)Kontinuitäten," in *Parteien,* ed. Oberndörfer and Schmitt, 39–64.

known pattern of interpretation considers regional fragmentation as a factor impeding the parliamentarization of the *Kaiserreich*.[15] For example, party-political studies view the Poles as a prime example of a "regional" party in the Second Empire. This classification corresponds to contemporaries' view of the Prusso-German authoritarian state in which the Poles, situated on the border with Russia, were seen as an element of strategic uncertainty. The Poles, however, did not consider themselves a regional movement within the German nation-state at all. Rather, their enormously successful efforts at political mobilization during election campaigns, and thus their ability to act as a leaven in the grassroots politicization of German society, were connected to their self-perception as a group whose common linguistic and national heritage spanned political borders.

Though less apparent, the nation is nevertheless very powerful as an analytical referent in the mainstream of regional history. Such analysis proceeds from a conception of the region that is geared toward the actions and sometimes the mentalities of protagonists in a certain area. But it hardly ever investigates the actors' *conception* of this territory in its own right. As noted previously, for a number of reasons scholars restrict the scope of historical problems they examine by using spatial criteria. They do so because some problems cannot be adequately examined on the macro level, because the source material does not sustain study on a grander plane, or because the researcher believes that in the selected region, a specific historical problem has manifested itself very conspicuously. In contrast to the construction of disparate political regions from a bird's-eye view, regional historians commonly claim that the demarcation of their subject area is historically justifiable due to the spatially concentrated interaction of the protagonists. In most cases, however, the selection of subject areas is based on the political, administrative, economic, or geographical specifics of the research project. For instance, the study may focus on communities, administrative districts, electoral constituencies, provinces, or federal states; but it may also focus on economic areas or "historical landscapes" (*historische Landschaften*).[16] For the most part, historians leave in doubt, or fail to ask, whether and to what extent inhabitants conceived of themselves as living in a "region": How did they actually act and interact with other protagonists inside this area — and also perhaps with those outside it? In short,

---

15. For a summary, see Gerhard A. Ritter, *Die deutschen Parteien, 1830–1914: Parteien und Gesellschaft im konstitutionellen Regierungssystem* (Göttingen, 1985), 30–32, 50, passim.

16. For a fruitful example of recent party history, see Lothar Gall and Dieter Langewiesche, eds., *Liberalismus und Region: Zur Geschichte des deutschen Liberalismus im 19. Jahrhundert* (Munich, 1995).

the construction of fixed "regions of interaction" may be indispensable as a question of practical investigative technique; but it cannot adequately compensate for the fact that people and organizations create not one but a "multiplicity of regions." Such regions "usually do not take the form of a well-ordered territorial mosaic, but rather reveal complex mutual overlappings and interpenetrations."[17]

III. Regional Political Culture as "Reality"

Currently, the most sophisticated theoretical reflections on studies of regional political culture have been advanced by Karl Rohe. He has raised the question of how specific sociocultural communities base their party-political preferences on their experiences, worldviews, habits, ways of life, and, not least, ideology proper. The chief assumption here is *not* that specific social structural features, which can usually be measured quantitatively, correspond to particular political preferences, but rather that these political preferences will be determined through a subjective interpretation of those features. The manner in which that subjective interpretation occurs, however, cannot be analyzed exclusively with quantitative methods (unless one is sounding current public opinion by means of polls). With respect to political culture, Rohe distinguishes this substantive aspect (*Inhaltsaspekt*) from the aspects of expression and process (*Ausdrucks- und Prozeßaspekt*). The aspect of expression denotes crystallizations of substance (content), for instance in the form of a certain political vocabulary or ritual. The aspect of process describes the updating and "maintenance" of political culture, especially by political elites.[18] Rohe emphasizes — rightly — the central role of elites in dealing with cleavages and in translating sociostructural conflicts into the political system.[19] He focuses therefore on the levels of mediation between parties and political elites on the one hand, and the sociomoral and cultural basis on the other. In this sense he speaks of "political coalitions" between voters and elites. He also distinguishes between practiced socioculture — the experienced, natural, internalized culture — and interpretive culture: the discursively generated, mediated, and conscious political culture that requires constant renewal.[20]

Using the example of the Ruhrgebiet, Rohe and many other scholars

---

17. Blotevogel, "Wege," 59.

18. Karl Rohe, "Politische Kultur und ihre Analyse: Probleme und Perspektiven der politischen Kulturforschung," *Historische Zeitschrift* 250 (1990): 321–46, esp. 338ff.

19. Karl Rohe, *Wahlen und Wählertraditionen in Deutschland: Kulturelle Grundlagen deutscher Parteien und Parteiensysteme im 19. und 20. Jahrhundert* (Frankfurt a. M., 1992), 24.

20. Rohe, "Politische Kultur," 341ff.

have focused on the long-term development of such a regional political culture. In particular, they have highlighted the continuity of the sociocultural "basis" and the discontinuity of party-political preferences. From the nineteenth century to the present, a nonparticipatory political culture prevailed. In the past, it was closely connected to the patriarchalism of heavy industry and mining. After 1945 it persisted as the unionized delegate system (*Stellvertretersystem*) based on the premise "I'm gonna take care of that for you" ("Ich mach dat für dich"). One cannot speak, however, of a regional identity among inhabitants of the Ruhrgebiet before the middle of the twentieth century. The party-political scene was initially heterogeneous, with the Center Party as the strongest force. But after 1945, the Social Democrats managed to become the guarantor of the welfare mentality (*Betreuungsmentalität*) and representative of the newly created regional consciousness of the Ruhrgebiet.[21]

IV.   The Mythical World of Regional Political Cultures

Karl Rohe champions an open, multilayered understanding of regional political culture. This includes "the respective regional or federal state consciousness, the political mentalities of the population, the well-established habits and usages of speech and action, and the interpretation of political reality, as they are put forward by political elites and intellectuals."[22] Rohe's work, though, clearly centers on socioculture, which in the final analysis is a variable of labor relationships and power structures. As a result, regional political culture acquires a natural bias: it becomes a cultural cage. Moreover, the openness of the concept halts abruptly at the frontier of the region itself. In the history of regional political cultures, the region remains an invariable quantity. The identity of the Ruhrgebiet after the Second World War is the telos of the history of a "region" that did not exist as such in the past. Even at the beginning of this century, the "Ruhrgebietler" did not perceive themselves as such: at that point, they were still Rhinelanders *or* Westphalians.

Such teleologies are hardly specific to the historiography of the Ruhrgebiet. A flood of recent *Landesgeschichten,* including studies of Germany's five new *Bundesstaaten,* works toward consolidating current "regional" identities that are the bread and butter of German

---

21. Cf. Karl Rohe, *Vom Revier zum Ruhrgebiet: Wahlen, Parteien, politische Kultur* (Essen, 1986); a more recent work, including an up-to-date bibliography, is Stefan Goch, " 'Der Ruhrgebietler' — Überlegungen zur Entstehung und Entwicklung regionalen Bewußtseins im Ruhrgebiet," *Westfälische Forschungen* 47 (1997): 585–620.

22. Karl Rohe, "Politische Kultur — politische Milieus: Zur Anwendung neuerer theoretischer Konzepte in einer modernen Landesgeschichte," in *Sachsen im Kaiserreich,* ed. Lässig and Pohl, 183.

federalism.[23] To overstate the case somewhat, one could say that such histories of regional political cultures are taken in by the mythical nature of their own subject matter, instead of challenging and "deconstructing" it. Regions can only become effective politically — that is, within the frameworks of power interests and conflicts, of mobilization and demobilization processes, and of participatory and representative cultures — if they are made "conscious." This means that they must be designated by name, and they should impart identity.

In this respect, myths play a special role. Myths mediate truths. However, they do so not rationally and in abstract terms, but suggestively and concretely. They pass off historical narratives as "natural," as divine providence or, for that matter, as an inevitable consequence of certain sociostructural, economic, or political circumstances. Events, too, are presented as fate. Myths may have a variegated substance: They can fall back on exemplary or traumatic events (as in the case of the Saar, which was constructed as a "region" only when it was severed from the Reich after the First World War). They can be oriented toward territories that have evolved over the course of time.[24] Or they can be based on principles of political behavior. Such principles may be a "healthy" spirit of subservience or a disposition toward opposition. Prussianism (perhaps the most consequential construct of a regional identity) on the one hand or the "special spirit" (*Sondergeist*) of the Bavarian Palatinate on the other suffice as examples of such dispositions.[25]

In recent research on nationalism,[26] it has become commonplace to observe that nations are — and always were — "imagined communities" (Benedict Anderson). Such communities are/were not only imagined; they require(d) continual "maintenance." What is far less often appreciated, however, is that this insight is even more applicable to regions than to nations, because regions' boundaries are much less fixed, both synchronically and diachronically. Identities or "interpretive cultures" based on territory have always been refracted in multiple ways. The same is true for interactive or "sociocultures."

---

23. Arno Mohr, "Politische Identität um jeden Preis? Zur Funktion der Landesgeschichtsschreibung in den Bundesländern," *Neue Politische Literatur* 35 (1990): 222–74. Cf. Ulrich Heß, "Sachsen im 20. Jahrhundert: Wiederentdeckung einer Region oder Neukonstruktion einer regionalen Identität?" *Informationen zur Raumentwicklung,* no. 11 (1993): 719–28.

24. Cf. Heinz Gollwitzer, "Die politische Landschaft in der deutschen Geschichte des 19./20. Jahrhunderts: Eine Skizze zum deutschen Regionalismus," *Zeitschrift für bayerische Landesgeschichte* 27 (1964): 523–52.

25. Ibid., 536.

26. For a research update, see Dieter Langewiesche, "Nation, Nationalismus, Nationalstaat: Forschungsstand und Forschungsperspektiven," *Neue Politische Literatur* 40 (1995): 190–236.

Historical stabilizations of particular spatial demarcations exist in the minds of people. They appear to develop most conspicuously by the application of external pressure, for instance through centralized power structures. They can also develop by means of more anonymous (or manipulative) processes of opinion-making. They favor spatially definable cohesion, and they result in the phenomenon we now call political regionalism but that contemporaries in the past—for instance, in the *Kaiserreich*—dubbed "particularism." The constitutive element of such phenomena was not necessarily the goal of national autonomy but rather the cultivation of certain political attitudes, norms of behavior, and social interactions that contrasted with the attitudes, behaviors, and interactions of the central authority. It was exactly these historically diverse constructions of "opposition" that constituted the liberal and democratic "traditions" of southern Germany before 1918—*not* the "special sociocultural perseverance of their advocates and content."[27] Put another way: "persistence"-constructs are the mythical clay from which very different political choices have been fashioned in different eras. During the Second Empire, the option of a democratic-progressive opposition evolved in southern Germany in opposition to a reactionary, centrifugal Prussia-Germany. In the late twentieth century, on the other hand, southern Germany presents itself as a kind of hindrance to political and cultural processes of "modernization."

V. Imagined Regions: Problems of Future Research

Historians of regional political cultures should not see their task in objectifying such territorial identities. Rather, they should make such identities transparent in the context of their historical and cultural contingency. They should problematize them, historically and culturally. From these observations, a number of central questions arise. How and to what end were regions made? For whom did they "exist," when, and in what form? As mental and social constructs, regions are not only an aspect of personal and social identity in politics, but also a medium of purposive rationality (*Zweckrationalität*) and power.[28] But it is important to clarify why and how certain regions have been constructed and others have not. More research is needed, therefore, into the role played here by institutional practices, spatially limited networks and social circles, economic and political interests, and symbolic or ideological representations.

---

27. This formulation is found in Lipp, "Heimatbewegung," 348f., who argues against the thesis that "regionalist movements are based on 'persistence.'"
28. Cf. Blotevogel, "Wege," 60.

The task of *historical* regional political cultural studies is also to historicize the region itself. It must be seen as a spatial construct of identification in order to break it down into its contemporary and often quite controversial interpretive variety.[29] The entities we investigate today as discrete regional political cultures—the Ruhrgebiet, Bavaria, Lower Saxony, Saxony, and so on—may in the past have had entirely different spatial coordinates. Nor should we forget that these demarcations were almost always intensely contested. Such "natural" boundaries as mountain ranges, rivers, state borders, territorial borders, administrative borders, diocesan borders; the boundaries that demarcate economic regions, languages, and dialects; and the boundaries of collective memories and myths—these and many other definitions of spatial constructs were never perfectly congruent; rather, they competed with each other and had to be continually redrawn (or reconfirmed).

In the nineteenth century, liberal parliamentarians claimed a virtual monopoly on the interpretation of spatial models of identification. These liberals differentiated between what they regarded as reasonable, "modern" patterns of spatial organization and outdated ones. Those patterns that were particularly useful to political opponents were held to be the most outdated; usually, they were identified with a parochial outlook (*Kirchturmshorizont*). Any historian of regional political cultures must pay attention to this intricate, convoluted amalgam of coexisting regional concepts in a particular historical situation, lest he or she be taken in by the hegemonial contemporary discourse on regions.

How, then, were regional identities endowed with meaning and substance in the past? What was the relation between regional identities and class identities, confessional identities, generational identities, and gender identities? From which other kinds of spatial concepts of identity were they differentiated? How did members of the political nation participate in the construction of regions? How did they attempt to infuse certain political biases into an already existing awareness of regional identity? Some examples of such processes are known. In 1866, the Kingdom of Saxony was at a crossroads, and its interpretation as a territory by nationalist-liberal, particularist-conservative, or German-democratic forces was highly controversial.[30] However, so far we know too little about other processes of identity formation. On what formal and informal levels of political activity were these regional identities

29. See Rohe, "Politische Kultur—politische Milieus," 182; for past periods, see, inter alia, Franz Irsigler, "Raumerfahrung und Raumkonzepte im späten Mittelalter und in der frühen Neuzeit," in *Region,* ed. Brunn, 163–74.

30. James Retallack, "'Why Can't a Saxon Be More Like a Prussian?' Regional Identities and the Birth of Modern Political Culture in Germany, 1866–67," *Canadian Journal of History* 32 (1997): 26–55.

constructed — in the state ministries, parliaments, parties, election meetings, newspapers, memorials, clubs, or at the local pub?

To be sure, regional historiography has not failed to pursue investigations at such levels. For example, Peter Steinbach's history of regional
elections examines the processes whereby regional identity was constructed. It does so by examining election themes, manifestos, programs,
and speeches, even including the image (-construction) of candidates and
deputies themselves. Through the example of the Principality of Lippe,
Steinbach has shown just how strongly regionally specific "ways of seeing" (*Deutungsmuster*) operated in history; he has also demonstrated that
one cannot speak of such ways of seeing as undergoing continual refinement (*Abschleifung*) in the direction of "nationalization" as understood
in classic modernization theory.[31] Steinbach's thesis that a (partial) re-
regionalization of politics occurred in the *Kaiserreich* nevertheless fails to
avoid all the pitfalls of modernization theory. When regionally specific
models of politics are defined by the historian in such a way that they are
placed in sharp opposition to national ones, this approach does not always
devote sufficient attention to the complex and contradictory nature of
contemporary constructions. Newer research on monuments, festivals,
and associational life, inspired by cultural-sociological concepts rather
than by modernization theory, has cast considerable doubt on the historical validity of this binary view.

It would be a grave mistake for scholars to perceive regions, regional
identities, and regional political cultures as derivatives of persistence and
continuity exclusively, in opposition, say, to constructs of the nation as the
engine of change.[32] On the contrary, in analytical terms regions should be
treated much like nations. Corresponding to the process of nation-
building, the process of "region-building" warrants critical investigation.
This would also be a logical extension of findings that Celia Applegate,
Alon Confino, Rüdiger Gans, and Detlef Briesen have derived from their
research on the Palatinate, Württemberg, and the Siegerland in the late
nineteenth and early twentieth centuries. Nor must comparative analysis
stop at the borders of Germany. As Xosé M. Núñez has written with
reference to Spain: "Nation-building may also imply region-building. . . .

---

31. Cf. above all Peter Steinbach, *Die Politisierung der Region: Reich- und Land-
tagswahlen im Fürstentum Lippe, 1866–1881*, 2 vols. (Passau, 1989); and idem, "Politisierung und Nationalisierung der Region im 19. Jahrhundert: Regionalspezifische Politikrezeption im Spiegel historischer Wahlforschung," in idem, *Probleme politischer
Partizipation im Modernisierungsprozeß* (Stuttgart, 1982), 321–49.

32. This is the basic presupposition of modernization theory, for instance as it is
formulated paradigmatically by Stein Rokkan in *Citizens, Elections, Parties: Approaches
to the Comparative Study of the Process of Development* (New York, 1970); cf. Kühne,
"Wahlrecht," 507.

Collective identities must be seen as a kind of concentric spheres, overlapping and complementing each other, from the family and even further, and as all forms of social identity, they are the result of dynamic historical processes. Nationalisms have contributed to reaffirm local and regional identities in order to make national identity take stronger roots among the population. . . . In other words, love for the 'Heimat' could mean, and did in fact mean, love for the fatherland."[33]

Of course, one must differentiate among different constructs of regional identity. On the one hand, around the turn of the century regional identity constructs were cemented at memorial ceremonies and other political celebrations geared toward national integration. In the same era, however, hard-fought election campaigns were serving to polarize social-economic groups within the nation and within the region. Not all forms of regional identity were in harmony with nationalisms and national identities. To probe further into the relationship between regional and other collective identities, their malleable substance, and their mutable frontiers, any history of regional political culture worthy of its name must seek to address these challenging issues squarely.

---

33. Xosé M. Núñez, "Region-Building in Spain during the 19th and 20th Centuries," in *Region,* ed. Brunn, 175–210, 176. Cf. Celia Applegate, *A Nation of Provincials: The German Idea of Heimat* (Berkeley, CA, 1990); Alon Confino, *The Nation as a Local Metaphor: Württemberg, Imperial Germany, and National Memory, 1871–1918* (Chapel Hill, NC, 1997); Rüdiger Gans and Detlef Briesen, "Das Siegerland zwischen ländlicher Beschränkung und nationaler Entgrenzung: Enge und Weite regionaler Identität," in *Wiederkehr,* ed. Lindner, 64–90. Cf. Heinz-Gerhard Haupt, "Die Konstruktion der Regionen und die Vielfalt der Loyalitäten im Frankreich des 19. und 20. Jahrhunderts," in *Region, Nation, Europa: Historische Determinanten der Neugliederung eines Kontinents,* ed. Günther Lottes (Heidelberg, 1992), 121–26; a systematic foundation for a cultural history of the region — which cannot be provided here — might be based on Georg Simmel, "Soziologie des Raumes" (1903), in idem, *Aufsätze und Abhandlungen, 1901–1908,* vol. 1, vol. 7 of *Gesamtausgabe* (Frankfurt a. M., 1995), 154–67; and idem, "Der Raum und die räumliche Ordnungen der Gesellschaft," in idem, *Soziologie: Untersuchungen über die Form der Vergesellschaftung* (1908), vol. 11 of *Gesamtausgabe* (Frankfurt a. M., 1992), 687–790; cf. Paul Nolte, "Georg Simmels Historische Anthropologie der Moderne: Rekonstruktion eines Forschungsprogramms," *Geschichte und Gesellschaft* 24 (1998): 225–47, esp. 237–41. See also the pathbreaking work of Peter Sahlins, *Boundaries: The Making of France and Spain in the Pyrenees* (Berkeley, CA, 1989).

The Boundaries of the Local
in Modern German History

Helmut Walser Smith

I. Introduction

Two decades ago, the author of a regional history defended the focus on the local by citing a modernist poet, Wallace Stevens:

> They said, "You have a blue guitar,
> You do not play things as they are."
> The man replied, "Things as they are
> Are changed upon the blue guitar."[1]

The local evoked a different texture, its own particular hues. Closer to life than national history, it seemed more authentic, a surer road to the heart of the real. For the early practitioners of *Alltagsgeschichte,* in practice often a German form of local history, the search for a deeper historical reality provided early studies with a forceful epistemological élan. Gert Zang, for example, postulated a crisis of the historical sciences, itself part of a wider societal crisis. This crisis in historical sciences had come about as a consequence of an alienation between ordinary people and a form of historical thinking and writing marked more by abstract social theorizing than by the hard, dirty work of sifting through the details of life. History, if it was to come out of its crisis, had to adopt a different tack — one that made more sense to ordinary people, one that said something more about their immediate background, where they were from, and how others like them thought. The closer proximity to life involved not only a higher degree of complexity, but also a different,

---

1. Cited by David Blackbourn, *Religion and Local Politics in Wilhelmine Germany: The Center Party in Württemberg before 1914* (Wiesbaden, 1980), ix. Although a local history, Blackbourn's work was not cast in the specific tradition of *Alltagsgeschichte.*

more authentic conception of historical reality. As Zang put it in bold print: "A transformed understanding of reality is the precondition for a meaningful regional history; a regional history [is] the precondition for a transformation of the conception of reality."[2]

As we sketch out the lines marking the contours of local and regional history, the resultant map will be without a utopian moment. We will not, I strongly suspect, argue that as a result of our labor a new understanding of reality will emerge, nor will the jargon of authenticity strike us as convincing. This is not just an epistemological problem. It also derives from a changed notion of what constitutes the local. To understand this change, it may be instructive to look at a similar debate within a neighboring discipline: anthropology, in particular cultural anthropology. Here the problem is especially acute, for in terms of disciplinary history, the village constituted the anthropologist's research site as surely as the archive has served as the locus of discovery for the historian. In "the simple and the distant," to borrow from Clifford Geertz, anthropologists could find "the royal road to recovering *les formes élémentaires de la vie sociale.*"[3] But a great deal of criticism — postmodern and postcolonial — has weakened the normative force of anthropology's claim to comprehend the essence of humans by understanding their simplest, most authentic ways of being.[4] The everyday experience of field research has further undermined the epistemological foundations of the field. James Clifford, one of the most productive critics of "modernist anthropology" (finding the universal in the local), reminds us of the stunning, vaguely unsettling image offered in Margaret Mead's study *The Mountain Arapesh*, in which "a local native [is] reading the index to the *Golden Bough* just to see if they had missed anything."[5] In this and in many other instances, the boundaries between

    2. Gert Zang, *Die unaufhaltsame Annäherung an das Einzelne: Reflexionen über den theoretischen und praktischen Nutzen der Regional- und Alltagsgeschichte* (Konstanz, 1985), 35. See also idem, ed., *Provinzialisierung einer Region: Zur Entstehung der bürgerlichen Gesellschaft in der Provinz* (Frankfurt a. M., 1978), 502. A similar, if more disciplined, tone was struck in 1979 by the Italian microhistorians. See Carlo Ginzburg and Carlo Poni, "The Name and the Game: Unequal Exchange and the Historiographic Marketplace," in *Microhistory and the Lost Peoples of Europe,* ed. Edward Muir and Guido Ruggiero (Baltimore, 1991), 4.

    3. Clifford Geertz, "Deep Hanging Out," *New York Review of Books* 45, no. 16 (22 Oct. 1998), 71.

    4. See Talal Asad, ed., *Anthropology and the Colonial Encounter* (London, 1973). For a spirited, if dated, analysis of developments in anthropology, see Sherry B. Ortner, "Theory in Anthropology since the Sixties," *Comparative Studies in Society and History* 26, no. 1 (1984): 126–66.

    5. James Clifford, *The Predicament of Culture: Twentieth-Century Ethnography, Literature, and Art* (Cambridge, MA, 1988), 232.

authenticity and accretion, local oral culture and global print capitalism, are no longer clear.

Mutatis mutandis, the question then becomes: What do we intend with the specific genre of local history? And what are the boundaries of the local? If the details themselves are not closer to God, then why write local history at all, except as a laboratory for larger questions? And if we try to go beyond the search for authenticity, what might be gained? In what follows, I suggest tentative defenses for approaches to local history that are not primarily about getting to the essence of local and regional identities. Rather, drawing mainly on recent work in other geographical contexts, I consider approaches to local history that destabilize these identities. In doing so, I argue that it is possible to widen and render more plural the conception of the local: who participates in it, where it begins, where it ends. To make these defenses, I discuss two research fields: (1) the local histories of working classes, and (2) analyses of the boundaries (ethnic and political) that shape regional identities. In both fields there are possibilities for methodological openings that, if they do not transform our sense of reality, may nevertheless change our notions of the legitimate boundaries of local and regional history.

II. Local History, Identity, and the Working Classes

Local history has two dimensions: geographical and chronological. In its most elementary form, local history is about people (and the products of human imagination and labor) in a physical space across time. Conceivably, these are the only necessary boundaries of local history as a genre. But, as Fernand Braudel famously reminded his readers in the beginning of his two-volume work *The Mediterranean and the Mediterranean World in the Age of Philip II:* "To draw a boundary around anything is to define, analyze, and reconstruct it, in this case select, indeed adopt, a philosophy of history."[6] The philosophy of history most typically adopted by professional historians working at the local level has been one of "metonymic freezing," where the purpose of the study has been to show how a specific identity became a dominant social fact and, as such, signified the whole.[7] This is especially true of the canonical works of labor history cast as local studies. Consider Hartmut Zwahr's work *Zur Konstituierung des Proletariats als Klasse,* which traced how one identity of the workers of Leipzig came to be the dominant identity; or Klaus Tenfelde's study *Proletarische*

---

6. Fernand Braudel, *The Mediterranean and the Mediterranean World in the Age of Philip II,* trans. Siân Reynolds, 2 vols. (New York, 1972), 1:18.

7. James Clifford, *Routes: Travel and Translation in the Late Twentieth Century* (Cambridge, MA, 1997), 24.

Provinz, which delineated the rise of a class-conscious radicalism among the miners of Penzberg, Bavaria, and then showed how this radicalism served as a buttress against the allure of National Socialism.[8] Both Tenfelde and Zwahr focused on, and explained, aggregative processes. But the aggregation of workers into a collective singular — the working class — was also imputed, distilled from an image of a quintessential worker with a specific, singular, social identity.[9] This identity then constituted a bridge between micro- and macrohistory, between the local and something larger. For it was not until their social identity became historically fixed that the subjects of local history could enter — via their representation as part of the collective singular called class — a larger historical field.[10]

But with the fixing of identity, the distilling of the authentic worker, a great deal got lost, as revealed by recent debates in labor history centered on criticism of E. P. Thompson's canonical *Making of the English Working Class.* Thompson's critics argued that the centrality of the question of class formation to studies of workers — local and otherwise — prefigured accounts that privileged worker solidarity and class cohesion above other socially constructed identities, such as race, ethnicity, gender, and religion, as well as above other kinds of experience: the experience of being uprooted, of having fought in war, and of having power, even if only to lord it over others. To be sure, historians who engaged in explaining the complexities of class took these other possibilities into account. But as Patrick Joyce, William Sewell Jr., Kathleen Canning, and Alf Lüdtke have since argued, the other possibilities were not foregrounded; they were of interest *"an sich"* but not *"für sich."*[11] The historiographical emphasis on the construction of class

8. Klaus Tenfelde, *Proletarische Provinz: Radikalisierung und Widerstand in Penzberg/Oberbayern, 1900–1945* (Munich, 1982); Hartmut Zwahr, *Zur Konstituierung des Proletariats als Klasse: Strukturuntersuchungen über das Leipziger Proletariat während der industriellen Revolution* (Berlin, 1978).

9. Sonya O. Rose, "Class Formation and the Quintessential Worker," in *Reworking Class,* ed. John R. Hall (Ithaca, NY, 1997), 133–68.

10. For a brilliant criticism of the way in which class is deployed, see Zygmunt Bauman, *Memories of Class: The Pre-history and After-Life of Class* (London, 1982). And for a spirited introduction to the state of the debate, see Patrick Joyce, ed., *Class* (Oxford, 1995), esp. 3–18.

11. William H. Sewell Jr., "How Classes Are Made: Critical Reflections on E.P. Thompson's Theory of Working Class Formation," in *E.P. Thompson: Critical Debates,* ed. Harvey J. Kaye and Keith McClelland (Oxford, 1987); Patrick Joyce, *Visions of the People: Industrial England and the Question of Class, 1848–1914* (Cambridge, 1991); Kathleen Canning, "Gender and the Politics of Class Formation: Rethinking German Labor History," *American Historical Review* 97 (1992): 736–68; Alf Lüdtke, "The Appeal of Exterminating 'Others': German Workers and the Limits of Resistance," in *Resistance against the Third Reich, 1933–1990,* ed. Michael Geyer and John W. Boyer (Chicago, 1992), 53–74.

also had profound effects on the shape of the story being told. Whether one considers the architectonic elegance of Klaus Tenfelde's work on the coal miners in the Ruhr, or E. P. Thompson's carefully constructed "biography" of the English working class, the narrative plot showed a progression (or maturation) from a condition of worker fragmentation to a state of unity, typically made manifest in collective action.[12]

This problem has also been at the center of critical reflection in the work of the Bologna school of microhistory and as part of the general reconsideration of the project of social history associated with the "crisis" of the *Annales* school. In both cases, a central issue has been how to overcome the ossification of social categories, like class, which historians and social scientists deploy more to fasten identities and secure them in a structural field than to imaginatively recreate the multiplicity of possibilities and histories that actually bear on a person's life at a given point in time. As the editors of the *Annales* put it in a programmatic article published in 1989 and entitled "Let's Try the Experiment": "[S]ocial objects are not things endowed with properties but, rather, sets of changing relationships within constantly adapting configurations."[13] This way of seeing social objects opens a number of analytic possibilities.

One possibility, pursued by historians who have taken the linguistic turn, is to focus on worker experiences without privileging a historical progression toward a unified class. This might entail, as William Sewell Jr. argued with respect to the workers of Marseilles, simply reconstructing "the words, metaphors, and rhetorical conventions that [workers] used to think about their experiences."[14] But as fecund as this approach has been, it has also severed labor history's materialist moorings, and with them the close-to-life reconstructions of local context that marked much of the best earlier work. Another possibility, advanced by historians and social scientists studying workers in East Asia, is to consider the way in which other identities dramatically complicated, perhaps even superseded, class identities. In a volume entitled *Putting Class in Its Place,* Elizabeth J. Perry summarized much of this research by arguing: "On the whole, workers in this part of the globe appear to have been more consumed with the politics of 'place' — a quest for social and cultural status entailing a desire to

---

12. Klaus Tenfelde, *Sozialgeschichte der Bergarbeiterschaft an der Ruhr im 19. Jahrhundert* (Bonn, 1977). For more detail with respect to this aspect of Thompson's *Making of the English Working Class,* see Helmut Walser Smith, "Zwischen den Fronten: Meisterwerke der Geschichtsschreibung und postmoderne Kritik," *Geschichte und Gesellschaft* 22, no. 4 (1996): 594–96; and Kaye and McClelland, *E.P. Thompson.*

13. "Tentons l'expérience," *Annales ESC* 44 (Nov./Dec. 1989): 1320.

14. William H. Sewell Jr., *Work and Revolution in France: The Language of Labor from the Old Regime to 1848* (Cambridge, 1980), 11. For a programmatic statement, see idem, "Toward a Post-Materialist Rhetoric for Labor History," in *Rethinking Labor History,* ed. Lenard R. Berlanstein (Urbana, IL, 1993), 15–38.

elude, rather than to embrace, the ranks of the proletariat — than with a 'class' struggle to further their interests qua workers."[15] This also opens possibilities, especially since "place" is conceivably an open series: one can feel attachments, of different kinds, to multiple places. But giving priority to "place" over "class" also fixes identities anew, while positing a place-class dichotomy deflects attention from attempts to theorize forms of hybridity. Nevertheless, in both instances, the general direction is to think through, as Kathleen Canning has put it, how "lines of differentiation — ethnicity, nationality, religion, and gender — . . . run 'next to, over, under or across class divisions.' "[16]

The process by which social identities are made and unmade has also come under critical scrutiny. For example, in his work on Turin around 1900, Maurizio Gribaudi has argued that worker turnover constituted a decisive social fact undermining a common experience of class, and that, instead of a powerful and unified process of class formation, a wide variety of ways to become a worker actually existed. In Gribaudi's view, workers negotiated their own "itineraries" to and away from fixed social identities; worker solidarities were often based less on social position than on similarity of positions within systems of relationships.[17] Two consequences follow: first, that when studying workers, one studies people in a specific point in a life course (or itinerary); and second, that the local contexts and lines of solidarity, which define what it is to be a worker (not the category but the person), are of immensely greater complexity than the ascription of social class suggests.

Gribaudi's solution — one of a number of possibilities — places movement in the center of the frame and suggests a possibility for writing a different kind of local history than a unifying narrative about class formation allows. Necessarily, Gribaudi's work emphasizes dislocation as much as rootedness, fragmentation as much as unity. And it plots the history of workers as a history of varied and different voices: histories — not history (in the sense of the crystallization of a single social identity).[18] Moreover, Gribaudi's work may be seen as part of a larger reorientation in the human sciences, especially evident in anthropology, in which movement, travel, living betwixt and between, has become a

---

15. Elizabeth J. Perry, *Putting Class in Its Place: Worker Identities in East Asia* (Berkeley, CA, 1996), 3.

16. Kathleen Canning, *Languages of Labor and Gender: Female Factory Work in Germany, 1850–1914* (Ithaca, NY, 1996), 5.

17. Maurizio Gribaudi, *Itinéraires ouvriers: Espaces et groupes sociaux à Turin aux début du XXe siècle* (Paris, 1987). See, as well, idem, "Espace ouvrier et parcours sociaux: Turin dans la première moitié du siècle," *Annales ESC* 2 (Mar./Apr. 1987): 243–63.

18. For some reflections on writing history in this way, see Peter Burke, "History of Events and the Revival of Narrative," in *New Perspectives on Historical Writing,* ed. idem (University Park, PA, 1991), 233–48.

more central fact of social life and social location. Indeed, to get a sense of the analytical distance involved one might compare Braudel's assumptions of the structuring force of physical environment with James Clifford's current attempts to develop "a view of human location as constituted by displacement as much as by stasis."[19]

What might this mean for local history in modern Germany or, more specifically still, Saxony? Here I would argue that we need to widen the lens, to—for a moment—take leave of narratives that are principally concerned with the making of unified social identities. Doing so opens a wider, more complex historical world. Consider the city of Chemnitz in 1907. According to Wolfgang Köllmann, most of the workers of Chemnitz had not been born in the city with which their socialization is principally identified. Of the workers in Chemnitz in 1907, only 33.2 percent were born in the city; a further 51.2 percent came from the surrounding areas of Saxony, mostly from the countryside; 5.9 percent came from further afield in the German Reich; and 9.7 percent from foreign lands, mostly from Czech and Polish areas.[20] Initial studies of German cities may have overestimated the transitory nature of the workforce. Yet it is nevertheless true that alongside a relatively stable population, a highly transitory pool of labor, mostly young men, came in and out of the cities.[21]

The point here is not merely to claim that movement is more important than stasis, but rather to call attention to the way it has been emplotted in local studies whose implicit narrative remained focused on explaining the construction of class and the phenomenon of collective action.[22] Thus David Crew, whose statistics for Bochum may have over-

---

19. Clifford, *Routes,* 2.

20. Wolfgang Köllmann, *Bevölkerung in der industriellen Revolution* (Göttingen, 1974), 117–24.

21. Stephen Bleek, "Mobilität und Seßhaftigkeit in deutschen Großstädten während der Urbanisierung," *Geschichte und Gesellschaft* 15 (1989): 5–33; Steven Hochstadt, "Migration and Industrialization in Germany, 1815–1977," *Social Science History* 5, no. 4 (1981): 445–68. Earlier work, inspired by the new urban history, tabulated persistence (*Seßhaftigkeit*) by comparing address books over ten-year periods without, however, sufficiently factoring in high mortality rates, thus resulting in extremely high rates of mobility, often over 50 percent. For this earlier work, see Stephen Thernstrom, *The Other Bostonians: Poverty and Progress in the American Metropolis, 1880–1970* (Cambridge, MA, 1973); and David F. Crew, *Town in the Ruhr: A Social History of Bochum, 1860–1914* (New York, 1979), 60–62. For more recent estimates, which downplay what Crew called "a remarkably volatile urban population," see, in addition to Bleek and Hochstadt, Friedrich Lenger, *Zwischen Kleinbürgertum und Proletariat: Studien zur Sozialgeschichte der Düsseldorfer Arbeiter und Handwerker, 1816–1878* (Göttingen, 1986).

22. Franz-Josef Brüggemeier, *Leben vor Ort: Ruhrbergbauleute und Ruhrbergbau, 1889–1919* (Munich, 1983), 267, makes a similar argument, showing that the emphasis of studies on class formation rendered as secondary research undertaken on the private sphere of workers.

estimated mobility, nevertheless structured his pathbreaking book in such a way as to make permanence (indexed by neighborhood residential patterns, the density of communal organizations, and personal and familial ties) the explanatory hinge for the book's penultimate chapter on collective action.[23] The point would be to reverse this telos and to consider instead the multiplicity of social identities as a matter of local history *für sich,* to reconstitute the range of horizons (geographic, ethnic, gendered) of workers at a given time in a physical space, to thematize the shifting configurations of social identities, and to incorporate this degree of diversity into a local history.[24] The result, I would suggest, would be a different understanding of the local, and, more importantly, a different understanding of whose history properly belongs to a genre called local history.

III.   Regional History: Contact Zones, Identities, and Boundaries

A similar set of concerns might be addressed with respect to regional history. Whose history do we write when we write about Saxony? And what are its boundaries? Here the antecedent is purposely ambiguous, as the boundaries of a state are not necessarily coterminous with the boundaries of the history of the people who live there or who, at some level of consciousness, strongly identify with it. Here too one might consider the centrality of movement to the larger historical frame: the movement of Polish and Czech workers to workplaces and dwelling places in Saxony, and the resultant interethnic constellations; the movement away from a region like Saxony of people who, nevertheless, maintained strong emotional ties; and, finally, the movement of boundaries, for Saxony, perhaps more than any other German state, has had a long history of changing border configurations.

The question of how to fit ethnic difference into a history of a German region is itself an issue of perspective, though also one of paramount importance. Our initial inclination, usually reinforced by linguistic hurdles, is to treat separate histories separately: the Poles who work in the sugar beet fields as properly part of either Polish labor history or the history of regional labor policy; the Sorbs as a separate part of the whole, living in Saxony to be sure, but having a history of their own. Here I do not wish to question that these groups have their own history; they most certainly do. Rather, I would suggest the analytical advan-

---

23. Crew, *Town in the Ruhr,* esp. 159–220.

24. For an exciting start in this direction, see Brüggemeier, *Leben vor Ort,* where movement is also placed at the center of the story. See also William H. Sewell Jr., *Structure and Mobility: The Men and Women of Marseille, 1820–1870* (Cambridge, 1985).

tages of considering a region — Saxony serves as a good example — as a space in which contact occurs, in which structures of hegemony and subordination are overdetermined by ethnicity, in which images of the other are generated, and in which identity (regional as well as national) is defined not just against Prussia but also in the spaces of daily contact, often against the ethnic foreignness encountered locally (as well, one should add, as the reverse).

Such a reorientation would open the field to a wider historiography concerned with the interaction of peoples in what Mary Louise Pratt has called "contact zones." Pratt defines contact zones as "social spaces where disparate cultures meet, clash, and grapple with each other, often in highly asymmetrical relations of domination and subordination."[25] The analytical vocabulary of "contact" is drawn from the field of linguistics and is concerned with the special idiom that results when speakers of different languages are forced into relationships, such as trade, that necessitate continual communication. Rather than a one-sided account of power, or a one-way narrative of cultural diffusion, this analytical tradition emphasizes "the spatial and temporal copresence of subjects previously separated by geographic and historical disjunctures."[26] The emphasis on copresence also involves posing different questions. As Greg Dening has written in his influential work *Islands and Beaches:* "To know a culture is to know its system of expressed meanings. To know cultures in contact is to know the misreading of meanings, the transformation of meanings, the recognition of meanings."[27]

The idea of a space as a contact zone has most fruitfully been applied to instances of contact that involve a great deal of asymmetry, such as occurred in the slave trade and in colonial encounters. Yet it also has important implications for conceptions of regional history. Two analogies from U.S. history serve to illuminate what I mean.[28] Not so long ago, the history of the American South was, in disciplinary terms, primarily a history of white Southerners. Trying to distill the authentic South, historians focused on groups they took to represent, metonymically, the larger whole. This approach had one great advantage: it allowed historians to write about "the South" in the collective singular, multifaceted to be sure, but with contours that everyone understood. Within this context, historians addressed slavery and racism, often with

25. Mary Louise Pratt, *Imperial Eyes: Travel Writing and Transculturation* (London, 1992), 4.

26. Ibid., 7.

27. Greg Dening, *Islands and Beaches: Discourse on a Silent Land, Marquesas 1774–1880* (Chicago, 1980), 6.

28. For a recent survey, see Edward L. Ayers et al., *All over the Map: Rethinking American Regions* (Baltimore, 1996).

a great deal of acuity; but African American life was researched within a separate disciplinary matrix, usually by historians who considered themselves African American historians. The two stories came together in terms of the history of policy and the history of white attitudes toward blacks, but not in terms of everyday life, and not in terms of contact.[29] Moreover, the story of the region called the South is no longer about blacks and whites in a dichotomous sense. Debates about the place of Floridian history (which in turn implicated debates about English settlement and Spanish influence, and whether Florida's pasts properly belonged to the South or to the Circum-Caribbean) necessarily forced a reorientation of the field, as did discussions about how multiethnic cities such as New Orleans fit in a history of the South.[30] The same may be said of Western history—for a long time a history of white settlement and Indian policy. Recently, however, Western history has embraced its own heterogeneity, with exciting results.[31] Thus Patricia Nelson Limerick concludes her study *The Legacy of Conquest* with an insight that is as salutary as it is simple: "Indians, Hispanics, Asians, blacks, Anglos, businesspeople, workers, politicians, bureaucrats, natives, and newcomers, we share the same region and its history."[32] Essentially, the new Western history conceives of the region as a zone of contact, not—in the first order—as a space of white expansion. This, in turn, has also had profound implications for our sense of the direction of Western history, as its grand narrative no longer self-evidently moves from east to west.[33]

Saxony is not the American West (though a trip to Radebeul might give one reason to pause). Yet certain historiographical preoccupations

29. The difference can be seen by comparing two texts, C. Vann Woodward, *The Origins of the New South, 1877–1913* (Baton Rouge, 1951), and Edward L. Ayers, *The Promise of the New South: Life after Reconstruction* (New York, 1992).

30. On Florida's place in American history, emphasizing its historical rootedness in the Circum-Caribbean, see Jane G. Landers, "Rebellion and Royalism in Spanish Florida: The French Revolution on Spain's Northern Colonial Frontier," in *A Turbulent Time: The French Revolution and the Greater Caribbean,* ed. David Barry Gaspar and David Patrick Geggus (Bloomington, 1997). On New Orleans, see Gwendolyn Midlo Hall, *Africans in Colonial Louisiana: The Development of Afro-Creole Culture in the Eighteenth Century* (Baton Rouge, 1992); and Kimberly S. Hanger, *Bounded Lives, Bounded Places: Free Black Society in Colonial New Orleans* (Durham, 1997).

31. For an exciting introduction, see Richard White, *"It's Your Misfortune and None of My Own": A New History of the American West* (Norman, OK, 1991). See also Donald Worster, *Under Western Skies: Nature and History in the American West* (New York, 1992); and William Cronon, George Miles, and Jay Gitlin, eds., *Under an Open Sky: Rethinking America's Western Past* (New York, 1992).

32. Patricia Nelson Limerick, *The Legacy of Conquest: The Unbroken Past of the American West* (New York, 1987), 349.

33. For a reflection on our sense of the direction of history, and how powerfully this can influence our images of historical topography, see James Clifford, "Fort Ross Meditation," in idem, *Routes,* 299–348.

have arguably obscured the degree to which Saxony, too, has been a zone of contact—for people on the move, and for ethnic coexistence (which can imply patterns of relation ranging from intermixing to segregation). The emphasis on the construction of milieus, cleavages, and camps, for example, has subordinated an interest in constellations of coexistence in common space to an explicit interest in the relationship of local civil societies to very specific political expressions.[34] The latter preoccupation is not illegitimate. Quite the contrary. But neither is there any a priori reason to subordinate the history of conflict and coexistence among groups in a region to the study of the social bases of high politics.

The constellations we have addressed to this point have resulted from in-migration to a common regional space. But the reverse is also possible and, especially in the twentieth century, an increasingly familiar part of our mental map. Thus it no longer seems strange, as it must have in the age of classical nationalism, that more Irish live in Boston than in Cork (and in the past, Dublin as well), more Slovenians live in Cleveland than in Ljubljana, and more Turks live in Berlin than in a whole collection of major Turkish cities. Far from erasing *Heimat* identities, migration has brought forth new kinds of attachment, governed less by "objective" criteria (birth, mother tongue, political citizenship) than by ways of *imagining* home. Those ways of imagining are often personally complex and mediated by new kinds of cultural occurrences. In recent German history, one might consider the constellation of new local histories whose title is some variation of "The Jews of My Hometown." Invariably written by young, post-Holocaust Germans, these books often provide occasion for German communities to invite Jewish survivors from the United States and Israel to return to "their" hometown in order to participate in the book's unveiling. As rituals of reaffirmation, such ceremonies dramatically complicate notions of what *Heimat* might mean, especially in a period—the middle of the twentieth century—in which political and racial cataclysms have dramatically severed connections between land and people.[35]

The experience of exodus has powerfully reshaped the geographical coordinates of national identity, rendering increasingly central what

---

34. See, for example, the prominence James Retallack gives to such studies in his wide-ranging review essay "Society and Politics in Saxony in the Nineteenth and Twentieth Centuries: Reflections on Recent Research," *Archiv für Sozialgeschichte* 38 (1998): 396–457.

35. For the European dimensions of this phenomenon, see Eugene Kulischer, *Europe on the Move: War and Population Changes, 1917–47* (New York, 1948). For Germany, and non-Jewish Germans, see Heinz Günter Steinberg, *Die Bevölkerungsentwicklung in Deutschland im Zweiten Weltkrieg* (Bonn, 1991). For the Jews of Europe, see Wolfgang Benz, ed., *Dimension des Völkermords: Die Zahl der jüdischen Opfer des Nationalsozialismus* (Munich, 1991).

Benedict Anderson has called "long-distance nationalism." The fact of exodus, combined with fluid capitalism, global television, and the potential of the Internet, have conspired, according to Anderson, to create the context for a kind of national engagement that "pries open the classical nation-state project."[36] For the most part, this is a phenomenon of second- and third-world communities with dwellings in exile in the first: Indians from the subcontinent, who, living in New York and Chicago, intervene in Hindu politics in New Delhi; Tamil communities in London and Toronto (the examples are Anderson's) who give financial and ideological support to the Tigers in Jaffna.[37] What they are creating — and this is of special relevance for us — are distinct kinds of communities of attachment in the context of displacement.[38]

These matters have not simply bypassed German history, even though German historians usually do not think within these terms of reference. One example might be the historiography of the expellees (*Vertriebene*), which is still largely cast in terms of questions of long-run assimilation. But might it not be more fruitful to reverse this telos as well and to consider the expellees as examples of distinct kinds of communities of attachment, marked, as much as other such groups, by the context of exodus and displacement? Then, rather than asking about the pace of assimilation, might it not be more propitious to consider the multiplicity of memories and experiences that they brought to a region (including the experience of living in ethnic borderlands)? This in turn would reshape not only the historiography of the expellees; it would also map the historiography of postwar German regions with high levels of in-migration from eastern Europe as zones of cultural contact and tension.

Finally, there is the question of borders and boundaries, marvelously ambiguous in German regional history. Some of the oldest journals, such as the *Zeitschrift für die Geschichte des Oberrheins,* nominally hold fast to natural boundaries. Other journals, however, are organized according to political borders. But both kinds of boundaries may be historically interrogated, especially for a state like Saxony, in which modern boundaries have undergone considerable flux, not only in terms of where they are drawn but also in terms of who is on the other side. Thus, to the south and east, borders that were once political are now exclusively ethnic. How, in this case, has the experience of shifting

---

36. Benedict Anderson, "Exodus," *Critical Inquiry* (winter 1994), 326–27. This essay has been revised and reprinted as "Long-Distance Nationalism," in idem, *The Spectre of Comparisons: Nationalism, Southeast Asia, and the World* (London, 1998), 58–76.

37. Ibid.

38. Clifford, *Routes,* 252, defines diaspora in terms that are highly illuminating for this general problem. "Thus the term 'diaspora' is a signifier not simply of transnationality and movement but of political struggles to define the local, as distinctive community, in historical contexts of displacement."

borders shaped regional as well as national identities? Do historical regions, such as the Erzgebirge, cut across hardened boundaries, creating a space in which common mentalities may be as revealing as the divisions between groups?

These kinds of questions have been at the center of some of the most innovative local studies in history and anthropology. Consider Peter Sahlins's pathbreaking work, *Boundaries: The Making of France and Spain in the Pyrenees.* Sahlins studied a border thought to be frozen since the Treaty of the Pyrenees in 1659 in order to examine the way in which two oppositional identities (one French, the other Spanish) came to mark the people of the Cerdaña. He concluded that the very act of constructing borders — a project participated in by administrators, lawyers, surveyors, and mapmakers from Paris and Madrid as well as by the more local engagement of the people of the Cerdaña — was central to the construction of identities thought of, each in their own way, as separate. Sahlins emphasized that these borders were in no sense natural. Nor do they demarcate two populations that, in terms of authentic qualities of Frenchness and Spanishness, could be thought of as different. Instead, Sahlins argued:

> National identity is a socially constructed and continuous process of defining "friend" and "enemy," a logical extension of the process of maintaining boundaries between "us" and "them" within more local communities. . . . In this sense, national identity, like ethnic or communal identity, is contingent and relational: it is defined by the social or territorial boundaries drawn to distinguish the collective self and its implicit negation, the other.[39]

For our purposes, Sahlins's argument is important for two reasons: first, because it suggests that the construction of boundaries can be studied most fully at the local level (and provides a model for how this might be done); and second, because it eschews a national teleology that plots national identity as something superseding local and regional identities.[40] Indeed, Sahlins argues that, in this border area, the local process of nation-building preceded the nationalization impulses emanating from the centers of Paris and Madrid. When one considers the modern-

---

39. Peter Sahlins, *Boundaries: The Making of France and Spain in the Pyrenees* (Berkeley, CA, 1989), 270–71. For an equally imaginative work examining two identities along one border, see John Borneman, *Belonging in the Two Berlins: Kin, State, Nation* (Cambridge, 1992).

40. For a recent work in the German context that also puts this hierarchy into question, see Alon Confino, *The Nation as Local Metaphor: Württemberg, Imperial Germany, and National Memory, 1871–1918* (Chapel Hill, NC, 1997).

ization paradigm of such canonical works as Eugene Weber's *Peasants into Frenchmen*, the considerable revisionist import of Sahlins's approach becomes evident. Moreover, the approach suggests exciting possibilities for local studies of a country, Germany, whose borders have undergone profound change—just as it does for a state, Saxony, whose borders have oscillated between the seemingly artificial and the seemingly natural, between borders defined by political lines and borders defined by ethnic lines. Definition by ethnicity, one should recall, is a recent invention, born of a different sense of demarcation and of a period of vast population transfers. As such, existing borders, far from constituting the given parameters of local and regional history, might, instead, be their object of study.

IV. Conclusions

Local history cannot bring us closer to the authentic. It can, however, sharpen our sense for changing patterns of people in common spaces. Seen against the earlier claims of historians who wished to get "at the heart of the real," this way of looking at the past may seem modest. Yet it conceivably places local histories at the center of important experiments in the humanities and social sciences. Consider the résumé of the current situation provided by the editors of the *Annales:*

> [R]esearchers in a number of areas are now moving away from the two great models that dominated the social sciences, the functionalist model and the structuralist model, and toward analyses in terms of strategies, which allow memory, learning, uncertainty, and negotiations to be reintroduced into the heart of social interaction.[41]

The editors go on to point out that the important issue is not the "constricting contrast between micro- and macroanalysis," but rather the fundamental problem of how to pose questions, and at what level of scale, that are important to the humanities and social sciences. Many of these questions may best be seen through a local lens. This is particularly true of questions that involve the interaction of groups in common space, the problems of dwelling in displacement, the negotiation of identities and allegiances in a complex field of affinities and antagonisms, and the ways in which borders are created and maintained. But the aperture of this lens, I have tried to argue, may need to be recalibrated to render a finer and more accurate image of the real heterogeneity of the local, *wie es eigentlich gewesen.*

---

41. "Tentons l'expérience," 1320.

Mapping Milieus Regionally: On the Spatial Rootedness of Collective Identities in the Nineteenth Century

Thomas Mergel

I. Introduction

"Bigger is better." Milieu theory is indebted to this kind of thinking.[1] Even though M. Rainer Lepsius's concept of sociomoral milieus has undergone considerable modification since it was introduced thirty years ago — so much modification, indeed, that one can hardly speak of "the" milieu theory any more — his canonical text nevertheless retains its essential validity: class and religion constitute the pillars of modern socialization (*Vergesellschaftung*) as it occurs in large groups on the national level (although, for Germany, in a characteristic pathology of dissociation). Thus, the particular stepchildren of German history, the workers and Catholics, receive a sort of belated vindication. Perhaps this point provides a clue to why milieu theory has found such resonance. Class and religious denomination are the decisive cohesive forces of the "social units" that Lepsius calls "milieus." Labor parties, Catholic parties, and liberal parties function as "political committees" of those milieus. Originally these parties were the principal focus of research, though lately such analysis has taken a back seat to the study of the cultural and social formations that made such political alliances possible in the first place.

However, religious denomination and class are not the only "structural dimensions" that constitute Lepsius's contextual framework of

---

1. M. Rainer Lepsius, "Parteiensystem und Sozialstruktur: Zum Problem der Demokratisierung der deutschen Gesellschaft," in idem, *Demokratie in Deutschland* (Göttingen, 1993), 25–50; this essay appeared originally in *Wirtschaft, Geschichte, Wirtschaftsgeschichte,* ed. Wilhelm Abel et al. (Stuttgart, 1966).

milieus. These other dimensions are relegated to the background in the course of Lepsius's argumentation. Apart from the ill-defined term "cultural orientation," they include "regional traditions." Lepsius concedes that "regional traditions" exist within all milieus except the workers' movement. Yet what they look like and how they function remains unclear. Milieu theory obviously intends to describe how class and religious affiliation transcend the pre-political backyard (*Hinterhof*) of regional socialization and become integrated on the higher—national—level of collectivity. It appears as though the people's parties of the West German Federal Republic represent the positive confirmation for Lepsius's concept: they are large political groupings that transcend social divisions, and they have clearly distinguishable worldviews; but they are not separated from each other by deep rifts.

The following reflections explore the tension between regional socialization and the formation of national milieus. Following a discussion of the function of the region in milieu theory, this essay will probe the regional rootedness of sociomoral milieus (II). Taking a step back in order to pursue the argument more systematically, I will then consider the ways and means by which regions are constructed (III). Overall, the analysis describes the relationship between regional socialization and the formation of national milieus as a strained relationship, *not* one in which a "before" evolves into an "after." This argument will be revisited briefly, rather than fully developed, in the conclusion (IV). The aim is to identify possible interconnections among disparate problems and to test new lines of argument. Since I have attempted to construct a systematic argument, I have refrained from including an elaborate scholarly apparatus of references.

II. Region as a Structural Dimension of Sociomoral Milieus

An imbalance exists within milieu theory. Whereas two pre-political factors, religion and class, are politically viable, region is not. This imbalance has had a far-reaching impact on the further elaboration of milieu theory, for the region has increasingly constituted the *arena* in which the formation of milieus is actively investigated. In recent years, researchers have proposed what might be called a regionalist reformulation of Lepsius's premises, without, however, systematically examining the function of the region in the formation of milieus. They have conducted research—to use Clifford Geertz's phrase—not *in* villages, but *about* villages. Hence the depiction of regional milieus is experiencing a boom.[2] Not only re-

---

2. See Siegfried Weichlein, *Sozialmilieus und politische Kultur in der Weimarer Republik: Lebenswelt, Vereinskultur, Politik in Hessen* (Göttingen, 1996); Jürgen Herres,

gions, but also local societies are described as "milieus."[3] Particularly in research on the middle classes, even circles of friends now have the honor of being called "milieus."[4] Theoretical attempts to generalize those efforts within the frame of micro-, meso-, and macromilieus have not proved very convincing. The same is true of attempts to differentiate between milieus centering on organizations and on persons.[5] Both approaches tend to overlook two important considerations.

First, they miss Lepsius's point that community formations of the milieu type are *theoretically unlikely*. Therefore their success is all the more surprising. Successful milieu formation constitutes an achievement of the first order: the entrenchment of coherent, stable sociomoral orientations and codes of behavior on a high level of collectivity. Such formation cannot be taken as a matter of course, especially considering the different target groups and the extended periods of time involved. Because of this unlikeliness, milieus deserve study. "Meso-milieus," in essence denoting regional socialization, are less surprising. Such community-formations are based on different mechanisms of cohesion as well as of differentiation; they also rely on other forms of communication.

Second, both attempts to generalize overlook the fact that milieus are about *politics*. National milieus derive part of their legitimacy from politicizing the loyalties they have established via class and religious denomination. Such a designation, however, requires that a milieu be able to formulate criteria valid beyond the accidental boundaries that

---

Städtische Gesellschaft und katholische Vereine im Rheinland, 1840–1870 (Essen, 1996); and Dietmar von Reeken, "Protestantisches Milieu und 'liberale' Landeskirche: Milieubildungsprozesse in Oldenburg, 1849–1914," in *Religion im Kaiserreich: Milieus — Mentalitäten — Krisen*, ed. Olaf Blaschke and Frank-Michael Kuhlemann (Gütersloh, 1996), 290–315.

3. See Antonius Liedhegener, *Christentum und Urbanisierung: Katholiken und Protestanten in Münster und Bochum, 1830–1933* (Paderborn, 1997); Doris Kaufmann, *Katholisches Milieu in Münster, 1928–1933: Politische Aktionsformen und geschlechtsspezifische Verhaltensräume* (Düsseldorf, 1984); Cornelia Rauh-Kühne, *Katholisches Milieu und Kleinstadtgesellschaft: Ettlingen, 1918–1939* (Sigmaringen, 1991); Stefan Goch, *Sozialdemokratische Arbeiterbewegung und Arbeiterkultur im Ruhrgebiet: Eine Untersuchung am Beispiel Gelsenkirchen, 1848–1975* (Düsseldorf, 1990); and Stephan Bleek, "Ein Wählermilieu in der Großstadt — Bemerkungen zum Durchbruch der SPD in einem Münchner Arbeiterviertel," in *Der Aufstieg der deutschen Arbeiterbewegung: Sozialdemokratie und Freie Gewerkschaften im Parteiensystem und Sozialmilieu des Kaiserreichs*, ed. Gerhard A. Ritter (Munich, 1990), 139–43.

4. Ursula Krey, "Von der Religion zur Politik: Der Naumann-Kreis zwischen Protestantismus und Liberalismus," in *Religion im Kaiserreich*, ed. Blaschke and Kuhlemann, 350–81.

5. Olaf Blaschke and Frank-Michael Kuhlemann, "Religion in Geschichte und Gesellschaft: Sozialhistorische Perspektiven für die vergleichende Erforschung religiöser Mentalitäten und Milieus," in *Religion im Kaiserreich*, ed. idem, 7–56; Karl Rohe, *Wahlen und Wählertraditionen in Deutschland: Kulturelle Grundlagen deutscher Parteien und Parteiensysteme im 19. und 20. Jahrhundert* (Frankfurt a. M., 1992), 19ff.

demarcate a neighborhood or a city. Milieus must be integrated in some way on a higher level of collectivity, preferably a national level. Moreover, they must facilitate "generalized communication" and possess qualified elites. Hence they have to have a public sphere defining those who belong and those who do not — not with respect to private persons, but to the social roles they play.[6] Therefore, circles of friends do not constitute milieus; they are merely friendship circles. Similarly, local milieus may pass as milieus, but in view of the four major milieus postulated by Lepsius, they are only places where loyalties are constituted, not where they achieve their real effectiveness.

Based on these observations, one should perhaps distinguish between an older and newer type of milieu. The older, local type is based on face-to-face communication and specifically *local* sets of roles. This is best illustrated in the early modern town. Here, conformity to the generally accepted norms was supported by an argument that went roughly as follows: "Elsewhere this type of behavior may be possible, but *here*, things are different; that's why we are special." In modern milieus, by contrast, the adherence to norms is explained by the fact that "here" (in, say, Catholicism) things are the same way *everywhere.* That is why things can be — and must be — the same way "here" (i.e., locally) as well. Modern milieus, in other words, set generalized norms of behavior, thereby enabling certainties of expectation. The fulfilling of these expectations made for the exhilaration experienced by itinerant Social Democratic journeymen or traveling Catholics when they found similar structures of rules and behavior wherever they went. They immediately felt "at home."[7]

Regions are unable to develop easily into integrated milieus because they lack one decisive characteristic: the potential to achieve the *political* reformulation of sociomoral norms (unless one simply defines political units such as the German *Länder* as "regions," which seems out of the question). For this very reason, the existence of a "conservative milieu" (the fourth of Lepsius's milieus, along with Catholics, the labor movement, and the middle class) can only be conceded with reservations. After all, the conservative milieu was a regional phenomenon. Its societal model, its structural frame, and the sets of roles it offered ap-

---

6. See Thomas Mergel, "Grenzgänger: Das katholische Bürgertum im Rheinland zwischen bürgerlichem und katholischem Milieu, 1870–1914," in *Religion im Kaiserreich,* ed. Blaschke and Kuhlemann, 166–92.

7. This was true in these two milieus at the supranational level as well. When Catholics and Social Democrats appraised Catholicism and Social Democracy abroad, they consistently praised those features that they regarded as most familiar. See, for example, the travel report of the ultramontane Heinrich Hansjakob from Baden, *In Frankreich: Reise-Erinnerungen* (Mainz, 1874).

plied only to Prussia east of the Elbe River. It is decisive for a milieu, however, that it be able to develop its sociomoral behavioral expectations in different social landscapes. The success of Catholicism — the same holds true for the workers' movement and, with qualifications, for the liberal middle classes — lay in the very fact that the various conceptions of what a "good society" should look like were persuasive in Bavaria, Silesia, Westphalia, or the Rhineland, even though people in these places had different traditions of a "good society." Modern milieus, in short, are distinguished by the fact that they produce common expectations of conduct, conceptions of society, and perceptions of the opponent, even in settings with entirely different social structures and political cultures.

My argument proper begins at this point. Lepsius's milieu theory was ultimately characterized by a conception of modernization that was based on increasing inclusion. By their power to integrate politically on a national level, both class and religion appear as factors of modernity, whereas region is stuck in the realm of premodernity. The following reflections are intended to show that the three milieus deserving of this label — Catholicism, the workers' movement, and the liberal middle-class milieu — were in essence also characterized by regionality. Moreover, it was the tension between national integration and regional attachment that constituted the very modernity of these milieus. In their own way, all three were minority cultures, and strictly speaking, all three functioned generically as a means to encompass different regional manifestations, which in some cases (e.g., the middle class) coalesced quite late in the day and which, despite considerable homogeneity, continued to display distinctive characteristics.

One can also identify several structural commonalities among these three milieus that might be considered under the (admittedly problematic) rubric of "cultural orientations." All three combined a legacy of collective deprivation with the confident notion that they held the key to the best of all possible worlds. In all three cases, this certainty stemmed from a theology of history that stylized the group in question as the avant-garde leading the way to a happy future. This confidence alone differentiated these milieus from conservatism. Moreover, each of these milieus relied on a special code of integration. These codes were inclusive to such a degree that they constantly had to be reformulated. What it meant to be "Catholic" was a perennial bone of contention, just as controversy raged within the labor movement on the question of what "socialism" was, and just as there was constant discussion in the *Bürgertum* about what it meant to be *bürgerlich*. Consequently, affiliation was not justified in terms of an "analytical" description of "Catholic" or "worker." Rather, it had to be reinforced by means of a *normative* description. Through the very act of transforming an objective characteristic into a subjective one (for example, by "*willing* to be Catholic"), these movements qualified as socio*moral* phenomena. It was not enough to be baptized a Catholic or to be born a worker; one had to put one's heart into it, so to speak. On this basis, all three milieus developed partial markets and socialized in exclusive associations. In each of them, the affiliation of the individual extended from "the cradle to the grave." For the middle class, however, these characteristics held true only in moderated form. Based on both its longevity and the hegemonic power of its particular interpretation of the world, the middle class won from the others a degree of respect that it did not reciprocate. The middle-class claim to represent the "universal estate" did not entirely lack persuasive sway over the two other social formations. As a result, its value system and its modes of sociability—for example, those fostered in voluntary associations—worked as models for the Catholics and the workers, too.

Catholicism

On the national level, German Catholicism exhibited impressive homogeneity. In the pomp and display associated with its biannual (after 1880, annual) Catholic conventions (*Katholikentage*), Catholicism presented itself as more cohesive than perhaps even Social Democracy. The large Catholic associations were structured in the same ways everywhere: this was above all true of the People's Association for Catholic Germany (Volksverein für das katholische Deutschland) but held for Kolping's Association of Journeymen (Gesellenverein) and for the numerous organizations targeting other kinds of social groups, such as mothers, husbands, and bachelors. Until the *Kulturkampf,* the administrative structure of the ecclesiastic hierarchy had been aligned to the Rhenish model. With the characteristic exception of Bavaria, the Center Party (Deutsche Zentrumspartei) presented much the same face throughout Germany. Indeed, Catholicism seemed so cohesive that it was difficult to rebut opponents' charges that it was subject to external manipulation, which in turn contributed to the legendary reputation of the Jesuits.

Nevertheless, Catholicism was essentially regional in character. The German variety of Catholicism is basically located in four core regions: the Rhineland, Westphalia, Silesia, and Bavaria. Only in these regions was Catholicism a majority culture; only here was Catholicism traditionally tied so closely to popular culture that it appeared as a natural way of life at school as well as in public festival culture. In other regions, Catholics were exposed to daily conflict with other denominations. In response they developed either an aggressive culture of defense, as happened in parts of Swabia, or a peaceful culture of negotiation, which prompted charges from the core regions that they were betraying the things most sacred to Catholics. This was the case in Baden, where a politicization of Catholicism occurred only late and with great difficulty.[8]

Among the core regions, the Rhineland was once again an exception. It was characterized by an urban, bourgeois, commercial culture, located in an area of conurbation that transcended political boundaries. Significantly, it was at the same time an old ecclesiastic territory. The other three regional strongholds showed a number of common features. They were rural in structure and had an influential nobility. Industrialization, where it occurred relatively early — as in Westphalia and Silesia — took place not in urban areas but in the countryside. Prosperity in these three regions was substantially lower than in the Rhineland.

These circumstances molded the different Catholicisms in the four core regions. In the Rhineland, an urban middle-class Catholicism developed with a pronounced social bent and with a basic tenor that was ideologically liberal. Compared to those living elsewhere, Rhenish Catholics were more conscious that they lived in a class society: they oscillated between a social Catholicism marked by anticapitalist instincts and a bourgeois Catholicism involving a highly developed self-confidence as laity in their church. Here connections to the liberal bourgeoisie were severed later and less abruptly than in other regions. Catholic members of the middle class showed themselves more open to modernity than elsewhere; but this did not preclude a burgher tradition of social thought that manifested itself in industrial districts as paternalist social welfare.

Silesia can be posited as an example lying at the opposite end of the spectrum. Its brand of Catholicism was dominated by nobles who were often mine owners, who generally favored industrial progress yet tended to be politically reactionary, and who exhibited even more characteristics

---

8. For Rhenish Catholicism, see Herres, *Städtische Gesellschaft;* Thomas Mergel, *Zwischen Klasse und Konfession: Katholisches Bürgertum im Rheinland, 1794–1914* (Göttingen, 1994); and Christoph Weber, *Aufklärung und Orthodoxie am Mittelrhein, 1820–1850* (Munich, 1973). For Westphalia: Wilhelm Schulte, *Volk und Staat: Westfalen im Vormärz und in der Revolution von 1848/49* (Münster, 1954); Heinz Reif, *Westfälischer Adel, 1770–1860: Vom Herrschaftsstand zur regionalen Elite* (Göttingen, 1979); and Jonathan Sperber, *Popular Catholicism in Nineteenth-Century Germany* (Princeton, NJ, 1984), which talks about both, but describes more the Westphalian than the Rhenish type. For Bavaria: Werner K. Blessing, *Staat und Kirche in der Gesellschaft: Institutionelle Autorität und mentaler Wandel während des 19. Jahrhunderts* (Göttingen, 1982); and Hermann Hörger, *Kirche, Dorfreligion und bäuerliche Gesellschaft* (Munich, 1978). Silesia is still terra incognita.

of living in a diaspora than Catholics living in other regions. After a long period of Catholic enlightenment, which included an extended history under the enlightened bureaucratic regimes of Austria and Prussia, Silesian Catholicism became decidedly clerical, though also closely tied to the state. Its social thought remained preindustrial.

Westphalian Catholicism was clerical but removed from the state; it did not exhibit an appreciable degree of enlightenment tradition. As a noble and agrarian Catholicism rooted in the strong aristocratic traditions of the seventeenth and eighteenth centuries, it showed an inclination toward revivalism and was ideologically probably the most intransigent. Deep down, Westphalian Catholicism was corporatist in a very traditional way: the acceptance of class society that came quite early to Rhenish Catholics took far longer here. Yet as with both Rhenish and Silesian Catholicism, Westphalian Catholicism grew in a territory acquired by Prussia. Hence religious and anti-Prussian sentiments blended to such an extent that it was difficult to distinguish one from the other.

Bavarian Catholicism, lastly, was above all pragmatic. This makes it similar to the Rhenish variety. However, two other features distinguished it as well. On the one hand, Bavarian Catholicism was supported by independent, propertied farmers, who also provided the most important pool for the recruitment of priests. On the other hand, reference to the dynastic state tradition was constantly invoked. Hence, in stark contrast to variants of Catholicism found in the other regions, Bavarian Catholicism incorporated traits of a state religion.

These regional distinctions within German Catholicism remained visible in the *Kaiserreich,* even on the level of semantic representation alone. When the *Katholikentage* were held alternately in the core regions (including Austria) — as they were most of the time — opening speeches often extended a welcome to representatives from the various "tribes" (*Stämme*) or "districts" (*Gaue*). Despite the rhetoric of unity, Catholic publicity mirrored such regional differences. As one traveled further east, the Catholic press displayed less awareness of social issues and class divisions, whereas clericalism increased. In general, Catholicism in western Germany proved to be more "bourgeois" but, at the same time, more socially conscious. The diverse social orientations of the Catholic workers' associations were also reflected in the differing regional centers. The People's Association for Catholic Germany, the Christian unions, and the closely associated Western German Union of Catholic Workers' Associations (Verband katholischer Arbeitervereine Westdeutschlands) — not to mention Kolping's Association of Journeymen — had their main centers of support in the Rhenish-Westphalian industrial region. By contrast, the antiunionist Union of Catholic Workers' Associations (Verband katholischer Arbeitervereine, Sitz Berlin) was strongest in Silesia.[9]

Two further areas of analysis can serve to illustrate regional differences within German Catholicism: the structure of clerical elites, and regional cultures of piety.

Formally, the training of priests after 1850 was essentially the same everywhere. But regional educational traditions and social cultures nevertheless gave the Catholic clergy differing sociocultural profiles. In the Rhineland, the image of the priest-bourgeois (*Priesterbürger*), cultivated in the era of Catholic enlightenment, persisted through the nineteenth century; there, seminary training was less "Roman" than in Bavaria. It made a great difference whether one studied theology at the University of Bonn, where after the doctrine of papal infallibility in 1869 most theology professors moved over to Old Catholicism (*Altkatholizismus*), or whether one received instruction from the conservative faculty at the University of Würzburg. Whereas in Bavaria the second-born sons of more affluent farmers were predestined to become priests, the clergy in the Rhineland was recruited mainly from the petty bourgeoisie in small or medium-sized cities, many of whom were employed in the public service. The *Habitus* of the quasi-bourgeois urban priest of the Rhineland was distinct from that of the "countrified" parish priest of rural Bavaria. Both, however, can be considered to have reflected their regional cultures. Thus a basic requirement was fulfilled for making clerics popular leaders, a role they rightly claimed for themselves.

Similar findings apply to cultures of piety. After the formation of piety through ultramontanism had displaced hundreds of local pilgrimage sites, regional centers of worship evolved: Kevelaer in the Rhineland, Telgte in Westphalia, Altötting in Bavaria. Saints and festival cultures also became regional in character: the equestrian parade in honor of Saint Leonhard was a Bavarian speciality, Saint Ludger was worshipped only in Westphalia. The pilgrimage to the Holy Frock in Trier, no matter how transregional it was in its instrumentalization of religious politics, remained in essence a regional pilgrimage. The worship of supraregional saints, however, laid different emphases according to region: In the Rhineland and Westphalia, and especially in the Ruhrgebiet, Saint Joseph was gradually stylized into a "worker." In Bavaria, however, he was a carpenter, and remained so. The reading matter

---

9. This union also had support in the Saar region. Not just with respect to Catholicism, the Saar played a special role from time to time due to its peripheral location; see, for example, Klaus-Michael Mallmann, "Ultramontanismus und Arbeiterbewegung im Kaiserreich: Überlegungen am Beispiel des Saarreviers," in *Deutscher Katholizismus im Umbruch zur Moderne,* ed. Wilfried Loth (Stuttgart, 1991).

available to Catholics was also regionally distinct. Whereas devotional literature had to deal with regional issues, the style of Catholic writings differed from region to region as fundamentally as did the content. The inflammatory literature of Friedrich Dasbach was popular primarily in the area around Trier, whereas the writings of Konrad von Bolanden enjoyed their greatest resonance in Bavaria.

Catholics were anything but unaware of these regional distinctions. Toward the end of the nineteenth century, a process of re-regionalization apparently took place. For example, to supplement the national Catholics' conventions, regional ones sprang up as well. The manner in which they were staged followed the same logic as the national displays; but in their image-cultivation and in their political demands, they referred to regional issues. Events surrounding the apparitions of the Virgin Mary in Marpingen not only exhibited anti-Prussian tendencies found elsewhere; they also pointed to the subregional character of what one might call a *Hinterland*-Catholicism in a mining region around Trier, which could not identify itself with the middle-class traditions of the Rhineland to which it belonged politically.

Catholics too did not always perceive themselves as belonging together. The Bavarian Center Party and its representatives in the Berlin Reichstag consistently played the role of outsiders: although they were Catholics, they were also Bavarians looking after Bavarian interests. To identify the modernizing wing in Catholicism with two Rhenish cities, Cologne and Moenchengladbach, made exceedingly clear what camp this direction belonged to. Hence the Catholic milieu was not as homogeneous nationally as it appeared from without. Nevertheless, the overall cohesion of Catholicism was high. On the one hand, relative homogeneity of iconography and ritual tended to paper over regional differences. On the other hand, major political conflicts made the Center Party a catalyst for Catholic unity. Finally, the opponents of Catholicism, perceived as a united hostile front, welded Catholics even more tightly together.

The Workers' Movement

The workers' movement also showed considerable regional disparities, most notably in the degree of organization, readiness to strike, potential for coalitions, and social culture. In general, one can speak of a north-south divide: the south was more moderate and reformist, the north, more radical and "proletarian." Similarities in daily routine, the gradual alignment of working conditions and legal positions across the Reich, and finally the role of the Social Democratic Party—these were all deter-

minants in the process of homogenization of the working classes.[10] However, this did not mean that the Ruhrgebiet even came close to being as
Social Democratic as, for instance, the structurally analogous strongholds in Berlin or Saxony. Regional differences stemmed primarily from
the fact that, in the course of industrialization, varying social groups
coalesced in areas with different legal and social traditions. Whereas
miners in the Ruhrgebiet had a long tradition of corporatist pride and
therefore had difficulty in committing to the proletarian identity of the
Social Democratic workers' movement, migrant workers were not en-
cumbered by such ties. For them, Social Democracy offered a home that
did not have to displace another home. Hence the Social Democratic
workers' movement in the Ruhrgebiet may be described as a culture of
migrants from afar. As such it became established as a "daughter of the
Catholic milieu" — the culture of the locals. In terms of its mechanisms
of cohesion, it imitated this older culture.[11]

By contrast, the workers' movement in Munich was primarily a
culture of migrants from the city's environs. In lower-class neighborhoods, a Social Democratic "culture of notables" soon developed, which
was not much different from that found among middle-class groups.
Saxony, on the other hand, may also be designated as a culture of locals.
Workers' changing ways of life were accompanied by a change in political attitudes. To this development may be ascribed the origins of Saxon
Social Democracy's inclination toward orthodoxy, which stemmed, first,
from a relationship between employer and employee freed of corporatist
residues and, second, from the broad cultural rootedness of the workers'
movement regionally: the Social Democrats were *the* Saxon party.[12]

These two different strands — corporatist traditions and migrant
traditions — at first determined the German labor movement's regionally
distinctive political cultures. Saxony's working classes were organized to
a much higher degree than were workers in the south. Workers in Berlin, too, or in the Hanseatic cities went on strike five to seven times more
often than their colleagues in Württemberg. To an even greater extent,
however, these traditions molded the *social* culture of the respective
regions. The tradition of the worker-farmer remained dominant in the

---

10. See the overviews in *Der Aufstieg der deutschen Arbeiterbewegung,* ed. Ritter;
and Gerhard A. Ritter and Klaus Tenfelde, *Arbeiter im Deutschen Kaiserreich, 1871–1914*
(Bonn, 1992).

11. Karl Rohe, *Vom Revier zum Ruhrgebiet: Wahlen, Parteien, politische Kultur*
(Essen, 1986).

12. See Karsten Rudolph, "Das 'rote Königreich': Die sächsische Sozialdemokratie im Wilhelminischen Deutschland," in *Sachsen im Kaiserreich: Politik, Wirtschaft
und Gesellschaft im Umbruch,* ed. Simone Lässig and Karl Heinrich Pohl (Weimar,
1997), 87–99.

Ruhrgebiet, right down to the level of residential development patterns: workers' colonies had small gardens, and "villages" were located around the colliery, with farms lying in between. In Berlin or Breslau, by contrast, urban living quarters soon predominated, featuring multiple backyards and several floors. Obviously this was connected to the different structures of industry. However, industry was only one factor in the process whereby the image of the working man in Germany was regionally constructed. In Saxony, Silesia, or Berlin, this image was based on the model of the urban proletarian. In the Ruhrgebiet or in Württemberg, however, it was based squarely on a "respectability" of middle-class provenance or the self-sustaining abilities of the farming worker — both ideas of independence.

Awareness of the degree to which the working-class milieu was regionally rooted also proved to be politically significant. Thus, for example, most SPD candidates came from the region in which they stood for election. Even though they might temporarily occupy posts as functionaries in other cities, they were generally nominated in constituencies close to where they lived or originated. Therefore, in the SPD, too, the cultural proximity of the candidate, substantiated by his regional attachment, appeared to be beneficial for the identification of voters with the entire party. In 1913, a newspaper representing Essen workers complained that "their" leader Otto Hue had to be elected in Berlin-Neukölln.[13] Bavarian Social Democrats — in a parallel way to the Bavarian Center — demonstrated that while they saw themselves as workers and Social Democrats, they were also Bavarians. In the major conflicts over SPD policy, regional characteristics also surfaced. The question of revisionism divided south German Social Democracy from its northern variant to such a degree that Albert Südekum distinguished between "our southern Germans" and "[August] Bebel and his Saxon bodyguards — or, more bluntly, his Committee of Public Safety."[14] When the Independent Socialists left the SPD in 1917, Karl Kautsky commented that "the differences of views" had been "not of a personal, but rather of a geographic, nature."[15]

As with the Catholic milieu, the homogeneity of the Social Democratic milieu was premised in large measure on the way it was seen by its opponents and on its members' self-stylization as outsiders and as repre-

---

13. Cited in Karl Rohe, "Die Ruhrgebietssozialdemokratie im Wilhelminischen Kaiserreich und ihr politischer und kultureller Kontext," in *Der Aufstieg der deutschen Arbeiterbewegung,* ed. Ritter, 330.

14. Cited in Karsten Rudolph, *Die sächsische Sozialdemokratie vom Kaiserreich zur Republik (1871–1923)* (Weimar, 1995), 76.

15. Cited in Ursula Mittmann, *Fraktion und Partei: Ein Vergleich von Zentrum und Sozialdemokratie im Kaiserreich* (Düsseldorf, 1976), 12.

sentatives of the "universal class" of the future. As with the Catholic milieu, it was the standardization of community-forming symbols, apparent for instance in the May Day celebrations, as well as the party's own homogenizing power, that led to a mental structure of "belonging together." Regional differences occasionally collided, but they generated no centrifugal momentum.

The *Bürgertum*

More markedly and for longer than Catholicism and the workers' movement, the German middle class retained its regional character. Until the end of the *Kaiserreich* it is probably more useful to speak of *Bürgertümer* in the plural. This points to the continuation of traditions from the early modern era. Regionally different urban forms and varied socioeconomic circumstances not only molded structurally different middle classes; they also shaped clear distinctions in self-awareness and worldviews.[16] The middle class of the Rhineland, a pioneer of the "modern" bourgeoisie, was constituted as an urban commercial and functional elite that maintained intensive contacts to neighboring regions and always received inflows of migrants. It viewed itself as an elite, clearly distancing itself from the *Mittelstand.* Liberalism, denominational tolerance, a consciousness of class society, and openness to industrialization were the defining features of this elite. By contrast, the southwestern German middle class was basically preindustrial. During most of the nineteenth century, it can be characterized as a small-town trade bourgeoisie (*kleinstädtisches Gewerbebürgertum*) that developed — sometimes with rigid religious boundaries — its own brand of liberalism. This liberalism was grounded in the distinctiveness of the hometown from the external world. It was also based on a relatively egalitarian structure of ownership and far-reaching forms of political participation that went back to early modern

---

16. See *Liberalismus und Region: Zur Geschichte des deutschen Liberalismus im 19. Jahrhundert,* ed. Lothar Gall and Dieter Langewiesche (Munich, 1995); and *Liberalismus im 19. Jahrhundert,* ed. Dieter Langewiesche (Göttingen, 1988). For the Rhenish middle class, see Rudolf Boch, *Grenzenloses Wachstum: Das rheinische Wirtschaftsbürgertum und seine Industrialisierungsdebatte* (Göttingen, 1991); Mergel, *Zwischen Klasse und Konfession;* and Friedrich Lenger, "Bürgertum und Stadtverwaltung in rheinischen Großstädten des 19. Jahrhunderts," in *Stadt und Bürgertum,* ed. Lothar Gall (Munich, 1990), 97–169. For southwest Germany, see Paul Nolte, *Gemeindebürgertum und Liberalismus in Baden, 1800–1850* (Göttingen, 1994); and Manfred Hettling, *Reform ohne Revolution: Bürgertum, Bürokratie und kommunale Selbstverwaltung in Württemberg, 1800–1850* (Göttingen, 1990). For Bavaria, see Dirk Schumann, *Bayerns Unternehmer in Gesellschaft und Staat, 1834–1914* (Göttingen, 1992); and Hans-Walter Schmuhl, "Bürgertum und städtische Selbstverwaltung im 19. Jahrhundert: Nürnberg und Braunschweig im Vergleich" (Habil. diss., University of Bielefeld, 1996).

principles of co-opting burghers into local government. In the Bavarian cities, however, where long-standing commercial traditions had solidified into corporatist privileges, there was a strong dominance of the patriciate and/or merchant community. Socially and culturally, this dominance was supported by mechanisms similar to those in the Rhineland; but the Bavarian middle class developed a more traditional attitude toward industrial society.

The middle classes also revealed cohesive mechanisms that related the social group to the region. Marriage circles that were already extended to the region in early modern times (just as the majority of migratory activity took place within the region) remained regionalized until the end of the nineteenth century. Only a small section of the upper bourgeoisie and the political class taking shape in the *Kaiserreich* socialized on a national level. For the groups in question, it was more probable that one would search for a wife in neighboring regions than further afield. These circles were a visible expression of business ties, too. Companies founded or managed by middle-class entrepreneurs were most commonly regional enterprises. Even if they were international firms and exported widely, their manufacturing sites usually remained in the vicinity where management and key business partners continued to live. The educated middle class was also regionally oriented. Apart from a few universities whose attraction was supraregional—Berlin and Marburg, for example—the majority of their sons studied, at least for most of their university years, at institutions nearby. Thus the University of Bonn can be considered to be where the educated middle class of the Rhineland was molded; the same was true for Breslau in Silesia.

The awareness of regional attachment and of the task to represent the region were two parts of the fundamental social ideology of the middle class. Pride in one's own *Heimat* and its cultural achievements; consciousness of one's own position as representative of the region; feelings of superiority vis-à-vis other middle classes and other regions— all these dispositions were especially pronounced in the Rhenish middle class. Consider how the lord mayor of Bonn, Leopold Kaufmann, described a circle of city magistrates in Aschaffenburg in 1861. "Those Bavarians are an incredibly crude lot," wrote Kaufmann. "They have a long way to go before they'll even come close to our level of general *Bildung*."[17] In short, what gave these regional middle classes the consciousness of belonging together was above all a similar *Habitus*. Grammar school and university, socializing style and the middle-class family:

---

17. Cited in Thomas Mergel, "Für eine bürgerliche Kirche: Antiultramontanismus, Liberalismus und Bürgertum, 1820–1850," *Zeitschrift für die Geschichte des Oberrheins* 144 (1996): 392–427, here 405.

these elements of a middle-class *Habitus* were not only ways of life; they also perpetuated ideologies that, despite being regionally rooted, nevertheless substantiated an awareness of a common social position and a common mission in the world. Such feelings and ideologies proved to be much stronger than the more narrow political guidelines set by the parties that claimed to speak for the middle class. Most of all, this awareness transcended religious denomination, enabling Catholics and Jews to participate in it as well.

III. Collective Identities and the Construction of Regions

As we see, those social groups and movements that managed to achieve integration on a national level and presented highly cohesive images of themselves were very diverse regionally. To say this is not to argue that the category of "milieu" ought to be discarded; rather, it reminds historians of their duty to describe as accurately as possible the function of the region in the process of milieu formation and milieu cohesion. On a regional level, milieus revealed structural similarities. The social qualities (*Neigungen*) in the Rhineland that molded Catholicism, the workers' movement, and, with some qualifications, the middle class, are one example. The pragmatism found in Bavaria is another; the revivalist strand in Westphalia, yet another. Precisely what is Rhenish, what Bavarian, what Westphalian about these movements, though? What constitutes their uniqueness?

Regions are clusters of social, political, and cultural communication. Economic history deals with such issues as the roadways, rivers, and similar conditions of production or reproduction.[18] However, these conditions are not themselves "natural." Mountains and rivers are often boundaries. Frequently, however, as in Swiss Graubünden or in Tyrol, they also function as a means to establish connections. In the ecclesiastical state of Cologne, the Rhine was a boundary; in that of Trier, it linked things together. Political boundaries, too, divide sovereign territories; but in so doing, they can just as well make new connections desirable. In the lands encompassing the territories of the Rhineland, Lorraine, Belgium, and Holland, it was the border itself that stimulated a more intensive flow of goods. In most cases, therefore, communicability within geographical spaces is established not only through similarity, but also through difference — differences, for instance, of social conditions or structures of power, both often fostering the leveling of legal distinctions. Seen as a social, cultural, and political interconnection of traditions, a region is a

---

18. See *Staat, Region und Industrialisierung*, ed. Hubert Kiesewetter (Ostfildern, 1985); and *Region und Industrialisierung*, ed. Sidney Pollard (Göttingen, 1980).

constructed entity, though the degree to which it is constructed may vary. Modern Bavaria was not created until the nineteenth century, by means of dynastic pageantry, standardization of secondary socialization (schools, the military, etc.), and federalist self-imaging. And whereas the preconditions for the development of the Rhineland had been created through legal-political integration by the French, only the common antipathy to Prussian rule after the Congress of Vienna launched the growth of a Rhenish identity. Even so, this identity could not have arisen had not another important historical prerequisite existed, which made the brief experience of French rule into a lasting, stable orientation: the fact that the largest part of the Rhineland consisted of the former ecclesiastical principalities of Cologne and Trier. Simplifying things somewhat, one can therefore say that the Rhineland was constituted of clerical rule plus French integration plus anti-Prussianism.

Moreover, one must contend with a number of structural conditions that distinguish a region. One such condition has been labeled *symbolische Ortsbezogenheit*:[19] individuals move within a space, but deeper structures determine how a space is conceived and shaped.[20] The dimensions of this space, in fact, are matters determined by one's mobility and perceptual horizon. How far afield does it make sense to cultivate continuous contacts? What degree of proximity enables a density of communication that may tie particular and lasting memories to a specific "there": the distance one can travel in a single day, perhaps? Answers to questions like these will depend on something more than concrete spatial mobility. Even the awareness of what a region is may change, and it may not be congruent with the finding that a shared structural affinity exists.

Consider: the Ruhrgebiet took shape out of legally, socially, and culturally disparate landscapes. Yet it eventually displayed similarities of production and lifestyle. Analytically, it can be described as a largely homogeneous region as early as the last third of the nineteenth century. However, as an object of identification, the Ruhrgebiet only came into being in the twentieth century. Indeed, a good argument could be made that the actual cultural homogenization of the "Ruhrpott" is only occurring now that its heyday has passed.[21] Thus we see that the concept of the "imagined community" is also applicable to the region, today prob-

---

19. Heiner Treiner, "Symbolische Ortsbezogenheit," *Kölner Zeitschrift für Soziologie und Sozialpsychologie* 17 (1965): 73–97, 254–97.

20. For example, friends from the Ruhrgebiet still say that my hometown of Regensburg "is not even a real city."

21. Only lately has identification with soccer clubs such as Borussia Dortmund and Schalke 04 shed its local connotations and begun to exhibit features of a regional identity; the chant "Ruhrpott" is only a few years old.

ably more than in the past. Radio and television now convey very concrete impressions of the region in which one lives. No fellow countryman would likely refute the thesis that the Westdeutsche Rundfunk is actively knitting together — constructing — a regional identity that has not existed for very long: the identity of an area we call North Rhine–Westphalia. Today, however, the regional space we generally speak of has become larger, due to changes in the scale of communication.[22]

A further structural feature facilitating the construction of regions — one that is too often neglected — is the family. Since the early modern period, the space in which a family socializes has most typically been the region. With the exception of the upper crust, even in the early twentieth century the mobility of familial formation should not be overestimated. For it too depends on the possibility of continual contact. Because families are always in the process of being "established," such contact is necessarily closely tied to other communicative options that are largely regional in nature: business relations, universities, associations, and so on.

Lastly, we must not forget two factors that are crucial to the construction of regions: language and historical memory. Dialects form clear boundaries, and they are long-lived. Even if they are only recognizable as slight linguistic colorations, as in most areas where North German *Plattdeutsch* is spoken, they act as sociological determinants, segregating those who belong from those who do not. This may be one reason that the Rhineland and Westphalia, despite their structural similarities, have always preserved a notable distinctiveness. Historical memory is naturally favored in the case of regions that have been integrated through the dynastic state. Bavaria is not the only German region that has been able to write its own history, to create its own dynastic myths. Where these possibilities do not exist, narratives of difference take place, setting the regional society against the state, which is then perceived as alien. These narratives may often draw on categories such as class or denomination for purposes of distinction. The Cologne Troubles of 1837–38 encoded a regional difference in religious terms. Later in the nineteenth century, that coding worked as a religious myth of self-invention for the Rhineland, whereby the fact was covered up that the region had actually been created by the actions of external forces (first the French, then the Prussians). That the demarcation of insiders and outsiders can result in the appearance of *regional* "friend-foe" dichotomies — of regional "Vaterländer der Feinde"[23] — comes as no surprise. In Bavarian historical memory, the war of 1866 is still considered the

---

22. For this argument, see Benedict Anderson, *Die Erfindung der Nation: Zur Karriere eines erfolgreichen Konzepts* (Frankfurt a. M., 1993).

23. Michael Jeismann, *Das Vaterland der Feinde: Studien zum nationalen Feindbegriff und Selbstverständnis in Deutschland und Frankreich, 1792–1918* (Stuttgart, 1992).

"most beautiful war" because it was the last in which one was allowed to shoot at Prussians.

In this context, it is not always clear from the outset which spaces have actually come to constitute "regions" and which have not. If Westphalia is to be considered a region, what then do the residents of the Münster region, of eastern Westphalia, and of the Ruhrgebiet have in common? This question can only be answered by asking which constructions of social, political, and cultural traditions are viable and "successful," and which ones are not. This in turn can only be answered from a perspective that is found too seldom in regional studies: the comparative dimension. Only by comparative analysis can one hope to determine exactly what is "Westphalian" about the Westphalians, or in what respect Rhenish Liberals and Catholics are closer to one another than Rhenish and Bavarian Catholics. These questions, of course, are also relevant to the study of Protestants.

IV. Conclusions

Social formations on a national level — not unlike sociomoral milieus, and not unlike nations themselves — are fairly abstract constructions. To a large degree they are dependent on imagination and can be linked to experience only in exceptional situations, as in wars, or, for Catholics, in *Katholikentagen*. Regions, for their part, allow for the imagination of communities without losing one's ground, so to speak: their very existence can be confirmed more easily through everyday experience. Idioms, social and political structures, and traditions, but also landscapes and climates — these things are constitutive of regional identities. The supraregional pattern of identification (be it class or religion) that characterizes milieus drew on the persuasive power of these regional patterns, even though the relationship between both levels was usually characterized by a certain tension. Generalized communication, which is typical of milieus but also of other functional systems (for example, the military), can only be understood if its referents draw on concrete experience. Only if one could be a Catholic or a Social Democrat without having to relinquish a Rhenish or Saxon identity — only then was it possible to augment one's identity without diminishing oneself in other respects. These regional majority cultures provided the self-confidence for Catholics or Social Democrats to survive on the national level, where they were a minority and lived on the margins of society. The accompanying process of politicization of class or religion revealed for these individuals that the daily conflicts of denominational struggle or class conflict, though carried out in their small worlds, were indeed "important." In this respect the discourse of milieu enforced regional identifications by demonstrating that this was a part of the world where significant things were going on. Milieu and region: both needed one another. From this perspective it seems plausible to suggest that the de-regionalization of collective identities that occurred in Germany in the wake of the First World War was related to the decline of the sociomoral milieu not long thereafter.

Part 2

EMANCIPATION, THE PUBLIC SPHERE, AND THE GERMAN BOURGEOISIE

Emancipation and Embourgeoisement: The Jews, the State, and the Middle Classes in Saxony and Anhalt-Dessau

Simone Lässig

I. Introduction

In France the emancipation of the Jewish minority was a child of the revolution. Confident in the integrating strength of bourgeois society, the French National Assembly saw no reason to demand that the Jews sacrifice their identity and lifestyle as compensation for being granted full civil rights. The question of how the minority should adapt itself to the majority in sociocultural terms could therefore be answered with reference mainly to the individual. The state did not demand collective acculturation, and until the second half of the nineteenth century this was not sought by the majority of Jews.[1]

In Germany, by contrast, the emancipation of the Jews was a child of bureaucratic reform — of the long-drawn-out development of bourgeois society, itself ridden with contradictions and "steered from above." Influenced and driven by the educational optimism of the German Enlighten-

---

1. See the excellent analysis in Phyllis Cohen Albert, "Israelite and Jew: How Did Nineteenth Century French Jews Understand Assimilation?" in *Assimilation and Community: The Jews in Nineteenth-Century Europe,* ed. Jonathan Frankel and Steven J. Zipperstein (Cambridge, 1992), 88–110. Cf. Paula E. Hyman, "The Social Contexts of Assimilation: Village Jews and City Jews in Alsace," ibid; Michael Graetz, *The Jews in Nineteenth-Century France* (Stanford, CA, 1996); Jacob Katz, ed., *Toward Modernity: The European Jewish Model* (New Brunswick, NJ, 1987); Pierre Birnbaum, "Between Social and Political Assimilation: Remarks on the History of Jews in France," in *Paths of Emancipation: Jews, States, Citizenship,* ed. idem and Ira Katznelson (Princeton, NJ, 1995), 94–127; and David Sorkin, "Religious Reforms and Secular Trends in German-Jewish Life," *Leo Baeck Institute Yearbook* 40 (1995): 169–84.

ment, some rulers and state officials developed programs for the cultural, social, and moral advancement of the Jews — that is, for their *bürgerliche Verbesserung*. The fulfilment of these expectations, however, was seen as a *prerequisite* to emancipation, or, rather, emancipation by stages. Whereas in Habsburg lands, in Baden, in Anhalt-Dessau, and in Prussia a conditional start to reform was discussed, and in part set in train, as early as the 1780s, the "Jewish question" remained a *noli me tangere* in other German states until well into the nineteenth century, when it finally fell under the rubric of "educational policy."

From the perspective of political and legal history, the specificity of this "German path to Jewish emancipation"[2] has been worked through fairly exhaustively.[3] As far as the origins of a "Jewish-German subculture" are concerned, the features of Jewish emancipation have also been sketched in.[4] Unaddressed in this literature, however, is the question whether differences in the course of emancipation among the various states were due to differences in the form and tempo of Jewry's own modernization in Germany's diverse regions.[5] Did the states' "Jewish policy" (*Judenpolitik*) influence the Jews' traditionalism or their readiness to acculturate? If so, one must then raise the question of what consequences this had for the cultural embourgeoisement (*Verbürgerlichung*) of the minority.[6] The comparison with France prompts the hypothesis that these processes were always interdependent. Having achieved their emancipation relatively early, French Jews developed a much

---

2. Walter Grab, *Der deutsche Weg der Judenemanzipation, 1789–1938* (Munich, 1991).

3. Among the pioneering studies, see Reinhard Rürup, *Emanzipation und Antisemitismus* (Frankfurt a. M., 1987); cf. Jacob Toury, *Der Eintritt der Juden ins deutsche Bürgertum: Eine Dokumentation* (Tel Aviv, 1972); idem, *Soziale und politische Geschichte der Juden in Deutschland, 1847–1871* (Düsseldorf, 1977); Jacob Katz, *Aus dem Ghetto in die bürgerliche Gesellschaft: Jüdische Emanzipation, 1770–1870* (Frankfurt a. M., 1986); and idem, *Zur Assimilation und Emanzipation der Juden* (Darmstadt, 1982). For a recent overview, see Michael Brenner, Stefi Jersch-Wenzel, and Michael A. Meyer, eds., *Deutsch-Jüdische Geschichte der Neuzeit*, vol. 2, *Emanzipation und Akkulturation, 1780–1871* (Munich, 1996).

4. David Sorkin, *The Transformation of German Jewry, 1780–1840* (New York, 1987).

5. The terms *modernizing* and *modernism* are used here to describe those profound challenges or changes — including all facets of everyday life — that arose from the Jews' incorporation into emerging bourgeois society. Both expressions are used in Brenner, Jersch-Wenzel, and Meyer, *Deutsch-Jüdische Geschichte*, vol. 2.

6. See Jacob Toury, "Der Eintritt der Juden ins deutsche Bürgertum," in *Das Judentum in der deutschen Umwelt, 1800–1850*, ed. Hans Liebeschütz and Arnold Paucker (Tübingen, 1977), 139–242; and Shulamit Volkov, "Die Verbürgerlichung der Juden: Eigenart und Paradigma," in *Bürgertum im 19. Jahrhundert*, ed. Jürgen Kocka, 3 vols. (Munich, 1988), 2:343–71.

weaker disposition toward reform and acculturation than their German counterparts who were still subject to "educational legislation" (*Erziehungsgesetzgebung*). Thus French Jews remained well behind German Jews in their level of embourgeoisement.

Contrary to the prevailing practice of writing German history from a Prussian or south German perspective, this analysis will examine the connection between emancipation and embourgeoisement in two less often studied, but very different, states: the Kingdom of Saxony and the Duchy of Anhalt-Dessau. Saxony was a medium-sized state that industrialized early, but, lacking an intermediate phase of enlightened despotism, it took up the question of Jewish emancipation very late; when it finally did so, its response was particularly hesitant. By contrast, the small, predominantly agrarian state of Anhalt-Dessau played a pioneering role in the development of a specifically German "educational policy." It seems fruitful, therefore, to analyze the driving forces, the structures, the leaders, and the timing whereby Jews in these two lands undertook their journey to modernity.

II.   Jews in Anhalt-Dessau

Under Prince Franz (1758–1817), Anhalt-Dessau was recognized as a model of religious toleration. This was a land, wrote Lebrecht Bäntsch in 1801, "where Protestants, Catholics, and Jews live together in peace and harmony [and] look after their own affairs; no one disturbs anyone else in the observance of his religion and his worship of his God."[7] In such an atmosphere, imbued with the spirit of the Enlightenment, Prince Franz's "educational optimism" was transferred at an early date to younger Jews who sought to put the state's liberal policy (*Beglückungspolitik*) into practice within the Jewish *Gemeinde*. Among these Jews' ideas for reform, a central place was occupied by the problem of *Bildung,* whose connotations include education, upbringing, and cultivation. The reformers deliberately latched on to the fact that education — even religious education alone — had always enjoyed special prestige among the Jews. Linking the traditional and the modern in this way, these young Jewish followers of the Enlightenment succeeded in opening a free school (*Freischule*) in Anhalt-Dessau as early as 1799.[8]

This was in several respects a novelty. On the one hand, the school —

7. Lebrecht Ludwig Baentsch, *Handbuch der Geographie und Geschichte des Fürstentums Anhalt* (Cöthen, 1801), 42.

8. Ludwig Horwitz, *Geschichte der Herzoglichen Franzschule in Dessau, 1799–1849* (Dessau, 1894); David Fränkel, *Die erste Errichtung einer jüdischen Freischule in Dessau* (Dessau, 1802); idem, *Nachricht von der jüdischen Haupt- und Freischule in Dessau* (Dessau, 1804).

soon highly regarded by Jews and Christians alike, even those outside Anhalt-Dessau — was run not only by individual highly engaged Jews, but by the whole *Gemeinde.* On the other hand, the institution felt the influence of the Dessau *Philanthropin* on its objectives, its curriculum, and its methods. Hence it came to perform a special function through the promotion of social integration and mobility. In contrast to most institutions of this kind, this was not a simple school for the poor. David Fränkel (1779–1865), prime initiator and director of the teaching institute, succeeded (with state support) in introducing compulsory school attendance and banning both private Talmud schools and small "hole-in-the-wall" schools (*Winkelschulen*).[9] Wealthy parents paid correspondingly higher school fees, although from 1815 onward the state also supported the project. As a result, poor Jewish boys could enjoy reform-oriented religious instruction as well as a secular education that was up-to-date and directed toward the achievement of a bourgeois lifestyle.[10] The boys were taught at first by self-educated followers of Enlightenment educational theory, and later by teachers who had themselves previously been pupils at the model school. Moreover, Christian secondary-school and grammar-school teachers showed their respect for the institution by themselves giving lessons at the Franz School (it was named after the prince himself).

The birthplace of Moses Mendelssohn, Dessau seems like a microcosm of enlightened absolutism.[11] Prince Franz strove to provide *all* his subjects with an upbringing that was inspired by Enlightenment practice and educational ideals. This goal was extremely attractive to a number of Jews. In 1806 the Christian pedagogue du Toit wrote that the "nation of Jews, under a noble, liberal government in Dessau, shows itself for what it is, both in a general way and also in its liberal thinking."[12] The reformers in the Jewish *Gemeinde* could be certain of the broad support of the state in pursuing their ideal. For after the *universal* attempt to realize the educational impetus and utopian goals of the Enlightenment had failed, officials saw a last opportunity to restore the impetus of

---

9. Fränkel came from an old Dessau/Berlin rabbinical family. He was director of the Franz School from 1800 to 1849, and from 1806 to 1848 also editor of *Sulamith.*

10. Landesarchiv (hereafter LA) Oranienbaum, Abt. Dessau, C 15 Nr. 21III, 81. Other Jewish schools existed in Anhalt-Dessau, in Gröbzig, Jeßnitz, Wörlitz, and Radegast. Fränkel founded the first Jewish school for girls in Dessau in 1806.

11. Erhard Hirsch, *Dessau-Wörlitz: Aufklärung und Frühklassik* (Leipzig, 1985); Hartmut Ross, "Die Kulturkreise Sachsen-Weimar-Eisenach und Anhalt-Dessau im Vergleich," in *Kleinstaaten und Kultur in Thüringen vom 16. bis 20. Jahrhundert,* ed. Jürgen John (Weimar, 1994), 221–31; Simone Lässig, "Reformpotential im 'dritten Deutschland'? Überlegungen zum Idealtypus des Aufgeklärten Absolutismus," in *Landesgeschichte in Sachsen: Tradition und Innovation,* ed. Rainer Aurig, Steffen Herzog, and Simone Lässig (Bielefeld, 1997), 187–215.

12. *Sulamith* 1, no. 1 (1806): 59.

Enlightenment thinking through the Jewish minority, among whom the claim for improvements in civil rights and *bürgerliche Verbesserung* had been raised to the demand for legal equality.

For this reason David Fränkel convinced Dessau government officials that they might be more than mere partners in the introduction of improved education for youth. At the same time he and his fellow campaigners skillfully used the authority of the state to oppose the efforts of Jews who excluded themselves from any modernization of Jewish life.[13] Officials and reformers based their alliance of interest on their common ideal of *Bildung,* which was understood by both sides to be essential for self-improvement (*Selbstveredelung*).[14] The government also looked favorably on other initiatives that targeted the cultural transformation of Jewish society. It was not by chance, therefore, that Dessau was the place of publication for the first German-language Jewish newspaper, *Sulamith,* from 1806 onward,[15] or that sermons in Dessau were *regularly* delivered in German after 1808 — another novelty in German lands.[16]

Thus the Jews in Anhalt-Dessau achieved significance on a European scale. As the Jewish Enlightenment (*Haskalah*) was transformed here from theory into practice, Dessau developed into one of the earliest centers of the Jewish reform movement. As early as 1811, David Fränkel expressed pride that "the Israelites in Dessau, as is well known, belong to that praiseworthy number who commendably distinguish themselves from many other of their German co-religionists through their higher level of culture and their communal organizations and institutions."[17] Although Fränkel remained silent about the resistance to change within the *Gemeinde,* mainly because he wanted to act as the disseminator of the new thinking, the Dessau example nevertheless illustrates how an enlightened policy of toleration could act as a powerful impulse to modernization beginning within the Jewish community. Focusing attention on two main issues — the realization of a modern educational plan, and the reform of

---

13. LA Oranienbaum, Abt. Dessau, C 15 Nr. 2, 22, 23, 25, 57.

14. On this general trend, see George L. Mosse, "Jewish Emancipation: Between Bildung and Respectability," in idem, *Confronting the Nation: Jewish and Western Nationalism* (Hanover, NH, 1993).

15. Siegfried Stein, "Die Zeitschrift Sulamith," in *Zeitschrift für die Geschichte der Juden in Deutschland* 7 (1937): 193–226; Werner Grossert, "Zur Geschichte der Emanzipation der Juden anhand der jüdischen Zeitschrift Sulamith," in *Kleinstaaten,* ed. John, 371–84.

16. David Sorkin, "Preacher, Teacher, Publicist: Joseph Wolf and the Ideology of Emancipation," in *From East to West: Jews in a Changing Europe, 1750–1870,* ed. idem and Frances Malino (Cambridge, 1990), 107–25; Alexander Altmann, "Zur Frühgeschichte der jüdischen Predigt in Deutschland: Leopold Zunz als Prediger," *Leo Baeck Institute Yearbook* 6 (1961): 3–59.

17. *Sulamith* 3, no. 2 (1811): 326.

religious practice—proved to be the correct strategy, for it allowed Jews in Anhalt-Dessau to work outward from a small, educated elite and in this way to propagate their views to other Jewish *Gemeinde*.[18] Because the defining principles of the culture toward which Jews were expected to work were set by the state bureaucracy—which was itself stamped with the values of the educated middle classes—in the first thirty years of the nineteenth century an increasing number of Jews adopted bourgeois values and attitudes. From this point of view, acculturation should be conceived not as a value-neutral means to move closer to mainstream society, but rather—and more precisely—as cultural embourgeoisement.[19]

III. Jews in Saxony

The life of the Jews in Saxony was defined by quite different conditions. The Enlightenment had gained no place in the practice of government. Consequently the introduction of an Enlightenment policy of toleration was hardly discussed, much less realized.[20] The Electorate of Saxony was reestablished in 1762–63, and although it was commercially already well developed, politically it remained fixed in its ways. Hence it believed it could do without a Jewish "substitute bourgeoisie" (*Ersatzbürgertum*).[21] Even during the phase of proto-industrial development, everyday Jewish existence in Saxony was burdened by laws that seemed almost medieval compared with the situation elsewhere in Germany. Apart from a few exceptional cases in Leipzig,[22] Jews had the right to settle only in Dresden, which had 735 Jewish residents in 1831—that is, almost as many as Dessau.[23] The Jewish minority in Saxony remained without

---

18. *Sulamith* developed into the most important medium for the propagation of a new religious and educational understanding. Its detailed reports on new Jewish schools were decisive in attracting children from outside the community; see LA Oranienbaum, Abt. Dessau, C 15 Nr. 21, Bd. 1.

19. According to Pierre Bourdieu, early cultural *Verbürgerlichung,* and with it the acquisition of "cultural capital," could promote socioeconomic elevation to bourgeois status. This would help to explain the different levels of *Verbürgerlichung* of the Jews in France and Germany. See Pierre Bourdieu, *Sozialer Sinn: Kritik der theoretischen Vernunft* (Frankfurt a. M., 1987); and idem, *Sozialer Raum und "Klassen": Leçon sur la leçon* (Frankfurt a. M., 1985).

20. See Simone Lässig, "Wie aufgeklärt war das Rétablissement? Religiöse Toleranz als Gradmesser," in *Sachsen, 1763–1832: Zwischen Rétablissement und bürgerlichen Reformen,* ed. Uwe Schirmer (Beucha, 1996), 40–75.

21. Stefi Jersch-Wenzel, *Juden und "Franzosen" in der Wirtschaft des Raumes Berlin/Brandenburg in der Zeit des Merkantilismus* (Berlin, 1978), 119.

22. In 1785 only 38 Jews lived there; in 1835 the total was 76.

23. In the town of Dessau, the figures were considerably higher: 807 Jews (8.7%) in 1818, and 763 Jews (7.2%) in 1830. Anhalt-Dessau had 1,645 Jews (3.1%) in 1818 and 1,614 (2.8%) in 1830. In Dresden, where the proportion of Jews in the population always

corporative rights, so that no *Gemeinde* in the traditional sense could be formed. This forced atomization of Dresden's Jews was emphasized through the ban on communal religious services. Whereas each of the larger *Gemeinden* in Anhalt-Dessau had its own synagogue, Dresden's Jews saw themselves restricted to small, private prayer rooms.

Dresden Jews were subject to greater restrictions than those in Dessau, not only in religious-cultural terms but also in social terms. The crafts remained banned to them, as did the acquisition of land and property. Even trade was restricted. Because Saxony did not overcome its political inertia even under Napoleonic influence, and because — unlike Prussia and Baden — it undertook no civic reforms, these heavy restrictions cemented the exclusion of Jews from urban society and remained in force during the period of the Confederation of the Rhine. The résumé on "the position of Jewish believers at this time" provided by Freiherr von Werthern in 1819 was that "their personal existence is oppressed, their business practices are subject to heavy restrictions, and the education of Jewish youth is terrible; lacking farsighted authorities, the Jews' prospects necessarily remain very unsatisfactory."[24]

A change in Saxon policy, prompting hopes for a move toward Jewish emancipation, came only in the mid-1830s. Saxony's 1831 constitution gave every inhabitant of Saxony full freedom of conscience and worship according to his belief but guaranteed equal civil and political rights only to Christians. For those of other beliefs, special laws were proposed. This proposition gave new relevance to the "Jewish question," which had been publicly discussed since 1828.[25] In the course of the ensuing debates, which were often emotional, it very soon became clear that the *Landtag* and the guilds were not the only bodies that refused to accept an equal position for the Jews; the majority of the representatives of the new bourgeoisie did so as well. Dresden's city council had already reached the conclusion that the anticipated "moral and civic emancipation" (*moralische und bürgerliche Vervollkommnung*) of the Jews was only to be achieved through a step-by-step improvement of their legal position. Yet the citizens of Dresden, in their revolutionary Catalogue of Demands (September 1830), had given a higher priority to

---

remained under 1%, they numbered 824 in 1817; 735 in 1831; and 882 in 1867. Only 1,022 Jews (0.05%) resided in all of Saxony in 1849.

24. Internal government report of 5 Feb. 1817, SächsHStA Dresden, Loc. 6583, 24.

25. See Wilhelm Traugott Krug, "Über das Verhältnis verschiedener Religionsparteien zum Staate und über die Emanzipation der Juden" (1828), in idem, *Ges[ammelte] Schriften* (Braunschweig, 1834), 4:459–82; Benvoglio [pseud. for Bernhard Beer], "Betrachtungen über die Regeneration der Israeliten," in *Die Biene* (1829), 284ff.; and Petition der Dresdner Judenschaft aus dem Jahre 1828, in SächsHStA Dresden, MdI Nr. 826c, 63–66.

the need for "protection from the Jews" than to any of their more general political objectives.[26] Even radical democrats such as Bernhard Moßdorf (1802–1833), leader of the Dresden Burgher Association (Bürgerverein), stated explicitly that citizenship rights should be granted only to Christians.[27] Accordingly, the Municipal Ordinance (*Städteordnung*) of 1832 denied Saxony's Jews civil rights. This extreme defensive posture — especially when compared with developments in Baden, Prussia, or Anhalt-Dessau — may also be due to the fact that no enlightened policy of toleration had been pursued in Saxony. Such a policy might have provided an opportunity to dismantle prejudices in the course of public debate and thus to prepare the ground for emancipation.[28]

Under these unfavorable conditions, it was left to those individuals close to state authority — as so often in German history — to take up this issue. In the *Landtag*'s elected lower house, opinions were sharply divided, but in the corporatist (*ständisch*) upper house, members quickly reached agreement that emancipation could no longer be refused on principle. Apart from the prominent liberal and philosopher Wilhelm Traugott Krug, who represented Leipzig University in the upper house and who vehemently supported Jewish demands for emancipation,[29] no one supported the granting of immediate equality. This position corresponded with the strategy of the government, which went back to the initial emphasis on education fifty years earlier. The government now declared that "moral improvement among the Jews, and especially their increasing proximity (*Annäherung*) to Christian usages and customs, must precede their civic (*bürgerlichen*) emancipation: one must in effect be a condition for the other."[30]

The Saxon government and members of the *Landtag*'s upper house agreed in 1834 to remove some particularly out-of-date regulations governing the Jews, especially those affecting residency, business practices, and taxation. Other legislation followed in 1837, regulating Jewish education and religious practices. The government continued to hope that these reforms would give a powerful impulse to the social and cultural integration of Jews. Whatever its shortcomings, this legislation represented real progress for Saxony's Jews, since they could now form a

26. M. B. Lindenau, *Geschichte der Haupt- und Residenzstadt Dresden,* 2 vols. (Dresden, 1862), 2:7.

27. Bernhard Moßdorf, *Constitution wie das sächsische Volk wünscht* [Dresden, 1831].

28. SächsHStA Dresden, Loc. 32556, Rep. XII, Nr. 456; Staatsarchiv Leipzig, Tit. LI Nr. 89, 1ff.

29. Moses Pinner, *Was haben die Israeliten in Sachsen zu hoffen? Und was ist ihnen zu wünschen? Mit einem Vorwort von Prof. Krug* (Leipzig, 1833).

30. SächsHStA Dresden, MdI Nr. 826c, 13.

Gemeinde with a public synagogue. Jewish education was now controlled by the ministry of education and cultural affairs, which generally
permitted Jewish children to attend Christian schools. Lastly, a law came
into force in 1838 that was regarded by the government as providing the
first step toward full civic (*staatsbürgerliche*) emancipation. This law,
however, gave Jews the status of being "shadow citizens" instead.[31] Jews
still enjoyed residency rights only in Dresden and Leipzig, and although
they could certainly obtain the civic rights necessary to conduct a business, they still lacked corresponding political rights.[32] Other restrictions,
including those affecting property, inheritance, and business activity,
indicate how far Saxony remained behind the other German states
on the issue of Jewish emancipation. It required the revolutions of 1848
and the proclamation of Basic Rights in Frankfurt effectively to emanci-
pate the minority. Until 1868, the right to conduct a business in Saxony
was confined to those few Jews who were already citizens of Saxony.
Saxon Jews achieved full emancipation only in the process of Saxony's
integration into the North German Confederation.[33]

IV. Paths to Emancipation

In the year 1839, the *Conversation-Lexikon der Gegenwart* noted: "Perhaps it is not without great advantage to the general and religious education of the Jews, especially the German Jews, that their emancipation is so
difficult for them to achieve. Pressure creates counter-pressure, and
through the dialectical struggle carried on now for so many years in Germany with such great effort, the Jewish spirit on the whole here has
developed with such solidity and strength as in hardly any other part of the
continent."[34] Whereas research has — rightly — emphasized the negative
consequences of conditional emancipation,[35] the *Allgemeine Zeitung des
Judentums* endorsed the opinion expressed in this passage. Obviously
even those Jews who strove publicly for emancipation, and thus were by
no means passive objects of state policy, were convinced that educational
legislation created an irresistible impulse to self-modernization within
Jewish society, and that because of this German Jewry had a pioneer role

---

31. According to Bernhard Beer's contribution to the *Allgemeine Zeitung des
Judentums* 7 (1843): 278.
32. *Gesetz- und Verordnungsblatt für das Königreich Sachsen* (1837), 66ff.; ibid.
(1838), 394–99.
33. See Rudolf Muhs, "Verfassungsgebung und Judenfrage," in *Dresdner Hefte zur
Kulturgeschichte*, no. 26 (1991): 31–36.
34. *Allgemeine Zeitung des Judentums* (1839), 624.
35. See Reinhard Rürup, "Kontinuität und Diskontinuität der 'Judenfrage' im 19.
Jahrhundert: Zur Entstehung des modernen Antisemitismus," in *Sozialgeschichte Heute,*
ed. Hans-Ulrich Wehler (Göttingen, 1974), 388–415, here 396.

in Europe. This contemporary interpretation leads directly back to the question posed at the outset, about the changing relationships among emancipation, acculturation, and embourgeoisement. Those relationships will henceforth occupy center stage in the analysis.

When one looks from this vantage point at regional specificities, the example of Anhalt-Dessau shows that the concept of "emancipation" does not *alone* explain very much. If the position of the Jews in society is considered simply on the basis of what is written in particular pieces of legislation, Saxony was not far behind Anhalt, where the first emancipation law was passed in 1848.[36] But one must not overlook the fact that Jews in Dessau had enjoyed freedoms since the eighteenth century that were conceded to Jews in Saxony only during the 1830s. One thinks here of freedom of religious expression, the unlimited right to form *Gemeinden* and to worship in a public synagogue, compulsory school attendance, a state subsidy for the Jewish school, the—albeit limited— opportunity to learn a craft, and the legal right to possess land and property. As early as 1800, Dessau had a policy of tolerance that extended further than in most other lands. Paradoxically, it was that very tolerance that prevented the state from appreciating the need for civic emancipation. When Baden and Prussia risked their first cautious steps toward legal equality, Anhalt-Dessau had already completed the most progressive phase of its *Judenpolitik*. The elderly prince's enthusiasm for reform was now dimmed, and his successor acted in accord with the reactionary tendencies of the period following the Congress of Vienna. For these reasons, the status of the Jews in Anhalt-Dessau remained virtually unaltered for several decades.

In spite of these deficits, conditions evolved differently in Anhalt-Dessau generally, and for the Jews in particular, than they did in Saxony. One can see these differences in the readiness of the Christian population to integrate Jews into their society. For example, whereas no Jewish teacher was appointed to a normal school in Saxony until 1918, there were already two Jews on the staff of the Dessau grammar school (*Gymnasium*) at the beginning of the nineteenth century. This was the result of years of cooperative effort at the Franz School and of the socialization of young, educated, middle-class citizens (*Bildungsbürger*) in a way that promoted the crossing of religious boundaries.[37] The revolutions of 1848 and their outcomes also showed the different paths taken. Although Saxony was a center of the democratic movement, neither the new government nor the revolutionary *Landtag* produced initiatives to pro-

---

36. Only the adoption of fixed family surnames was conceded in 1822 and, in 1834, the free choice of domicile.

37. *Das Friedrichs-Gymnasium, 1785–1935* (Dessau, 1935), Stadtarchiv Dessau Nr. 1636.

mote equality for the Jews.[38] Jews were excluded from the suffrage when city council elections were planned for November 1848 in Leipzig and Dresden. The Jews in Saxony were finally emancipated not by their own state, but—in March–April 1849[39]—by the recognition of the Basic Rights of the German People in Frankfurt. By contrast, the immediate emancipation of the Jews had been one of the first demands of the revolutionary bourgeoisie in Dessau. As early as March 1848, 339 Christian citizens signed a petition along these lines, which led on 22 April 1848 to the government and Duke Leopold IV Friedrich giving approval to a law granting the Jews complete equality.[40] The powerful after-effects of such toleration policies can be seen from "insignificant" decisions made outside the realm of high politics. The Jewish writer Wilhelm Wolfsohn (1820–65), planning to marry a Christian girl from Leipzig, sought from 1840 onward to win Saxon citizenship. His efforts were in vain. After other German states had also declined his applications, Anhalt-Dessau finally awarded him citizenship (*Bürgerstatus*) in 1851.[41]

Anhalt-Dessau developed differently from Saxony in terms of its level of acculturation and of the Jews' cultural *Habitus*. This difference may be explained by the long tradition of toleration during the period of enlightened absolutism and the readiness of the majority to integrate. The Franz School had not only brought the enlightened Jews in Dessau the respect of educated Christians, and through this entry into educated middle-class society; it had also become an important center for social integration. As such, it transmitted to a whole generation of Jews the essential factual knowledge and relevant speaking skills essential to middle-class life. But it also inculcated in them genuine bourgeois values. Hence, at least the younger group of Jews acquired the cultural competence and the *Habitus* that allowed them to move closer socially (*vergesellschaften*) to the non-Jewish *Bürgertum*.

This development was strengthened by pioneering reforms in the religious sphere, for which the Franz School—in conflict with the numerous orthodox Jews who remained in the *Gemeinde*—was the foundation and starting point. Such reforms included not only the delivery of sermons in German, but also the successive removal of incomprehensible

---

38. In *Dr. Bernhard Beer: Ein Lebens- und Zeitbild* (Breslau, 1863), 183f., Zacharias Frankel, chief rabbi of Saxony from 1836 to 1854, noted that the majority of Democrats had refused to include the Jews in their demands, not daring to go against public opinion.

39. Basic rights came into effect in Saxony on 2 March 1849. The government then issued an executive decree on 20 April 1849 that guaranteed equality of rights for the Jews.

40. August Habicht, *Das politische Leben in Anhalt*, 1. Heft (Leipzig, 1948), 17ff.

41. Erhard Hexelschneider, "Wilhelm Wolfsohn ein jüdischer Kulturmittler zwischen Rußland und Deutschland," *Dresdner Hefte*, no. 45 (1996): 58–62.

Hebraic prayers and the introduction of prayers in German; choir singing with instrumental accompaniment; and the establishment of confirmation celebrations for young Jews. These reforms were all aimed at
"refining" (*veredeln*) the religious service, whose traditional forms had
always been regarded by Christians as synonymous with a foreign, repellent, and immoral Jewish lifestyle.

These changes in religious practice, seeking to achieve moral perfec-
tion, inner spirituality, and a new aesthetic, should in no way be conceived only as a passive reaction to the state's education policy. Nor
were they mere copies of Christian practices. Their basic intention can
only be understood if one realizes how strongly the protagonists of
reform — whether in Dessau or, as later, in Dresden and numerous other
German towns — *already* saw themselves as educated middle-class citizens. Because their own thoughts and actions were already attuned to
the middle-class value system, the rites they opposed as outdated surviv-
als from the past simply did not correspond any longer with their new
cultural self-perception. An academically uneducated "Polish rabbi,"
for example, now appeared repellent, not only to non-Jews but to Jews
themselves. Because such repellent examples of older practices affected
the establishment of their own cultural ideals in the broader community,[42] they were considered detrimental. Nevertheless, when Fränkel
vigorously defended the demand that all brothers of the faith should be
educated and thus "blessed" (*beglücken*), he encountered strong resistance within the *Gemeinde*.

Otherwise the results of the struggle for reform were impressive
indeed. Besides such members of the first enlightened generation as
Fränkel, Moses Philippson (1775–1814),[43] and Joseph Wolf (1762–
1826),[44] together with several other qualified doctors and teachers,
within a short time the Jewish communities of Anhalt-Dessau produced
a collection of important Jewish scholars. This latter group included
Gotthold Salomon (1784–1862), a brilliant preacher in demand throughout Germany; Ludwig Philippson (1811–89), who, after studying philosophy and philology, worked in Magdeburg and became known above
all as founder and publisher of the *Allgemeine Zeitung des Judentums;*
and the philosopher and philologist Heymann Steinthal (1823–99), who
together with Moritz Lazarus later founded the subdiscipline of eth-
nopsychology (*Völkerpsychologie*). Among the economic bourgeoisie
(*Wirtschaftsbürgertum*) too, increasing numbers of Jews gained recogni-

---

42. LA Oranienbaum, Abt. Dessau, C 15 Nr. 35, 37.
43. Gotthold Salomon, *Lebensgeschichte des Herrn Moses Philippsfon* (Dessau,
1814).
44. Sorkin, "Preacher."

tion for their honest and successful business activities: the door-to-door peddler, so often criticized, became a rare sight. Parallel to this cultural and economic embourgeoisement ran the social embourgeoisement of Anhalt-Dessau's Jews. This process revealed itself particularly in the participation of many Jews in middle-class associations and, after 1848, in their election to parliamentary bodies.[45] These developments certainly did not come without tensions and ruptures. Nevertheless, the example of Dessau clearly demonstrates that a policy of toleration derived from Enlightenment principles promoted an openness even among the Christian middle classes toward the integration of Jews, just as it helped the Jewish minority become members of the middle classes in cultural terms. The inverse of this proposition is equally clear: in Saxony, the intolerant posture of the state must have delayed or hindered the same historical processes.[46]

Because of Saxony's quasi-medieval restrictions (outlined previously), little had happened by the beginning of the nineteenth century to change the traditional picture of the Jew as a peddler, a haggler, and thus somehow a threat. Because sustained contact between Jews and Gentiles did not develop, neither did the foundation for Jewish integration into society. A kind of two-way blockage existed: on the side of the majority and on the side of the Jewish minority. For Saxony's Jews *as a group,* the will to break out of the traditional Jewish world was much less evident than in Dessau.

The ban on founding *Gemeinden* and the state's continuing restriction of Jews to private prayer rooms must be seen as two of the most important reasons for this lack of development. These stipulations not only accentuated turmoil within the Jewish minority; they also favored the extension of the cultural hegemony of the synagogue proprietors, who formed an elitist group and who defended their own interests. This defense of their social and cultural exclusivity by a small group of Jews also had an effect on educational policy within the *Gemeinde.* The way these issues were handled suggests that the process of acculturation was carried through on an individual basis, not a group basis, much longer in Dresden than in Dessau. The relatively few wealthy Jewish families in Dresden engaged private teachers or already sent their children to Christian schools.[47] They were vehemently opposed to the construction of general intercommunal schools with qualified teachers. Consequently, even in 1820 most Jewish children had to attend small private schools

---

45. For the association's membership, see the lists in LA Oranienbaum, Staatsministerium Dessau 1.

46. See further details in Lässig, "Reformpotential."

47. Cf. Willy Richter, "Matrikel der Kreuzschule, Gymnasium zum Heiligen Kreuz in Dresden, 1654–1848/49" (MS, 1963).

providing only religious education.[48] Bernhard Hirschel, who attended such a cheder in Dresden until 1823 and who later took up the medical profession, later characterized his school as "very bad, even shocking. Most of the pupils were children of not only poor, but also uneducated, people. In those days, the *Gemeinde* had a poor idea of education."[49]

Because of the fractured nature of Jewish society, the impetus and scope for reform remained very restricted. Nonetheless, the winds of change emanating from certain reform-minded *Gemeinden* finally reached Dresden. At the end of the 1820s, a small group of reformist Jews gradually coalesced in Dresden, thanks primarily to the initiative of the young (private) scholar, Bernhard Beer (1801–61).[50] In 1828 Beer gave the first sermon in the German language in a private synagogue. A year later he won the support of a considerable number of Jews — including some wealthy ones — to establish the Mendelssohn Association, whose aim was to promote the training of Jews in the arts, sciences, and handicrafts. His goal was to provide an answer to the demand of Saxon officials for "productive activity" among the Jews. In 1833, Beer organized the first confirmation celebrations in Dresden, and finally in 1834 he produced a tract entitled *Grundzüge eines Entwurfs zur Regulierung des Kultur und des Schulwesens der Israeliten* (Principles of a proposal for the regulation of the Israelites' religious practices and schooling).[51]

Saxony's ministry of education and cultural affairs took up Beer's draft with considerable goodwill. It thereby indicated — more clearly than through the provision of state support for the Mendelssohn Association — that different interests were beginning to converge. State officials and Jewish reformers now saw eye to eye on the need for new educational strategies and, in essence, more bourgeois conceptions of morals, ethics, and aesthetics among Saxony's Jews. Building on these cultural affinities, a kind of alliance of interests was formed,[52] similar to what had occurred previously in Dessau. After 1835–36, this alliance took on

---

48. Details are in Emil Lehmann, *Aus alten Acten* (Dresden, 1886); cf. Simone Lässig, "Vom Mittelalter in die Moderne? Anfänge der Emanzipation der Juden in Sachsen," *Dresdner Hefte,* no. 45 (1996): 9–18.

49. Bernhard Hirschel, "Memoiren" (MS), found among memoirs in the archive of the Leo Baeck Institute, New York.

50. He was a member of the *Gemeinde*'s governing board (with a short interruption) in 1837–61; cf. Frankel, *Beer.*

51. SächsHStA Dresden, MfVB Nr. 11131, 16ff.

52. Twelve non-Jewish members, almost all of them high-ranking civil servants, had joined the Mendelssohn Association; SächsHStA Dresden, MfVB Nr. 11130. Such officials also participated in the first confirmations in Dresden, in examinations at the Jewish school, and in the laying of the foundation stone and the consecration of the synagogue.

a new quality with the election of Zacharias Frankel as first chief rabbi (*erster Oberrabbiner*) of Saxony.

V. The Contribution of Zacharias Frankel

Zacharias Frankel (1801–75) originally came from Prague. He had completed his doctorate at the University of Pest and then worked as chief rabbi in Treplitz. As the first rabbi in Bohemia who preached regularly in German, he soon became widely known as the representative of a moderate reformed Judaism. He came to the attention of officials in the Saxon ministry of education and cultural affairs through a wide-ranging report he provided on the organization of contemporary Jewish religion. In advocating "refinement through education" and "an approach to the spirit of the times," but also in the religious service itself, Frankel saw the Jews contributing to a society "in which Christian and Jew can live freely together as brothers." "A mingling of feelings, while preserving differences of belief," wrote Frankel, " — this is the watchword of an enlightened century."[53] The ministerial officials were impressed by the rabbi's solid scientific learning and his cultural knowledge. Therefore they successfully aligned themselves with those in the *Gemeinde* who supported the choice of Frankel.

Two factors hindered realization of Frankel's proposals: the slow progress of the emancipation debate, and the situation inside the *Gemeinde*. Frankel complained vigorously against the fragmentation of religious life, the generally low educational and cultural standards of the time, and a "lack of unity and noble thinking." The current situation, he wrote, was characterized by "apathy and dull despair, which paralyze action and foster a renunciation of anything better." The main cause of this, according to Frankel, was the "domineering vanity of the prayer-room proprietors" and their spirit of opposition to each and every improvement.[54] To be sure, Frankel knowingly exaggerated here. His aim was to convince the government of the absolute necessity of his reform program. Nevertheless, his statements show that the state's long-standing reluctance to adopt an active Jewish policy in fact favored the preservation of traditional forms of Jewish life and held up modernization within the Jewish *Gemeinde*.

From this perspective it seems surprising that the face of Dresden's *Gemeinde* actually changed rapidly. This was due principally to the fact that the government shared the fundamental aims of the forces for

---

53. SächsHStA Dresden, MfVB Nr. 11131, 42ff.
54. Ibid., 196, 210f.

reform among the Jews and sought in different ways to increase their authority. State officials had already demonstrated this position in the course of negotiations over the rabbi's chair, when Frankel's application for the post seemed about to fail because of his high salary demand.[55] The government was interested in this particular rabbi because it considered him (on the basis of his report) to be "well-meaning and pious," "educated and deep thinking." As the Saxon government considered Frankel to be the only available candidate capable of carrying through the necessary improvements, it awarded him personally an additional sum of 170 *Thaler.* Frankel also obtained state support when he was wrestling with the changes in religious practice that he considered necessary—in addition to the founding of schools—in order to bring Judaism into the modern age. In the future, he believed, the religious service should be both "modern" and "noble": whereas it should illustrate the Jews' new cultural self-perception, it should do so without a radical break from Jewish tradition or by copying the Protestant liturgy.

An adaptation to Christian ways was by no means the principal aim of the reformers. The driving force behind their efforts, rather, was the conviction that traditional Judaism was increasingly antipathetic to the needs and aesthetic sensibilities of middle-class society. This antipathy affected not only outward characteristics of religious services—such as the loud outcries and the eternally long, incomprehensible sermons—but above all the formalism of the old Judaism, which defined laws and norms of action externally. Middle-class religiosity, by contrast, was believed to orientate itself to self-directed individuals. It addressed not only their feelings but also their intellect. Because reformers such as Frankel already shared the self-perception of the educated middle classes, and because they wanted to be seen to do so within their own environment, the traditional forms of Jewish religiosity collided not only with the expectations of the majority Christian society, but also with its own norms, values, and feelings. Hence, just as the middle classes had initially wanted to transfer their cultural model to other levels in society, those Jews who had already become middle-class attempted to influence the whole of their minority. This strategy had its limits, however, and mechanisms of exclusion remained. For example, Frankel pleaded in 1836 that the "religious fusion should be extended only to German Israelites." "The Poles," he wrote, were to be excluded because "their morals and usages are too strongly differentiated from ours."[56]

Frankel came a large step nearer his goal when the state agreed to

55. Stiftung Neue Synagoge Berlin, Gemeinde Dresden, Dr. 75 A, Nr. 1; Sächs-HStA Dresden, MfVB Nr. 11131, 116ff.; and for the following.

56. SächsHStA Dresden, MfVB Nr. 11131, 197b.

his request that private synagogues be banned. The significance of this action, which called into question the traditional hegemony of the old Jewish elites, can hardly be overestimated. If one seeks to explain why Jewish acculturation now proceeded more rapidly, several consequences of the ban on private synagogues can be identified. Because emancipation had already begun, existing elites quite quickly gave up their massive initial resistance to the erosion of their traditional positions of power. Now the prospect of entry into middle-class society opened up new opportunities for them to accumulate social and cultural capital. Moreover, reform-oriented Jews for the first time were in a position to influence Jews occupying different social levels, encompassing them within their project for "cultural refinement." The fact that until then there had been no *Gemeinde* as the vehicle for a traditional Jewish group existence turned out now to be an advantage, for the path forward — however rocky in other respects — was not impeded by the need to dissolve it. The formation of a *Gemeinde* in Dresden and Leipzig was thus first made possible through the beginning of emancipation: it was a child of the modern age. The reforms for which Jews in other lands had fought so arduously were now carried through in a fashion that appreciated the risks involved but, on the whole, proceeded without conflict.

The Jewish school established in 1836, soon regarded even by non-Jews to be "one of the best schools in Dresden," could now build on the commitment of the whole *Gemeinde*.[57] The same was true of the Dresden synagogue, constructed between 1838 and 1840 according to the design of Gottfried Semper. This synagogue represented one of the first Jewish bourgeois public buildings in Germany. A new form of religious service was also devised to match this architectural novelty: tightened up to conform with the times, this service was based on inner devotion and edification. Its central features were a short lecture by the rabbi in German; the introduction of choral singing — another innovation — and a few short prayers in German; and the main prayers, which were retained in Hebrew. In short, far-reaching but cautious changes were made to the content of the service and to its aesthetic effect (as demonstrated, for instance, by the absence of an organ until 1870). Frankel was able to generate wide agreement for these changes within the *Gemeinde* — certainly an accomplishment of the first order. According to Beer, writing in 1840, the *Gemeinde* was made up "almost entirely of so-called pious Israelites, whose domestic life is conducted according to the laws of Jewish ritual." Beer continued: "Dresden may be the only *Gemeinde* that

---

57. For the history of the Jewish community school in Dresden, see *Monatsschrift für Geschichte und Wissenschaft des Judentums* (1862), 297; SächsHStA Dresden, MfVB Nr. 11134, 316ff.

combines enthusiastic and regular synagogue-goers, among whom grey-haired Talmud scholars are also to be found, and whose members, young and old, take part in the new rites with joy and devotion."[58]

The Dresden Jews around Frankel and Beer, together with those involved with the Mendelssohn Association, had hoped that the promotion of educational endeavors and the reform of religious practice would signal to the Saxon state and to Saxony's middle classes that the Jewish minority was worthy of immediate emancipation. This proved to be an illusion. Seen in the proper historical perspective, however, we can acknowledge that the efforts of the Jewish reformers, because they were directed to molding middle-class attitudes, initiated and then accelerated a very important process of social-cultural change — one, moreover, that went well beyond religious questions, as middle-class Christians also appreciated. As the *Morgenblatt für gebildete Leser* reported in 1851:

> In times past, in the *Neumarkt* one could sense — indeed, with virtually all five of the senses, because one *felt* seized by some importunate person — something of the ghetto or of Prague's Jewish quarter. Roguish faces and raggedly clothed figures hung around by the dozens, carrying dirty bundles in their arms, haggling loudly or in whispers, and to a greater or lesser extent annoying every passerby. Now, hooked noses and black beards have not completely disappeared from the old accustomed meeting places, but the groups have become smaller and more respectable: at most, one in ten of these people is dressed in soiled frocks [*im unsauberen Kittel*].[59]

VI. Conclusions

Comparing developments in the two states examined here, one clear difference comes to the fore. In Anhalt-Dessau, emancipation came at the end of the cultural and socioeconomic integration of the Jews into middle-class society. In Saxony, by contrast, the process of acculturation got under way only when the state moved toward emancipation: the two processes proceeded along parallel lines. To the degree that synchronization occurred between the German states in setting the framework of Jewish ways of life, regional differences as to the degree of acculturation achieved were reduced over time. How successfully the Jews were able to move toward middle-class status in "latecomer regions" can be seen in

---

58. *Allgemeine Zeitung des Judentums* (1840), 376.
59. *Morgenblatt für gebildete Leser* (1851), 737.

the educational progress of the Jews in Saxony. As early as 1876 — that is, hardly more than a generation after the founding of the first modern Jewish school in the state — 34 percent of Jewish pupils attending schools of any sort in Saxony went on to some form of secondary education. By contrast, fewer than 2 percent of Protestants did so.[60]

The decisive phase in the process of cultural embourgeoisement of course came with the completion of the emancipation process in the 1860s. By that time, when equal rights were established throughout Germany, the Jewish minority had already freed itself from the bonds of traditional Judaism: in terms of culture, of *Habitus,* and — soon — of social status, it had moved closer to the middle classes. Enjoying equal rights in all German states, Jews now enjoyed opportunities that a small town like Dessau had provided for many years. From this point onward, many Jews sought and found their greatest educational and professional opportunities in the large cities. In Saxony this development can be seen in the enormous growth of the Jewish population of Leipzig.[61]

Many of the problems addressed in this essay require more systematic research. The comparison between Anhalt-Dessau and Saxony indicates that historians should direct their attention to the problem of how "emancipation by stages" determined the prospects for Jewish acculturation in Germany. To integrate a study of these two processes — acculturation and embourgeoisement — in two or more states, one must consider the different starting points in each one, as well as the options available at any particular time and the long-term consequences of these processes' reciprocal effects. In these ways, among others, the Prussocentric view of nineteenth-century German history may eventually be modified and broadened to cover more than just elites. Future researchers might also pursue the question of whether regional variations in the emancipation process could have had consequences for the

---

60. *Bericht über den Stand der dem Ministerium des Cultur und öffentlichen Unterrichtes unterstellten Unterrichts- und Erziehungsanstalten im Königreiche Sachsen* (Dresden, 1876). The assessments were somewhat inflated insofar as almost all Jewish pupils lived in large towns, whereas comparable figures for Protestant pupils were derived from the whole kingdom.

61. The number of Jewish inhabitants increased as follows: in Dresden — 1867: 870; 1875: 1,956; 1890: 2,595; 1900: 3,029; and in Leipzig — 1858: 713; 1871: 1,768; 1880: 3,265; 1890: 4,136; 1900: 6,171. In both cities, the percentage of Jewish inhabitants hovered around 1 percent. In Saxony as a whole, a rapid increase occurred between 1867 and 1875, with the number of Jewish inhabitants rising from 2,103 to 5,360. For Leipzig, this increase was the result not only of the in-migration of German Jews, but also of Jews arriving from abroad. See Erich Berger, *Das natürliche und konfessionelle Gefüge der Bevölkerung im Königreich Sachsen* (Halle, 1912); and Solvejg Höppner, "Migration nach und in Sachsen," in *Sachsen und Mitteldeutschland,* ed. Werner Bramke and Ulrich Heß (Weimar, 1995), 287ff.

sociocultural integration of the Jews as a whole into the society of the early German empire. It might then become more clear whether or not the state's role in fostering resentment toward the Jews explains the strength of the antisemitic movement. Even if this assumption were to prove false, such a perspective would be salutary. By considering developments over the *longue durée,* and by integrating approaches used by social, cultural, and political historians, it may be possible to stimulate further research into the political culture of the German Empire.

Models of Political Participation in the Beust Era: The State, the Saxon *Landtag,* and the Public Sphere, 1849–1864

Andreas Neemann

I. Introduction

"Time has been unkind to the reaction. After dwelling with painstaking detail on every obscure putschist of the revolution, the scholar usually dismisses the Fifties with a few remarks about obscurantist tyranny and hurries on to grapple with the Bismarckian enigma."[1] This statement (1958) by Theodore Hamerow was intentionally exaggerated. However, for many years it characterized the state of German historiography, especially in the form of general narratives of the era.[2] The 1850s were generally treated briefly, and mainly as the sad epilogue to the revolutions of 1848–49. As indicated by the term *Reichsgründungsjahrzehnt* — the founding decade of the Reich — historians examined the politically more turbulent 1860s mainly with undisguised anticipation for the subsequent foundation of a *kleindeutsch* nation-state.

Recently, however, Wolfram Siemann has examined the years 1849–71 as an autonomous and contingent "period of formation," one that demonstrates substantial social and political dynamism.[3] Whoever

---

1. Theodore S. Hamerow, *Restoration, Revolution, Reaction: Economics and Politics in Germany, 1815–1871* (Princeton, NJ, 1958), 199.
2. Cf. Thomas Nipperdey, *Deutsche Geschichte, 1800–1866: Bürgerwelt und starker Staat* (Munich, 1983). Nipperdey devotes only ten pages (pp. 674–84) to the 1850s.
3. Wolfram Siemann, *Gesellschaft im Aufbruch: Deutschland, 1849–1871* (Frankfurt a. M., 1990). Karl Rohe, *Wahlen und Wählertraditionen in Deutschland: Kulturelle Grundlage deutscher Parteien und Parteiensysteme im 19. und 20. Jahrhundert* (Frankfurt a. M., 1992), 57, labels the 1860s a "period of incubation of the German party system."

adopts this viewpoint initially abandons analytical referents from an older historical tradition that until recently seemed secure. Rather than focusing on the Prusso-Austrian dualism in the German Confederation, and rather than emphasizing the inevitability of developments leading to 1866, the interpretation favored by Siemann now requires a more differentiated viewpoint. Such a viewpoint takes account not only of national affairs but also of the internal politics of the individual German states. On the one hand, each of the federal states faced political challenges resulting from enormous economic and social change after 1850. On the other hand, whereas the great powers Prussia and Austria certainly tried to shore up their power and autonomy through domestic and cultural reforms as well as with their diplomacy, the same strategies were pursued by the states constituting the so-called Third Germany: Baden, Bavaria, Württemberg, Hanover, and Saxony.[4]

This change in perspective also requires a more intensive investigation of individual German states and their evolving political cultures. The Kingdom of Saxony is a case in point. In Saxony, the political system established in 1850 experienced unusual longevity. Whereas some of the reactionary governments in other states of the German Confederation resigned or were reshuffled during the "political thaw" (*Tauwetterphase*) after 1858, the government of Saxony held on to power until 1866. Even then, only two ministers stepped down as a result of the military defeat by Prussia, and not because of any internal crisis but due to external pressure. Until that point, the Saxon government had not repealed any of the draconian laws of 1850 curbing political clubs, political meetings, and the press.

Nevertheless, enforcement of those laws had been relaxed over the previous years. Nor should it be supposed that the superficial "success" of the reactionary government in Saxony depended on the total lack of a bourgeois class. Saxony was not an agrarian state dominated by large estate owners. On the contrary, it constituted one of the most industrialized and densely populated regions of Germany, with a high degree of urbanization even outside the two large centers of Dresden and Leipzig.[5] Examining Saxony's legislative record after 1850 also reveals that regression and stagnation by no means predominated. The agrarian reforms, initiated in the 1830s and merely accelerated in 1848, continued after 1850. The extension of a state-owned transportation network, especially modern railroads, progressed markedly between 1850 and 1866. A lib-

---

4. On Bavaria, see Manfred Hanisch, *"Für Fürst und Vaterland": Legitimationsstiftung in Bayern zwischen Revolution von 1848 und deutscher Einheit* (Munich, 1991).

5. Cf. Hubert Kiesewetter, *Industrialisierung und Landwirtschaft: Sachsens Stellung im regionalen Industrialisierungsprozess Deutschlands im 19. Jahrhundert* (Cologne, 1988).

eral freedom of occupation law (*Gewerbegesetz*) was passed in 1861, and further reforms of the justice system followed on the heels of the judicial and administrative reform of 1854, which had abolished patrimonial jurisdiction (a contentious noble privilege). Lastly, after lengthy preparation, in 1865 the first Civil Code (*Bürgerliches Gesetzbuch*) enacted in any German state came into effect in Saxony.

This impressive catalogue of Saxon reforms is hardly unknown in the literature. Historians have long been aware that moderate and liberal reforms occurred in the spheres of economics and infrastructure at the same time that state administration was extended and severe political repression was undertaken under the auspices of the Saxon premier, Count Friedrich Ferdinand von Beust. To date, however, historians have provided only relatively crude hypotheses as to why the political system established in 1850 managed to persist for so long, and why this remarkable survival story occurred in a state with a substantial bourgeoisie. The richness of archival sources now available to scholars underscores the need to reconsider those hypotheses.

Heinrich von Treitschke was one of the first to reflect on why the Saxon bourgeoisie lacked a will to power. According to Treitschke, the liberal economic reforms of the Beust regime provided the bourgeoisie with material affluence and security from social revolutionary encroachments by the lower-middle classes but in the process broke its liberal backbone.[6] Of course we should not take Treitschke's pronouncement at face value. The principal aim of this essay is to examine the frameworks of opportunity and constraint within which political activity in Saxony unfolded during an era when a part of society was politically engaged. To be sure, this political participation did not yet meet — or no longer met, as in 1848 — "modern" democratic standards. Nevertheless, it is too easy to forget that a parliament existed in Saxony in the 1850s and early 1860s, and that in this parliament sat elected deputies who debated and voted on government bills. Though not entirely free, a political press survived in the kingdom, and individual cities had institutions of local self-government. Which social groups made use of their rudimentary participatory rights, and what kinds of political yardsticks did they apply to their actions? To what extent were the party-political boundaries of 1848–49 diluted as a result of this? To address these questions, the

---

6. Heinrich von Treitschke, "Die Zustände im Königreich Sachsen unter dem Beustschen Regiment," in *Historische und politische Aufsätze* (Leipzig, n.d.), 4:97–110. Treitschke spoke of the "demoralization" of the bourgeoisie. His explanatory model was adopted in a similar form by Marxists and evaluated as a class-based constriction of the bourgeois claims to emancipation after the revolution of 1848–49; see Roland Zeise, "Die bürgerliche Umwälzung: Zentrum der proletarischen Parteibildung, 1830–1871," in *Geschichte Sachsens,* ed. Karl Czok (Weimar, 1989), 297–387.

analysis will center not on government decision making alone, but on the interplay between the government, parliament, and a "tamed" (*gezähmte*) public.[7]

II. Politics and the Public Sphere

The revolution of 1848–49 was particularly fierce in Saxony. Apart from the events in Baden, the Dresden Uprising in May 1849 was one of the bloodiest conflicts in the course of the revolution's second wave. It highlighted just how rapidly the political parties had become entrenched in the popular consciousness after 1848, and how the fault lines of social conflict now also determined options for the formation of political parties. The political bourgeoisie was split in its political objectives: The democrats favored a transformation of the state "from below" through universal suffrage; they also advocated the arming of the population and the toppling of the traditional elites. The liberals advocated moderate reforms "from above" and a settlement with the monarchy. In Saxony these two factions collided in the *Landtag,* where the expanded suffrage of 1848 had given the democrats an overwhelming majority. The liberals operated and exerted influence primarily through the government, to which the king had appointed some prominent liberals in 1848. One year later, in March 1849, however, the liberal government had already resigned in conflict with parliament, having been caught between the conservative court and the democratic majority in the *Landtag.* The king appointed a conservative-bureaucratic cabinet under the direction of Count von Beust, who headed the ministries of foreign affairs and culture. Beust's cabinet ended up refusing to recognize the Imperial Constitution in May 1849 and thus precipitated the May Uprising in Dresden.

After the violent suppression of this rebellion, the conflict between the *Landtag* and the government resumed under somewhat different circumstances. Following the ban of the Democratic Party and the subsequent reelection of the *Landtag,* the liberals constituted the majority party in parliament. Now they pursued a stance of determined opposition vis-à-vis the conservative government. On the one hand, the liberals wished to tie the Saxon government to Prussia, whose foreign minister Joseph Maria von Radowitz had already made an attempt at *kleindeutsch* national unification in 1850. On the other hand, they pushed hard to accelerate the pace of reform in Saxony itself.

---

7. The model of a "defensive modernization" initiated by the bureaucracy reduces the process to the intentions of the government and prematurely discounts parliamentary and public discussion as powerless "acclamation"; cf. Hans-Ulrich Wehler, *Deutsche Gesellschaftsgeschichte,* 3 vols. to date (Munich, 1995), 3:205.

In July 1850 the Saxon government escaped the mounting political pressure through a coup d'état. It dissolved the democratically elected *Landtag* without, however, arranging for new elections. Instead it reconvened the prerevolutionary *Landtag*. The so-called June Decrees changed the basis of constitutional law and conferred on the government sweeping administrative powers. Freedoms of the press, of assembly, and of association were all abolished by decree, and existing courts meant to decide by jury over "press infractions" were dissolved.

Even before these decrees were issued, the government bureaucracy had begun to discipline the civil service politically. Civil servants who had sympathized with the revolution were temporarily or permanently suspended. Obviously the authorities applied a double standard, especially with respect to the ministerial bureaucracy. A number of the revolutionary "March ministers" had emerged from the ranks of the higher civil service and continued to serve there even after 1850.[8] As well, some of the ministers who had tried in May 1849 to push the king into acceptance of the Imperial Constitution by threatening resignation remained in important ministerial positions after 1850: they retained responsibility for the liberal reforms listed previously.[9] It would certainly be too simple to imply that in the period after 1850 these bourgeois bureaucrats adhered to liberal or even democratic principles. Indeed, one can ask whether they even held such convictions in 1849. However, the influential reformer Albert Christian Weinlig, already well known both in government circles and among the general population before 1848, was deliberately used by his minister after 1850 as a popular figure of integration, in order to demonstrate the government's social conscience and its willingness to proceed with further reforms.

The coup d'état of 1850 represented a turning point in Saxon history, particularly with respect to constitutional law and the parliamentary suffrage. A few examples may serve to illustrate this point: The upper house of the *Landtag* was not an elected house but a chamber of peers, whose members were eligible for appointment by virtue of their office or birth. The lower house consisted of deputies who were divided among four

---

8. For example, the former justice minister, Dr. Karl Alexander Braun, who became district governor (*Amtshauptmann*) in Plauen. Or the interior minister in 1848–49, Martin Oberländer, who was well known for his contacts to the network of democratic clubs; Oberländer remained a ministerial administrator in the interior ministry, responsible for administering the public fire insurance corporation.

9. Albert Christian Weinlig, interior minister in 1849, is an example. He prepared the bills for the occupational law of 1857 and 1861; Gustav Friedrich Held, previously justice minister, prepared the code of criminal procedure and the civil code; Karl Wolf von Ehrenstein stayed on as the right hand of the postrevolutionary minister Behr, who had little knowledge of financial matters.

"estates" (the nobility, farmers, representatives of the cities, and members of commercial and industrial circles). The suffrage, even in the cities, was conditional on the ownership of landed property, and elected deputies had to reside in their constituency. One might guess that the coup d'état would have completely changed the social and political composition of the lower house in comparison to the democratically elected parliaments of 1849 and 1849–50. One look at the deputies after 1850, however, reveals many familiar faces. Thirty-eight percent of the members of the lower house in 1849 won reelection to the *Landtag* between 1850 and 1866. An even higher proportion (50 percent) of the deputies in the upper house in 1849 rejoined state politics in this capacity. On the other hand, many individuals also refused any further participation in the *Landtag*. They did so in protest against the coup d'état, and among them were many liberal conservatives such as the Leipzig publisher Heinrich Brockhaus and the prominent industrialist Gustav Harkort. The Saxon democrats, though already banned in 1849, had been active in a number of successor organizations until 1850. Now most of them ceased all (party-) political activities. Nonetheless, some democratic deputies continued to maintain a high public profile and retained the loyalty of their former party colleagues and voters even after 1850. The coup d'état of 1850, in short, did *not* result in the wholesale replacement of the parliamentary elite, as historians have regularly but incorrectly suggested.[10]

The year 1850 constitutes an even more distinct caesura with respect to the public sphere in Saxony, which was now gagged more effectively and severely than in the pre-March era.[11] Almost all press and publication organs were subjected to strict press laws, threatening even minor "offenses" with such exorbitant penalties that a repeat infraction would clearly result in the economic ruin of the enterprise. The existence of all clubs and permission for public meetings—whether with or without a political hue—were dependent on the arbitrary judgment of the government authorities. After 1850 they used their powers to dissolve all political and quasi-political clubs in Saxony and to forestall the founding of new ones. As a result, the party divisions of 1848–49 separating liberals, democrats, and conservatives declined in significance. Parties no longer provided the organizational platform linking parliamentary politics with the formation of public opinion. Nevertheless, organizations resembling po-

---

10. Here I am relying on the more comprehensive analysis found in Andreas Neemann, *Landtag und Politik in der Reaktionszeit: Sachsen, 1849/50 bis 1866* (Düsseldorf, 2000).

11. Cf. "Allerhöchste Verordnung, das Vereins- und Versammlungsrecht betr.," *Gesetz- und Verordnungsblatt für das Königreich Sachsen vom Jahre 1850,* 137–42; "Allerhöchste Verordnung, einige Zusätze zum Preßgesetze vom 18.11.1848 betr.," ibid., 142–44. Both decrees were subsequently submitted to and approved by the *Landtag*.

litical parties continued to exist even during the 1850s. Several arch-conservative members of the *Landtag*'s upper house founded a Saxon Association (Sachsenverein), which maintained a press organ.[12] This organization, combining antiliberalism and anticapitalism, contributed mainly to the negative integration of the middle-class public in that it became a focal point of bourgeois hostility. The invocation of this conservative bogeyman was among those factors leading to a merger of the previously hostile democrats and liberals, to whom some independents attached themselves as well.

One must also remember that municipal councils throughout Saxony—not only in the large cities—became an important reservoir and forum of political activity for liberals who had withdrawn from the state-level legislative arena in frustration over the coup d'état.[13] Municipal councilors and administrators were certainly subject to strict controls by the state authorities. The government also implemented further changes to the municipal suffrages to undermine opposition. Yet especially in Leipzig, Chemnitz, and Dresden, these measures failed to prevent former liberals and democrats from taking up their seats in city parliaments.[14]

This brief sketch suggests that the various elements of political life—the government, parliament, and the public sphere—remained closely intertwined during the reactionary era. Thus it should come as no surprise that city councilors made up a considerable proportion of deputies in the lower house of the *Landtag*. As in the prerevolutionary era, parliamentary motions could once again be supported and even carried by corresponding petitions from the cities. On the other hand, the government also sought to influence the public, not only by sup-

---

12. This daily newspaper, the *Freimütige Sachsenzeitung,* was edited by Hugo Häpe and Emil Eduard Eckert, two middle-class editors with liberal pasts. Häpe later switched to the Saxon interior ministry, where he was in charge of police surveillance of the press and production of the government organ, the *Dresdner Journal;* see *Der "Polizeiverein" deutscher Staaten: Eine Dokumentation zur Überwachung der Öffentlichkeit nach der Revolution von 1848/49,* ed. Wolfram Siemann (Tübingen, 1983), 28, 70.

13. After 1850, Karl Biedermann initially continued to sit in the Leipzig parliament, as did Heinrich Brockhaus; see Richard Bazillion, *Modernizing Germany: Karl Biedermann's Career in the Kingdom of Saxony, 1835–1901* (Frankfurt a. M., 1990), 248–49. Biedermann, however, had to leave this body in 1851, because he had moved his residence to Lindenau, near Leipzig; *Sächsische Constitutionelle Zeitung,* no. 220 (16 Jan. 1851), 877.

14. This is demonstrated if we consider liberals who even in the early 1850s were elected chairmen of Saxony's most important municipal parliaments: in Leipzig, Dr. Hermann Joseph, and in Chemnitz, Franz Xaver Rewitzer, both former democrats and deputies in the Frankfurt Parliament. In Dresden's municipal parliament, a stronger conservative trend prevented former liberals and democrats from gaining a majority; but they remained a strong minority in which another prominent democrat, Franz Jacob Wigard, continued his political work.

pressing freedom of the press but also by extending the scope and effectiveness of government newspapers and journals, which became quasi-modern instruments of propaganda.[15] Whether these interrelated factors tended to support the government or the opposition, and why, is the subject of the following sections, which discuss three key areas of public policy after 1850.

III.   Cultural Policy

For early German liberals, political emancipation was always tied up with issues of education and self-cultivation (*Bildung*). As a result, the pursuit of religious freedom and control over internal church matters by parishioners gained political momentum as important issues of liberal politics at a relatively early date. In Saxony, a state with a rationalist ecclesiastical tradition, this tendency had preceded the 1848–49 Revolutions in the form of the German Catholic and Free religious communities (*Deutschkatholiken, Freien Gemeinden*). Even before 1848, conservative members of the government sought to counter these groups by combining state administration of the church with the orthodox Protestant movement.[16] After the coup of 1850, the state government leaned increasingly in this direction. The strategy of combining clerical antirationalism with political conservatism can be read from the text of a sermon delivered upon the opening of the reactivated *Landtag* in late July 1850. The sermon was given by the principal court preacher, Gottlieb Christoph Adolf Harleß, who was known for his Orthodox convictions. As a dean, he was not a member of the government, but in his role as a churchman, he cooperated closely with it. In this sermon, Harleß condemned man's quest for a better future — which he claimed was doomed to failure — because such striving was not linked to an unconditional belief in God. Corresponding to "the damnable customs of the time," Harleß stated, "people emancipated their conscience from the fear of God and from the oath of allegiance sworn to Him." Instead — "oh, for

---

15. In the face of the landslide election victory of the democrats, in early 1849 the liberal revolutionary government founded a second government newspaper, the *Dresdner Zeitung,* to supplement the *Leipziger Zeitung.* Beust's reactionary government retained this second organ despite occasional resistance from the *Landtag;* it also sought to gain influence over a plethora of minor official newssheets (*Amtsblätter*) in the provincial cities.

16. Günther Kolbe, *Demokratische Opposition im religiösen Gewande und anti-kirchliche Bewegung im Königreich Sachsen* (Leipzig, 1963); Hans Rosenberg, "Theologischer Rationalismus und vormärzlicher Vulgärliberalismus," in idem, *Politische Denkströmungen im Deutschen Vormärz* (Göttingen, 1972). On Orthodoxy in Saxony, see Helmar Junghans, "Die Berufung von Gottlieb Christoph Adolf Harleß nach Leipzig und die Erneuerung des Luthertums in Sachsen," *Jahrbuch für Regionalgeschichte* 14 (1987): 282–300.

shame" — they allowed (political) leaders and "self-elected chiefs" to dictate what they ought to say and think.[17] Contemporaries found Harleß's sermon explosive, not only because of the place and occasion chosen to deliver it, but also because of Harleß's proximity to governmental authority. In fact the two objections merged into one, because this sermon, though delivered at the opening of parliament, was issued in print form and read aloud in every church across the state. The liberal response came swiftly. The Leipzig public-school teacher Eduard Sparfeld printed a pamphlet at his own expense — it was initially published anonymously — to express his outrage at what he believed to be a dangerous public pronouncement. Sparfeld's two most pointed complaints against the Orthodox court preacher drew an important linkage that is also doubly interesting for historians. On the one hand, he criticized the almost exclusive use of passages from the Old Testament in Harleß's text. According to Sparfeld, the severe tone found in Old Testament language relegated the "message of love" and "reconciliation" to the background: the insistence on unconditional and submissive faith was not compatible with liberal church tradition in Saxony. Sparfeld objected, second, to the undisguised political content of the sermon, which he judged to be highly inappropriate in the politically tense summer of 1850: "Through the lamentable confusions of these times," wrote Sparfeld, "the path of wisdom, wisely taken, is hindered and interrupted, the popular sense of justice is violated, and the bonds of love and trust, which for so long have girdled the prince and the people to the glory and pride of both, are loosened. Thousands have had to moan in the dungeons of the land, thousands yearn for reconciliation, thousands seek the alleviation of their torments."[18]

Sparfeld's pamphlet was immensely successful, reaching three editions. Of course Harleß felt bound to issue a reply, and his reply in turn was answered by Sparfeld (again anonymously). Finally, the state

---

17. [G. Ch. A. Harleß], *Was unserem Volk in dieser Zeit Noth thue: Predigt zur Eröffnung des Landtags am 22.VII.1850* (Dresden, 1850), 9. The leitmotif of the sermon was a passage from the Old Testament (Zech. 10:1–2): "Ask ye of the Lord rain in the time of the latter rain; so the Lord shall make bright clouds, and give them showers of rain, to every one grass in the field. For the idols have spoken vanity, and the diviners have seen a lie, and have told false dreams; they comfort in vain: therefore they went their way as a flock, they were troubled, because there was no shepherd."

18. [Eduard Sparfeld], *Der Prophet Sacharia auf der Kanzel der evangelischen Hofkirche in Dresden: Ein offenes Wort an Herrn Oberhofprediger Dr. Harleß . . .* (Dresden, 1850), 14. The theologians Friedrich von Ammon (1766–1849) and Franz Volkmar Reinhard (1753–1812) were Harleß's predecessors as principal court preachers and deans, as well as prominent representatives of an ecclesiastical liberalism that was influential beyond Saxony. See *Allgemeine Deutsche Biographie* (Leipzig, 1875), 1:405–6, (Leipzig, 1889), 28:32–35.

authorities brought the controversy to an end. After identifying Sparfeld as the author, they ousted him from his teaching post and added to his difficulties with multiple lawsuits. This outcome is much less important, however, than what the Harleß-Sparfeld controversy revealed about older (in this case, clerical-religious) points of reference in Saxon political discourse. Even in an age of reaction, these referents retained undiminished interpretive power over people who were evaluating their political options, as it were, in the "here and now." Such weighing of options did not need to revisit the lessons of 1848–49 to reach the conclusion that the government was pursuing a reactionary course. Even without having to make explicit reference to the revolutionary and democratic attainments of the recent past, Sparfeld and other liberals were able to criticize and delegitimate the actions of the Saxon government, judging them against standards provided by older traditions.

A second example shows a similar course of events. In 1853 the minister for education and cultural affairs, Baron Johann Paul von Falkenstein, intended to prohibit the use in church of some prayer books that were deemed to be liberal. This time a conservative *Landtag* deputy, the middle-class estate owner Karl August Rittner, vehemently protested this form of "book burning" by the ministry.[19] Rittner's protest was endorsed by other moderate conservative and liberal deputies; he also received supporting letters from the general population. Rittner had not merely criticized the antirationalist course of the Saxon ministry but also denounced its actions as illegitimate. He thus precipitated a debate over the Saxon church constitution that lasted for over a decade and in 1868 — after an abortive attempt in 1863 — resulted in a Saxon church constitution with a state synod, a form of ecclesiastical parliament.

The Saxon government tried after 1850 to strengthen and invigorate Saxon regional and traditional consciousness as much as possible, believing this to be the natural support of its reactionary policies. Yet very frequently, this tactic came to nothing because liberal traditions persisted tenaciously. On occasion, they were apt to endanger or even thwart the political plans of the government. A further example in this context is the debate concerning the municipal militias (*Kommunalgarden*) that had been established after 1831. Because some of these armed units had sided with the insurgents in 1849, the government wanted to reorganize them after 1850. Above all, the formally autonomous "general command" was to be disciplined through incorporation into the war ministry. However,

---

19. *Mitteilungen über die Verhandlungen des (außer)ordentlichen Landtags im Königreich Sachsen, 1854,* II. Kammer: 10 (16 Oct. 1854). Rittner used the Spanish expression *autodafé,* recalling the Inquisition. The volumes in question were by Dinter, Tischer, and Schuderoff.

this move also met with vigorous resistance, even from conservative deputies who preferred to see the militias abolished entirely rather than have their historic autonomy removed.[20]

IV. Administrative Reform

The reform of judicial administration in 1854 sheds further light on the political climate in Saxony during the era of reaction.[21] The blueprint for judicial reform had a long prehistory, dating back to the 1830s. In the wake of inaugurating the Saxon constitution, the state's administration had been fundamentally restructured. The judicial and administrative organs, having been united until then, were separated on the level of the ministries and intermediary authorities, but not in the lowest echelons. As yet private patrimonial judges (*Patrimonialrichter*), who were predominantly owners of knightly estates (*Rittergutsbesitzer*), operated as the local extension of the state administration, presiding, for example, over the courts of first instance.[22] During the 1840s, more far-reaching reforms were planned, but they failed due to vigorous noble resistance from the upper house of the *Landtag*. Finally, in 1848 the government and the *Landtag* abolished many of the older administrative structures, beginning with the patrimonial courts. However, with a view to a possible future national constitution, they did not create any new structures. After the 1850 coup, a strong conservative faction, consisting mainly of nobles, established itself in the upper chamber. It immediately began to agitate publicly against the reform plans of the government. Taking account of the opinions of these arch-conservative nobles, the government had already removed many of the more liberal features in the draft administrative reform, even before legislation was introduced (one example is the provision for trial by jury, which had been guaranteed in 1848). The revised blueprint for administrative reform nevertheless still insisted on the abolition of the patrimonial courts. Certainly previous patrimonial judges were offered compensation: they would be allowed to continue local police functions as "justices of the peace." But they were now to be subject to the overall supervision of state authorities. This concession could not hide the fact that the government was intent

---

20. *Mitteilungen über die Verhandlungen . . . des Landtags . . . 1851/52*, II. Kammer: 1781–1814 (5 Feb. 1851).

21. See Heinz-Georg Holldack, *Untersuchungen zur Geschichte der Reaktion in Sachsen, 1849–1855* (Berlin, 1931).

22. They did not preside over the court themselves but had to engage legal experts as so-called court directors; Gerhard Schmidt, *Die Staatsreform in Sachsen in der ersten Hälfte des 19. Jahrhunderts* (Weimar, 1966).

on bringing jurisprudence and administration — even in the lowest echelons of the judicial system — under strict state control. Nor could contemporaries fail to see that the holders of older corporatist legal titles,
whether representatives of the privileged cities or the nobility, would
now take second place behind this authority.

The political wing of the Saxon aristocracy was by no means content
with this revision of the judicial system and threatened to block passage of
the reform in the *Landtag*. Liberal deputies of the lower house, too, could
not be counted as certain supporters of the motion, due to their disappointment over the scrapping of the trial-by-jury provision. Moreover,
until this point the liberals had not played a prominent role in parliamentary legislation because the government had continually avoided relying
on their support. In the case of the motion for the administrative reform,
however, this outsider role was changed. The liberal minority now once
again had an important function in achieving a majority. Equally important, the liberals could now rely on public debate that concerned itself not
only with the judicial reform but also with other issues close to liberal
hearts. Liberal support for the government was more forthcoming, because liberals realized that strong opposition would only benefit the conservative nobles. From the liberal perspective, cooperation with the government and with the moderate conservatives in the lower house of the
Landtag held the best hope for real gains in the long term.

Thus the liberal movement to the government's side, which facilitated passage of the administrative reform (*Behördenorganisationsge-
setz*) of 1854, was characterized by practical considerations, and it was
aimed above all at the arch-conservatives. However, this political alliance, arising in 1854 from a crisis situation, was not consolidated across
the board. While parts of the public continued to voice demands for liberalization of the political system as a whole, the liberal *Landtag* deputies
developed an increasingly cooperative relationship to the government
that precluded such a policy. This partnership underscored the retrospective affinity of the 1850s to the 1830s, another era of intensive reforming
activity. This viewpoint was represented in the political creed of the president of the lower house, Heinrich Haase, who had already sat in the first
constitutional *Landtag* in 1833 and who declared on the floor of the
Landtag in 1854:[23] "Progress turns everywhere into regression — in state
and civic institutions as well as in the trades, the arts, and in science — as
soon as one leaves it at that. Therefore the legislation of a country must
also progress, not only because the sciences are supported by it, but also
because the genuine task of the legislator is to keep pace with the change

---

23. *Mitteilungen über die Verhandlungen . . . des Landtags . . . 1854*, II. Kammer:
154 (10 Nov. 1854).

and augmentation of institutions in the country and to regulate the new circumstances that arise as a consequence of those changes."

Haase's words suggest how, in the context of the 1850s, "progress" was stripped of its politically emancipatory connotations. Haase's general line of reasoning went so far as to defend the "good" revolution (of 1830) against the "vicious" revolution of 1848–49, mirroring an evolution within liberal thought that had already become apparent during debate over the municipal militias. Outside the *Landtag*, however, this consciousness of the need for liberals to align themselves with a reforming state authority did not manage to attain lasting influence. For liberal journalists and councilors sitting in municipal parliaments, the laws initiated in 1848 continued to serve as ideological litmus tests and regulative yardsticks alike. Of special importance in this regard were the Frankfurt Catalogue of Basic Rights and the struggle for national unification. The liberal-conservative majority in the Saxon *Landtag*, by contrast, wished to regard the same laws as a kind of legislative grab bag (*Verfügungsmasse*) at the disposal of a government whose legitimacy was undiminished.

V. Promotion of the Trades

For large segments of the political public in Saxony during the 1850s, the German nation remained little more than a glimmer of hope on the horizon, even though it contrasted sharply with the deficiencies of particularistic government at home. Not until the foundation of the German National Association (Deutscher Nationalverein) in 1859 was the nation — in the form of a *kleindeutsch* federal state — again seen by some Saxon liberals as a viable goal of political action. However, by this time the Beust government had learned how to accommodate the opinions and interests of those who were not represented (or were underrepresented) in the *Landtag*. In the process Beust had even learned how to bypass parliament itself, as he did during the early phase of consultations that eventually led to enactment of the freedom of occupation legislation in 1861.

This reform completed an older legislative project initiated in 1848. At that time, the interior ministry had instructed a democratically elected "commission of inquiry" to gather the opinions and wishes of people throughout the kingdom concerning the planned legislation.[24]

---

24. This was the Kommission zur Erörterung der Gewerbs- und Arbeitsverhältnisse im Königreich Sachsen; although it was called in shorthand the Arbeiter-Kommission, this was a misnomer, because the commission dealt with all problems of contemporary trades, especially with the future of the crafts.

Even this process of opinion gathering (or opinion making) proved to be extremely difficult, because the party divisions of 1848–49 were also reflected in the commission. For the democrats, the maintenance or extension of the traditional guild system constituted the best means to ensure the welfare of the general population. Accordingly, they were opposed to freedom of occupation, which was preferred by the less numerous middle-class liberals in and outside the government. The issue thus became polarized along partisan lines. The Saxon government did not submit any bill at all until 1850, hoping to avoid a further escalation of political tension. But the coup of 1850 brought about a curious constellation of political groups: The conservative hard-liners, who now occupied a strategic position in the *Landtag,* spoke out in favor of maintaining the existing guild constitution—just as the democrats had in the past. They romanticized the guild system as the divinely ordained, organic social order. The reality in Saxony, however, had long since changed. Since the seventeenth century, royal privileges and concessions had undermined existing obligations to join a guild. The overall result had been the advance of "modern" forms of occupation—initially, manufactures; then, since the beginning of the nineteenth century, home crafts and industry—and the weakening of the existing guilds. The desire for a clearly regulated occupational law thus remained strong both among the crafts sector and in industry.

When the Saxon interior ministry drew up a bill, it sought to accommodate the recommendations of the "commission of inquiry" but also take account of the current constellation of parties, and possible majorities, in the *Landtag.* Consequently, the draft completed in 1857 attempted with its veritable flood of statutes to transfer corporatist structures to industry and home crafts. The draft bill never reached the *Landtag,* however. To everyone's dismay, the government published the entire draft instead. At the same time it invited expert commentary from the public, which it said would subsequently be evaluated by the state council (*Staatsrat*)—a deliberating constitutional body that convened very infrequently. The public response elicited by the draft showed that no one was really satisfied with the bill as it was, neither the supporters of the guild constitution nor its opponents. Yet reading the public statements about the government's draft bill reveals some striking dimensions to this debate. The conservative opponents of freedom of occupation, who might well have constituted a *Landtag* majority, played only a peripheral role in this debate. Liberal voices dominated instead, and they almost universally advocated complete freedom of occupation. But their arguments were multilayered. Above all, they viewed freedom of occupation as a means of securing the survival of middle-class artisans in an industrial environment where the remnants of guild constitutions and the expanding system of concessions no longer impeded the advance of modern industrial practices.[25]

Particular conceptions of a future German nation also played a role in all this. In a period of continual exchange of goods and expanding free trade, the argument went, a country without freedom of occupation would inevitably fall behind. In this context, the Saxon economic liberals were not thinking only of Prussia; they also pointed to Austria, where in the late 1850s a reform of the guild constitution was initiated as well. This notion of substituting (partial) national "standardization" for the (political) national unity that was still lacking—thereby starting the motor of reform in the individual states of the Confederation—was actually endorsed by the Saxon government. Beust's ministry subsequently submitted to the *Landtag* and got legislative approval for a bill providing almost complete freedom of occupation in accordance with the liberals' demands. References to the government's inability to find a public consensus after 1857 and to the "proven impossibility" of integrating the guilds in a modern economic system finally undercut the opposition of *Landtag* deputies who argued for continued guild support.

In the end, even this willingness to recognize the "sign of the times" was not sufficient to keep Beust in the good graces of the growing national movement in Saxony. Beust, too, realized that the political momentum generated by the German question could not be checked by partial reforms. He did not express this insight publicly, but in private diplomatic conversations he clearly indicated that "if one does not wish to see these [national] sentiments satisfied by Prussia and at the cost of the middle-sized states, these states will have to join together firmly and do something on their own to meet those demands that are legitimate."[26]

VI. Saxony on the Eve of Unification

A state government jealously protecting its sovereignty; a parochial, conservative, and philistine bourgeoisie; and a national, liberal opposition: this picture of the main protagonists in Saxon political life in the 1850s and 1860s, drawn by Treitschke and adopted by too many of his successors, is no longer tenable. Certainly a variety of political currents remained in

25. Cf. Kiesewetter, *Industrialisierung und Landwirtschaft*, 167f.; and Paul Horster, *Die Entwicklung der sächsischen Gewerbeverfassung, 1780–1861* (Crefeld, 1908), 34–36. The status of Saxon industry, which could already rely on royal privileges and concessions, was not affected by the freedom of occupation legislation. Therefore it is difficult to accuse the liberal spokesmen of representing bourgeois "class interests."

26. Report of the Austrian envoy in Dresden, Baron Josef von Werner, to the Austrian foreign minister, 7 May 1860, in *Quellen zur deutschen Politik Österreichs, 1859–1866*, ed. Heinrich Ritter von Srbik, 5 vols. (Berlin, 1934), vol. 1, no. 133.

play during these decades. But they joined together, influenced each other, and thus changed. The liberals on the one hand accepted partial reforms of government; but on the other hand they demanded a degree of political codetermination. The government maneuvered between authoritarian domestic politics and voluntary concessions to groups it considered supportive of the state. But this strategy, too, required attention to the quest for national unity, one of the great aims of middle-class liberalism in Germany. Regional consciousness and national consciousness, liberal traditions and conservative traditions—these things often could not be distinguished in the 1860s. Hence it was in this decade that the government, instead of relying on ambiguous regional traditions as an ideological backbone for its rule, found a more effective and attractive strategy to undercut political liberalism: it adopted some of the liberals' own goals. This strategy eventually became evident during the Schleswig-Holstein crisis of 1863–64. The great powers Prussia and Austria subordinated the demands of the national movement for self-determination of the two duchies to their own power-political interests. This might have been Beust's finest hour, for he made a concerted effort to defend the right of the two duchies to self-determination by means of a coalition of the middle German states.

Beust achieved real popularity for a time. Like other leading German statesmen in similar circumstances, he welcomed the support he received from the German national movement. To be sure, he stopped short of addressing the nationalists' larger demands, whereas Bismarck proceeded without much hesitation. Nevertheless, one should not draw too sharp a picture of Beust and his fellow reactionaries standing in opposition to the national movement's political demands (and, in particular, steadfastly resisting their demand for a democratically elected all-German parliament). Indeed, the argument can be made that Bismarck's "revolution from above" was actually the recognition of a line of development that during the 1850s and the 1860s had quietly unfolded in the individual German states at least as clearly as at any supraregional level. As the Saxon case suggests, one of the most important aspects of this development was the silent integration of middle-class interests and models for political participation into the practices of state governance.

Saxon Forty-eighters in the Postrevolutionary Epoch, 1849–1867

Christian Jansen

I. Introduction

In addition to Berlin, Vienna, and southwestern Germany, Saxony was a center of revolutionary activity in 1848–49.[1] That it quickly became a stronghold of left-wing politics is reflected in the outcome of elections to the German National Assembly: of the twenty-four electoral constituencies in the Saxon kingdom, twenty (later twenty-one) were represented in Frankfurt's Paulskirche by politicians who joined left-wing caucuses.[2] The radicals received broader support only in the Rhineland-Palatinate and in several small states.

After the May 1849 rebellion in Dresden had been put down with Prussian help, a strong wave of repression began against the Saxon Forty-eighters. Two-thirds of the representatives in Frankfurt were affected by it as well.[3] Contrary to the view that the revolutionaries of 1848–49 simply retreated from politics to economic activities or to pri-

---

1. See also Andreas Neemann, "Kontinuitäten und Brüche aus einzelstaatlicher Perspektive: Politische Milieus in Sachsen, 1848 bis 1850," in *Die Revolutionen von 1848/ 49: Erfahrung—Verarbeitung—Deutung,* ed. Christian Jansen and Thomas Mergel (Göttingen, 1998), 172–89.
2. See Heinrich Best and Wilhelm Weege, *Biographisches Handbuch der Abgeordneten der Frankfurter Nationalversammlung, 1848/49* (Düsseldorf, 1996); and, for a more detailed definition of the term *left,* Christian Jansen, *Einheit, Macht und Freiheit: Die Paulskirchenlinke und die deutsche Politik der nachrevolutionären Epoche (1849–1867)* (Düsseldorf, 2000), chap. 1. See also Thorsten Tonndorf, "Die wahl- und sozialpolitische Zusammensetzung der sächsischen Paulskirchenvertreter," *Zeitschrift für Geschichtswissenschaft* 42 (1994): 773–94.
3. On the persecution and emigration of the Paulskirche leftists, see Jansen, *Einheit,* chap. 2.

vate life, the majority of the former Paulskirche representatives stayed politically active in spite of persecution or returned to political life after imprisonment or emigration. This applies especially to Saxony. Except for Württemberg, in no other German state before 1871 was the liberal opposition so dominated by Forty-eighters as in the kingdom on the Mulde and the Elbe.[4]

The Saxon case thus provides an opportunity to study the complex evolution of Germany's bourgeois left after its fundamental defeat at midcentury. Even a cursory examination of the political paths taken by selected Saxon Forty-eighters reveals some of that complexity. Twenty years after the revolution, the Leipzig democrat Hermann Joseph found himself in the National Liberal Party (Nationalliberale Partei), together with his former political opponent, the left liberal Karl Biedermann. The *großdeutsch* left liberal Heinrich Wuttke and the democrat Emil Adolph Roßmäßler belonged to the first intellectuals in the 1860s who joined the labor movement. In these four cases, former comrades drew different conclusions from the failure of the revolution, ending up in opposite camps where they joined forces with former opponents. On the other hand, the Dresden democrats Franz Jakob Wigard and Wilhelm Michael Schaffrath, as well as Franz August Mammen, quarreled side by side for twenty years, beginning with their activities in the Paulskirche caucus known as the Deutsche Hof and extending up to the establishment of a Progressive caucus in the North German Reichstag.

Behind these different political careers one can discern the basic issues on which intra-German affairs turned in the 1850s. The left agreed, for the most part, that their national-democratic program — defined as the simultaneous quest for national unity, a European position of power, and political freedom — had failed, largely because of the balance of power in Europe. These leftists therefore sought to adapt this program to new political realities. Within the bourgeois left, various factions emphasized different aspects of the ideas of 1848. Some leftists were finally ready to collaborate with the reactionary regimes in Berlin or in Vienna in order to gain national unity and power. Others wanted to concentrate initially on the achievement of a parliamentary government and the rule of law in the individual states; these leftists generally trusted in a gradual, federal union of liberal German states. A third faction, which is particularly relevant to the Saxon case, perceived the explosive power of the social question, whose contours had become

---

4. This is demonstrated by the index listings in the meticulous study by Herbert Jordan, *Die öffentliche Meinung in Sachsen, 1864–66* (Kamenz, 1918), 248. On Saxon political culture before 1871, see also "Ein Beitrag zur Geschichte des Sächsischen Politik," *Preußische Jahrbücher* 34 (1874): 550–81.

clear to them in 1848. These leftists strove above all for the political emancipation of workers.

The following analysis examines the problems and conflicts within Saxon liberalism between 1849 and 1867, identifying three crucial turning points. It considers, first, the Saxon constitutional conflict of 1849–50, which forced the left into a defensive position for years to come. Second, it explores the left's failed hopes for the political constitution of a "Third Germany" during the Schleswig-Holstein crisis of 1863–64. And third, it analyzes the disputes among Saxon leftists in the wake of the Austro-Prussian War[5] of 1866, when Saxony joined the North German Confederation under Prussian domination. This last turning point brought Saxony closer to the national unity longed for by the bourgeois left, but not in accordance with their ideals of 1848.

II.   The Saxon Constitutional Conflict

After the failure of the 1848 Revolution, the Saxon government initially pursued a course of reform, as did most middle-sized German states. After May 1849 the government faced large majorities in the *Landtag* under the leadership of radical Paulskirche representatives who stuck to the principles of 1848. The German princes, however, increasingly led state governments on a reactionary course. Thus there arose major constitutional conflicts in Saxony as well as in Bavaria, Württemberg, Hesse, and several smaller states; these conflicts "were conducted stubbornly and bitterly with all legal means."[6] The nature of the showdown between liberals and the various governments was the same almost everywhere: The chambers tried to prevent antirevolutionary measures and implement further reforms by means of various kinds of constitutional pressure — for example, by interpellating government ministers or by refusing to approve the state's budget. If, as a consequence, the chambers were dissolved, voters tended to reelect the liberal majorities. If ministers resigned because of votes of no confidence, however, they were more commonly replaced by reactionaries, a process that further intensified the confrontation. The ministries of the middle-sized states finally governed unconstitutionally by means of an emergency decree, without a budget, and after coups d'état, whereby they abrogated the constitutions and suffrage laws to which they had agreed during the

---

5. Christian Jansen quite legitimately prefers the term "German-Prussian war" of 1866. For consistency, however, "Austro-Prussian War" is used throughout this volume. —Ed.

6. Manfred Botzenhart, *Deutscher Parlamentarismus in der Revolutionszeit, 1848–1850* (Düsseldorf, 1977), 725; Ernst Rudolf Huber, *Deutsche Verfassungsgeschichte seit 1789,* 3d ed. (Stuttgart, 1988), 3:182.

revolution. These electoral laws were either replaced by older, estate-bound (*ständisch*) statutes, or new ones were imposed that generally worsened the liberals' chances of reelection. By 1851 these measures had resulted in the establishment of submissive chambers in all German states.

In Saxony, the constitutional conflict effectively came to an end with the coup d'état of 1 June 1850. Three prominent Paulskirche leftists — Karl Biedermann, Hermann Joseph, and Franz Mammen — played major roles in defending the rights of the *Landtag*. They represented the three factions of the liberal-democratic spectrum in Saxony: Biedermann represented the left liberals, who supported the government as long as it followed a political course compatible with the *kleindeutsch* German Union. Joseph represented the moderate and *kleindeutsch* democrats. And Mammen, who was elected president of the *Landtag*'s upper chamber, represented the radical, anti-Prussian left. The democratic Forty-eighter Franz Wigard[7] joined the latter group when he was elected to the lower chamber of the Saxon *Landtag* in February 1850. The three factions of the bourgeois left together had large majorities in both chambers of the Saxon parliament.[8] They greatly outnumbered conservative deputies, who were themselves divided into *kleindeutsch* and particularist factions. However, consensus was elusive even on the left.[9] Disunity was particularly evident in debates on intra-German affairs: the same difficulties in decision making and consensus building that had hamstrung the left in the Paulskirche when the national question was debated in 1848–49 cropped up subsequently in the Saxon *Landtag*.

In early 1850, fierce conflicts arose within the Saxon left about whether and under what conditions the country should join the German Union (the Union had been proposed by Prussia after rejection of the Imperial Constitution). Anti-Prussian democrats such as Mammen and Wigard opposed the Union steadfastly. They stuck to the *großdeutsch* ideal and demanded new elections for a National Assembly. That assembly, they believed, should carry out the revision of the Imperial Constitution that had become necessary after Frederick William IV refused the imperial crown. The moderate democrats under Joseph's leadership had no patience for debates that would lead to decisions the *Landtag* could not

---

7. Cf. Ruth Fuchs, "Franz Jacob Wigard: Ein Beitrag zur Geschichte der kleinbürgerlichen Demokratie im 19. Jahrhundert" (Ph.D. diss., University of Leipzig, 1970), 121.

8. Until the coup d'état of 1850, both chambers consisted mainly of elected members; see Botzenhart, *Parlamentarismus*, 230.

9. *Mitteilungen über die Verhandlungen des Landtags im Königreich Sachsen* (hereafter *Sächs. LT*), I. Kammer 1849/50, 24; ibid., II. Kammer, 42; Fuchs, "Wigard," 121; Botzenhart, *Parlamentarismus*, 28 (and for the following paragraph).

implement. They therefore proposed a declaration that the Frankfurt Catalogue of Basic Rights (*Grundrechtekatalog*) and a "freely elected parliament" (*Volksvertretung*) should be inalienable preconditions of the German agreement. The disagreement among the left in Saxony's upper chamber, however, led to a stalemate, so that no resolution of the issue was possible.

In the lower chamber, in which the left liberals held a majority, Biedermann was able to obtain passage of a declaration in favor of a German federal state with a directly elected representative body of the people and a parliamentary government. This proposal resembled Joseph's petition to the upper chamber and was only rejected by the conservative minority. The lower chamber pronounced itself in favor of joining the Union if the southern German states also took part, so that in fact the entire non-Austrian federal territory would have been unified under Prussian leadership. In other words, Saxon *Landtag* debates about the German Union revealed a constellation that Bismarck later used in establishing the German Empire. After the Paulskirche democrats had split over the question of the imperial crown for Prussia, some of them — especially north Germans and Hegelians — were ready to put aside demands for freedom in favor of unification under Prussian leadership, because they expected the economic and political modernization of Germany as a result.

The various factions on the Saxon left appraised these different options in part according to how likely each one considered a revival of the revolution to be. The radicals refused any agreement with the government and insisted strictly on the validity of the Frankfurt Imperial Constitution. According to this apparently legalistic, but actually revolutionary, position, this constitution could only be altered by a democratically elected successor parliament. The *kleindeutsch* democrats did not insist on the wording of the Imperial Constitution, but on its basic principles. Even this demand could only be realized by a new revolution. The left liberals in particular no longer expected another revolution, and they were willing to accept the Union project. While Biedermann, Joseph, and their friends were still thinking about the conditions under which the *kleindeutsch* left could participate in the building of the German Union, however, the German governments abandoned this unification project altogether.

By following a pro-Austrian policy of reestablishing former federal institutions, the Saxon government aggravated the confrontation with the *Landtag* in the spring of 1850. Saxon ministers also became more and more provocative in their disregard of the *Landtag* deputies' wishes, for example in such constitutional issues as the enforcement of parliamentary prerogative or the validity of the Basic Rights of the German

People, which Saxony had put into force in 1849. The factions in the *Landtag* thereafter moved closer to each other and put aside their quarrels. Thus, the lower house unanimously accepted Wigard's petition directed against Minister of the Interior Ferdinand von Zschinsky, who wanted to retain only those Basic Rights that the government considered "healing and beneficial to the fatherland."

In mid-1850 the lower house of the *Landtag* endorsed an address drafted by Biedermann, which reminded the king of the reforms promised in the throne speech delivered in late 1849. Disappointed by the reactionary politics of the state ministry and by its rejection of a program leading to unification along *kleindeutsch* lines, more and more *Landtag* deputies adopted a policy of resolute opposition to the government. When Foreign Minister Count Friedrich Ferdinand von Beust announced the reestablishment of the Bundestag, even Biedermann proposed a tax boycott, thereby indicating his willingness to resort to the strongest means available within the constitutional system to pressure the government. To preempt such a motion, the *Landtag* was dissolved the next day. In the following days, freedoms of the press, of assembly, and of association were repealed; the death penalty was reestablished; and the estate-bound (*ständisch*) constitution of 1831 was reinvoked.[10]

Consequently, Biedermann, the head of the left-liberal majority in the lower house, took another remarkable step. In a political pamphlet he protested against "the re-summoning of the former estates in Saxony." After having demonstrated the unconstitutionality of the governmental measure and having refuted the existence of a state of emergency, Biedermann posed a question that was rarely asked by a German liberal: did Saxons have the right to resist their government's actions? According to Biedermann, because the coup d'état had been a "thoroughly revolutionary" measure, further revolutionary action was not only likely to occur, but was morally justified. Hence "resistance to the government's incursions against the constitution is not only a constitutional, but above all a conservative, duty." Biedermann believed that members of the former *Landtag* should refuse en bloc to accept their mandates, especially because they had agreed upon constitutional reform two years earlier.

10. *Sächs. LT,* I. Kammer, 636; II. Kammer, 1500, 1641 (quotation from Zschinsky), 1718; Karl Biedermann, *Fünfzig Jahre im Dienst des nationalen Gedenkens: Aufsätze und Reden* (Breslau, 1892), 59; idem, *Mein Leben und ein Stück Zeitgeschichte,* 2 vols. (Breslau, 1886), 2:13; idem, *Die Wiedereinberufung der alten Stände in Sachsen, aus dem Gesichtspunkte des Rechts und der Politik beleuchtet* (Leipzig, 1850), esp. 66 and 85; Fuchs, "Wigard," 123; Joachim Müller, "Karl Biedermann und die preußische Hegemonie in Deutschland: Vom Liberalismus zum Bonapartismus" (Ph.D. diss., University of Leipzig, 1972), 211.

Biedermann's argument did not stop there. Even "the authorities," he wrote, were obliged to resist illegal governmental action. In a situation that represented the "to be or not to be of the entire constitutional order," argued Biedermann, every citizen — and in particular every civil servant — had "to be ready to take responsibility for legality and constitutional propriety [*Recht und Gesetz*] with everything he is and everything he owns." Even though Biedermann did not demand self-sacrifice from every civil servant, he expected them to present their doubts concerning the coup d'état to their employer, just as laid down in the Law for Public Servants. Biedermann also advised Saxon citizens to pay only those taxes that had been passed lawfully. In doing so, he implicitly called for a boycott of all taxes passed by the reestablished *Landtag*. Biedermann himself came to the conclusion that his proposals were hardly suitable "to force the government to return to the constitutional path." However, he also pointed out that the fundamental politicization of German society in the revolutionary era had inalterably changed the relationship between state and society. After emancipation of the citizen, a return to authoritarian rule as in the prerevolutionary era no longer seemed possible.

Not legal convictions alone, but also the fear of a second, possibly uncontrollable revolution, led Biedermann to this comprehensive formulation of a right of resistance, which went beyond the German liberal tradition. He concluded with the "confident" hope that "our King" will let himself, through "public opinion," be pulled out of his present "deception" about the politics of his government. In other words, whereas he argued unambiguously that the Saxon coup d'état had been illegal, Biedermann fell back on the image of the "good king" being manipulated by his government into political positions diametrically opposed to the interests of his people. Biedermann's definition of resistance, like that of other Forty-eighters, was deeply rooted in premodern thinking.[11] Yet ironically — and, again, like other politicians of the left who protested the coup d'état — Biedermann badly overestimated the power shift from monarchy to parliament that had occurred in 1848–49.

The weakness of the resistance against the Saxon government's coup d'état is most notable if one compares it to Electoral Hesse, where

---

11. *Protokolle über die Verhandlungen in den Sitzungen der [2. sächsischen] Kammer,* 23 and 24 July 1850; *Sächs. LT,* I. Kammer, 22 July 1850; II. Kammer, 28 July 1850: 20; Biedermann, *Wiedereinberufung,* esp. 78. Against this background, the picture of Biedermann the modernizer, which Richard J. Bazillion draws in *Modernizing Germany: Karl Biedermann's Career in the Kingdom of Saxony* (New York, 1989), seems too one-dimensional. For the rootedness of the 1848 Revolution in early modern traditions, see Jonathan Sperber, "Eine alte Revolution in neuer Zeit: 1848/49 in europäischer Perspektive," in *Revolutionen,* ed. Jansen and Mergel, 14.

most civil servants and members of the officer corps opposed the government, and where their resistance could be broken only by the intervention of a federal army. In Saxony, the wounds of the bloody Dresden Uprising in May 1849 and the wave of repression that followed it seemed too fresh to be forgotten. Moreover, conflicts seething within the Saxon left remained particularly strong, which rendered it incapable of united political action. Because leftist politicians sought power in a constitutional system where they lacked strong public support and legislative power, their politics were confined mainly to symbolic acts of protest, even as they attempted to rally public opinion to put more pressure on the Saxon monarch.

The radical Saxon left continued its boycott of *Landtag* proceedings, reestablished after the coup d'état of 1850, until the 1860s—longer than in any other German state. When the Paulskirche leftist Mammen returned to the Dresden lower chamber in November 1863, he felt obliged to explain in his very first address to the house that taking up his seat did not signify recognition of the conditions established by the coup d'état.[12] The radical left's parliamentary boycott, which lasted more than ten years, led not only to political paralysis, but also to an ongoing confrontation between government and opposition. In the southern German states, where the left continued to be represented in state parliaments, political structures dating from the revolutionary era were retained, despite reactionary association laws. In Saxony and Prussia, however, the left had to await the abandonment of the political boycott before it reorganized itself as the Progressive Party (Fortschrittspartei). Even then, the prior reaction and the long-standing boycott had impeded the promotion of younger political thinkers within left-wing ranks. This was one of the reasons Forty-eighters once again took on leadership roles after the left began to play a part in Saxon and Prussian politics.

Taking account of these diverse experiences of reaction among German states, one might say that liberals adhered to a general pattern: the more confusing the political perspectives, the greater their political readiness to take risks. That readiness, found frequently in south German constitutional states, was in turn the prerequisite for other aspects of a reorientation in left-wing politics, involving not only a fundamental rethinking of political goals but also a willingness to experiment politically:

---

12. [Heinrich Wuttke, "Korrespondenz aus Leipzig,"] in *Allgemeine Zeitung,* 22 Apr. 1863, 1854f.; Fuchs, "Wigard," 133, 192; *Sächs. LT,* 10 Nov. 1863. Cf. Franz v. Mammen, *Franz August Mammen in Plauen: Leben und Wirken eines sächsischen Industriellen* (Dresden, 1935), 289. Although moderate democrats in Saxony, as in Prussia, opposed the tactical use of boycotts (see Neemann, "Kontinuitäten"), Wuttke complained that his Paulskirche comrades (Schaffrath and Joseph) stood as Landtag candidates; *Augsburger Allgemeine Zeitung,* 22 Apr. 1863.

to deal flexibly with reactionary authorities, to discern the limits and opportunities of continued resistance, and to develop new political strategies.[13] By contrast, in those states where the reaction prevailed most fully — in Prussia, Austria, Saxony, Electoral Hesse, and Mecklenburg — the bourgeois left continued to hope for a second revolution. There it acquired a dichotomous political perspective, which tended to see only two possible victors: on the one hand, the reaction, together with its opportunistic fellow travelers from the ranks of the constitutionalists and liberals; on the other hand, the radical, politically persecuted opposition.

III. The Schleswig-Holstein Crisis

The radical left returned to the political stage in Saxony at a moment when the escalation of the Schleswig-Holstein conflict led to a temporary convergence of left-wing forces. After a public meeting in Leipzig, where the *kleindeutsch*-oriented Biedermann had given the main speech, a Schleswig-Holstein Association came into being, which was headed by Biedermann and the *großdeutsch*-oriented democrat Wuttke. When at the beginning of 1864 nineteen Schleswig-Holstein associations from all over Saxony appointed a regional steering committee, Biedermann shared the chair with the Dresden democrat Wigard. These alliances not only show that the liberal movement in Saxony was led for a very long time by veterans of the Paulskirche; they also demonstrate that Forty-eighters who differed on many other political issues found new reasons to cooperate during the Schleswig-Holstein conflict.[14] Not least because the Schleswig-Holstein issue was deemed to be central to liberal ideology in general, veterans of the 1848–49 Revolution were elected almost everywhere in Saxony as heads of local committees and as delegates to the national movement. As in 1848, liberals' euphoria about the surprising success of their efforts at political mobilization masked differences over policy and strategy.

The Schleswig-Holstein question was also discussed intensely in the Saxon *Landtag*. Franz August Mammen was the moving spirit behind

---

13. In the south German constitutional states, civil liberties and a public sphere survived the reaction to a far greater extent than in Prussia, Austria, Saxony, Electoral Hesse, etc.; reforms were partially continued, and the bourgeois left continued to be represented in many *Landtage*. Here one could find the most sophisticated strategic debates on national affairs, and it was here that August Ludwig von Rochau wrote a work entitled *Grundsätze der Realpolitik* (1853), in which he coined a term, *Realpolitik*, that came to stand for a new way of thinking about how to define and implement the "right" political course. Cf. Jansen, *Einheit*, chap. 11, sec. 1.

14. Jordan, *Meinung*, 99; Müller, "Biedermann," 256. On Schleswig-Holstein, cf. Jansen, *Einheit*, chap. 17.

these debates. He introduced the relevant motions on the floor of the house, and he served as secretary to the special committee that was struck to discuss the question. Mammen's attitude changed over the course of time, however, from one that was in broad agreement with the government to an increasingly critical viewpoint. This change of views is typical of the rising frustration on the democratic-federalist left in Germany, whose members tried to use the Schleswig-Holstein movement as the means to push state governments toward a more decisive German policy.

As in the Württemberg *Landtag,* and in particular contrast to the two great powers in Germany, the members of the Saxon *Landtag* achieved fundamental consensus on the Schleswig-Holstein problem. All factions in both houses of the Saxon *Landtag* agreed with Beust's government—though not always for the same reasons—that the aim of German policy in Schleswig-Holstein should be to create a new middle-sized state through federal action against Denmark.[15] This consensus was the object of scorn from some quarters. Carl Vogt, one leader of the Paulskirche left who had emigrated, scoffed at the willingness of liberals in the middle-sized states to cooperate with state governments on the national question. With the perspicacity of the outsider, Vogt wrote: "The movement that stopped at the foot of the throne in 1848 is now working behind the thrones, trying to push them forward." That same national movement, continued Vogt, now cheered every nationalist statement of the monarchs and wished for "nothing but to act with their princes' and ministers' consent." To Vogt, Saxony seemed to provide the most obvious example of this unpolitical "smoothing of inner quarrels," for it was in Saxony that national-minded liberals celebrated a minister president (Beust) whom Vogt labeled a rigid reactionary and the "loyal squire of Austria."[16]

In the spring of 1864, when the middle-sized state governments shrank from a military confrontation over Schleswig-Holstein, the mood of the Saxon *Landtag* became impatient with Beust. An interpellation formulated by Mammen asked how the former parliamentary decisions had been implemented on a federal level, why the questions of succession still had not been solved in favor of Frederick von Augustenburg, and why the troops of the "states loyal to the federation" had not been mobilized. After months of tactical reserve, Mammen now openly accepted his role as leader of the German nationalists in the Saxon *Landtag.* He immediately expressed the suspicion that the great powers "had a plan for the

---

15. *Sächs. LT,* 11 Dec. 1863, 45; 16 Dec. 1863, 155; 17 Dec. 1863, 194; 29 Jan. 1864, 436 (cit. 441, 455).

16. Carl Vogt, *Andeutungen zur gegenwärtigen Lage* (Frankfurt a. M., 1864), 58; see also Jordan, *Meinung,* 98.

division of Germany" and that the Germans might share the fate of the Poles. Mammen also expressed the nationalists' demand for the appointment of a "German parliament." Mammen could no longer count on the consensus achieved earlier, either from the government side or from a united *Landtag*. Yet for that very reason a more determined policy was called for. Thus Mammen addressed another area of conflict that pitted German nationalists against their state governments and that was also closely linked to the Schleswig-Holstein problem: the issue of restrictive association laws, which circumscribed the organization of gymnastic and shooting clubs and, the nationalists believed, thereby hindered the effectiveness of paramilitary forces. According to Mammen, German state governments, preferring secret diplomacy to cooperation with the nationalist movement, "still mistrusted the people."[17]

Mammen was not the only member of the Saxon *Landtag* at this time to identify the liberals' main dilemma: how to transform the mobilization of public opinion into real political influence. A *großpreußisch*[18] minority was now developing among Saxon liberals, led by Biedermann and Joseph. In their opinion, Bismarck's strong leadership and the power of the Prussian army, proven in Denmark, made up for the deficit of liberalism in Berlin politics. As with the federalist and *großdeutsch* majority in the national movement, there was also disappointment about the inability of the middle-sized states to act decisively. These differences of opinion between *großpreußisch* and *großdeutsch*-federalist leftists in Saxony boiled down to a single question: Was the Prussian government an ally of the national movement, or was Bismarck's fall necessary to achieve the left's political aims?[19]

IV. The Aftermath of 1866

Saxony's defeat by Prussia during the Austro-Prussian War of 1866 split the Saxon liberal movement. Quarrels culminated as early as mid-August 1866, resulting in the formation of the National Liberal Party in

---

17. Müller, "Biedermann," 259; *Sächs. LT,* 3 Mar. 1864, 885, cit. 888 (Mammen's speech was also printed as a supplement to Biedermann's *Deutsche Allgemeine Zeitung* [hereafter *DAZ*] on 5 Mar. 1864); 29 Feb. 1864, 842.

18. In contrast to the *kleindeutsch* proposals to solve the German question, which resurrected the constitutional compromise in the Paulskirche and strove for nation-building without Austria and under a Prussian political leadership, I label as *großpreußisch* those initiatives in the 1860s that favored nation-building in the form of annexation by Prussia. The North German Confederation and the German Reich were in this sense also *großpreußisch* solutions, since Prussia dominated the German states after 1866 to a fundamentally greater extent than would have been possible under the *kleindeutsch* constitution of 1849. Cf. Jansen, *Einheit,* chap. 10, sec. 2.

19. Cf. Jordan, *Meinung,* 112.

Saxony. Even thereafter, though, all liberal factions in the state were headed by Forty-eighters, almost all of whom had belonged to the Paulskirche left. Joseph led the faction that wanted union with Prussia; this group was supported by the historian Heinrich von Treitschke. Biedermann represented a mediating, "federalist" policy, whereas Roß-mäßler, Schaffrath, and Wigard stood at the head of the democratic-federalist, anti-Prussian movement.[20]

One factor that led to the quick escalation of the conflicts among liberals in Saxony was the impending annexation by Prussia after the defeat. This crisis forced politicians from all camps to issue clear statements of policy regarding the future of the Saxon state. During Prussia's lengthy peace negotiations with Saxony, which lasted until mid-October 1866, the different liberal factions tried to influence the outcome by convening public rallies and private conferences. One of the meetings called by Biedermann to discuss the relation of Saxony to the North German Confederation was boycotted by the *großdeutsch*-federalist democrats, who were incensed that only a small number of their representatives had been invited, in contrast to a greater number of conservatives. That Biedermann's organizing committee put considerable effort into finding a means to cooperate with the conservatives while excluding the radical bourgeois left reveals the change of viewpoint among Saxon liberals. Those who gravitated to what came to be called the National Liberal group no longer strove for the unity of liberalism, which had provided the basis for the progressive parties; indeed, they opted for closer ties to the reformist conservatives, who had come to accept the fundamental principles of constitutionalism. Roßmäßler, Schaffrath, and Wigard, however, charged publicly that the "Biedermann-Josephsche *Landesversammlung*" had wrongly laid claim to this name; they therefore called for a countermeeting, of democrats only.[21] In fact the lines of communication between the former leftist comrades had been thin for quite a while, even before the Saxon democrats withdrew — half excluded, half isolated — to their position of principled protest. In Weberian terms the split can be

---

20. Cf. the Dresden Resolution, signed by — among others — Schaffrath, Wigard, and the "Saxon *Turnvater*" and Paulskirche leftist Otto Leonhard Heubner. This resolution once again demanded a national state established on the basis of the imperial constitution and a new national assembly; *Mitteldeutsche Volkszeitung*, 25 July 1866, cited in Fuchs, "Wigard," 248; cf. Jordan, *Meinung*, 124.

21. Müller, "Biedermann," 275; Biedermann, *Mein Leben*, 286. Cf. James Retallack, "Antisocialism and Electoral Politics in Regional Perspective: The Kingdom of Saxony," in *Elections, Mass Politics, and Social Change in Modern Germany: New Perspectives*, ed. Larry Eugene Jones and James Retallack (New York, 1992), 63. Wigard and Schaffrath did not join the Saxon People's Party, established at a regional meeting of the democrats in Chemnitz on 19 August 1866, but they worked closely together with it and shared similar views on the German question; see Fuchs, "Wigard," 177.

described as the decision between the ethic of responsibility and the ethic of ultimate ends.[22] A similar development occurred some months later in Württemberg and — over the issue of indemnity for the unconstitutional government of Bismarck — in Prussia.

Even in the National Liberal camp, differences of opinion continued to exist. Biedermann was in favor of a close connection to Prussia, but contrary to Joseph, he did not think annexation was possible. Therefore he advocated caution. Biedermann wrote to Treitschke that Saxony should transfer sovereignty rights to Prussia for the sake of national unification. However, the idea of a possible annexation of Saxony to Prussia should not be openly discussed, he believed, because "the number of those who oppose annexation at the moment is substantially greater. This term ["annexation"] would become very uncomfortable for us in Saxony, probably disastrous, especially for me and my comrades, and would drive me once again into exile."[23]

The regional assembly (*Landesversammlung*) of Saxon liberals that convened on 26 August 1866 passed a resolution that expressed Biedermann's viewpoint. It advocated a federalist position, thereby complying not only with the views of conservative monarchists who favored the continued existence of the Saxon dynasty, but also with those of Saxon democrats in attendance, whose anti-Prussian convictions were well known. The assembly elected a committee that organized the establishment of the National Liberal Party in Saxony. Biedermann remained chairman of that party until 1876. The new party demanded that Saxony should "transfer all common administration, especially in matters of transportation, to the institutions of the Confederation's central authority and parliament." Saxony was also to "cede its military sovereignty and its diplomatic representation to the Prussian crown."[24] With the successful passage of this resolution, Biedermann the pragmatist had asserted himself against the radical annexationist views of the right wing of the party around Joseph and Treitschke.[25] In particular, the demands about federal competence went far beyond what was projected in Bismarck's constitutional draft. Those demands corresponded roughly to the legislative measures liberals finally carried against the wishes of the German princes during the constitutional negotiations in the Constituent North German Reichstag in early 1867.

---

22. Cf. Max Weber, *Politics as a Vocation* (originally published 1919) (Philadelphia, 1965).

23. Biedermann to Treitschke, 30 Aug. 1866, cited in Müller, "Biedermann," 279.

24. Biedermann, *Mein Leben,* 287; cf. Jordan, *Meinung,* 181.

25. In August 1867, the radical annexationists close to Joseph once again unsuccessfully attempted to assert themselves against Biedermann's movement. Cf. Müller, "Biedermann," 280.

The Reichstag elections in February 1867 revealed that Biedermann was more than justified in worrying about the Saxon public's response to a policy favoring Prussian supremacy in Germany. Only with a concerted effort were the Saxon democrats Schaffrath, Wigard, and Roßmäßler able to assert themselves against more determined oppositional elements on the left who wanted to boycott the elections altogether: these three agreed with leaders of the labor movement in favoring a policy of electoral participation. The National Liberals, who had strong support only among Leipzig's bourgeoisie, nominated their own candidates in no more than a handful of constituencies, and none of those candidates was elected.[26] Making a virtue of necessity, they overlooked their remaining differences of opinion with the men of the Progressive Party and assisted seven of them, including Wigard and Schaffrath, to victory.[27] Although these deputies had been elected to the North German Reichstag with the support of Saxon liberalism as a whole, they actually belonged to the principled opposition: just as in the Saxon *Landtag,* they continued the long-standing ritual of demanding the reestablishment of the 1849 Imperial Constitution. In their opinion, a new national assembly provided the means to solve problems of domestic politics. Yet the fact that eleven of the twenty-three Saxon Reichstag deputies rejected the North German constitution when it came up for approval in April 1867 shows once again that Saxony, despite its status as the second-largest state in the North German Confederation, was home to relatively few sympathizers of the *großpreußisch* option. Apart from a deeply rooted *Landespatriotismus,* the insensitive Prussian occupiers had contributed to the National Liberals' unpopularity by favoring the pro-Prussian politicians around Biedermann in a partisan way during the occupation. In doing so, the Prussian authorities actually undermined the National Liberals' political legitimacy in the eyes of Saxon voters.[28]

---

26. The National Liberal defeats were especially bitter in their only Saxon stronghold, Leipzig. In the municipal elections of December 1866, the list headed by Biedermann and Joseph failed to win a majority for the first time since 1849; cf. Jordan, *Meinung,* 231.

27. James Retallack, " 'Why Can't a Saxon Be More Like a Prussian?' Regional Identities and the Birth of Modern Political Culture in Germany, 1866–67," *Canadian Journal of History* 32 (1997): 26–55, here 48; Jordan, *Meinung,* 185. In a number of other constituencies, Paulskirche veterans (Joseph, Schaffrath, Wuttke) had been nominated but were not elected. Mammen turned down the mandate he won in February 1867 but accepted it after the Reichstag elections of August 1867; Mammen, *Mammen,* 334. See also the reports in Brandenburgisches Landeshauptarchiv Potsdam, Rep. 30 Berlin C 12576, report of 14 Mar. 1867, and 15534, report of 26 Jan. 1867; *Sächsische Zeitung,* 24 Apr. 1867; and *DAZ,* 25 Jan. 1867.

28. Cf. Jordan, *Meinung,* 181, 207; "Beitrag," 574; Siegfried Weichlein, "Sachsen zwischen Landesbewußtsein und Nationsbildung," in *Sachsen im Kaiserreich: Politik, Wirtschaft und Gesellschaft im Umbruch,* ed. Simone Lässig and Karl Heinrich Pohl (Dresden,

V. Conclusions

The Kingdom of Saxony was not only a center of the revolution and a stronghold of radicalism; after 1849 it even eclipsed Prussia as — in James Retallack's words — the "playground of authoritarianism."[29] Firmly opting for repression over reform, the government tried to paper over the fact that the dynasty was unpopular and that the regime had been able to defeat the revolution only with the help of its powerful neighbor to the north, Prussia. The authoritarian regime led by Beust and the radical Saxon left adopted a stance of mutual suspicion and hostility in the postrevolutionary epoch. One result of this situation was the near-total decline of political life in the state, which in turn helps explain both the lack of flexibility among Saxony's leading left-wing politicians and the unusually long domination of Saxon liberalism by veterans of the 1848–49 Revolution.

As in Prussia, whose political culture was also imprinted by similar conflicts, a debilitating split occurred within the liberal movement, separating pragmatists from those interested in pursuing principled opposition. After 1866, the pragmatists, especially Joseph and Biedermann, sought to move closer to Prussia and its successful power politics. In the process they increasingly disassociated themselves from the "ideas of 1848." The "opposition of conviction," including such men as Mammen, Schaffrath, and Wigard, generally displayed more steadfastness and political courage. Their policies, however, appear to have been just as sterile as those of the pure pragmatists, in that they refused to accept new realities in national affairs and ascribed legitimacy only to the 1849 constitution. Nevertheless, whereas clashes between National Liberals and democratic federalists were inevitable, they found themselves in fundamental agreement on many questions of Saxon domestic politics (which cannot be dealt with here). It should also be remembered that, as late as 1866, Biedermann stood by his fundamental rejection of the constitution imposed in 1850, agreeing to the democrats' demand for reestablishment of the suffrage law of 1848.[30]

Also as in Prussia, the Saxon liberals did not succeed in finding a way to integrate the labor movement, which developed initially within the liberals' own ranks. The liberals in both states displayed paternalist

---

1997), esp. 252; Richard Dietrich, "Preußen als Besatzungsmacht im Königreich Sachsen, 1866–1868," *Jahrbuch für die Geschichte Mittel- und Ostdeutschlands* 5 (1956): 273–93, esp. 282 for the proof that Biedermann et al. took action against unpopular Saxon bureaucrats by deliberately denouncing them to the Prussian occupying forces.

29. Retallack, "Antisocialism," 55.

30. Cf. [Karl Biedermann], *Die reactivirten Stände und das verfassungsmäßige Wahlgesetz in Sachsen* (Leipzig, 1866).

arrogance, but fundamental conflicts of interest also inclined those who sought to defend workers' interests to favor the establishment of independent workers' organizations. The Forty-eighters Roßmäßler and Wuttke represent interesting exceptions to this general pattern insofar as they were liberal intellectuals but sided decisively with the early labor movement.

All in all, the division within Saxon liberalism had large implications. An authoritarian, nationalistic party representing mainly the interests of the bourgeoisie diverged from a democratically inclined Progressive Party. Although both movements remained important in Saxon political life, by failing to work together they never proved capable of forming a durable liberal majority. At the same time, the early emergence of an independent labor party in Saxony hindered the development of realistic policies directed toward compromise and reform. In the postrevolutionary epoch and during the imperial period, these promising signs were much more apparent in southern Germany. Nevertheless, both there and in Saxony, the German and European constellations that led to the *großpreußisch*-military unification of 1867–71 prevented the stabilization of a democratic-republican milieu that transcended class divisions and that might have developed the ideas of 1849. The party-political branch of this milieu was the "people's parties" (*Volksparteien*), which vanished in the Reich's founding era but flourished for a short period during the 1860s.

Liberalism and the Making of the "New Man": The Case of Gymnasts in Leipzig, 1845-1871

Páll Björnsson

I. Introduction

During the winter of 1854–55, the Leipzig professor, publicist, and former Forty-eighter Karl Biedermann co-organized weekly lectures for upper-class women in Leipzig; the themes were history, literature, art, and science.[1] Biedermann later explained his dilemma in organizing this undertaking: "Nothing is more difficult than to find the right measure and method to introduce history to women and girls, so that the abundance of information does not overwhelm their memories or confuse

For their critiques of drafts of this essay, I am grateful to Celia Applegate, Robert Beachy, and James Retallack.

1. "Vorträge für Frauen," *Leipziger Tageblatt,* no. 310, 6 Nov. 1854. A year later Biedermann published the lectures as Karl Biedermann, *Frauen-Brevier: Kulturgeschichtliche Vorlesungen für Frauen* (Leipzig, 1856), and in 1881 a revised edition appeared. Attendance at these lectures was socially exclusive, as the price for the whole cycle was 3 *Thaler* per person. By comparison, a maid earned approximately 1 *Thaler* per month, and a male railroad worker earned between 10 and 20 *Thaler* per month. See Michèle Schubert, "Soziale Lage und politisches Handeln Leipziger Dienstmädchen während der industriellen Revolution," *Jahrbuch für Regionalgeschichte* 18 (1991–92): 107–23; and Suzanne Schötz, "Städtische Mittelschichten in Leipzig während der bürgerlichen Umwälzung (1830–1870)" (Ph.D. diss., University of Leipzig, 1985), 57. Karl Biedermann (1812–1901) was one of the leading liberals in Leipzig and a member of the city parliament after 1846; he also belonged to the Frankfurt Parliament, the Saxon *Landtag* (1849–50 and 1869–76), the German Reichstag (1871–74), and various local associations. In August 1866 he organized the foundation of the liberal-national party in Leipzig, which later became a part of the German National Liberal Party. See Richard J. Bazillion, *Modernizing Germany: Karl Biedermann's Career in the Kingdom of Saxony, 1835–1901* (New York, 1990); and Joachim Müller, "Karl Biedermann und die preußische Hegemonie in Deutschland: Vom Liberalismus zum Bonapartismus" (Ph.D. diss., University of Leipzig, 1972).

their minds, but still informs them about things that are of general interest for every human being."[2] Clearly Biedermann not only meant to educate women; he also sought to reinforce a cultural system in which women's subjugation was central. A difference between masculinity and femininity was pivotal in his worldview:

> If one can divide human life into two fundamental features, one characterized by excitability or receptivity to external impressions, the other by an inner ability to act independently and to process received impressions, then it seems as though these two features got divided between the two sexes: the man—to a larger degree than women—is inherently accustomed to acting on his own, whereas a woman is distinguished by excitability and sensitivity. Physiology has shown that the biological reasons for this difference lie in the larger size of the masculine brain compared to the female one, and in the organization of the whole female body, which is more tender than muscular, more soft and flexible than hard and sturdy.[3]

Furthermore, Biedermann claimed that only masculine men were able to think analytically—that is, to combine ideas, observations, and experience in a systematic way—whereas women mainly acted according to their instincts and heart. Women were also naturally dependent on others and tended to surrender to alien authorities.[4] In these ways Biedermann's lectures revealed just how fundamental gender was to the liberals' cultural web of meaning—an aspect of German liberalism that most of its students have neglected.[5]

Biedermann regarded masculinity as a synonym for *Bildung,* selfless-

---

2. Biedermann, *Frauen-Brevier* (1881), vi–vii.

3. Biedermann, *Frauen-Brevier* (1856), 73–74.

4. Ibid., 75, 402. Believing in the superiority of the "white" man, Biedermann ascribed characteristics to "colored" people of both genders that were very similar to those he ascribed to "white" women; ibid., 64.

5. Dieter Langewiesche is one of the few scholars who has complained about the missing gender-link in studies of German liberalism. See Langewiesche, "Liberalismus und Region," in *Liberalismus und Region: Zur Geschichte des deutschen Liberalismus im 19. Jahrhundert,* ed. Lothar Gall and Dieter Langewiesche (*Historische Zeitschrift,* Beiheft 19) (Munich, 1990), 16–17; and Langewiesche, "The Nature of German Liberalism," in *Modern Germany Reconsidered, 1870–1945,* ed. Gordon Martel (London, 1992), 115. In his own work, however, Langewiesche largely fails to explore gender. For an innovative study of liberalism and gender, see Dagmar Herzog, *Intimacy and Exclusion: Religious Politics in Pre-revolutionary Baden* (Princeton, NJ, 1996). For a discussion of gender and men's history, see, inter alia, Thomas Kühne, "Männergeschichte als Geschlechtergeschichte," in *Männergeschichte—Geschlechtergeschichte: Männlichkeit im Wandel der Moderne,* ed. idem (Frankfurt a. M., 1996), 7–30.

ness, and rationality.[6] To these virtues he attributed a political dimension. Biedermann claimed that liberalism should block egoism, blind instincts, and irrationality; such blockage, he believed, was a precondition for the rise of a constitutional state. Consequently, "irrational" people were not entitled to exert political power — to become burghers.[7] Leipzig liberals, however, who dominated the city council and parliament, did not suggest that the "cultural" level of the candidates needed to be tested, for they believed that this level correlated to the amount of property people owned.[8] In mid-nineteenth-century Leipzig, all women were excluded from the political public, and only about a quarter of the male population older than twenty-one had enough resources to pay for citizenship. Only the German city-states demanded higher citizenship dues than Leipzig.[9]

Because liberalism is often associated with people's social and political liberation, it is crucial to analyze how liberals justified this entrance barrier into the political public. One logical place to begin might be with a definition of liberalism. But James J. Sheehan has noted that "no term within the vocabulary of politics is more difficult to define than *liberalism.*" One reason for this, Sheehan suggests, is that "[l]iberalism never found its Marx."[10] The historiography of German liberalism reflects these difficulties: some scholars have regarded it exclusively as a consti-

---

6. See, for instance, Biedermann, *Frauen-Brevier* (1856), 492. In his first lecture for the Leipzig women in 1854, Biedermann defined *Bildung* as "spiritual health," and he emphasized that it was not a mass of information. See ibid., 3–4. Translating *Bildung* is difficult, as it comprises education, cultivation, and "appropriate" behavior. See Rudolf Vierhaus, "Bildung," in *Geschichtliche Grundbegriffe,* ed. Otto Brunner et al., 7 vols. (Stuttgart, 1972), 1:508–51.

7. Karl Biedermann, "Der Liberalismus und der Kommunismus: Briefwechsel zwischen dem Herausgeber und einem Kommunisten. II," *Der Herold: Eine Wochenschrift für Politik, Literatur und öffentliches Gerichtsverfahren,* no. 81, 10 Oct. 1846.

8. See, for instance, Karl Biedermann, "Sozialistische Bestrebungen in Deutschland: Zweiter Artikel: Der praktische Sozialismus," *Unsre Gegenwart und Zukunft* 2 (1846): 235, 239; and Moritz Schreber, *Die deutsche Turnkunst in der Gegenwart und Zukunft: Wesen, Bedeutung und Grundregeln bei Ausübung derselben: Ein den versammelten 13 ländlichen Turnvereinen des Leipziger Umkreises am 5. Dezember 1860 gehaltener Vortrag* (Leipzig, [1860]), 12. At least one European liberal suggested that an examination would be the best way of testing people's "cultivation," as their property alone would be an imperfect criterion for measurement. See John Stuart Mill, "Consideration on Representative Government," in idem, *Collected Works,* 33 vols. (Toronto, 1963–91), 19:474–75.

9. In Leipzig, applicants' occupation and family relations to other Leipzig burghers determined the price of citizenship for each applicant. See "Acta, die Bürger- und Schutzrechtsgebühren betr., Vol. I (1852–67), Vol. II (1867–71)," Stadtarchiv (hereafter StadtA) Leipzig Tit. XXXIV 41.

10. James J. Sheehan, "Some Reflections on Liberalism in Comparative Perspective," in *Deutschland und der Westen: Vorträge und Diskussionsbeiträge des Symposions zu ehren von Gordon A. Craig,* ed. H[enning] Köhler (Berlin, 1984), 44–45.

tutional movement, whereas others have seen its goal in improving people's lives.[11] Students of liberalism agree that the individual represents the basic unit of any liberal society. Generally, however, they have focused on liberalism's belief in the sanctity of the individual in the face of state power. Of course, guaranteeing individual rights *was* crucial to liberals; it still is today. But in order to explain why German liberals in the nineteenth century believed that "cultivated" men alone should enjoy participatory rights, one has to develop a new concept—the image of an ideal "new man"—and then explore the liberals' attempts to implement this ideal. One reason this issue has escaped the attention of most scholars is that the historiography of German liberalism has been skewed by concentration on high politics, especially in the arena of national politics. By studying liberals in their local environments, however, one can access certain elements of liberal culture more easily than on the national plane, not least because German liberals generally had more influence locally than nationally.

The "new man" is a powerful analytical tool. It highlights, first, the liberals' preoccupation with the building of character. Second, it illustrates how fundamental gender is to any definition of liberalism. And third, it undermines the notion that whereas liberalism takes people's virtues and vices as "given," only other political "isms" seek to form a new character. According to this argument, instead of remaking people, liberals sought only to change state and society, to construct a political system of checks and balances.[12] Deploying the concept of the "new man" calls for a fundamental revision of this view.

II. Liberals and Leipzig's Gymnasts

Karl Biedermann's sociocultural views were broadly typical of those held by other liberal men in Leipzig around the middle of the nineteenth

---

11. See, for example, Lothar Gall, "Liberalismus und 'bürgerliche Gesellschaft': Zu Charakter und Entwicklung der liberalen Bewegung in Deutschland," *Historische Zeitschrift* 220 (1975): 324–56, here 325; and Dieter Langewiesche, *Liberalismus in Deutschland,* (Frankfurt a. M., 1988), 7. Langewiesche borrowed his definition from Ralf Dahrendorf, *Die Chancen der Krise* (Stuttgart, 1983), 37.

12. Consider, for instance, Stephen Holmes, *Benjamin Constant and the Making of Modern Liberalism* (New Haven, CT, 1984), 168, 222; Anthony de Jasay, *Choice, Contract, Consent: A Restatement of Liberalism* (London, 1991), 63; Stephen Macedo, *Liberal Virtues: Citizenship, Virtue, and Community in Liberal Constitutionalism* (Oxford, 1990), 3; Susan Mendus, "Liberal Man," *Philosophy and Politics* (Royal Institute of Philosophy Supplement), vol. 26, ed. G. M. K. Hunt (Cambridge, 1990), 55; and Brian Barry, *Political Argument* (London, 1965), 66. In contrast to these interpretations, scholars have claimed that liberals did indeed try to change people's character, but in most cases they have tended to focus on the inculcation of national loyalty. See, for example, Gary Gerstle, "The Protean Character of American Liberalism," *American Historical Review* 99 (1994): 1043–73.

century. These men were convinced that at least some "uncultivated" men could be socialized into full-fledged citizens by making available to them images of appropriate role models. This might also be accomplished by creating situations in which the "uncultivated" could meet with their models and imitate them. Besides "traditional" instruments of educational instruction (e.g., the public schools), liberals advocated the use of the civic guard (*Kommunalgarden*), festivals, playgrounds, lectures, and publications.[13] Biedermann, for one, condemned authors who failed to provide their readers with proper role models. He even criticized Goethe for using male characters who were weaklings, egoists, slaves of their emotions, or men of soft sentimentality.[14] Last but not least, the liberals recommended public meetings and voluntary associations as other means to inculcate suitably "manly" values.

Scholars agree that voluntary associations not only fostered an emerging civil society in Germany, but were also crucial for the development of liberalism itself. Liberals used associations to implement and perpetuate their system of cultural and political hegemony.[15] As an instrument of such hegemony, voluntary associations were particularly useful because many of them were open to everyone — or, rather, every man. Moreover,

---

13. Leading liberals sought to make the public schools (*Volksschulen*) more "democratic" by abolishing altogether tuition fees that had varied considerably from school to school. Such liberals believed that the mixing of social classes would improve children's character. These attempts failed, however, due to resistance among the school principals and within the city council. For the liberals' ideas about playgrounds, see, for example, Moritz Schreber, "Die Jugendspiele in ihrer gesundheitlichen und pädagogischen Bedeutung," *Gartenlaube*, no. 26 (1860): 414–16; and Ernst Innocenz Hauschild, *Vierzig pädagogische Briefe aus der Schule an das Elternhaus* (Leipzig, 1862), 44, 64. These authors were convinced that playgrounds would prepare boys to become citizens. A few years after Schreber's death, Hauschild founded the first *Schreberverein* in Leipzig to promote the opening of playgrounds. Later, Schreber's name became synonymous with the German allotments movement (*Kleingartenbewegung*). See Marion Bähr, "Erziehung zur Lebenstüchtigkeit durch harmonisches Miteinander von Körper und Geist des ersten deutschen Schrebervereins," *Leipzig: Aus Vergangenheit und Gegenwart: Beiträge zur Stadtgeschichte*, no. 7 (1990): 59–76.

14. See Biedermann, *Frauen-Brevier* (1856), 492. We should not be surprised that in all three of the dramas he wrote, Biedermann had masculine heroes play the leading role.

15. See, for example, Thomas Nipperdey, "Verein als soziale Struktur in Deutschland im späten 18. und frühen 19. Jahrhundert: Eine Fallstudie zur Modernisierung I," in idem, *Gesellschaft, Kultur, Theorie: Gesammelte Aufsätze zur neueren Geschichte* (Göttingen, 1976), 174–205. Cf. Manfred Hettling, "Von der Hochburg zur Wagenburg: Liberalismus in Breslau von den 1860er Jahren bis 1918," in *Liberalismus und Region,* ed. Gall and Langewiesche, 253–76; and Dieter Bellmann, "Der Liberalismus im Seekreis (1860–1870): Durchsetzungsversuch und Scheitern eines regional eigenständigen Entwicklungskonzepts," in *Provinzialisierung einer Region: Regionale Unterentwicklung und liberale Politik in der Stadt und im Kreis Konstanz im 19. Jahrhundert,* ed. Gert Zang (Frankfurt a. M., 1978), 183–263.

each association represented the constitutional state in miniature, a locus where men would learn to obey laws and govern their own affairs. Liberals advocated many kinds of voluntary associations as vehicles to achieve these aims—for example, workers' associations, artisans' associations,[16] singing societies, and gymnastics clubs.[17] By considering just one of these examples—the activity of liberals in the gymnastics movement—one can at the same time illuminate the symbiosis between liberalism and voluntary associations and specify liberals' attempts to "cultivate" masculine men through a combination of organized physical exercise, social gatherings, lectures, excursions, and festivities.

The founding fathers of Leipzig's General Gymnastics Association (Allgemeiner Turnverein, or ATV) included Karl Ernst Bock, Moritz Schreber, and Karl Lampe. Bock (1809–74) was a professor of medicine at Leipzig University and author of a number of popular works on medicine. He was a member of the city parliament in 1846–48, active in the Schriftstellerverein and Verbrechertisch, and a candidate for the Progressives in the *Landtag* elections of 1864. He co-organized the Leipzig lectures for women in 1854–55 with Biedermann, whose views resembled his own. For example, Bock also believed that women had smaller brains than men. Schreber (1808–61) was a medical doctor and wrote a number of popular pedagogical works. He was a member of the liberal Deutscher Verein in 1848–49, of the Harmonie club, and of the Nationalverein, and one of the founders of the Pädagogische Gesellschaft in 1861; he also was elected to the city parliament on the liberal ticket in 1847–51, serving as its deputy president in 1850–51. Lampe (1804–89) was a businessman and one of the founders of the Leipzig-Dresden Railway Company. He was a city councilor 1834–38, and active in the Kunstverein, the freemason

---

16. Some Leipzig liberals were active in workers' and artisans' associations—for example, the Gesellenverein (1848–54), the Gewerblicher Bildungsverein (founded in 1861 and later called the Arbeiterbildungsverein), and the Bauhütte (founded in 1866).

17. Even though the gymnastic movement was one of the largest social movements in nineteenth-century Germany, until recently scholars have neglected it. For a short survey, see Dieter Langewiesche, " '. . . für Volk und Vaterland kräftig zu würken . . .': Zur politischen und gesellschaftlichen Rolle der Turner zwischen 1811 und 1871," in *Kulturgut oder Körperkult? Sport und Sportwissenschaft im Wandel,* ed. O[mmo] Grupe (Tübingen, 1990), 22–61. For a book-length survey, see Michael Krüger, *Körperkultur und Nationsbildung: Die Geschichte des Turnens in der Reichsgründungsära—eine Detailstudie über die Deutschen* (Schorndorf, 1996). However, both Krüger and Langewiesche overlook the impact of gender on the gymnastics movement. For studies in which gender plays a central role, see Daniel A. McMillan, "Germany Incarnate: Politics, Gender, and Sociability in the Gymnastics Movement, 1811–1871" (Ph.D. diss., Columbia University, 1996); Teresa Sanislo, "The Dangers of Civilization: Defending Masculinity in the Age of Enlightenment and National Liberation" (Ph.D. diss. in progress, University of Michigan, Ann Arbor); and Svenja Goltermann, *Körper und Nation: Habitusformierung und die Politik des Turnens, 1860–1890* (Göttingen, 1998).

lodge Minerva, Harmonie, the Vertraute Gesellschaft, the Lutheran Gustav-Adolf-Verein, and the Deutscher Verein.[18] In July 1845 these men called together some twenty other prominent individuals.[19] The liberals who played a leading role in this group were convinced that gymnastics could help the male population to acquire the virtues needed to participate in a political public. Such virtues included *Bildung,* masculinity, independence, initiative (*Selbsttätigkeit*), and civic sense (*Gemeinsinn*). Representing these opinions, Biedermann pointed out that every man could easily become a member of a gymnastics club, as it did not require a minimum amount of *Bildung.* Indeed, such participation would be wholesome for the "uncultivated" — morally, mentally, and physically.[20] Moritz Schreber maintained that gymnastics could bring men of different social backgrounds together more effectively than any other means: as he put it, everyone who had arms and legs could join the clubs. Being together would foster the civic sense of the members in reciprocal ways: the less "cultivated" would be elevated, and the highly "cultivated" would learn to respect the lower classes. By engaging in physical exercise, Schreber added, members would overcome hindrances to self-confidence, courage, vigor, determination, steadfastness, and stamina. Physical exertion, in other words, would ennoble one's will and energy; attaining these qualities was the precondition for spiritual freedom.[21] Lastly, the

---

18. See Bock, *Das Buch vom gesunden und kranken Menschen* (Leipzig, 1855), 47; and Karsten Hommel, "Karl Lampe: Ein Leipziger Bildungsbürger, Unternehmer, Förderer von Kunst und Wissenschaft zwischen Romantik und Kaiserreich" (Ph.D. diss., Humboldt University Berlin, 1998).

19. The provisional council of the club was dominated by well-known liberals. See F. Rudolf Gasch, *Festschrift zur fünfzigjährigen Jubelfeier des Allgemeinen Turnvereins zu Leipzig, 1845–1895* (Leipzig, 1895), 2–3. In the 1848–49 Revolution and the following decades, the same group of men played leading roles in the liberal movement.

20. Biedermann, "Sozialistische Bestrebungen in Deutschland," 206–67. Cf. anon., "Politische und commerzielle Uebersicht," *Deutsche Monatsschrift für Literatur und öffentliches Leben* 1 (1843): 76.

21. See Schreber, *Turnkunst,* 12–14; and idem, *Kallipädie oder Erziehung zur Schönheit durch naturgetreue und gleichmäßige Förderung normaler Körperbildung, lebenstüchtiger Gesundheit und geistiger Veredelung und insbesondere durch möglichste Benutzung spezieller Erziehungsmittel* (Leipzig, 1858), 176. Similar arguments are found in Karl Ernst Bock, "Vortheile und Nachtheile des Turnens," *Deutsche Turn-Zeitung,* no. 1 (1856): 2. Schreber's younger son, Daniel Paul Schreber, has become a subject of many works in psychoanalysis. Many authors have made the father and his pedagogy responsible for the mental illness of the son. The most recent interpretation of this kind is in a German film of 1997, directed by Jan Peter and Jury Winterberg, *Neue Menschen aus Schreberschen Geist;* the directors even claim that Moritz Schreber was a proto-Nazi and a proto-communist who sought to turn people into machines — an interpretation the sources rule out. For a critical survey of the literature, see Han Israëls, *Schreber: Vater und Sohn: Eine Biographie* (Munich, 1989).

liberals believed that the goal of every man was to live under the laws he had legislated himself — laws that themselves embodied liberal virtues.[22]

Not only were liberals the initiators of the gymnastics club; its foundation in turn helped give birth to an organized liberal movement. Before 1845, liberals had organized themselves only intermittently, for instance to advocate the independence of Greece and Poland or to support the seven professors expelled from the University of Göttingen in 1837. Hence one can hardly speak of a liberal movement in Leipzig before 1845.[23] In that year, however, Leipzig's liberals organized themselves both politically and socially: they fielded their own list of candidates for election to the city parliament, they organized a *Stammtisch* (the "Maikäfer"), and they founded a private social club.[24] In each case the nomenclature chosen by local liberals was significant: they named their ticket "Truth and Justice" (*Wahrheit und Recht*), a designation they were still using in the 1870s, and they named their club "Museum" (*Museum*). The "Museum" was actually a salon with reading rooms for affluent men. It was open every day from 8 A.M. until 10 P.M., and it subscribed to some 300 newspapers and journals devoted to political, scholarly, and literary subjects. The annual membership fee was 8 *Thaler,* but a one-day ticket cost 5 *Neugroschen.*

In the autumn of 1845 many of the same liberals who were involved in these initiatives also participated in the protest against the Dresden government that followed the riots (*Gemetzel*) of 12 August, when

22. See, for example, the speech of Eduard Stephani, the deputy mayor of Leipzig, at the Leipzig festival of the German gymnastic firefighters in 1865: "Der VI. deutsche Feuerwehrtag zu Leipzig," *Deutsche Turn-Zeitung,* no. 36 (Sept. 1865). Stephani (1817–85) was a lawyer, a member of the city parliament in 1848–54, Leipzig's deputy mayor in 1865–74, a member of the North German Reichstag in 1867, and a member of the German Reichstag in 1871–84. He was also active in the first Turnrat of the ATV, the freemason lodge Minerva, Harmonie, the liberal *Stammtisch* "Kitzing," and the Gustav-Adolf-Verein; he served as manager of the latter from 1847 to 1865.

23. See Roland Jäger, "Deutsche Liberale im hannoverschen Verfassungskampf (1837–1843)" (Ph.D. diss., University of Leipzig, 1986); and Winfried Löschburg, "Wilhelm Traugott Krug und der nationale Befreiungskampf des griechischen Volkes," in *Karl-Marx-Universität Leipzig, 1409–1959: Beiträge zur Universitätsgeschichte,* 2 vols., ed. Ernst Engelberg (Leipzig, 1959), 1:208–22. For a sketchy survey of Saxony's pre-March liberal movement, see Stephanie Vogel, "Die liberale Bewegung in Sachsen, 1830–1849 (unter besonderer Berücksichtigung des politischen Zentrums Leipzig)" (Ph.D. diss., University of Bonn, 1993).

24. See *Deutsche Allgemeine Zeitung,* no. 285, 7 Dec. 1870, supplement; and *Deutsche Allgemeine Zeitung,* no. 269, 15 Nov. 1868. Cf. Friedrich Boettcher, *Eduard Stephani: Ein Beitrag zur Zeitgeschichte, insbesondere zur Geschichte der nationalliberalen Partei* (Leipzig, 1887), 4; Karl Biedermann, *Mein Leben und ein Stück Zeitgeschichte,* 2 vols. (Breslau, 1886), 1:205–7, 214; "Museum," *Leipziger Tageblatt,* no. 270, 27 Sept. 1845; and "Das Museum in Leipzig," *Grenzboten* 4 (1845), 1. Sem., Vol. 1:124–27.

Saxon soldiers killed seven people. These riots broke out during the visit of the king's brother, Prince Johann, but their chief impetus was the religious and political tension between the Catholic court in Dresden and the overwhelmingly Lutheran population of Leipzig.[25] During the weeks following the riots, the opponents of the Dresden regime organized public meetings and dispatched numerous petitions — not as a unified front, however, but separately as democrats and liberals.[26] A polarization between the two groups was coming to light, forming the partisan political constellation that later characterized the 1848–49 Revolution and its aftermath. Yet as the foundation of the General Gymnastics Association reveals, it would be misleading to argue that the Leipzig liberal movement was simply a product of the riots.[27]

This alliance between liberalism and the gymnastics club was strengthened through the policy of the liberal city government. In the spring of 1846, the city allowed the club to use its gymnastics field. The following year, as the club founded a joint-stock corporation to finance the construction of a gymnasium, the city's chief of police — who was also a member of the city council — became the chairman of this corporation. Moreover, near the end of 1846, the city fathers agreed to subsidize the club with 200 *Thaler* yearly; this subsidy continued during the following decades. (In 1848, the Leipzig gymnastics club did not disappoint its supporters: unlike many other clubs in Saxony, it took a stand against the revolution.)[28] In the early 1860s, when the need for a

---

25. For a survey of the riots, see Richard J. Bazillion, "Urban Violence and the Modernization Process in Pre-March Saxony, 1830–31 and 1845," *Historical Reflections* 12, no. 2 (1985): 279–303; cf. *Aktenstücke über die Leipziger Augustnacht: Vollständige Sammlung sämmtlicher über die Ereignisse des 12. August 1845 ergangenen Adressen und officiellen Bekanntmachungen, nebst den commissarischen Erörterungen* (Leipzig, 1845).

26. For the liberals' plans to organize public meetings, see "Acta, die von Hrn. Prof. Biedermann und den gebetene Erlaubniß zu Veranstaltung einer öffentlichen Versammlung im Schützenhause hier, ergangen 1845," StadtA Leipzig II. Sektion (k) B.1885.

27. The history of the ATV also demonstrates a close personal relation between the club and the liberal movement. Until 1871, most of its chairmen were liberals. Biedermann, for instance, became its first chair in 1845, and one year later, Schreber replaced him and led it until 1851. The next chairmen were J. Ch. Hentze and F. Freiesleben. From 1862 to 1867, Paul Bassenge occupied the chair, and from 1869 to 1871, Julius Müller. Hentze and Freiesleben were members of the liberal Deutscher Verein. Paul Bassenge was a merchant, a member of the Turnrat in 1853–67 and of the Gesellschaft Erholung, a liberal representative in the city parliament in 1862–67, a city councilor in 1867–68, and a member of the Saxon *Landtag* in 1885 and 1891. Müller (1812–84) was a lacquerer, a member of the ATV after 1845, and a member of the Turnrat from 1855 to 1884; he also belonged to the Gesellenverein and the Deutscher Verein. Representing liberals in the city parliament from 1849 to 1868 (including a few years as an alternate), he was also a member of Leipzig's (national-) liberal *Stammtisch* "Kitzing."

28. Justus Karl Lion, *Zur Geschichte des Allgemeinen Turnvereins zu Leipzig* (Hof, 1885), 5, 8.

larger gymnasium had become urgent, the city itself built a new one and rented it to the ATV. Finally, when the club hired a technical manager in 1862, the city paid more than half of his salary (his duties included supervising the gymnastic exercises of the city's pupils).[29] Given the Saxon government's skepticism toward the gymnastics movement, this generous level of support and cooperation reflects the strength of liberalism in Leipzig. It also shows how seriously liberals were prepared to commit their time and money toward attempts to construct the "new man."[30]

A relatively large proportion of Leipzig's male population welcomed the club and embraced its activities. By the end of 1845, approximately 170 men had become members, many of them professionals.[31] By the summer of 1846, the club had approximately 500 full members and some 200 associated members, mostly students.[32] The membership fee was relatively low; hence more affluent workers could afford to join it. In 1845, the monthly charge was 5 *Neugroschen;* for the whole winter cycle it was 1 *Thaler.* Less affluent men could receive a rebate or were exempted from paying altogether.[33] In 1849 the price was raised to 7.5 *Neugroschen* per month and 1.5 *Thaler* for a cycle (dues remained at this level until 1867).[34] In the 1850s, the club continued to grow: near the end of the decade, membership reached 1,000, peaking in 1863 with

---

29. H. Wortmann, *Dr. Justus Carl Lion: Sein Wirken für die deutsche Turnkunst* (Leipzig, 1887), 49–50. The ATV hired Justus Karl Lion, a liberal who once described himself as a member of "the cultivated class of the German nation." See Justus Karl Lion, *Sein Briefwechsel mit Alwin Martens und anderes von ihm,* ed. Rudolf Gasch (Leipzig, 1929), 54.

30. For example, in the summer of 1846, Leipzig's district governor asked the city council to report to him about the new gymnastic club. The council assured him that the club had not shown any political tendencies whatsoever. See Stadtrat to Kreisdirektion (24 July 1846), 19–20; and Kreis-Direktor Schurmann to Stadtrat (30 June 1846), 1, both in "Acta, die wegen des hiesigen Turnvereins angestellten Erörterungen betr. 1846," StadtA Leipzig II. Sektion T (kap) no. 1005. See also the Dresden government's critique of the Leipzig police for not spying on a gymnastic social gathering in 1861, in "Acta, Oeffentl. Versammlungen und Vorlesungen, 1857–91," SächsHStA Dresden, Ministerium des Innern Nr. 11039, 65–79.

31. The 167 members were divided among the following occupations: 15 lawyers, 7 doctors, 2 officials, 17 artisans, 87 merchants, 8 artists, 5 teachers, 3 technicians, 5 professors, 6 writers, and 17 students. See "Ueber das sächsische Turnwesen," *Der Herold,* no. 33, 23 Apr. 1846. Another source identifies 187 members; Lion, *Geschichte,* 5.

32. See "Verzeichniß der stimmberechtigten Mitglieder," 7–17, which listed 531 names of full members, although 40 had already resigned; and Stadtrat to Kreisdirektion (24 July 1846), fol. 19, both in "Acta, die wegen des hiesigen Turnvereins angestellten Erörterungen betr. 1846," StadtA Leipzig II. Sektion T (kap) no. 1005.

33. August Schürmann, *Zur Geschichte des Allgemeinen Turnvereins in Leipzig* (Leipzig, 1871), 36; *Leipziger Tageblatt,* no. 306, 2 Nov. 1845.

34. See *Leipziger Adressbuch,* 1849–67.

2,550 members. Thus the ATV became the largest club in German territories.[35]

Although the club's healthy growth was part of a national trend, many new members were attracted by the third German gymnastics festival, which the ATV organized in Leipzig in 1863.[36] Hosting 20,000 participants was no small achievement in a city of only 85,000 inhabitants. However, Leipzig's liberal city fathers made it possible to stage a festival on such a grand scale by subsidizing it with 29,000 *Thaler.* (The ATV estimated total expenses to be about 75,000 *Thaler;* by comparison, the city's entire school budget amounted to about 48,000 *Thaler.*)[37] Combining sports shows with social gatherings and political propaganda, the festival's program reveals the dominance of the liberals. Indeed, their speeches read rather like a (national-) liberal manifesto.[38] By displaying symbols like Germania and the tricolor German flag, these liberals expressed not only their preference for a united Germany but also their hostility toward the Saxon government in Dresden. No doubt this festival enabled Leipzig's liberals to address a larger German audience — larger, certainly, than other media alone permitted. Yet we should not forget that the event was edifying for the individual participant too. As a reporter for the liberal journal *Grenzboten* pointed out, such a participant learned to practice self-government and self-control.[39]

Using the ATV as their vehicle, Leipzig's liberals sought to inculcate masculinity and other liberal virtues into "uncultivated" members. Besides supervised exercises according to prescribed rules, the gymnasts also came together to drink beer or to travel outside Leipzig on excursions. In the mid-1850s, sometimes more than 400 members took part in such gatherings. Alwin Martens, the leading trainer of the club, pointed out that these activities drew in a wide cross-section of Leipzig's male population, including professors, craftsmen, school principals, errand boys, artisans, and shop assistants. But "of course," he added, "the

35. "Heute vor zwanzig Jahren wurde der Leipziger ATV gegründet," *Leipziger Tageblatt,* no. 204, 23 July 1865.

36. After the festival, many left the club; in 1865 the total membership was about 1,500. See "Bericht über die Frequenz des Turnvereins," *Leipziger Tageblatt,* no. 308, 4 Nov. 1865.

37. The expenses turned out to be lower than estimated, and the income higher; thus the city's contribution was reduced to 17,500 *Thaler.* See Schürmann, *Geschichte,* 28; "Verhandlungen der Stadtverordneten am 10. April 1863," *Leipziger Tageblatt,* no. 109, 19 Apr. 1863; and Ernst Barth, *Das Schulwesen in großen Städten mit besonderer Beziehung auf Leipzig: Eine financiell-statistische Studie* (Leipzig, 1873), 10.

38. For a collection of the speeches and an overview of the festival itself, see *Blätter für das dritte allgemeine deutsche Turnfest zu Leipzig, 2.–5. Aug. 1863* (Leipzig, 1863).

39. "Tagebuchsblätter vom leipziger Fest," *Grenzboten* 22 (1863), 2. Sem., Vol. 4:167.

members form groups according to their inclinations and acquaintances, which means the professor must not be afraid of having to talk to the worker during the evening; but the atmosphere inspires everyone, and a feeling of unity transcends the social barriers."[40] As Martens's oblique reference to professorial circumspection suggests, the liberals apparently had not fully implemented their ideal of having different social classes mingle without distinction. Not only were the role models able to avoid the "uncultivated" at the social events; even the club's rules quietly facilitated social exclusivity. No better example of this can be found than the provision that better-off members could exercise with only their social peers during the day by paying double the monthly fee (15 instead of 7.5 *Neugroschen*). These extra payments may have undermined the alleged universality of the club's activities, but they certainly strengthened the club financially, allowing it, for example, to hire a technical manager in 1862.

The position of the manager sparked a conflict in the gymnastics club in the mid-1860s. Ultimately, this dispute was the consequence of tensions between the club's executive body (*Turnrat*) and its mainly young trainers (*Vorturnerschaft*). These tensions had been building since the early 1860s. At the 1863 festival, the young trainers refused to perform in public under the supervision of the manager. In 1864, they refused again. Finally, part of the *Vorturnerschaft* broke away and founded its own club in 1867, the Leipzig Gymnastics Association (Leipziger Turnverein, or LTV).[41] Soon this new organization had some 300 members; one year later, the membership reached almost 500. The social structure of the ATV also changed between 1865 and 1868. For instance, the number of manual laborers (*Handarbeiter*) and market assistants (*Markthelfer*) decreased by more than 90 percent, from about 270 to about 25.[42] The number of artisans and merchants also decreased. Because the statistics do not distinguish between apprentices and shop owners, one cannot determine whether only

---

40. Martens to Lion (21 Jan. 1855), in Lion, *Sein Briefwechsel*, 44.

41. See, for example, the "Protocolle der Leipziger Vorturnerschaft, vom Jahre 1864 ab bis zu 14. Dec. 1866. Vol. II," in Sportmuseum Leipzig; and *Der Conflict im Allgemeinen Turnverein zu Leipzig: Ein Beitrag zur Geschichte des deutschen Turnwesens* (Leipzig, 1867). Cf. Jochen Hinsching, "Der Trennungsprozeß der demokratischen von den liberalen Kräften im Allgemeinen Turnverein Leipzig unter besonders Berücksichtigung des Wirkens von Oswald Faber und Alwin Martens," *Wissenschaftliche Zeitschrift der Hochschule für Körperkultur*, no. 9 (1964): 23–38. Hinsching, however, does not provide any evidence for his thesis that the founders of the LTV were democrats.

42. *Geschäfts- und Rechnungsbericht auf die Zeit vom 1.10.1864 bis 30.9.1865, erstattet an die Ordentliche Hauptversammlung des Allgemeinen Turnvereins zu Leipzig den 9. December 1865 durch den Turnrath*, 5–6, in "Acta, Turn-Verein betr. Vol. IV. 1863–1919," SächsHStA Dresden, Kreishauptmannschaft Leipzig, Nr. 282; and "Jahresbericht des ATVs," *Leipziger Tageblatt*, no. 345, 10 Dec. 1868.

lower-class members left the club. Nevertheless, the newer LTV had more craftsmen (*Gewerbetreibende*) than the ATV and just as many workers;[43] hence one can say that the character of the new club was conspicuously more petty-bourgeois than that of the ATV, even though the membership fee was the same for both.[44]

The first chairman of the new gymnastics club was Rudolf Schmidt, an active liberal.[45] He was also one of the founders of the Städtischer Verein, a liberal association with left-liberal tendencies that had been founded only a day before the LTV.[46] There are some indications of a division between left-wing liberalism and national liberalism in the two gymnastics clubs.[47] However, one year after the breakup, the two clubs had buried their differences.[48] In any event, the goal of the new club was the same as that of the old one: to make a "new man."[49]

The breakup of the ATV was not simply a process of social differentiation; it must also be considered in the broader context of political developments in the mid-1860s. After a decade of postrevolutionary reaction, political activities in Leipzig began to gain momentum at the end of the 1850s. The foundation of the German National Association (Deutscher Nationalverein) and the Schiller festival in 1859 were mile-

---

43. One in two members of the LTV belonged to one of these social categories.

44. See "Nachtrag," *Leipziger Tageblatt,* no. 359, 24 Dec. 1868; and "Verschiedenes," *Leipziger Tageblatt,* no. 95, 5 Apr. 1867. Cf. *Geschichte des Leipziger Turnvereins (Westvorstadt): Festschrift zur Feier des 25. Stiftungsfestes* (Leipzig, 1892).

45. Rudolf Schmidt, a lawyer, took an active part in the public meetings in Leipzig between 1863 and 1867; he gave lectures in workers' associations; he was a member of the Nationalverein and of the liberal shooting club (Schützenbund); he was one of the founders of the liberal-national party in the autumn of 1866 (in 1871 he sat on its board); and in 1870 he became a member of the city parliament after having served for a few years as an alternate.

46. *Deutsche Allgemeine Zeitung,* no. 80, 5 Apr. 1867; and "Verschiedenes," *Leipziger Tageblatt,* no. 95, 5 Apr. 1867. In 1872 Schmidt became the chairman of the Städtischer Verein.

47. Besides Rudolf Schmidt, two well-known left-wing liberals were members of the LTV council: Ferdinand Vieweg and Karl Wilhelm Häckel. Vieweg (died 1871) was a master basket-maker, a member of the city parliament from 1849 to 1863 and 1868 to 1870, and active in various associations, including the Deutscher Vaterlandsverein, Gesellenverein, Blumverein, Erheiterung, Verbrechertisch, Nationalverein, the liberal Schützenbund, the Fortschrittsverein, and Städtischer Verein. Häckel was a master tinsmith and the chairman of the Board of Trade (*Gewerbekammer*). He was a member of the city parliament from 1854 to 1865, a city councilor from 1866 to 1875, and was elected to the Saxon Landtag in 1871 and 1873. He was also active in the Deutscher Verein, Erheiterung, the Vorschußverein, and the Städtischer Verein; in the latter he served as chairman between 1867 and 1872.

48. See *Deutsche Allgemeine Zeitung,* no. 82, 7 Apr. 1868.

49. See *Deutsche Allgemeine Zeitung,* no. 125, 30 May 1867; and "Verschiedenes," *Leipziger Tageblatt,* no. 149, 29 May 1867.

stones in this process. Much the same can be said of the two most prominent national festivals of 1863: the gymnastics festival and the fiftieth anniversary of the Battle of the Nations of 1813.[50] Furthermore, a number of public meetings were held in Leipzig between 1863 and 1867 on various issues: for example, the Schleswig-Holstein question, possible revision of the structure of local government, and elections to both national and local parliaments.

One aspect of this process of increasing political activity was the drive of working-class associations — especially the Arbeiterbildungs-verein — toward independence. In the mid-1860s, the personal contact that some leading liberals had established with this association was broken off.[51] The process of separation was sparked in the early 1860s by a debate about the level of membership fees workers should pay within the Nationalverein. Most liberals spoke against lowering the fees, preferring that workers not become full members. Debates about fees also took place within the General Gymnastics Association: in 1864, a majority of the "full" members turned down a motion that would have lowered the fees.[52]

III. Conclusions

These debates about membership fees are particularly interesting and important in this era of German history because they reflected a tension built into liberal ideology and politics. In theory, both liberalism and liberal politics were universal. But in practice, both tended to be exclusive.[53] The goal of the liberals in Leipzig (but not only there) was to liberate those persons whom they classified as "uncultivated" and prepare them for political participation. However, everyone who did not meet the liberals' expectations was prevented from participating. In making this distinction, the liberals in effect turned the political public into a political private. Instead of liberating individuals, they ended up creating two cultural classes: the "cultivated" and the "uncultivated." It

---

50. In Leipzig, the Nationalverein had fewer than 200 members. See Heyner to Streit (20 Nov. 1861), in Bundesarchiv, Abteilungen Potsdam, 61 Na 2, Deutscher Nationalverein, Vol. 23, 340.

51. See, for instance, Biedermann, *Mein Leben,* 2:212–13.

52. See "Die ordentliche Hauptversammlung des ATV," *Leipziger Tageblatt,* no. 348, 13 Dec. 1864. In order to cast a vote in the ATV (or become a "full" member), one had to be at least 21 years old and to have been a member for at least six months during the current year. In September 1864, only about 560 out of 1,690 members were "full" members. See *Deutsche Turn-Zeitung,* no. 38 (Sept. 1864): 303.

53. This tension is mentioned in James J. Sheehan, "Wie bürgerlich war der deutsche Liberalismus?" in *Liberalismus im 19. Jahrhundert: Deutschland im europäischen Vergleich,* ed. Dieter Langewiesche (Göttingen, 1988), 28–44, here 38.

was precisely in this act of excluding the "uncultivated" from the "public" that one can discern the crystallization of the liberal belief in the hegemony of "cultivated" males, premised on the image of the "new man." Hence liberals believed that the ideal form of government had to correspond to the level of people's "cultivation." For example, their republican ideal required a large number of "cultivated" men. Because this precondition was not fulfilled in the nineteenth century, liberals preferred a constitutional monarchy.[54]

Although this essay has focused on public men, it enhances our understanding of women's situation as well. "One way to read women back into politics," one scholar has claimed, "is to identify the ways in which a particular politics involves measures of exclusion."[55] As we have seen, it is possible to illuminate such measures by analyzing those qualities that liberals ascribed to the "new man" and by examining the liberals' preoccupation with the process of making him. We can conclude, on the one hand, that distinctions between the masculine and the feminine were fundamental to nineteenth-century liberalism. Just as significant, on the other hand, is a recognition that the interrelated processes of emancipation and exclusion, of political reform and social control, were actually two sides of a single coin, both of which imprinted liberal culture in nineteenth-century Leipzig.

---

54. See, for example, Karl Lampe, "Republik und Monarchie auf demokratischer Basis, welcher Unterschied?" *Leipziger Tageblatt,* no. 178, 26 June 1848; and *Aus den Tagebüchern von Heinrich Brockhaus,* 5 vols. (Leipzig, 1884–87), 2:162.

55. Eve Rosenhaft, "Women, Gender, and the Limits of Political History in the Age of 'Mass' Politics," in *Elections, Mass Politics, and Social Change in Modern Germany: New Perspectives,* ed. Larry Eugene Jones and James Retallack (New York, 1992), 158–59.

Saxons into Germans: The Progress of the National Idea in Saxony after 1866

Siegfried Weichlein

I. Region and Nation: Approaches and Dilemmas

Before German unification in 1871 and for some time thereafter, regional identities were viewed as particularistic and therefore incompatible with a sense of national identity. German states such as Bavaria and Württemberg had invested an enormous amount of energy in reforming their societies and administrations after the Napoleonic period. They were fairly successful in generating loyalty to the dynasties and the states, which were in some cases composed of hundreds of older historical regional units. At the center of their reform efforts stood the churches, the military, and the educational system. At the same time, older allegiances to subregional communities continued to play an important role.[1] Consequently, two forms of political regionalism affected the political culture of nineteenth-century Germany: the interstate regionalism of the territorial states themselves, and the intrastate regionalism of territories that were swallowed up by the newly constituted states after 1803. Intrastate regionalism had its stronghold in southern Germany, with its long tradition of imperial cities: it often took the form of localism.[2] Research on the relationship between region and nation must

---

1. Cf. Helmut Berding, "Staatliche Identität, nationale Integration und politischer Regionalismus," in idem, *Aufklären durch Geschichte: Ausgewählte Aufsätze* (Göttingen, 1990), 284–309; Hans Gollwitzer, "Die politische Landschaft in der deutschen Geschichte des 19./20. Jahrhunderts: Eine Skizze zum deutschen Regionalismus," *Zeitschrift für bayerische Landesgeschichte* 27 (1964): 523–52.
2. Cf. Wolfgang Hardtwig, "Nationalismus — Regionalismus — Lokalismus: Aspekte der Erinnerungskultur im Spiegel von Publizistik und Denkmal," in *Lieux de mémoire, Erinnerungsorte*, ed. Etienne François, Cahier no. 6 (Berlin, 1996), 91–104; idem,

therefore address different territorial levels: the national, the regional, and the local.

Whereas up to 1871 German nationalism conveyed a sense of antagonism between regional and national identities, this changed in subsequent decades with the declining influence of the monarchies. Previously, monarchies had provided the symbolic backbone of particularistic identities. But as Wolfgang Hardtwig has written: "With the shriveling of the monarchical functions in the German Empire, the rivalry between the nation and the states diminished in significance. It seems to be more important that national consciousness came to be based on particularistic identities; the supportive aspect overshadowed the rivalry. You were German because you were a Berliner, a Catholic Rhinelander, or a Protestant Nuremberger. National pride derived more and more from regional and local pride."[3] The turning point in this process lay in the period between 1866 and 1890, when the exclusionary logic of region and nation turned inclusionary.

This transformation is the focus of two recent studies that analyze regional and national identities in Germany. Both take as their starting point the idea of *Heimat*. Alon Confino has examined the *Heimat* concept in Württemberg as a way to connect local and national identities. Methodologically he suggests "expanding the notion of national memory . . . with the aid of the notion of imagined community so that memory can tell us not only what people remember of the past, but also how they internalize an impersonal world by putting it in familiar and intelligible categories. . . . By combining the notions of national memory and imagined community we can understand how people construct a common denominator between local and national memory."[4] Empirically Confino finds *Heimat* in diverse vehicles of memory, including *Heimat* books (*Heimatbücher*), *Heimat* studies (*Heimatkunde*), *Heimat* museums, beautification societies (*Verschönerungsvereine*), regional *Heimat* associations, and—from 1904 onward—the German League for Heimat Protection (Deutscher Bund Heimatschutz). He identifies distinct aspects of the concept of *Heimat:* history, nature and folklore, and ethnography.[5]

The *Heimat* idea represented the impersonal concept of the nation

"Nation—Region—Stadt: Strukturmerkmale des deutschen Nationalismus und lokale Denkmalskulturen," in *Das Kyffhäuser-Denkmal, 1896–1996: Ein nationales Monument im europäischen Kontext,* ed. Gunther Mai (Weimar, 1997), 53–84.

3. Hardtwig, "Nationalismus," 101.

4. Alon Confino, "The Nation as a Local Metaphor: Heimat, National Memory, and the German Empire, 1871–1918," *History and Memory* 5 (1993): 45; see also idem, *The Nation as a Local Metaphor: Württemberg, Imperial Germany, and National Memory, 1871–1918* (Chapel Hill, NC, 1997).

5. See Confino, "Nation," 50.

in an understandable and communicable way and in a local context. Its impact on nation-building after 1871 can be seen in at least three ways: First, *Heimat* was closely related to family values. According to contemporary gender role models, *Heimat* reaffirmed the role of women through a rhetoric that established linkages between *Heimat,* home, coziness, and women. The nationalization of women in the *Kaiserreich* seems at a certain stage to have been closely related to the *Heimat* discourse. Second, the *Heimat* idea provided a means to bridge the gap between urban and rural areas, insofar as it gave the rural population access to the national discourse. This access was by no means restricted to the written word: for example, it encompassed the invention of traditional costumes (*Trachten*). By reaffirming rural identities, the *Heimat* discourse was socially attractive, since it underpinned rural identities in a new political environment. Third, the *Heimat* idea provided an opportunity, both semantic and real, to communicate the national text within local contexts, not least by sidestepping the dichotomy of "nation" or "region." *Heimat* conveyed a sense of national equality—every German had a *Heimat*—but also local diversity. Diversity, in short, could exist within a concept of nationalism that was nominally egalitarian. Thus *Heimat* made the processes of standardization palatable, not only in the economic and political realms but also to a certain degree in the idioms and customs that accompanied the implementation of the nation-state.

A few years earlier, Celia Applegate came to similar conclusions in her study of the *Heimat* idea in the Palatinate.[6] Applegate emphasized the mediating function of *Heimat* between national and local identities. Her case study—the Bavarian Palatinate, on the west bank of the Rhine—was a complete anomaly within Bavarian state-building after 1815: it was distinct from the Bavarian "mainland" confessionally and, more important still, territorially. Herein lay the seeds of German nationalism locally, because the population of the Palatinate could not look to Munich or the Bavarian state to address its economic grievances. From the local population's point of view, improvement could come only from a new German nation-state. Thus localism and nationalism coexisted comfortably in the Palatinate: the people would ensure national unification by themselves, not with the help of the state or the bureaucracy. Indeed, the local Pfälzer—inhabitants of the Palatinate—drew rather radical consequences from this. As the Forty-eighter Carl Schurz put it,

---

6. Celia Applegate, *A Nation of Provincials: The German Idea of Heimat* (Berkeley, CA, 1990); idem, "Localism and the German Bourgeoisie: The 'Heimat' Movement in the Rhenish Palatinate before 1914," in *The German Bourgeoisie: Essays on the Social History of the German Middle Class from the Late Eighteenth to the Early Twentieth Century,* ed. David Blackbourn and Richard J. Evans (London, 1991), 224–54.

"it is understood by the Pfälzer themselves that if the King of Bavaria does not want to be German, then the Palatinate must cease to be Bavarian."[7]

The special relationship of the Bavarian Palatinate to the German nation-state was underlined with the rise of the *Heimat* movement in the 1880s. The ensuing cult of Pfälzer peculiarities did not contradict national enthusiasm. As Applegate wrote: "Identification with the nation did not, in other words, require that all peasants, hometownsmen, and other unregenerate localists shed themselves of their premodern burden of provincial culture. Nationalism could embrace their smaller worlds; Germanness could encompass their diversity."[8]

Building on Applegate's pioneering work, Confino goes a step further in his analysis. For him, *Heimat* is not only the mediation between nation and localism, but a metaphor for the nation itself, an "interchangeable representation of the local, the regional and the national community."[9] Not only is the nation represented in local contexts, but the nation itself is portrayed in the imagery of *Heimat*. Put another way, *Heimat* works as an emotional part of the national discourse itself. Thus *Heimat* is commonly addressed through use of the second person singular, *Du,* in German, so that the reader, too, becomes part of the *Heimat* narration.

Nevertheless, we should not generalize too quickly from these conclusions. The analytical payoff promised by this new approach may be more limited than we have imagined. In particular it may be applicable only to industrial latecomer regions such as those investigated by Applegate and Confino. Several other cautionary observations may also be introduced.

The *Heimat* idea seems to have had historical force mainly in areas originally lacking the homogenizing force of industrialization. This is not to argue that industrialization took place in the same way everywhere in Germany, but rather that similar experiences of uprootedness, migration, and proletarianization went along with a growing economy, underpinning the need for secondary integration through forms of organization and ideology. Furthermore, the *Heimat* movement paid special attention to the hardships and anxieties stemming from migration, depopulation, and the problems of underdevelopment. It often did so through a harsh critique of industrialization and in the form of agrarian romanticism. *Heimat* referred not to a social entity as the focal point for common

---

7. Carl Schurz, *Vormärz in Deutschland,* ed. Herbert Pönicke (reprint, Munich, 1948), cited in Applegate, *Nation of Provincials,* 28.

8. Applegate, *Nation of Provincials,* 13.

9. Confino, "Nation," 50.

memories and social cohesion, but to nature and a pastoral landscape, especially after 1890, when Germany made its transition from an agrarian to an industrial society. Thus, as Hardtwig has observed, "[A]s time went on, the 'Heimat' concept on the one hand tended increasingly to bridge the gap between region and nation, but on the other hand it deepened the friction in German society between the critics and the supporters of modernity. Thereby it undermined its own original integrative effort."[10]

We have enough evidence from other studies to conclude with confidence that rapid industrialization transformed the connection between local and national identities in a range of ways.[11] We should not underestimate the impact of mass migration, population growth, and increasingly similar patterns in the formation of social identities, all of which changed local identities and realigned social groups in ways other than strictly territorial ones. *Heimat* may be most useful, therefore, as an analytical tool to study underdeveloped areas and to investigate the period before Germany's transformation to an industrial society.

Heimat is a concept or a mental pattern (*Bewußtseinsfigur*). Its strength derives from its capacity to translate characteristics of the nation-state into local concepts. Nevertheless, ideas are rarely generated by other ideas in isolation from experience. Concepts such as *"Heimat"* or "region" both emerge from and define ways of experiencing. *Heimat* is a valuable concept if it is understood as part of a dialectic of experience and consciousness. Therefore, in order to evaluate concepts such as *"Heimat,"* "nation," and "region," we have to take into account not only regional and national *consciousness*, but also the *experience* of the region and the nation.[12]

Moreover, the inclusion of the region into the nation essentially comes down to the dialectic of establishing equality on a national level and thereby legitimizing diversity or inequality in the regions and subregions. Thus equality between co-nationals not only tolerates but can actually legitimize inequality between different regions within one nation. From this situation arose a competition among regions—for example, between Prussia and Saxony—to determine whose citizens were "most German." Whereas Prussia could always point to its leading role in German unification, Saxons were anything but shy in 1889 when they used the occasion of the 800th anniversary of the House of Wettin to

---

10. Hardtwig, "Nationalismus," 57.

11. For example, Dieter K. Buse, "Urban and National Identity: Bremen, 1860–1920," *Journal of Social History* 26 (1993): 521–37.

12. For this general argument, see Reinhart Koselleck, " 'Erfahrungsraum' und 'Erwartungshorizont' — zwei historische Kategorien," in idem, *Vergangene Zukunft*, 3d ed. (Frankfurt a. M., 1984), 349–75. Cf. idem, *Futures Past: On the Semantics of Historical Time,* trans. Keith Tribe (Cambridge, MA, 1985).

argue that their dynasty was much older than the Hohenzollern one and, therefore, more deeply embedded in German history.[13]

We can trace this trajectory from exclusion to inclusion on a number of levels: for instance, as it was reflected in politics, constitutional debates, elections, and political culture;[14] through the emergence of new networks of mass communication (newspaper subscriptions, printed matter, mass transportation);[15] and by means of the representation of the nation and the region in elementary school lessons.[16] Nevertheless, we should not overemphasize the linearity of this process, as though there were no alternatives. Until the outbreak of the First World War, the inclusionary logic of the nation-state could not overcome certain limitations, most evidently in Alsace-Lorraine, but also in Polish territories in the east. The nationalization of the region never fully succeeded where regionalism was underpinned by counternationalism. Therefore, we should not rely on a false Hegelian teleology, as if the nation were negated, suspended, and elevated in the nation state ("sublation"). When analyzing these processes we would do better to look for shifting balances and bipolar identities.

The next section of this essay offers some hypotheses about the interplay of the region and the nation in Saxony in the political and electoral process. Saxony is an extremely revealing subject for research on these matters — and not just because it has been the focus of so much pioneering regional history in the 1990s. Unlike Bavaria and Württemberg, regional identity in Saxony was so strongly developed before 1866 that the state was willing to fight a war against its northern neighbor, Prussia. Yet Saxony also provides examples of German radical nationalism as early as 1878–79.[17] In Saxony, therefore, we can follow in chronologically foreshortened form an important development that took much

---

13. Cf. Hermann Ferdinand Criegern, *Der Leumund der Sachsen: Festschrift zur Jubelfeier der 800jährigen Regierung des Hauses Wettin über das gegenwärtige Königreich Sachsen* (Leipzig, 1889).

14. See also Peter Steinbach, "Politisierung und Nationalisierung der Region im 19. Jahrhundert: Regionalspezifische Politikrezeption im Spiegel historischer Wahlforschung," in *Probleme politischer Partizipation im Modernisierungsprozeß*, ed. idem (Stuttgart, 1982), 321–49.

15. Compare Karl Deutsch, *Nationalism and Social Communication: An Inquiry into the Foundations of Nationalism*, 2d ed. (Cambridge, MA, 1966); and Peter Katzenstein, *Disjoined Partners: Austria and Prussia since 1815* (Berkeley, CA, 1976).

16. Alfred Kelly, "The Franco-Prussian War and Unification in German History Schoolbooks," in *1870/71–1989/90: German Unifications and the Change of Literary Discourse,* ed. Walter Pape (Berlin, 1993), 37–60.

17. See also Heinrich A. Winkler, "Vom linken zum rechten Nationalismus: Der deutsche Liberalismus in der Krise von 1878/79," *Geschichte und Gesellschaft* 4 (1978): 5–28; compare Ludwig Bamberger, "National," in *Nation,* 22 Sept. 1888, reprint in idem, *Politische Schriften,* 5 vols. (Berlin, 1897), 5:203–37.

longer in other parts of the German Empire: the transformation from an exclusively regional and local identity into a vibrant German nationalism.

II.   Regional and National Politics in Saxony after 1866

In contrast to Rudy Koshar's description of Marburg, Saxony did not wear different faces for different audiences, as a good actor should.[18] Saxony's long-standing reputation for fierce political regionalism was invigorated in 1866 after it fought with Austria on the losing side in the Austro-Prussian War. The onerous Prussian occupation in the autumn and winter of 1866–67 provided more fuel for the particularistic fire.[19] Earlier differences between conservatives and liberals on the one hand, and between liberals and socialists on the other, were overshadowed for a time by common anti-Prussian resentment. Politics and election campaigns took on the form of referenda, based on plebiscitary yes-or-no alternatives. Two questions became particularly prominent.

In the first few months after the defeat at Königgrätz, political debate in Saxony presented Saxons with the choice between outright Prussian annexation (as had been the fate of Hanover, Electoral Hesse, Nassau, and the free city of Frankfurt) and Saxony's continued independence. The annexationist cause was by no means limited to Prussian occupiers. National Liberals in Leipzig joined forces with colleagues outside Saxony to demand an end to Saxony's outdated particularism. The Saxon-born Heinrich von Treitschke, who held a professorship in Leipzig before relocating northward, was uncompromising in stating his vision of Saxony's future: "These three dynasties (Hanover, Saxony, and Electoral Hesse) are ready — more than ready — for their rightful annihilation; their reestablishment would be a threat to the security of the new German Confederation, a sin against national morality."[20]

After the territorial integrity of Saxony was narrowly preserved in the treaties of Nikolsburg (26 July 1866) and Prague (23 August 1866), another political alternative was posed: for or against active participation in the North German Reichstag. Once again voices from the bour-

---

18.   Cf. Rudy Koshar, *Social Life, Local Politics, and Nazism: Marburg, 1880–1935* (Chapel Hill, NC, 1986), 23. For the following, see Siegfried Weichlein, "Sachsen zwischen Landesbewußtsein und Nationsbildung, 1866–1871," in *Sachsen im Kaiserreich: Politik, Wirtschaft und Gesellschaft im Umbruch,* ed. Simone Lässig and Karl Heinrich Pohl (Dresden, 1997), 241–70; and James Retallack, " 'Why Can't a Saxon Be More Like a Prussian?' Regional Identities and the Birth of Modern Political Culture in Germany, 1866–67," *Canadian Journal of History* 32 (1997): 26–55.

19.   Richard Dietrich, "Preußen als Besatzungsmacht im Königreich Sachsen, 1866–1868," *Jahrbuch für die Geschichte Mittel- und Ostdeutschlands* 5 (1956): 273–93.

20.   Heinrich von Treitschke, *Die Zukunft der norddeutschen Mittelstaaten* (Berlin, 1866), 8.

geoisie spoke clearly in favor of an active role for Saxons in the North German Confederation. They feared that if such a role were not taken up, Saxony would lose economic privileges derived from the Prussian-led Zollverein. One commentator accused the Saxon government of betraying its own people: "The Saxon government finds it easy to subject its country to such an ordeal and make it drain the bitter cup of particularistic syphilis to the last drop. If a people such as the Saxons wish to uphold the glory of its dynasty for reasons of loyalty and submissiveness, thereby defying reason and their own national interest, we consider this either foolish or shameful."[21] As a scenario to be avoided at all costs, critics of Saxon particularism pointed to the legacy of the American Civil War and the fight over states' rights in the postwar United States. It is striking how well-informed even Saxons living in small villages were about the American war and its aftermath.[22]

In both of these plebiscitary debates, self-proclaimed Saxon "patriots" emphasized the need to defend Saxony's independence. In a flood of pamphlets, they directed their venom against National Liberals, who advocated annexation. Nevertheless, they cautiously accepted the principle of participation in the North German Reichstag—but only if this served Saxony's own interests and strengthened the rights of the federal states. After the Nikolsburg agreement was signed, and then again some months later when the king returned to Dresden (October 1866), Saxony's political camps (*Lager*) were realigned. In the summer and autumn of 1866, Saxon identity still underpinned a sense of political unity. In fact the group of Saxon loyalists grew larger as the constitutional debates in the North German Confederation approached. Anti-Prussian feeling created a coalition that went far beyond the boundaries of particularistic feelings: it included conservative patriots organized in the Saxon Electoral Committee (Sächsisches Wahlcomité), left-liberal democrats (known as *Fortschrittler*), and the *großdeutsch* socialists newly organized in the Saxon People's Party (SVP) led by August Bebel.

The common element binding together this very heterogeneous group was a defense of the principle of "equality" in the emerging Germany. The members of the group gave "equality" a range of meanings, some of which merged with the related terms "parity" and "equity." The later Federalist-Constitutionalists (Bundesstaatlich-Konstitutionelle) feared that the military imbalance of power in the Prussian-led Confederation would only increase, further disadvantaging Saxony in its attempt to defend its remaining sovereignty. These Federalists were afraid of a growing disparity among members of the Confederation. The

---

21. Eduard Löwenthal, *Deutschlands neustes Schmerzenskind* (Dresden, 1866), 5.
22. See, for example, reports in the *Buddissiner Nachrichten,* passim.

großdeutsch democrats feared both the authoritarian character of the Prussian military state and forced separation from the south German states and Austria. Like the conservatives and the Federalist-Constitutionalists—groups that cannot be neatly separated—the *großdeutsch* democrats in Saxony opposed any element of disparity among the member states of the Confederation or, for that matter, between the states already integrated into the Confederation and those remaining outside. But they went further in stressing equal individual rights, especially rights of political participation, such as those that had been granted during the revolution. The Forty-eighter and left-liberal candidate Franz Wigard embodied this position. Like his colleague Emil Roßmäßler, Wigard at first declined to become a candidate in 1867 on the grounds that his mandate from 1848 had not expired.[23] August Bebel's Saxon People's Party emphasized even more strongly the importance of Austria's participation in the national state. By including Austria, the socialists wanted to counterbalance Prussian influence. Their key strategic goal was not to guarantee state rights, but to destroy Prussian-based militarism and to secure individual rights. Left-liberal candidates who subscribed to this platform were supported by Bebel's party.

The dominance of these issues is shown by the rift they created in the ranks of the working-class parties. The Saxon People's Party was unwilling to join forces with the Saxon Lassalleans, whose ranks were dominated by the Hatzfeldtian branch of the movement. The Lassalleans accepted the outcome of the Austro-Prussian War.[24] But even their *kleindeutsch* outlook was not sufficient to facilitate cooperation with the pro-Prussian National Liberals, who in turn found no common ground with the *großdeutsch* left liberals.[25]

Fragile as this coalition of anti-Prussian forces was, it was remarkably successful in Reichstag elections and by-elections held between 1867 and 1869. In the elections to the Constituent North German Reichstag held on 12 February 1867, anti-Prussian candidates won all twenty-three seats in Saxony. Fourteen fell to the conservatives, seven to the left liberals, and two to the Saxon People's Party. The latter two deputies were by far the fiercest opponents of Prussian domination in the North German Confederation.

In those elections of February 1867, Saxon voters were generally presented with only two options: they could cast a vote either for or against a North German Confederation under Prussian hegemony. Vot-

---

23. See also Christian Jansen's contribution to this volume.
24. See the Lassallean platform in the *Deutsche Allgemeine Zeitung*, 25 July 1866.
25. Klaus-Erich Pollmann, *Parlamentarismus im Norddeutschen Bund, 1867–1870* (Düsseldorf, 1985), 113; *Nationalzeitung*, no. 597, 19 Dec. 1866; *Vossische Zeitung*, no. 7, 9 Jan. 1867.

ers had to choose among three candidates when both wings of the workers' movement—the Lassalleans and the SVP—contested a seat, or when a democratic committee fielded a local candidate. Only in Leipzig was there a contest among four parties: the National Liberals, the conservatives, the *großdeutsch* democrats, and the candidate of the Saxon People's Party. In the runoff ballot, law professor Carl Wächter of the conservatives won with the help of the democrats and the socialists. His National Liberal opponent, Leipzig's deputy mayor Eduard Stephani, had captured an astounding 48.4 percent of the vote in the first round of balloting, but he narrowly missed winning an absolute majority in the runoff elections.[26]

The high voter turnout in the elections of February 1867 suggests the extraordinary politicization of Saxony after 1866. Seven of ten eligible voters went to the polls—a percentage not surpassed until the *Kartell* elections of 1887.[27] Voter turnout in Saxony was higher than the average in the North German Confederation and in Prussia, where 64.9 percent of the eligible voters cast ballots. Only Prussian constituencies with a large ethnic Polish population showed a comparable turnout. There the enfranchisement of a national minority was used to create a highly visible national representation.[28] High participation worked in Saxony in favor of the conservatives. In general one can say that the higher the turnout in a constituency, the greater the likelihood that a conservative would be elected.

There was an important institutional aspect to the changing relationship between regional and national politics in the late 1860s. Issues of particular importance for Saxony's sovereignty were hotly debated in the local and regional press. Broad communication networks served as institutional backbones for all major players: for conservative particularists, for Progressives, and for National Liberals striving to achieve a unitary state (*Einheitsstaat*). High diplomacy dealt with these questions, but the most important institutional mediation between region and nation was provided by the democratically elected constitutional assembly, the North German Reichstag. It was here that staunch Saxon particularists made peace with the new state, joining forces with other regionalists in the Federalist Constitutional Union (Bundesstaatlich-Constitutionelle Vereinigung).

---

26. Pollmann, *Parlamentarismus,* 137, 151.

27. Albert Richter, "Die öffentliche Meinung in Sachsen vom Friedensschlusse 1866 bis zur Reichsgründung" (Ph.D. diss., University of Leipzig, 1922), 75; Gerhard A. Ritter with Merith Niehuss, *Wahlgeschichtliches Arbeitsbuch: Materialien zur Statistik des Kaiserreiches, 1871–1918* (Munich, 1980), 89.

28. In the Prussian province of Poznan, voter turnout in February 1867 was 86.6 percent; Pollmann, *Parlamentarismus,* 529.

It was mainly the federal structure of the North German Confederation that calmed many of the conservatives' fears. Antagonism became skepticism. The constitution not only secured Saxony's state rights but had certain attractive features for the average Saxon voter. The third article of the constitution established freedom of movement and the unrestricted right to settle anywhere in the North German Confederation. Before the promulgation of the constitution, Saxon residents had been prevented by local restrictions (*Heimatrecht*) from exercising such rights even in Saxony, much less in the entire area of the North German Confederation. This was especially important to individuals who chose, or were forced, to seek work outside their hometowns. The civic rights of Saxon Jews were also enhanced: previously, Jews were permitted to settle only in Dresden or Leipzig.

On the other hand, these constitutional changes also gave Germans from outside Saxony the right to move to Saxony, to take jobs there, and to receive public support in case of impoverishment. National standards were developed for compulsory secondary training (*Berufsschule*), for university diplomas, and — not to be underestimated in an age of mass migration — to determine which local community had to provide welfare for persons on relief (*Unterstützungswohnsitz*). Of particular interest was the debate whether Saxony had to accept theologians with a theology diploma from neighboring Reuß and give them pulpits in the kingdom.[29] The regulations on free movement also had to be brought into line with compulsory military service requirements. Since Saxony was a net importer of labor, these provisions had an explosive character for the working classes. Up to the outbreak of the Franco-Prussian War in the summer of 1870, the Saxon public hotly debated these thorny questions concerning military service and welfare requirements.[30]

Modernizing reform efforts went well beyond the level of the newly founded North German Confederation; they could be felt on the local level too. Saxony introduced a new suffrage law for the lower house of the Saxon *Landtag* and restructured the state administration.[31] Until 1868 the lower house had a suffrage based on occupational estates.[32] The suffrage reform bill of 1868 lowered the census to an affordable 1 *Thaler* (3 marks) and redivided the constituencies along urban (45 constituen-

---

    29. "Der Norddeutsche Bund und seine Angehörigen," *Deutsche Allgemeine Zeitung,* no. 151, 2 July 1867.

    30. SächsHStA Dresden, Ministerium des Innern Nr. 9599, Verfassung des Deutschen Reiches, 1867–1917, passim.

    31. Cf. Richard Dietrich, "Die Verwaltungsreform in Sachsen, 1869–1873," *Neues Archiv für Sächsische Geschichte und Altertumskunde* 61 (1940): 49–85.

    32. See also James Retallack's contribution to this volume.

cies) and rural (35) lines. To secure legislative continuity, one-third of the *Landtag*'s deputies were to be elected every two years.

Prussia honored Saxony's independence in the Franco-Prussian War and gave its army significant responsibilities in the campaign of 1870–71. Regional pride in the Saxon army focused on their victory at St. Privat. This battle was central for the Saxon memory of the war, more than Sedan or Weißenburg. Ceremonies in public squares, schools, and town meetings continually reiterated Saxony's military contribution to the victory over France, reaffirming Saxons' military pride in the German nation-state and thereby compensating for its defeat in 1866. Dresden and other Saxon cities welcomed their troops back home with a *via triumphalis,* as did Munich and Stuttgart.[33] Conversely, though, Saxon newspapers took little notice of the coronation of the German Kaiser on 18 January 1871. Saxons' collective memory of the war of 1870–71 emphasized instead Saxony's glory and pride within (not outside of) the common victory over an exaggerated "evil enemy." Thus Saxony's glory shone all the brighter. Indeed, Saxons entered a kind of competition with other states to decide who had contributed the most to German unification: Bavarians, Prussians, or Saxons? A language of exclusion had given way to an inclusionary one, though one that had no place for Bebel's socialists, who had disavowed the German war effort after the victory at Sedan. Whereas the democrats switched sides, socialists in the Saxon People's Party stayed firm in their belief that only Großdeutschland could legitimately address the questions of freedom and equality.

National elections in March 1871 reflected this change in mood. Candidates of the National Liberal Party (Nationalliberale Partei) captured a quarter of all votes cast in Saxony, gaining seven seats to the Reichstag. The Progressives, who by now had reconciled themselves to the national state, won eight seats. Thus the supporters of unification won a clear mandate from Saxon voters. The strongest opponents of unification, the socialists, held just two seats. Elections in 1874 showed once again that two strong political camps had emerged in Saxony's political culture. Between 1866 and 1869, elections had been plebiscites between pro- and anti-Prussian forces, with the socialists in the anti-Prussian camp. Socialists' votes were decisive in several hotly contested runoff elections, where their support helped tip the balance toward conservatives (as in Leipzig) or left liberals. After unification, however, this camp disintegrated at the same time that the socialist party grew. In 1874, socialists won 35.4 percent of all votes cast in Saxony, eclipsing the overall vote for any other party for the first time. Six socialists repre-

---

33. See the reports of the *via triumphalis* in the *Constitutionelle Zeitung,* 13 July 1871.

sented Saxony in the Reichstag. As a general rule, high voter turnout now worked to the advantage of the socialists, whereas seven years earlier it had benefited the Saxon conservatives.[34] By the mid-1870s, election campaigns had become essentially a two-party competition between a governmental and a revolutionary party (*Ordnungspartei* versus *Revolutionspartei*). In the runoff ballots, the establishment parties usually combined forces, defeating the socialists.

For the establishment of a nationalist camp in Saxony, two developments were decisive. First, earlier than in other parts of Germany, the Saxon conservatives sided with the governmental parties. They had definitively switched sides as early as April 1877. The program of the Conservative State Association (Conservativer Landesverein) called for a coalition of all antisocialist forces.[35] In order to maintain their political influence in parliament under the existing suffrages in Saxony and the Reich, conservatives joined forces with the other nonsocialist parties, thus forging antisocialist solidarity. The Saxon antisocialist *Kartell* also found allies outside the kingdom, since its governmental orientation worked on the national as well as on the regional level. Second, the Saxon socialists were able to establish a monopoly over the long tradition of *großdeutsch* nationalism, which dated back to the campaign for an Imperial Constitution in 1849. The political shift of left liberals in Saxony over to the government side proved to be ambivalent. Saxon Progressives soon entered an informal coalition with the National Liberals (leaving the Social Democrats to fill the vacuum on the left). The Progressives' dramatic move to the right was harshly criticized by their national leader Eugen Richter, who referred to the Saxon branch of left liberalism scornfully as the *Kammerfortschritt.*

One result of this division of the political landscape into two antagonistic camps was that the government parties — which soon entered a formal agreement regarding the running of candidates — showed a tendency to become both more governmental and more nationalist over time. These features became a fundamental element of their electoral profile. For much the same reason, the socialist party became virtually the sole critic of the national state. For a good portion of the population of Saxony, an anti-Prussian consensus had been transformed into an antisocialist one. This bipolar structure of politics in Saxony was distinc-

---

34. See also Wolfgang Schröder's contribution to this volume; and idem, "Wahlkämpfe und Parteientwicklung: Zur Bedeutung der Reichstagswahlen für die Formierung der Sozialdemokratie zur politischen Massenpartei (Sachsen, 1867–1881)," *Mitteilungsblatt des Instituts für die Erforschung der europäischen Arbeiterbewegung,* no. 20 (1998): 1–66.

35. *Leipziger Zeitung,* 16 Apr. 1877; Wolfgang Schröder, "Die Genese des 'Conservativen Landesvereins für das Königreich Sachsen,'" in *Sachsen im Kaiserreich,* ed. Lässig and Pohl, 149–74.

tive. For in most other parts of Germany, the presence of a substantial Catholic population — of which at least a portion was also stigmatized as an "enemy of the Reich" — prevented the socialists from becoming isolated as the sole representatives of anti-Prussian sentiment. It is hard to overestimate the impact of a relatively homogeneous Lutheran population for the development of the Saxon party system, where socialists were the only fundamental critics of the newly founded nation-state. This distinguished the Saxon case from regional party systems in the Rhineland or in Silesia.

III. Conclusions: Negative Integration and Antisocialism

The relationship between regional and national consciousness in Saxony, as in the other small- and medium-sized German states, cannot be seen as simply a matter of one mental pattern (nationalism) displacing another (regionalism). Saxon patriotism did not have to diminish as a new national consciousness grew. In fact a strong regional patriotism often was accompanied by strong national feeling. Saxon patriotism was not destroyed by the defeat of 1866, but rather strengthened. The plebiscitary nature of the 1867 Reichstag elections, as well as the high level of grassroots politicization, favored those in the anti-Prussian camp. The more anti-Prussian one was, in fact, the more "Saxon" one felt. The early growth of the Social Democratic Party in Saxony was due in large measure to its uncompromising anti-Prussian position.

How, then, did Saxons become Germans? While the concept of negative integration has generally been used to characterize the position of Social Democrats in Wilhelmine Germany,[36] the concept fittingly describes the position of the governmental parties in Saxony after 1871. It was through their increasingly strident antisocialism that these parties came to be integrated into Bismarck's new Reich, which otherwise seemed so distasteful to them. To defend Saxony's sovereignty with increasing vehemence and consistency meant to oppose the "forces of revolution" in the same ways. As a result, Saxon antisocialists discovered a strong affinity with antisocialists in Prussia and other German states. Thus antisocialism became a defining element of German nation-building — not only after passage of antisocialist legislation in 1878, but well before.

---

36. See Dieter Groh, *Negative Integration und revolutionärer Attentismus: Die deutsche Sozialdemokratie am Vorabend des Ersten Weltkrieges* (Frankfurt a. M., 1973).

Community Values, Democratic Cultures? Reflections on Saxony's Place in the German Cooperative Movement, 1849–1933

Brett Fairbairn

I. Introduction

One face of Saxony is that of the bellwether region, frequently ahead of the German trend. Saxony was first to industrialize, and first to turn "red" in turn-of-the-century Reichstag elections. Indeed, it turned darker red than most, with Communists organizing there in the 1920s. As Benjamin Lapp recently reminded us, it was also the first state to turn "brown."[1] Saxony appears to have remained in the vanguard recently, too, especially when one considers the importance of the peaceful demonstrations in Leipzig in preparing the way for the *Wende* of 1989. It seems, then, that Saxony was the first German region to be socialist, the first to be antisocialist, and the first to be postsocialist—a simplistic generalization, to be sure, and one that belies a complicated and turbulent history.[2]

This essay looks at the social landscape of Saxony through what might be considered a narrow or a broad window, depending on one's point of view. This is the window provided by the history of cooperative organizations. Cooperatives are enterprises owned and democratically controlled by their customers or by their employees. In the nineteenth and twentieth centuries, they spread in almost every country under the sponsorship of farmers' and workers' movements. Cooperatives by them-

---

1. Benjamin Lapp, *Revolution from the Right: Politics, Class, and the Rise of Nazism in Saxony, 1919–1933* (Atlantic Highlands, NJ, 1997).

2. In this essay, "Saxony" includes both the Kingdom of Saxony and the adjacent Prussian province of Saxony, which was annexed by Prussia in 1815.

selves are just one kind of business and one kind of community institution; as such they have been marginalized in economic and social history.[3] However, by virtue of their dual nature as democratic associations of people and as competitive enterprises, cooperatives straddle the boundary between market economy and social movement. Indeed, cooperatives represent the largest social movement in history.[4]

Saxony holds a significant distinction as a birthplace of the German cooperative movement. It was in Saxony in the late 1840s that some of the first cooperatives in Germany emerged, as part of the early labor movement. It was in the Prussian province of Saxony that Hermann Schulze-Delitzsch popularized cooperatives in a way that brought them to the attention of his contemporaries and linked them to the German *Mittelstand*. And it was in Saxony, beginning in the 1880s, that self-consciously proletarian and Social Democratic consumer cooperatives emerged. Thus Saxony has a claim to be a birthplace of German cooperatives in general, of *Mittelstand* cooperatives, and of Social Democratic consumer cooperatives. Because of its leading role in the development of industry, of labor, of liberal movements, and of cooperatives, Saxony has been characterized as the "Lancashire of Germany."[5] This provocative comparison may raise as many questions as it resolves. What does the history of cooperatives tell us about how progressive Saxony really was?

To ask such a question immediately forces an unpacking of assumptions behind narratives of progress. Cooperatives were used by those who, like the liberals, had an explicit concept of progress or improvement and who sought to realize this modernizing program in concrete institutional forms. But cooperatives were also used by those who contested dominant notions of "the modern": by some who opposed what they saw as modernity altogether, and by others who embraced it selectively and sought to articulate versions of modernity that better reflected alternative values and identities. Thus, to choose to view German history within a Saxon frame is to highlight social and political conflict, but also to highlight the variety and diversity of social projects and possibilities.

---

3. On the historiography of German cooperatives before 1914, see Brett Fairbairn, "History from the Ecological Perspective: Gaia Theory and the Problem of Cooperatives in Turn-of-the-Century Germany," *American Historical Review* 99 (1994): 1203–39, esp. 1216 and fn. 49.

4. The International Co-operative Alliance, a UN-affiliated nongovernmental organization based in Geneva, claimed in 1995 to represent 575 million cooperative members in 740,000 cooperatives in 69 countries. In 1993 German cooperatives claimed nearly twenty million members. See DG Bank, *Die Genossenschaften in der Bundesrepublik Deutschland, 1994*, 10.

5. Johnston Birchall, *The International Co-operative Movement* (Manchester, 1997), 11.

II. The Origins and Development of Cooperatives before 1914

Cooperatives grow directly out of local circumstances. They are rooted in local communities of face-to-face interaction. And yet at the same time they are part of national and international movements. If there is a tendency among historians to regard "local" as meaning "traditional," and "national" (or "international") as meaning "modern," then cooperatives squarely straddle these distinctions. While cooperatives are, as a result of their local/community orientation, quite diverse, they also work together in federations, and they agree on common statements of principles.[6] Prominent among the common purposes of cooperatives are ideas of democratic process and the education of members, leading toward greater control of their own situations. The immediate purposes are usually direct and practical: better prices, more appropriate services, more trustworthy products, and so on. But usually, where cooperative movements become large, there is a wider social or community vision behind these economic benefits. The economic benefits are conceived as accruing to a group, not only to individuals. Moreover, this group is conceived as having some important purpose in the larger state or society. In short, local identity and economic benefit are tied to an ideological conception and to a class, occupational, or national identity.

The formation of cooperatives requires not only a group identity but also an economic need and conditions of civil society conducive to the creation of democratic associations. In Germany, these circumstances first came together, other than in Berlin and a few other centers, in Saxon towns in the 1840s. Groups who saw themselves adversely affected by social-economic change formed cooperatives to improve their economic positions and to advance their interests in the industrializing economy. It is not true, as is sometimes still claimed, that the first cooperative in Germany was founded in Chemnitz in 1845.[7] It is accurate to say, however, that working-class associations in the 1840s were beginning to articulate a common identity and to address the needs of working-class groups. Such efforts multiplied following the 1848 revolutions with the development of the General German Workers' Fraternity (Allgemeine deutsche Arbeiterverbrüderung). The vision of the Arbeiterverbrüderung was a socialization of the economy through reorganiza-

---

6. See Ian MacPherson, *Co-operative Principles for the Twenty-first Century* (Geneva, 1996).

7. The Spar- und Konsum-Verein "Ermunterung." Cf. Paul Göhre, *Die deutschen Arbeiter-Konsumvereine* (Berlin, 1910), 32; and Erwin Hasselmann, *Geschichte der deutschen Konsumgenossenschaften* (Frankfurt a. M., 1971), 47–48.

tion into a broad system of productive and consumer cooperatives.[8] The national movement founded its first known cooperatives in Berlin. But it found a special resonance in Saxony. The most important of the early foundings was the October 1849 General Association (*Allgemeine Association*) in Chemnitz, which soon had 1,500 members, its own warehouse, and its own coffee-roasting plant.[9]

It is worth stressing that these early cooperatives were individually small and that they were widely scattered, for several reasons. First, despite great attention to the person of Hermann Schulze-Delitzsch, cooperatives in Germany were not created by "great men." The movement really did develop initially "from the bottom up," on a highly localized level of activity, and from working-class, artisanal roots. Second, these local initiatives were inspired and coordinated almost from the beginning through wider regional and national movements such as the Arbeiterverbrüderung, whose most important function was to provide a network that popularized and legitimized the cooperative idea. Third, the first wave of cooperatives in Saxony and elsewhere is noteworthy because of its marginal success—these early movements did not "take off." Michael Prinz concludes that the democratic nature of the early cooperatives isolated them from the state and the authorities, while their willingness to demand social reforms through state action isolated them from the liberal movement. This left them without allies.[10]

The associationist idea was in the air in the 1840s, in England, France, Italy, and Germany. The accomplishment of Schulze-Delitzsch was to articulate a form of associationism that was acceptable to his fellow liberals, and eventually to the governing authorities. In doing so, he initiated a tradition of *Mittelstand* cooperativism that, again, found special resonance in Saxony. Schulze-Delitzsch became acquainted with the problems of artisans in his capacity as a judge in the town of Delitzsch and, even more so, when as a deputy to the Berlin National Assembly of 1848 he chaired a committee to investigate the problems in the artisanal economy.[11] Schulze-Delitzsch concluded that the emergence of a competitive, modern economy was threatening to ruin the

8. See Christiane Eisenberg, *Frühe Arbeiterbewegung und Genossenschaften: Theorie und Praxis der Produktivgenossenschaften in der deutschen Sozialdemokratie und den Gewerkschaften der 1860er/1870er Jahre* (Bonn, 1985), 25.

9. Michael Prinz, *Brot und Dividende: Konsumvereine in Deutschland und England vor 1914* (Göttingen, 1996), 131.

10. Ibid., 137.

11. On Schulze-Delitzsch, see Rita Aldenhoff, *Schulze-Delitzsch: Ein Beitrag zur Geschichte des Liberalismus zwischen Revolution und Reichsgründung* (Baden-Baden, 1984).

livelihoods of wide groups of people upon whom the liberal movement and German civilization were dependent. "Remember that the German *Mittelstand,*" Schulze-Delitzsch said, "whose economic independence we have undertaken to strengthen, has the great task of being one of the chief bearers of the culture and political development of our father-land."[12] The threat that the *Mittelstand* would be torn apart — poorer artisans becoming proletarianized, others turning to support conserva-tive policies — was a threat both to liberalism and to Germany. What liberals needed was a solution to the social question that was consis-tent with liberalism — in other words, a solution that did not involve state intervention. "Instead of complaining about the inroads made by the factory and by commerce, about the excessive power of capital, one should instead empower oneself with the advantages of factory-like, businesslike enterprise and put capital at one's own service," wrote Schulze-Delitzsch in 1853. To the members of the Reichstag he later justified his cooperatives as "the guilds of the future," that is, as guilds suited to the modern economy and "destined to play as powerful a role in the social development of the near future as the old guilds did in their own time."[13]

It may be permissible to see Schulze-Delitzsch's ideas as a projec-tion onto the German stage of particularly Saxon realities. The wide-spread artisanal economy, its economic crisis, and the spreading impact of factories and large-scale production were more apparent in Saxony in the late 1840s and 1850s than in most other places. One might also say that it was due to Saxony, as well as to Schulze-Delitzsch, that the German cooperative movement was decisively impelled at an early stage toward forms of cooperatives suited to the *Mittelstand:* above all, credit cooperatives — *Volksbanken* — in which Schulze-Delitzsch was a pioneer. That this type of cooperative was dominant at this early stage sets Ger-many apart from almost every other country.[14]

It is true that Schulze-Delitzsch also wanted to help wage laborers; he promoted the concept of consumer cooperatives partly for their bene-fit. The first indisputable consumer cooperative in Germany was the 1850 association in Eilenburg, established with Schulze-Delitzsch's inspi-

---

12. Speech to Allgemeiner Verband meeting in Potsdam, 1862, cited in Eberhard Dülfer, "Das Organisationskonzept 'Genossenschaft' — eine Pionierleistung Schulze-De-litzschs," in *Schulze-Delitzsch: Ein Lebenswerk für Generationen,* ed. Deutscher Genos-senschaftsverband (Schulze-Delitzsch) (Wiesbaden, 1987), 59–126.

13. Bundesarchiv (hereafter BA) Berlin, Reichstag, Nr. 406. The phrase *Innung der Zukunft* (guild of the future) goes back at least to Schulze-Delitzsch's *Assoziations-buch* of 1853, p. 56, and also appeared in the title of a newsletter he published in the 1850s.

14. Except Italy, where Luigi Luzzatti promoted ideas very similar to Schulze-Delitzsch's.

ration.[15] At root, however, his vision of cooperatives was less one of helping the proletarian working class than one of preventing the formation of a proletarian working class in the first place. Schulze-Delitzsch developed practical models for various kinds of cooperatives, including credit, input-purchase, warehousing, production, marketing, and consumer cooperatives, most of which were designed to help self-employed artisans. These multiplied in the 1860s—especially the credit cooperatives, followed by the consumer associations. At the end of August 1867, Schulze-Delitzsch counted 1,571 cooperatives in Germany, of which 1,122 were credit cooperatives, 250 were consumer cooperatives, and 199 were raw-materials-purchasing cooperatives and other artisanal types. The known consumer associations were located mainly in the more industrialized parts of Germany, notably the Kingdom of Saxony (39), the Rhine province (33), and Brandenburg (27).[16] The spread of cooperatives proved problematic in terms of Schulze-Delitzsch's original vision, however, for increasingly the members did not come from the *Mittelstand*. It was estimated at the time of Schulze-Delitzsch's death in 1882 that perhaps two-thirds of the members of his most successful kinds of cooperatives—the credit and consumer associations—were made up not of artisans but of groups such as farmers, industrial workers, and civil servants.[17] Once again, these developments were most pronounced in Saxony.

The 1880s were the start of what has been called the "Saxon special case" (*Sonderfall Sachsen*) in the German workers' movement.[18] A number of consumer cooperatives were created under the influence of local members of the Social Democratic Party, who saw in them a tool for advancing the material interests of working people. In pursuing this strategy, Saxon Social Democrats were going squarely against the party line, which—following from the debates of Marx against Lassalle over the question of production cooperatives—was averse to cooperatives of any kind as a distraction from the class struggle. A key step came with the founding in 1884 of the Leipzig-Plagwitz consumer cooperative by a group of Social Democrats who were angry with local retail merchants for having publicly opposed the SPD in the 1881 Reichstag elections.[19]

15. Hasselmann, *Geschichte der deutschen Konsumgenossenschaften,* 68–69.

16. "Statistische Uebersicht über Zahl und Geschäftsresultate der Deutschen Genossenschaften in den letzten Jahren," Reichstag des Norddeutschen Bundes, I. Legislatur-Periode, Sitzungs-Periode 1868, Nr. 60, attachment.

17. "Schulze, Franz Hermann S.," in *Allgemeine Deutsche Biographie* (Leipzig, 1891).

18. Prinz, *Brot und Dividende,* 250.

19. A. Bammes, *Der Konsumverein Leipzig-Plagwitz: Seine Entstehung, Entwickelung und sein gegenwärtiger Stand* (Leipzig, [c. 1903]). See also Prinz, *Brot und Dividende,* 253; and Göhre, *Die deutschen Arbeiter-Konsumvereine,* 122ff.

The Leipzig-Plagwitz association long remained one of the strongest consumer cooperatives in all of Germany, and one that was under the most solid Social Democratic management. One writer enthused that "the whole enterprise is pure business, built on a commercial basis [*kaufmännischer Grundlage*], . . . a truly proud and admirable creation of Saxon proletarians!" Other associations followed, including the Vorwärts consumer association in Dresden in 1887, further demonstrating the potential for working-class consumer cooperatives to expand in big industrial centers.[20]

These associations were innovative in adopting an explicit working-class orientation, but they remained small, localist in orientation, dependent on voluntary leadership, and traditional in their marketing techniques. In Leipzig-Plagwitz, for example, members objected to sales and shop-window displays as "deceit" and "waste."[21] Despite this no-frills consumer fundamentalism — or because of it — Saxon cooperatives were also known as exceptionally successful in financial terms, offering their patrons high refunds at year-end. Refunds were as high as 20 percent of the total purchased by each member.[22] Since cooperatives sold at prevailing prices (or at least were meant to do so), refunds of this magnitude massively undercut nearby private retailers. Not surprisingly, it was also in Saxony that organized opposition of private retailers to consumer cooperatives emerged.

As more predominantly working-class cooperatives were created, they fit less comfortably within the liberal Schulze-Delitzsch federation. The consumer cooperatives went on to construct even larger enterprises, such as the 1894 Wholesale Society of German Consumer Associations (Grosseinkaufsgesellschaft deutscher Konsumvereine, or GEG), a wholesale company based in Hamburg and owned by the retail cooperatives. They also built even larger, comprehensive local cooperatives, such as the new Produktion cooperative launched in 1899 in Hamburg. Mammoth enterprises were logical as far as the consumer cooperators were concerned, since they offered economies of scale and market power. But to the leaders of the Schulze-Delitzsch movement, these innovations crossed an important line. Instead of helping the *Mittelstand,* the new cooperatives were *replacing* artisans and shopkeepers with consumer-owned enterprises. The fact that the consumer cooperatives were associated with Social Democracy did not help. To their critics, the large consumer cooperatives began to look like tools designed by a Marxist movement in order to eliminate the *Mittelstand.*

---

20. Adolph von Elm, *Die Genossenschaftsbewegung* (Berlin, 1901), 10.
21. Prinz, *Brot und Dividende,* 264.
22. Ibid., 254.

Eventually Schulze-Delitzsch's successor, Hans Crüger, brought a motion to the 1902 meeting of the Schulze-Delitzsch cooperative federation (the Allgemeiner Verband) in Kreuznach stating that cooperatives hostile to the *Mittelstand* had no place in the federation. This resulted in the expulsion of ninety-eight consumer cooperatives, estimated at the time to have a membership that was 78 percent working-class.[23] They organized their own umbrella federation, the Central Federation of German Consumer Associations (Zentralverband deutscher Konsumvereine, or ZdK) in 1903. When it came into existence, the new federation was strongest in the Kingdom of Saxony.[24] The ZdK swiftly surpassed the Schulze-Delitzsch movement in the number of people and volume of business it represented, to become (after Britain's) the second-strongest consumer cooperative movement in the world. The ZdK cooperatives looked pointedly not to Schulze-Delitzsch for inspiration, but rather to the British cooperative movement originating from Rochdale, and to social-democratic ideas.

The growth of consumer cooperatives as self-consciously working-class institutions forced a rapprochement with Social Democracy on the national level. In 1899 at the SPD party conference in Hanover, consumer cooperatives were widely debated for the first time. Cooperative supporters faced criticism from figures such as Rosa Luxemburg on the left of the party. The Hanover conference finally passed a resolution stating that "the party is neutral toward the creation of cooperatives."[25] Eventually the SPD's Magdeburg party conference of 1910 encouraged party members to be involved in consumer cooperatives. In return, cooperatives were to provide jobs, support striking workers, provide model working conditions, and train the working class to manage its own enterprises.[26] According to some, the workers' movement now rested on three completely independent but equally important pillars: the party, the trade unions, and the consumer cooperatives. Still, it had taken a quarter century for the Saxon developments of the mid-1880s to be reflected in the national labor movement.

Growing support for consumer cooperatives by Social Democrats

---

23. Heinrich Kaufmann, *Kurzer Abriß der Geschichte des Zentralverbandes deutscher Konsumvereine* (Hamburg, 1928), table, 341.

24. Preussische Central-Genossenschafts-Kasse, *Mittheilungen zur deutschen Genossenschaftsstatistik für 1900. Bearbeitet von Dr. A. Petersilie . . .* (Berlin, 1902), table 3. See also Dieter Fricke, *Die deutsche Arbeiterbewegung 1869 bis 1914* (Berlin, 1976), 774.

25. Hermann Fleißner, *Genossenschaften und Arbeiterbewegung,* 2d ed. (Jena, 1924), 21.

26. Heinrich Kaufmann, *Die Stellungnahme der Sozialdemokratie zur Konsumgenossenschaftsbewegung* (Hamburg, 1911), 40–49; Arnulf Weuster, *Theorie der Konsumgenossenschaftsentwicklung: Die deutschen Konsumgenossenschaften bis zum Ende der Weimarer Zeit* (Berlin, 1980), 164, 235; Elm, *Genossenschaftsbewegung,* 16–18.

was complemented by mounting hostility from other quarters. Saxony was one center of Germany's newer, more radical, and more right-wing *Mittelstandspolitik* in the 1890s (and especially after 1900). Associations of small retailers defended shopkeepers' interests and influenced politicians and public opinion. Some of these associations were political, for example, the *Schutzverbände*. Others combined economic and political action, as did the *Rabattsparvereine*, which helped shopkeepers offer discounts to compete with the cooperatives. Among the leaders and activists of these organizations were ultranationalists and antisocialists.[27] The campaigns of such *Mittelstand* groups were given publicity, ideas, and legitimacy by middle-class writers and officials, among whom the most prolific was likely Professor E. Suchsland, a senior teacher of Latin from Halle.[28] Governments at all levels responded to the *Mittelstand* lobby by taking incremental steps to restrict consumer cooperatives. At the Reich level, the cooperative law was amended in the 1890s to criminalize sales by consumer cooperatives to nonmembers. This measure was suited to intimidating and harassing cooperatives and their staff. Consumer cooperatives in rural areas — which sold predominantly to farmers — were exempted from the legislation.[29] In Prussia and the Kingdom of Saxony, state officials were forbidden to serve on cooperative boards of directors or even to join cooperatives. The *Magistrat* (senate) of Dresden's municipal government did not permit trolley supervisors to join consumer cooperatives.[30]

Piecemeal measures did not satisfy *Mittelstand* activists, who maintained continuous pressure on the Saxon ministry of the interior. The government position — defended by government leader Count Wilhelm von Hohenthal und Bergen in the lower house of the *Landtag* on 3 March 1908 — was that the ministry of the interior would "observe complete neutrality" and that "the competition of consumer associations against shopkeepers and small business was not to be favored either

---

27. Robert Gellately, *The Politics of Economic Despair: Shopkeepers and German Politics, 1890–1914* (London, 1974), 70–71.

28. Among others, E. Suchsland, *Notwahrheiten über Konsumvereine: Eine Diskussionsrede vom Kampfplatz mit der Sozialdemokratie* (Halle a. S., 1904); and idem, *Los von den Konsumvereinen und Warenhäusern: Eine Mahnung und eine Bitte an alle Vaterlandsfreunde zur Erhaltung des gewerblichen Mittelstandes in Stadt und Land, als des Fundamentes unseres Staatswesens und unserer Kultur* (Halle a. S., 1904).

29. The parliamentary debates became earnest with the government's bill of December 1895 (*Stenographische Berichte über die Verhandlungen des Reichstages* 9. Legislaturperiode, IV. Session 1895/96, Nr. 34). See the minutes, motions, and petitions in BA Berlin, Reichstag, Nr. 412.

30. Cited in Klaus Kluthe, *Genossenschaften und Staat in Deutschland: Systematische und historische Analysen deutscher Genossenschaftspolitik bezogen auf den Zeitraum 1914 bis zur Gegenwart* (Berlin, 1985), 84.

directly or indirectly."[31] This meant that consumer cooperatives of officials would not be allowed free rent or utilities in public buildings, and civil servants would not be allowed to work on paid time for the cooperatives. These policies closely paralleled Prussian policies. Despite the pressure, government officials did not, at this time, go further. The ministry was caught between the *Mittelstand* lobby and the economic interests of its own officials: after all, leaving consumer cooperatives alone might make for more contented officials and, hence, lower salary demands. Hence the Saxon government, even though it sympathized with the *Mittelstand,* dragged its feet. Only in 1918 did it radicalize its policy, responding favorably to a petition that officials be ordered to distance themselves from consumer cooperatives and "instead patronize the useful establishments involved in the *Rabattsparvereine.*"[32]

Mittelstand activists also demanded special taxes to restrict consumer cooperatives, and in this sphere Saxony was a national leader. Saxon shopkeepers petitioned in 1895 for a special tax of 3 percent of gross sales on every chain store, which would include large cooperatives because of their branch systems. Similar proposals were taken to state governments in Prussia and Bavaria at the same time, but Saxony was the first to give in.[33] In 1896 the Saxon government passed a series of ordinances permitting municipalities to impose special taxes on consumer cooperatives. These took the form of special taxes on businesses that had large sales volumes (which hit consumer cooperatives because they were larger than their competitors), special taxes on businesses that operated numerous branches (which hit consumer cooperatives because they were centralized multiple retailers), and special taxes on warehouses (consumer cooperatives were large enough to operate their own warehousing networks). As the context makes clear, *Mittelstand* activists wanted to use such taxes to drive consumer cooperatives out of business. "When the business tax was brought in, the [cooperative] store could not make it and was closed again," one activist was reported to have told the Saxon legislature about his local experience. "Then one was able to remove the business tax, since its purpose had been achieved."[34]

While consumer cooperatives were increasingly opposed by public-policy measures, *Mittelstand* cooperatives were officially and materially

31. Beschluß des Ministeriums des Innern (hereafter MdI) vom 29. Mai 1912 (reaffirming the 1908 stance), in SächsHStA Dresden, Justiz-Ministerium Nr. 967.

32. Copy from MdI, 16 Aug. 1918, ibid. The *Kreishauptmannschaften* were directed, "die ihr unterstellten Behörden im Sinn der Bestrebungen des Verbandes sächsischer Rabattsparvereine in geeigneter Weise zu verständigen."

33. Johannes Wernicke, *Umsatzsteuer und Konsumvereine* (Berlin, 1898), 15.

34. Hermann Fleißner, *Zur Geschichte der Umsatzsteuer in Sachsen: Nebst Urteilen und Gutachten über die Umsatzsteuer* (Hamburg, 1904), 18.

encouraged. The Kingdom of Saxony assembled a support fund of 2 million marks in 1897, later expanded to 6 million marks. Of the eventual total, 3 million was earmarked for assistance to agricultural cooperatives and 3 million for artisanal cooperatives.[35] After the end of the First World War, the fund was doubled to 12 million marks, two-thirds of which was meant for small business and trades.[36] In proportion to its population, Saxony made more money available to the *Mittelstand* than did other states. But it appears that, rather than revolving, most of the Saxon funds were tied up in long-term debts or loans to enterprises that had difficulty repaying.[37] The statistics on creation of new artisanal (*Handwerker*) cooperatives were dismal. Compared to 433 such enterprises in Prussia and 100 in Bavaria, the Kingdom of Saxony could count only 11 in 1905 — that is, eight years after creating the special fund.[38] Deputies complained of the lack of a "pervasive organization encompassing the entire state."[39] By this they meant a central institution such as the Prussian Central Cooperative Bank, or Preußenkasse, created in 1895 by Finance Minister Johannes von Miquel, architect of social-protectionist *Sammlungspolitik*. The Preußenkasse was capitalized with state funds and acted as an autonomous bank, accepting deposits from cooperatives and relending the additional capital. The centralized Preußenkasse provided for a much more concerted intervention. Saxony's special funds may have made political capital, but they created few cooperatives.

Where artisanal cooperatives failed to thrive, shopkeepers' cooperatives slowly and fitfully took off. Saxony was one focus for the emergence of a new and distinctively German kind of cooperative: cooperatives of small retailers, who conducted wholesaling functions in common. The first retailers' purchasing association was founded in Görlitz, Lower Silesia, in 1888, to combat the local consumer cooperative. Others soon followed.[40] In 1892 the movement attempted to establish its central buying committee in Leipzig, backed by the Leipzig *Kolonialwaren-Zeitung;* but this attempt failed. As it turned out, shopkeepers had difficulty forming a national organization. From 1898 to 1903 they instead formed re-

35. See the documents in SächsHStA Dresden, Finanzministerium (hereafter FinM) Nr. 5452. Originally the MdI wanted to lend the money at rates as low as 1 percent, but the finance ministry resisted.

36. Note from Finanzbuchhalterei, 22 July 1920, in SächsHStA Dresden, FinM Nr. 5453.

37. See note from Finanzbuchhalterei, dated 13 Feb. 1912, in SächsHStA Dresden, FinM Nr. 5452.

38. Wilhelm Peters, *Zur neuesten Entwicklung des Genossenschaftswesens in Handwerk* (Ph.D. diss., University of Marburg, 1905, publ. 1906), 40.

39. See MdI to finance ministry, 11 Dec. 1917, citing comments of Dr. Böhme during the budget debate, in SächsHStA Dresden, FinM Nr. 5453.

40. See the *Jubiläumsschrift, EDEKA, 1907–1957* (Hamburg, 1957), 12.

gional purchasing associations of grocers, which in 1904–7 were brought together to form a Federation of German Shopkeepers' Cooperatives (Verband deutscher kaufmännischer Genossenschaften). In 1911 this federation acquired the Edeka trademark, previously developed in Berlin by the Einkaufszentrale der Kolonialwarenhändler, or EdK. The Edeka cooperatives remained disproportionately strong in Saxony until the 1930s. Among all districts of the country, the Edeka-Zentrale's highest volume of business was in Chemnitz, with Leipzig and Dresden fourth and fifth after Hamburg and Breslau.[41]

Overall, then, the Kingdom of Saxony was a willing but not particularly leading participant in *Mittelstandspolitik*. The Saxon state did intervene in support of artisanal cooperatives in the 1890s, but not effectively. The only kind of *Mittelstand* cooperative that thrived — the Edeka movement — did so more or less without government help. There was only one sphere in which the Saxon state truly followed the desires of the *Mittelstand* activists and became a leader in Germany: this was in the negative side of *Mittelstand* policy, the active hindering of working-class consumer cooperatives. The Saxon political elite demonstrated that whereas its actual *Mittelstandspolitik* was conceptually bankrupt, its antisocialism was alive and well.

III.   Twentieth-Century Challenges

Prior to the First World War, separate and economically powerful cooperative movements had developed in Saxony to represent a liberal vision of a competitive society based on small independent producers, a conservative ideal of harmonious, state-supporting traditional orders, and a social-democratic goal of proletarian liberation through occupational solidarity. These alternative visions were all based on community-level associations networked into wider federations and central economic agencies such as wholesales and banks. While all had some political and social influence, the consumer cooperatives had the largest membership.

Through the disruptions of the First World War and the long postwar economic crisis, consumer cooperatives did not fare badly, largely because they generally dealt in the necessities of life. Saxon cooperative leaders could boast in 1931 that they still led the country, for example by such measures as average sales per member (a measure of individual loyalty) and percentage of goods purchased through the GEG wholesale

---

41. Edeka, *Jahresbericht 1932*, 25–26. The Edeka organizations survived the Second World War and operated for a time in the Soviet occupation zone. The Edeka and related REWE stores, now among the largest wholesale/retail enterprises in Germany, were reintroduced in the east after 1990.

(a measure of local cooperatives' loyalty to the national institutions).[42] Only in the late 1920s did matters grow truly serious, when the onset of the Depression coincided with the National Socialists' effective revival of the Mittelstand-oriented, anticooperative campaign. But by then the consumer cooperatives, especially in Saxony, were also busy dealing with new foes from within.

After the German Communists split from the majority Social Democrats in 1919, Communist activists contested the control of local working-class institutions. Their aim was to wrest from the Social Democrats the legitimate claim to speak on behalf of workers. Whereas Communists did not gain control of the cooperative movement as a whole, they did score successes in electing "opposition" delegates within many of the cooperatives, and in taking control of a few of them, particularly in eastern Germany. The "cooperative opposition" attacked the weak points of the now large, aging, and rather bureaucratic SPD-led institutions — for example, they attacked their record as employers. At the turn of the century, the consumer cooperatives had made a point of having unionized staff and offering model contracts; now they found it difficult to maintain this leadership.[43] The opposition also made important efforts to recruit women activists into leadership positions in the cooperative movement, for women constituted an important group of "outsiders" who had not effectively been integrated by the old SPD consumer leaders. In securing the election of women into cooperative bodies, the Communist Party (KPD) was especially successful in Saxony, Sachsen-Anhalt, and Thuringia (where its influence was greatest).[44]

Communists argued that the cooperatives and their Social Democratic leadership were betraying the working class. These attacks became vociferous after the onset of the Depression, when many cooperatives felt forced to cut back. Social Democratic cooperatives were accused of "wage theft" (Lohnraub) when they rolled back wages.[45] The influence of the Communist opposition peaked when its candidates won control of the Halle and Merseburg consumer cooperatives. Both were subsequently shut out of the consumer cooperative movement for what were said to be bad business practices; loans were recalled by the cooperative central institutions; and both cooperatives went bankrupt in 1931. The Commu-

42. "Den Genossenschaftern zum Gruß! Zum Verbandstag der Sächsischen Konsumvereine, Klaus Zweiling," in BA Berlin, Bestand 95, Materialsammlung "Geschichte der Konsumgenossenschaften," Nr. 13.

43. Ernst Grünfeld, Das Genossenschaftswesen, volkswirtschaftlich und soziologisch betrachtet (Halberstadt, 1928), 308–9.

44. Autorenkollektiv, Zur Geschichte der deutschen Konsumgenossenschaften: Von den Anfängen bis 1945, Verband Deutscher Konsumgenossenschaften (n.p., 1974), 63.

45. See clippings from 1931 in BA Berlin, Bestand 95, Nr. 13.

nist version of the history of the Halle cooperative blamed its demise on "the traitorous right-wing SPD leadership clique," who drove it into bankruptcy. This account also compared the Social Democrats' policies to Chancellor Heinrich Brüning's attacks on the working class.[46]

The infighting between Communists and Social Democrats was cut short by the Nazi seizure of power in 1933. Most associations continued to function for some years. Managers and elected leaders who were not arrested for political activity could continue in their posts, as long as they did not overtly fight with the Nazi appointees who had been added to the management and board of directors. Some associations, seeing the handwriting on the wall, chose to dissolve themselves; this was the fate of the historic Chemnitz association. The chronicles of the association, kept since 1870, came to an end in 1933 with a motion to dissolve the cooperative.[47] Elsewhere — as in the historic Leipzig-Plagwitz cooperative — Social Democratic leaders managed to maintain intact a network throughout the Nazi years, only to see it broken in show trials under the Communists in 1949–50. While space does not permit a recounting of the turmoils of the Saxon cooperative movement after 1933, it is interesting to note that today (1998) some of the most successful consumer cooperatives in united Germany are in historic centers such as Leipzig and Eilenburg. This suggests that some local continuities persist after more than half a century under two dictatorships.[48]

IV.   Conclusions

Other states in the German empire had greater numbers of cooperatives than did Saxony. Statistics show that in 1907 the Kingdom of Saxony and the Prussian province of Saxony together counted 7.9 percent of all the cooperatives in the German Empire. But these Saxon cooperatives were large, with about 500,000 members, or 12.4 percent of the national total.[49] This meant that the two Saxonys had more members than all of Bavaria, more than the Rhine province, more than any other two provinces put

---

46. BA Berlin, Bestand 95, Nr. 154.

47. Ibid., Nr. 142.

48. DG Bank, *Die Genossenschaften in der Bundesrepublik Deutschland,* 59. The incorporation of reorganized enterprises from the former GDR into overall German cooperative statistics also brought a large increase in the total number of trade (*gewerbliche*) cooperatives, housing cooperatives, and agricultural cooperatives starting in 1993, the first year these were included. Unfortunately, limits of space do not allow me to discuss these types of cooperatives.

49. Calculated from Preußische Central-Genossenschaftskasse, *Mitteilungen zur deutschen Genossenschaftsstatistik für 1907,* bearbeitet von Dr. A. Petersilie, *Sonderabdruck aus dem XXIX. Ergänzungshefte zur Zeitschrift des Königlich Preußischen Landesamts* (Berlin, 1909), table 1a.

together. These statistics reflect the predominance in Saxony of the larger and more urban kinds of cooperatives, the Schulze-Delitzsch credit cooperatives and the consumer cooperatives. Ultimately, however, the greatest importance of Saxon cooperatives was not in their numbers, but in their character and, above all, their ideological orientations.

To return to the question posed at the outset: Does the history of cooperatives suggest a Saxony that led Germany in economic and social development, in formal organization and integration? Or did Saxony, on the contrary, lag behind or deviate from some ideal path? Perhaps the short answer is "both." The entrenched — perhaps "unmodern"? — polarizations in Saxon society were what, in part, drove the widespread development of cooperatives (themselves a modern form of organization) while the high degree of development of cooperatives contributed in part to the antagonistic dualism that may make Saxony appear exceptional. As broad, popular organizations that were also formal and market-oriented, cooperatives were poised on a knife-edge of ambiguities.

First and foremost, cooperatives suggest that it is futile to try to separate local movements or cultures from regional and national movements and events. Cooperatives were in essence *local* institutions; yet at the same time they were strongly integrated into regional and national movements, associated with ideological social-economic groupings, and influenced by larger-scale political developments. It is difficult to correlate "modern" with national (or central) and "backward" with local (or peripheral): the local embodied the national. Hence one can only hope for more studies of how individual cooperatives negotiated conflicting demands: of localism and universalism, of tradition-bound neighborhood hierarchies and sweeping democratic ideals, of hostility to capitalist retailing and adoption of modern merchandising.

Second, the history recounted here suggests that Saxony's distinctive artisanal and industrial structure in the nineteenth and early twentieth centuries had a great deal to do with the particular forms and ideological content of Saxony's social and political movements.

Third, looking at the history of cooperatives reinforces the impression that the deep antagonism between those who claimed to speak for the working class and those who claimed to speak for the *Mittelstand* was a driving force in Saxon public life from the 1880s on. No other cleavage so decisively affected the Saxon cooperative movement as this one. Arguably, it was the articulation of this particular cleavage that represents the Saxon cooperative movement's greatest contribution to the wider German scene.

Fourth, the Saxon case highlights the vulnerability of democratic mass movements to political and social turmoil. From the turn of the century onward, cooperatives in Saxony faced repeated disruptions from war, radical right-wing movements, and polarized social-political conflict. No national history more conspicuously than Germany's, and within Germany no regional history more conspicuously than Saxony's, makes clearer the painstaking process of building and defending popular organizations, and the extent to which such organizations are dependent upon a functional and stable civil society.

Fifth and last, the contested history of cooperatives in Saxony makes clear that social movements do not follow a linear narrative of modernism; they cannot be neatly slotted into a bipolar dualism as either wholehearted advocates or opponents of progress. Cooperative movements reflected efforts by broad and divergent social groups, not to implement the modern or the antimodern, but to achieve futures that were in their judgment better than what they saw developing without their intervention. Members of cooperatives embraced a pluralism of conceptions of society and of future social and economic orders. Saxony's largest and most distinctive cooperative movements sought to remake what their members believed to be an emerging social order, to explore alternatives and to pursue variations. In doing this they freely combined formal, market-oriented institutions with efforts to perpetuate and revive solidarity based on community or on social status. Of course, the curtain that fell in 1933 is a reminder that such explorations can be cut short. Words and ideologies really do matter—so do power relationships. Voices can be silenced; simplistic dualisms can be imposed by force. One outcome is that some of Saxony's and Germany's largest social movements have nearly been forgotten.

Part 3

AUTHORITARIANISM, DEMOCRACY, AND THE "DANGEROUS CLASSES"

On the Disappearance of a Political Party from German History: The Saxon People's Party, 1866–1869

Karsten Rudolph

I. The Three Connotations of "People's Party" in German History

When someone in Germany today speaks of a "people's party" (*Volkspartei*), this denotes a type of politically regulative organization that began an exceptional success story in Germany in the 1960s but encountered a serious crisis in the 1980s.[1] The term describes the concept or the construction of a political party that on the one hand attempts continuously to attach traditional members and current voters to the party but on the other hand also strives to make inroads into the social and political recruitment pool of other parties. In contrast to its predecessors — the ideologically committed parties of mass integration — the people's parties, or "catch-all parties," have a tendency to relinquish basic ideological, programmatic, and confessional convictions in order to maximize votes or to achieve political compromise.[2]

But there is usually more at stake than elevating the principle of vote maximization to the raison d'être of the party itself. The great promise of the "genuine people's party"[3] lay (and lies) in the transcen-

---

1. Gordon Smith, "The German Volkspartei and the Career of the Catch-All Concept," in *Party Government and Political Culture in Western Germany*, ed. Herbert Döring and Gordon Smith (London, 1982), 59–76.

2. Otto Kirchheimer, "Der Wandel des westeuropäischen Parteiensystems," *Politische Vierteljahresschrift* 6 (1965): 20–41.

3. This term derives from the "Bergheimer Memorandum," the product of a circle of young Westphalian Social Democrats who formerly belonged to the Hitler Youth and who, after the defeat of the SPD in the 1953 federal elections, demanded that traditional-

dence of milieu boundaries and class barriers, by means of an adaptation to social and economic change. This promise is anticipated in the suggestion that this "new type of party"[4] harmonizes the relationship between party and people, between state and society. Every party in the German Federal Republic fears the stigma of being a party catering to special interest groups instead of a people's party. In historical perspective, the Social Democratic Party first accomplished the transformation from a party of mass integration to a modern people's party. The legendary Godesberg party manifesto of 1959 inscribed this transformation verbatim: "The Social Democratic Party represents freedom of conscience. It is a community of people who originate from different confessional and intellectual backgrounds. . . . The Social Democratic Party has developed from a workers' party into a party of the people."[5]

Moving backward in time, we find that the term "people's party" during the Weimar Republic stood in opposition to the concept of a class or confessional party. In the 1920s, the German Center Party (Deutsche Zentrumspartei) also called itself a "Christian People's Party," which indicated its initial interconfessional tendencies. These tendencies only came to fruition in the Christian Democratic Union and the Christian Social Union after the Second World War. The conservative currents in Germany united after the revolution of 1918 and adopted the appellation German National People's Party (Deutschnationale Volkspartei), not least in order to shed the appearance of being an old, regionally narrow, Prussian Junker party — an image that would have been a hindrance in the era of modern democracy. Finally, the National Liberals, who after 1918 operated under the name of German People's Party (Deutsche Volkspartei), adopted the term "people" from the Progressive People's Party (Fortschrittliche Volkspartei), which had been founded in 1912 by bringing together Prussian National Liberals with central and southern German left liberals. The adoption of these party names by no means signaled avowal of the democratic tradition of 1848. Rather, they helped propagate the fiction of a "people's community" (*Volksgemeinschaft*), which

---

ism in the party be put aside. Everhard Holtmann, "Die neuen Lassalleaner: SPD und HJ-Generation nach 1945," in *Von Stalingrad zur Währungsreform*, ed. Martin Broszat et al. (Munich, 1988), 205–8.

4. On the normative substance of this concept, see Hermann Kaste and Joachim Raschke, "Zur Politik der Volkspartei," in *Auf dem Weg zum Einparteienstaat*, ed. Wolf Dieter Narr (Opladen, 1977), 30–31. More recent party research has been trying to focus attention on the fact that the concept of a "people's party" represents a problematic academic term, an instrument of internal and external party conflicts, and a constructed myth cultivated by the parties themselves; Alf Mintzel, *Die Volksparteien: Typus und Wirklichkeit* (Opladen, 1984).

5. "Grundsatzprogramm der SPD, beschlossen vom a.o. Parteitag in Bad Godesberg 1959," in Susanne Miller and Heinrich Potthoff, *Kleine Geschichte der SPD: Darstellung und Dokumentation*, 7th rev. ed. (Bonn, 1991), 408, 420.

was conceived to stand in opposition to the "democratic people's state" of the Social Democratic workers' movement. Only the left liberals recalled the tradition of 1848. After 1918 they named their new party the German Democratic Party (Deutsche Demokratische Partei).[6]

Lastly, in the 1860s the term "people's party" stood for the "party-political manifestation [*Parteiung*] of (federalist) democracy,"[7] which in essence was based on a political alliance of workers, small master artisans, and journeymen, as well as politically oriented burghers. This tradition encompassed the Democratic People's Party (Demokratische Volkspartei; 1863–66), the German People's Party (Deutsche Volkspartei; 1868–1910), and the subject of this essay: the Saxon People's Party (Sächsische Volkspartei, or SVP; 1866–69). Within this tradition, the parties in question based their opposition to authoritarianism on the will of the people. They distanced themselves with just as much determination from the customary liberal party of notables (*Honoratiorenpartei*), such as the German Progressive Party (Deutsche Fortschrittspartei), as from the autocratically led and centrally directed type of workers' party represented by the General German Workers' Association (Allgemeiner Deutscher Arbeiterverein, or ADAV).[8] As far as the political orientation of these new people's parties was concerned, the Mannheim Workers' Education Association formulated the following paradigmatic statement at the beginning of 1868: "[T]he democratic party must cease to be merely a political party; it must make its duty the transformation of social disparities [and] the elevation of the working classes and deprived fellow citizens — it ought to become a people's party in the true sense of the word."[9] These were almost exactly the words the Prussian democrat

---

6. Detlef Lehnert, "Zur historischen Soziographie der 'Volkspartei': Wählerstruktur und Regionalisierung im deutschen Parteiensystem seit der Reichsgründung," *Archiv für Sozialgeschichte* 29 (1989): 3.

7. Richard Stöss, "Einleitung: Struktur und Entwicklung des Parteiensystems der Bundesrepublik — Eine Theorie," in idem, *Parteienhandbuch: Die Parteien der Bundesrepublik Deutschland,* special ed. (Opladen, 1986), 1:122.

8. Rolf Weber, "Demokratische Volkspartei: 1863–1866," in *Lexikon zur Parteiengeschichte: Die bürgerlichen und kleinbürgerlichen Parteien und Verbände in Deutschland, 1789–1945,* ed. Dieter Fricke et al., 4 vols. (Cologne, 1983), 1:504–13; Ludwig Elm, "Deutsche Volkspartei (DtVp): 1868–1910," in *Die bürgerlichen Parteien in Deutschland: Handbuch der Geschichte der bürgerlichen Parteien und anderer Interessenorganisationen vom Vormärz bis zum Jahr 1945,* ed. Dieter Fricke et al., 2 vols. (Berlin, 1968), 1:637–44; Friedrich Payer, "Die deutsche Volkspartei und die Bismarck'sche Politik," in *Patria: Bücher für Kultur und Freizeit* (Berlin, 1908), 1–19.

9. "Zuschrift in der Deutschen Arbeiterhalle vom 7.2.1868," cited in Andrea Hoffend, "Verhinderte Sozialdemokraten: Die Rolle des Mannheimer Linksliberalismus im Emanzipationsprozeß der deutschen Arbeiterbewegung nach 1860," in *Sozialismus und Kommunismus im Wandel (Hermann Weber zum 65. Geburtstag),* ed. Klaus Schönhoven and Dietrich Staritz (Cologne, 1993), 129.

Johann Jacoby had used when he addressed his voters only a few days before.[10]

II.   The Long Shadow of Borussian Historiography

The history of all these people's parties — particularly that of the Saxon People's Party — has been relegated to the periphery of German historiography. This unfortunate state of affairs is not due only to shifts in terminology. Traditional conservative and national historiography considered such party formations outdated phenomena after the failure of the 1848–49 Revolutions, the Danish conflict of 1864, the Austro-Prussian War of 1866, and the unification of the German Reich under Prussian leadership in 1871. In this scholarly tradition, such parties were not merely outdated; they were aberrations — flickering flares that illuminated nothing — in German history.

This dismissive viewpoint was particularly characteristic of the writings of Johann Gustav Droysen, the founder of the *kleindeutsch* historiographical tradition. After the mid-1860s, the position of politically active historians who opposed Bismarck became very tenuous. It was symptomatic that the Prussian court historian, Heinrich von Treitschke, went further even than Bismarck with his demands that the small- and medium-sized states be annexed. Bismarck, for his part, preferred a federalist solution, though one that assured Prussian hegemony in the North German Confederation. Theodor Mommsen spoke apodictically of the "bankruptcy of particularism," while Hermann Baumgarten and Heinrich von Sybel either openly supported the policies of the Prussian minister president or portrayed their *kleindeutsch* outcome — as do their disciples today — as inevitable.[11]

Unofficially, the year 1866 was stylized in this historical writing as the "fateful year" in which German liberals concluded their about-face during the Prussian constitutional crisis, a crisis whose resolution also signaled the coming-apart of the struggle for constitutional freedom. In the new chapter of German history that allegedly began in 1866, Saxony's political development appeared strangely regressive. The Saxon People's Party in particular seemed little more than a sorrowful relic of the dashed hopes of 1848.[12] Even today, a historian such as Hans-Ulrich

---

10. Johann Jacoby, *Gesammelte Schriften und Reden* (Hamburg, 1872), 338.

11. Thomas Nipperdey, *Deutsche Geschichte, 1866–1918,* 2 vols. (Munich, 1992), 2:24; Hans-Ulrich Wehler, *Deutsche Gesellschaftsgeschichte,* 3 vols. to date (Munich, 1995), 3:236ff.

12. The notion of the "Schicksalsjahr 1866" can be found, for instance, in Gustav Mayer, "Die Lösung der deutschen Frage im Jahre 1866 und die Arbeiterbewegung," in *Festgaben für Wilhelm Lexix* (Jena, 1907; reprint, Frankfurt a. M., 1989); see also Hagen

Wehler regards this outcome as so inevitable that the central and south German movement for a democratic people's party can be reduced to the "particularist" SVP—that is, to a prologue anticipating the founding of the Eisenach wing of Social Democracy.[13]

In contrast to this interpretation, Theodor Schieder has described the reorganization of Germany after 1866 into three spheres of political power, "whose interrelationship remained unclear": the North German Confederation led by Prussia, the states located south of the Main River, and the Austrian Empire.[14] Even though the withdrawal of Vienna from German politics strongly favored developments leading toward the *kleindeutsch*-Prussian nation-state, the external political constellation appeared to be anything but unequivocal, and certainly not complete. In Bavaria, Catholic particularism among the peasants regenerated itself and, after 1868, fed the activities of the Patriots' Party. In Württemberg, the federalist-democratic forces, most of whom were petty bourgeois, joined the People's Party. Lastly, "petty-bourgeois democracy" in central Germany kept a foothold in the Thuringian People's Party and particularly in the Saxon People's Party. Although Saxony had already been forced into the North German Confederation, federalist-democratic convictions were sustained by the hope that a *großdeutsch*-democratic bridgehead could be formed there.[15]

Historians like Baumgarten or Treitschke were not genuinely representative of National Liberal policy. Baumgarten on principle denied the bourgeoisie any capacity for constructive political innovation. Treitschke advocated a realignment of bourgeois political demands in favor of a "social monarchy" capable of suppressing the discontented masses. Moreover, many liberals saw plenty of room for maneuver even within the *kleindeutsch* solution to the German question. Hence one need not speak

Schulze, *Der Weg zum Nationalstaat: Die deutsche Nationalbewegung vom 18. Jahrhundert bis zur Reichsgründung,* 2d ed. (Munich, 1986), 118f. Wehler's *kleindeutsch* viewpoint has been appropriately criticized in John Breuilly, "Auf dem Weg zur deutschen Gesellschaft? Der dritte Band von Wehlers '*Gesellschaftsgeschichte*,'" *Geschichte und Gesellschaft* 24 (1998): 136–68. This orientation is particularly recognizable in the chapter on the revival of the political parties in the course of unification, where Wehler ignores the SVP and instead follows the outline of Michael Stürmer's account in *Die Reichsgründung: Deutscher Nationalstaat und europäisches Gleichgewicht im Zeitalter Bismarcks,* 3d ed. (Munich, 1990), 49ff.

13. See Wehler, *Deutsche Gesellschaftsgeschichte,* 3:348.

14. Theodor Schieder, *Vom Deutschen Bund zum Deutschen Reich,* 3d ed. (Munich, 1975), 176ff. See also Klaus Erich Pollmann, "Vom Verfassungskonflikt zum Verfassungskompromiß: Funktion und Selbstverständnis des verfassungsberatenden Reichstages des Norddeutschen Bundes," in *Gesellschaft, Parlament und Regierung: Zur Geschichte des Parlamentarismus in Deutschland,* ed. Gerhard A. Ritter (Düsseldorf, 1974), 189–203.

15. On the Thuringian People's Party, see Ursula Herrmann and Karl Brundig, "Die Agitationsreise August Bebels durch Thüringen im Juni 1869: Zur Vorbereitung der Sozialdemokratischen Arbeiterpartei," *Zeitschrift für Geschichte* 18 (1970): 906.

one-sidedly of their "resignation." For both National Liberals and pro-gressive liberals, 1866 did not signify or necessitate a hiatus in their quest for national and constitutional goals. Rather, it represented the *starting point* for a remarkable liberal ascent in Germany. This helps explain why Ludwig Bamberger's slogan — "through unity to liberty" — found such an echo, not only among liberals but also among workers.[16] In the North German Reichstag, the president of the ADAV, Johann Baptist von Schweitzer, claimed to speak in favor of the impending reforms "within the newly forming fatherland," whereas the faction led by August Bebel and Wilhelm Liebknecht allegedly stood "outside of it."[17] In short, the decisive break in *this* liberal tradition did not occur in 1866, but rather twelve years later, when the various liberal currents gradually came to worship an integrative type of nationalism and when a defense of the industrial bourgeoisie's class interests came to the fore. After 1878, the political influence of these liberals began to wane once and for all.[18]

In this malleable political constellation, which has been sketched only in outline here, the Saxon People's Party appears as anything but anachronistic. In contrast to the conservative champions of an out-of-date brand of Reich patriotism, who regarded 1866 as a catastrophe because Bismarck had committed a kind of treason against his class, the Saxon People's Party provided a ray of hope for the "little people" — the commit-ted liberals and the middle-class democrats — who still strove for the de-mocratization, parliamentarization, and federalization of Germany. Jo-hann Jacoby concluded that Bismarck had played into the hands of the democrats, and that they would "make hay while the sun shines."[19] Wil-helm Liebknecht went so far as to call on the south German representa-tives at the Nuremberg convention of the workers' associations in 1868 to tear up the military treaties with Prussia in case of a war and to make the

---

16. Cf. the motto of the Erfurter ADAV general meeting in late December 1866; *Der Social-Democrat*, 28 Oct. 1866.

17. *Stenographischer Bericht über die Verhandlungen des Reichstags des Nord-deutschen Bundes*, 1. Legislaturperiode, Session 1867 (Berlin, 1867), 1:471.

18. See Heinrich August Winkler, "1866 und 1878: Der Liberalismus in der Krise," in *Wendepunkte deutscher Geschichte, 1848–1990*, ed. Carola Stern and Heinrich August Winkler, rev. ed. (Frankfurt a. M., 1994), 50ff.; Wolfram Siemann, *Gesellschaft im Aufbruch: Deutschland, 1849–1871* (Frankfurt a. M., 1990), 221; and the survey in Helga Grebing, *Der "deutsche Sonderweg" in Europa, 1806–1945: Eine Kritik* (Stuttgart, 1986), 96ff. See also the older study by Karl-Georg Faber, "Realpolitik als Ideologie: Die Bedeutung des Jahres 1866 für das politische Denken in Deutschland," *Historische Zeit-schrift* 203 (1966): 1–45. For Saxony, see Richard J. Bazillion, "Liberalism, Moderniza-tion, and the Social Question in the Kingdom of Saxony, 1830–90," in *In Search of a Liberal Germany: Studies in the History of German Liberalism from 1789 to the Present*, ed. Konrad H. Jarausch and Larry Eugene Jones (New York, 1990), 87–110.

19. Jacoby, *Schriften und Reden,* 339.

"war of the Caesars into a war of resurrection of the peoples."[20] In the histories of the workers' movement, this appeal usually disappears behind the resolution to join the International Working Men's Association, the "First International," which in turn is alleged to have signified the "break with the democratic wing of liberalism."[21] In retrospect, such hopes for the national revolutionary movement may seem to have been wholly unrealistic. Yet for Bebel and Liebknecht, even after the Battle of Königgrätz, it appeared to be a more obvious course than national political capitulation, political resignation, or escape into social revolution.

III.   The Saxon People's Party in the Historiography of the Workers' Movement

The dominant motif in histories of the German workers' movement dates from Schweitzer's pronouncement of 1865: "Prussian bayonets or German proletarians' fists—we do not see a third option."[22] Franz Mehring, the Social Democratic historian and editor of Schweitzer's political writings, concurred with this point of view. In the Leipzig SPD's commemorative volume published in 1903, Mehring considered the path of a people's party to be a one-way street, or at best a marginal development in the history of the German workers' movement.[23] Mehring popularized the Prussian military solution not only by portraying it as the lesser evil in comparison to Austrian supremacy, but by labeling it a decisive historical advance in the development of a capitalist economy on a national scale.

An orthodox conception of how German Social Democracy was formed as an independent class movement was cultivated for forty years by historians in the German Democratic Republic. As such it severed the continuity of the radical democratic-federalist tradition, which extended through the Saxon People's Party and the Social Democratic Workers' Party to the modern German workers' movement. Thus GDR historiogra-

---

20. *Bericht über den 5. Vereinstag der deutschen Arbeitervereine zu Nürnberg, 1868* (Leipzig, 1928), 27.

21. Cf. Gustav Mayer's pioneering study, *Die Trennung der proletarischen von der bürgerlichen Demokratie in Deutschland, 1863–1870* (Leipzig, 1912), reprinted in idem, *Radikalismus, Sozialismus und bürgerliche Demokratie*, ed. Hans-Ulrich Wehler, 2d ed. (Frankfurt a. M., 1969), 108–78; Wolfgang Abendroth, *Einführung in die Geschichte der Arbeiterbewegung*, vol. 1, *Von den Anfängen bis 1933* (Heilbronn, 1985), 100; and Miller and Potthoff, *Kleine Geschichte der SPD*, 39.

22. Cited in Mayer, "Lösung," 235.

23. Franz Mehring, "Die Leipziger Arbeiterbewegung, 1862–1867," in *Die Gründung der deutschen Sozialdemokratie: Eine Festschrift der Leipziger Arbeiter zum 23. Mai 1903* (Leipzig, 1903), 40ff.

phy represented the latter as essentially Marxist in inspiration and distinct from the ADAV. Of course, there were nuances within this general interpretation. Rolf Weber, for instance, viewed the alternative solution of the German question under Austrian hegemony as a complete illusion. Weber also considered the Habsburg Empire even "more reactionary than the Prussian Bonapartist state." In his view, the formation of a German people's party might have been possible only between 1864 and 1866; this opportunity, however, was destroyed during the Battle of Königgrätz.[24] Some years later, official GDR historiography was more lenient in its judgment of Bebel and Liebknecht. It nevertheless portrayed them crudely as adhering to a fictitious proletarian-socialist line. Now Johann Jacoby was depicted as a hopeless idealist who, even after 1872, believed in the fundamental "congruity of the petty bourgeoisie and the workers' party."[25] Hartmut Zwahr, in his study of the formation of the Leipzig proletariat as a class—a pioneering work of GDR scholarship—does not mention the Saxon People's Party at all.[26] Instead the substance of the proletariat's political and ideological vision is aligned with a teleological conception of class formation to suggest that in 1869 the proletariat fit neatly into the framework of a proletarian party based on Marxist principles. In GDR scholarship, then, anything that upset this monolithic but distorted interpretation was simply ignored: the anti-Prussian dispositions of Bebel and Liebknecht, the workers' movement as part of the national movement, the decision to form a people's party, and so on. Only the East German biographer of Bismarck, Ernst Engelberg, refused to follow the simplified view inaugurated by Schweitzer and continued by so many GDR historians. In the late 1980s Engelberg stood up for Bebel's and Liebknecht's attempt to set in motion an "anti-Bismarckian people's movement." Engelberg also expressed doubts as to whether the "workers' movement" could be distinguished easily from "that of the petty-bourgeois masses."[27]

Social Democratic historiography, too, even though it fixes the founding of the party in 1863, has rarely granted the Saxon People's Party any significance other than having served as a radical-democratic

---

24. Rolf Weber, "Das kleinbürgerlich-demokratische Element in der deutschen Nationalbewegung vor 1866," in *Probleme der Reichsgründungszeit, 1848–1879,* ed. Helmut Böhme, 2d ed. (Cologne, 1972), 72ff.

25. See Dieter Fricke, ed., *Deutsche Demokraten: Die nichtproletarischen demokratischen Kräfte in Deutschland, 1830 bis 1945* (Cologne, 1981), 70.

26. See Hartmut Zwahr, *Zur Konstituierung des Proletariats als Klasse: Strukturuntersuchung über das Leipziger Proletariat während der industriellen Revolution* (Munich, 1980), 204ff.

27. Ernst Engelberg, "Sozialisten und Demokraten am Vorabend des Krieges von 1866," in *Demokratie, Antifaschismus, Sozialismus in der deutschen Geschichte,* ed. Helmut Bleiber and Walter Schmidt (Berlin, 1988), 190, 192f.

cocoon from which the Eisenach wing burst in 1869 as "the second workers' party in Germany" (the ADAV having been the first).[28] Social Democratic revisionism never went as far as turning the idea of the old people's party into a viable concept of the future, although it would have stood to reason. Indeed, everything that existed apart from the ADAV or before the Social Democratic Workers' Party (Sozialdemokratische Arbeiterpartei, or SDAP) appeared relegated to the dim and distant past of the socialist movement. That it came to this was partly Bebel's own doing. He contributed to the legend that the Saxon People's Party constituted something of a disguised preliminary stage of the SDAP. Thus Bebel later portrayed the decision to abstain from a declaration of socialist principles at the founding of the SDAP as a purely tactical move.[29] In 1877 — before Bismarck's antisocialist laws were passed, and before the reorganization of the Social Democratic "party of the people" into a "class party of industrial workers" had occurred — Karl Holthof complained in the weekly *Die Waage* about how rapidly the shadow of the rising political workers' movement, unified at Gotha in 1875, was casting a shadow over the Saxon People's Party: "Today, any true and righteous Social Democrat is not allowed to know that, before his party, a democratic one existed."[30]

No one has highlighted this sharp turn more accurately than Arthur Rosenberg. Rosenberg emphasized that socialist workers in the *Kaiserreich* no longer had any living connection to 1848: the SPD by that point had come to represent a new brand of protest party — a party, moreover, composed mainly of skilled industrial workers — that was far removed from the "people's party of 1848 provenance." According to Rosenberg, Marx and Engels never fully understood this fact.[31] From the perspective of revolutionary democracy, the development of the European workers' parties since the 1860s appeared as a structural aberration: they had retreated from active revolutionary politics in favor of representing the occupational interests of (a part of) the proletariat. And despite growing organizational strength, they had isolated themselves politically as well. As a result, "the gesture of protest and isolation vis-à-vis capitalist society . . . had become a vital necessity for most workers."[32]

28. For the "classic" account, see Abendroth, *Einführung;* also Miller and Potthoff, *Kleine Geschichte der SPD,* 39.

29. Brigitte Seebacher-Brandt, *Bebel: Künder und Kärrner im Kaiserreich* (Bonn, 1988), 87.

30. Karl Holthof, "Zur Geschichte der deutschen Volkspartei," *Die Waage* 5 (1877): 505–6.

31. Arthur Rosenberg, *Demokratie und Sozialismus: Zur politischen Geschichte der letzten 150 Jahre* (1935–37; reprint Frankfurt a. M., 1962), 185, 250, 253.

32. Ibid., 265.

The history of the people's party movement in the 1860s, then, has remained obscured in three ways. Besides the long shadow cast by Borussian historiography, it is overshadowed by the notion of a socialist class party of industrial workers and clouded by historians' interest in organizational history. This latter interpretive focus conceives of the separation of bourgeois democracy from proletarian democracy primarily as an organizational split or as an escape of the proletarian party from a tactical political alliance with the democratic petty bourgeoisie. It shows little interest either in alternative processes of party formation or in exploring the room for maneuver that sociopolitical movements directed against unification "from above" actually still enjoyed in the 1860s.[33]

IV. Regional Preconditions for the Transformation of the Democratic Movement

In a comparative regional study, Dieter Dowe has perceptively analyzed the "development of class movements in place of people's movements that transcended classes" between the 1840s and the late 1860s. Focusing on the Prussian Rhine Province and the Kingdom of Württemberg, Dowe rightly suggests that political and economic regions need to be considered more concretely in historical research. He has worked out two substantially different lines of attack.[34] On the one hand, he notes that the Rhine Province, artificially created in 1815, took a pioneering role in the industrialization of Germany, combining a rapid expansion of paid labor, the experience of exploitation, and a particularly backward political constitution. On the other hand, the kingdom in southwest Germany, having doubled its territory in 1806, was characterized by small-scale industry, by "divided enterprises," by workers' strong attachment to their own plot of land, and by a politically progressive constitution. In the 1848–49 Revolution, the bourgeoisie in the Rhineland remained loyal to Prussian authori-

---

33. See Mayer, *Trennung;* Wolfgang Schieder, "Das Scheitern des bürgerlichen Radikalismus und die sozialistische Parteibildung in Deutschland," in *Sozialdemokratie zwischen Klassenbewegung und Volkspartei,* ed. Hans Mommsen (Frankfurt a. M., 1974), 17–34; and, most recently, Roswitha Wieczoreck, "Zur Trennung der proletarischen von der bürgerlichen Demokratie: Die sozialistische Parteibildung in Dresden," in *Demokratie und Emanzipation zwischen Saale und Elbe: Beiträge zur Geschichte der sozialdemokratischen Arbeiterbewegung bis 1933,* ed. Helga Grebing, Hans Mommsen, and Karsten Rudolph (Essen, 1993), 26–41.

34. Dieter Dowe, "Deutschland: Das Rheinland und Württemberg im Vergleich," in *Europäische Arbeiterbewegungen im 19. Jahrhundert,* ed. Jürgen Kocka (Göttingen, 1983), 77. See also Siemann, *Gesellschaft,* 231ff.; and Dieter Langewiesche, "Liberalismus und Region," in *Liberalismus und Region: Zur Geschichte des deutschen Liberalismus im 19. Jahrhundert,* ed. Lothar Gall and Dieter Langewiesche (Munich, 1995), 1–18.

ties and welcomed the king's constitutional coup d'état of December 1848. In Württemberg, by contrast, the Swabian middle classes split into a liberal and a democratic wing. The Rhineland was characterized by a continuity in the workers' association movement, which in turn was rooted in the 1848–49 Revolution and in the local chapters of the Communist League; by strong class tensions and a massive strike movement; and by the absence of a reasonably consistent, nonproletarian democratic movement. In Württemberg, on the other hand, the workers' movement showed a uniformly liberal-democratic tendency. The first major strike took place only in 1872. Until the 1870s, the ADAV remained a marginal phenomenon, because the democratic-federalist, anti-Prussian People's Party had forged a close bond between workers and burghers. And even after the late subsequent division of proletarian and bourgeois democracy, the SDAP and the People's Party frequently worked together on the local level.[35]

Integrating Saxony into this comparative sketch suggests that it represented a kind of middle (or even mediating) position between the Rhenish and Württemberg poles. In terms of socioeconomic development, Saxony resembled the Rhineland; it also experienced the early detachment of the proletarian workers' movement from the liberal-democratic movement. However, the appearance of class conflict cannot be reduced to socioeconomic determinants alone. In Saxony, and particularly in Leipzig, the separation of the proletariat from the bourgeoisie occurred in the course of intense debates about national issues, though the "German question" had implications for domestic and economic policy as well. Ernst Engelberg has written that Austria had already experienced its "economic Königgrätz" in 1865, upon the conclusion of the trade treaty with the Zollverein. Against this backdrop, and in terms of its constitutional and national options, Saxony was closer to Württemberg than to the Prussian Rhine province.[36] The establishment of the Saxon People's Party initially served to block the formation of an independent class party of workers; subsequently, it tended to retard its development. Above all, the creation of the SVP was a response to specific regional circumstances and the particular nature of the democratic movement in the Kingdom of Saxony.

---

35. See also the essential work by Dieter Langewiesche, *Liberalismus und Demokratie in Württemberg zwischen Revolution und Reichsgründung* (Düsseldorf, 1974).

36. See Roland Zeise, "Zur Rolle der sächsischen Bourgeoisie im Ringen um die wirtschaftspolitische Vormachtstellung in Deutschland in den fünfziger und sechziger Jahren des 19. Jahrhunderts," in *Die großpreußisch-militaristische Reichsgründung, 1871: Voraussetzungen und Folgen,* ed. Horst Bartel and Ernst Engelberg, 2 vols. (Berlin, 1971), 1:233–70; and Karsten Rudolph, *Die sächsische Sozialdemokratie vom Kaiserreich zur Republik (1871–1923)* (Weimar, 1995), 34ff.

V. The Formation of the Saxon People's Party and the Rise of the Democracy Movement

In Saxony, defeat at Königgrätz on 3 July 1866 did not spell the demise of the idea of a people's party. On the contrary, the outcome of Königgrätz gave it real impetus. It is not at all clear that one can speak — even for Saxony alone — of a whirlwind of change blowing through Germany in 1866–67, one that fundamentally restructured the rules of political culture in the direction of new processes of nation-building, new forms of political mobilization, new ("modern") cultural orientations, and new perceptions of the democratic idea that included equal and free male suffrage.[37] Was not quite a different form of nation-building being organized, especially in Saxony but elsewhere, too? Did not political mobilization occur along more familiar paths already trodden by popular movements seeking to square the circle "from below"? At any rate, some skepticism is always appropriate when fundamental processes of change are said to have occurred in just a few months, and in this instance such skepticism seems very much called for. Considering the political threshold that is said to have been crossed on 3 July 1866, it is rather surprising that the protagonists of the Saxon People's Party tenaciously clung to their basic political concept and vigorously embarked on an effort to reorganize the regional democracy movement along lines first formulated in 1848. In contrast to the spokesman of the First International, Johann Philipp Becker, the SVP's leaders did not at all perceive German democracy to have been defeated alongside Austria at Königgrätz; that defeat came some years later.[38]

In May 1869, Wilhelm Liebknecht addressed the members of the Democratic Workers' Association in Berlin and declared that the Social Democrats still had to distance themselves from two "socialist" competitors. On the one side stood "Prussian court socialism" around Hermann Wagener, a conservative advisor of Bismarck who advocated universal suffrage, the implementation of sociopolitical reforms, and the dispensing of favors to socialists of Ferdinand Lassalle's ilk, all "in order to paralyze democracy." On the other hand, Social Democrats had to distinguish themselves from the kind of "National Liberal socialism" advocated by Johannes Miquel, who subsequently would rise to the top of the Prussian state as minister of finance. Liebknecht contrasted these two currents with "democratic socialism which, setting out from the insepara-

---

37. This is the argument found in James Retallack, "'Why Can't a Saxon Be More Like a Prussian?' Regional Identities and the Birth of Modern Political Culture in Germany, 1866–1867," *Canadian Journal of History* 32 (1997): 26–55, esp. 29.

38. Mayer, "Lösung," 267.

bility of the political and the social question, proudly rejects any endorsement of the status quo and intends to fight for the democratic state by means of a society organized along socialist lines." Thus Liebknecht in effect provided the rallying cry for a German Social Democratic People's Party, just a few weeks before the creation of the SDAP. Liebknecht suggested that socialist and democratic tendencies should no longer compete; instead they should strengthen and complement one another and thereby create a "serious, magnificent social democratic movement."

Far from being a cry in the wilderness, Liebknecht's appeal built upon the pronouncements of others who had advocated much the same thing for years. For example, at a workers' convention of the Maingau in July 1865 — that is, at the height of the campaign for the amalgamation of the People's Party with the ADAV and the Union of German Workers' Associations (Verein Deutscher Arbeitervereine, or VDAV) — Ludwig Eckhardt had expressed similar sentiments.[39] Since the establishment of the Saxon People's Party on 19 August 1866 in Chemnitz, Bebel and Liebknecht had continuously striven for the same goal.[40] And nothing less than Liebknecht's "magnificent" social democratic movement was sought by Johann Peter Eichelsdörfer, the long-standing leader of Mannheim's Workers' Education Association, when he joined with the south German democratic leader Leopold Sonnemann to keep open the possibility of merging the SDAP, the ADAV, and the People's Party.

Therefore we can legitimately ask whether Dowe is really describing the "development of class movements in place of people's movements that transcended classes" outside the Prussian Rhine provinces. Did the workers' movement really break away from the general democratic movement?[41] Or was it not the bourgeoisie instead that gradually withdrew from it? Did central and southern Germany not actually witness, albeit for the last time, the surge of a people's movement that transcended classes?[42]

At any rate, the Saxon democracy movement became immensely popular during the summer of 1866. In February 1862, the new Prussian envoy in Dresden had reported that the Saxon king believed Saxony did not lack democrats but that they were "clearly in the minority" — an

---

39. Wilhelm Liebknecht, *Über die politische Stellung der Sozialdemokratie,* 9th ed. (Berlin, 1893), 18–19, 22; Fricke, *Deutsche Demokraten,* 56.

40. The assessment in Hoffend, "Verhinderte Sozialdemokraten," 111, goes amiss insofar as it suggests that Bebel and Liebknecht regarded the people's party only as a "transitional phase on the path to an independent class organization of labor."

41. Dowe, "Das Rheinland und Württemberg im Vergleich," 78.

42. See the balanced assessment by Dieter Langewiesche, *Liberalismus in Deutschland* (Frankfurt a. M., 1988), 120.

appraisal that was immediately questioned in Berlin.[43] Three years later, however, the meetings organized by Saxon democrats were filled to bursting—as, for instance, when Liebknecht specifically called on workers in Chemnitz, the "Saxon Manchester," to organize because "the fate of Germany . . . and the future of democracy . . . rested above all in their hands."[44]

To speak of these developments as a "revolutionary crisis"—as GDR historians tended to do[45]—is certainly an exaggeration, if only because the democratic movement was highly differentiated by region. In Saxony, the ADAV and large parts of the liberal bourgeoisie adopted a stance that was either explicitly pro-Prussian or favored neutrality in the approaching Prussian-Austrian showdown. Bebel and Liebknecht, however, did not want anything to do with a full-fledged "people's war" (August Röckel) as it was propagated by Ludwig Büchner and other radical democrats. They advocated a *großdeutsch* policy of armed neutrality—which was also favored, incidentally, by the provisional general council of the First International and by liberals in the German southwest. Hence Bebel and Liebknecht did not join Leopold Sonnemann in siding with Vienna; instead they agitated against the "German fratricidal war" (*deutscher Bruderkrieg*).[46] In other words, central Germany was the place where diverging national movements collided so abruptly that they had a striking impact on postwar political developments.[47] Not only were the overtures between the ADAV and VDAV that had begun during the spring of 1866 suddenly stopped; they were soon banished to the dustheap of history. The last opportunity to escape

---

43. Geheimes Staatsarchiv Preußischer Kulturbesitz (hereafter GStAPK), Berlin-Dahlem, Nr. III. 762, 47–48.

44. Cited in Engelberg, "Sozialisten und Demokraten, 1866," 192.

45. See Günter Benser, *Die Herausbildung der Eisenacher Partei* (Berlin, 1956), 13.

46. See the text of the "Resolution der Volksversammlung zu Leipzig am 8. Mai 1866," in August Bebel, *Schriften, 1862–1913,* ed. Cora Stephan (Frankfurt a. M., 1981), 1:27f.

47. On Thuringia, see the informative article "Die Stimmung in Thüringen," *Süddeutsche Presse,* 22 Oct. 1869 (ed. Julius Fröbel), in GStAPK Berlin-Dahlem, Rep. 81 Gesandtschaft Weimar Nr. 24, 80; on Anhalt and Dessau, see the recent portrait in Torsten Kupfer, *Der Weg zum Bündnis: Entschieden Liberale und Sozialdemokraten in Dessau und Anhalt im Kaiserreich* (Weimar, 1998), 30ff. See also Benser, *Eisenacher Partei,* 59ff.; Klaus Erich Pollmann, "Arbeiterwahlen im Norddeutschen Bund, 1867–1870," *Geschichte und Gesellschaft* 15 (1989): 166ff.; Wolfgang Schröder, "'. . . zu Grunde richten wird man uns nicht mehr': Sozialdemokratie und Wahlen im Königreich Sachsen, 1867–1877," *Beiträge zur Geschichte der Arbeiterbewegung* 36 (1994): 5f.; Dieter Langewiesche, "Zur Frühgeschichte der deutschen Arbeiterbewegung: Unbekannte Briefe von August Bebel und Wilhelm Liebknecht aus den Jahren 1866, 1867 und 1869," *Archiv für Sozialgeschichte* 15 (1975): 301–21; and Fricke, *Deutsche Demokraten,* 58ff.

these mutually hostile positions was the creation of the Saxon People's Party, which could immediately rely on the support of the overwhelming majority of workers' associations amalgamated in the VDAV, as well as that of the *großdeutsch* democrats. After the SVP's successful showing in the February 1867 elections, the party's leaders set in train the founding of new people's associations, which primarily recruited workers and artisans. It was no accident that the program of the Saxon People's Party began with the democrats' perennial renunciation of any war that was precipitated by particularist and dynastic interests. According to the SVP program, such a war would inevitably destroy the common welfare and exacerbate the division of Germany. The program then included the pledge to uphold the old political program and to defend it in the North German Reichstag. Here the program identified the goal of convening a constituent assembly, to which all German states would send delegates. Only *then* did the program go on to present the "demands of democracy," beginning with full political self-determination by the people.[48]

The Saxon People's Party represented the only viable strategic option for the regional democracy movement. With its campaign for electoral rights, it contributed to the movement that eventually resulted in the Saxon *Landtag*'s passing of a liberal electoral law in 1868, which abolished corporatist divisions within parliament and allowed direct elections. Clearly, then, the party was able to point to major successes. However, it came under pressure primarily due to external factors: the continued absence of a democratic party in Prussia, the restriction of the People's Party to southern Germany and Württemberg, and the Franco-Prussian War of 1870–71. The founding of the Social Democratic Workers' Party nevertheless has to be viewed first of all as a reorganization rather than a refounding. This view is supported not only by study of the SDAP's program but also by continuities in the party's social constituency (workers and skilled craftsmen), by the fact that the idea of a pure workers' party only slowly gained ground among workers, and finally by the adoption of older middle-class associational traditions.[49] In the early years, the SDAP was still far removed from the type of a socialist class party, until amalgamation with the ADAV resulted in a decisive break with the tradition of the people's party.

---

48. Fricke, *Deutsche Demokraten,* 97ff.

49. See Rosenberg, *Demokratie und Sozialismus,* 137–38, 141; Toni Offermann, "Das liberale Vereinsmodell als Organisationsform der frühen deutschen Arbeiterbewegung in den 1860er Jahren," in *"Der kühnen Bahn nur folgen wir . . .": Ursprünge, Erfolge und Grenzen der Arbeiterbewegung in Deutschland,* ed. Arno Herzig and Günter Trautmann (Hamburg, 1989), 1:51f.

VI.   The Return of the People's Party

In line with the analysis of Gustav Mayer, recent scholarship has depicted the history of the German democracy movement between the 1848–49 Revolution and unification in 1871 too much as a history of successive division or exclusion. As a result, historical moments that held back these developments are pushed to the margins. The ways in which this marginalization has occurred are numerous. According to their own lights, historians have chosen to focus on the social question (as did Mayer), on democratic issues (as did Shlomo Na'aman),[50] or on the "preeminence of the national question for both wings of the German workers' movement in the 1860s,"[51] as did Werner Conze and Dieter Groh. Some premised their analyses on a combination of these factors, as did Theodor Schieder. And some have sought to establish stronger contextual connections between regional political traditions and socioeconomic lines of conflict, as did Dowe. Whatever the method of analysis, the conclusion is almost always the same: the social democratic people's party originally pursued by Bebel and Liebknecht remains either anachronistic or merely transitory. Now that German reunification in 1990 has provided better access to archives of the former GDR, it is high time that historians turned to the history of the people's party movement, which except for the case of Württemberg has never been researched systematically, let alone surveyed in outline. Even a glance at the people's parties in the German Federal Republic reveals that their conceptual origins and the roots of their exceptional regional diversity do not lie in the party formations of the Wilhelmine era, or even with the first parties of mass integration. They lie, instead, in the people's parties of the 1860s. In this respect, the Saxon People's Party long ago returned, albeit unnoticed, to real currency in German historiography.

---

50. Shlomo Na'aman, *Demokratische und soziale Impulse in der Frühgeschichte der deutschen Arbeiterbewegung der Jahre 1862/63* (Wiesbaden, 1969).

51. Werner Conze and Dieter Groh, *Die Arbeiterbewegung in der nationalen Bewegung: Die deutsche Sozialdemokratie vor, während und nach der Reichsgründung* (Stuttgart, 1966), 47.

Suffrage Reform, Corporatist Society, and the Authoritarian State: Saxon Transitions in the 1860s

James Retallack

> *[T]he taming of chance by statistics does not introduce a new liberty. . . . The bureaucracy of statistics imposes not just by creating administrative rulings but by determining classifications within which people must think of themselves and of the actions that are open to them.*[1]

I. Introduction

In world history the 1860s was a decisive decade. It was a decade of political renewal, dominated by reformist conservatives who sought to sidestep the revolutionary aspects of political modernization.[2] If we think initially of Bismarck in Prussia and Cavour in Italy, we are soon prompted to consider Napoleon III in France, Disraeli in England, Lincoln in America, John A. Macdonald in Canada, and the oligarchs behind the Meiji Restoration in Japan. Even in the calmer corners of

---

1. Ian Hacking, "How Should We Do the History of Statistics?" in *The Foucault Effect: Studies in Governmentality,* ed. Graham Burchell, Colin Gordon, and Peter Miller (Chicago, 1991), 181–95, here 194.
2. Works pointing to this historical moment include David Blackbourn, *The Fontana History of Germany, 1780–1918: The Long Nineteenth Century* (London, 1997), 244; Theodore S. Hamerow, "The Origins of Mass Politics in Germany, 1866–1867," in *Deutschland in der Weltpolitik des 19. und 20. Jahrhunderts,* ed. Imanuel Geiss et al. (Düsseldorf, 1973), 105–20, esp. 105; and Geoff Eley, "Liberalismus, 1860–1914: Deutschland und Großbritannien im Vergleich," in *Liberalismus im 19. Jahrhundert,* ed. Dieter Langewiesche (Göttingen, 1988), 260–76.

central Europe—in the cantons of Switzerland,[3] in Vienna,[4] in the Württemberg *Landtag*[5]—we find transitions to more democratic forms that involved the fundamental realignment of parliamentary suffrages.[6]

In this era, reformist conservatives were remarkably successful in drawing (or redrawing) the boundaries of new nation-states, in revitalizing the sources of state legitimation, or in overseeing the redefinition of national electorates. Some of them did all three things at the same time. As David Blackbourn has recently pointed out, most of these developments that "laid the basis of a modern state" unfolded against a common background of "growing national sentiment, argument over sovereignty, and civil war."[7] Yet when we consider how "argument over sovereignty" actually unfolded, we discover a striking incongruity. Many reformist conservatives did not stake their new claims to legitimacy on arguments, wars, and the battle of interests at all. Instead they proclaimed the existence of a broad consensus that made political reform irresistible.[8] Often referring to "the new requirements of the age" or "the sign of the times," such arguments were used during the debates that preceded the reform of Saxony's *Landtag* suffrage in 1868.[9] This essay considers how

3. See the definitive study by Erich Gruner, *Die Wahlen in den schweizerischen Nationalrat, 1849–1919,* 3 vols. in 4 (Bern, 1968).

4. See Pieter M. Judson, *Exclusive Revolutionaries: Liberal Politics, Social Experience, and National Identity in the Austrian Empire, 1848–1914* (Ann Arbor, MI, 1997), 81–83; Maren Seliger and Karl Ucakar, *Wahlrecht und Wählerverhalten in Wien, 1848–1932* (Vienna, 1984); and John Boyer, *Political Radicalism in Late Imperial Vienna* (Chicago, 1981), 273ff.

5. See Rosemarie Menzinger, *Verfassungsrevision und Demokratisierungsprozeß im Königreich Württemberg* (Stuttgart, 1969); and Hartwig Brandt, *Parlamentarismus in Württemberg, 1819–1870* (Düsseldorf, 1987), 162ff., on the 1868 suffrage reform.

6. See Markus Mattmüller, "Die Durchsetzung des allgemeinen Wahlrechts als gesamteuropäischer Vorgang," in *Geschichte und politische Wissenschaft,* ed. Beat Junker, Peter Gilg, and Richard Reich (Bern, 1975), 213–36; and Jürgen Kohl, "Zur langfristigen Entwicklung der politischen Partizipation in Westeuropa," in *Vergleichende europäische Wahlgeschichte,* ed. Otto Büsch and Peter Steinbach (Berlin, 1983), 377–411. On the extreme flux in the German party system following 1866, see Klaus-Erich Pollmann, "Parlamentseinfluß während der Nationalstaatsbildung, 1867–1871," in *Regierung, Bürokratie und Parlament in Preußen und Deutschland von 1848 bis zur Gegenwart,* ed. Gerhard A. Ritter (Düsseldorf, 1983), 56–75; and Margaret Lavinia Anderson, "Voter, Junker, Landrat, Priest: The Old Authorities and the New Franchise in Imperial Germany," *American Historical Review* 98 (1993): 1448–74.

7. Blackbourn, *Fontana History of Germany,* 244.

8. Cf. Niels-Uwe Tödter, "Die deutschen parlamentarischen Klassenwahlrechte im 19. und 20. Jahrhundert" (Jur. Diss., University of Hamburg, 1967), esp. 67–86, 94–119.

9. See Simone Lässig, "Wahlrechtsreformen in den deutschen Einzelstaaten: Indikatoren für Modernisierungstendenzen und Reformfähigkeit im Kaiserreich?" in *Modernisierung und Region im wilhelminischen Deutschland: Wahlen, Wahlrecht und politische Kultur,* ed. Simone Lässig, Karl Heinrich Pohl, and James Retallack, 2d rev. ed. (Bielefeld, 1998), 127–69; Gerhard Schmidt, "Der sächsische Landtag, 1833–1918: Sein

Saxon suffrage reform specifically, and suffrage reform debates in general, illuminate broader cultural responses on the part of states to the challenges of social, economic, and political change. This essay's working hypothesis is that suffrage reform in Saxony was not untypical in revealing both positive and negative reactions to two closely interconnected developments: the transition from a corporatist society of occupational estates (*Stände*) to one of interests and classes; and the transition of German political culture from one that identified and balanced group rights to one where the rights of individuals, although far from paramount, were given a more positive weight. Strong evidence suggests that Saxon statesmen, like reformist conservatives elsewhere in the world, appreciated the opportunity, and not just the threat, inherent in the need to align Saxon political culture with new realities. The final section of the essay suggests that only comparative and long-term analyses can reveal whether we should evaluate this response principally in terms of continuity or discontinuity.[10]

In nineteenth-century Germany, state legitimization on the basis of "rights" was often problematic. What we might call the "modernization project" of German liberals frequently cited individual rights as sacrosanct or transcendent in the construction of a modern civil society. But the liberals' universalizing vision had no place for rights they designated as "particularist" or parochial. On no issue were liberals more vulnerable than on the extension of the suffrage to the common man (let alone woman).[11] Conversely, conservatives did not oppose only individ-

---

Wahlrecht und seine soziale Zusammensetzung," in *Beiträge zur Archivwissenschaft und Geschichtsforschung*, ed. Reiner Groß and Manfred Kobuch (Weimar, 1977), 445–65; Wolfgang Schröder, "Wahlrecht und Wahlen im Königreich Sachsen, 1866–1896," in *Wahlen und Wahlkämpfe in Deutschland: Von den Anfängen im 19. Jahrhundert bis zur Bundesrepublik*, ed. Gerhard A. Ritter (Düsseldorf, 1997), 79–130; and idem, "Sozialdemokratie und Wahlen im Königreich Sachsen, 1867–1877," *Beiträge zur Geschichte der Arbeiterbewegung* 36, no. 4 (1994): 3–18. See also James Retallack, " 'Why Can't a Saxon Be More Like a Prussian?' Regional Identities and the Birth of Modern Political Culture in Germany, 1866–67," *Canadian Journal of History* 32 (1997): 26–55.

10. See the important study by Elfi Bendikat, *Wahlkämpfe in Europa, 1884 bis 1889: Parteiensysteme und Politikstile in Deutschland, Frankreich und Großbritannien* (Wiesbaden, 1988). Cf. Brett Fairbairn, *Democracy in the Undemocratic State: The German Reichstag Elections of 1898 and 1903* (Toronto, 1997); Stanley Suval, *Electoral Politics in Wilhelmine Germany* (Chapel Hill, NC, 1985); Thomas Kühne, "Wahlrecht — Wahlverhalten — Wahlkultur: Tradition und Innovation in der historischen Wahlforschung," *Archiv für Sozialgeschichte* 33 (1993): 481–547; Karl Rohe, *Wahlen und Wählertraditionen in Deutschland* (Frankfurt a. M., 1992); and Peter Steinbach, *Die Zähmung des politischen Massenmarktes*, 3 vols. (Passau, 1990).

11. For a contemporary view, see Friedrich von Raumer, *Über die geschichtliche Entwicklung der Begriffe von Recht, Staat und Politik*, 3d ed. (Leipzig, 1861; reprint, Aalen, 1971), 306–7. For two recent offerings among many others, see Thomas Bridges, *The*

ual rights: they, too, could condemn special "entitlements" because entitlements undermined the notion of a hierarchical, organic society. As the Saxon case demonstrates, when it came to incorporating individual and group rights into suffrage legislation, Saxons on both the left and the right expressed fears that granting voting rights to individuals (as under the Reichstag suffrage) would undermine social collectivities, group cohesion, and Saxon identity itself. But if only social groups were to have rights, what made a particular group legitimate in the eyes of the state? Social preeminence, education, or property ownership? Annual tax payment? Other service to the state? These questions became acute when legislators and state ministers tried to peg suffrage thresholds at levels that rewarded "state-supporting" citizens and excluded the "dangerous classes." Yet far from dipping their toes into unfamiliar democratic waters with fear and loathing, as historians have generally argued,[12] Saxon state ministers — not unlike the other reformist conservatives mentioned at the outset — understood that reform offered the best prospects for state legitimization if it was not forced upon them but was freely given.

II.   The Suffrage Reform of 1868: A Thumbnail Sketch

Only a few lines are required to set up the political context of Saxony's suffrage reform and to outline the principal revisions implemented in the legislation of 1868. After Saxony's defeat alongside Austria in 1866 and her forced entry into the Prussian-dominated North German Confederation, a new set of government ministers inaugurated what has been called Saxony's only liberal era, which lasted until the mid-1870s. The government leader was Baron Richard von Friesen, who replaced the much-hated Count Friedrich Ferdinand von Beust. Friesen's somewhat pedantic emphasis on fiscal discipline and administrative propriety lacked the flair of his hotheaded predecessor. But Friesen shared the liberals' familiarity with Saxony's dynamic industrial economy; he also sympathized with their preference for undertaking (and thus controlling) constitutional experiments legally and rationally.

The most conspicuous change actually enacted in the reform of 1868 was abandonment of representation according to occupational estates

---

Culture of Citizenship: Inventing Postmodern Civic Culture (Albany, 1994), esp. 5–15; and Caroline Daley and Melanie Nolan, eds., *Suffrage and Beyond: International Feminist Perspectives* (Auckland, 1994). Still useful is Jacques Droz, "Liberale Anschauungen zur Wahlrechtsfrage und das preußische Dreiklassenwahlrecht," in *Moderne deutsche Verfassungsgeschichte (1815–1918)*, ed. Ernst-Wolfgang Böckenförde (Cologne, 1972), 195–214.

12.   Andreas Neemann's contribution to this volume is a notable exception to this consensus.

(*ständische Vertretung*).[13] Under the old *Landtag* suffrage, the 80-member lower house was composed of 20 deputies representing large estate owners, 25 representing farmers, 25 representing town dwellers, and 10 representing commercial and industrial circles. The 1868 reform substituted a system whereby 45 deputies were elected from rural constituencies and 35 from urban ones. Saxony's suffrage also became direct, secret, and nearly universal. Apart from relatively minor exclusions, all male citizens over the age of 25 who paid at least 1 *Thaler* (3 marks) in state taxes annually were allowed to vote.[14] This threshold corresponded to an annual taxable income of about 600 marks. Whereas it is difficult to gauge the size of the Saxon electorate before 1868, about 245,000 Saxon males (or about 10 percent of the population) were entitled to vote after the suffrage reform.[15] Yet one in two Reichstag voters was still disqualified from *Landtag* voting even after the reform of 1868.[16]

III. Rationales for Reform

Baron von Friesen's *Landtag* suffrage reform provided the cornerstone for major administrative, judicial, press, and educational reforms in the early 1870s.[17] If we swallow liberal pronouncements we might believe that the force of public opinion alone had compelled Friesen to accept these changes. As a liberal member of Saxony's lower house put it early in the process: "The call for reform of our constitution and of our suffrage is no longer a demand voiced merely by one political party in the land. It is voiced by all classes and strata of the people without distinction according to party line. It is rooted in the requirements of the age [*Bedürfnissen der Zeit*], and it has received nourishment and legitimization through the

13. E. Otto Schimmel, *Die Entwicklung des Wahlrechts zur sächsischen Zweiten Kammer und der Zusammensetzung derselben in parteipolitischer und sozialer Hinsicht* (Nossen, 1912), 79–87.

14. That is, unless they were disqualified by active military service, withdrawal of citizen rights through a court sentence, residency of less than three years (a major exclusion), indebtedness, bankruptcy, receipt of poor relief, etc.

15. This figure of 10 percent corresponds almost exactly to the proportion of Saxons entitled to vote for the Frankfurt parliament in 1848; Theodore S. Hamerow, "Die Wahlen zum Frankfurter Parlament," in *Moderne deutsche Verfassungsgeschichte*, ed. Böckenförde, 215–36, here 231.

16. In 1871 about 18.5 percent of Saxony's total population was enfranchised for Reichstag elections. The *Landtag* electorate, due to rising wages, tax reform, and inflation, roughly doubled between 1869 and the mid-1890s, when it stood at about 500,000. The increase in the Reichstag electorate was somewhat smaller: roughly 744,000 Saxons were enfranchised in 1893.

17. Richard Dietrich, "Die Verwaltungsreform in Sachsen, 1869–1873," *Neues Archiv für Sächsische Geschichte* 61 (1940): 49–85; see also Wolfgang Schröder's contribution to this volume.

mighty transformation . . . [of] 1866."[18] Yet one can argue that Friesen, recognizing that Saxon political culture was still in its formative stage, saw a more vigorous state parliament as an inherent good—as a means to share power with, and thus co-opt, potential enemies of the state.[19] Of course such a sharing of power was possible only if state ministers did not become formally responsible to parliament. Nevertheless, in 1870, in the final days of the first session elected under the new suffrage, Friesen acknowledged that a positive new spirit had invigorated the *Landtag*. "We have drawn nearer to each other," he told the liberals, "and a great deal of mistrust has been removed."[20]

How do we explain Friesen's willingness not only to accommodate but actually to embrace suffrage reform? Of special relevance here is a recent observation by Larry Diamond: "We observe during democratic consolidation the emergence of an elite political culture featuring moderation, accommodation, restrained partisanship, system loyalty, and trust. These norms enhance the predictability and mitigate the intensity of political conflict." Here we should recall that Friesen had come to ministerial office just in time to assist in the suppression of the Dresden Uprising in May 1849; he had left Beust's cabinet in the 1850s in protest over his more repressive measures; and in September 1866 he witnessed firsthand in Berlin how Bismarck overcame the determined opposition of liberals in Prussia's House of Deputies. Hence Friesen was well aware of the dividends to be reaped by mitigating the intensity of political conflict.

To what extent was suffrage reform premised on new ideas about the relationship between the state and civil society? The strategies deployed by Friesen and other reformist conservatives suggest that state and society were no longer seen only as rivals. Rather, social groups and the parties that soon came to represent their interests were considered legitimate participants in everyday political life: not just in the sense of overseeing or controlling the state, but in cooperating with it and helping to set its agenda. Conversely, suffrage reforms allowed states to draw their legitimacy and their security more explicitly from such participation. Voting rights in the 1860s were often appraised as a kind of reward for service (*Gegenleistung*). Eventually such service to the state came to include a new and more abstract sense of national loyalty. But long

18. *Landtags-Mitteilungen* (hereafter *LT-Mitt.*) 1866–68, II. Kammer, Bd. 3, 2636, Heinrich Theodor Koch (23 Mar. 1868).

19. Larry Diamond, cited in Fairbairn, *Democracy*, 28.

20. *Constitutionelle Zeitung*, 3 Mar. 1870; *Leipziger Zeitung*, 25 Feb. 1870; cf. *Deutsche Allgemeine Zeitung*, 24 Feb. 1870, all cited in Albert Richter, "Die öffentliche Meinung in Sachsen vom Friedensschlüsse 1866 bis zur Reichsgründung" (Ph.D. diss., University of Leipzig, [1922]), 137.

before new ideas of national citizenship became key elements of political legitimacy, the undertaking of novel social and economic tasks on the part of the state was seen to lie not in opposition to society, but rather as an opportunity for the state to extend its hegemony in new and more far-reaching ways.

Antonio Gramsci's distinction between "hegemonic" and "coercive" forms of rule may be relevant here in explaining the willingness of reformist conservatives to eat away at local autonomies and traditional privileges on the one hand and, on the other, to favor "a politically more modern but still hegemonic form of political control." Thus Gramsci might almost have been describing the Saxon suffrage reform of 1868 when he wrote: "In the ancient and medieval state alike, centralization, whether political-territorial or social . . . , was minimal. The state was, in a certain sense, a mechanical bloc of social groups. . . . The modern state substitutes for the mechanical bloc of social groups their subordination to the active hegemony of the directive and dominant group, hence abolishes certain autonomies, which nevertheless are reborn in other forms, as parties, trade unions, cultural associations."[21] As Michael Warner has noted, new public figures in the age of mass politics appealed to universal interests rather than particular estates, classes, or other sets of persons: in such an age, "what you say will carry force not because of who you are but despite who you are."[22]

And yet suffrage reform was highly contentious from the very outset. On the one hand, a remarkable array of suffrage schemes were proposed by democrats, liberals, conservatives, and government bureaucrats before a final compromise was hammered out.[23] These proposals range from the prescient to the harebrained. On the other hand, it is no accident that Friesen first acknowledged the desirability of suffrage reform at the moment when Saxony's sovereignty was most threatened, in mid-September 1866. Writing from Berlin while awaiting the Prussians' peace proposals, Friesen observed that "next to a federal parliament elected under universal suffrage, a *Landtag* based on the principle of occupational estates cannot exist."[24] Friesen was hardly thinking of dis-

---

21. Cited in Geoff Eley, "Nations, Publics, and Political Cultures: Placing Habermas in the Nineteenth Century," in *Habermas and the Public Sphere*, ed. Craig Calhoun (Cambridge, MA, 1992), 289–339, here 324.

22. Michael Warner, "The Mass Public and the Mass Subject," in *Habermas and the Public Sphere*, ed. Calhoun, 377–401.

23. See Wilhelm August Gersdorf, *Einige Sätze in Betreff eines neuen Wahlgesetzes für das Königreich Sachsen* (Crimmitschau, 1867). These schemes cannot be discussed here due to limits of space.

24. Letter of 15 Sept. 1866, in Richard von Friesen, *Erinnerungen aus meinem Leben*, 3 vols. (Dresden, 1880–1910), 2:288.

mantling the Saxon *Landtag*. Quite the contrary: he did everything in his power to ensure that Saxony's parliament *not* become redundant. Thus he made sure that the *Landtag* voting scheduled for the autumn of 1866 proceeded according to plan. Why? By demonstrating the continued independence of Saxony's own state parliament, Friesen believed that the Saxon people would see him as the determined defender of Saxon interests just when the Prussian occupation was most onerous and when rumors were flying that Saxony would be annexed outright.[25] However, these elections convinced no one that Saxony's sovereignty remained fully intact. Public interest in the *Landtag* campaign remained very low.

During 1867 Saxon liberals relentlessly drew the contrast between the Reichstag's universal male suffrage and the *Landtag*'s restricted suffrage. This made Saxony's homegrown parliament seem more anachronistic than ever. As Karl Biedermann, a former Forty-eighter and later leader of the Saxon National Liberals, asked pointedly: "Is not the common weal of the individual state inextricably linked to that of the Confederation? . . . Can this larger body tolerate a diseased limb?"[26] For sixteen years, since the government's coup d'état of 1850, wrote Biedermann, the reactionary *Landtag* in Dresden had condemned Saxon political life to "deathly silence" (as Beust himself had famously boasted). This silence had not retarded economic modernization, Biedermann conceded; but it had prevented the attainment of civil liberties and religious tolerance:

> When have these reactivated estates ever demonstrated any understanding for timely reform? Where can one find a single law passed [by parliament] that corresponds to the people's legitimate claim for the protection of those rights without which a true and genuine political life is unthinkable? . . . Have the old reactivated [assembly of] estates protected freedom of religion? The law of July 1852, which restricted the Jews to Leipzig and Dresden and resurrected the medieval law of 1838, says enough about that. Have the estates protected the rights of the press or recognized the freedoms of expression and assembly? Not in the least!

---

25. See Richard Dietrich, "Preußen als Besatzungsmacht im Königreich Sachsen, 1866–1868," *Jahrbuch für die Geschichte Mittel- und Ostdeutschlands* 5 (1956): 273–93; and Retallack, "'Why Can't a Saxon?'"

26. [Karl Biedermann], *Die reactivirten Stände und das verfassungsmäßige Wahlgesetz in Sachsen* (Leipzig, 1866), 12. Compare Karl Biedermann, *Die Wiedereinberufung der alten Stände in Sachsen aus dem Gesichtspunkte des Rechts und der Politik betrachtet* (Leipzig, 1850).

In the *Landtag* session of 1866–67, another liberal complained that the "glaring" discrepancy between the *Landtag* and Reichstag suffrages "screamed" for immediate redress. One of his colleagues proposed a motion designed to address "the legitimate wishes of the people for a progressive widening of the threshold for the active and passive suffrage, and for a more up-to-date [*zeitgemäßer*] composition of parliament." And a university professor representing Leipzig declared in the upper house: "Political wisdom dictates that one not only have a finger on the pulse of the times but also take into account the healthy, moral spirit of the people and seize the initiative accordingly in a timely, honorable fashion."[27]

Saxon liberals offered innumerable variations on this basic theme. Writers in the *Constitutionelle Zeitung* and the *Grenzboten* argued that dismantling the upper house of the *Landtag* would streamline legislation and eliminate "the bastion of particularism, governmental complacency, and agrarian interests." The prominent Progressive deputy Hermann Schreck declared in the lower house that the estate-bound suffrage was "unfit for the requirements of the day." He therefore called on the government to dissolve the *Landtag,* submit a new suffrage reform package, and seek a bill of indemnity. Such a bill would exactly parallel Bismarck's indemnity bill that was passed by the Prussian *Landtag* in September 1866. The National Liberal Moritz Heinrich Lorenz ostentatiously resigned his Saxon *Landtag* seat, declaring that he did not recognize the legality of *Landtag* proceedings since 1850.[28] Leipzig's liberal mayor told the upper house that the *Landtag* should confine itself to the passing of the two-year budget and a new suffrage bill. After a dissolution, he added, Saxony "should be governed *ad interim* according to the constitution of the North German Confederation."

In contrast to National Liberal agitation, petitions sent to the *Landtag* by democrats and social democrats stressed the minimum level of voting rights necessary to transform the *Landtag* into a "true people's parliament."[29] Conservatives of course disagreed with both positions. One of them argued that even the most moderate among the liberals' motions for reform was "not as harmless as it appears." What exactly is "up-to-date?" asked this speaker, and what are the "legitimate wishes" of the Saxon people? Another conservative opposed plans to "adapt" Saxony's suffrage to the North German Confederation, predicting that individual *Landtage* would soon be reduced to "mere provincial parlia-

27. *LT-Mitt.* 1866–68, I. Kammer, Bd. 1, 96–98, debates of 6 Dec. 1866.
28. See Andreas Neemann's contribution to this volume.
29. From the resolution of 1 Nov. 1867, SächsHStA Dresden, Gesammt-Ministerium, Loc. 63, Nr. 4, 266.

ments." These provincial parliaments, rather than concerning themselves with great national issues, should focus their attention on "questions of practical importance." Because "practical businessmen" were best suited to such debates, this speaker added, the universal suffrage was wholly unsuitable for Saxony.[30]

In the course of 1867, Saxon liberals became even further convinced that *Landtag* suffrage reform was the sine qua non for further reforms in state and society. An article published in the *Preußische Jahrbücher* in mid-1867, which may well have been written by Heinrich von Treitschke, hammered home the point: "Freely elected representatives of the people will prevail not only over the sort of cranky particularism that so contemptuously abuses the name of patriotism, but also over the spirit of serfdom and servility that suffuses almost the entire civil service in Saxony and has even found its way into the circle of burghers who appear outwardly independent." Indulging in the rhetorical excess that was so characteristic of Treitschke, this writer continued: "Individuals and parties must . . . demonstrate manly courage and resolution, they must unlearn the vacillation and seesawing, the glances to left and right, the fear of unfriendly looks from above and of unpopularity from below. . . . Into their soft, pliant, submissive Saxon natures they must bring some steel. . . . If this regenerative process is completed, then Saxony will be one of the brightest pearls in the crown of our great German Fatherland. May God grant it!"[31]

Did these debates influence Friesen and his colleagues when they met in the autumn of 1867 to draw up the reform bill? Any answer must note that at this time a pro-reform petition campaign was set in motion by groups stretching from social democrats on the extreme left to National Liberals in the middle.[32] We must not overestimate the cohesion of this campaign or its immediate impact.[33] Yet Joseph Crowe, the British consul in Leipzig, was impressed enough to predict that "this Saxon agitation is the prelude to change throughout the whole of Germany." In following up this observation, Crowe obviously believed the National

---

30. *LT-Mitt.* 1866–68, I. Kammer, Bd. 1, 27–35, 81–101 (esp. 81–88), 4 and 20 Dec. 1866.

31. "Zur Charakteristik des öffentlichen Geistes in Sachsen," *Preußische Jahrbücher* 20, no. 2 (1867): 195–215.

32. SächsHStA Dresden, Gesammt-Ministerium, Loc. 63, Nr. 4, 269 (*LT-Akten* 1866/68, Abt. 1, Bd. 3, 155ff., No. 77, Decret an die Stände . . . 19 November 1867, esp. "Motiven," 170–82); also in SächsHStA Dresden, Ständeversammlung, Nr. 5948, esp. 22–40v. This file (together with ibid., Nr. 5904, esp. 32ff.) also contains the numerous petitions discussed below, handwritten minutes of committee meetings, and the printed protocols of parliamentary debate in both houses between March and May 1868.

33. See the police report in SächsHStA Dresden, Ministerium des Innern (hereafter MdI), Nr. 11039, 169.

Liberals had already convinced many Germans about the compelling need for a more thoroughly integrated system of political representation in the new Germany: "Nothing can be more clear than that the tendency of German thought at this time is to admit the superiority of the one-chamber over the two-chamber system" (by which Crowe meant a national Reichstag and independent *Landtage,* not an upper and lower chamber). "A powerful party in Germany favours the absorption of all legislative power into this body [the Reichstag] by gradually degrading the old chambers to the rank of provincial assemblies. The first step in this direction would be the assimilation of the electoral laws in Kingdoms and principalities to that of the federation; and the German press sounds the key note of agitation when it points out the anomaly of universal suffrage and a single parliament being enforced for the whole whilst restricted franchise and dual chambers govern the parts."[34]

Saxony's interior minister, Hermann von Nostitz-Wallwitz, also felt it was important to see Saxony's reform in a federal context.[35] Nostitz insisted that the North German Confederation's new constitution had no *direct* implications for the individual states, and he refuted the charge that the current *Landtag* represented only privileged estates. The Saxon *Landtag,* he declared, was already more representative than the English parliament and much more so than the Belgian parliament, with its tax threshold of approximately 11 *Thaler* (33 marks).[36] Nostitz also observed that most other German electoral laws included tax thresholds, residency requirements, or three-class voting as in Prussia. Yet Nostitz also conceded the Confederation's *indirect* impact:

When a number of people live together in a large house, certainly each one has the right to furnish his own room according to his tastes. But in doing so he will have to take into account

---

34. Public Record Office, London (Kew), Foreign Office (hereafter PRO Kew, FO) 68, Nr. 147, General no. 10, Joseph Crowe, Leipzig, to FO, 2 Dec. 1867. At this time Crowe enjoyed close relations with Leipzig's most prominent National Liberals. See also Bayerisches Hauptstaatsarchiv (hereafter BayrHStA) Munich, Abt. II, MA III, Nr. 2841, reports no. 101 and 105, 3 and 8 Nov. 1867.

35. Here I am drawing on Nostitz's arguments during debates a year earlier, that is, before Disraeli's Second Reform Act had passed; *LT-Mitt.* 1866/67, II. Kammer, 110–11, 6 Dec. 1866.

36. Cf. John K. Walton, *The Second Reform Act* (London, 1983); Francis B. Smith, *The Making of the Second Reform Bill* (Cambridge, 1966); Maurice Cowling, *1867: Disraeli, Gladstone, and Revolution: The Passing of the Second Reform Bill* (Cambridge, 1967); Gertrude Himmelfarb, "The Politics of Democracy: The English Reform Act of 1867," *Journal of British Studies* 6 (1966): 97–138; and Bruce L. Kinzer, "The Ballot Question in English Politics, 1830–1872" (Ph.D. diss., University of Toronto, 1975). The Belgian constitution of 1831 was regularly cited by nineteenth-century German liberals as exemplary.

certain structural features of the building, and if he is to live in peace with his fellow lodgers, he cannot prevent their customs and habits from influencing his own. I believe that in many respects we find ourselves in a similar relationship to the federal constitution.

The preamble (*Motiven*) to the government's suffrage bill rehearsed Nostitz-Wallwitz's remarks. The Reichstag and individual *Landtage,* it stated, necessarily "influenced and complemented" each other. Therefore it was "advisable" that the two parliaments not differ greatly in their composition.[37] But each tier of government required its own suffrage. The distance between national and local affairs was so great, the preamble argued, that the universal suffrage could not be extended either to *Landtag* or to local elections:

> The more universal in nature interests represented in the Reichstag have become, . . . the wider it has been possible to set the limits of voting rights for Reichstag elections. By contrast, the main tasks of the *Landtag*e in individual federal states will continue to lie in the conscientious overseeing of the state budget and the prudent improvement of existing society and its institutions. Therefore the prerequisites for attaining the right to vote will be different. . . . [A]lthough no classes of the population are to be excluded from voting, only those persons can be included whose status as burghers [*bürgerlichen Verhältnissen*] allows one to assume that they demonstrate the necessary concern for the tasks at hand.

Here we can see that although social and economic modernization called for new tasks at each level of government, the "new requirements of the age" could be given a positive spin to favor a particular kind of reform: one that "modernized" legislatures at all three levels, to be sure, but one that did *not* subordinate them to a single vision of democracy or one based on natural rights.

IV.   A Balance Sheet

How do we draw up a balance sheet of the ways in which the 1868 suffrage bill reflected traditional and newer (if not necessarily "mod-

---

37. Yet to those liberals who advocated abolishing Saxony's upper house, the Saxon government responded that a two-chamber system would give Saxony's "national [*vaterländischen*] institutions the character of an independent state organism." "Motiven," 172–75.

ern") conceptions of civil society? We might begin with the Saxon government's most conspicuous break with the past: its endorsement of direct rather than indirect voting. There was "no doubt," the preamble stated, that the more direct procedure "expresses the will of the voters more completely and with less falsification" than indirect voting. The Saxons probably shared Bismarck's conviction that Prussian liberals profited from indirect voting under the three-class system. Thus they may have hoped to eliminate the liberals' successful mobilization (or "falsification") of public opinion through their emerging network of constituency-level associations. Nevertheless, on balance the Saxon government appears to have been more confident than Bismarck that conservatives would profit from the deployment of local influence at election time. Second, the proposed bill broke with the traditional requirement that candidates must run in their home constituency — the so-called *Bezirkszwang,* long a target of liberal attacks.[38] Third, each house was now empowered to examine the propriety of its own members' election, and each could respond as it saw fit to charges of electoral chicanery. Fourth, the grounds on which voters or candidates could be excluded from the voters' list were considerably narrowed.[39]

When we consider the less progressive features of the government's bill, we might distinguish between relatively clear-cut efforts to hold back the tide of democracy on the one hand and, on the other, more ambivalent or ambiguous measures that cannot be so neatly categorized. Prominent among the former category would be provisions for grouping together urban constituencies that were not contiguous. As one sees immediately when looking at one of the rare maps of Saxon *Landtag* constituencies, as many as fifteen towns were deemed to constitute a single urban riding. Floating like islands in the larger sea of rural constituencies, these towns proved to be — as the bill's drafters intended — especially susceptible to conservative influence. The relatively underdeveloped network of local liberal associations was inadequate to organize a coherent campaign involving communication and travel across vast distances. The Saxon administration, however, together with police, local councils, pastors, foresters, and even railway officials, could distribute propaganda and ballots in these far-flung locales.[40]

The same conservative tendency is evident in the bill's preservation

---

38. A candidate could represent another occupational estate or come from another part of Saxony.

39. It is also important to take note of those relatively progressive aspects of the existing suffrage that were left untouched by the government's bill. Limits of space prevent a full discussion here.

40. See Schröder, "Wahlrecht," esp. 94–102; for Austria, cf. Judson, *Exclusive Revolutionaries,* 88.

of the so-called rolling renewal of the *Landtag*. Under this system, one-third of *Landtag* seats were contested every two years (formerly three). The lack of general elections, plus the fact that the constituencies contested in any given year were scattered throughout the land, necessarily dampened the enthusiasm of both voters and their elected representatives. In any given year no political issue, however contentious, could produce a landslide or change the whole complexion of the house. Moreover, at least two-thirds of every *Landtag* would be composed of incumbents, thus smoothing the business of legislation and ensuring the "cautious consideration" of legislation. Why would any government *not* wish to preserve this congenial situation?

Among the more ambiguous features of the government's bill was the elimination of formal representation according to occupational estates. Even Friesen's conservative colleagues recognized the fruitlessness of holding to the outworn idea of an estate-bound suffrage.[41] Yet one historian has suggested that the goal of preserving *ständisch* society was abandoned not in 1868 but much earlier, in the suffrage of 1831. That earlier reform, together with other far-reaching policy changes implemented in the 1830s, had recognized (and accelerated) the gradual but unstoppable disintegration of *ständisch* society.[42] This interpretation is bolstered by noting that the government's preamble itself conceded that a minor suffrage reform in 1861 — which had increased the number of industrial and commercial representatives from five to ten — had demonstrated that the lower house already represented *interests,* not social estates. In fact, Prussian bureaucrats had discovered while drafting their own suffrage reform in 1849 that it was impossible to "draw up appropriate categories to designate corporative or occupational groups as the basis for elections according to occupational or corporative 'interests.'" As one constitutional expert wrote, "the distinction between urban and rural constituencies was no longer conceived as representation according to estates or interests, but rather as a practical stipulation corresponding to the actual proclivities [*tatsächlichen Neigungen*] of the people."[43] The

---

41. See the minutes of the cabinet meetings of 27 Sept. and 5 Nov. 1867, and 23 Feb. and 26 Mar. 1868, SächsHStA Dresden, MdI Nr. 5372, 6–11, 17–21, 118d–e, 119b–c.

42. See Axel Flügel, "Sozialer Wandel und politische Reform in Sachsen: Rittergüter und Gutsbesitzer im Übergang von der Landeshoheit zum Konstitutionalismus, 1763–1843," in *Wege zur Geschichte des Bürgertums,* ed. Klaus Tenfelde and Hans-Ulrich Wehler (Göttingen, 1994), 36–56, esp. 40–42. Cf. Günter Grünthal, *Parlamentarismus in Preußen, 1848/49–1857/58* (Düsseldorf, 1982), 68, 72–77; and Klaus-Erich Pollmann, *Parlamentarismus im Norddeutschen Bund, 1867–1870* (Düsseldorf, 1985).

43. C[arl] V. Fricker, ed., *Die Verfassungsgesetze des Königreichs Sachsen* (Leipzig, 1895), 65 n. 2. The idea of *ständisch* representation did not die easily; see, e.g., Ludwig von Hirschfeld, "Die proportionale Berufsklassenwahlrecht: Ein Mittel zur Abwehr der sozialistischen Bewegung," *Grenzboten* 44, Bd. 4 (1885): 1–16, 65–82, 113–33.

British chargé d'affaires in Dresden saw things in a similar light. One could of course argue that he was insufficiently attuned to the fine distinctions German constitutional theorists made between "estates," "interests," and "classes." Nevertheless, the chargé felt strongly that "[t]he fundamental principle that every class interest shall be represented has in all material points been adhered to." Thus he reported to the Foreign Office that the changes inaugurated by Saxony's suffrage reform were "not numerous."[44]

V. Suffrage Reform and Democratization: Comparing Regions Internationally

The most interesting aspect of this particular suffrage debate — and arguably the aspect most amenable to cross-national comparisons — is the issue of a tax threshold, below which contemporaries believed the so-called dangerous classes would be enfranchised. Limitations of space do not permit a full discussion here. Instead it may be helpful to identify some ways to address this and similar issues comparatively.

The first way is to study the *process* whereby bureaucrats and legislators amend initial proposals and come up with often quite different interpretations of "safe" thresholds. We know that the government's proposal in 1867 envisaged a tax threshold of 2 *Thaler*. This was reduced to 1 *Thaler* by conservatives who feared that craftsmen and small producers paying between 1 and 2 *Thaler* would vote for the liberals. The parallel thinking undertaken by Bismarck, Disraeli, and other conservatives, but also by the middle-level bureaucrats who actually drafted their reform bills, cries out for detailed analysis. More than a few legislators in history have had their best-laid plans confounded by faulty statistical forecasts.

Second, we might consider the *context* of other suffrage stipulations that allowed tax thresholds to be pegged very low. Many of these stipulations offset the universal or near-universal nature of new suffrages by ensuring that certain social groups would enjoy privileges through extra votes, parallel chambers, nomination rights, and so on. The redrawing of electoral boundaries, the publication of parliamentary debates, per diem allowances for deputies, the length of parliamentary periods, plans for future tax reform — these were practical issues that reformers invariably considered in tandem with tax thresholds. One can argue, for example, that in 1867 Disraeli and Friesen effectively abandoned urban

---

44. J. Hume Burnley to FO, no. 3, 26 Feb. 1868, addendum, in PRO Kew, FO 68, Nr. 149.

constituencies to the liberals only because other features of their reforms tightened the conservatives' hold on rural seats.

Third, the *cultural* significance of tax thresholds can be gauged by considering the determination of reformist conservatives to "measure up" as modern statesmen in the constitutional era. In 1867 Friesen shared with Saxon liberals a determination to draw up a suffrage law that would not only stand up to international yardsticks of fairness, but also erase the lingering embarrassment of backwardness and pliability from the Beust era. Those yardsticks were always calibrated according to particular traditions. As we have seen, federalism was a key issue for German reformers in 1867 — far more decisive, for obvious reasons, than in Britain or Japan. Nevertheless, national and international comparisons grew more significant as time went by. After 1900 Saxon ministers commissioned dozens of studies of suffrage reforms passed in neighboring lands. Far from remaining behind closed doors, these comparisons infused public debate about electoral fairness. Thus in late 1905, not long after the Tsar handed down his October Manifesto, Social Democrats demonstrating in favor of suffrage reform declared ominously that they had learned to "speak Russian." Everyone knew exactly what they meant.

Turning the coin over, how did foreign observers report back to their superiors on reforms undertaken elsewhere? Here it seems relevant to know that Disraeli's Second Reform Act of 1867 had already passed when the British chargé d'affaires in Dresden reported to London that "the qualifications of a vote [in Saxony] are made it appears to me as low as are consistent with safety, the line of one Thaler or 3 Shillings of taxation bringing it down almost to the Proletariat class."[45] In October 1869 the chargé reported: "[T]he Suffrage qualification has been put as low as it possibly can be without calling in the actual proletariat class." This assessment was about right: although conservative diehards complained that the 1-*Thaler* threshold would throw parliament into the arms of the "communists," Saxony's interior minister claimed that this threshold would give "any worker who distinguishes himself through talent, intelligence, and hard work the opportunity to attain the vote." Such a prospect, he added tellingly, would in turn "also enliven the interest of the well-off classes of the population in the elections."[46]

One last example may suggest why far-flung comparisons need not

---

45. Ibid. Burnley continued: "It is not safe to say what the aspect of the Chamber will be at present, one thing however seems very certain that it will be decidedly more democratic than its predecessor"; Burnley to FO, no. 34, 5 Oct. 1869.

46. Interior Minister von Nostitz-Wallwitz, speaking in the lower house on 23 Mar. 1868, cited in Schröder, "Wahlrecht," 99 n. 54. See also report no. 101, 3 Nov. 1867, in BayrHStA Munich, Abt. II, MA III, Nr. 2841.

be far-fetched. Might it not be important to know which European capitals other than Berlin were visited, and which constitutional experts were consulted besides Rudolf von Gneist, Hermann Roesler, and Lorenz von Stein, by the Meiji reformers before they drafted Japan's constitution of 1889? One wonders: if they had learned to "speak Saxon" before returning to Tokyo, would they still have set the tax threshold for Japan's diet at 15 yen?[47]

We know that Saxon legislators, emphasizing practicality over theory at every turn, seldom referred to Stein or any other expert. Yet as Colin Gordon has written, elements of Stein's teachings have a relevance that extends beyond the German context. Stein was impatient for German administrators to move away from the "archaic" and "fragmented" polity of corporatist society, toward what he called a "social state" but what in essence was a society of classes. One can debate whether this society was a fully bourgeois, liberal one, or whether it bore the hallmarks of a "social monarchy." For this reason, among others, we should not locate such a state of classes unequivocally at the end point — for us, the near end — of the telos of modernization. As the passage cited at the outset of this essay suggests, the "taming of chance by statistics" does not necessarily introduce liberty. Similarly, the taming of accidents of birth by formal democratization does not necessarily introduce "modern" ideas of fairness, and the taming of regional particularities by a national parliament does not necessarily introduce "modern" ideas of loyalty to a larger, more powerful ideal. Nevertheless, as Gordon notes, the vision that reformers took from Stein was a powerful one: it was "the vision of a liberal state as active historic partner in the making of civil society; an exacting appraisal of the inner consistency of the social fabric; and, perhaps most strikingly, a tabling of the question of class formation as part of the state's agenda — a condition, one might add, of the state's security."[48]

---

47. My preliminary understanding of the Meiji Restoration is based on the following reading: Nobutaka Ike, *The Beginnings of Political Democracy in Japan* (Baltimore, 1950); George M. Beckmann, *The Making of the Meiji Constitution: The Oligarchs and the Constitutional Development of Japan, 1868–1891* (Lawrence, KS, 1957); Joseph Pittau, "Ideology of a New Nation: Authoritarianism and Constitutionism, Japan: 1868–1890" (Ph.D. diss., Harvard University, 1962), esp. chap. 7; George Akita, *Foundations of Constitutional Government in Modern Japan, 1868–1900* (Cambridge, MA, 1967); and Robert A. Scalapino, *Democracy and the Party Movement in Prewar Japan: The Failure of the First Attempt* (Berkeley, CA, 1967). The Japanese "Law of Election for the Members of the House of Representatives, February 11, 1889" was consulted in Centre for East Asian Cultural Studies, *The Meiji Japan through Contemporary Sources*, vol. 1, *Basic Documents, 1854–1889* (Tokyo, 1969), 131–52.

48. See Colin Gordon, "Governmental Rationality: An Introduction," in *The Foucault Effect*, ed. Burchell, Gordon, and Miller, 1–51, here 30–31.

VI. Conclusions

Saxony's suffrage debate alerts us to the danger of accepting at face value either unsubstantiated historical claims about the force of public opinion upon lawmakers, or undifferentiated contemporary arguments about an irresistible *Zeitgeist* in favor of democracy. It is less important to paint the Saxon suffrage reform of 1868, or any other, as either "modern" or "unmodern" than to consider in specific ways how it contributed to the transformation of electoral and political cultures. In the 1860s, hierarchical society based on occupational estates was not only disintegrating, it was *seen* to be disintegrating. And yet what M. Rainer Lepsius described as sociomoral milieus had not yet come into focus for contemporaries. Nor had the modern mass parties formed that would later rely on these milieus for their stability. The extraordinary degree of flux in the German party system generally, and its electoral culture specifically, necessarily determined the nature of suffrage reforms— those only contemplated, and those actually implemented. In particular, the inadequacy of traditional or "natural" arguments in favor of estate-bound suffrages was patently obvious to contemporaries. But equally compelling and comprehensive alternatives were elusive. Hence a simpler electoral law was conceived on the basis of "rewarding" those who provided wealth or service to the state. Even this partial solution was only one step on Saxony's odyssey toward democracy. The term "odyssey" connotes a grand and epoch-making journey, one into uncharted territory. Yet as Friesen, Bismarck, and many of their world contemporaries stated explicitly, and as the liberals would have agreed, it is preferable to make revolutions than to suffer them.

This essay has also tried to suggest the value of making explicit comparisons among states whose leaders were working with, working through, and reworking again long-held assumptions about the bases of state legitimacy. Württemberg's suffrage reform, enacted at exactly the same time and broadly with the same result as Saxony's reform, provides another particularly revealing example of how German statesmen in this era accommodated social, economic, and political change in the interests of system stabilization. Württemberg's interior minister Ernst von Geßler recognized that a modern state could no longer be based on the support of traditional (agrarian) elites alone. This conservative reformer was not going to sacrifice the vital interests of the state on the altar of nationalism or liberalism. Yet Geßler was convinced that any struggle against the forces of change could never repeat the victory of 1848–49: therefore the modern state should never attempt one. Instead, timely suffrage reform should be conceived as the means to sidestep such a crisis. As Geßler wrote in a memorandum that had previously made reference to universal suffrage at Frankfurt in 1849, in the Reichstag after 1867, and in the Second French Empire: "In consideration of these factors, I believe it is more prudent to initiate the step required by the logic of circumstances quickly and comprehensively at the outset, rather than to let it be wrung from us by stages in a struggle that the government will have to undertake not on its own behalf but for particular classes of citizens who have long enjoyed special privileges — a struggle, moreover, in which the government might well be abandoned by these classes at the decisive moment and would therefore have to take the entire weight of battle upon its own shoulders." In a strikingly similar argument and at virtually the same time, Friesen observed that Saxon Conservatives lacked both the energy and the necessary organization to provide the government with the support it required. Hence Friesen was prepared, with liberal support, to embark on a course of reform that virtually ensured broader and more lasting support for the authoritarian state.[49]

Lastly, the preceding argument has suggested that when we look at these "revolutions from above," when we peel back the rhetoric of class harmony, constitutional propriety, and administrative nonpartisanship, we often find disturbing images of pedantry, prejudice, and the abuse of power. Such abuse is rarely mentioned in historical accounts of how states modernized by accepting the progressive expansion of voting rights. One of the foremost authorities on the subject, Karlheinz Blaschke, has suggested that of Saxony's three major suffrage reforms enacted in 1868, 1896, and 1909, it was unequivocally the *first* of these reforms that pulled the Saxon *Landtag* into the modern era. According to Blaschke, after 1868 the lower house became the "locus of real political opinion formation and political decision making by a plurality of groups in constant touch with public opinion."[50] Yet the Social Democratic leader August Bebel, who was not lacking in firsthand knowledge, described the Saxon *Landtag* during the 1880s in the most bitter terms:

> A very considerable proportion of the chamber was made up of rural deputies whose political horizons were as narrow as the boundaries of their own constituency. [These were] people who had only the most laughable conceptions of what we Social Democrats actually wanted. Along with them went a number of small-town mayors who lived in a *spießbürgerlich*

49. See Menzinger, *Verfassungsrevision,* 56–68, esp. 60; Friedrich von Eichmann to Otto von Bismarck, no. 95 (confidential), 18 Dec. 1867, in Politisches Archiv des Auswärtigen Amtes, Bonn, Sachsen 39, unfoliated.

50. Karlheinz Blaschke, "Die Verwaltung in Sachsen und Thüringen," in *Deutsche Verwaltungsgeschichte,* vol. 3, *Das deutsche Reich bis zum Ende der Monarchie,* ed. Kurt G. A. Jeserich et al. (Stuttgart, 1984), 781.

milieu and thought the same way. The remaining deputies were made up of some government officials, a few industrialists, and a large component of lawyers. With only a few exceptions, the deputies were Saxon particularists of the narrowest sort, wherein the so-called Progressives could hardly be distinguished from the Conservatives. There wasn't a single day when it was a pleasure to sit in such a chamber.[51]

In the end it is less important to choose between the positive and negative appraisals offered here by Blaschke and Bebel than to develop a more nuanced, contingent picture. What were reformist conservatives actually trying to achieve when they sought to enhance the governmentality of their societies? In exploring the contentious nature of electoral rights, this essay has attempted to recapture the ambivalence, but also the variety and boldness, of their reform proposals. The picture that emerges suggests that liberals *and* reformist conservatives each developed compelling strategies for political renewal, accommodating economic development and social upheaval in the interest of system stabilization. The middle ground upon which liberals and conservatives met was often narrow and shifting. But it should not be ignored. Both groups of reformers developed ideas that were diverse and complex, and both may have been more in tune with "the spirit of the times" than scholars tend to admit. If this is so, then Germany's political culture in this watershed era surely remains a high priority for comparative research in the future.

---

51. August Bebel, *Aus meinem Leben* (Berlin, 1961), 784.

Saxony's "Liberal Era" and the Rise of the Red Specter in the 1870s

Wolfgang Schröder

I. The Context

It was a rare occurrence in the history of parliaments: When the Saxon *Landtag* convened in November 1866 for the first time after the Austro-Prussian War, one quarter of the eighty deputies in the lower house — supported by a campaign of public meetings and petitions — demanded the immediate dissolution of parliament and the holding of new elections, in accordance with the electoral law of 15 November 1848. The motion was defeated by the overwhelming conservative majority in the house. However, the issue of reform by no means disappeared from the parliamentary agenda. On the contrary.

The episode in November–December 1866 was the symptomatic expression of a conflict that had been simmering for two decades. Having won a share in political power through the royally sanctioned electoral law of November 1848, the Saxon bourgeoisie had been abruptly excluded from this (albeit circumscribed) legislative role by the government's coup d'état against the *Landtag* on 1 June 1850. The previously abolished *Landtag* was reactivated. Both the upper and lower houses of the *Landtag* were now structured along corporatist lines, and therefore they were once again dominated by absolute conservative majorities. During the 1850s, this constellation came to be seen increasingly as inappropriate to the social and economic structure of the Saxon kingdom. Therefore, by the early 1860s the question of *Landtag* suffrage reform constituted a central conflict zone in Saxon domestic politics, pitting a conservative state government against the political representatives of the Saxon bourgeoisie.[1] In the era of reaction, the Saxon authorities had also attempted to curb conflict through a mixture of repressive measures, the careful provision of economic reform to safeguard middle-class economic interests, and minimal political concessions. Chief among the economic reforms that had implications for all levels of political life was the introduction of occupational freedom in 1861. It was no accident that this economic reform was accompanied in 1861 by a suffrage reform. But the new suffrage was a stopgap palliative at best: it neither encroached on the prerogatives of the upper house nor radically altered the corporatist character of the lower house. Its provisions were limited to increasing (from five to ten) the number of lower-house deputies representing the social "estates" of trade and manufacturing.[2] As a result, the liberal bourgeoisie was still condemned to remain a perennial minority in the Saxon parliament.

If this situation was precarious even in "normal times," it became highly explosive when the "catastrophe of Königgrätz" (3 July 1866) called into question the very existence of the Kingdom of Saxony. The challenge to the status quo came not only from influential Prussian circles, but also from an important part of the Saxon bourgeoisie, whose leaders had tried to stir up resentment against the war with Prussia in part because such a war would directly damage their economic interests. After Saxony's defeat at the side of the Austrian forces, these Saxon burghers demanded — though far from unanimously — the closest possible association of Saxony with the Hohenzollern state. Some of them even demanded that Saxony be annexed outright by Prussia. These aspirations emanated from Leipzig, the "secret capital" of Saxony, which since the partition of Saxony at the Congress of Vienna in 1815 had come to be located on the extreme northwestern periphery of the kingdom. In terms of trade politics, it was natural that Leipzig entrepreneurs should not only look mainly toward their Prussian neighbor to the north, but also demand a strong national state. Such a state, they argued, would help them find markets as far afield as the New World; it would also contribute to the increasing uniformity of markets within Germany. These national political interests of the Saxon bourgeoisie

---

1. Rolf Weber, *Die Revolution in Sachsen, 1848/49: Entwicklung und Analyse ihrer Triebkräfte* (Berlin, 1970); Roland Zeise, "Zur Rolle der sächsischen Bourgeoisie im Ringen um die wirtschaftspolitische Vorrangstellung in Deutschland in den 50er und 60er Jahren," in *Die großpreußisch-militaristische Reichsgründung, 1871,* ed. Horst Bartel and Ernst Engelberg, 2 vols. (Berlin, 1971), 1:233ff.; Andreas Neemann, "Landtag und Politik in der Reaktionszeit: Sachsen, 1849/50 bis 1866" (Ph.D. diss., University of Tübingen, 1998).

2. Of the 80 deputies, 20 were elected by direct vote from among owners of knightly estates (*Rittergüter*), 25 indirectly in urban ridings, 25 in agrarian ridings, and 10 by trading and manufacturing circles (*Handels- und Fabrikstand*).

naturally collided with the particularism found among many small and medium-sized German states at this time. The axis of this conflict pointed in the same direction as the polarity between the force of Bismarck's "revolution from above" and the particularist defensive stance of the Saxon conservatives. Bismarck, aided by the Prussian military, fulfilled fundamental bourgeois demands, which helped to stabilize Hohenzollern rule. But Saxon particularists vehemently opposed — whether openly or covertly — the incorporation of Saxony into the emerging national state.

II. New Departures after 1866

Decisive in determining the outcome of this conflict were the peace treaties Saxony was forced to conclude with Prussia in October 1866. Other factors conditioning these developments should not be neglected, however. When King Johann returned to Saxony immediately after the peace agreement, his journey from the Saxon-Bohemian border town of Bad Schandau into Dresden turned into a triumphal procession, accentuated by anti-Prussian sentiment. This demonstration of "loyalty and devotion" to the "ancestral ruling house" by very broad strata of the population became an important factor in the tense political situation of the day, for it became obvious now that the mass of Saxon citizens did not blame the sovereign for the misguided policy that had led to the costly war against Prussia and the disastrous defeat. To be sure, the monarchy had had to accept a grievous diminution of its sovereignty in the agreement with Prussia. Yet it mastered the domestic political crisis without damage. As a result, the entire system of governance remained intact, including the state apparatus dominated by Saxon conservatives. Paradoxically, the traditionally strong leftist opposition in Saxony contributed to this. For although left-wing liberals and democrats pushed for a *großdeutsch* federalism and voiced vehement opposition on the basis of democratic principles to antidemocratic, militarist rule in Prussia, they also made a stand against any *kleindeutsch* unitary state. As a result, members of the National Liberal Party (Nationalliberale Partei) in Saxony were seriously isolated. Demonized by the conservatives as "annexationists," as proponents of the "archenemy" Prussia, and as traitors to the "fatherland," these National Liberals were utterly ostracized in Saxon politics. Their status as pariahs was so clear that they did not even dare to nominate their leader, Karl Biedermann, as a candidate for the Constituent Reichstag of the North German Confederation.[3]

---

3. The entire process is perceptively analyzed in James Retallack, " 'Why Can't a Saxon Be More Like a Prussian?' Regional Identities and the Birth of Modern Political

Retaining some elements of its previous sovereignty, but bound and gagged in many other respects, Saxony was integrated into the emerging Germany, even while Prussian troops continued to occupy its soil. Essential rights were ceded either to Prussia or to the Confederation. Sovereignty in military and foreign affairs was given up outright, whereas the loss of autonomy in judicial, trade, and other economic matters was more drawn out. Saxony also lost control over its very lucrative postal and telegraph system, as it did over indirect taxes and customs revenues. Thus weakened, the Kingdom of Saxony had hardly any influence on political decisions made in Berlin. With a territory of roughly 15,000 square kilometers and a population of almost 2.6 million (1871), Saxony was the largest member of the North German Confederation after Prussia, but it was virtually overwhelmed by the latter, whose area of 350,000 square kilometers outstripped Saxony's by more than twenty-three times, and whose population of 25 million exceeded Saxony's tenfold. The Reichstag deputies elected in Saxony had just as little influence: the twenty-three seats accorded to Saxony were completely dwarfed in the plenary assembly of the North German Reichstag, where 297 deputies sat. The same situation prevailed in the postunification German Reichstag, which numbered 397 seats after 1874.

In light of the precarious situation vis-à-vis the Berlin center, the conflict simmering in Saxony between the monarchical-conservative government and the liberal bourgeoisie for two decades was extremely threatening: it increasingly endangered the domestic political stability of the kingdom and its already weak position in the North German Confederation. The threat was only increased by the continuing rapid development of Saxon trade and industry. The census of 1871 indicated that only 16 percent of the Saxon population was engaged in agriculture, compared to 52 percent engaged in industry and crafts and 10 percent in trade and transportation.[4] Other than Belgium, Saxony was the most industrialized state in Europe. Despite severe structural crisis, the bourgeoisie had an

---

Culture in Germany, 1866–67," *Canadian Journal of History* 32 (1997): 26–55. Cf. Siegfried Weichlein, "Sachsen zwischen Landesbewußtsein und Nationsbildung, 1866–1871," in *Sachsen im Kaiserreich: Politik, Wirtschaft und Gesellschaft im Umbruch,* ed. Simone Lässig and Karl Heinrich Pohl (Dresden, 1997), 241–70.

4. "Die Verteilung der Bevölkerung des Königreichs Sachsen nach Haupt-Berufs- und Erwerbsklassen auf Grund der Volkszählung vom 1. December 1871," *Zeitschrift des K. Sächs. Statistischen Bureaus* 31 (1875): 39ff. as well as the supplement, 1ff.; Rudolf Forberger, *Die Industrielle Revolution in Sachsen, 1800 bis 1861,* 2 vols. (Berlin, 1982); for the period before 1871, see also Hubert Kiesewetter, *Industrialisierung und Landwirtschaft: Sachsens Stellung im regionalen Industrialisierungsprozeß Deutschlands im 19. Jahrhundert* (Cologne, 1988). The most recent study of industrial development in Saxony after 1871 is a century old: Heinrich Gebauer, *Die Volkswirtschaft im Königreiche Sachsen,* 3 vols. (Dresden, 1893).

extraordinarily broad economic basis in Saxony, for a rapidly expanding population relied on it for its livelihood, foodstuffs, and clothing. The political domination of slightly more than 1,000 owners of knight's estates (*Rittergutsbesitzer*) must have seemed all the more anachronistic in this context. As a social group, these estate owners occupied key positions in the state apparatus; they also dominated the upper house of the *Landtag* and frequently bent political opinion in the lower house to their will. Economically strong, but politically weak, the liberal bourgeoisie was relegated to a minor role in the legislative process.

To resolve the conflict over Saxony's *Landtag* suffrage law through cosmetic reforms was no longer feasible after 1866, because Bismarck had chosen to provide universal Reichstag suffrage without any property qualifications. In fact, he had done so against the explicit opposition of the Saxon government. Bismarck had recognized in universal suffrage the means to break dynastic resistance to German unification. The elections to the Constituent Reichstag of the North German Confederation in February 1867 revealed just what kind of appeal and mobilizing potential were represented by universal suffrage: fully two-thirds of eligible voters in Saxony trooped to the polls to cast their ballots. Another innovation in February 1867 was that although Conservatives and Liberals stood as candidates, so did members of the fledgling workers' movement. Candidates of the Saxon People's Party even won a majority in two of the twenty-three Saxon constituencies. This experience inevitably acted as an additional impulse that fueled the existing bourgeois opposition to the corporatist suffrage. In fact, in Leipzig and in the industrialized Erzgebirge in particular, workers' and people's associations (*Arbeiter-* and *Volksvereine*) demanded a democratic suffrage for the *Landtag*. They also called explicitly for the abolition or thorough reform of the feudal upper house.[5] The sum of these factors suggests why Saxon public opinion felt so strongly that the corporatist suffrage was untenable. Reluctantly, in 1867–68 the conservative Saxon government had to consent to a real electoral reform.[6]

III. Electoral Reform and Its Consequences

The new electoral law of 3 December 1868 abolished the previous corporatist structure of the *Landtag*'s lower house and granted a direct rather

---

5. SächsHStA Dresden, Ministerium des Innern Nr. 5372, 24ff.

6. Gerhard A. Ritter with Merith Niehuss, *Wahlgeschichtliches Arbeitsbuch, Materialien zur Statistik des Kaiserreichs, 1871–1918* (Munich, 1980), 163ff.; Wolfgang Schröder, "Wahlrecht und Wahlkämpfe im Königreich Sachsen, 1866–1896," in *Wahlen und Wahlkämpfe in Deutschland: Von den Anfängen im 19. Jahrhundert bis zur Bundesrepublik*, ed. Gerhard A. Ritter (Düsseldorf, 1997), 79ff.

than indirect (or two-stage) electoral procedure. All male citizens aged 25 and over were enfranchised, provided they paid at least 1 *Thaler* (3 marks) in direct taxes or owned a property with a dwelling on it.[7] (Other minor provisions excluded a small proportion of such males.) At a stroke, Saxony had the most progressive *Landtag* franchise of any individual German state, granting the vote to about 10 percent of the population. The moderate property qualification, however, excluded half of the citizens already eligible to vote in Reichstag elections. Furthermore, not only was the upper chamber's existing position and composition left practically unchanged; a corporatist remnant was grafted onto the lower chamber in that its eighty deputies were elected in thirty-five urban and forty-five rural ridings. On the one hand, this provision ensured the predominance of deputies from the countryside. On the other hand, many small and medium-sized towns that served as the central point of district (political) cultures were torn from their natural surroundings. An extreme case was the extensive fifth urban constituency, encompassing fifteen smaller towns with completely different local interests. It was exceedingly difficult to find a candidate who was known in this local multitude and who enjoyed a good reputation everywhere. Conversely, the rural constituencies were extended by this stipulation to include up to 150 villages. The liberal parties were usually incapable of distributing even ballot papers everywhere in such districts, let alone their own propaganda. The only institution with an overview of the dozens of villages was the government, which acted — partly in secret, partly publicly — as the driving force behind conservative election campaigns.[8]

The new electoral law provided for the one-time replacement of all eighty deputies. This first "integral renewal" of the lower house was effected in the elections of 4 June 1869. Each subsequent *Landtag* election, however, saw only one-third of constituencies contested at biennial intervals. As a result, the election campaign was broken down further, in addition to being fragmented into rural and urban constituencies. If the preceding elections had automatically ensured an agrarian-conservative three-quarters majority, in 1869 the liberal movement for

---

7. In accordance with this regulation, impoverished villagers in the countryside (*dörfliche Häusler*) were also eligible to vote; the government considered them to be conservative elements. Even in small and medium-sized towns, eligibility resulted primarily from house ownership. For example, in Taucha, 283 (10.9%) of 2,597 inhabitants (in 1867) had the right to vote; of these, 238 (84%) were enfranchised by virtue of owning a house or a farm, whereas only 45 (16%) by virtue of meeting the tax limit. Sächsisches Staatsarchiv Leipzig, Stadt Taucha, Nr. 2006, Landtagswahlliste 1869.

8. The Prussian envoy in Dresden even believed "that the organization of the Saxon Conservative Party at this time only existed in the civil service." Geheimes Staatsarchiv Preußischer Kulturbesitz Berlin-Dahlem, Rep. 81 Dresden IV A Nr. 29a, 243, Friedrich von Eichmann to Otto von Bismarck, report no. 95, 18 Dec. 1867.

the first time had a chance of achieving a majority, at least in the lower house. Despite insufficient party and electoral organization, it indeed attained a slim majority there.[9] To be sure, Zittau's conservative mayor, Daniel Haberkorn, was once again elected president of the lower house: the regional solidarity of deputies from Upper Lusatia tipped the scales in his favor. Moreover, considerable differences still existed between the two wings of the liberal camp: the National Liberal wing and the left-liberal Progressive wing. Nevertheless, the formation of a common (if not quite united) liberal caucus materialized in the *Landtag*. In this caucus the left liberals (*Fortschrittler*) held the numerical advantage, while the National Liberals (*Nationalliberalen*) possessed the outstanding political mind in Karl Biedermann, editor of the *Deutsche Allgemeine Zeitung*.

IV. Dawn of the "Liberal Era"

The liberal deputies, having agreed on a common election platform that called for reforms in central areas of domestic politics, specified their demands in a series of motions that were submitted soon after the *Landtag* convened.[10] The government, however, after anxiously awaiting the election result, limited itself essentially to the constitutional requirement that it put its proposed budget before the *Landtag*. The government wanted to avoid "bringing such questions to debate on which a principled disagreement among the parties could be expected."[11] After some hesitation, and not without heated discussions in cabinet meetings, the government followed the arguments of the interior minister, Hermann von Nostitz-Wallwitz, who had been responsible for the previous suffrage law of 1861 but who now signaled a readiness to move closer to the liberals' position. That the liberal awakening was beginning to take root is also suggested by the popular contemporary designation of the *Landtag* session of 1869–70 as the "motion *Landtag*" (*Antragslandtag*).

In the *Landtag* elections in the fall of 1871 the liberal camp won an

---

9. Determining the exact party grouping of the *Landtag*'s lower house is complicated by the malleable caucus boundaries. According to voting behavior, approximately 37 deputies can be placed in the liberal camp, 43 in the conservative one.

10. *Leipziger Tageblatt*, no. 125, 5 May 1869, 4167f.; *Leipziger Zeitung*, no. 123, 26 May 1869, 3177. When it came to concrete proposals, the "necessary advance of our internal constitutional affairs" postulated in the election program — including expansion of the suffrage, abolition of the electoral distinction between town and country, and removal of the two-chamber system — was relegated to the background. Priority was given to the reform of local government and of schooling.

11. Richard von Friesen to the Prussian envoy in Dresden, as reported in Politisches Archiv des Auswärtigen Amtes (hereafter PA AA) Bonn, R 3193, Eichmann to Bismarck, 31 Aug. 1869.

additional two seats, which strengthened its slim majority over the conservatives. For the first time, a left-liberal deputy and former Forty-eighter, Dr. Wilhelm Michael Schaffrath, was elected president of the lower house. Against the background of a significant economic upturn during the postunification era — which also included a plethora of fraudulent companies — the liberals continued on the offensive. The "motion *Landtag*" of 1869–70 became the "reform *Landtag*" of 1871–73. How did this happen in the face of resistance from the still-conservative Saxon government?

The regime in Dresden considered the liberals' reform package from two points of view. First, Saxon ministers could not ignore the fact that the apparently provisional arrangement of the North German Confederation had turned out to be a permanent and final decision, entrenched as a result of the victory against France in 1870–71 and the founding of the *Kaiserreich* in 1871. These developments had shattered the Saxon government's hopes that the addition of Bavaria, Württemberg, and Baden would also bring concessions to Saxon sovereignty. The treaty stipulations concluded in the aftermath of the "catastrophe of Königgrätz" in 1866 were not eased one iota. Second, the more perceptive government ministers viewed the liberal reform bills as an opportunity to serve the interests of the entire state by removing the considerable backlog of necessary reforms that had built up in the reactionary era after 1848–49. Such ministers were motivated by the expectation that they could at the same time stabilize the existing conservative regime by means of domestic reform but also take the wind out of the liberal opposition's sails. In any case, they were aware that the government could not provoke any internal political conflicts by insisting on a "do-nothing" stance: in light of liberal developments in the Reich, such a policy would have reflected badly on Saxony when compared to Bismarck's course. Even when compared to other smaller and medium-sized states, Saxony lagged behind the Bismarckian "revolution from above."

V.   The Reform of Local Government and Education

Although the reforms set in motion by liberal initiative were far-reaching, that they took shape at all was due to the cooperation of the conservative Saxon government, as well as the determination of the liberal majority in the lower house to overcome the stubborn resistance of the "aristocratic" upper house. The starting point was a revision of the rural municipal act (*Landgemeindeordnung*) of 1838. The prevailing statutes had long since become untenable because of the previous removal of feudal dues and other related changes that necessitated a

"true, radical reform."[12] The new provisions granted Saxon rural municipalities, which numbered approximately 2,000, greater autonomy and
extended functions in municipal affairs, though under the supervision of
the authorized government office. This offer of greater independence
for local government was associated with the additional financial burdens incurred by the Saxon state as the result of the transfer of functions
previously exclusive to the state (for example, the partial assumption of
police powers). This development in turn created the (financial) prerequisite for freeing the one hundred or so Saxon courts of justice from
their administrative tasks. As lower organs of state authority, these
courts had been both exercising judicial functions and administering
their districts. Unless delegated to the municipalities, administrative
functions now became the responsibility of the twenty-five newly created district administrations (*Amtshauptmannschaften*). By implement-
ing the separation of the judiciary and the administration at this time (at
least for the lower echelons of state authority), the government addressed the old liberal demand for a state ruled by law (*Rechtsstaat*).
This was the first step on a long road—largely precipitated by imperial
legislation—that eventually included the reorganization of the judicial
apparatus in Saxony and a modernization of legal proceedings.

Under the direction of their arch-conservative president, Ludwig
von Zehmen, the aristocrats in the upper house tried to block this
reform package with all means at their disposal. They did not even draw
back from speculating on a shift in policy due to a rumored change on
the Saxon throne. To be sure, they resented the extension of functions of
the rural municipalities and the removal of the district administrations
from their direct sphere of influence; however, the peers also strove to
undermine cooperation between the conservative interior minister Nostitz-Wallwitz and the liberal majority in the lower house, because they
perceived this precedent as dangerous. The attempt failed, however, in
part because the conservatives in the lower house refused to follow the
lead of their comrades in the upper house. Responsible for this "defection" was a group of younger district governors (*Amtshauptleute*) who
were convinced of the need for an administrative reform and who believed that such a reform, even one passed under liberal auspices, would
actually stabilize conservative dominance. This indeed proved to be the
case. A more effective administrative hierarchy was achieved by institut-
ing a clear division of power among (from top to bottom) the Saxon
cabinet (*Gesamtministerium*), the regional government (*Kreishauptmannschaft*), district government (*Amtshauptmannschaft*), and munici-

---

12. "Regierung und Landtag des Königreichs Sachsen, II," in *Die Grenzboten,* I.
Quartal (1873): 313.

palities, each of which retained a markedly conservative personnel policy. The position of district governor was without exception filled by conservative officials, about half of whom came from noble ranks. The local representational bodies (*Bezirksvertretungen*) assigned to them were hailed by the liberals as a "parliamentarization" of the administrative organs despite undemocratic election procedures. Yet they usually proved to be a conservative instrument in the hands of the respective district governors.

Connected to this modernization of Saxony's internal administration was an equally significant reform of the state's elementary school system, which had long been demanded by the liberals. The elementary school bill (*Volksschulgesetz*) introduced by the newly appointed minister of education and cultural affairs, Carl von Gerber, signified a substantial improvement from the liberal viewpoint. Previously, schools (and particularly rural schools) had been under the thumb of the churches; they were simultaneously subject to the patronage of the manorial lord. Now the principle of expert state supervision of schools was established; the training and status of teachers was improved; and a curriculum oriented more toward secular needs was supplemented with obligatory further schooling subsequent to the eight-year compulsory education. Lastly, responsibility for schools, including financial responsibility, was transferred to the municipalities. These fundamental innovations were nevertheless coupled with regulations against which the liberals protested vehemently. These concerned, for instance, the demand approved by the First State Synod in 1871 that the church continue to supervise not only religious instruction but all "ethical-religious education," together with the insistence on confessional schools, the obligation that children of dissenters take religious instruction, and the commission of clerics as inspectors of small rural schools.

The upper house used the elementary school law as a test of strength with the lower house: the peers wanted compensation for their glaring defeat over administrative reform. This time they succeeded, largely because they secured the allegiance of conservatives in the lower house. The bill was narrowly defeated by the lower house, but it was passed almost unanimously in the upper house, and after it was published it came into effect. This procedure actually represented a turning point that ensured the continued existence of the semifeudal "chamber of peers." A contributor to the *Grenzboten,* a liberal journal edited by Hans Blum (as the successor to Gustav Freytag), spoke of a decisive "setback in Saxony." The appraisal was correct. For this turn of events had demonstrated the hollowness of exaggerated liberal hopes that the conservative state government, still unchallenged in its authority, would orient itself primarily toward the liberal majority in the lower, "elected chamber," and that the upper chamber, which still stood in crass contradiction to the social structure of Saxony, would be relegated to the background. Subsequent developments also contributed to turning the liberal dawn into disillusionment.

VI. Party Politics in the "Liberal Era"

Two fundamental processes can be identified in this respect. In the economic sphere, a "Great Depression" followed the boom of the founding years. With a certain time lag, after 1875 it precipitated a drastic decline in trade and industry in the highly industrialized Saxony, followed by widespread unemployment and decreasing purchasing power. The *Gründerkrise* not only weakened the economic position of the bourgeoisie in Saxony; it generally threw into question the liberal concept of society. These doubts were exploited by the conservatives in their effort to demolish liberalism. In the political sphere, the Reichstag elections of January 1874 witnessed the emergence of the Social Democrats as the strongest party — the first occasion of such a victory in any German state. The Social Democrats had not held a single seat in the *Landtag,* but in the Reichstag voting they won 35 percent of votes cast in Saxony, and six of twenty-three Saxon seats.[13] In comparison to 1871, the number of Social Democratic voters had tripled, from 36,600 to almost 97,000. The Social Democratic Workers' Party (Sozialdemokratische Arbeiterpartei, or SDAP) founded in Eisenach had not only overcome the existential crisis precipitated by the Franco-Prussian War of 1870–71 and the imprisonment of their leaders; in an age of growing social and economic conflicts, it had also been able to consolidate its mass appeal. The government's counterattack against the socialists, culminating in the trial of August Bebel and Wilhelm Liebknecht for high treason in March 1872,[14] proved futile. In conflict with the General German Workers' Association (Allgemeiner Deutscher Arbeiterverein, or ADAV) founded by Ferdinand Lassalle in 1863, the "Bebel-Liebknecht wing," with its headquarters in Leipzig, had triumphed in Saxony. August Geib, Julius Vahlteich, Johann Most, August Bebel, Julius Motteler, and Wil-

---

13. Gerhard A. Ritter, "Das Wahlrecht und die Wählerschaft der Sozialdemokratie im Königreich Sachsen, 1867–1914," in *Der Aufstieg der deutschen Arbeiterbewegung,* ed. idem (Munich, 1989), 49–101, esp. 62ff.; Wolfgang Schröder, "'. . . zu Grunde richten wird man uns nicht mehr': Sozialdemokratie und Wahlen im Königreich Sachsen, 1867–1877," *Beiträge zur Geschichte der Arbeiterbewegung* 4 (1994): 3–18.

14. Bebel and Liebknecht were each sentenced to two years' confinement in a fortress. Karl-Heinz Leidigkeit, ed., *Der Leipziger Hochverratsprozeß vom Jahre 1872* (Berlin, 1960); Ursula Herrmann and Volker Emmrich, *August Bebel, Eine Biographie* (Berlin, 1989), 125ff.; August Bebel, *Aus meinem Leben* (Berlin, 1983), 336ff.

helm Liebknecht were Eisenachers who represented Saxony in the Reichstag.

The election results showed that Social Democracy had become a political and social factor of the first order. The increasingly well-organized and disciplined socialist movement gave a voice to the "common man" and represented a social and political alternative—both bourgeois-democratic and socialist in character—to the existing economic and political systems.[15] In the process, though, the bipolar relationship between the conservative and liberal camps (both of which were internally divided) had also mutated, becoming now a triangular relationship. Ignoring the innovative potential of Social Democracy and unnerved by the Paris Commune of 1871, the propertied classes and their political representatives, both liberal and conservative, resorted to an unproductive conflict with the socialist left. However, they patently failed in their attempt to dislodge the Saxon SPD from its growing mass base. The National Liberals reacted to the shock of the Reichstag elections of 1874 by mutating into an Imperial Association for Saxony (Reichsverein für Sachsen). The declared purpose of this new organization was to "combat all enemies of the Reich and of the social order."[16] These enemies of socialism attempted to occupy the "political center" in Saxony, hoping that they might tip the scales of power within the liberal camp against the Progressive Party (Fortschrittspartei). One reason for the animosity between National Liberals and Progressives was that the latter had refused to support the "military compromise" during the dispute over army appropriations (the *Septennat*) in the Reichstag.

These disagreements within the liberal camp had a direct effect on parliamentary life in the Saxon *Landtag*. In the (one-third) elections in the autumn of 1875, the liberals managed to retain their majority. But due to abstention by the National Liberals, Zittau's conservative mayor, Haberkorn, replaced the Progressive Schaffrath as president of the house.[17] This was a symptom of far-reaching changes in the political power constellation in Saxony. Until that point, fear of the National Liberals' "unifying tendencies" had created a virtually unbridgeable chasm between the right wing of the liberal camp and the conservatives, who had repeatedly collaborated with the *großdeutsch* Progressive Party

---

15. Karsten Rudolph, *Die sächsische Sozialdemokratie vom Kaiserreich zur Republik (1871–1923)* (Weimar, 1995), 34ff.; Wolfgang Schröder and Inge Kiesshauer, *Die Genossenschaftsbuchdruckerei zu Leipzig, 1872–1881* (Wiesbaden, 1992).

16. Karl Biedermann, *Fünfzig Jahre im Dienste des nationalen Gedankens* (Breslau, 1892), 124.

17. *Mittheilungen über die Verhandlungen des ordentlichen Landtags im Königreich Sachsen während der Jahre 1875–1876*, I. Kammer, Allgemeine, die Ständeversammlung betreffende Nachrichten, I, 9ff., 2. Präliminarsitzung der II. Kammer vom 13. Okt. 1875.

out of particularist considerations. Now this polarity was increasingly transcended by a strongly antisocialist policy, which provided a bridge between the National Liberals, previously branded as "annexationists," and the conservatives. In this way, the National Liberals managed to make themselves "respectable" in Saxony.

This trend nevertheless collided with the reorganization of the conservative camp, which in April 1875 had formed the Conservative State Association for the Kingdom of Saxony (Conservativer Landesverein für das Königreich Sachsen). This founding, one should note, occurred one year prior to the founding of the German Conservative Party (Deutschkonservative Partei), supported by Bismarck, on a national basis. The founding manifesto of the Conservative State Association included the statement that "[o]ur form of conservatism is far removed from any antifederal particularism." The manifesto also declared that Saxon Conservatism "does not trust uncritically in official [state] policy, does not acquiesce automatically to it, and does not inevitably oppose the healthy aspirations of the parties calling themselves liberal."[18] Notwithstanding the characteristic negativity of these formulations, this was not just empty rhetoric. In practice, Conservatives knew full well that deliberations in the Saxon Landtag, always closely monitored by the government, usually ended in compromise. In policy matters, however, the Conservatives now established themselves as a more coherent, more united party, standing decidedly to the right of the government line (though not always without its support), and increasingly organized in local associations across the state.

This (re)organization of Conservative forces had a twofold effect: First, the establishment of the new party was calculated to spearhead a Conservative offensive against the "liberal terror." It was specifically aimed at achieving a Conservative majority in the lower house. Second, by planting the Conservative pole firmly, this new organization dragged the center of the political power constellation to the right. This in the long run paved the way for a corresponding shift of the entire center of gravity in Saxon politics. Pressure in this direction increased significantly when in 1877 the Conservative Association for the Leipzig District (Conservativer Verein für den Leipziger Kreis) was founded under the direction of a noble estate owner living just south of Leipzig, Baron Heinrich von Friesen-Rötha. The new association represented an entirely new organizational structure, intended to create a Conservative ring around Leipzig and thus besiege the (National-) liberal bastion there. This

---

18. *Leipziger Zeitung*, no. 155, 2 July 1875, 2034; Wolfgang Schröder, "Die Genese des 'Conservativen Landesvereins für das Königreich Sachsen,'" in *Sachsen im Kaiserreich*, ed. Lässig and Pohl, 152–74.

tightly organized association, whose jurisdiction encompassed one-quarter of Saxony, became a personal instrument that allowed Friesen to wield power — in a decisively antiliberal direction — within the State Association for one and a half decades.[19] On the other side of the spectrum, the ADAV, with approximately 16,000 members, and the SDAP, with about 9,000 members under Bebel and Liebknecht, amalgamated into the German Socialist Workers' Party (Sozialistische Arbeiterpartei Deutschlands) at the Gotha congress in 1875. At last the division within the workers' movement was overcome.[20] The unification at Gotha not only survived the severe test of the antisocialist laws, which Bismarck whipped through the Reichstag in 1878. It also created the preconditions for the socialist triumphs that led to and followed the Iron Chancellor's departure from office in 1890.[21]

Thus the liberal bourgeoisie was no longer either the sole opponent of the Conservatives or the sole partner of the Saxon government. Instead, in this triangular constellation of parties, it was caught between the political fronts. Hence it was forced onto the defensive vis-à-vis both the growing workers' movement and the reorganized Conservative Party. In contrast to its adversaries on the left and the right, the Saxon liberals were not unified; they remained divided into the National Liberal wing and the left-liberal Progressive Party. Both wings remained essentially parties of notables, and both possessed only a loose organizational structure. Nevertheless, together or apart, they exerted considerable influence on the Saxon political landscape, especially because of their strong presence in the media. Economically weakened by the Great Depression, they also lost their backing in federal politics, which shifted from a liberal to a conservative course.[22] The hopes from the early 1870s for a new "liberal era" faded quickly. Instead the liberals were thrown increasingly into defensive engagements. This altered posi-

---

19. Wolfgang Schröder, " 'Die Armee muß organisiert sein, ehe der Krieg beginnt': Die Entstehung des Conservativen Vereins für den Leipziger Kreis," *Leipziger Kalender* (1996), 140–65; James Retallack, *Notables of the Right: The Conservative Party and Political Mobilization in Germany, 1876–1918* (London, 1988); idem, "Die 'liberalen' Konservativen? Konservatismus und Antisemitismus im industrialisierten Sachsen," in *Sachsen im Kaiserreich*, ed. Lässig and Pohl, 133–48.

20. Wolfgang Schröder, "Der 'Berliner Entwurf' des Vereinigungsprogramms von 1875 und seine Stellung im Vereinigungsprozeß von SDAP und ADAV," *Jahrbuch für Geschichte* 21 (1980): 169ff.

21. Horst Bartel, Wolfgang Schröder, and Gustav Seeber, *Das Sozialistengesetz, 1878–1890: Illustrierte Geschichte des Kampfes der Arbeiterklasse gegen das Ausnahmegesetz* (Berlin, 1980), 37ff.

22. Gustav Seeber et al., *Deutsche Geschichte*, vol. 5, *Der Kapitalismus der freien Konkurrenz und der Übergang zum Monopolkapitalismus im Kaiserreich von 1871 bis 1897* (Berlin, 1988), 179ff.

tion become apparent relatively early in one important area of Saxon domestic politics where, as with the earlier administrative reform, a fundamental impetus for modernization still existed: tax reform.

VII. Tax Reform

If in the period 1869–73 the programmatic zeal and practical initiatives of the liberal camp resulted in overcoming the existing reform backlog, this did not apply to the bitter battles fought over the equally overdue tax reform. These battles, which lasted almost a decade, were largely precipitated by two factors. On the one hand, state revenues were placed under a substantially heavier strain after 1867. They were further weakened by the fact that indirect taxes went into the federal budget: state finances now had to rely on direct taxes above and beyond other fiscal revenues. These direct taxes in turn were made up of property, business, and personal taxes, assessed on completely different scales, and they were antiquated by virtue of the freedoms and leniency they accommodated. Still, the Saxon agrarians were incensed by the proportion of property and business taxes they paid, even though one-third was carried by the cities. Their ire only increased during the flourishing boom after 1871, which revealed an unexpectedly large amount of mobile capital. The agrarians used this fact to support their rebellion against the existing system of taxation, organizing a campaign of public meetings and petitions. This campaign, too, helped stabilize the Conservative camp and forced the liberal side onto the defensive. The result of these conflicts, in the course of which myriad complicated tax scenarios were considered and rejected, was a compromise between "city" and "country." On the basis of the first statewide estimate of income in 1875 (in which it was reported that almost one million actual and legal persons achieved a total annual income of slightly over 1 billion marks), an income tax was finally introduced in 1877–78. This tax was only minimally progressive, and it came into law in conjunction with a substantially reduced property tax. It nonetheless provided Saxony with the bulk of its tax revenues in subsequent decades.

VIII. Electoral Politics, Parliamentary Life, and the Onset of Reaction

One unanticipated and unwelcome consequence of tax redistribution was that workers whose annual income amounted to only 500 marks now also met the required property qualification for *Landtag* elections, which was pegged at 3 marks (or 1 *Thaler*) of direct state taxes (surtaxes were not taken into account). As a result, the voting potential of the

Social Democrats increased considerably. In the highly industrialized districts, more than one district governor complained as a result that "we have almost reached universal suffrage." In fact, until 1895 the number of voters eligible for the *Landtag* elections had risen from 10 to about 15 percent of the population.

On this basis, the Social Democrats saw good reason to participate actively in the election campaigns — in contrast to their policy in other states. In 1877, the Leipzig lawyer Emil Otto Freytag became the first Social Democrat to win a seat in the lower house of the Saxon *Landtag*. In 1879 and 1881, respectively, the leading minds of German Social Democracy, Wilhelm Liebknecht and August Bebel, also gained admission to the *Landtag*.[23] Once again, among all German states it was in Saxony that such inroads were first made at the level of state politics. Social Democracy, though persecuted by the antisocialist laws, thus obtained a new, legal arena for action. By 1895–96, the SPD caucus in the *Landtag* numbered fifteen deputies — almost one-fifth of all seats. The propertied classes were no longer "on their own" (*unter sich*) in Dresden's parliament. Instead, fresh faces and impertinent tempers now "interfered" regularly in domestic politics. This was a new type of opposition, unfamiliar in the halls of the lower house, for it articulated the consequences of social divisiveness and thereby breached the elitist atmosphere that had previously prevailed in the house. The severity of the indictments that Social Democratic deputies hurled at legal injustices and arbitrary policy powers is reminiscent of the revolutionary period of 1848–49. But the Social Democratic deputies did not stop there. Rather, they submitted a plethora of proposals pushing for feasible reforms in various areas, concerning, for example, further reform of the school system, mining legislation, or revision of a statute for domestic and rural servants. Some of these positions had been supported in the past by the liberals. But the novelty of the Socialist Party's demands is demonstrated by Bebel's suggestion that the premises used by Saxony's diplomatic envoy in Berlin should be made available to Reichstag deputies from Saxony, irrespective of the party they represented, in order to reduce costs and streamline the business of politics.

The stenographic reports of Saxon *Landtag* debates amply demonstrate with what obstinacy and ignorance the majority responded to even the most innocuous motions from SPD benches. The representatives of the "established parties" practiced a rigorous strategy of ostracizing their Social Democratic colleagues. Until 1909 not a single one

---

23. See the brief overview in Mike Schmeitzner and Michael Rudloff, *Geschichte der Sozialdemokratie im Sächsischen Landtag: Darstellung und Dokumentation, 1877–1997* (Dresden, 1997), 13ff.

of them was admitted to one of the *Landtag*'s committees, which were responsible for debating and making preliminary decisions on pending bills. In plenary debates, Socialist speeches were regularly cut short by motions to end the day's deliberations — that is, when the established parties had not agreed beforehand to forgo debate on Social Democratic motions altogether. Obviously, such resistance made the work of SPD deputies exceedingly difficult.

But the Social Democrats were not the only victims of such practices. By joining the common line of the Conservatives and National Liberals, the deputies of the Progressive Party (known as the Sächsischer Fortschritt) virtually relinquished their own position in the house and abandoned their political platform. The left-liberal opposition, which in 1866 had still been a relatively strong force in the lower house, was reduced by the 1880s to a mere shadow of its former self. By concentrating its entire effort on the enemy to the left, the Progressive Party was caught in the embrace of the right and paralyzed. The clearest expression of this self-subordination was a declaration by a factory owner from Mitweid, Kurt Starke, in January 1883, on behalf of the Progressives. "Even today," declared Starke, Saxon Progressives stood "firmly on the principles and program of the German Progressive Party [Deutsche Fortschrittspartei], and will always keep in mind its ideals." He added, however, that the Progressives appreciated "that a considerable part of our wishes and ideals have been fulfilled through the benevolent support of our government or are about to be realized, so that, at least in Saxony, we have no reason whatsoever to act in fundamental opposition . . . to this government." Starke then expressed his hope that the time would come when Saxon parliamentarians would "have nothing to do any more" with Social Democracy as a factor in politics, "and when we shall be able again to proceed on the basis of reasonable progress and hopefully in step with the government (vigorous shouts of approval from all sides of the House)."[24] The Austrian envoy stationed in Dresden evaluated this declaration as "welcome proof that party politicking has been patriotically subordinated to the great aims of the state."[25]

This was grist for the Conservatives' mill. After a few setbacks, their antiliberal offensive brought them their first majority in the *Landtag* elections of 1881 — a majority that was extended in subsequent elections. In 1877, the Conservative newspaper edited by Eduard von Ungern-

---

24. *Mittheilungen* 1883/84, II. Kammer, 1. Bd., 562, 36th session, 28 Jan. 1884. A motion to end debate, passed with only 15 nays, cut short Bebel's and Liebknecht's statements.

25. Österreichisches Staatsarchiv Vienna, Haus-, Hof- und Staatsarchiv, PA V/43, Baron von Herbert to Count Kálnoky, 19 Feb. 1884.

Sternberg declared: "Despite everything, we are growing constantly." Haughtily predicting that Conservatives would soon break the back of Saxon liberalism, Ungern-Sternberg added: "In a few years you will have no choice but to join us."[26] In other words, it was from a *strategic* position of strength and independence in the *Landtag* that Saxon Conservatives entered into election agreements with the National Liberal Party and the Progressive Party. Far from diluting the essence of conservatism, in their view such alliances were merely *tactical* compromises.

Political developments during the 1880s were dominated by the "*Kartell* of parties supporting the state" (*Kartell der staatserhaltenden Ordnungsparteien*). Beginning with the runoff elections to the Reichstag in 1874, this coalition — despite its many contradictions and conflicts — lasted for about twenty-five years, that is, into the early twentieth century. By contrast, the Bismarckian *Kartell* of Conservatives and National Liberals at the national level lasted only from 1887 to 1890. Gradually, the Saxon *Kartell* was extended to the *Landtag* elections, where Bismarck's antisocialist laws were rigorously invoked to gag the adversary (including, for instance, the confiscation of ballots). Without shaking the Social Democrats' mass base, these measures temporarily minimized the ability of Social Democrats to achieve *Landtag* victories. The bourgeois parties generally agreed before the election on a common candidate who had the best prospects for defeating a Social Democratic rival. In order to concentrate votes on this compromise candidate, the nominee often had to make substantial concessions. If a Conservative was nominated, he would have to hold out a few carrots to liberal voters; if a Progressive candidate was chosen — sometimes the best strategy to reduce the potential number of Social Democratic votes — he had to take into consideration Conservative and National Liberal wishes. In practice, the Conservatives usually emerged victorious from the wrangling over compromises. Strategically *and* tactically, then, the Saxon *Kartell* was a "compromise on conservative terms."[27] It misled both liberal "partners" into positions they would not otherwise have adopted, and it distorted the kingdom's political culture in general.

---

26. *Neue Reichs-Zeitung,* no. 8, 12 Jan. 1877; lead editorial, ibid., no. 19, 14 Jan. 1877.

27. This is the term used by James Retallack in "Politische Kultur, Wahlkultur, Regionalgeschichte: Methodologische Überlegungen am Beispiel Sachsens und des Reiches," in *Modernisierung und Region im wilhelminischen Deutschland: Wahlen, Wahlrecht und politische Kultur,* ed. Simone Lässig, Karl Heinrich Pohl, and James Retallack, 2d rev. ed. (Bielefeld, 1998), 15ff. The development and impact of *Kartellpolitik* is also analyzed in Gerhard A. Ritter, "Wahlen und Wahlpolitik im Königreich Sachsen, 1867–1914," in *Sachsen im Kaiserreich,* ed. Lässig and Pohl, 29–86.

As a last point, it should be noted that the social composition of the *Landtag*'s lower house differed considerably from that of any other German parliament, including the Reichstag. Almost half of all *Landtag* deputies were larger or smaller entrepreneurs, constituting more than 200 of about 440 deputies who sat in parliament from 1869 to 1909. A reciprocal effect was at work here. With the rise of the Ruhr district as the center of heavy industry in Germany, together with the rapid development of industry in Upper Silesia and Berlin, Saxony lost its singular role as an industrial pioneer. Extremely dependent on raw materials and exports, it was largely sustained by medium- or even small-scale enterprises. It was therefore particularly prone to crises. Apart from Leipzig's cosmopolitan commercial bourgeoisie, the political self-conception of these entrepreneurs, often dispersed in remote valleys, was dependent on a few general political principles. The entanglement of the Saxon Progressives with the Conservatives and National Liberals in antisocialist tactics deprived many of these entrepreneurs of any political point of reference from which they might have recaptured some measure of independence and influence. This signified an immense change in the overall nature of Saxon parliamentary life. In 1869 the typical industrialist or businessman who won a seat in the *Landtag* was a member of the oppositional left liberals. A quarter of a century later, an industrialist or businessman was even more likely to be a Conservative than a National Liberal. Having degenerated into a caricature of itself, the Saxon Progressive Party displayed none of the radicalism commonly associated with Eugen Richter's more determined left liberals in the Reichstag (thus Richter's dismissive reference to the Saxon Progressives as the *Sächsischer Kammerfortschritt,* which today might carry the connotation of "closet Progressives"). In Saxony, left liberalism had decimated its own base.

IX.   Conclusions

Even before 1881, when the Conservatives regained their majority in the lower house of the *Landtag,* the "liberal era" in Saxony had definitively ended. Under the auspices of the particularly severe Saxon variant of *Kartellpolitik,* the National Liberal and Progressive parties gradually shifted to the right and became junior partners of their actual adversaries. The entrenchment of a starkly antisocialist policy in Saxony proved to be a slow poison, infecting the substance of liberalism and finally leading in 1896 to a dramatic reversal of the *Landtag* suffrage introduced in 1868. The relatively open suffrage of 1868 was abolished with the votes not only of Conservative deputies but of most liberals as well. In its place was erected a three-class voting system similar to the one that prevailed in Prussia.[28] This Saxon "coup" emboldened antidemocratic forces elsewhere in Germany. Kaiser Wilhelm II asked imperiously: "This has to be tried here [in Berlin]. . . . Who can attend to it?"[29] In Saxony, however, the conservative trend continued to such an extent that the Conservatives won a two-thirds majority in the *Landtag* after 1900; this put them in the commanding position of being able to amend the Saxon constitution unilaterally. Conservative domination of Saxon political affairs became a burden even to the conservative Saxon government and led eventually to a breakup of the *Kartell*. After a lengthy tug-of-war, the cardinal mistake of 1896 had to be corrected in 1909, through the introduction of a more equitable pluralistic suffrage.

These later developments notwithstanding, in the first half of the 1870s the short-lived "liberal era" in Saxony achieved a substantial and innovative advance over the system of government that had prevailed during the 1850s and early 1860s. However, neither the basic prerogatives of the feudal upper house nor the conservatism underlying the overall system of governance was challenged in its essence. Therefore, the brief flowering of liberalism was followed by an era in which liberalism itself was paralyzed by its fear of the "red specter." That fear in turn permitted Saxon Conservatives to score some tangible victories in their battle against liberalism. The reestablishment of the Conservative *Landtag* majority in 1881 went hand in hand with the extinction of any innovative potential originating from the Saxon parliament. Once again, as in the 1850s, a reform backlog began to build, and once again this ultimately weakened Saxony's position within the German federation.

---

28. These issues are examined comprehensively in Simone Lässig, *Wahlrechtskampf und Wahlreform in Sachsen (1895–1909)* (Weimar, 1996); and James Retallack, " 'What Is to Be Done?' The Red Specter, Franchise Questions, and the Crisis of Conservative Hegemony in Saxony, 1896–1909," *Central European History* 23 (1990): 271–312. See also Karl Heinrich Pohl, "Die Nationalliberalen in Sachsen vor 1914," in *Liberalismus und Region: Zur Geschichte des deutschen Liberalismus im 19. Jahrhundert,* ed. Lothar Gall and Dieter Langewiesche (Munich, 1995), 195–215.

29. PA AA Bonn, R 3292, marginalia of Wilhelm II on a report by the Prussian envoy in Dresden, 24 Apr. 1896.

How Proletarian Was Leipzig's Social Democratic Milieu?

Thomas Adam

I. Introduction

In the last third of the nineteenth century, Leipzig, more than any other large German city, became the stronghold of the workers' culture movement (*Arbeiterkulturbewegung*).[1] Here, between the 1870s and the 1930s, a dense and broadly diversified Social Democratic organizational network developed that enveloped its members, as the saying goes, from the cradle to the grave, penetrating nearly all areas of life. After the prohibition of the Social Democratic Party in 1878, a multitude of theater and choral societies emerged, whose members were recruited from among Social Democrats. About two years later over forty such organizations already existed in Leipzig, with approximately 1,600 members. At the center of this organizational network was the Workers' Continuing Education Society (Fortbildungsverein für Arbeiter). Led by Friedrich Bosse, this organization—officially—was to promote "the continued education of the worker, to the exclusion of every political or religious bias."[2] Courses were offered in such subjects as arithmetic, bookkeeping, and English. From the beginning, it controlled the sections for gymnasts and singers. These activities, however, could not hide the fact that the association was a kind of legal substitute for the outlawed Social Democratic organization in Leipzig.[3]

After the lapse of the antisocialist laws in 1890, cultural workers' associations sprouted like mushrooms in the city. In 1893, fifteen work-

---

1. This essay draws on Thomas Adam, *Arbeitermilieu und Arbeiterbewegung in Leipzig 1871–1933* (Weimar, 1999).

2. *Der Arbeiterverein Leipzig, seine Entstehung und seine Entwicklung: Eine Festschrift zum 25jährigen Stiftungsfest* (Leipzig, 1904), 7.

3. Fritz Staude, *Sie waren stärker: Der Kampf der Leipziger Sozialdemokratie in der Zeit des Sozialistengesetzes, 1878–1890* (Leipzig, 1969), 64–67.

ers' gymnastics clubs with over 1,000 members could be counted. In 1907 the Workers' Choral Society (Arbeitersängerbund) in Leipzig had over 2,700 members in sixty men's choirs and six mixed choirs. Until the mid-1920s, a multitude of new cultural associations were added, and membership figures of the individual organizations grew enormously. The Consumers' Cooperative (Konsumverein) of Leipzig-Plagwitz included 76,000 members in 1926, while approximately 12,000 athletes were organized in thirty-eight gymnastics clubs and sports clubs for workers. Nowhere else did such a tightly knit network of workers' cultural organizations develop as in the *Messestadt*. This network provided support for the Leipzig member from his birth to his death: cared for by the *Kinderfreunde*, he eventually reached the age where he would join the Social Democratic youth organization, which in turn conveyed him to the SPD and/or a trade union.[4] In this way arose an apparently self-contained proletarian counterpart to bourgeois culture.

These developments, together with the exceedingly rich source material available, predestined Leipzig to become an exemplary case study for investigations into the origins and growth of the Social Democratic milieu in Germany. Whereas almost all existing work on the concept of milieus examines them in their (alleged) prime — in the Weimar Republic — their origins remain obscure, as Arnold Sywottek complained as long ago as 1984.[5] For this reason the following analysis concentrates on the last third of the nineteenth century: the period during which the Social Democratic milieu developed. Two principal questions are addressed here: What were the preconditions for the emergence of such a tightly knit network of workers' associations in the *Messestadt*? And why did Leipzig, not Berlin or Hamburg, become a stronghold of the workers' culture movement at such an early date? To answer these questions, the working hours and the wage levels of the Leipzig workforce are examined. The Leipzig example seems to suggest that an increase in leisure time and high wages were the indispensable preconditions for the emergence of such a broadly diversified Social Democratic associational network.

In almost all previous work on the Social Democratic milieu, the labor movement and the Social Democratic milieu have been conflated

---

4. Hans Dieter Schmid, "Der organisierte Widerstand der Sozialdemokraten in Leipzig, 1933–1935," in idem, *Zwei Städte unter dem Hakenkreuz* (Leipzig, 1994), 26–70, here 27–28; see also Karsten Rudolph, *Die sächsische Sozialdemokratie vom Kaiserreich zur Republik (1871–1923)* (Weimar, 1995); and Frank Heidenreich, *Arbeiterkulturbewegung und Sozialdemokratie in Sachsen vor 1933* (Weimar, 1995).

5. Arnold Sywottek, "Konsumverhalten der Arbeiter und 'sozialistische' Konsumgenossenschaften: Zur Geschichte der Arbeiterbewegung in der Weimarer Republik," in *Studien zur Arbeiterkultur*, ed. Albrecht Lehmann (Münster, 1984), 59–102, here 59.

uncritically. The Göttingen political scientist Franz Walter, for example, consistently uses the two concepts synonymously.[6] Therefore we need to pose the question: Was the Social Democratic milieu in fact socially homogeneous—that is, was it proletarian? Or was it, similar to the Catholic milieu, socially heterogeneous? The argument below suggests that the Social Democratic milieu of Leipzig, as in comparable large cities with pronounced service sectors (for example, Frankfurt am Main), was not a homogeneous, proletarian milieu. It was heterogeneous. The distinctions supporting this argument are to be examined by analyzing the social composition of the membership structure of two workers' sports clubs.

The construction of a Social Democratic associational network embracing nearly all areas and all stages of life implies the emergence of a socialist counterculture.[7] Did the workers' culture movement in Leipzig produce its own cultural agenda or program? Was this culture an alternative culture, as Franz Walter and Peter Lösche (among others) claim for the period of the Weimar Republic?[8] Or was it an integral part of the culture of the whole society, as Dieter Groh suggested with his thesis of "negative integration" or as Detlef Lehnert and Klaus Megerle have also argued?[9] What, if anything, was specific enough about the content of workers' culture to distinguish it clearly from bourgeois culture?

II. Opportunities for Leisure

Leisure time, to be sure, was not a product of the industrial revolution. However, industrialization first enabled its extension to underprivileged social strata. Along with the separation of residence and workplace came the strict distinction between work time and free time. As work time and leisure time became strictly separated from one another, the workday was rearranged so that the largest possible blocks of time be-

---

6. Franz Walter and Helge Matthiesen, "Milieus in der modernen deutschen Gesellschaftsgeschichte: Ergebnisse und Perspektiven der Forschung," in *Anpassung, Verweigerung, Widerstand: Soziale Milieus, politische Kultur und der Widerstand gegen den Nationalsozialismus in Deutschland im regionalen Vergleich,* ed. Detlef Schmiechen-Ackermann (Berlin, 1997), 46–75.

7. Cf. Antonio Gramsci, "Das Problem der politischen Führung bei der Bildung und Entwicklung der Nation und des modernen Staates in Italien: Aufzeichnungen aus den Jahren 1934/35," in idem, *Zu Politik und Kultur: Ausgewählte Schriften* (Frankfurt a. M., 1980), 277–303, here 277; see also Heidenreich, *Arbeiterkulturbewegung,* 9–12.

8. Cf. Walter and Matthiesen, "Milieus."

9. Dieter Groh, *Negative Integration und revolutionärer Attentismus: Die deutsche Sozialdemokratie am Vorabend des Ersten Weltkriegs* (Frankfurt a. M, 1973); Detlef Lehnert and Klaus Megerle, *Politische Teilkulturen zwischen Integration und Polarisierung: Zur politischen Kultur in der Weimarer Republik* (Opladen, 1990).

came available for both pursuits. Whereas successive phases of work and leisure had previously stood in close proximity—they had affected each other and penetrated each other—now the daylight was generally reserved for work, while the evening and nighttime were given over to leisure.[10]

Beginning in the 1880s, the hours of work at factories in two of Leipzig's western suburbs, Plagwitz and Lindenau, still totaled between ten and twelve hours per day.[11] To this was added a daily commute that might total between one and two hours, depending on what local public transport was used. The hours of work in the businesses of Leipzig and its suburbs extended from 6 A.M. to 8 P.M.; they were interrupted only by a lunch break of one to two hours. Because of the various work schedules, the worker spent over half the day either in the factory or on the commute to work.[12] Gradually, however, the temporal range of factory working hours diminished through more intensive production methods and shorter breaks. In the mid-1880s, the typical workday was still ten hours in the engineering works and iron foundries of Leipzig's suburbs.

In 1898 the so-called English workday, lasting from 7 A.M. to 12:30 P.M. and from 1 to 5 P.M., was finally introduced for the first time in some Leipzig enterprises. Within twenty years, therefore, the workday in most firms decreased by about two to three hours. From then on it totaled about nine to ten hours per day. Employees in the printing trades already enjoyed a nine-hour workday around 1900. The end of the workday was pushed forward as a rule from 8 P.M. in 1880 to 5 P.M. at the turn of the century. In this way, leisure time had noticeably advanced into the daylight hours.[13]

The phenomenon of "free time" invited workers to think about how they could use it. The range of options was limited, however, both

---

10. Wolfgang Nahrstedt, *Die Entstehung der Freizeit: Dargestellt am Beispiel Hamburgs: Ein Beitrag zur Strukturgeschichte und zur strukturgeschichtlichen Grundlegung der Freizeitpädagogik* (Bielefeld, 1988), 249–61; E. P. Thompson, "Time, Work, and Industrial Capitalism," *Past and Present,* no. 91 (1967): 56–97; Mark Harrison, "The Ordering of the Urban Environment: Time, Work, and the Occurrence of Crowds, 1790–1835," *Past and Present,* no. 110 (1986): 134–68.

11. Plagwitz and Lindenau were incorporated into Leipzig in 1891.

12. *Jahresberichte der Königlich Sächsischen Fabriken- und Dampfkessel-Inspektionen für 1879–1900, ab 1884 Jahresberichte der Königlich Sächsischen Gewerbe- und Berg-Inspektoren, ab 1887 Jahres-Berichte der Königlich Sächsischen Gewerbe-Inspektoren* (hereafter *Jahresbericht*); Vorstand des Deutschen Buchbinder-Verbandes, *Statistische Erhebungen in den Buchbindereien und verwandten Berufen Deutschlands im Jahre 1900* (Stuttgart, 1902), 164.

13. *Jahresberichte; Statistische Erhebungen über die Lohn- und Arbeitsverhältnisse der in der Metallindustrie Leipzigs u. Umgegend beschäftigten Arbeiter und Arbeiterinnen: Winterhalbjahr 1896/97* (Leipzig, 1897), 18, 26ff.

by the amount of free time available and by the financial resources of the worker. On balance, the workforce of the *Messestadt* was granted more free time, and its wages rose more rapidly, than in other developed industrial centers and cities.[14] In the last third of the nineteenth century, workers' wages steadily increased in the various branches of Leipzig industry because of an economic cycle interrupted by only a few crises. Feeding the same trend were the growing strength of the unions and the almost continuous shortage of labor. Between 1877 and 1885 alone — years that are regarded as crisis years for German industry — the average earnings of employees in the Leipzig metal and textile industries rose by approximately 7 to 20 percent.[15] In 1885, the average weekly wage paid to industrial workers within the constituency of Leipzig factory inspectors (*Gewerbeinspektion Leipzig*) can be broken down as shown in table 1. The average earnings listed in the table say little, however, about individual circumstances. Individual incomes could lie either far above the average or far under it. In 1889, workers in Leipzig bookbinderies received weekly wages of up to 55 marks for a thirteen-hour workday. Such a high wage was unparalleled at this time.[16]

These findings concerning wage growth are all the more remarkable because they contradict the argument found in older research that Germany (as a whole) suffered a deep economic crisis between 1873 and 1895 — a crisis that Hans Rosenberg named the Great Depression.[17] Leipzig, obviously — but also other parts of Saxony, such as the Chemnitz, Zwickau, and Bautzen industrial regions — was not as badly affected by this crisis as historians have assumed until now.[18] Certain Leipzig industries did experience setbacks in the economic cycle in 1873, 1885–86, and 1890–92. But these were not nearly as strongly felt as they

---

14. For general developments in the German Empire, see Gerhard A. Ritter and Klaus Tenfelde, *Arbeiter im deutschen Kaiserreich, 1871 bis 1914* (Düsseldorf, 1992), 360–71, 475–506.

15. *Jahresbericht* (1885), 64–65.

16. *Jahresbericht* (1889), 88.

17. Hans Rosenberg, *Große Depression und Bismarckzeit, 1873–1896* (Berlin, 1966); Hans-Ulrich Wehler, *Das Deutsche Kaiserreich, 1871–1918* (Göttingen, 1988), 41ff.; Knut Borchardt, "Wirtschaftliches Wachstum und Wechsellagen, 1800–1914," in *Handbuch der deutschen Wirtschafts- und Sozialgeschichte,* ed. Hermann Aubin and Wolfgang Zorn (Stuttgart, 1976), 2:198–275; idem, *Die Industrielle Revolution in Deutschland* (Munich, 1972), 69–70.

18. Compare the assessment of the economic situation in Saxony in the *Jahresberichten der Königlich Sächsischen Gewerbe- und Berg-Inspektoren für 1884–1886; Jahres-Berichte der Königlich Sächsischen Gewerbe-Inspektoren für 1887–1895;* see also Paul Bramstedt, *Die Krisis der sächsischen Industriewirtschaft* (n.p., 1932), 3.

TABLE 1.   Average Weekly Wages Paid to Leipzig Industrial Workers, 1885 (marks)

Industrial Branch	Males	Females
Stone, clay	13.60	6.80
Metallurgy	14.80	6.60
Metalworking, machinery, toolmaking	16.30	7.10
Chemicals	14.50	—
Heating	14.60	—
Textiles	14.50	7.20
Paper and leather	14.70	7.10
Wood	13.50	—
Food, luxury items	14.30	6.80
Clothing	13.45	7.20
Polygraphic trades	17.50	7.80

Source: *Jahresbericht der Königlich Sächsischen Gewerbe- und Berg-Inspektoren* (1885), 64.

were elsewhere in the empire. Like Hamburg,[19] the *Messestadt* was spared because of the particular nature of the postunification economic crisis, which above all struck the foodstuff, semiluxury foods, and tobacco industries, the agricultural equipment industries, and the metal industry.[20] The crisis actually improved the material position of Leipzig workers in comparison with those in Germany's industrial regions. It also meant they could afford membership in the numerous working-class cultural associations, for a worker could join and pay dues to such an association only if some disposable income was left over after providing for life's necessities. The leisure activities in the association or in the allotment garden (*Kleingarten*), as well as the membership in a cooperative, were cost intensive. As a rule, the monthly membership fee for cultural associations amounted to 50 pfennigs. For a share in the consumers' cooperative, 50 marks had to be raised; in a building cooperative, at least 300 marks.

Until the turn of the century, the wages paid in Leipzig factories continued their upward trend. The survey of workers' earnings in table 2, conducted by the Leipzig medical insurance program, illustrates this development. The number of workers who earned more than 15 marks per week almost doubled between 1889 and 1896. This group of better-paid workers attained weekly wages of up to 30 marks or more. By 1900 the wages paid in Leipzig industries topped those paid elsewhere in

---

19. Helga Kutz-Bauer, *Arbeiterschaft, Arbeiterbewegung und bürgerlicher Staat in der Zeit der Großen Depression: Eine regional- und sozialgeschichtliche Studie zur Geschichte der Arbeiterbewegung im Großraum Hamburg, 1873 bis 1890* (Bonn, 1988).

20. Ernst Hasse, *Die Stadt Leipzig und ihre Umgebung geographisch und statistisch beschrieben, Verwaltungsbericht für die Stadt Leipzig für die Jahre 1866–1877* (Leipzig, 1878), 326–28.

TABLE 2. Weekly Earnings of Leipzig Workers, 1889–96

	1889	1892	1896
Over 15 marks	30,628 (51.3%)	38,458 (61.5%)	57,923 (70.6%)
12–15 marks	12,670 (21.2%)	9,183 (14.7%)	8,585 (10.5%)
9–12 marks	8,941 (15.0%)	6,331 (10.1%)	6,963 (8.5%)
Below 9 marks	7,458 (12.5%)	8,611 (13.7%)	8,535 (10.4%)

Source: Jahresberichte der Königlich Sächsischen Gewerbe- und Berg-Inspektoren (1879–1900).

Germany, with the exception of Berlin, Hamburg, and Munich.[21] An inquiry prepared for the British monarch in 1908 also noted Leipzig as an anomaly within Saxony: "Wages are comparatively very high in Leipzig—much higher than in any other town in Saxony."[22] Table 3 illustrates these points.

Leipzig's high wage-rate leveled off in the 1920s, in part due to the comprehensive wage agreements. Soon wage levels in the *Messestadt* differed hardly at all from those in the surrounding countryside or in other large cities. This trend was evident, for example, in the metal industry and the printing trades. Nevertheless, a December 1927 comparison of the hourly wages established by unions in eight large cities of central Germany (Chemnitz, Dresden, Gera, Halle, Leipzig, Magdeburg, Plauen, and Zwickau) reveals that the highest average hourly wages were paid in Leipzig.[23]

These statistics illustrate two important points. First, the thesis that Saxony was an area of low wages is correct only if one looks at the average for all of Saxony.[24] Hidden behind the aggregate figures are

---

21. Compare Vorstand des Deutschen Buchbinder-Verbandes, *Statistische Erhebungen*, 160; idem, *Statistische Erhebungen über Lohn- und Arbeitsverhältnisse in Buchbindereien, Kontobuchfabriken, Liniieranstalten, Album-, Etuis-, Kartonnagen-, Galanterie- u. Lederwaren-, Luxuspapier- u. Papierwarenfabriken und ähnlichen Betrieben in Deutschland: Aufgenommen im November 1910* (Berlin, 1912), 416; *Statistische Erhebungen über die Lohn- und Arbeitsverhältnisse der Bauklempner und Installateure Deutschlands: Veranstaltet und zusammengestellt vom deutschen Metallarbeiter-Verband* (Stuttgart, 1907), 12, 34–35.

22. *Cost of Living in German Towns: Report of an Enquiry by the Board of Trade into Working Class Rents, Housing, and Retail Prices, Together with the Rates of Wages in Certain Occupations in the Principal Industrial Towns of the German Empire* (London, 1908), 305.

23. *Leipziger Volkszeitung*, 29 Feb. 1928.

24. This thesis is presented most pointedly in Werner Bramke, ed., *Sachsens Wirtschaft im Wechsel politischer Systeme im 20. Jahrhundert* (Leipzig, 1992); and idem, "Die Industrieregion Sachsen: Ihre Herausbildung und Entwicklung bis zum Ende des zweiten Weltkrieges," in *Industrieregionen im Umbruch: Historische Voraussetzungen und Verlaufsmuster des regionalen Strukturwandels im europäischen Vergleich*, ed. Rainer Schulze (Essen, 1993), 291–317.

TABLE 3. Index of Workers' Incomes in Selected Cities and Industries, 1908 (Berlin = 100)

City	Construction		Machine Building		Printing Trades	
	Skilled	Unskilled	Skilled	Unskilled	Skilled	Unskilled
Hamburg	102	125	97	96	100	93
Berlin	100	100	100	100	100	100
Düsseldorf	85	103	98	103	90	93
Remscheid	83	85	97	108	88	91
Leipzig	88	95	95	96	96	89

Source: *Cost of Living in German Towns: Report of an Enquiry by the Board of Trade into Working Class Rents, Housing, and Retail Prices, Together with the Rates of Wages in Certain Occupations in the Principal Industrial Towns of the German Empire* (London, 1908), 305.

industrial regions with very different wage structures. The findings for Leipzig clearly illustrate that workers' wages in particular industrial regions of Saxony were exceptionally high. The three large cities of Dresden, Chemnitz, and Leipzig, but much of western Saxony too, were regions with a markedly high income level. Tending to offset these high levels were the cottage industries in the Erzgebirge and the Vogtland, where very low wages were paid. Given these disparities, historians would be well advised to abandon sweeping generalizations about Saxony as a region of low wages; they might move instead toward an examination of income levels differentiated by district. Second, a stratum of relatively highly paid workers was able to establish itself in Leipzig.[25] This stratum was composed of skilled specialists in different branches of industry, but above all in the printing and metal industries, where it was often possible to live relatively comfortably, to invest in savings accounts, or to acquire shares in consumer or building cooperatives. Of course one should not overlook the fact that another stratum of workers lived at the subsistence level. Nevertheless, even a growing number of such workers could afford membership in the numerous cultural and political organizations.[26]

---

25. The concept of "labor aristocracy" should not be used here because it does not adequately represent reality and is not theoretically well-founded. Compare Hans Wilhelm Winzen, "Arbeiteraristokratie," in *Historisch-kritisches Wörterbuch des Marxismus,* ed. Wolfgang Fritz Haug (Hamburg, 1994), 1:422–28; by contrast, see the discussion in Ritter and Tenfelde, *Arbeiter,* 464–65; and Gerhard Beier, "Das Problem der Arbeiteraristokratie im 19. und 20. Jahrhundert: Zur Sozialgeschichte einer umstrittenen Kategorie," in *Herkunft und Mandat: Beiträge zur Führungsproblematik in der Arbeiterbewegung* (Frankfurt a. M., 1976), 9–71.

26. "Die Sparkasse der Stadt Leipzig, 1913–1920" [Geschäftsbericht, MS], in Stadtarchiv (hereafter StadtA) Leipzig, Kap. 30 Nr. 30; Hubert Kiesewetter, "Zur Entwicklung sächsischer Sparkassen, zum Sparverhalten und zur Lebenshaltung sächsischer Arbeiter

III. Workers' Sports Activities

The gradual reduction of the daily hours of work and the growing income of workers were essential preconditions for the emergence of a diverse array of clubs, organizations, and societies. Nevertheless, these material prerequisites do not suffice to explain the phenomenon, because ultimately only a minority of those well-remunerated Leipzig workers became involved in an association. This can be illustrated using the example of two workers' sports clubs: the Gymnastics and Sports Club of Leipzig-Probstheida (Turn- und Sportverein Leipzig-Probstheida) and the Knautkleeberg Athletic Association (Verein für Leibesübung Knautkleeberg).[27]

Workers' sports remained up to the end of the Weimar Republic first and foremost a male preserve. Only 22 percent of members in the Probstheida club, and about 10 percent of the Knautkleeberg Athletic Association members, were women. Women often left these and other associations soon after marriage, in order to dedicate themselves to their household and family. But for them, the solidarity generated in the gymnastics and athletic clubs had considerably greater significance than it did for men, precisely because far fewer possibilities for relaxation and conviviality were open to them. As housewives they were isolated, or as working women they were doubly burdened. The husband's local pub remained barred to them, and work within the party or trade union was male-dominated.[28]

Sport was also a matter for the young. An analysis of the age structure of the Probstheida club reveals that sixteen- to twenty-six-year-olds predominated from the outset. Before and after the First World War, about 60 percent of members were in this age group. This finding applies not only to the gymnastics clubs, but also to other workers' cultural associations. From the 1890s onward, the available leisure opportunities were used principally by the second generation of workers — that is, the first generation of a proletariat that knew no other existence. Because members of this second generation of factory workers were born and raised in the city, their socialization differed fundamentally

---

im 19. Jahrhundert (1819–1914)," in *Arbeiterexistenz im 19. Jahrhundert: Lebensstandard deutscher Arbeiter und Handwerker,* ed. Werner Conze and Ulrich Engelhardt (Stuttgart, 1981), 446–86.

27. For the Turn- und Sportverein Leipzig-Probstheida, see Sächsisches Staatsarchiv Leipzig, PP-V 1406, 3613; for the Verein für Leibesübungen Knautkleeberg, see StadtA Leipzig, NL Paul Kloß Nr. 9.

28. Gertrud Pfister, "'Macht euch frei.' Frauen in der Arbeiter-Turn- und Sportbewegung," in *Illustrierte Geschichte des Arbeitersports,* ed. Hans-Joachim Teichler and Gerhard Hank (Berlin, 1987), 48–57, here 52.

from that of their parents' generation, which had grown up mostly in rural areas or small towns. More and more people, above all the young, were ready to spend the money necessary to take advantage of the myriad forms of leisure on offer. Coming from patriarchal households, these youths were determined to enjoy new freedoms and new (urban) lifestyles.[29]

This generation, together with the one that followed, did not mimic the gymnastics activities of their fathers (girls could not join such organizations until 1908). Instead, they indulged in soccer matches on the meadows outside the city, despite the fact that soccer had long been frowned upon as un-German and bourgeois. This was a twofold protest, directed not only against paternal authority, but against tradition itself. It was a generational conflict, but it was more besides: by abandoning the previously typical German interest in gymnastics in favor of "English" soccer, this generation of workers was abandoning typically German values as well. Here one can agree with Norbert Elias and Eric Dunning, who have interpreted the advance of sport as part of the process of defeudalization—a process that led to a state of self-determination and independence.[30] In contrast to gymnastics, which in the workers' gymnastics clubs was never geared toward competition, the newer preferred sports such as soccer reflected the mechanisms of the capitalist order, not least by introducing players to the need to develop a competitive edge on the playing field.

Whereas evidence about the age structure of the members of both these associations confirms previous research, analysis of the occupational structure of the Probstheida club produces a more unexpected result. Only 43 percent of its members were workers. No less than 39 percent were white-collar workers (*Angestellte*) and officials (*Beamte*).[31] Hence this club was by no means a homogeneous workers' association. Although Fritz Kühn has postulated such social heterogeneity as typical of bourgeois sports clubs,[32] no one has previously raised the same issue with respect to workers' sports clubs. This may be due to a lack of

---

29. Nils Minkmar, "Vom Totschlagen kostbarer Zeit: Der Gebrauch des Kinos in einer Industrieregion (1900–1914)," *Historische Anthropologie* (1993), 431–50, here 436; Hartmut Zwahr, "Zur Konstituierung des Proletariats als Klasse: Strukturuntersuchung über das Leipziger Proletariat während der industriellen Revolution," in *Die Konstituierung der deutschen Arbeiterklasse von den dreißiger bis zu den siebziger Jahren des 19. Jahrhunderts,* ed. idem (Berlin, 1981), 361–411, esp. 364–70, 397–98.

30. Norbert Elias and Eric Dunning, *Sport im Zivilisationsprozeß* (Münster, 1983), 12–13.

31. In 1927 the association numbered 170 members. The occupation of 101 members could be established.

32. Fritz Kühn, *Die Arbeitersportbewegung: Ein Beitrag zur Klassengeschichte der Arbeiterschaft* (Rostock, 1922).

sources or a lack of original thought. In any case, the social heterogeneity that is evident in the Probstheida club can be ascribed, first, to the admission of new members who were already officials and, second, to the promotion of white-collar workers and officials of lesser rank to positions of relatively high status during their membership period. Despite such ascending career paths and the higher social status that went with them, these members evidently remained in the workers' sports clubs and did not move into corresponding bourgeois associations. By contrast, analysis of the Knautkleeberg Athletic Association produces a very different picture. With a membership composed of 80 percent workers, the Knautkleeberg club illustrates such a clear dominance of workers that one can speak of a nearly homogeneous workers' association.[33]

To sum up this section: The members of workers' cultural organizations in Leipzig were first and foremost young people; but they were not only workers. The consumer and building cooperatives in particular were anything but homogeneous workers' organizations. Whereas at least one-third of the members of the Leipzig-Plagwitz consumer cooperative were not workers, workers represented between 40 and 50 percent of the total membership in the building cooperatives. These important organizations — for cooperatives typically had larger memberships than other segments of the workers' cultural movement — were nevertheless integrated into the Social Democratic milieu not later than the 1920s.[34] The Social Democratic milieu of Leipzig was thus a socially heterogeneous and relatively open one. To this extent it revealed characteristics found in other large cities with pronounced service sectors, including Munich,[35] Frankfurt am Main,[36] and Berlin.

IV. "Workers' Culture" and the Social Democratic Milieu

The workers' culture movement developed from the 1890s onward partly in opposition to the Social Democratic movement. The friendly societies in Leipzig had not been founded to offer the workers an opportunity for

33. In 1924 the association had 178 members. The occupation of 136 could be established.

34. The milieu concept of M. Rainer Lepsius was based on this general argument. See M. Rainer Lepsius, "Parteiensystem und Sozialstruktur: Zum Problem der Demokratisierung der deutschen Gesellschaft," in idem, *Demokratie in Deutschland: Soziologisch-historische Konstellationsanalysen: Ausgewählte Aufsätze* (Göttingen, 1993), 25–50.

35. Karl Heinrich Pohl, *Die Münchener Arbeiterbewegung: Sozialdemokratische Partei, Freie Gewerkschaften, Staat und Gesellschaft in München, 1890–1914* (Munich, 1992).

36. Andreas Wolf, *Arbeiterkulturelle Aspekte in der Weimarer Republik: Teilkulturelle und solidargemeinschaftliche Ansätze in Frankfurt am Main, unter Einbeziehung eines städtetypologischen Vergleichs zu Leipzig* (Frankfurt a. M., 1992).

leisure activity, but rather to preserve the forbidden SPD organization under the guise of social gatherings. After its legalization in 1890, the SPD no longer needed these associations. However, it was impossible to convince the workers to leave them or to dissolve them completely. The gymnastics, choral, and theater associations had awakened the workers' need for attractive and affordable leisure activities. These aims had never been a priority for party strategists, and they had not calculated that these sociable associations would very quickly achieve popularity among Social Democrats—and others. After the lapse of the anti-socialist laws, the SPD leadership vehemently dissociated itself from the workers' cultural associations: it believed that workers who joined such associations would sooner or later be lost to the proletarian struggle. Their activity was branded *Vereinsmeierei* (association nonsense) and rejected. However, because numerous followers and even functionaries of the SPD were already integrated into these associations, the party leadership could not exclude them out of hand. Thus the SPD attempted, from the middle of the 1890s onward, to achieve a kind of hegemonic position over party members (and fellow travelers) who were organized in these associations. It did this reluctantly, on the understanding that if one could no longer get rid of the cultural associations, one should gain control over them.

Little by little the SPD integrated the individual organizations into its milieu. The first pillar of the Social Democratic movement—the party—was supplemented by the trade unions as the second pillar and the workers' gymnastics clubs as the third. These three pillars formed the nucleus of the Social Democratic milieu, into which further associations and organizations were integrated up until the mid-1920s: the consumer cooperatives around the turn of the century, the workers' sports clubs (including soccer clubs) between 1911 and 1919, and the building co-operatives between 1910 and 1925. We see, thus, that the Social Democratic associational network was by no means already completely developed in the 1890s. It grew until the period of the Weimar Republic, quantitatively and qualitatively, through an increasing breadth of offerings. In this respect, one can concur with Peter Lösche and Franz Walter: quantitatively, the peak of the workers' cultural movement clearly lay in the early 1920s.[37] Less clear, though, is whether all the so-called milieu organizations of the prewar period were countercultural organizations (*gegenkulturelle Sonderorganisationen*).[38] Here the evidence seems to

---

37. Peter Lösche and Franz Walter, "Zur Organisationskultur der sozialdemo-kratischen Arbeiterbewegung in der Weimarer Republik," *Geschichte und Gesellschaft* 15 (1989): 511–36.

38. Ibid., 512.

support Hartmann Wunderer, who has noted a depoliticization of the Social Democratic milieu.[39] This trend is revealed most clearly in the sphere of adult education, where the milieu-associated organizations were abandoned in favor of nonpartisan adult education.[40]

The analysis of the membership structure of the various workers' organizations confirms the thesis that the Social Democratic milieu in large cities with pronounced service sectors was not socially homogeneous (therefore proletarian). Rather, it was socially heterogeneous, and therefore comparable to the Catholic milieu. The exceedingly high proportion of workers in garden allotment societies as well as in building cooperatives, when considered in conjunction with the opening of the consumer associations and workers' sports clubs to white-collar workers, officials, and other strata of the bourgeoisie, contradicts standard accounts about where these organizations recruited their members. Neither allotment gardens nor building cooperatives were supported exclusively by civil servants and the petty bourgeoisie; conversely, one does not expect to find officials and white-collar workers in a workers' sports club, but their presence in such organizations is undeniable. Evidently, then, Leipzig workers' relatively high incomes made it possible for them to enter associations that demanded a significant financial commitment. Existing studies verify that the Social Democratic–oriented associations exercised a great appeal for white-collar workers, officials, and small entrepreneurs, particularly after 1918. The reason for this may lie in the diverse offerings of the associations and their material achievements in the form of clubhouses, playing fields, gymnasiums, etc. These associations' festivals and processions were also calculated to maximize their public appeal, as happened, for example, during the first workers' gymnastics and sports festival of 1922.

In short: the concept of "workers' culture" (*Arbeiterkultur*) had become problematic for Leipzig by the middle of the 1920s at the latest. What remains of the concept, then, if the so-called workers' associations and organizations were not always dominated by workers? And what was the specific content of workers' culture, in contrast to bourgeois culture? Certainly workers' sports activities differed hardly at all from bourgeois sports once the prohibition on competitions had been reversed and after sports with Anglo-American origins had been heartily taken up by workers. In the end, only the organizational structure

---

39. Hartmann Wunderer, *Arbeitervereine und Arbeiterparteien: Kultur- und Massenorganisationen in der Arbeiterbewegung, 1890–1933* (Frankfurt a. M., 1980), 74–75, 224.

40. Thomas Adam, "Leipzig — Die Hochburg der Arbeiterkulturbewegung," in *Wirtschaft und Gesellschaft in Sachsen im 20. Jahrhundert,* ed. Werner Bramke and Ulrich Heß (Leipzig, 1998), 229–67, esp. 247ff.

handed down from the *Kaiserreich* era appeared to separate bourgeois sport from workers' sport.[41]

In the fields of art and education, too, Leipzig's Social Democrats failed to produce a new socialist culture. Their cultural activities were limited to the consumption of bourgeois art, which admittedly underwent a partial reinterpretation. The Workers' Educational Institute (Arbeiter-bildungsinstitut, or ABI), unique in Germany, developed into an association of mere spectators, organizing theater performances and concerts for subscribers. Here the spectators as a rule absorbed bourgeois works of art, even though they were subject to reinterpretation by means of introductions in the journal, *Kulturwille*. An acquisition of bourgeois cultural goods (*bürgerliche Kulturgüter*) took place insofar as the partici-pants read the introductions and absorbed their content. In this way the cultural work of the Workers' Educational Institute moved into the prob-lematic realm of imitation and appropriation. In contrast to the *Volks-bühne* movement, however, the ABI did not claim to be creating an independent proletarian culture.[42] Social Democrats in Leipzig never developed an independent cultural program. Hence it is all the more astonishing to find that they were able to erect and preserve a nearly complete network of workers' associations covering people from the cradle to the grave. Yet if bourgeois culture, albeit in a somewhat altered form, was simply transmitted to the workers, then this also effected their integration into existing society. Whether consciously or unconsciously, Leipzig's Social Democrats ultimately pursued an integrative concept.[43]

In a period of just twenty years (1890–1910), the Leipzig labor movement, based on a solid stratum of high-wage earners, had estab-lished a range of material accomplishments that was unique in Germany. The establishment of numerous workers' libraries, the building activity of the Leipzig-Plagwitz consumer cooperative, and the erection of the Volkshaus (People's House) — the largest and finest in Germany — testify to this. The workers were proud of these achievements, which had been accomplished through their own powers, and they derived from them a self-confidence and an identification with the Leipzig labor

---

41. Dieter Langewiesche, "Politik-Gesellschaft-Kultur: Zur Problematik von Ar-beiterkultur und kulturellen Arbeiterorganisationen in Deutschland nach dem 1. Welt-krieg," *Archiv für Sozialgeschichte* 22 (1982): 259–402, here 380.

42. On the controversial concept of "socialist culture," cf. Gramsci, "Problem," 277–79.

43. This concept was most pervasive in adult education. After the founding of the city's *Volkshochschule,* party-controlled general adult education in the ABI was discontin-ued in favor of "open and party-neutral adult education" in the communal *Volkshoch-schule.* This was made much easier for the SPD because the leadership of the city's *Volksbildung* office was entrusted to a Social Democrat. See Adam, "Leipzig — Die Hochburg," 250ff.

movement. They mediated a working-class identity that was linked to Leipzig's Social Democratic milieu and yet made possible its integration into the city's society.

This conclusion points to the existence of a Social Democratic movement that leaned toward a reformist position and that wanted to prepare the way for a new social order through building up its own institutions in miniature. One should not expect a revolutionary position to be adopted by a party that owned numerous party buildings and facilities, because — as Simone Lässig has rightly noted — such a party has a great deal to lose in the event of a revolutionary conflict.[44] To be sure, Leipzig's Social Democrats adhered to a radical Marxist position even into the 1920s, despite revisionist temptations. Yet if one examines the radicalism of Leipzig's Social Democrats more closely, one sees that it was mainly verbal, not a radicalism of action. On average, Leipzig workers were very well read: they regarded themselves as "enlightened workers," superior to both unenlightened workers and the bourgeoisie. Compared to workers in other Social Democratic strongholds, a special Leipzig type of Social Democrat can be identified: highly educated, but adhering to Marxist doctrine like a religion — that is, somewhat complacently — and waiting for the great *Kladderadatsch*. Until that day, whose arrival for Leipzig Social Democrats was so natural that it needed no active instigation, one had to do nothing more than to make the existing organizations larger and stronger.[45]

V. Conclusions

The construction of the Social Democratic milieu occurred through a long process that began in the case of Leipzig in the 1860s and was not complete until the mid-1920s. In the *Messestadt*, the antisocialist laws were of decisive significance for the construction of the milieu. Between 1878 and 1890, the kernel of the Social Democratic milieu emerged; it was then enlarged and perfected in the following decades. Whether this development was similar to those occurring in other German regions has hardly been investigated until now. Some recent research, however, suggests that in several regions of Germany, the antisocialist laws had no impact on the emergence of Social Democratic cultural organizations that first appeared after 1890.[46]

---

44. Simone Lässig, *Wahlrechtskampf und Wahlreform in Sachsen (1895–1909)* (Weimar, 1996), 177.

45. Michael Rudloff, Thomas Adam, and Jürgen Schlimper, *Leipzig — Wiege der deutschen Sozialdemokratie* (Berlin, 1996), 99–101.

46. See further Thomas Adam and Werner Bramke, ed., *Milieukonzept und empirische Forschung* (Leipzig, 1999).

Two hypotheses can be suggested to explain why Leipzig became a stronghold of the workers' cultural movement at such an early date (before Berlin, Hamburg, and Munich). On the one hand, a reduction in the number of hours worked each day took place in Leipzig earlier than elsewhere. Hence Leipzig workers enjoyed a larger block of free time much sooner, which allowed them to organize and expand a range of cultural associations. Second, exceptionally high wages made it possible for a large proportion of the Leipzig workforce to afford such activities.

The Social Democratic milieu of Leipzig proved to be a socially heterogeneous milieu, in which not only workers, but also white-collar employees, officials, and even small entrepreneurs were integrated. To describe this milieu, therefore, as either a workers' milieu or a proletarian milieu would be unwise. This milieu's character was far less proletarian than previously supposed, and it was far more bourgeois than previously suspected. Leipzig was not the only German city with a socially heterogeneous Social Democratic milieu, however. Frankfurt am Main, Berlin, and Munich also had Social Democratic movements that included workers and members of other social strata. Hence the results of this case study of Leipzig are significant for other local and regional studies, especially those focusing on large cities with a highly developed service sector.

The culture of the Leipzig labor movement, when seen in relation to the ruling bourgeois culture, cannot be described as a counterculture. Rather, it was a component culture (*Teilkultur*): it had an integrative function, and it did not claim to be developing a consistently socialist cultural program. For this reason, Leipzig clearly differs from Berlin, where a proletarian counterculture developed from the mid-1920s onward. Indeed, the question might be raised whether Berlin, with its strong Communist Party, might not be considered to be the real anomaly in the development of a proletarian counterculture, rather than the typical case that it has been considered until now. From this perspective, perhaps the Leipzig example is much closer to the norm after all.

Reports of a Cop: Civil Liberties and Associational Life in Leipzig during the Second Empire

Marven Krug

I. Introduction

If we are to understand the political culture of Saxony, or indeed of any society, then the respective civil liberties environment must form an integral part of our analysis. Political culture is shaped in part by the conception that the citizenry enjoys certain fundamental liberties. Political mobilization and maturation both depend upon liberal freedoms of assembly and association, among other things. The growth of a healthy public sphere necessitates limits upon the power of the state. The ability of public opinion to influence politics depends in turn upon a thriving public sphere marked by a free press. The examination of civil liberties, in other words, is not a peripheral undertaking; rather, it must be a central component of any effort to understand political culture.

Let us remember that political decisions made in Berlin, Dresden, and other cities were eventually translated into specific actions carried out by police, prosecutors, judges, and censors. In this way they came to have a direct impact on the everyday lives of ordinary Germans. Conversely, developments at the grass roots of society were translated into political pressure through the intermediaries of public opinion, the press, and elected politicians. In this way they came to have an impact on the decision makers.

In this essay we go right down to street level — to the direct interaction between Leipzig's police and the city's citizens — in order to see what events there can tell us about political culture. We are able to do this thanks to a unique set of documents. Like most major German police departments toward the end of the nineteenth century, the Leipzig police department had a special division, known as the political police, that was in charge of assemblies and associations, the press, political parties, and trade unions. In 1894, the Leipzig political police began writing annual reports on political and union activity in the Reichstag electoral districts of Leipzig-City and Leipzig-County (Leipzig-Stadt and Leipzig-Land). In those reports they offered their assessment of the general political situation in the Leipzig area, with particular emphasis on the role of the Social Democratic Party. They also enumerated the cases in which police had acted against associations and publications. These reports were prepared each year until the end of the *Kaiserreich*. For most of this period, they were written by the perceptive Leipzig police inspector Förstenberg.

II. Reports of a Cop

Förstenberg's reports[1] constitute a remarkable series of snapshots of association rights in Saxony. They provide both a statistical overview of associational life in the Leipzig area and a description of the key events of each year. Together they constitute an evolving picture of political, social, and economic developments in Saxony as seen through the eyes of agents of state authority and order. This picture is one of a city in which the vast majority of voluntary associations and thousands of assemblies were completely untouched by police interference. In most years, the number of assemblies banned or dissolved could be counted on one hand. The reports show clearly that associational life became more dynamic each year, and that police interference in this activity was relatively modest (see table 1).

For part of this period, until May 1908, associational life in Leipzig was regulated by the Saxon association law, one of the most reactionary state association laws in Germany. Under this law, the police had considerable powers to ban meetings in advance and to dissolve meetings in progress. Such actions did, however, have to be made public, and they were thus exposed to scrutiny. Moreover, under the Saxon law, all associations that served political purposes were subject to more stringent controls than nonpolitical ones. The SPD often complained that progovernment clubs were treated more leniently in this regard than opposi-

---

1. For this essay, the following reports were used: for 1896: SächsHStA Dresden, Kreishauptmannschaft (hereafter KHM) Leipzig Nr. 253, 66–101; for 1899: SächsHStA Dresden, Ministerium des Innern (hereafter MdI), Nr. 10991, 2–38; for 1900: ibid., 97–156; for 1901: SächsHStA Dresden, MdI Nr. 10992, 74ff.; for 1902: ibid., 275–330; for 1903: SächsHStA Dresden, MdI Nr. 10993, 21–68; for 1904: ibid., 105–43; for 1905: ibid., 247–301; for 1906: SächsHStA Dresden, MdI Nr. 10994, 17–91; for 1907: ibid., 135–315; for 1908: ibid., 329ff.; for 1912: SächsHStA Dresden, KHM Leipzig Nr. 254, 561–743; for 1917: ibid., Nr. 255, 247–78. The entire series of reports stretches from 1894 to 1917.

TABLE 1. Associational Life in Leipzig, 1896–1917

Year	New Clubs (New Political Clubs)	Total No. of Political Clubs	Clubs Supervised by Police	Meetings Registered with Police	Meetings Supervised by Police (of Those, SPD Meetings)	Bans or Dissolutions of Meetings
1896	135 (25)	226	297	—	1,024 (161)	12
1899	118 (45)	301	409	—	851 (128)	10
1900	151 (38)	323	422	—	766 (89)	4
1901	132 (35)	332	435	—	706 (81)	4
1902	125 (21)	336	448	1,572	664 (97)	1
1903	107 (29)	379	473	1,670	711 (127)	1
1904	103 (31)	398	492	1,764	752 (100)	4
1905	94 (30)	417	494	1,777	827 (97)	6
1906	113 (50)	444	530	1,946	868 (126)	14
1907	132 (60)	473	555	1,899	860 (159)	3
1908	102 (15)	—	609	1,511	488 (—)	0
1912	—	—	838	437	218	—
1917	—	—	—	1,281	554	0

tional ones.[2] Lastly, all outdoor meetings, whether political or not, required police permission. Under section 12 of the law, police could ban all meetings that posed an acute threat to public peace, order, or safety. The police liked to use this section to ban meetings on the grounds that the meeting place was too small to accommodate the expected crowd.

Perhaps the most heavily criticized provision of the Saxon association law was section 5, which forbade meetings that "constituted illegal or immoral acts, encouraged such acts, or were likely to make someone inclined to commit such acts." One might well ask — as the victims of this provision often did — how the police could determine whether a meeting would have such a character before it even took place. Eventually the Saxon association law was amended in 1898 to allow clubs to cooperate

---

2. See, for example, August Bebel's complaints in the official protocol of the Saxon *Landtag* session of 19 March 1888, 960ff.

with one another and to bar minors from attending political meetings. Even then, however, police retained considerable powers. As we will see below, Förstenberg's reports help us to understand how these powers were used in practice.

III. Civil Liberties in Comparative Perspective: Saxony and Baden

Before turning to Förstenberg's reports, we should first consider both the Saxon political environment in which they were written and the place of Saxony in the wider German context. Looking at Germany as a whole, it is clear — given the absence of a Reich association law before 1908 — that little effort was made to harmonize police practices in the area of association rights on a national level. As a result, the degree of freedom in associational life varied considerably from state to state. The Baden police, to use an example that stands in stark contrast to Saxony, were remarkably tolerant of oppositional statements made at political meetings, reflecting both the liberal Baden association law and the Baden civil service's strong liberal tradition. Verbal outbursts that would lead to the dissolution of a meeting in any other state — and particularly in Saxony — were permitted in the liberal *Musterländle*.

Two specific cases from Baden illustrate this. In 1893, a Conservative Party speaker — Inspector Wettstein from Karlsruhe — was able to make very dubious assertions about Baden's government and civil service.[3] In one town he said that all local government officials and policemen were obliged to give political support to the liberals. In another town, Wettstein said that senior civil servants were forced to vote liberal for fear that the interior minister would transfer them to less desirable posts if they did not.[4] At a third meeting, he went so far as to claim that the minister had actually ordered the public service to vote liberal. This was an outright fabrication, yet it was tolerated. At the other end of the political spectrum, the Radical party's Oskar Muser was allowed to state in a public meeting, also held in 1893, that both feudal privileges for the nobility and the upper house of the Baden *Landtag* were grossly undemocratic.[5] Like Wettstein, Muser claimed that the

---

3. Police station Mosbach to *Bezirksamt* (administrative district) Mosbach, 18 June 1893 (also forwarded to interior ministry), in Generallandesarchiv (hereafter GLA) Karlsruhe, Abt. 236, Nr. 17125, 223–24. On the oppositional stance of Baden Conservatives, see James Retallack, "Anti-Semitism, Conservative Propaganda, and Regional Politics in Late Nineteenth-Century Germany," *German Studies Review* 11 (1988): 377–403.

4. Police station Fahrenbach to police district Mosbach, 8 June 1893, in GLA Karlsruhe, Abt. 236, Nr. 17125, 214–15.

5. Police station Boxberg to *Bezirksamt* Tauberbischofsheim, 15 Oct. 1893, ibid., 230–34.

government bureaucracy blatantly campaigned for the National Liberal Party (Nationalliberale Partei, or NLP). According to a police report, Muser spent ninety minutes at one meeting criticizing the Baden government, its civil service, and the NLP. Yet the same report concluded with the comment that there were no disturbances at the meeting, and no comments insulting to the government.

Compare this to the climate in Saxony. In early 1890, the Saxon *Landtag* was forced by the Social Democrats to consider the matter of alleged illegalities in a Reichstag electoral district.[6] The SPD's formal complaint in the *Landtag* described two incidents during the official campaign period in which SPD electoral meetings had been banned by police officials. Wilhelm Liebknecht quoted from the actual bans, which both stated that electoral meetings featuring Liebknecht as speaker could not be permitted, since he was a "notorious, influential socialist agitator." He then pointed out that he had given hundreds of speeches in Saxony, most of them between elections, and that only one of these meetings had ever been banned, excepting the two bans in question. Liebknecht next reminded his colleagues that the Reichstag committee in charge of supervising elections had previously ruled that the antisocialist laws could not be used to silence the political voice of the SPD, and especially not during elections. Specifically, meetings could not be banned solely because they were SPD meetings or because a socialist was listed as a speaker. Liebknecht finally asked what the government intended to do about the two illegal bans. The minister who replied to the question said that he could not comment definitively until decisions taken at the district level were appealed to the Saxon ministry of the interior; he added, however, that he did not believe the bans would be overturned. This deferral to the formal appeal process was a typical tactic of Saxon ministers faced with uncomfortable questions in parliament.

We can examine attitudes toward May Day as another means to set the political stage. All outdoor meetings and processions in Saxony on 1 May 1890 were expressly forbidden.[7] Contraventions of this ban were to be severely punished. The decree made public in the Saxon government gazette stated that "it is expected that the majority of order-loving workers will avoid and prevent anything liable to disturb the public peace." It also warned that "the government is obliged to preserve public peace and order with all means available." Clearly, Saxon officials — particularly in 1890, when the antisocialist legislation was due to expire — were very concerned by the prospect of massive gatherings

---

6. August Bebel et al., interpellation no. 98 to the *Landtag,* 10 Feb. 1890; *Landtag* session of 15 Feb. 1890, 87ff., both in SächsHStA Dresden, MdI Nr. 11039, 340–48.

7. Decree of the Saxon interior ministry, 26 Apr. 1890, ibid., 40; it was also published in the *Dresdner Journal.*

of Social Democrats. Just as clearly, they were willing to mobilize the full machinery of state power to prevent them.

On the other hand, the attitude of police toward May Day celebrations did relax somewhat after the expiry of the antisocialist laws. This change can be observed in the rules governing Dresden's May Day celebrations in 1891.[8] As the year before, processions on public streets were to be denied permission. But now festivities at other locations would be tolerated. Police may have sensed that the socialists were no longer as staunchly opposed to the established order, now that their activities had been legalized. On the other hand, it may simply have been the case that the expiry of the antisocialist laws robbed police of the tools they needed to repress May Day celebrations in the way they wished. At any rate, as in the previous year, all gatherings were to be supervised by police, and dissolved if they were used for political activity.

When we turn to Förstenberg's reports on associational life in Leipzig, below, we will be faced with the question of whether conditions in Leipzig were symptomatic of Saxony as a whole. Only a systematic comparison with other districts could give us a definitive answer, of course. However, one can say that the Saxon interior ministry repeatedly attempted to ensure that association rights were uniform throughout the state. This concern lay behind a ministry directive to all district administrators in 1891 on the implementation of the Saxon association law.[9] The ministry acknowledged that the increasing complexity of associational life, including the increasing number of public meetings, made it more difficult to implement the law. The ministry also conceded that local authorities retained complete decision-making powers: the ministry could only make suggestions, not issue implementation guidelines. Nevertheless, the ministry suggested that officials would find their task easier if they applied the provisions of the association law equitably in all political directions and if they did not favor or thwart the activities of particular parties. The directive stressed that officials should resist the temptation to treat the SPD differently from the "parties of order" (*Ordnungsparteien*). Officials were reminded that under current law — unlike under the now-lapsed antisocialist laws — meetings could not be dissolved. Nor could clubs be banned solely because they pursued Social Democratic aims. Lastly, the directive stated that the ministry had recently been forced to overturn the ban of a SPD meeting because there had been no basis for the police assumption that the law would be broken. If these suggestions

---

8. Report of the *Amtshauptmannschaft* (district administrative precinct) Dresden/ Altstadt to local police authorities, 27 Apr. 1891, in SächsHStA Dresden, MdI Nr. 10989, 205–8.

9. Saxon interior ministry to all *Kreishauptmannschaften* (regional administrative precincts), 11 Feb. 1891, in SächsHStA Dresden, MdI Nr. 11040, 4–6.

were taken to heart by police officials, the directive's author concluded, then such embarrassing incidents might be avoided in the future.

Indeed, the Saxon interior ministry was constantly in touch with local officials in an effort to ensure some degree of consistency throughout the state. In 1894, interior ministry officials became concerned about the imprecision that was creeping into registration of public meetings.[10] At a public meeting in Harthe, for example, speakers had been permitted to discuss the character of Jesus, the nature of the Bible, and the question of human origins. When the meeting was registered with the police, however, these topics had been buried under the vague program point "discussions and questions." The ministry felt that if the topics had been accurately described, the meeting would have been banned on the grounds that it was likely to cause religious or moral offense. If the practice of imprecise registration were allowed to continue, virtually any topic could be brought forward for discussion at a public meeting without the police knowing what was going on. This was illegal, declared a ministry official, because section 2 of the Saxon association law obliged organizers of meetings to describe the purpose of the meeting to police: implicitly, the law demanded an accurate and detailed description. Thus, the interior ministry ordered police forces to reject the registration of such a vague topic as "discussions and questions" and to prevent unregistered topics from being discussed.

These Saxon concerns stand in sharp contrast to liberal Baden, where there was no such obsession with micromanaging associational life, and where the police were more relaxed about public meetings. This becomes clear from an examination of the reports filed by Baden police officers sent to supervise meetings. Three reports from the second half of 1894 are typical for Baden.[11] Two of the meetings were organized by Baden left liberals, whereas the third was an all-party meeting. All three meetings were held in pubs. Each officer dispassionately described the speeches at the meeting he was supervising. Some of these assertions were inflammatory, but they were recorded without comment by the officers. Each report ended with the terse observation that the meetings proceeded without incident and gave no cause for police intervention. Police in Baden were obviously more concerned with the format of meetings than with the content.

A look at Saxony's capital city can also help to put Förstenberg's

---

10. Saxon interior ministry to *Kreishauptmannschaft* Leipzig, 25 Oct. 1894, ibid., 127.

11. Police station Eberbach to police district Eberbach, 15 July 1894; police station Offenburg to police district Freiburg, 5 Dec. 1894; and police station Schwetzingen to police district Mannheim, 17 Dec. 1894, all in GLA Karlsruhe, Abt. 236, Nr. 17125, 242–43, 250–51, 254–55.

Leipzig reports into perspective. Consider, for example, a petition sent to the Saxon *Landtag* in 1894 by forty-two local government leaders in the Dresden area.[12] The municipal leaders complained that life in Dresden's satellite communities had become "intolerable" for "worthy, pro-monarchist citizens" as a result of the "anarchy and nihilism" displayed by the local socialists. According to the petition, decent people could no longer walk the streets for fear of encountering gangs of young men who "insulted opponents of revolution," sullied the honor of women, and sang revolutionary songs while blocking traffic. Furthermore, these gangs allegedly occupied respectable dance halls, forced the bands to play revolutionary songs, and caused nonsocialists to leave the dance floor. Often they ordered a large number of beverages and left without paying for them. On occasion, the socialist supporters also prevented people from celebrating the Kaiser's birthday, from showing patriotism through the display of flags, and even from attending church. Allegedly, business people were forced, through the use of boycotts, to adopt a sympathetic attitude toward socialism. All of these activities, complained municipal leaders, had the effect of eroding respect for the state, the Church, and the social order. In order to make their communities livable again, the local politicians demanded a significantly expanded police presence.

The committee of the Saxon *Landtag* charged with the task of considering these complaints reacted sympathetically.[13] The "social ills" found in the Dresden area, wrote the committee, were merely "one link in the chain of disturbing excesses" found among the socialist, working-class masses. The committee felt it was speaking for the majority of Saxons when it stated: "Many people find it incomprehensible that we have allowed things to go this far." Of course, it was not the staunchly conservative Saxon government that had "allowed" this, but rather the dangerously liberal Reichstag, whose will could only be blocked through a coup d'état (*Staatsstreich*). The committee hoped that the Saxon government would make full use of the powers available to it in the battle against socialism. Above all, however, it wished that "the Reich government would give up its hesitant, passive stance toward these destructive elements and these increasingly undisguised, disturbing symptoms, and energetically support the repression of the enemies of legal authority and the revival of the faded belief in the protection of civil society." The *Landtag* committee therefore asked the Saxon government to make representations in Berlin along these lines. As for the specific request

---

12. Report of the petition committee of the upper chamber of the Saxon *Landtag*, 10 Jan. 1894, in SächsHStA Dresden, MdI Nr. 10989, 198–99.

13. Ibid.

for more policemen, the committee noted that this decision was up to the finance committee. The upper house of the *Landtag* decided to approve the committee's recommendations.[14]

Compare these exaggerated Saxon fears to the calmer assessments emanating from Baden. The Baden government's analysis of developments after the expiry of the antisocialist laws was remarkably less alarmist than those of the Prussian, Bavarian, and Saxon governments.[15] The Badenese did acknowledge that the influence of Social Democracy had expanded after 1890. This could be seen in the increasing number of votes garnered by SPD Reichstag candidates in Baden. However, the state government did not believe that all SPD voters were in fact followers of socialist ideology. It recognized that some people voted SPD because they favored the individual candidate, because they wanted to send a message of protest to the incumbent, or because they were upset with a particular government policy. Moreover, the rate of increase in votes cast for the SPD was actually less after 1890 than in the period 1887–90: the expiry of the antisocialist laws may even have dampened enthusiasm for the party in Baden.

The government in Karlsruhe thus remained unperturbed, for a number of reasons.[16] First, it believed that the majority of the Badenese population, and especially the portion that lived in the countryside, was "state-supporting" (*staatserhaltend*) and governmental. Second, the police had noticed a calming of the SPD's agitational style since October 1890 (the month in which the antisocialist laws formally ended). Third, while the police missed the powers of the antisocialist laws, they were finding that the Baden association law and the Reich criminal code did constitute useful tools for combating socialist excesses. Fourth, the fear that socialist publications would flood the state after October 1890 had turned out to be unfounded. Even three years later, only two SPD newspapers were published regularly in the state. All in all, the tone of the Baden government's analysis signaled optimism, not despair, about the ability of the state to deal with Social Democracy. This tone may have had a great deal to do with the fact that the socialist problem faced by the Baden government was much smaller than that faced by its counterparts in Prussia and Saxony. On the other hand, the government's reasonable attitude may have encouraged Baden's Social Democratic leaders in turn to adopt a calmer approach than their colleagues elsewhere. For example, the SPD caucus in the Baden *Landtag* was increas-

---

14. Protocol of the debates in the upper house of the Saxon *Landtag,* 18 Jan. 1894.

15. Memorandum from the Baden foreign ministry to Karl von Eisendecher, the Prussian envoy in Karlsruhe, 19 Jan. 1894, in Bundesarchiv Potsdam, 15.01, Nr. 13687, 115ff.

16. Ibid.

ingly given opportunities to participate fully in parliamentary business. In Saxony, by contrast, SPD deputies were completely shut out of the *Landtag* committees by the dominant Conservatives and their National Liberal allies.[17] In historical perspective it seems legitimate to suppose that the moderate revisionist wing of Social Democracy might have been given an invaluable boost in Saxony if the SPD had been treated more positively by the other parties and by the regime in power. Indeed, the Saxon government appears to have been aware that relations between the SPD and the state did not have to be as strained as they were.

That conclusion resonates through a report written in 1898 by the Saxon envoy (*Gesandter*) to Bavaria, who was writing about Social Democracy in southern Germany.[18] He noted that in the south, SPD voices in the press and in the legislatures were not as hostile toward the state governments as in northern Germany. In parliamentary debates, southern socialists were always polite and were even willing to praise the government when it did something to their liking. Even southern trade unionists were well-behaved in that they avoided politics and stuck to economic issues. The envoy reported with amazement that southern socialists were seen by governments and by bourgeois politicians not just as "worthy of doing business with" (*verhandlungsfähig*), but also as "worthy of associating with" (*gesellschaftsfähig*). He was equally amazed when he learned in discussions with "leading personalities" in the south that the SPD was seen not as a threat, but as just another political party.

Predictably, however, the Saxon envoy did not draw the same conclusion from these observations as might be drawn by the modern observer. Wholly resistant to the notion that the SPD, when treated with respect, might respond in kind, the envoy concluded that southern Germans were simply different from northerners.[19] For one thing, southerners were by nature more democratic and had a greater social conscience. Hence they were more favorably disposed toward Social Democracy in the first place. Further, social cleavages were less deep in southern society. The envoy had realized this, he claimed, when he observed rich and powerful Bavarians drinking in the same beer halls as lowly laborers. Even the bearing of the wealthy southerners was "less exclusive and autocratic" than that of the northern upper classes, he wrote; as a result, poor southerners felt less resentment. Lastly, the Saxon envoy noted with apparent envy (and more than a hint of regional bias) that the southern Germans were less interested in public affairs and more inter-

---

17. This state of affairs was heavily criticized in "Vom sächsischen Landtage," *Vorwärts,* 28 Nov. 1895.

18. Saxon envoy in Munich to Saxon foreign ministry, 22 Mar. 1898, in SächsHStA Dresden, MdI Nr. 10990, 93–95.

19. Ibid.

ested in the joys of life. The envoy's report may have prompted his superiors in Dresden to wish that Saxons were more like Bavarians; but there is no evidence whatsoever that it induced them to reconsider their policies to combat socialism.

IV. Monitoring or Repressing the Socialists?

Having set the political stage, let us now turn to the reports prepared by Inspector Förstenberg.[20] Förstenberg's annual report for 1896 is an interesting starting point because that year was marked by debate over a bill to reform the Saxon *Landtag* suffrage. The report shows that, politically, the beginning of the year was dominated by agitation against this reactionary bill, which had been introduced by the Conservatives in December 1895. Economically, Leipzig was prospering; this had led to the growing strength of the Social Democratic trade unions. However, this did not necessarily translate into political advantages for the SPD, whose influence stagnated in 1896, as Förstenberg noted in his report. The SPD was able to organize a number of very large meetings in January and February to protest the suffrage reform bill. At a beer garden on the outskirts of Leipzig, crowds of up to ten thousand people gathered to hear August Bebel and others speak. As the meetings dispersed and the crowds filed back to the city, minor disturbances occasionally provoked the police into making a small number of arrests.

In February, opponents of the suffrage bill formed a Suffrage League (Wahlrechtsliga) that used petitions, demonstrations, and printed materials to express its opposition. Just two weeks after its founding, though, the League was banned under the Saxon association law. Although the League's statutes pledged to use "only legal means" to achieve its goals, its advertising in the Social Democratic *Leipziger Volkszeitung* recommended using "any and all means." The League's membership cards also contained phrases that in Förstenberg's eyes could be considered insulting to nonsocialist *Landtag* deputies and to the Saxon government. The League appealed the police ban to the district authorities, but to no avail. The police were also well-informed about the SPD's "agitation committee," which was responsible for electoral and other propaganda. They knew, for instance, that the committee's weak leader retained his job only because he was a good friend of the editor of the *Leipziger Volkszeitung*. In 1896 he was having no luck finding pubs in which Social Democrats could meet. The party tried using boycotts to persuade recalcitrant pub owners, but it was hampered when police turned to the tactic of charging boycotters with causing a public disturbance (*grober Unfug*).

---

20. For the relevant reports, see n. 1.

Due mostly to the increase in trade union activity, the Leipzig police supervised more assemblies in 1896 than in the previous year. Of the thousand or so meetings supervised—85 percent were open public meetings and 15 percent were closed club meetings—about one in ten had a Social Democratic character, according to Förstenberg. Topics discussed at these meetings included wages, working conditions, internal SPD matters, suffrage reform, and May Day celebrations. Due to a new moderation among SPD speakers and organizers, though, the number of meetings actually dissolved by the police decreased from the previous year to just eight. All eight were union meetings. Only four assemblies were banned in advance in 1896: three anarchist meetings and one assembly of the roofers' union. The two largest assemblies of 1896 were both Social Democrat in character, and both went off without incident or significant police intervention. The May Day procession attracted about seven thousand people, and the trade union festival in August 1896 drew twelve thousand participants. Naturally, there were also many Social Democratic funerals during the year, but these led to only a single arrest when a man tried to lay a wreath with an illegal red banner. All in all, then, associational life in Leipzig in 1896 was very lively, but it was neither violent nor directly threatening to the state. More than one hundred new clubs were registered in Leipzig in 1896, including two dozen that dealt with public affairs. The total number of political clubs thereby reached 226. The only club to be banned in this year was the Suffrage League. A total of almost three hundred clubs stood under police observation during the year.

Let us now jump ahead one decade for our next sample of the views of the Leipzig political police. The reports for 1905 and 1906 are some of the most dramatic of all those written by Förstenberg. They reflect the political upheavals in Leipzig caused by the Saxon *Landtag* elections in the autumn of 1905, the Russian Revolution, and the *Landtag* suffrage reform issue, which began to reach a boiling point in November and December of 1905 and climaxed in early 1906. Toward the end of 1905, the Second International called on Germans and others to organize meetings for January 1906 that would show solidarity with the Russian proletariat. In Leipzig, the SPD responded to this call by planning fourteen meetings for 21 January 1906. The meetings were to deal both with the Russian Revolution and the Saxon suffrage reform issue. However, the Leipzig police were directed by the Saxon interior ministry to assume that the meetings would constitute a threat to public safety and order, and therefore to ban them. This the police did. The bans were appealed but ultimately upheld. Förstenberg noted that "it was not the intention of the Leipzig police department to hinder the peaceful discussion of suffrage matters" but pointed out that even the SPD's own publicity for the banned meetings did not attempt to hide the party's intention to use them as vehicles for revolutionary propaganda. From the police point of view, the bans turned out to be successful in that 21 January 1906 was a quiet day in Leipzig.

The suffrage reform movement continued to dominate Leipzig politics and associational life through the remainder of 1906. There were also municipal elections, and the Reichstag was dissolved near the end of the year. Förstenberg noted that the SPD's associational life, though very active and focused on suffrage reform, largely took an orderly course and rarely gave cause for police intervention. Aside from the banned SPD meetings on 21 January, the police banned only two other meetings in 1906. Of the almost two thousand meetings registered in Leipzig in 1906, the police decided to supervise about eight hundred, including over a hundred that were purely Social Democratic in nature. Thus, both the total number of meetings in Leipzig and the number supervised by police were rising on a yearly basis.

Inspector Förstenberg's report for 1908 shows the effect of the Reich association law, which replaced the Saxon association law on 15 May 1908. Förstenberg complained that the new law made it much more difficult to supervise the Social Democratic movement, and he explained that his reports could no longer be as detailed as in previous years. The Reich association law represented a considerable improvement in the association rights of Saxons. It entrenched the right of all inhabitants of the Reich to meet and form associations for lawful purposes, and it clearly defined the circumstances under which police could override this right. The law removed all nonpolitical meetings from police supervision. Organizers of political meetings now needed only to announce these meetings to the police; explicit permission was no longer required. Police could no longer observe meetings covertly, and no more than two officers could attend a meeting. It was much more difficult for police to ban meetings in advance, and the power to dissolve meetings already in progress was also reduced significantly.

In the four and a half months before the Reich law came into effect, eight hundred meetings were registered with the Leipzig police, who supervised about half of them. In the remaining two-thirds of the year, however, only 350 meetings were either registered or announced publicly,[21] and the police supervised only eighty-five of them. These numbers clearly show that the new law had a dramatic impact. This impression is reinforced by the fact that there were no successful bans whatsoever of clubs or meetings in Leipzig in 1908. The police attempted to ban one meeting, a lecture by a Swiss professor on "racial

---

21. The new law allowed the latter option.

degeneration and racial improvement," but their ban was overturned by the interior ministry. Inspector Förstenberg, who had so meticulously collected statistics on Leipzig associational life, now had to rely on the SPD's own statistics for much of his report. According to those figures, the party held about 1,200 meetings in Leipzig in 1908.

The police report for 1917 — the last to be considered here, and written not by Förstenberg but by his successors — shows the overriding importance of wartime circumstances on the effort to monitor associational life in Leipzig. The main task of the police in this fourth year of the war was to prevent revolution and to attempt to maintain an atmosphere of law, order, and justice. According to the report's authors, these tasks were made especially difficult by the problematic and unfair distribution of food and by the unscrupulous practices of war profiteers. Politically, the year 1917 was marked by the steadily growing support of the Independent Social Democratic Party (Unabhängige Sozialdemokratische Partei Deutschlands, or USPD). The police attempted to combat the USPD's drive toward a Russian-style revolution by intense surveillance of the party's leaders, repression of their pamphlet printers and distributors, and the gathering of intelligence among the workers. The police used a strategy of immediate and harsh intervention as soon as a strike or demonstration occurred. This strategy had a palpable deterrent effect. Yet even the police recognized that if conditions got bad enough, no amount of deterrence could be effective. Hence the political police had plenty to do in 1917. There were three large strike waves in Leipzig, with the most serious one affecting the armaments industry in April. There were also two large antiwar demonstrations, in July and November. These led to a total of fifty-two arrests and treason charges. In addition to maintaining order during strikes and demonstrations, the police also had to keep track of the three thousand "hostile foreigners" (citizens of enemy countries) in the city. This group generated few real problems but a great amount of paperwork. Lastly, every journey during wartime — even a short trip to a neighboring town — required a permit, and the political police got bogged down in issuing these special travel papers.

Despite the war, Leipzig's associational life remained remarkably vibrant in 1917. No fewer than 1,300 meetings took place during the year. Of these, the police directly supervised about five hundred. No meetings at all were banned in advance. There were twenty-one large public meetings that dealt with political issues, of which eighteen were organized by the USPD and two by the SPD. All other meetings dealt with industrial or religious issues or were held for entertainment purposes. The two large SPD assemblies were both held in January in beer halls and attracted about two thousand participants each. At both meetings, speakers argued for an immediate peace and, more specifically, for a definition of possible peace terms on the side of the German government. The police did not intervene, which is surprising given the dramatic military situation and the general prerevolutionary atmosphere. May Day in 1917 was anticlimactic, since the army high command had held talks with the trade unions and the SPD and convinced them that a work-free day, especially in the defense sector, would amount to treason. The only significant event in Leipzig on 1 May was a rally organized by the USPD and held in a theater outside of working hours. It attracted about 1,200 people and dealt largely with peace issues. In August and September 1917, the movement to use a general strike as a means to force the German government to the peace table gathered strength. According to the police report, the police had to intervene "energetically" in August to prevent marches in support of a desired general strike; about forty arrests were made.

The socialist youth movement was particularly active during the late-summer weeks of general strike agitation. As a result, the political police paid particular attention to this movement, closely supervising its publications and meetings. They even arrested seven minors, which was unusual. The commanders of the local 19th Army Corps debated banning socialist youth organizations altogether, but eventually they decided that this would make it too difficult to observe the movement: in the generals' view, open protest was less dangerous than underground protest. This attitude did not last very long, however. On 24 November the army leadership "suggested" that meetings likely to advocate an immediate end to the war be banned in advance. The Saxon government took up this suggestion and issued the appropriate decree. The only surprising thing about this step is that it came so late. In Leipzig, no one even bothered to organize such a meeting once the decree had been issued, so the political police did not need to issue any actual bans. Still, it is worth emphasizing that until this late date, it was possible for Leipzigers to gather by the thousands in public places: they could protest against the government's foreign and defense policy without fear of police repression, let alone treason charges.

V. Conclusions

The analysis based on these Leipzig political police reports yields several conclusions. The number of clubs in the city that concerned themselves with public affairs increased steadily. This increase was reflected in the number of clubs supervised by police. The number of public meetings registered with police also showed a gradual rise. However, the reports penned by Inspector Förstenberg and his successors also reveal that although police kept a close eye on associational life in Leipzig, the majority of clubs and meetings were untouched by police interference. In most of the years in question, a mere handful of the thousands of planned meetings were banned or dissolved. And each year, less than half of the public meetings that took place were actually supervised by police. Taking into account the fact that Saxony had the most repressive association law in Germany, at least among the larger states, it is reasonable to conclude that in the rest of Germany, an even larger majority of clubs and meetings were allowed to carry on unhindered. After the passage of the Reich association law in 1908, associational life in Leipzig and elsewhere became even freer than before. Even after three years of war, the freedoms of assembly and association remained much more liberal than one would expect. In short: between 1896 and 1917, it was generally possible — albeit with some exceptions — for citizens of Leipzig to assemble peacefully and discuss virtually any topic, including those that were sure to cause discomfort for the government.

Part 4

THE NEW LEFT, THE NEW RIGHT, AND GERMANY'S DYING MIDDLE

Power in the City: Liberalism and Local Politics in Dresden and Munich

Karl Heinrich Pohl

I. Introduction

Local politics play a remarkable role in the history of Wilhelmine Germany. On the one hand, local politics encompassed political, economic, and cultural events and therefore merit just as much consideration as similar events at the state and national levels. On the other hand, political problems typical of the *Kaiserreich* are seen in local contexts as though under a magnifying glass (*Brennglas*). This perspective is particularly enlightening when used to consider the simultaneous existence of progressive and regressive factors in German political life.[1] As many historians have stressed,[2] local politics provided the arena in which problem-solving strategies could be developed and, at least to some extent, implemented, often long before they were tried at the state and national levels. Local politics are very often summed up under the heading of "municipal socialism." By this historians mean policies that were oriented toward the general good and marked by elements of social

---

1. The most up-to-date analysis of the concept of modernization is found in Thomas Mergel, "Geht es weiterhin voran? Die Modernisierungstheorie auf dem Weg zu einer Theorie der Moderne," in *Geschichte zwischen Kultur und Gesellschaft: Beiträge zur Theoriedebatte,* ed. idem and Thomas Welskopp (Munich, 1997), 203–232; cf. Hans-Ulrich Wehler, "Modernisierungstheorie und Geschichte," in idem, *Die Gegenwart als Geschichte: Essays* (Munich, 1995), 13–59; on Saxony see Karl Heinrich Pohl, "Das sächsische Unternehmertum und der VSI: Ein 'moderner Weg' industrieller Interessenvertretung zu Beginn des 20. Jahrhunderts?" in *Blätter für deutsche Landesgeschichte,* forthcoming.

2. See the summary in Karl Heinrich Pohl, " 'Einig', 'kraftvoll', 'machtbewußt': Überlegungen zu einer Geschichte des deutschen Liberalismus aus regionaler Perspektive," *Historische Mitteilungen der Ranke Gesellschaft* 7 (1994): 61–80.

reform.[3] Such policies in particular were conceived in opposition to the private profit motive and self-centered party politics, in order to protect the interests of all strata of the population. Against this background, the following observations address the question of how local politics developed in Dresden and Munich.[4] Which city was more prepared to carry through "modern" policies of "municipal socialism"? To what do we ascribe similarities and differences between them?

A comparative sketch of the two cities can be drawn quite easily. They were of similar size. Both were typical provincial capital cities, important as cultural centers and hence meccas for tourists. And the populations of both were considered open-minded. Industrialization came slowly and relatively late in each city, though later in Munich than in Dresden. Neither city was particularly marked by a large working-class population. In Munich—as in Bavaria as a whole, and in contrast to Saxony and Dresden—neither Conservatism nor antisemitism played any role. Instead, the Center Party (Deutsche Zentrumspartei) dominated the scene, enjoying a commanding position in the lower house of the Bavarian *Landtag,* just as the Conservatives did for many years in Saxony.

A few brief observations about the general political scene in each city are in order.[5] Saxony was the classic German industrial region. Overwhelmingly Protestant but with a Catholic ruling house, Saxony roused itself as from a long, deep sleep after the turn of the century and began a very slow journey to modernity. However, the massive resistance of the Conservatives and the antisemitic Reform Party (Deutsche Reformpartei) must not be underestimated. This resistance was all the

3. See Jürgen Reulecke, *Geschichte der Urbanisierung in Deutschland* (Frankfurt a. M., 1985); Wolfgang R. Krabbe, *Kommunalpolitik und Industrialisierung: Die Entfaltung der städtischen Leistungsverwaltung im 19. und frühen 20. Jahrhundert: Fallstudien zu Dortmund und Münster* (Stuttgart, 1985); and Dieter Langewiesche, *Liberalismus in Deutschland* (Frankfurt a. M., 1988).

4. A modern study of Dresden is not available; for a preliminary study of Saxon Social Democracy, see Karsten Rudolph, *Die sächsische Sozialdemokratie vom Kaiserreich zur Republik (1871–1923)* (Weimar, 1995). On Munich see, inter alia, Friedrich Prinz and Marita Krauss, eds., *München—Musenstadt mit Hinterhöfen: Die Prinzregentenzeit, 1886–1912* (Munich, 1988); Karl Heinrich Pohl, *Die Münchener Arbeiterbewegung: Sozialdemokratische Partei, Freie Gewerkschaften, Staat und Gesellschaft in München, 1890–1914* (Munich, 1992); and Gerhard Neumeier, *München um 1900: Wohnen und Arbeiten, Stadtteile und Sozialstrukturen, Hausbesitzer und Fabrikarbeiter, Demographie und Mobilität* (Frankfurt a. M., 1995).

5. On Saxony, see Karl Czok, ed., *Geschichte Sachsens* (Weimar, 1989); and Simone Lässig and Karl Heinrich Pohl, eds., *Sachsen im Kaiserreich: Politik, Wirtschaft und Gesellschaft im Umbruch* (Weimar, 1997). On Bavaria, besides works cited in n. 4, see Wolfgang Zorn, *Bayerns Geschichte im 20. Jahrhundert: Von der Monarchie zum Bundesland* (Munich, 1986).

more important because the Conservative Party (Deutschkonservative Partei) dominated both chambers of the Saxon *Landtag* until 1907; in fact it had been able to put its stamp on Saxony for decades previously. Besides the (numerically) strong Social Democratic Party, which won a sensational victory in 1903 by capturing twenty-two of the twenty-three available Reichstag seats in Saxony, and the various industrialists' interest groups — in particular the League of Saxon Industrialists (Verband sächsischer Industrieller, or VSI) — it was the National Liberal Party (Nationalliberale Partei) that played a major role in opening up the land to change. It was this party that most conspicuously promoted "modernization" in Saxony. Bavaria, though still predominantly agricultural at the beginning of the twentieth century, also found itself on the road to modernity, though this development began to stagnate in 1912 with the advent of the government headed by Count Georg von Hertling. In contrast to their comrades in Saxony, the Social Democrats in Bavaria were broadly (albeit reluctantly) accepted as legitimate players in the regional political culture. Functional alliances between the SPD and the Center and regular coalitions between the SPD and the liberals were already possible in Bavaria at a time when such things were still unthinkable in Saxony. That Social Democrats visited the royal palace in Munich was unusual, even in Germany's liberal south.[6] In short, the political culture of the land, together with the government's demonstrated understanding for workers' demands (and even for their political and economic organizations), created a moderate, pro-reform atmosphere. Even though the Center Party's unbreakable domination firmly put the brake on educational and cultural reform in Bavaria, positive developments in other spheres were assisted by the fact that the organized workers' movement had no chance of achieving political power (which was more conceivable in Saxony). Thus the fear that the "reds" would seize power was very small in Bavaria.

II. Dimensions of Local Politics

Among the many perspectives from which one might compare local politics in Munich and Dresden, two in particular are highlighted in the following analysis. The first examines the exercise of political power in areas of local authority that were influenced by the local suffrage and by changes made to it before the First World War. This issue concerns the problem of participation in local politics in a broader sense. How far were the wishes of the lower classes and of their political organizations

6. Heinrich Hirschfelder, *Die bayerische Sozialdemokratie, 1864–1914*, pt. 2, *1878–1914* (Erlangen, 1979), 489.

(perhaps *the* political problem of the time) appreciated by local city politicians? To what extent was a form of local politics "for all" and "by all" in fact implemented? To what extent should we believe the liberals' vehement assertions that they pursued a policy directed toward the "general good"? And to what extent were Social Democrats actually involved in local politics? The answers to these questions are important insofar as they are generally answered in the negative when other tiers of politics are considered. It is therefore all the more interesting to discover whether—and if so, how successfully—such efforts were made at the local level. This investigation will also permit us to see what barriers continued to obstruct recognition of the Social Democratic workers' movement as a legitimate representative of the working classes.

The prerequisites for such a "modern" policy were lacking in almost all German municipalities. Each was characterized by an extremely restricted suffrage, which—in contrast to most other countries—was hardly expanded at all over time. On the contrary, the already undemocratic suffrage was often "worsened."[7] In this respect it mattered little whether the local elite was liberal, reformist, or conservative.[8] The configuration of local suffrages everywhere entailed an out-and-out undemocratic strategy directed at the retention of power by the municipal elites. It often happened that this strategy was coupled with a very specific understanding of "local parliamentarism." Local politics were generally defined as "unpolitical," that is, as an enterprise that—in contrast to the national and state levels—was dominated by expertise and that consisted of the dutiful and dispassionate dispatch of objective matters within the framework of existing laws. Nevertheless, some cities had embarked on a course toward recognizing the equal rights of all town councilors elected in (still circumscribed) local elections, to involve them in municipal work and to foster cooperation across party lines. In various localities shortly before the First World War, one can discern something approaching a "functioning parliamentary system," with coalitions that included all parties, even the Social Democrats. Whether or not one wants to label this a full-fledged "parliamentary culture," one cannot deny that the political climate in such areas was very advanced—in any event, much more advanced than in the Reichstag or in most *Landtage.*

---

7. Karl Heinrich Pohl, "Kommunen, kommunale Wahlen und kommunale Wahlrechtspolitik: Zur Bedeutung der Wahlrechtsfrage für die Kommunen und den deutschen Liberalismus," in *Modernisierung und Region im wilhelminischen Deutschland: Wahlen, Wahlrecht und Politische Kultur,* ed. Simone Lässig, Karl Heinrich Pohl, and James Retallack, 2d rev. ed. (Bielefeld, 1998), 89–126.

8. See Merith Niehuss, "Strategien zur Machterhaltung bürgerlicher Eliten am Beispiel kommunaler Wahlrechtsänderungen im ausgehenden Kaiserreich," in *Politik und Milieu,* ed. Heinrich Best (St. Katharinen, 1989), 60–91.

The second aspect to be considered comprises selected features of local politics, specifically here the issue of labor or employment exchanges (*Arbeitsvermittlung*). In the period before 1914, the significance of employment exchanges is difficult to judge.[9] In contrast to today, unemployment in this era seems not to have been a mass phenomenon. The principal task of the employment exchanges was to reconcile the interests of the two main participants in the labor market: employers and workers. Whoever controlled the employment exchange possessed a real advantage over the other in dominating the labor market. Consequently employers, trade unions, and local authorities fought bitterly for influence over these institutions.[10] The degree of influence that could be exerted in this respect provides a rough indicator of the disposition of power in a locality. Domination by one party illustrated its hold on power, whereas equal participation suggested a balance of power and perhaps even a balance of interests. A "progressive" employment exchange policy therefore signified a municipal policy that had as its objective not so much the removal of conflicts of interests between the participants in the labor market as their reconciliation and pacification. The goal being striven for was not only an improvement in the efficiency of the exchanges and the transparency of the exchange procedure, but also the simultaneous achievement of a balance in the power structure, so that neither worker nor employer dominated the other. Hence this arena of local politics provides a kind of litmus test for the functioning of "modern municipal socialism."

III. Munich

In spite of its primarily Catholic population, Munich had always been middle-class in its ways and liberal in its politics.[11] A broad spectrum of liberal thought developed there, ranging from the dominant National Liberals on the right to the few left-wing liberals around Ludwig Quidde. The spectrum of liberal parties effectively controlled local politics in Munich until the end of the nineteenth century. The common

9. Ewald Frie, "Wohlfahrtsstaat Sachsen? Das Königreich und Preußen im Vergleich," in *Sachsen im Kaiserreich,* ed. Lässig and Pohl, 343–70; idem, *Wohlfahrtsstaat und Provinz: Fürsorgepolitik des Provinzialverbandes Westfalen und des Landes Sachsen, 1880–1930* (Paderborn, 1993).

10. Anselm Faust, *Arbeitsmarktpolitik im deutschen Kaiserreich: Arbeitsvermittlung, Arbeitsbeschaffung und Arbeitslosenunterstützung, 1890–1918* (Stuttgart, 1986); Karl Heinrich Pohl, *Zwischen protestantischer Ethik, Unternehmerinteresse und organisierter Arbeiterbewegung: Zur Geschichte der Arbeitsvermittlung in Bielefeld von 1887 bis 1914* (Bielefeld, 1991); Frie, "Wohlfahrtsstaat Sachsen?" 343ff., and for the following paragraph.

11. The following account is derived from Pohl, *Die Münchener Arbeiterbewegung.*

enemy was the clerical Center Party rather than the reformist Social Democrats. The Center acted rather like an external force that held the divergent elements among the liberals together. The largest group of organized Munich liberals was based squarely in the middle-class business community (*Wirtschaftsbürgertum*). An almost equally important role was played by the *Mittelstand,* which in Munich comprised principally master craftsmen. Around the turn of the century, this group still made up about one-quarter of all liberal sympathizers. Increasingly, the liberals had to compete with the Center for the allegiance of this latter group, and over time they were less and less successful. Members of the educated middle classes, who grew more influential, composed about one-fifth of the potential liberal support. All sections of the civil service were represented among this group, including even army officers — a situation that would have been unthinkable in Prussia.[12] Liberal local politics and the organization of local election campaigns were arranged by the forty-member committee of the Association of Liberal and Non-ultramontane Voters (Verein der liberalen und nichtultramontanen Wähler). Middle-class businessmen and the middle-class intellectual elite had a dominant position on the committee. By contrast, the home- and landowners' lobby (*Haus- und Grundbesitzer*) had very limited influence on liberal policy in Munich.[13]

In the mid-1890s, Munich liberals faced growing competition from the Social Democrats and Catholics. Consequently the city's ruling elite allowed the Social Democrats some share of power: they preferred to cooperate with Munich's reformist Social Democrats (with whom they had much in common) rather than to concede greater influence to the Center.[14] Something of a social-liberal model of local politics developed subsequently. This model was distinguished by its social and educational policies, which were directed principally against the Center, and by its attempts to defuse conflicts between capital and labor. This development was not affected by the fact that the Center — which gained tighter control over Bavarian policy after the 1906 suffrage reform — lurched toward right-wing policies, characterized by the rejection of almost all facets of political "modernization" and by deep mistrust toward the social-liberal experiment in Munich. To be sure, the local liberal oligarchy in Munich fought a dogged battle (though

---

12. Manfred Hettling, "Politische Bürgerlichkeit: Der Bürger zwischen Individualität und Vergesellschaftung in Deutschland und der Schweiz von 1860 bis 1918" (Habil. diss., University of Bielefeld, 1997), 117ff., and for the following paragraph.

13. Elisabeth Angermair, "Münchner Kommunalpolitik: Die Residenzstadt als expansive Metropole," in *München,* ed. Prinz and Krauss, 36–43; Merith Niehuss, "Parteien, Wähler, Arbeiterbewegung," ibid., 44–53.

14. See Pohl, "Kommunen," 89–126.

mainly unsuccessfully) against the democratization of the suffrage.[15] But the dam broke with the local suffrage reform of 1908, which was pushed through jointly by the Bavarian ministry, by the Center Party, and by the Social Democrats. As a result of this reform, the composition of Munich's municipal parliament (*Gemeindebevollmächtigtenkollegium*) began to shift in favor of the Social Democrats and the Center. After elections in 1911, the sixty-member representative committee consisted of twenty-four liberals, fourteen Center Party members, two "house agrarians" (*Hausagrarier*), one antisemite, and nineteen Social Democrats. A further increase in the number of Social Democrats seemed inevitable.[16]

From this point onward there existed in Munich a kind of "municipal parliamentarism" in which the Social Democrats were (nearly) treated as equals. In the municipal parliament the former collier Sebastian Witti was elected as the deputy president (he became president during the war). Social Democrats held the position of chairman in the committees for administration, trade, finance, building, schools, and medical services, and they made up one-third of the membership of these committees. They were also represented on the local school commission and on the council for the care of the poor. Indeed, their collaboration was actually encouraged by the other parties. Only medals of honor were (so far) refused by Social Democrats. Otherwise they were fully integrated into municipal politics.

Such a development should not come as a complete surprise. In the area of school policy, the extent of such cooperation is perfectly understandable, as is the vehemence with which the Center opposed it.[17] A common policy in the areas of economic and social affairs, on the other hand, does prompt genuine astonishment. Yet in such matters as the promotion of wage agreements, Munich may rightly be regarded as having stood in the vanguard. The rationalization of industrial relations and the gradual predominance of contractual rules instead of short-term solutions wrung from one's opponents by strikes or lockouts—these features of modern industrial policy were evident in

---

15. Annelise Kreitmeyer, "Zur Entwicklung der Kommunalpolitik der bayerischen Sozialdemokratie im Kaiserreich und in der Weimarer Republik unter besonderer Berücksichtigung Münchens," *Archiv für Sozialgeschichte* 25 (1985): 103–35.

16. In the last elections where one-third of parliamentary deputies were chosen, the liberals won five seats and the Center six, but the Social Democrats won eight seats; see Pohl, *Die Münchener Arbeiterbewegung*, 426ff., and for the following paragraph.

17. Karl Heinrich Pohl, "Sozialdemokratie und Bildungswesen: Das 'Münchner Modell' einer sozialdemokratisch-bürgerlichen Schulpolitik und die Entwicklung der Volks- und Fortbildungsschulen im Bayern der Jahrhundertwende," *Zeitschrift für bayerische Landesgeschichte* 53 (1990): 79–101.

Munich from the beginning of the twentieth century onward. In fact they led to real hope among contemporaries that industrial relations would soon be based on a policy of solid cooperation: each of the parties involved understood that in economic matters a policy of limiting potential conflicts promised real rewards. Such a strategy is usually referred to in German historiography as "modern."[18]

It is certainly unusual that as early as 1907, two-thirds of all employed workers (male and female) in Munich had working conditions controlled by collective wage agreements. No other city had such a high proportion of workers covered by such agreements.[19] Dresden, with a level of 17 percent, can hardly even compare with Munich.[20] There are various reasons for Munich's unique position here,[21] but the political will of the community (and of the state) is among the most decisive. Both the state government, which declared in 1905 that it specifically welcomed wage agreements and that it would support their creation by any possible means,[22] and the local authorities in Munich can be regarded as driving forces behind this development. On several occasions, local authorities stood up to Munich's big industrialists when they refused to enter into regulated wage agreements.

In Munich, this system of collective bargaining soon proved its value. Each time an industrial dispute produced bitter conflict between rival parties, either the local authorities or the Bavarian state stepped in at the decisive moment to smooth the waters. Most often it was the Reconciliation Office (*Einigungsamt*) of the Munich industrial court, whose members were elected in equal number from workers and employers, that took up the case and played the role of arbitrator. The authority it gained in doing so soon enabled it to defuse conflicts on a regular basis. The modifying influence of the local authorities was particularly evident in the printing industry: Here it conformed completely with the Social Democratic demand that state printing contracts were to be given out only to firms prepared to recognize the wage agreement. Because no

---

18. Here one can consult only Klaus Schönhoven, "Arbeitskonflikte in Konjunktur und Rezession: Gewerkschaftliche Streikpolitik und Streikverhalten der Arbeiterschaft vor 1914," in *Streik: Zur Geschichte des Arbeitskampfes in Deutschland während der Industrialisierung,* ed. Klaus Tenfelde and Heinrich Volkmann (Munich, 1981), 177–93.

19. The average for the Reich in 1912 was about 15 percent.

20. Alfred Hahn, "120 Jahre Dresdner Gemeindevertretung: Kommunerepräsentanten und Stadtverordnete, 1830–1950" (MS, Dresden, n.d.), 33.

21. Pohl, *Die Münchener Arbeiterbewegung,* 263ff.; Elisabeth Jüngling, *Streiks in Bayern, 1889–1914: Arbeitskampf in der Prinzregentenzeit* (Munich, 1986), 27; idem, "Arbeitskämpfe der Jahrhundertwende: Zwischen polizeilicher Observierung und staatlichen Schlichtungsbemühungen," in *München,* ed. Prinz and Krauss, 54–57.

22. Letter from the Bavarian foreign ministry to the local district administrations, 2 Mar. 1905, Bayerisches Hauptstaatsarchiv (hereafter BayrHStA) Munich, M Arb 861.

exceptions were allowed, companies were in practice forced to accept the agreement.[23]

Without exaggeration, then, one can speak of a climate in Munich that was, in social and political terms, as "mild" as it was parliamentarily "advanced." This climate had been created, above all, because local authorities, the Bavarian state, employers, trade unions, liberals, Social Democrats, and even the Center were all able to work beside each other, and with each other, on an equal footing. These various parties were able to clear up many disputes in their initial phase or minimize their negative consequences. In this respect at least, free trade unions and Social Democrats were recognized and respected as partners, not enemies, even though they had to continue to fight arduously for equality of status.

IV. Dresden

Developments in Dresden looked rather different, in spite of the liberals' dynamic new understanding of social issues after the turn of the century. For Dresden, unlike any other German city, was ruled until roughly 1900 by a coalition of Conservatives and antisemites. The latter, generally known as "Reformers" in the vocabulary of local politics because many of them belonged to or sympathized with the antisemitic German Reform Party, dominated this coalition. Meanwhile, Dresden's liberals and (later) the Social Democrats waited in the anteroom of power.

As in Munich, a variety of citizens' and district associations (*Bürger- und Bezirksvereine*), rather than formal parties, constituted the basis of local politics and organized the election of city councilors in Dresden.[24] In contrast to Munich, however, the Home-Owners Association (Hausbesitzerverein) held sway in Dresden, representing over 4,000 members at the turn of the century. One of Dresden's well-known liberal politicians complained that the Home-Owners Association, "supported by the Reform Association [also the Conservative Association — *KHP*] and by the citizens' and district associations — which for the most part hold the same political views as the Reformers — exert such great influence that they can keep awkward candidates off the list [of nominees for the city council]."

The social structure of the Conservative-Reformer group and their

---

23. Pohl, *Die Münchener Arbeiterbewegung,* 284f., and for the following paragraph.
24. For example, a Conservative-Reformer election manifesto from the year 1904 was supported by nearly fifty associations of the most different political hues; *Dresdner Neueste Nachrichten,* no. 113, 16 Nov. 1904, 13; for the following, 117.

liberal opponents can be described as follows.[25] Most support for the Conservative-Reform alliance, perhaps 42 percent or more, came from the *Mittelstand*. By contrast, only 17 percent of their sympathizers were upper-middle class.[26] Self-employed workers, journeymen, master craftsmen, and independent master craftsmen were the backbone of the Conservative-Reform coalition, representing about half of its support. Craft workers, who played a subordinate role among all shades of liberals with only a 5 percent representation, made up almost one-third of the coalition's support. Members of the civil service, who at 35 percent represented a very substantial proportion of liberal support, constituted only one-fifth of the Conservative-Reform following. On balance, therefore, the Conservative-antisemitic alliance was shaped to a large degree by independent master craftsmen, who may be included under the rubric of the *Mittelstand*. The core of this alliance was represented by the classic "old" *Mittelstand*.

The liberal opposition certainly had its sympathizers, perhaps 40 percent, among the lower-middle classes. However, it recruited its followers above all (about 30 percent) from the upper-middle classes. Within liberal ranks one finds hardly any workers at all — perhaps 2 percent. Journeymen, master craftsmen, self-employed independents, or self-employed master craftsmen still formed a bloc making up a quarter of the liberals' clientele, slightly fewer in number than the civil servants (26 percent), but more numerous than the salaried workers (about 18 percent). What is particularly striking about the liberal camp, however, is the social affiliation of the different wings of the party. Supporters of the Young Liberals (Jungliberalen) in Dresden — the "modern" wing — came disproportionately (45 percent) from the ranks of the *Mittelstand;* by contrast, only about 24 percent of Young Liberals were drawn from the upper-middle classes. There were a few more workers (about 5 percent) among the Young Liberals than among all liberal forces, but fewer self-employed, journeymen, master craftsmen, and self-employed master craftsmen (a mere 18 percent). The "new" *Mittelstand,* mainly salaried employees, were overrepresented. The upper-middle classes, on the other hand, about 15 percent of Young

---

25. These categories are derived from the model used in Reinhard Schüren, *Soziale Mobilität: Muster, Veränderungen, Bedingungen im 19. und 20. Jahrhundert* (St. Katharinen, 1989). This class analysis is based on the list of signatories among a total of 2,732 supporters of liberal candidates in Dresden *Landtag* constituencies: Hettner (Young Liberal), Vogel, and Heinze. See *Dresdner Neueste Nachrichten,* no. 287 (21 Oct. 1909): 22ff.; ibid., no. 23 (24 Jan. 1907): 12–14.

26. Again, these categories correspond to those used in Schüren, *Soziale Mobilität; Dresdner Neueste Nachrichten,* no. 285 (19 Oct. 1909): 12, which provides a list of signatories among 383 sympathizers.

Liberals, were only half as strongly represented as they were among the "old" liberals, where they constituted a good 25 percent of supporters.

Two events in Dresden, occurring almost simultaneously after the turn of the century, suddenly brought movement to local politics, thereby threatening the apparently stable power structure in the Saxon capital. The first was the "storming" of local electoral politics by the Social Democrats, whose efforts began in 1900 and were capped with success just three years later. The second was the determination of National Liberals to strike out in a new direction—the sign of things to come.

Dresden's municipal elections of 1904 brought the Social Democrats a considerable increase in their total vote. This development was in turn partly the result of the SPD's phenomenal success in the Reichstag elections of 1903. On both occasions, the Social Democrats astounded everyone by attracting the support of many middle-class voters. Certainly Dresden's Social Democrats had not yet succeeded—in contrast to the situation in Munich—in converting this success into a corresponding number of seats in the municipal parliament. It was clear, however, that they were destined to achieve further victories in the next elections. In the face of this perceived danger, the majority parties on the Dresden city council acted with lightning speed in 1905 to change the suffrage. Their sole aim was to keep the Social Democrats out of municipal politics. The new suffrage (known as an *Abteilungs- und Klassenwahlrecht*) segregated voters into two voting "divisions," depending on the length of time they had possessed civil rights (the dividing point was pegged at ten years). These two "divisions" were then subdivided into four occupational "classes," designating voters who were considered to be without a profession (*Berufslose*), workers (*Arbeiter*), officials (*Beamte*), and employers (*Unternehmer*). In the first voting division, voters elected 12, 12, 24, and 36 city councilors respectively. In the second voting division, they elected six councilors in each category. This complicated system was meant to achieve one simple goal: to make it impossible for Social Democrats to gain the number of parliamentary seats that corresponded to their proportion of the popular vote.[27] This objective, however—similar to the outcome when the *Landtag* suffrage was altered a few years later—was achieved only in part. As the Bavarian envoy in Dresden observed in a report to his superiors in Munich: "This calculation [the exclusion of the Social Democrats] has not been successful; Mayor [Otto] Beutler, who rules as autocratically in Dresden's city hall as Privy Councilor [Paul] Mehnert [leader of Saxony's Conservatives] does in the lower house of the *Landtag*, is about to suffer a great failure;

---

27. All workers were included in only one "class" in order to restrict their influence.

his splendid, loyal majority is about to come to an end."[28] The envoy's prediction was not far off the mark. Despite the intentions of the framers of this suffrage revision, in 1906 six Social Democrats entered Dresden's municipal parliament for the first time. Four more councilors followed in 1907, and then another four in 1908, so that the Social Democrats soon held fourteen of eighty-four seats.[29]

Simultaneously, National Liberals in Dresden, in alliance with the League of Saxon Industrialists, began their ascent from oblivion, gradually freeing themselves from the grasp of the Conservatives. The importance these men placed on achieving success in local politics can be seen from the fact that three of their leaders (Gustav Stresemann, Paul Wilhelm Vogel, and Rudolf Heinze) sat on the city council. As was stated openly in a manifesto issued by the National Liberals, these men's objective was to provide municipal administrators and advisors drawn from only "those men who, by virtue of their education and position, are best qualified to serve [or, one might say, to serve their own supporters wherever possible—*KHP*] and to bring a greater number of such men into the most important municipal committees." "It would be severely damaging," this manifesto added, "not only for the citizens of Dresden but for the whole of Germany, if healthy progress in a city such as Dresden were held up by the Reform Party, and if instead of social freedom the city were to experience the ruthless autocracy of one economically motivated party."[30]

The liberal onslaught achieved striking success. The city council in 1905 was still composed of 36 Reformers, 20 Conservatives, only 3 National Liberals, no Social Democrats, and a few independents, who more or less sympathized with the Conservatives and Reformers. This picture was dramatically changed in just a few years. By 1909, the ruling bloc of 20 Conservatives, 7 Home-Owners, and 13 Reformers already faced 27 liberals of all shades and 15 Social Democrats. The presence of two independents, who leaned toward the Reformers, meant that the scales were still tipped against the liberals.[31] The liberals nevertheless immediately sought to capitalize on their initial success. They claimed,

28. Montgelas report of 2 Dec. 1905, in BayrHStA Munich, MA 98679.

29. It remains an open question whether these developments can best be interpreted as the start of "modernization" or as a "democratic refusal." If one takes seriously the latest trends in research on Saxony, emphasis should be placed on the modernizing aspects of this suffrage reform, because they followed the trend initiated by the *Landtag* suffrage reform of 1909.

30. Manifesto (*Aufruf*) of the National Liberal Party (n.p., n.d.), in the Stadtarchiv Dresden, PA, Alldeutscher Verband, Bd. 26, p. 291.

31. *Nationalliberales Vereinsblatt* 4, no. 24 (15 Dec. 1909): 243; *Sächsische Nationale Blätter* 1, no. 16 (15 Jan. 1910): 365.

not just for themselves but also for the Social Democrats, fairer representation on the city's managing board and on the city council's committees. In fact, thanks to the support of the liberals, a Social Democrat soon sat on the city council executive body (*Direktorium der Stadtverordneten*). Dresden's entrenched power elite was beginning to lose its dominating position.[32] The liberals themselves proclaimed that partial collaboration between liberals and Social Democrats was no longer ruled out. As the National Liberals' leading newssheet declared: "There may still exist a *deep, wide chasm* between the views of the *liberals* and *Social Democrats;* but no one with insight would now dispute that parliamentary bodies should admit Social Democratic members as collaborators and that they should offer them the opportunity to make full use of their parliamentary mandate. The liberal group in our city council, adopting a just and reasoned viewpoint, has unanimously agreed to allow the Social Democrats two seats on each committee."[33]

That is where things remained, however. The integration of the Social Democrats into everyday municipal politics in Dresden was only in its infancy. When one compares developments in Dresden with those in other cities of the Reich—and above all with Munich—the Saxon capital obviously remained politically backward. "Municipal parliamentarism" arrived hesitantly and slowly; it was certainly not established before the First World War. To be sure, future development in a positive direction could no longer be ruled out either. One symbol of liberal and Social Democratic solidarity may be seen in the fact that the "Red Cyclist" bicycle repair workshop advertised its services in the National Liberals' newspaper, the *Sächsische Nationale Blätter;* no doubt it hoped, and perhaps expected, to win liberal custom.[34] Nevertheless, and again in obvious contrast to Munich, the formulation and enactment of local policies in the interest of workers was subordinated in Dresden to policies that favored master craftsmen and other social groups who exercised influence through the powerful Home-Owners' Association. These social groups were, and remained, convinced opponents of the organized labor movement, of the trade unions, and above all of wage agreements. Any notion of entering into a partnership with the "enemies of the state" was for them still unthinkable.[35] Accordingly, Dresden politicians remained virtually bound to deal with economic reforms only—for

---

32. See the unsigned letter from Dresden addressed to Gustav Stresemann in 1915, in Politisches Archiv des Auswärtigen Amtes, Bonn, NL Gustav Stresemann, 144.

33. *Sächsische Nationale Blätter* 1, no. 16 (15 Jan. 1910): 366; emphasis in the original.

34. *Sächsische Nationale Blätter* 5, no. 19 (10 May 1913): 138.

35. See "Das Handwerk und die Tarifverträge," *Correspondenzblatt* 22, no. 42 (19 Oct. 1912): 621–23.

example, to work wholeheartedly to prevent the establishment of a central employment exchange.[36] *Mittelständler* carried a motion forbidding the city's workers from either forming trade or economic cooperatives or even participating in such organizations.[37] In short, a softening of political fronts in Dresden hardly even lay on the horizon before the First World War.

V.   The Employment Exchange in Dresden

"Probably in no other German city have so many difficulties been placed in the way of the opening of public employment offices as in Dresden," noted Erdmann Graack in his history of employment exchanges in the Elbe metropolis.[38] Indeed, Dresden's progress toward a modern "independent" employment exchange system was exceptionally protracted. It thus serves to show what great obstacles were placed in Dresden's path to modernity. One cause of this slowness was the city's late industrialization, which meant that this question was addressed seriously only at the end of the 1880s.[39] Until that point, municipal efforts to combat poverty and begging had sufficed,[40] rendering unnecessary the creation of a municipal employment exchange. Another reason for this "delay" was the polarization of forces in the city and of the parties involved in its economic life. The employers' associations in Dresden were set up relatively late, although they were soon well-organized and their employment exchange offices had a considerable clientele. The effectiveness of these associations as a political and economic weapon against the workers was sufficient that no one imagined that they would be voluntarily given up.[41] The peculiar feature of Dresden's industry was that it needed special skills; therefore the advantage of having a central employment office that could provide unskilled and semiskilled workers could hardly be called into question. This, together with their enduring mistrust of trade unions and the Social Democrats, meant that the majority of Dresden's employers regarded such municipal employment offices with extreme skepticism. Ironically, skepti-

---

36. Paul Gregor (liberal) to a Herr Vetter, chairman of the "Verband zur Förderung von Dresden rechts der Elbe," 7 Nov. 1911, in Stadtarchiv Dresden, 13.29, Verband zur Förderung der Neustadt, 5.

37. See the report of the Bavarian envoy in Dresden, 23 Oct. 1903, in BayrHStA Munich, MH 12732.

38. Erdmann Graack, *Ein deutscher Arbeitsnachweis und seine geschichtliche Entwicklung* (Dresden, [1915]), 102.

39. The initial attempt at a solution by the social reformer and National Liberal Victor Böhmert dates from this time.

40. In any event, all workers' organizations firmly declined to cooperate in 1888.

41. For this and the following, see Pohl, *Zwischen protestantischer Ethik*, 222ff.

cism was also found, although not to the same extent, among the trade unions and the Social Democrats. They regarded the new proposals, sponsored by Christian and charitable interests, as no alternative to their own similarly well frequented offices. Charitable organizations, Christian organizations, and those motivated by middle-class compassion — these were all designed to deliver welfare to the poor, not to help people help themselves. Hence, for the Social Democrats, such organizations offered no alternative to organizing the workers themselves; nor did they hold the prospect of breaking the power of the employers. To this was added a third factor. In contrast to the resolute centralization of employment offices in the southern and southwestern states of Germany, and although the south German governments (and Prussia) had been active in the field since 1894,[42] Dresden felt no impetus from the Saxon state to provide a municipal employment exchange for many years. Things began to change only after 1906, as a result of the slow liberalization of Saxon domestic politics. By 1914, though, state initiatives had had no visible effect.

A fourth factor was perhaps the decisive one in determining Dresden's hesitancy to establish a municipal employment exchange: the lack of a dynamic impulse from within municipal government itself. This was again the result of the fact that Dresden's parliament was dominated by artisans organized in the *Handwerkskammer,* which was resolutely opposed to a municipal employment exchange. Its members saw such an institution solely as an opening to the "reds." As one of the biweeklies addressing the interests of artisans stated in 1902: "One must fear that, instead of promoting a more congenial relationship between employer and worker, a communal employment exchange system would give certain workers — specifically, those *whose efforts are directed to the overthrow of the existing state and social order* — a new field of operation for their activities."[43] Corresponding to this viewpoint, Dresden's guild authorities would only agree to such a system if parity were removed from a municipal employment exchange. But the free trade unions would not agree to any institution on which they not only lacked equal representation, but on which "national" workers would have a seat and equal rights.[44] On this issue, even the initiatives of the Association of Saxon Industrialists exhausted themselves in the face of stubborn resis-

---

42. Frie, "Wohlfahrtsstaat Sachsen?" 353.

43. *Der Arbeitsmarkt—Halbmonatsschrift der Centralstelle für Arbeitsmarkt-Berichte* 5, no. 11 (1 Mar. 1902): 202–3; emphasis in the original.

44. See the materials prepared for the Dresden municipal council session of 4 Nov. 1908, in Stadtarchiv Dresden, Stadtverordneten-Kanzlei, A 69I, together with points made on this topic by the National Liberal deputies and the VSI functionary Johannes März in the session of 20 June 1912, in *Sächsische Industrie* 8, no. 19 (10 July 1912): 293–94.

tance from the Conservatives.[45] This disappointing outcome also high-lighted the diversity of interests within the VSI, whose Dresden chapter declined to support an employment exchange that was set up with any-thing approaching parity for representatives of the free trade unions. For all these reasons, then, the movement for a municipal labor ex-change came relatively late, at the beginning of 1909, and even then only outside Dresden. Thus an unusual situation arose in Saxony where the district authorities (*Kreishauptmannschaft*) took the initiative. They put pressure on the municipality to take in hand the task of setting up a central employment exchange system; indeed, they even enticed it to do so with financial incentives.[46] Dresden's municipal leaders took this prob-lem in hand only in 1912, and then only because the municipal power constellation began to change in favor of the liberals (and the Social Democrats). But even at this late date, no unambiguous approval was given to an employment exchange system with equal representation.

When Dresden's employment exchange office finally opened in 1912, representational parity was not achieved. Instead it proved to be an instrument of the conservative municipal administration and of the em-ployers, both of which opposed the interests of workers in the free trade unions. The employers' own employment exchanges retained the lion's share of the business. The strike clause was modified so that it corresponded to the ideas of the VSI's relatively conservative local chapter. And the supervisory administrative council of the employment exchange was constituted in such a way that, on the workers' side, representatives of the "national" workers were given equal consider-ation beside the free trade union cartel,[47] ensuring that Dresden's em-ployers always enjoyed a two-thirds majority on these committees. In short, Dresden's employment exchange office corresponded to the clas-sic model of an employment office cut to the cloth of employers' inter-ests, obstructing the emancipation of workers organized in the free trade unions. Thus Dresden took its place at the bottom of the list of German cities ranked by efficiency, parity of representation, and local political support for municipal reform. Until the outbreak of the First World War, it was not possible to reconcile the opposing industrial interest groups in Dresden or to conduct "modern" local politics, at least not when the contentious issue of labor exchange offices was under debate. Even with the best will in the world, one cannot speak here of a modern political culture.

---

45. See Pohl, "VSI"; idem, "Wirtschaft und Wirtschaftsbürgertum im Königreich Sachsen im frühen 20. Jahrhundert," in *Sachsen und Mitteldeutschland,* ed. Werner Bramke and Ulrich Heß (Weimar, 1995), 319–36; and Frie, "Wohlfahrtsstaat Sachsen?" 359.

46. Frie, "Wohlfahrtsstaat Sachsen?" 356.

47. Graack, *Arbeitsnachweis,* 294.

VI.   The Opposite Pole: Munich

In Munich, the problem at hand was not significantly different, but its treatment certainly was. The rising economic tide in Munich demanded a higher quota of skilled workers and a regularization of the hitherto chaotic employment exchange system. Although this situation provided pressure for agreement, conflicting political objectives and hesitation were evident both on the side of employers and among representatives of the trade unions. The free trade union cartel in Munich fought for power in the employment exchanges, because this was where job seekers and job vacancies came together. The hope among Munich union leaders was that "[d]irect pressure should be brought to bear on the employers, or pressure exerted on the flank by demands and measures for industrial action,"[48] whereby they conceived such pressure being exerted by a free trade union monopoly of employment exchanges and through regulation (and, if necessary, the limitation) of the supply of labor. Employers wanted to weaken the position of the trade unions by controlling employment exchanges themselves. In this way a (potentially) powerful weapon would be taken out of the unions' hands. Both sides were nevertheless determined to try to solve the basic problem at hand.

In this situation the attitude of the municipality proved to be decisive, and it is here that the contrast between Munich and Dresden is most evident. Whereas Dresden's municipal authorities constantly prevaricated, the Munich city council went on the offensive. Under its dominant influence, the foundation of municipal employment exchanges was carried through in what seems almost a modern fashion. After the trade unions had made the first initiative in 1890, the Munich city council took up the proposal in 1893. At that time it requested that the participating interests — the free and Christian trade unions on the one side, and the trade association (representing the employers) on the other — each produce an expert opinion. Such a procedure would have been impossible in Dresden at this time.

The Social Democrats approved the proposal but set a number of conditions. They demanded equal representation for employers and workers.[49] To aspire to such parity of representation would have been a

---

48. Anselm Faust, "Arbeitsmarktpolitik in Deutschland: Die Entstehung der öffentlichen Arbeitsvermittlung, 1890–1927," in *Historische Arbeitsmarktforschung: Entstehung, Entwicklung und Probleme der Vermarktung von Arbeitskraft,* ed. Tony Pierenkemper and Reinhard Tilly (Göttingen, 1982), 253–73, here 260.

49. Karl Hartmann, *Die gemeindliche Arbeitsvermittlung in Bayern: Mit besonderer Berücksichtigung der Verhältnisse bei dem städtischen Arbeitsamte München* (Munich, 1900); Wolfgang Schwarz, "Die Wirksamkeit des Arbeitsamtes München — innerhalb der unter Gemeindeverwaltung stehenden Geschäftsperiode von 1895 bis 1928" (Ph.D. diss., University of Munich, 1945).

utopian dream in Dresden, but it signified no insuperable obstacle in Munich. More serious was the demand that the future employment exchange should cease to operate during strikes (but not during lockouts). The significance of this demand was twofold. To grant this demand would have indirectly signified that a municipal institution recognized the unions' competence to act during a strike. It would also have positioned the municipal authorities in the unions' camp. Understandably, from the employers' point of view, under these circumstances the principal function of the employment exchange would have been dramatically altered, putting it squarely on the side of the free trade unions in the event of industrial action. Although the attitude of Munich employers was less uniform than that of the trade unions, most of them feared that such an employment exchange office would become a playground for socialist agitators. Therefore the majority of employers favored rejection. Again, however, differences of opinion within the various groups should not be dismissed; nor should we forget that everyone remained ready to talk.

In view of this stalemate, the actions of the municipality again took on paramount importance. Its pressure on the various parties finally resulted in the setting up of a municipal commission, which included participation by the Social Democrats. Defying the resistance of members (*Magistratsräte*) sitting in the municipal parliament's upper chamber as well as representatives who favored the guilds, this commission prepared a draft proposal outlining the "ideal" model for a future exchange. In the discussion of this draft, the deputies' arguments focused on the so-called strike paragraph in the proposal. Both the majority of the municipal representatives and the Bavarian state government supported an agreement that would be fair to the unions' interests. The majority of Munich's city councilors, however, who were more directly under the influence of employers, still rejected such an agreement, though only by a slim majority. These differences notwithstanding, the parties were eventually forced by the pressure of events to reach an agreement. A compromise formula stated that all job seekers should be informed by the exchange about every strike or lockout, without in principle the exchange's work being stopped. This system proved to be so effective that discussion of the strike paragraph soon died away. The municipal employment exchange swiftly appropriated to itself four-fifths of all employment transactions before the First World War,[50] and a city official who enjoyed the confidence of both workers and employers became manager of the office.[51] In the course of the twentieth century,

---

50. *Geschäftsbericht des Städtischen Arbeitsamtes München* 18 (1913): 26.
51. *Geschäftsbericht des Städtischen Arbeitsamtes München* 1 (1895–96): 2.

this labor exchange evolved into a fiefdom of the free trade union movement. Thus a coalition of rational men drawn from the city council, the trade unions, and state authorities (including Bavaria's state government), together with municipal deputies representing the Center, the liberals, and the Social Democrats, had succeeded in setting up an employment exchange in the face of strong resistance from the employers and from those council members close to the guilds. This employment exchange may be said to have conducted its operations in a completely unbiased way, thus corresponding in its structure and activities to exchanges existing today.

VII. Conclusions

On the face of it, the question of whether developments in Munich or Dresden were more "modern" calls for a simple answer. Clearly Munich was more "progressive" than Dresden, and clearly it showed itself more prepared to carry through a "municipal socialist" policy. Progressive local politics were evident only in Munich, not in Dresden. A more important question, however, concerns the factors that account for such different developments in such similar cities.

Local power relationships played a conspicuous and decisive role, because municipal rule was a refuge of German liberalism. It was in the cities that liberalism had been founded in the early nineteenth century, and when liberalism's power at the national and regional levels began to decline, it was to the cities that it retreated, still with considerable strength, at the end of the century. There the liberals — and they alone — created a new, "modern" politics. "Modern" local politics in this respect was no general and universal peculiarity of all cities, as some have argued; rather, it was a specific achievement of municipal liberalism. The phenomenon called "municipal socialism" was an original product of liberal local politics, as the Munich example demonstrates perhaps better than any other. In Dresden, by contrast, an anomalous situation arose in that the liberals had no decisive influence; municipal power lay in the hands of the Reform Party and the Conservatives, who were massively opposed to a policy of "municipal socialism." Above all, they refused to cooperate with Social Democrats, for they did not consider the SPD to represent legitimate interests. Hence municipal parliamentarism could develop in Munich, but not in Dresden.

One must also acknowledge that the wider political context played a role in both cities. Local politics in the *Kaiserreich* seems to have been autonomous of wider political movements only to a certain, limited degree. Even without discarding the notion of the relative autonomy of the municipality, it would be foolish to argue that the political stagnation evident in Dresden was not in part the product of a powerful and rigid antisocialist consensus among Conservatives and the Reform Party at the state level. That liberalism developed so late in Dresden was also due to the fact that the Kingdom of Saxony, at least until the early twentieth century, was even more robustly conservative than Prussia. This conservative ethos was demonstrated most strongly in the *Residenzstadt* Dresden, although one has to assume that liberal rule was quite possible in other Saxon towns such as Chemnitz or Leipzig. In Dresden, however, where the threads of conservative state power came together, political roadblocks impeded both the spread of liberal thinking and the "modernizing" developments that might have arisen from such thought.

Things were very different in Munich. Modern liberalism succeeded there in spite of a strictly antireformist political undercurrent. Center Party policy and the regional influence of Catholicism in Upper Bavaria could only put a partial brake on local politics. Municipal politics in Munich was largely autonomous of such external influences. This circumstance certainly has much to do with the fact that the Munich experiment was promoted over a long period by the liberal state government. When Hertling's "Catholic government" assumed power from the liberals in 1912, the Munich system was already so firmly in place that the city remained positively disposed toward reformist policies. It succeeded in defending its political autonomy against onslaughts from the Bavarian state government.

In Dresden, on the other hand, change set in only after 1900, partly as a result of changes in state-level politics, but also because change was endorsed on principle by local liberals. Now the coalition of Reformers and Conservatives could no longer repress progressive sentiments that originated with the Saxon National Liberal Party but also found support from many Saxon businessmen and even the Social Democrats. Although change was late in coming, local liberalism began gradually to grow in strength in Dresden shortly before the outbreak of war in 1914. Hence what applies generally to Saxony—that it lagged far behind the Kingdom of Bavaria in its overall development and in its political culture—also applies to local politics in its capital city. In spite of Dresden's cultural flowering, its educational policy, and its structural renewal, such decisive problems of "modernity" as the defusing of tensions between workers and employers could not be adequately addressed during the imperial period. Whereas "social-liberal" Munich promoted the extension of wage bargaining, set up an employment exchange with equal representation, and integrated the Social Democrats into the city's institutions, the alliance of Reformers and Conservatives who dominated Dresden's local political scene succeeded in impeding any such progress.

Saxon Politics during the First World War: Modernization, National Liberal Style

Christoph Nonn

I. Introduction

Whether the authoritarian monarchy of Wilhelmine Germany could have evolved into a modern parliamentary democracy is a long-debated and still open question. Recent research on Saxony, important in its own right, has contributed to both sides of the debate. According to some historians, the kingdom on the Elbe witnessed the emergence of a new political culture at the turn of the century, based on compromise and cooperation between parties and the social groups they represented, which contrasted sharply with the confrontation and repression characteristic of the old regime. Thus some have pointed to the collapse of the liberal-conservative *Kartell* that had dominated Saxon politics since the 1880s, pitting the "parties of order" against "revolutionary" Social Democracy; to the Saxon liberals' opening to the left, following the discovery of common urban-industrial interests between middle and working classes; and to the democratization of the *Landtag* suffrage in 1909. Others have maintained that despite these developments, rigid class divisions nevertheless remained the basis of Saxon domestic politics. Indeed, no firm alliance of liberals and Social Democrats replaced the old liberal-conservative cartel, which arguably persisted in the field of social policy. The 1909 democratization of the suffrage merely reversed the conservative 1896 reform. No positive steps toward a formal parliamentarization of the political system were taken.[1]

---

1. The debate can now best be approached through Simone Lässig and Karl Heinrich Pohl, eds., *Sachsen im Kaiserreich: Politik, Wirtschaft und Gesellschaft im Umbruch* (Weimar, 1997), especially via the contributions of the two editors (for the "new political culture" thesis) and those of Karsten Rudolph and Ewald Frie (for the "class divisions"

Until now, most research has concentrated on the period between the two suffrage reforms of 1896 and 1909. By contrast, the last years of the Saxon monarchy have so far attracted little attention. This essay therefore takes a closer look at domestic events during the First World War. The subject merits attention both in its own right and as a contribution to the ongoing debate about the modernization of Saxony and Germany. Due to lack of space, only selected key developments can be highlighted. Special attention is therefore devoted to the liberals, since they were the decisive force in the power triangle of Saxon politics.[2] This essay focuses on the development of socioeconomic cleavages — class conflict and the urban-rural divide — and on the more culturally defined concepts of regional identity and national unity.[3] Developments both in "high politics" (government and party leadership circles) and "low politics" (the problems and protests of the people) will be considered.

II. The *Burgfrieden* and Beyond

As in the other German states and in Berlin, all conflict in Saxon politics was suspended in August 1914 by the parties' agreement to a "domestic truce" (*Burgfrieden*). However, in "low politics" this truce began to show cracks as early as 1915. Scarcity and high food prices were central to these developments. The introduction of government controls and rationing in 1914–15 could mitigate the problem but not solve it. As a highly industrialized state, Saxony was hit very early and severely when the allied blockade cut Germany off from the import of foodstuffs upon which the country depended. It was the first region to witness violent hunger riots, starting in 1915. The military had to intervene in October 1915 to quell the looting of shops in Chemnitz, and again in May 1916

---

thesis). I have taken an intermediate position, stressing the importance of both class and rural-urban conflict. I argue that Saxony on the eve of the First World War was on the move, but not in the direction of a social democracy: Christoph Nonn, "Arbeiter, Bürger und 'Agrarier': Stadt-Land-Gegensatz und Klassenkonflikt am Beispiel des Königreichs Sachsen," in *Demokratie und Emanzipation zwischen Saale und Elbe: Beiträge zur Geschichte der sozialdemokratischen Arbeiterbewegung bis 1933,* ed. Helga Grebing, Hans Mommsen, and Karsten Rudolph (Essen, 1993), 101–13.

2. James Retallack is currently preparing a major study of party politics and electoral culture in Saxony. In addition, see the account of Saxony during the First World War from a Social Democratic perspective: Karsten Rudolph, *Die sächsische Sozialdemokratie vom Kaiserreich zur Republik (1871–1923)* (Weimar, 1995), esp. 86–188. Despite some major disagreements, the following analysis is much indebted to this pioneering work.

3. Readers familiar with Stein Rokkan's cleavage theory will realize my indebtedness to his methodological approach: cf. Seymour Lipset and Stein Rokkan, "Cleavage Structures, Party Systems, and Voter Alignments: An Introduction," in *Party Systems and Voter Alignments: Cross-National Perspectives,* ed. idem (New York, 1967).

due to hunger riots in the suburbs of Leipzig. Here thousands of people, mainly women, also demonstrated peacefully in front of the town hall against the shortage of potatoes. In November, a similar demonstration took place in Dresden.[4]

Strikes set in only later. They remained isolated incidents during 1916, with only a few hundred participants at most. Moreover, they too centered on the issue of food shortages. When finally, in April 1917, more than 10,000 workers went on strike in Leipzig alone, the district governor reported to his superiors in Dresden that it was not really better working conditions the strikers wanted, but food and peace. Indeed, the first thing the workers' resolution asked for was to provide the population with sufficient food at reasonable prices. Once economic demands were met, the strike quickly dissipated.[5] Although scarcity of food was the ultimate reason for the protest, this problem was aggravated by the existence of a black market. Peasants who sidestepped state controls and sold their produce on the black market could make huge profits, allowing the affluent to improve significantly upon their meager rations. Some state officials, especially those at lower levels, were willing to tolerate this injustice. Some even shared in the profits.[6]

Of special importance here is not the extent of this black market, but how it was perceived by the people. In a memorandum of April 1917, an official of the Saxon ministry of the interior contended that "the people rather stubbornly persist in their conviction that there are more than enough foodstuffs in the countryside" but that the peasants were holding them back under protection of the pro-agrarian conservative government. When the ministry received a deputation of Dresden hunger marchers in November 1916, the protesters demanded a more just distribution of food between town and country. However, it was not only the urban-rural divide they complained about. They also demanded a fairer distribution between rich and poor. At home, and at the front as well, this sort of class injustice was a central focus of complaints. Soldiers of different social standing and political sympathies bombarded their deputies with letters complaining about the unjust distribution of rations: allegedly,

---

4. Klaus-Peter Reiss, *Von Bassermann zu Stresemann: Die Sitzungen des national-liberalen Zentralvorstandes, 1912–1917* (Düsseldorf, 1967), 286, on unrest as early as February 1915; Stephan Pfalzer, "Der 'Butterkrawall' im Oktober 1915," in *Demokratie und Emanzipation*, ed. Grebing, Mommsen, and Rudolph, 196–201; SächsHStA Dresden, Ministerium des Innern (hereafter MdI) Nr. 11070.

5. SächsHStA, MdI Nr. 11071, esp. 111f. for the report of Leipzig's district governor (*Amtshauptmann*) dated 17 May 1917; Rudolph, *Sozialdemokratie,* 136–40.

6. There is still no comprehensive modern study of Germany's food economy in the First World War; but see Gerald D. Feldman, *The Great Disorder* (New York, 1993); Robert G. Moeller, *German Peasants and Agrarian Politics, 1914–1924* (Chapel Hill, NC, 1986); and Avner Offer, *The First World War: An Agrarian Interpretation* (Oxford, 1989).

officers were amply provisioned with meat, butter, and fat, whereas they had to make do with marmalade and salted herring.[7]

III. Defending the Fatherland . . . and Saxony

The irregularities and injustices of food distribution were ultimately blamed on the government. Step by step, this undermined trust in the old regime. As in the Reich, Prussia, and other German states, the authoritarian regime in Saxony increasingly lost its legitimacy.[8] However, rather than exploiting this erosion of loyalty among the population for a full-scale attack on conservative hegemony, Social Democrats and liberals held back, for the sake of the common war effort. The scarcity of food during the war perpetuated and even widened the cleavages that had prevented a firm anticonservative alliance between the workers' movement and the bourgeoisie before 1914. Whereas the rural-urban cleavage united Social Democracy and liberalism as town-based movements against agrarian conservatism, class conflict divided them, inducing the liberal middle classes to seek the support of the conservatives against workers' demands. Thus conflicts and cleavages in Saxon "high politics," and the corresponding division into three main political camps, remained essentially the same as before the war. For these reasons, harnessing the issue of food to the cause of political reform in the Dresden *Landtag,* despite its importance in the minds of the people, proved to be extremely difficult.

But there was at least one aspect of the food question on which Social Democrats and liberals in Saxony could agree: the conviction that the central government in Berlin did not allocate to Saxony its fair share of the agrarian surplus harvested in the Prussian east. Antipathy toward the "Prussians" had a long tradition in Saxony as well as in southern Germany, although, arguably, this particularist expression of regional identity had withered since the foundation of the *Kaiserreich* in 1871. Now it was back with a vengeance. Not only in Bavaria were tourists compelled to stress that they were not Prussian to assure themselves a friendly welcome. In Saxon pubs, too, the locals were likely to fall silent upon the entrance of strangers "who were said to be from Germany's leading state." On one such occasion, because visitors from the tiny

---

7. Memo of 7 Apr. 1917, in SächsHStA Dresden, MdI Nr. 11071, 10f.; memo of 2 Nov. 1916, ibid., MdI Nr. 11070, 49–51; Nitzsche-Leutzsch to Saxon ministry of war, 10 May 1916, in Ernst Johann, ed., *Innenansichten eines Krieges* (Frankfurt a. M., 1968), 194f.; also *Sächsischer Volkswart,* July 1915.

8. See also the splendid study on Baden by Klaus-Peter Müller, *Politik und Gesellschaft im Krieg: Der Legitimitätsverlust des badischen Staates, 1914–1918* (Stuttgart, 1988).

Thuringian principality of Reuß did not announce distinctly enough that they were *"Reußen,"* they were initially mistaken by the Saxon locals to be *"Preußen"* (Prussians). "Thank God, they had simply misheard: The 'P' in front had to go. . . . And cheerfully they raised their beer mugs together."[9]

In the extraordinary session of the Saxon *Landtag* in 1915–16, liberals and Social Democrats demanded "an improvement of Saxony's economic position in the Reich." In parliament, the food issue took precedence over all other problems brought about by the war. With the explicit aim of defusing popular protest, leftist deputies introduced motions not only for a fairer distribution of food within Saxony, but also among the federal states of Germany. The kingdom on the Elbe, they claimed, was deliberately being disadvantaged by Berlin. As the most thoroughly industrialized region in Germany, it was dependent on the import of foodstuffs, which could be supplied by the surplus from the agricultural Prussian east. But the conservative Junkers in Prussia were allegedly hoarding grain in order to profit from the black market.[10]

Saxon politicians at first tried to solve this perceived problem by lobbying the Reich authorities through their national party executives in Berlin. Each new outburst of popular unrest in Saxony was followed by an intensification of these efforts in Berlin. After the first major hunger riots in Chemnitz, the Reichstag in late 1915 set up a committee to advise the government on the food question. The May 1916 riots and demonstrations in Leipzig prompted a remodeling of the committee into a far more powerful War Food Office.[11] But the situation did not improve. Not only Saxon Social Democrats, but National Liberals as well developed the impression that the Prussian conservatives—holding a dominant position in the Reich government as well as the Federal Council (*Bundesrat*)—deliberately obstructed all efforts for a fairer distribution of food. The day after the great strike of April 1917 began, a contributor to the National Liberals' official newssheet in Saxony wrote sarcastically that "Prussian food policy has not exactly made any moral conquests in Saxony." Joined by the Social Democrats, the National Liberals went on to demand a reform of the Prussian suffrage. Subsequently the two parties also agreed to ask the Saxon government "to work through its representative in the Federal Council for the quick introduction of a liberal and democratic new order in the Reich."[12]

---

9. *Sächsische Umschau,* 17 Apr. 1917.

10. *Landtags-Akten von den Jahren 1915/17: Berichte der zweiten Kammer,* passim, and *Mitteilungen über die Verhandlungen . . .* , esp. 23 Nov. 1915; *Nationalliberale Blätter: Deutsche Stimmen* (1915), 518–21, 1136; (1916), 622, 781f.

11. Reiss, *Von Bassermann zu Stresemann,* 284–89.

12. *Sächsische Umschau,* 17 Apr. 1917; *Landtags-Akten,* no. 427 (12 June 1917).

Despite the *Burgfrieden,* the people's economic grievances had finally led to demands for political modernization. So far, however, this
spillover into politics had consequences only in Berlin. Whereas members of the Saxon National Liberal Party (Nationalliberale Partei) — who
held a decisive position in the Saxon *Landtag* — advocated substantial
constitutional reform, especially suffrage reform, in the Reich and Prussia, they did not do so at home. Of course one reason was that in a
parliamentary democracy they feared being pressed to the wall by a
Social Democratic majority.[13] But was this the only reason? If so, why
did Saxon National Liberals push for constitutional reform on the national level? In fact they could argue with some justification that if the
disastrous food supply was to be improved at all, the key to this solution
lay in Berlin and not in Dresden. It is important to note that it was
indeed only in Berlin that some sort of parliamentarization of government took place after the summer of 1917. In contrast to the Reich and
Prussia, whose government bureaucracies overlapped to a considerable
extent, parliamentarians in Saxony, Bavaria, Württemberg, and Baden
were invited to join ministries of state either not at all or only shortly
before the outbreak of revolution in November 1918.[14] This lag can be
explained largely by the relative unimportance of the federal states in
the management of food supplies during the war. Whereas parliamentarization and democratization were already deemed inevitable in
Berlin, the Saxon National Liberals still did not see these reforms as
necessary to defuse popular unrest at home.

That constitutional reform became a subject in Saxony at all was
largely due to the conservative-dominated upper house of the *Landtag,*
which vetoed the lower house's resolution asking the government to
press for Reich reform in the Federal Council. As a result, a majority of
Social Democrats and liberals demanded supremacy of the lower over
the upper house and a restructuring of the latter. After the government
refused, the same majority then introduced a motion calling for a
strengthening of the parliament vis-à-vis the executive. In the wake of
new strikes in January 1918 and after much internal wrangling, the National Liberals even decided to speak up for a further democratization of
the Saxon suffrage, though not for the "one man, one vote" principle
favored by the Social Democrats.[15]

---

13. This is the direction of the argument in Rudolph, *Sozialdemokratie.*

14. See inter alia Müller, *Politik und Gesellschaft,* on Baden; Willy Albrecht,
Landtag und Regierung in Bayern am Vorabend der Revolution von 1918 (Berlin, 1968), on
Bavaria; and Manfred Scheck, *Zwischen Weltkrieg und Revolution* (Cologne, 1981), on
Württemberg.

15. *Landtags-Akten 1915/17,* nos. 490, 498, Reports of the parliamentary committee struck to debate the "new order" (8 and 12 Oct. 1917); *Landtags-Akten 1917/18,* nos.

IV. Saxon Political Reform and the "New Order"

Despite this political movement, the cause of political reform did not advance much further in Dresden. The conservatives in the upper house of the *Landtag* continued to veto all progress, while the conservative-dominated Saxon government made only minor concessions.[16] What is more, neither liberals nor Social Democrats pressed for reform in a resolute manner. For example, they accepted the government's decision to adjourn the *Landtag* in May 1918.[17] Moreover, they then exerted no pressure to reconvene parliament before the end of hostilities became imminent in October. We can discern two reasons for this laxity.

First, the paths of popular protest and high politics diverged again after the first great strike wave of April 1917. The complicated blueprints for reform of the *Landtag*'s upper house did not animate the general population. The problem they had with their diet was not one of suffrages, but of potatoes and turnips. Once the impression had taken root that the food supply could only be improved through pressure in Berlin, interest in Saxon politics dwindled. After May 1917, even the grotesquely misnamed organ of the conservative middle classes, *Der Fortschritt* (Progress), reduced the number of pages it devoted to politics, choosing instead to advise its readership on how to grow edibles instead of flowers and conjure nourishing meals out of sparse rations. The second great strike wave of January 1918, in which the issue of political reform played a much more important role than before, had very few participants in Saxony. Rather, it was strongest in Berlin, where around 150,000 workers temporarily laid down work.[18] When in May 1918 a democratization of the Saxon suffrage was debated in the Dresden *Landtag,* one conservative speaker pointed to the empty public galleries to drive home his claim that the population showed little interest in the subject. Liberals and Social Democrats in effect assented to this interpretation by agreeing meekly to adjourn parliament.[19]

Second, and perhaps even more important, the vast majority of political leaders agreed to postpone domestic quarrels for the sake of the common war effort. Liberals and Social Democrats may have asked for

---

189, 300 (9 Apr. 1918, 14 May 1918); *Sächsische Umschau,* passim. See also Rudolph, *Sozialdemokratie,* 141–43.

16. This undermines the assertion in Rudolph, *Sozialdemokratie,* 143, that "the National Liberals proved to be the central obstacle to a thoroughly reformist policy."

17. *Landtags-Akten 1917/18,* nos. 300, 303; *Mitteilungen* (16 May 1918); Rudolph, *Sozialdemokratie,* 157.

18. SächsHStA Dresden, MdI Nr. 11073; Ingo Materna, ed., *Dokumente aus geheimen Archiven IV* (Berlin, 1989); Rudolph, *Sozialdemokratie,* 151f.

19. *Landtags-Akten 1917/18, Mitteilungen,* 16 May 1918, 2082f. (Deputy Schmidt).

the rudder to Saxony's ship of state; but they did not rock the boat when their request was denied. Neither did the great majority of the population. Even before the strike wave of April 1917, the government realized that it did not have the means to crush a revolution. However, the revolutionary agitation of the radicals, who split off from the left wing of the SPD to form the Independent Social Democratic Party (Unabhängige Sozialdemokratische Partei Deutschlands, or USPD), was not very successful. In April 1917, the strikes subsided after economic demands had been fulfilled. The Independent Socialists' subsequent calls for political mass strikes were followed by no more than a few hundred protesters at most, even in USPD strongholds.[20] By contrast, the Majority Social Democrats' call for hunger marches in September 1918 attracted 20,000 supporters in Dresden alone. On this occasion, Saxon protesters reiterated the well-worn litany of complaints against Berlin regarding the distribution of food.[21]

To be sure, from late 1916 onward the demand for food was increasingly joined by a call for peace. But as with the demand for reform of the Prussian suffrage, the call for peace served largely functional purposes. Suffrage reform meant reducing the influence of Prussian agrarians in the central government of the Reich, which in turn promised a fairer distribution of surplus grain from east of the Elbe River. Peace meant an end to the allied blockade, which in turn promised renewed food imports and the end of hunger. Moreover, it was not an unconditional peace that most people wanted. After the summer of 1917, when the German Reichstag passed its famous Peace Resolution — to which the allies replied with their demand for surrender — the strike movement lost all momentum for several months. The food question still fueled class protest, consumer complaints, and Saxon particularism. Bickering between town and country and between rich and poor continued. But these conflicts remained within limits. Vested agrarian and capitalist interests still had little to fear, for the conservative regimes in the individual federal states were not seriously challenged. Paradoxically, protests had the greatest effect in Berlin, where they contributed to the parliamentarization of the Reich. But even here, national unity for the war effort was perceived to be of paramount importance, so that parliamentarians subordinated themselves to the authority of the army's Supreme

---

20. SächsHStA Dresden, MdI Nr. 11072, 103, 123–36, 173–75; ibid., MdI Nr. 11073, 9, 26, 36–45. Rudolph, *Sozialdemokratie,* 136–40, 144–53, follows GDR historiography by ascribing this to the Saxon government's policy of repression and cooperation with Majority Social Democrats. This tends toward the "betrayal-of-the-workers" argument and does not square with developments in Berlin, where — under much the same conditions — a mass strike *did* take place in January 1918.

21. Rudolph, *Sozialdemokratie,* 158.

Command, as always in the "national interest." In return, the military accepted reformist window-dressing as compensation for a catastrophic food situation that it saw no way of improving.[22]

It was symptomatic of this arrangement that a Social Democratic speaker in the Saxon *Landtag* stated in mid-1917 that his party wanted peace, "but not peace at any cost."[23] Such patriotism was shared even by those who loudly voiced protests over the economic situation. Thus, in June 1917, striking industrial workers in Chemnitz "saw that it was necessary to stick it out; they were patriotic, . . . [but] they just could not go on working because of hunger and could not go on seeing their families starve."[24] In short, despite its many cracks, the *Burgfrieden* agreed upon in August 1914 remained essentially intact until October 1918. Like other Germans, Saxons decided to "stick it out" and postpone serious domestic quarreling for the future as long as there remained some hope of winning the war.

V. Political Modernization, National Liberal Style

A dam broke in October 1918, therefore, when the initiation of negotiations for an armistice signaled the futility of such hopes. The conservative Saxon regime had lost its legitimacy long before that date, but it had been protected by the *Burgfrieden*. Now, under massive pressure from Social Democrats and liberals alike,[25] the authoritarian regime began to crumble. On 26 October 1918 the Saxon king appointed the National Liberal Rudolf Heinze as government leader. Heinze proceeded to bring more liberals and two Social Democrats into the government; he retained three conservative ministers. For three weeks, Saxony was the only German state where a de facto parliamentary government ruled, before being swept from power by the revolution.[26] In Bavaria and Württemberg, the co-opting of parliamentarians into state governments was decided upon much later, and neither here nor in Baden was this evolutionary parliamentarianism ever tested in action. Only in Berlin was parliamentary rule achieved at the same time as in Dresden. On the very day that Heinze was appointed government leader in Dresden, the

22. See Gerald Feldman, *Army, Industry, and Labor in Germany, 1914–1918* (Princeton, NJ, 1966), 369.

23. Julius Fräßdorf, statement of 3 July 1917, reprinted in *Sächsische Umschau,* 19 Aug. 1917.

24. SächsHStA Dresden, MdI Nr. 11072, 12–14 (as reported by Chemnitz police headquarters, 30 June 1917).

25. See Rudolph, *Sozialdemokratie,* 159; and *Nationalliberale Blätter: Deutsche Stimmen* (1918), 731–34.

26. The Heinze administration was ousted on 15 November 1918.

Reich government shook off the supremacy of the Supreme Command. In Berlin, however, this was at least partly the result of external pressure applied by U.S. president Woodrow Wilson. Hence it is to the last weeks of imperial rule in Saxony, unadulterated by foreign influences, rather than to the death throes of the Hohenzollern empire, that we should look for clues to what the political system of the *Kaiserreich* might have become.

Saxony in late October and early November 1918 also provides an ideal litmus test to determine the behavior of German liberals once in power. For it was only in Dresden that National Liberals indisputably seized the reins of power when the conservatives relinquished them under the pressure of popular protest and rival political parties. Outside Saxony, National Liberalism had to compete for power with the Center Party (Deutsche Zentrumspartei) and left liberals. This helps explain why — especially in southern Germany — conservative governments took longer to fall: they often bought time by playing Center and liberal parties off against each other. In Saxony, which was almost completely Protestant, the Center Party was virtually nonexistent. Moreover, left liberals were very weak in Saxony, and the old conservative elites did all they could to prevent the Social Democrats from gaining control. Thus power almost naturally fell to the National Liberals.

What did they do with it? At first sight, not very much. The Heinze administration devoted itself mainly to addressing the interests of state officials; it decreed cost-of-living bonuses for civil servants and made sure they got paid. On the day the co-optation of parliamentarians into government was decided upon, only one other resolution came up for discussion in the *Landtag:* the familiar demand that Berlin attend to the catastrophic food supply.[27] Many contemporaries, and some historians, have poured scorn on this "idling," arguing that the immediate introduction of far-reaching constitutional reform could have prevented the outbreak of revolution.[28] The revolution of November 1918, however, had little to do with constitutional reform. It broke out in Berlin, where parliamentarization and democratization of the political system had been pushed much further than in Dresden, but also in Baden and elsewhere in southern Germany, where reform had hardly begun. When revolution came, it came because the population was tired of war, food shortages, and injustice. As a contemporary observer remarked, the scarcity of food and the resulting influenza epidemic created fertile

---

27. *Staatszeitung,* no. 254, quoted in Herbert Schönebaum, "Die Umwälzung in Sachsen nach dem Kriege," in *Sachsen in großer Zeit: Gemeinverständliche sächsiche Kriegsgeschichte und vaterländisches Gedenkwerk des Weltkrieges in Wort und Bild nach amtlichen Quellen,* ed. Johann Edmund Hottenroth, 3 vols. (Leipzig, 1923), 3:369.

28. See Rudolph, *Sozialdemokratie,* 167f.

ground for a coup: any change was a welcome alternative to this desperate situation.[29]

Surrender to the allies was a matter that could be decided only in Berlin. Therefore, the only practical thing the Heinze government could do was to keep the wheels of the state bureaucracy well oiled, not for its own sake but because it was indispensable to the maintenance of the economy and the food supply. Nevertheless, the new National Liberal administration also formulated a political program. In his inaugural address to the Saxon *Landtag* on 5 November 1918, Heinze offered a detailed blueprint of the political system he intended to strive for.[30] This system was neither democratic nor authoritarian, but a delicate mixture of both, with a corporatist flavor. In this system it was assumed that the liberals would retain their leading position by exploiting the differences between the old elites and the Social Democrats.

Heinze and his friends announced the introduction of a democratic suffrage for the lower house of the Saxon *Landtag*. That suffrage would be universal, equal, secret, and direct; it would also include proportional representation.[31] The first elections under the new suffrage were expected to take place in mid-1919—certainly not earlier than the conclusion of peace and demobilization. The government would stand "in closest possible contact" with the people's representatives. Heinze declared it impossible under the new system for a minister to remain in power if he were to lose the support of parliament. Exactly what prerogatives the *Landtag* would enjoy concerning the appointment of government ministers, however, remained open.

Obviously the governing National Liberals intended to maintain or introduce institutions that would keep in check the power of the *Landtag*'s lower house, which under a democratic suffrage could be expected to have a Social Democratic majority. One of these institutions was proportional representation. Explicitly introduced "in order to protect minorities,"[32] this innovation squared with democratic principles. Other provisions fit less well, however. The upper house would not be abolished; instead it would remain a corporatist "assembly of estates," though now with representatives of industry, civil servants, and organized labor added to those of the landed gentry. Its members would also be eligible for ministerial office. The exact relationship between the

---

29. Schönebaum, "Umwälzung," 375. See also Rudolph, *Sozialdemokratie,* 169–80 and passim, for details of the revolutionaries' demands.

30. *Landtags-Akten 1917/18,* 2185ff.

31. These questions definitely did not "remain open," as Rudolph contends in *Sozialdemokratie,* 166.

32. This had already been demanded by Nitzsche-Leutzsch in *Nationalliberale Blätter: Deutsche Stimmen* (1918), 732f., and was repeated in Heinze's inaugural address.

popularly elected lower house and the corporatist upper house remained open, as did the issue of their relative powers. This indeterminacy was also true for the position of the government vis-à-vis the legislature. Here Heinze declared only that the government leader would "be more responsible to the *Landtag*" than he had been in the past.

This system corresponded to the Saxon National Liberals' conviction that parliamentary rule in Saxony and Germany would not be introduced by law but would evolve naturally, as it had in England.[33] Of course these proposed reforms also served the interests of the party that held the central posts of government leader and minister of the interior in the present administration. A strong government could be counted on as another effective check to an expected Social Democratic majority in the lower house. The provisions also had strongly corporatist traits, such as those that assured representation of the industrial middle classes, the workers' movement, and the old conservative bureaucracy. Liberal ministers were to be given virtually free rein in the fields of industry and commerce, and the Social Democrats were to be given control of a ministry of labor and an employment exchange run by the state. Thus both liberals and Social Democrats got what they had long craved, while conservative ministers from the old regime kept a certain degree of autonomy in the classic bureaucratic domains of justice, finance, and culture. In theory, problems were to be solved cooperatively in cabinet. But in practice, if conflicts proved unavoidable, the liberals would be in a position to tip the balance in their own favor.

VI. Conclusions

This concept of governance, developed but not realized by the short-lived Heinze administration, is interesting not just as an experiment in hypothetical, counterfactual history. It also lends insight into the liberal concept of modernization itself. The ongoing debate about whether Saxony was evolving toward a modern political system after 1900 — and, if so, whether this "new course" corresponded to National Liberal intentions — actually becomes rather moot when one takes into account the renowned slipperiness of the term "modern." To put it another way: The authoritarian political system in Saxony probably would have evolved; by the end of the war it *did* evolve. But at least for a transitional period, the end point of that evolution was not necessarily a parliamentary democracy. Whereas the Majority Social Democrats regarded a parliamentary system as modern, the National Liberals applied that label to a corporatist system. Nor were these two conceptions of

---

33. *Landtags-Akten 1917/18*, no. 498 (12 Oct. 1917).

democracy the only ones available at the time. The Independent Social Democrats regarded a system of councils (*Räte*) as the ideal solution to the problem of popular representation. Not surprisingly, in each of these models, the respective advocates of these concepts would have been the greatest beneficiaries of their realization.[34]

The failure of the corporatist concept advanced by the liberals in the last weeks of the monarchy also had a considerable impact on events that followed. It was not the Heinze government that provoked the revolution. But when the revolution came, it dealt a hard blow to the fragile pattern of cooperation that had developed between the workers' movement and the liberal middle classes since 1900. In contrast to what happened in the other German states (excepting Berlin), in Saxony the liberals were not included in the revolutionary government: they were distinctly tainted by virtue of having compromised with the conservatives in the preceding weeks. Thus, during the crucial first months of the Weimar Republic, and again after the short interlude of a social-liberal coalition between 1920 and 1923, Saxony was governed solely by working-class parties. This "republican project of the left" has been credited with a thorough modernization and democratization of politics and society. It has even been called a "Saxon alternative" to the continuity that characterized the transition from monarchy to republic elsewhere — a continuity that is often regarded as singularly inauspicious for the future development of the Republic.[35] But the era of working-class dominance in Saxon politics also severely antagonized the middle classes. This, too, proved to be a handicap for the future, especially since the cleavage between town and country lost much of its relevance with the end of agrarian conservative political dominance, whereas class conflict correspondingly gained in significance. In any case, Saxon political culture once again became ingrained with the patterns of conflict and confrontation that had characterized it before the turn of the century. The beginnings of a new political culture based on cooperation and compromise were submerged in the revolutionary earthquake.

---

34. Later, during debates on a new Saxon constitution in 1919, the Majority SPD leader Georg Gradnauer opted for a strong president — a post he had a good chance of filling himself. His party, on the other hand, preferred a parliamentary democracy to a presidential democracy; Rudolph, *Sozialdemokratie,* 213–14.

35. Ibid., passim.

Remembering the Year 1923 in Saxon History

Benjamin Lapp

I. Introduction

The year 1923 was a significant turning point in the history of the Weimar Republic. In this year, the hyperinflation destroyed the German currency, and with it the savings of the German middle classes. In retrospect, the long-term political implications were ominous. Adolf Hitler became a national figure as a result of the failed Beer Hall Putsch of 8–9 November 1923. In the same year, the *Reichsexekution* (federal intervention by force) against Saxony followed the entry of Communists into the state government.

Until the Nazi seizure of power, references to 1923 continued to play an important role in Saxon politics. This essay examines the implications of that year for Saxon history. It argues that "1923" came to signify the hegemony of the Left for Saxon bourgeois elites. Saxony's bourgeois parties placed the responsibility for the political turmoil of 1923 firmly on the SPD's shoulders. In the *Landtag* elections of 1926, an electoral pamphlet of the German People's Party (Deutsche Volkspartei, or DVP) announced that a revival of the "Zeigner system" would lead to the dissolution of Saxony's political and cultural structure, the "collapse of the Saxon economy," and the politicization of the administration. A socialist victory would mean "terroristic conditions" leading to a "second invasion by the Reichswehr" and the "total collapse of Saxony."[1] In the state elections of 1929, the nationalists warned of "[t]he terror of the red hundreds [that is, the *Proletarische Hundertschaften*] in the city and

This essay is based on material from Benjamin Lapp, *Revolution from the Right: Politics, Class, and the Rise of Nazism in Saxony, 1919–1933* (Atlantic Highlands, NJ, 1997).

1. *Pirnaer Anzeiger,* 25 Sept. 1926.

in the country, the plundering of shops, the forced requisition of food from farmers, . . . and amnesty for thieves."[2] "Never Again a Soviet Saxony!" was undoubtedly the most heard campaign slogan of the bourgeois parties until the Depression, and their hostility toward the SPD in fact precluded any possibility of a Great Coalition. Their attempt to instrumentalize this memory for their own political purposes, however, proved a dismal failure.

II. Left and Right in Saxony

In 1923, Saxon Social Democracy entered into a coalition with the Communist Party (Kommunistische Partei Deutschlands, or KPD). In response, Reich Chancellor Gustav Stresemann sent in the Reichswehr to forcibly remove the cabinet of the Socialist minister president in Saxony, Erich Zeigner. These events led to the withdrawal of the SPD from the national government and the collapse of the Great Coalition in Weimar. Following the *Reichsexekution,* the SPD split into two factions, with a majority of the membership (but not of the *Landtag* deputies) rejecting coalitions with the middle-class parties. The right wing of the party (represented by twenty-three of the forty socialist deputies in the *Landtag*) broke off from the SPD and formed the "Old Socialist Party" (Alte Sozialdemokratische Partei Sachsens) in 1926. It thereby committed itself to alliances with the bourgeois parties, but ultimately it embraced an ultranationalist plank associated with renegade socialists such as Ernst Niekisch and August Winnig.[3] After 1923, the Socialist Left, though it had its stronghold in Saxony, would never exercise political power in the state.

The use of "1923" as a reference point in bourgeois political propaganda was in part a political strategy aimed at discrediting the socialists. It must be emphasized, however, that the virulent opposition of the bourgeois parties and bourgeois elites to the Saxon SPD predated Zeigner's term as minister president. Their call for a *Reichsexekution* in 1923 represented the culmination of a political and cultural conflict between Saxon Social Democracy and the bourgeois electorate that had been simmering since the revolution of 1918–19.

Karsten Rudolph has provided a convincing description of the modernizing, democratizing trends of Saxon Social Democratic policies,

---

2. *Chemnitzer Tageblatt,* 21 Apr. 1929.

3. On the split within the Saxon Social Democratic Party, see Christopher Hausmann, "Die 'Alte Sozialdemokratische Partei,' 1926–1932: Ein gescheitertes Experiment zwischen den parteipolitischen Fronten," in *Demokratie und Emanzipation zwischen Saale und Elbe,* ed. Helga Grebing, Hans Mommsen, and Karsten Rudolph (Essen, 1993), 273–94; and Benjamin Lapp, "A 'National' Socialism: The Old Socialist Party of Saxony, 1926–1932," *Journal of Contemporary History* 30 (1995): 291–309.

particularly after the *Landtag* elections of November 1920.[4] Under the leadership of Minister President Wilhelm Buck and Minister of the Interior Richard Lipinski, Rudolph argues, the Saxon SPD regained the initiative of the 1918 Revolution and abandoned the defensive political strategies characteristic of the more conservative national party. Economic and political reforms were introduced that challenged the persistent power of traditional elites and provided a potential model for the embattled Weimar Republic. In contrast to the Prussian Social Democrats, who were constrained by their dependence on the Center Party (Deutsche Zentrumspartei) and the Democrats (Deutsche Demokratische Partei), Saxon Social Democracy attempted to construct a firm foundation for the republic as a defense against its opponents. Throughout the years 1921–22, the Saxon government made remarkable progress in the areas of educational policies, democratization of the civil service, the police, and the judiciary, the struggle against counterrevolutionary organizations, and the attempt to fight chronic unemployment through public works. Not surprisingly, these policies met with the resolute hostility of the bourgeois parties and their constituencies. Thus, socialist measures limiting the influence of the church on education were alleged to represent a "modern persecution of Christendom."[5] The replacement of conservative, antidemocratic civil servants with committed democrats represented "an attempt to introduce a dictatorship of the proletariat."[6] And the Saxon government's rigorous application of the Laws to Protect the Republic by prohibiting nationalist and rightist organizations such as the Stahlhelm were viewed by the bourgeois parties as yet another example of a class-based infringement on bourgeois patriotism. In short, according to the bourgeois view, the state had become allied with "the street": the middle classes were subject to the partisan rule of socialists set on overthrowing the traditional order.

The gap separating the bourgeois parties from the Social Democrats was clarified in the emotional conflict over the decision of the government in April 1922 to make 1 May and 9 November state holidays. The first of May was of course the traditional day of celebration for the working classes; 9 November was the anniversary of the 1918 Revolution and the day on which Germany was declared a republic. In contrast to their national counterparts, Saxon Social Democrats—who were not dependent on bourgeois coalition partners—were in a position to affirm their political worldview in the proclamation of state holidays. For the

---

4. See Karsten Rudolph, *Die sächsische Sozialdemokratie vom Kaiserreich zur Republik (1871–1923)* (Weimar, 1995).

5. *Zwickauer Tageblatt,* 25 Nov. 1922.

6. *Leipziger Neueste Nachrichten,* 19 July 1921.

Socialists, the two celebrations had enormous symbolic significance. May Day represented the celebration of international proletarian solidarity. More provocatively, 9 November celebrated the collapse of the *Kaiserreich,* thereby emphasizing the revolutionary origins of the Weimar Republic. The bourgeois parties were unanimous in their rejection of the two memorial days, and the celebration of 9 November was rejected with particular vehemence. Speaking of the proposed May Day celebration, the Democratic deputy Peter Reinhold argued that such a holiday highlighted class tensions: "If this day is celebrated, it will only be to show who has the power and that this power will be used to denigrate the *Bürgertum.*" Reinhold felt that 9 November was not a day that should be celebrated either. The gist of his argument, widely quoted in the bourgeois press, is surprisingly similar to the rhetoric of the political Right. Reinhold and his party colleagues disapproved "of the fact that in an hour of spiritual and physical collapse, the German people threw down their weapons, and by this cowardly deed led Germany to the miserable abyss in which it now finds itself." To declare 9 November a holiday, he concluded, would represent an act of national indignity.[7] The parties to the right of the Democrats took a similar position. The representatives of the German People's Party and the German National People's Party (Deutschnationale Volkspartei, or DNVP) condemned the internationalism of the May Day celebration as illusory. Moreover, they associated 9 November with cowardice, treachery, and national disgrace — in short, with the stab-in-the-back legend in its entirety. The central role and power of these symbolic representations were reflected in the angry debates concerning the issue of political holidays. According to the mayor of Leipzig, if 9 November were to be celebrated as a public holiday, it would lead to outbreaks of violence among Leipzig's middle classes.[8] Furthermore, the hostility to the holidays sparked a petition campaign to initiate a referendum, which in turn would lead to the dissolution of parliament and new elections. The petition in question received 818,797 signatures — well over the 276,000 signatures required to put the question on a ballot. The strength of this support provided clear evidence of the depth of hostility to the policies of the Socialist government among Saxony's bourgeois electorate.

The elections of November 1922 simply reaffirmed the status quo. The bourgeois parties lost one seat and the Communist Party gained four. Together the SPD and the KPD had fifty seats — a slim majority. The Socialists pronounced their satisfaction with the results and viewed

---

7. *Landtagsverhandlungen,* 30. Sitzung, 2 Mar. 1921.
8. Mayor Roth to ministerial director Schulz, 22 June 1922, Stadtarchiv Leipzig, Kap. 72/17/62.

the election as a mandate to continue the policy of reform. However, a parliament divided into two camps by seemingly irreconcilable differences, and a government dependent on the unreliable support of the Communist Party, were ill-equipped to deal with the social and economic upheavals of 1923.

III.   Violence and Memories of Disorder

In 1922, the Communist Party came to adopt a "united front" policy of cooperation with other working-class organizations. The Communists' intent was to force a revolutionary crisis. Thus, the party leadership decided to create workers' governments in those states where the possibility existed and to emphasize such militant organs as proletarian control commissions and armed workers' units. Saxony (along with neighboring Thuringia) provided an ideal environment in which to test this policy, because the Socialist minority government was already dependent on the toleration of the KPD. Neither Lipinski nor Buck was an advocate of closer cooperation with the Communists, however, and in January 1923, the KPD withdrew their support, forcing the cabinet to resign. Lengthy negotiations led to the election of a new government in March 1923. It was headed by Zeigner, who was a highly idealistic Social Democrat, a former minister of justice, and committed to the left-Socialist policy of democratization. Hermann Liebmann replaced Lipinski as minister of the interior. The new cabinet agreed to specific Communist demands, the most controversial of which were the creation of proletarian control commissions for monitoring profiteering and the proletarian defense units (*Hundertschaften*) ostensibly designed to combat fascism.

Erich Zeigner took office at a particularly critical moment in the history of the Weimar Republic. In 1923 the passive resistance against the French occupation of the Ruhr sparked disastrous hyperinflation. Motivated by feelings of genuine outrage as well as by the desire to maintain some authority over the most radical elements of the workers' movement, Zeigner used his position to attack specific national policies. Among these were the policy of secret rearmament and the collaboration of the Reichswehr with illegal rightist paramilitary organizations. Zeigner's revelations brought upon him the wrath of the bourgeois parties, the Reichswehr, and the minister of defense, Otto Gessler. Zeigner's remarks about national and foreign policies were made in part to unite his own divided supporters and to encourage working-class solidarity. Given the rapidly deteriorating economic situation and the social unrest that inevitably resulted, however, his best efforts proved woefully inadequate. The German hyperinflation had particularly disastrous implications for Saxony, as the rapid currency depreciation was accompanied by unemployment rates more than twice the national average. By April 1923, there were 70,000 unemployed and up to 200,000 underemployed (*Kurzarbeiter*). By October 1923, the number had risen to 112,000 unemployed and 350,000 underemployed.[9] The results were predictable: a dramatic increase in economic violence and class tension.

The response of the Saxon government to the crisis was in keeping with its stated solidarity with the working classes. Even in May and June 1923, food riots and plundering had become common occurrences in Saxony's cities. During debate in the *Landtag* in June concerning food riots in Dresden and Leipzig, the Democratic deputy Dr. Kästner demanded to know what steps the government would take to preserve order. The response of Interior Minister Liebmann must have astonished the liberal and conservative deputies. The real guilt for the hunger riots, Liebmann stated, lay with the financial policies of the Reich, policies that were designed to further the interests of the bourgeoisie. Prior to the November revolution, he continued, the police had been an instrument of the class state, used to suppress the workers. But under the leadership of the Socialists, Liebmann announced, the police would no longer brutalize the hungry. Instead they would serve the Republic. While the police would do their best to preserve order, they would as a matter of policy avoid firing on unarmed demonstrators.[10] In the same vein, the government's extremely controversial policy of providing amnesty to those accused of illegally performing abortions and of crimes committed out of need and poverty, as well as the proletarian control committees designed to ensure a "fair price," represented an attempt to legislate an ideal of justice that took as its first priority the interests of the poor. From the perspective of the propertied classes, however, the Socialists seemed to have abandoned all pretense to governmental nonpartisanship (*Überparteilichkeit*). In a representative statement, the editor of the *Leipziger Neueste Nachrichten* argued that Liebmann's speech represented a "direct threat to all citizens who love order."[11]

By the summer and fall of 1923, the cycle of violence resulting from the genuine misery engendered by the catastrophic combination of hyperinflation and unemployment had spiraled out of control. The control committees and the Red Hundreds came increasingly under the influence of the KPD. Zeigner's government found itself caught between a groundswell of uncontrolled and increasingly radicalized activism "from below" and the harsh antagonism of the bourgeoisie. The bitterness of Saxon

9. See Gerald D. Feldman, "Saxony, the Reich, and the Problem of Unemployment in the German Inflation," *Archiv für Sozialgeschichte* 27 (1987): 102–44.

10. *Landtagsverhandlungen*, 1923, Bd. 2, 42. Sitzung, 1099–1100.

11. Letter from Arno Gunther to Chancellor Cuno, 23 June 1923, Bundesarchiv (hereafter BA) Koblenz, R43 I, 2307, 326–28.

burghers was intensified immeasurably by the political rhetoric of a government that placed its loyalties firmly on the side of the working-class victims of the inflation.

Both in letters to the Reich ministry of the interior and in personal pleas to Gustav Stresemann (who had replaced Wilhelm Cuno as chancellor on 13 August 1923), the Saxon Rural League (Sächsischer Landbund), the League of Saxon Industrialists (Verband sächsischer Industrieller, or VSI), and an assortment of middle-class organizations described a situation in which lawlessness and disorder reigned. In their view, the state government was not providing adequate protection to its middle-class citizens. Thus, wrote a representative of the DNVP, "the mob is indulging in all sorts of violent actions; . . . plundering, kidnapping, and robbery are the order of the day."[12] Representatives of Saxon industry related horror stories of the "terror" of the proletarian brigades.[13] In fact, as Walter Fabian has pointed out, Saxony was not unique: violence was widespread in Germany during the hyperinflation.[14] Nevertheless, the pattern of social and political unrest in Saxony had distinguishing characteristics that lend some credence to bourgeois expressions of anxiety and helplessness.

A peculiarity of economic violence in Saxony at this time was the spontaneous development of popular forms of justice. Employers in small and medium-sized firms were subjected to well-patterned degradation rituals because they were viewed as profiting unethically from currency depreciation and unemployment. The choreography of the ceremony followed a predictable pattern: The employer would be forced to march in a demonstration, often carrying either a red flag or a sign on which was inscribed the words "I am a scoundrel." A variation on the same theme was for demonstrators to force the object of their ridicule to sit on a cart and be led through the town while being taunted. As a result of such degradation rituals, employers were often forced to negotiate new wage agreements with their employees. This was frequently the outcome even when actual physical violence did not occur, although in one instance a sixty-year-old metal industrialist in the Erzgebirge was nearly beaten to death.

Significantly, these types of attacks on employers were centered in the Vogtland and the Erzgebirge, where smaller firms predominated and where the unions historically had the least influence. One industrial man-

---

12. Letter of the DNVP Landesverband Sachsen to Gustav Stresemann, 10 August 1923, BA Koblenz, R43 I, 2308, 169–70.

13. "Besprechung mit Vertretern des Verbandes Saechsischer Industrieller," 19 June 1923, in *Akten der Reichskanzlei: Das Kabinett Cuno,* 590 (Boppard a. R., 1968), Doc. 197.

14. For Fabian's perspective, see his *Klassenkampf um Sachsen* (Berlin, 1972).

ager in the Erzgebirge bemoaned the spiraling process of radicalization that was rendering local industry "completely uncompetitive." "Some workers," he wrote, "are already demanding an hourly wage of 180,000 Marks. The trade unions have lost their leadership!"[15] Given this intense class hostility, industrialists even came to view the proletarian *Hundert-schaften* (which they generally condemned as communist terrorist organizations) as a restraining force; sometimes they were even praised for their "will to preserve order."[16] But the prevailing sentiment among Saxony's employers was one of helplessness and rage at the state government for not providing adequate protection. Thus, Hans Weiland, the owner of a construction firm in Aue who had been "taken away by strangers under threat of force" without being provided "the least bit of protection" by state officials, declared his refusal to pay taxes. An accompanying letter to the Saxon interior ministry from a city councilor (*Stadtrat*) in Aue stated that Weiland's sentiment was shared by many middle-class residents of his city.[17]

Artisanal and shopkeeper organizations also felt victimized by the street violence and unprotected by the Saxon government. During hunger riots, which were common occurrences in the summer and fall of 1923, small stores with food stocks were often plundered. The local police force was frequently overwhelmed by massive food riots (instigated mainly by the unemployed), and they were largely incapable of protecting small shopkeepers. Such activity was not uncommon in Germany during the period of hyperinflation. However, the official sanction of control committees by the Saxon government meant, according to the organization representing Saxon artisans, that small businessmen were subjected to unrelenting interference. Just as the industrialists had been forced to negotiate high wages, shopkeepers were being forced to sell at low prices, and in ways that they perceived to be disrespectful and demeaning: "They come into the shoe-repair shop . . . and force the artisan to relinquish a piece of his work at a price that barely pays for the time spent at labor," stated one report.[18] At the Saxon artisans' congress (*Handwerkertag*) held in Dresden on 9 September, speaker after speaker condemned the policies of the Socialist government. The conservative *Ministerialdirektor* Dr. Schulze was booed when he attempted to speak, because of his position within the state government.[19]

---

15. Gerald D. Feldman, "Labor Unrest and Strikes in Saxony," *Estratta da Annali della Fondazione Giangiacomo Feltrinelli* (1990–91), 319.

16. Ibid., 320.

17. Letter from the Aue *Stadtrat* to the Saxon ministry of the interior, 23 July 1923, SächsHStA Dresden, Ministerium des Innern (hereafter MdI) Nr. 11112, 241–45.

18. *Sächsische Innungsbote*, 31 Oct. 1923.

19. *Leipziger Neueste Nachrichten*, 9 Sept. 1923.

As in the case of small industrialists in the Erzgebirge, artisans and shopkeepers felt that the model of justice and legality espoused by the control committees and proletarian brigades victimized middle-class citizens and producers. From their perspective, the government was acting in close alliance with the mob. The traditional role of the state had been turned on its head.

Whereas in the cities food shops were the first to be plundered, in the countryside the farmers were subjected to widespread confiscation of food products. This action testified to the genuine want and widespread hunger in Saxony. From the city of Zittau came a report that the astronomical rise of food prices had created a mood among consumers that bordered on despair.[20] The unfortunate result of such desperate circumstances was a dramatic rise in conflict between unemployed workers and the rural *Mittelstand*. Reports from all corners of the state document an exceptionally large increase in crop thefts. The attempt by the authorities to protect farms proved unable to stop the "well-organized bands that usually arrive at night by bicycle."[21] Attempts at resistance by the farmers themselves had equally poor results. In the village of Trebsen, near Leipzig, a farmer who observed a group of men gathering crops from his field shot a pistol in the air to frighten them away. Instead he was disarmed by several men, beaten up, and forced to come to Trebsen, where — in a repetition of the degradation ritual — he was paraded in front of the townspeople. At the conclusion of the demonstration, the traumatized farmer agreed to relinquish two pigs for the benefit of the town's unemployed.[22] A farmer and his wife in the district of Stollberg, after sarcastically referring to striking miners by remarking (in a play upon the term *Hundertschaft*) "Here comes the *Hungerschaft*," had their clothes torn off by a large group of furious workers.[23] Most farmers, by contrast, were understandably pliant. "The agrarian population is totally intimidated and passively accepts everything," noted one report.[24] The *Sächsische Bauernzeitung* openly pleaded for the intervention of the Reich, suggesting that the plight of farmers was a matter of indifference to the Saxon government.[25]

---

20. Report of the district of Zittau to the *Polizeipräsidium* Dresden, 13 Oct. 1923, SächsHStA Dresden, Staatskanzlei, Nr. 128, 250–54.

21. *Amthauptmannschaft* (district administrative precinct) Dresden-Altstadt to MdI, 4 Sept. 1923, SächsHStA Dresden, Staatskanzlei, Nr. 128, 6061.

22. Report of the *Polizeipräsidium* Leipzig, 23 Aug. 1923, SächsHStA Dresden, MdI Nr. 11108, 108–10.

23. See Gerald D. Feldman, *The Great Disorder: Politics, Economics, and Society in the German Inflation, 1914–1924* (New York, 1997), 702.

24. SächsHStA Dresden, MdI Nr. 11108, 114–18.

25. *Sächsische Bauernzeitung,* 23 Aug. 1923.

IV. The *Reichsexekution*

Reichswehr intervention was to come in October 1923, following the entry of Communists into the Saxon government on October 10. In fact, despite the revolutionary intentions of the KPD, Saxony did not provide the Communists with a revolutionary situation. This became clear on 21 October when the Communist Heinrich Brandler called for an immediate general strike to protest the state of emergency and the occupation of Saxony by Reichswehr troops. Brandler's call to arms received only lukewarm support. The Communists' attempt to launch a revolution from Saxony ended, in the memorable words of August Thalheimer, with a "third-class funeral." Nevertheless, plans for the *Reichsexekution* went ahead. On 27 October, following the occupation of Dresden by the Reichswehr, Stresemann presented Zeigner with an ultimatum demanding the withdrawal of his cabinet and the construction of a new government, sans Communist participation. In the event that Zeigner did not agree to the conditions, Stresemann threatened, a *Reichskommissar* would take over the government administration "until the restoration of conditions that accord with the Constitution" under the provisions of Article 48. Zeigner refused. Hence, on the morning of 29 October, Reichswehr troops occupied the government ministries in Dresden and forced the cabinet ministers out of their offices — all to the accompaniment of a military band.

To become *Reichskommissar,* Stresemann chose Rudolf Heinze: Saxony's last government leader before the November revolution, member of the DVP's Reichstag delegation from Saxony, and previously minister of justice in the Reich. Heinze had his own agenda, which did not entirely match that of Stresemann. He hoped to use his powers to exclude the Socialists from any new government and appoint the cabinet without parliament's consent. Heinze and the leadership of the Saxon DVP viewed the *Reichsexekution* as a means of effectively ending parliamentary government in Saxony until a bourgeois government could be guaranteed. Stresemann intervened and prevented Heinze from appointing a new cabinet without the consent of the *Landtag.* On the following day, Karl Fellisch formed a Socialist minority government with the support of the Democrats. This was a solution born of a lack of alternatives. Given the hostility between the bourgeois parties and the Social Democrats, it was not likely to last long.

The reason the *Reichsexekution* became virtually the sole alternative did not lie exclusively in the pleas of angry and intimidated *Mittelständler* and entrepreneurs, however much those pleas might have influenced Stresemann. More immediate political considerations played a central role. By removing the Zeigner government, Stresemann would eliminate Bavaria's excuse for mobilizing troops against the "red" threat on its borders. He would also appease right-wing critics of his own domestic policies. Stresemann's decision to remove the Saxon government forcibly while leaving the outspokenly antirepublican Bavarian government untouched was undoubtedly politically expedient. It nevertheless left in its wake a legacy of intense bitterness on the part of working-class activists. This bitterness was fed by the often brutal treatment of protesting workers by Reichswehr troops. In the city of Freiberg, twenty-three demonstrators were killed and scores wounded on 27 October 1923. The prevailing feeling among Saxony's organized working classes was resentment at the use of force against a government that represented proletarian interests.

By contrast, the military occupation of the state was welcomed by the propertied classes. According to the American consul in Dresden, the Saxon bourgeoisie greeted the *Reichsexekution:*

> The entire life in the towns suddenly took on another aspect. The shops which had previously closed their show-windows throughout the day, opening, if at all, merely the entrance door in order to be able to shut down at once in case of a repetition of the daily riots of the unemployed, again displayed their goods. . . . In Dresden . . . the public spirit seemed entirely changed . . . the streets became full of life, more cheerful and crowded, quite in contrast with the situation when everyone hurried away from the center of the town in order not to be molested by occasional riots. The reintroduction of the change of guard of the Reichswehr was cheered by thousands, throwing flowers on the soldiers, who seemed a protection to them and a guarantee for the discontinuance of the frequent riots which had occurred.[26]

No historian could ask for a more telling witness to the gulf that separated the Zeigner government from its bourgeois constituents. Little wonder, then, that the Saxon bourgeoisie greeted the Reichswehr troops as an army of liberation.

V. The Aftermath

Despite their best efforts, the attempts of the bourgeois parties to benefit from the "memory" of 1923 proved a failure. To be sure, hostility to

---

26. Report of Consul Louis Dreyfus, 2 Nov. 1923, U.S. National Archives, Washington, D.C., 862.00, 1361.

the SPD remained the sine qua non of bourgeois politics. In the words of the Democratic politician Richard Seyfert, "large portions of the Saxon bourgeoisie, including industrialists, the *Mittelstand,* civil servants, and intellectuals, . . . view the suppression of Social Democracy as the be-all and end-all of politics."[27] But the negative appeal of anti-Marxism was not in itself enough to maintain popular support. The upheavals caused by hyperinflation and the harsh policy of stabilization that followed convinced the *Mittelstand* that the traditional parties were dominated by big industry and big agriculture and hence were unresponsive to middle-class interests. Thus, the three parties that claimed to represent the bourgeois voter found themselves losing their constituencies to a variety of special-interest parties in the mid-1920s. Ultimately, the Nazi Party benefited most from the "dissolution of the bourgeois party system."[28]

Like the bourgeois parties, the Nazis proclaimed "Never Again a Soviet Saxony!" But the Nazis could claim to be more aggressive and consistent in their opposition to Social Democracy. Josef Goebbels accused the Saxon bourgeois parties of upholding the same political system with which Social Democracy was identified: their anti-Marxism was merely rhetorical, he claimed. For the National Socialists, by contrast, "Never Again a Soviet Saxony!" was not merely a slogan; it represented a concrete course of action. Thus, according to Goebbels, the Nazis would cleanse Saxony of the "Zeigner-filth." In the rhetoric of Nazism, "Zeigner" came to represent all that was flawed with the Republic: corruption, economic crisis, class conflict, and the failure of the Left.[29]

Of course, the bourgeois parties also condemned "Zeigner" ceaselessly as the centerpiece of the left-Socialist project. But those parties continued to be linked in the popular imagination with the crises and failures of the Weimar Republic. The Nazis, by contrast, presented themselves as a radical alternative. In the *Landtag* debates of October 1929 concerning the abolition of the 9 November holiday, the bourgeois parties reiterated their arguments of 1922. They believed that 9 November was still a day to be mourned. They also declared their continued determination to challenge the legitimacy of a celebration that had been imposed on the Saxon bourgeoisie by a small minority. The arguments of the National Socialists were distinctly different from those of the bourgeois deputies. The National Socialist Manfred von Killinger derisively dismissed 9 November as a "work disturbance," during which one

27. Richard Seyfert, "Sachsen," in *Zehn Jahre Deutsche Republik,* ed. Anton Erkelenz (Berlin-Zehlendorf, 1928), 192.

28. Larry Eugene Jones, "The Dissolution of the Bourgeois Party System," in *Social Change and Political Development in Weimar Germany,* ed. Richard Bessel and E. J. Feuchtwanger (London, 1981), 268–88.

29. *Der Angriff,* 8 June 1930.

set of managers was substituted for another. The so-called revolutionaries of 1918 were not nearly ruthless enough, he charged: "Revolutions look entirely different. . . . The Revolution of a Kemal Pascha, the French Revolution . . . — those are Revolutions!" When thousands of workers marched on Berlin, Killinger concluded, and when the heads of the Social Democratic "bosses" (*Bonzen*) were chopped off, *that* would be a day for celebration. As far as the May Day celebration was concerned, it would indeed be celebrated in the future National Socialist state. It would not, however, celebrate internationalism, but rather the national will, the antithesis of Social Democracy. The National Socialists thus presented themselves as the truly revolutionary party that would initiate a transformation of Germany according to the tenets of radical nationalism. The Social Democrats were pseudo-revolutionaries and traitors, whose loyalties belonged to an anti-German internationalism. As for the bourgeois parties, the clear implication was that they, too, were caught up in an older style of politics: they were simply too "reactionary" and too committed to the interests of a particular class to lead the way. The coming Nazi revolution, in contrast to 9 November, would be a genuine social revolution that would unify the nation.

With this message already exhibiting considerable popular appeal, National Socialists were poised to reap the benefits when the Depression hit Saxony with particular force.[30] As middle-class voters flocked to the Nazis, memories of 1923 continued to play a part in confirming the lack of alternatives. This mind-set among the Saxon *Bürgertum* was illustrated by a police report of 1931 noting that farmers were looking to the Nazi storm troopers to help them defend "against the type of plundering that occurred in 1923."[31] Similarly, in response to a socialist interpellation in parliament that concerned Nazi hooliganism, a NSDAP deputy referred to the "time of Zeigner, when middle-class people were forced to carry red flags in Marxist demonstrations."[32] Although the bourgeois parties still tried to draw on the memory of 1923 to emphasize the vulnerable position of the middle classes, the Nazis were better able to represent themselves as the party most capable of defeating the political Left. Moreover, in contrast to the liberal or conservative parties, the Nazis were able to mobilize a significant portion of the working classes who felt disillusioned with the Republic. Hence, whereas the events of 1923 had revealed the limits of Social Democratic reform, the Nazis now finally seemed to offer a truly radical alternative. They successfully tran-

---

30. Unfortunately, I was not able to consult the recent book by Claus-Christian Szejnmann, *Nazism in Central Germany: The Brownshirts in 'Red' Saxony* (Oxford, 1999).

31. Report of the *Amtshauptmannschaft* Bautzen, 12 Mar. 1931, in SächsHStA Dresden, MdI Nr. 19807, 72.

32. *Landtagsverhandlungen,* 7 Oct. 1930, 21.

scended the largely negative tone of bourgeois politics, and they promised the realization of the "people's community" (*Volksgemeinschaft*). For Saxons who identified the Republic primarily with class conflict and economic crisis—not only the conflicts and crises of 1929–33, but also those powerfully conjured up by memories of 1923—the Nazi utopia seemed an attractive alternative to Weimar.

Saxony, 1924–1930: A Study in the Dissolution of the Bourgeois Party System in Weimar Germany

Larry Eugene Jones

I. Introduction

The dissolution of the Weimar party system and the rise of National Socialism proceeded at an uneven pace from one part of Germany to the next. In certain regions the collapse of the bourgeois middle parties and the resultant polarization of the German party system into two mutually antagonistic camps anticipated developments at the national level, while in others this process occurred at a much slower pace than it did elsewhere. This distinction is particularly relevant for the state of Saxony, where the absence of a substantial Catholic population meant that the German Center Party (Deutsche Zentrumspartei) was not available to perform its customary role as a mediator between different social classes in the interest of political stability. As a result, the process of fragmentation and polarization that ultimately led to the collapse of the bourgeois party system in Germany as a whole was much more advanced in Saxony than in states like Prussia, Württemberg, or Bavaria, where the respective Catholic parties—the German Center Party or, in the case of Bavaria, the Bavarian People's Party (Bayerische Volkspartei)—were able to mediate between middle-class and working-class elements in such a way as to inhibit the process of political polarization that led to the collapse of effective parliamentary government at both the state and national levels by the end of the 1920s.

The purpose of this essay is to examine the fragmentation and polarization of the Saxon party system from 1924 to 1930 as a case study in the dissolution of the bourgeois party system of the Weimar Republic.[1] It will

---

1. In the interests of economy, references to secondary works have been omitted whenever possible. Much of the following on Saxon political history in the Weimar Repub-

begin by examining the failure of the established bourgeois parties to maintain their hold over Saxony's nonsocialist electorate in the face of increasingly formidable challenges from parties that represented the interests of specific sectors of the Saxon middle class. At the same time, it will examine the response of Saxony's paramilitary Right to the increasing fragmentation of the Saxon party system and the failure of the more established bourgeois parties to provide Saxony's nonsocialist voters with the political cohesiveness they needed to keep the Saxon Left at bay and to prevent a recurrence of what had transpired in 1922–23. This, in turn, had a radicalizing effect upon the Saxon Right and helped create an increasingly volatile situation into which the National Socialist German Workers' Party was able to insinuate itself with consummate skill. If the outcome of the 1926 Saxon *Landtag* elections revealed the great disarray in which Saxony's nonsocialist forces found themselves and intensified the desire for greater bourgeois cohesiveness in the face of the Saxon Left, then the results of the 1929 and 1930 state elections suggested that the party with the greatest chance of satisfying this desire was none other than the NSDAP.

II. The Challenge of Special Interests

In no other part of Germany, with the possible exception of Bavaria, did the "specter of communism" loom more menacingly than in Saxony. In December 1920 the Majority and Independent Socialists had formed a governmental coalition whose policies did much to aggravate middle-class fears throughout the state. The unification of the two socialist parties in September 1922 and the gains that the local Communists scored in the Saxon *Landtag* elections on 5 November 1922 did little to allay these fears. The principal casualty of these developments was the German Democratic Party (Deutsche Demokratische Partei, or DDP), which suffered a series of electoral reverses in the first half of the 1920s and was never able to function as an effective mediator between the socialist Left and Saxony's middle classes.[2] In the meantime, the Saxon middle classes regrouped in the German People's Party (Deutsche Volkspartei, or DVP) and the German National People's Party (Deutschnationale Volkspartei, or DNVP), both of which were adamantly opposed to the socialist domination of Saxon political life and employed

---

lic is taken without further attribution from Benjamin Lapp, *Revolution from the Right: Politics, Class, and the Rise of Nazism in Saxony, 1919–1933* (Atlantic Highlands, NJ, 1997).

  2. On the history of the DDP in Saxony, see Richard Seyfert, "Sachsen," in *Zehn Jahre Deutsche Republik: Ein Handbuch für republikanische Politik,* ed. Anton Erkelenz (Berlin-Zehlendorf, 1928), 189–96.

the rhetoric of class conflict to mobilize their supporters against the policies of the state government. This, in turn, set the stage for a bitter confrontation between Left and Right in the fall of 1923, when the SPD's decision to invite the Communists into the government left Berlin with no alternative but to order the Reichswehr into Saxony in order to depose the state government and restore federal authority.

Federal intervention left the Saxon Left deeply divided and dealt it a blow from which it never really recovered. In the meantime, the more moderate bourgeois parties — namely, the DDP and DVP — were able to regain a measure of influence by joining the Social Democrats in a cabinet of the "Great Coalition" under the leadership of the SPD's Max Heldt. As the only nonsocialist opposition party, the DNVP attacked the DDP and DVP as traitors to the Saxon middle class and repeatedly called for new elections to the state legislature.[3] But the DNVP's effectiveness as an opposition party in Saxony was undercut by the fact that in January 1925 the Nationalists had entered the national cabinet under the chancellorship of Hans Luther. The DNVP's entry into the Luther cabinet was part of a comprehensive attempt by Germany's most prominent bourgeois politician, the DVP's Gustav Stresemann, to stabilize the Weimar Republic by co-opting the more moderate elements on the German Right. These efforts, which drew much of their impetus from influential economic interest organizations such as the National Federation of German Industry (Reichsverband der Deutschen Industrie, or RDI) and the National Rural League (Reichs-Landbund, or RLB), found little resonance in Saxony, which remained something of an economic backwater during the Weimar Republic and never shared in the economic benefits of Germany's short-lived "return to normalcy" in the second half of the 1920s. As a result, first special-interest parties like the Business Party of the German Middle Class (Wirtschaftspartei des deutschen Mittelstandes, or WP) and the Reich Party for People's Justice and Revaluation (Reichspartei für Volksrecht und Aufwertung, or VRP), and then patriotic associations like the Stahlhelm — League of Front Soldiers (Stahlhelm — Bund der Frontsoldaten) and the Young German Order (Jungdeutscher Orden), sought to fill the vacuum created by the DNVP's inability to establish itself in Saxony as a credible opposition party.

From the outset, Saxony was one of the Business Party's most important regional strongholds. After a disappointing showing in the 1922 *Landtag* elections, the WP polled 2.8 and 4.7 percent of the popular vote in the three Saxon electoral districts in the May and December 1924 Reichstag elections respectively, figures that compared favorably to the

3. J. Siegert, *16 Monate sächsischer Landtag: Ein politischer Überblick,* Schriften der Deutschnationalen Volkspartei in Sachsen (Arbeitsgemeinschaft), no. 2 (Dresden, 1924).

1.8 and 2.3 percent of the national electorate the party received in the same two elections. In no other large German state did the Business Party fare as well in the 1924 national elections as it did in Saxony.[4] The bulk of the WP's support in Saxony, as in other parts of the Reich, came from organized housing interests and the economically independent elements of the German middle class. The party's impressive performance in West Saxony, where it polled over 7 percent of the popular vote in the two 1924 elections, stemmed directly from the strong support it received from the leaders of the local homeowners' organization.[5] By no means, however, was the Business Party the only party competing for the votes of Saxony's disaffected middle class. In the autumn of 1924 Reinhard Wüst, a lawyer from Halle, helped launch the German Revaluation and Recovery Party (Deutsche Aufwertungs- und Aufbaupartei) as a protest against the revaluation provisions of the Third Emergency Tax Decree, which had taken effect the preceding February.[6] Although the new party's impact in the December 1924 Reichstag elections was negligible, its emergence underscored the frustration that an increasingly large segment of Germany's middle-class electorate began to feel over the terms of Germany's political and economic stabilization in the second half of the 1920s.[7]

The Saxon *Landtag* elections on 31 October 1926 provided Germany's middle-class splinter parties with an excellent forum for validating themselves as legitimate voices of middle-class discontent. In the summer of 1925 the Business Party had rebaptized itself the Reich Party of the German Middle Class (Reichspartei des deutschen Mittelstandes) in an attempt to escape the odium of special interest and to broaden its appeal among Germany's middle-class voters. The following July the WP held its annual party congress in Görlitz — no doubt with an eye to the upcoming *Landtag* elections — and used the occasion to launch a new party program called the "Görlitzer Richtlinien." As the work of Saxon party leader Walther Wilhelm, the "Görlitzer Richlinien" sought to embellish the party's ideological profile by reformulating the traditional demands of homeowners, artisans, and small businessmen in the lan-

---

4. See the tables in Martin Schumacher, *Mittelstandsfront und Republik: Die Wirtschaftspartei — Reichspartei des deutschen Mittelstandes, 1919–1933* (Düsseldorf, 1972), 228, 230–31.

5. Ibid., 101.

6. In this respect, see the two pamphlets by Reinhard Wüst, *Das Aufwertungsproblem und die 3. Steuernotverordnung: Eine gemeinverständliche Betrachtung* (Halle, 1924), and *Im Aufwertungskampf für Wahrheit und Recht gegen "Luthertum" und "Marxismus": Eine gemeinverständliche Auseinandersetzung mit den Trugschlüssen und Schlagworten der Aufwertungsgegner* (Halle, 1924).

7. For further details, see Larry Eugene Jones, "Inflation, Revaluation, and the Crisis of Middle-Class Politics: A Study in the Dissolution of the German Party System, 1923–28," *Central European History* 12 (1979): 143–68.

guage of German corporatism.[8] With the adoption of the new party program, the Business Party's transformation from a party easily stigmatized as an agent for organized housing interests into one that claimed to represent the German middle class in all of its social and economic heterogeneity was essentially complete. All of this, including the choice of Görlitz as the site where this transformation supposedly culminated in the promulgation of a new party program, was part of a calculated effort to position the WP as advantageously as possible in the campaign for the upcoming Saxon state elections. In the meantime, the various revaluation groups that had surfaced throughout the country since the enactment of the Third Emergency Tax Decree had begun to coalesce into a national revaluation party. These efforts, which capitalized upon the sense of betrayal that Germany's middle-class investors felt toward the DNVP as a result of its role in the passage of the 1925 revaluation law, reached a climax in late August 1926 with the founding of the Reich Party for People's Justice and Revaluation at a national delegate conference of the Savers' Association for the German Reich (Sparerbund für das Deutsche Reich) in Erfurt.[9] Speaking in Erfurt, onetime DNVP patriarch Count Adolf von Posadowsky-Wehner assailed the more established bourgeois parties for having betrayed the trust of Germany's small investor and exhorted those who had been victimized by this betrayal to seek their revenge at the polls.[10]

By using the Saxon campaign to thrust themselves into the national political spotlight, the WP and VRP transformed the campaign for the 1926 Saxon *Landtag* elections into a referendum on the future of the more established, ideologically oriented parties like the DDP, DVP, and DNVP. The Democrats responded to this challenge by trying to divert attention from the agitation of the special-interest parties to the role they had played in containing the threat of the radical Left in 1922–23 and in restoring effective constitutional government with the formation of the "coalition of the middle" in January 1924.[11] Stresemann and the

---

8. Reichspartei des deutschen Mittelstandes, *Die Satzungen und Görlitzer Richtlinien der Reichspartei des deutschen Mittelstandes e.V. (Wirtschaftspartei)* (Berlin, [1929]), 18–31. For an excellent statement of the WP's "middle-class ideology," see Walther Waldemar Wilhelm and Willy Schlüter, *Die Mission des Mittelstandes: 99 Thesen für das schaffende Volk,* ed. Eugen Fabricus (Dresden, 1925).

9. Adolf Bauser, "Notwendigkeit, Aufgaben und Ziele der Volksrechtspartei," in *Für Wahrheit und Recht: Der Endkampf um eine gerechte Aufwertung: Reden und Aufsätze,* ed. idem (Stuttgart, 1927), 90–91.

10. Speech by Posadowsky-Wehner, "Ansprache, gehalten auf der Reichsdelegiertentagung des Sparerbundes zu Erfurt am 28. August 1926," in idem, *Die Enteignung des Gläubiger-Vermögens: Eine Sammlung von Aufsätzen* (Berlin, [1928]), 42–46.

11. DDP Leipzig, "Vom Klassenstaat zum Volksstaat: Vier Jahre sächsischer Politik, 1922–1926" [Oct. 1926], Bayerisches Hauptstaatsarchiv, Munich, Abt. V, Flugblätter-Sammlung, F62/1926.

leaders of the DVP, on the other hand, took a more aggressive stance, denouncing the emergence of the WP and VRP as a symptom of the increasing fragmentation of the national electorate into vocational groups that placed their own special interests before the welfare of the nation as a whole. As Stresemann warned in an open letter to Fritz Kaiser, the Saxon minister of culture and a member of the DVP *Landtag* delegation, this development not only isolated the German middle class from those parties that were committed to the defense of its legitimate social and economic interests; more importantly, it frustrated the formation of a viable domestic consensus for the articulation and conduct of national policy at home and abroad.[12] The same refrain echoed through the campaign appeals of the DNVP, though here it was tinged by the party's obsession with the need for greater bourgeois cohesiveness in the struggle against Marxism. The WP's efforts to unite the German middle class into a single political party were dismissed as a frivolous distraction that only undermined the effectiveness with which the DNVP could defend the interests of its middle-class constituents.[13] By the same token, the Nationalists argued that single-issue parties like the VRP could not defend the interests of their supporters as effectively as a larger party like the DNVP.[14]

The emergence of special-interest parties constituted a direct threat to the tenuous grip on power that Saxony's bourgeois parties had held since the beginning of 1924, and it aroused widespread concern well beyond the parties that were directly affected by this process. This was particularly apparent in the case of the paramilitary Right, which had discovered in Saxony a fertile breeding ground for its own brand of antisystem politics. The Stahlhelm had been active in Saxony ever since the summer of 1919 and had built up a strong state organization under Theodor Duesterberg, a determined and resolute opponent of Weimar parliamentarism with close ties to the right-wing DNVP.[15] By the same token, the Young German Order chose Leipzig as the site of its first national rally in recognition of the strong resonance that its efforts had

---

12. Stresemann to Kaiser, 27 Oct. 1926, in the unpublished Nachlaß of Gustav Stresemann, Politisches Archiv des Auswärtigen Amtes, Bonn, vol. 97, pp. 173325–34 (hereafter PA AA Bonn, NL Stresemann, 97/173325–34).

13. "Entwurf zu einer Diskussionsrede in Versammlungen der Wirtschaftspartei," n.d., in SächsHStA Dresden, NL Albrecht Philipp, 20.

14. Philipp, "Aufwertung und Landtagswahl," *Leipziger Abendpost,* 16 Oct. 1926, no. 242.

15. On the early history of the Stahlhelm in Saxony, see Stahlhelm, Landesverband Mitteldeutschland, *Sechs Jahre Stahlhelm in Mitteldeutschland* (Halle, 1926), esp. 23–50. See also Stahlhelm, Landesverband Sachsen, *10 Jahre Dresdner Stahlhelm, 1924–1934* (Dresden, 1934), 13–14.

found among the Saxon middle classes.[16] Having cooperated in the presidential campaign of war hero Paul von Hindenburg in the spring of 1925, both the Stahlhelm and the Young German Order lamented the fragmentation of Germany's political culture and sought to rebaptize German political life in the spirit of the so-called front experience.[17] Fearful that the upcoming Saxon *Landtag* elections would produce an even greater fragmentation of Germany's bourgeois forces, the leaders of Saxony's paramilitary organizations called upon the so-called patriotic parties to set aside their differences and unite in a crusade to free Saxony—and, by extension, Germany—from the insidious yoke of Marxism.[18] When this effort at "bourgeois consolidation from below" foundered on Stresemann's refusal to countenance any electoral alliance that might jeopardize the prospects of the "Great Coalition" in the Reich,[19] the Saxon Citizens' Council (Sächsischer Bürgerrat), with strong support from the League of Saxon Industrialists (Verband sächsischer Industrieller) and other bourgeois interest organizations, tried to salvage what it could of the campaign for bourgeois unity by proposing the creation of an electoral truce for the duration of the campaign.[20] This attempt at "bourgeois consolidation from above" was much less threatening to Stresemann and the DVP's national leadership than the initiative of the paramilitary leagues. It eventually produced an agreement to which the DVP, DNVP, and Business Party all adhered.[21]

The various proposals for bourgeois solidarity in the campaign for

---

16. Further details are in Fritz Otto von Stieglitz, "Die Entwicklung des Jungdeutschen Ordens in Sachsen," in *Jungdeutscher Tag zu Leipzig am 6. u. 7. Brachet 1925: Eine Fest- und Erinnerungsschrift,* ed. Rudolf Vesper (Leipzig, [1925]), 13–15.

17. In this respect, see Richard Bessel, "The 'Front Generation' and the Politics of Weimar Germany," in *Generations in Conflict: Youth Revolt and Generation Formation in Germany, 1770–1968,* ed. Mark Roseman (Cambridge, 1995), 121–36.

18. Brückner (Stahlhelm, Landesverband Sachsen) to the DVP, Wahlkreisverband Leipzig, 29 July 1926, PA AA Bonn, NL Stresemann, 96/173150–51. See also Frank to Stresemann, 9 Aug. 1926, ibid., 173144–46. On the role of the Young German Order, see the memorandum of a conversation between Artur Mahraun and Otto Bornemann from the Young German leadership and Stresemann's secretary Henry Bernhard, 16 Aug. 1926, ibid., 173179–82.

19. For Stresemann's reaction, see his letter to Johannes Dieckmann, chairman of the DVP district organization in East Saxony, 25 Aug. 1926, PA AA Bonn, NL Stresemann, 96/173225–28.

20. For further details, see Frank to Stresemann, 24 Aug. 1926, PA AA Bonn, NL Stresemann, 96/173213–14; and Dieckmann to Stresemann, 24 and 28 Aug. 1926, ibid., 173221–24, 173236–43, as well as the memorandum of the meeting organized by the Saxon Citizens' Council in the offices of the League of Saxon Industrialists, 22 Aug. 1926, ibid., 96/173215–17.

21. Arthur Graefe, *3 Jahre Aufbaupolitik: Zu den Sachsenwahlen 1926,* ed. Sächsische Wahlkreisverbände der Deutschen Volkspartei (Dresden, 1926), 59–62. The phrases "consolidation from below" and "above" are from Lapp, *Revolution,* 143–50.

the October 1926 Saxon *Landtag* elections represented a direct response to the fragmentation of the Weimar party system and the threat this posed to the tenuous hegemony of Saxony's nonsocialist forces. In the final analysis, however, the more modest attempt at "bourgeois consolidation from above" proved inadequate and failed to protect the Saxon bourgeoisie from the centrifugal forces that more than a decade of economic hardship had unleashed within its midst. For the outcome of the 1926 Saxon *Landtag* elections revealed just how powerful the appeal of special-interest parties was and how powerless the more established bourgeois parties were to insulate their followers against this appeal.[22] When the votes were all counted, the DDP, DVP, and DNVP had suffered losses amounting to 42.0, 28.7, and 37.6 percent of what they had each received in Saxony in the December 1924 Reichstag elections. The Business Party, on the other hand, more than doubled the number of votes it had received in 1924, from 124,193 to 237,462 (10.1%), and entered the newly elected *Landtag* with a complement of ten deputies. The fledgling People's Justice Party polled 98,258 votes (4.2%) and received four *Landtag* mandates.[23] The implications of this were not lost upon Germany's national political leaders. As Stresemann lamented in an article written for the *Deutsche Stimmen:*

> The most distressing thing about the present situation in Germany is the tendency to overemphasize the purely economic and vocational aspect of the political struggle. Should the principle behind the Business Party triumph, then the political fabric of Germany's national life would soon fragment to the point where we would have agricultural groups here, industrial groups there, the civil servants and white-collar employees somewhere else. But in the midst of all this, the spiritual cement necessary to fuse these elements into a dynamic and organic whole would be sadly missing.[24]

III. The Crisis of the Saxon DNVP

Nowhere was Stresemann's lament over the outcome of the 1926 Saxon *Landtag* elections more pregnant with meaning than in Saxony itself. The

---

22. See Dieckmann to Stresemann, 30 Sept. [*sic;* Oct.] 1926, PA AA Bonn, NL Stresemann, 299.

23. *Wirtschaft und Statistik* 6, no. 21 (18 Nov. 1926): 783–84. See also Rademacher, "Zur Frage der Aufwertung," 19 Nov. 1926, in the private papers of Kuno Graf von Westarp in the possession of Friedrich Freiherr Hiller von Gaertringen (hereafter NL Westarp).

24. Gustav Stresemann, "Die Gegenwartsaufgaben des nationalen Liberalismus," *Deutsche Stimmen* 38, no. 23 (5 Dec. 1926): 553–58.

fragmentation of the Saxon party system meant that efforts to form a new government were to drag on for the next seven months. The final result — a cabinet that depended upon the support of no fewer than seven different parties — was hardly reassuring. The new cabinet, headed once again by the dissident socialist Max Heldt, rested upon a broad, but inherently unstable, parliamentary coalition that extended from Heldt's own group of supporters to the DNVP on its extreme right wing and that included both the WP and VRP. Saxony was in fact the first state in which the Business Party was represented in the government, in this case by Hugo Weber as minister of finance and Walther Wilhelm as minister of economics, though the latter was obliged to surrender his post when the DNVP finally joined the cabinet in July 1927. For the DNVP the critical question was whether or not it would be able to stem the defection of its supporters to special-interest parties like the WP and VRP. But as events were to show, this was a problem that did not merely affect the DNVP's relations with its urban electorate; it also held profound implications for the future of the party's place in the Saxon countryside.

As the largest of Saxony's nonsocialist parties, the DNVP had always relied upon the support of the Saxon Rural League (Sächsischer Landbund, or SLB) to win the votes of the Saxon peasantry. In 1924, as in 1920, the DNVP and SLB had worked closely to secure the election of Nationalist deputies who regarded the defense of agricultural economic interests as an essential ingredient of conservative politics.[25] But this alliance, which was reaffirmed in the 1926 Saxon *Landtag* elections and no doubt helped shield the DNVP from even more serious losses than those it actually suffered,[26] was severely threatened by developments at the end of 1927 in the neighboring state of Thuringia. In November 1927 the leaders of the Thuringian Rural League (Thüringer Landbund) petitioned the RLB's national leadership in Berlin on behalf of a national agrarian ticket for the Reichstag elections that were set to take place early the next year. Although this proposal was shelved at a meeting of the RLB executive committee on 14 December 1927 in favor of a resolution that left the question of electoral strategy to the discretion of the RLB's state and regional affiliates, this did little to deter the leaders of the Thuringian Rural League from going ahead with their plans for a national agrarian party. On 17 February 1928 they announced the founding of the Christian-National Peasants and Farmers' Party (Christlich-nationale Bauern-

25. Alwin Domsch and Albrecht Philipp, *Sächsische Landwirtschaft und Reichstagswahl 1924: Ein Rückblick und Ausblick,* Schriften der Deutschnationalen Volkspartei in Sachsen (Arbeitsgemeinschaft), no. 6 (Dresden, [1924]), 13–15.

26. Rademacher to Westarp, 24 Mar. 1928, NL Westarp.

und Landvolkpartei, or CNBLP). The party's official founding took place in the Thuringian capital on 8 March 1928.[27]

The leaders of the Saxon DNVP and Saxon Rural League followed the developments in Thuringia closely. The leaders of the DNVP at both the state and national level were concerned that the widespread sympathy that the founding of a new agrarian party in the neighboring state of Thuringia had evoked among the Saxon peasantry might inflict a defeat upon their party even more severe than the one it had suffered in the 1926 Saxon *Landtag* elections.[28] The leaders of the Saxon Rural League, most of whom remained committed to the alliance with the DNVP,[29] tried to halt the spread of the new party by nominating their own slate of candidates on a list entitled the Saxon Landvolk (Sächsisches Landvolk). They did so on the twofold condition that those who were elected on this ticket affiliate themselves with the DNVP Reichstag delegation and that all *Reststimmen* not required for the election of these deputies be credited to the DNVP's national slate of candidates, or *Reichswahlvorschlag*.[30] This arrangement, however, did little to ease tensions between the party and the SLB; instead it ended up pitting rural and urban interests against each other in the nomination of candidates on the two tickets.[31] The ensuing deadlock was only broken when the SLB yielded to pressure from the RLB's national leadership and agreed to nominate DNVP Reichstag deputy Albrecht Philipp, an articulate and outspoken advocate of agricultural interests,[32] to a secure candidacy despite criticism from within the SLB that he was not a working farmer.[33] Though fraught with tensions that made

---

27. For further details, see Larry Eugene Jones, "Crisis and Realignment: Agrarian Splinter Parties in the Late Weimar Republic, 1928–1933," in *Peasants and Lords in Modern Germany: Recent Studies in Agricultural History,* ed. Robert G. Moeller (Boston, 1986), 198–232.

28. For example, see Rademacher to Beutler, 7 Mar. 1928, appended to Rademacher to Westarp, 10 Mar. 1928, and Rademacher to Westarp, 24 Mar. 1928, all in NL Westarp.

29. For example, see the letter from the SLB's Otto Feldmann to the TLB's Höfer, 27 Mar. 1928, NL Westarp.

30. Lüttichau to Westarp, 24 Mar. 1928, NL Westarp. See also "Warum: Sächsisches Landvolk?" *Sächsische Bauern-Zeitung: Amtliches Organ des Sächsischen Landbundes e.V.* 35, no. 17 (22 Apr. 1928): 166–67.

31. For further details, see Philipp to Schiele, 10 and 19 Apr. 1928; and Philipp to Westarp, 12 and 17 Apr. 1928, all in SächsHStA Dresden, NL Philipp, 20.

32. Albrecht Philipp, *Die Zukunft der deutschen Landwirtschaft: Nach einer Rede gehalten am 30. April 1928 zu Geithain auf der Generalversammlung des Landbundes Borna,* Schriften der Deutschnationalen Volkspartei in Sachsen (Arbeitsgemeinschaft), no. 26 (Borna, 1928).

33. For example, see the letter from ten members of the SLB to the organization's headquarters in Dresden, 21 Apr. 1928, SächsHStA Dresden, NL Philipp, 20.

Philipp's renomination unlikely in the future, the alliance nevertheless accomplished its main objectives by holding the CNBLP's gains in Saxony to slightly more than 17,000 votes, thus enabling the DNVP to hold on to two mandates that might otherwise have been lost if the CNBLP had succeeded in establishing a foothold among the Saxon peasantry.[34]

Although the DNVP's alliance with the SLB made it possible for the Nationalists to retain their hold on the Saxon countryside, the party failed to recapture the support it had lost to middle-class splinter parties in the 1926 *Landtag* elections: it saw its share of the popular vote in the three Saxon electoral districts slip from 20.5 percent in December 1924 and 14.5 percent in 1926 to 9.3 percent in May 1928. Compared to the results of the October 1926 Saxon *Landtag* elections, these losses indicated that the DNVP's decline among urban voters continued unabated, though at a somewhat less frenetic pace than had been the case between 1924 and 1926.[35] In any event, the DNVP's losses in Saxony greatly exceeded those of the two liberal parties, both of which emerged from the election in relatively good shape. The DVP, for example, saw its percentage of the popular vote in the three Saxon districts fall from 15.4 percent in the December 1924 Reichstag elections and 12.4 in the 1926 Saxon *Landtag* elections to 11.6 percent in the May 1928 Reichstag elections, while the DDP actually increased its share of the Saxon vote from 4.7 percent in October 1926 to 5.4 percent in May 1928. The WP and VRP, on the other hand, received 232,052 (8.5%) and 87,545 (3.2%) votes respectively in the three Saxon districts—or only slightly more than what they had received in the 1926 *Landtag* elections. While there may have been no significant shift in the relative strengths of Saxony's nonsocialist parties between 1926 and 1928, the more established, ideologically oriented parties like the DNVP, DVP, and DDP continued to lose support to such special-interest parties as the WP and VRP, though perhaps not as dramatically as between 1924 and 1926.[36]

The DNVP's losses in Saxony in the May 1926 Reichstag elections were part of a much broader pattern of electoral decline that cost the party over a quarter of the popular vote it had received in the December 1924 Reichstag elections and 30 of the 103 seats it had held in the Reichstag. The magnitude of the DNVP's defeat in the 1928 Reichstag elections brought to a head the crisis that had been brewing within the

34. Rademacher to Westarp, 21 May 1928, NL Westarp.

35. Albrecht Philipp, *Bilanz und Aufgaben deutschnationaler Arbeit 1928: Eine politische Übersicht*, Schriften der Deutschnationalen Volkspartei in Sachsen (Arbeitsgemeinschaft), no. 27 (Dresden, 1928), 4–8.

36. Supporting statistics are found in *Wirtschaft und Statistik* 6 (1926): 783–848; 8 (1928): 383–84.

party ever since its entry into the fourth Marx cabinet in January 1927. In June 1928 Count Kuno von Westarp resigned as the DNVP's national chairman. In October he was succeeded by Alfred Hugenberg, an unrelenting opponent of the so-called Weimar system who was determined to free the party from the grip of the special economic interests he held responsible for its ill-advised experiments at government participation in 1925 and 1927. Hugenberg's hostility toward the role that organized economic interests had played in Weimar's political and economic stabilization since 1924 placed him and the DNVP on a collision course with the National Rural League and its newly elected president Martin Schiele, himself a member of the DNVP Reichstag delegation. This, in turn, was to have profound consequences for the party organization in Saxony and its relations with Saxon agriculture. For although the leaders of the Saxon DNVP were quick to reassure the new party leader of their full and undivided support,[37] the conflict between Hugenberg and the RLB placed a heavy strain upon relations between the Saxon DNVP and the Saxon Rural League and exposed the party to a new round of attacks from the rival Christian-National Peasants and Farmers' Party.

The difficulties in which the leaders of the Saxon DNVP suddenly found themselves became abundantly clear as the party prepared for new *Landtag* elections in the spring of 1929. Although initially the leaders of the SLB had voted to renew their organization's alliance with the DNVP for the upcoming *Landtag* elections, they suddenly reversed their position on 9 April and announced that the SLB would field its own slate of candidates in the elections scheduled for the following month.[38] In the meantime, Hugenberg's opponents in the DNVP's Saxon organization launched a concerted effort to purge the party's executive committee of his supporters and to block their nomination for election to the *Landtag*.[39] The resulting turmoil within the party organization severely hampered its efforts in the campaign and only reinforced the determination of the SLB leadership to go its own way in the upcoming state elections. At the same time, the leaders of the DNVP's Saxon organization complained that Hugenberg's *Katastrophenpolitik* left their party defenseless against charges by the DVP and WP that the DNVP had

37. For example, see Philipp, *Bilanz und Aufgaben,* 9–13.

38. Kurt Philipp to Albrecht Philipp, 11 Apr. 1929, SächsHStA Dresden, NL Philipp, 23.

39. In this respect, see Reyher to Bang, 30 Mar. 1929, as well as the long letter to DNVP Reichstag deputy Paul Bang, 4 Apr. 1929, both in the unpublished records of the Alldeutscher Verband, Bundesarchiv Berlin-Lichterfelde (hereafter BA Berlin-Lichterfelde, ADV), 219/12–24; and the memorandum "Zu den Vorgängen im Landesverband Ostsachsen," n.d., ibid., 29–30.

abandoned the German middle class in an all-or-nothing strategy aimed at bringing about the fall of the Weimar Republic. The net effect of all this was to inflict a severe defeat on the DNVP in the May 1929 Saxon *Landtag* elections. The party lost 36.0 percent of the votes it had received in the 1926 *Landtag* elections and 14.2 percent of the votes it had received in the three Saxon electoral districts in the May 1928 Reichstag elections. As a result, the DNVP saw its share of the Saxon electorate reduced from 14.5 percent to 8.1 percent between 1926 and 1929.[40] If the DNVP had been the largest nonsocialist party in the Saxon *Landtag,* it now stood behind both the DVP and WP, which between 1926 and 1929 increased their share of the Saxon electorate from 12.4 to 13.5 percent and 10.1 to 11.3 percent respectively. At the same time, the Saxon Landvolk received 5.2 percent of the popular vote and entered the newly elected *Landtag* with five seats of its own. The most surprising development of all, however, was the fact that the Nazi Party, an altogether negligible factor in 1926 and 1928, emerged from the elections with 4.9 percent of the popular vote and five seats in the *Landtag.*[41]

IV.   Fragmentation and Radicalization of the Saxon Right

Following the DNVP's defeat in the May 1929 Saxon *Landtag* elections, Hugenberg's supporters launched a determined campaign to gain control of the Saxon party organization and to purge it of the faction led by DNVP Reichstag deputy Albrecht Philipp. In this regard, Hugenberg received crucial support from the leaders of the Dresden chapter of the Pan-German League (Alldeutscher Verband, or ADV), who worked tirelessly on his behalf to undercut the position of Philipp and his supporters.[42] Like Hugenberg, the Pan-Germans were adamantly opposed to any sort of accommodation with the existing system of government: they sought to return the DNVP to the course of unconditional opposition to the Weimar Republic that had served it so well between 1918 and 1924. At the same time, the Pan-Germans sought to forge closer ties at both the national and local levels between the DNVP and other right-wing organizations, including the NSDAP.[43] Here Hugenberg's supporters were aided by the fact

40. For a thoughtful discussion of the reasons for the DNVP's defeat, see Philipp to Beutler, 16 May 1929, SächsHStA Dresden, NL Philipp, 23.

41. *Wirtschaft und Statistik* 9 (1929): 436.

42. For further details, see Kretschmar to Claß, 5 June 1929, BA Berlin-Lichterfelde, ADV, 219/33–36; and Guratzsch to Traub, 20 Oct. 1932, in the unpublished Nachlaß of Gottfried Traub, Bundesarchiv Koblenz (hereafter BA Koblenz), 50/35–38.

43. Heinrich Claß, "Alldeutsche Ziele für Deutschlands Erneuerung," *Deutschlands Erneuerung* 12, no. 10 (Oct. 1928): 575–80. On the ADV after 1926, see Barry A. Jackisch, "'Make the Right Wing Strong!' The Pan-German League and Right-Wing

that in June 1929 the national leadership of various right-wing organizations from the RLB and CNBLP to the DNVP, ADV, and NSDAP joined
forces in the National Committee for the German Referendum (Reichs-
ausschuß für das deutsche Volksbegehren) in an attempt to block ratification of the Young Plan by popular referendum. This was followed by the
creation of a state committee (*Landesausschuß*) for Saxony in which the
DNVP, SLB, ADV, Stahlhelm, and NSDAP were all represented.[44] But
hopes that this might pave the way for the creation of a united German
Right quickly evaporated as a bitter conflict erupted on the national
level over the wording of the proposed "Freedom Law" with which the
leaders of the National Referendum Committee hoped to block implementation of the Young Plan. Not only did this pit the National Rural
League and its regional affiliates against Hugenberg and his allies from
the Pan-German League; it exacerbated tensions within the DNVP to the
point where in December 1929 twelve members of the DNVP Reichstag
delegation resigned from the party in protest against the style and substance of Hugenberg's political leadership.[45]

The conflict within the DNVP Reichstag delegation had immediate
repercussions upon the party's situation in Saxony. For although none of
the six members of the DNVP Reichstag delegation from Saxony took
part in the secession, the leaders of the Saxon DNVP stubbornly refused
to give Hugenberg the vote of confidence his supporters were seeking
from the DNVP's state and local organizations throughout the country.[46]
The leaders of the Saxon Rural League gave Hugenberg's supporters a
measure of relief when they refused to follow the RLB and CNBLP in
resigning from the National Referendum Committee after the defeat of
the "Freedom Law" in the Reichstag in December 1929.[47] Yet their
relations with the DNVP were ultimately strained to the breaking point
when, in April 1930, Hugenberg tried to block passage of an emergency
farm bill that Martin Schiele, himself a member of the DNVP Reichstag
delegation and the minister of agriculture in the newly installed cabinet
of Centrist Heinrich Brüning, introduced with the full authority of the

---

Politics in the Weimar Republic" (Ph.D. diss. in progress, State University of New York at
Buffalo).

44. In this respect, see Berthold to Beutel, 31 Aug. 1929, in the unpublished records of the Dresden chapter (Ortsgruppe) of the Pan-German League, Stadtarchiv
Dresden, 12.

45. For further details, see Elizabeth Friedenthal, "Volksbegehren und Volks-
entscheid über den Young-Plan und die deutschnationale Sezession" (Ph.D. diss., University of Tübingen, 1957).

46. Kurt Philipp to Albrecht Philipp, 13 Dec. 1929, SächsHStA Dresden, NL Philipp, 20.

47. *Sächsische Bauern-Zeitung* 37, no. 4 (26 Jan. 1930): 33.

Reich President behind him.[48] The fact that the government's agrarian bill eventually passed with the support of a substantial majority within the DNVP Reichstag delegation did little to allay the sense of betrayal this turn of events had produced among the leaders of the SLB,[49] who now found themselves locked in a bitter fight to prevent their organization from being taken over by those favorably disposed to the CNBLP.[50] As a result, the leaders of the Saxon Rural League tried to place as much distance as possible between themselves and the DNVP in the campaign for the new *Landtag* elections that had been set for 22 June 1930.[51]

The 1930 Saxon *Landtag* elections represented another important moment in the dissolution of the Saxon party system. Not only had the Saxon Rural League effectively terminated its alliance with the DNVP; the leaders of the Young German Order had become so concerned about the fragmentation of the political middle that they decided to enter the campaign themselves. In late 1927 the Young Germans had launched a highly publicized crusade to free German political life from the tyranny of organized economic interests through the "reactivation of the German middle" and its consolidation into a new party of *"staatsbürgerliche Sammlung."* This crusade reached a preliminary climax in April 1930 when Artur Mahraun, the enigmatic High Master of the Young German Order, announced the founding of the People's National Reich Association (Volksnationale Reichsvereinigung, or VNR) after several months of intensive preparation.[52] Mahraun and his supporters continued to insist that they had no intention of founding a new party of their own.[53] Nevertheless, they did not hesitate to criticize the more established bourgeois parties—in particular the DNVP and DVP—for having fallen under the spell of special economic interests to the extent that they were no longer capable of providing the dynamism necessary to fuse a badly

---

48. For further details, see Dieter Gessner, *Agrarverbände in der Weimarer Republik: Wirtschaftliche und soziale Voraussetzungen agrarkonservativer Politik vor 1933* (Düsseldorf, 1976), 183–99.

49. For example, see Georg Bachmann, "Neue Fundamente," *Sächsische Bauern-Zeitung* 37, no. 16 (20 Apr. 1930): 152–54; and O. F. [Otto Feldmann], "Zur Lage," ibid., no. 17 (27 Apr. 1930): 162–63.

50. On the situation within the SLB, see Philipp to Schiele, 18 Apr. 1930, SächsHStA Dresden, NL Philipp, 24.

51. For example, see Otto Feldmann, "Die Politisierung des Sächs. Landbundes," *Sächsische Bauern-Zeitung* 37, no. 24 (15 June 1930): 237. See also Landbund Borna, Rundschreiben Nr. 25/30, 4 June 1930, SächsHStA Dresden, NL Philipp, 24.

52. Cf. Volksnationale Reichsvereinigung, *Der erste Reichsvertretertag am. 5. und 6. April 1930* (Berlin, 1930), 14–59.

53. Mahraun to Koch-Weser, 23 Apr. 1930, NL Erich Koch-Weser, BA Koblenz, 101/165–66.

fragmented German middle into a cohesive political force.[54] Alarmed by the advanced state of disintegration in which the Saxon party system found itself, Mahraun and the national leaders of the VNR chose to leave the decision as to whether or not the VNR should intervene in the upcoming Saxon *Landtag* elections in the hands of the organization's local leadership.[55] Accordingly, the Saxon state committee (*Landes-ausschuß*) of the VNR announced on 23 May 1930 that the situation in Saxony was so desperate, and the threat of National Socialism so great, that it had no choice but to enter the upcoming state elections in an attempt to salvage what it could from the ruins of the Saxon party system.[56] Over the next month, Mahraun and the Young Germans were to make the Saxon campaign their highest national priority. They threw the full weight of their organization behind the VNR and its efforts to mobilize the Saxon *Staatsbürgertum*.[57]

The VNR's entry into the campaign for the 1930 Saxon *Landtag* elections came at a time when not just the DNVP but also the DDP and, more significantly, the DVP were reeling from severe internal crises. Stresemann's death in the autumn of 1929 had triggered a bitter struggle for control of the party. That struggle was only temporarily resolved with the election of Ernst Scholz (chairman of the DVP Reichstag delegation and the candidate of the party's right wing) as Stresemann's successor in December 1929.[58] Scholz's election came as a great disappointment to the leaders of the party's young liberal movement, who since the spring of 1929 had begun to work more and more closely with the Young German Order in the struggle to bring about a reform and realignment of the German party system.[59] In the campaign for the 1930 Saxon *Landtag* elections, the leaders of the VNR tried to drive a wedge be-

---

54. For the VNR's political objectives, see Artur Mahraun, *Der Aufbruch: Sinn und Zweck der Volksnationalen Reichsvereinigung* (Berlin, 1930).

55. Mahraun to the local chapters (*Kreisgruppen*) of the VNR, 21 May 1930, in the NSDAP Hauptarchiv, BA Berlin-Lichterfelde, Bestand NS 26, vol. 875. See also Kurt Pastenaci, "Sachsenwahlen," *Der Jungdeutsche*, 22 May 1930, no. 118.

56. *Der Jungdeutsche*, 24 May 1930, no. 120.

57. Artur Mahraun, "Volksmacht gegen Finanzmacht: Um die Entscheidung in Sachsen," *Der Jungdeutsche*, 24 May 1930, no. 120. See also Jungdeutscher Orden, Anordnung Nr. 1 für ein Eingreifen in den Wahlkampf, 25 May 1930; and VNR, Landesverband Sachsen, Rüstzeug Nr. 1 für die Redner, 3 June 1930, both in the unpublished records of the Jungdeutscher Orden, BA Koblenz, Bestand R 161, vol. 5.

58. Larry Eugene Jones, *German Liberalism and the Dissolution of the Weimar Party System, 1918–1933* (Chapel Hill, NC, 1988), 348–49.

59. Larry Eugene Jones, "Liberalism and the Challenge of the Younger Generation: The Young Liberal Struggle for a Reform of the Weimar Party System, 1928–30," in *Politische Jugend in der Weimarer Republik*, ed. Wolfgang R. Krabbe (Bochum, 1993), 106–28.

tween the DVP party leadership and the reform-minded elements on the party's left wing. They did so by attacking Scholz and his supporters as instruments of the "anonymous plutocratic forces" that were intent upon thwarting the popular will in its demand for a reform of the existing party system.[60] These attacks greatly exacerbated the party's internal crisis and severely impaired its effectiveness in the Saxon campaign.[61] The situation was hardly any better in the DDP, where party leaders found themselves embroiled in a bitter dispute over their party's precise role in the movement for bourgeois consolidation. In deference to the close ties that Mahraun enjoyed with the Democratic party, however, the VNR leadership refrained from criticizing the DDP in the campaign for the Saxon elections with the same venom it reserved for the DVP, DNVP, and NSDAP.[62]

The outcome of the 1930 Saxon *Landtag* elections underscored the fragility of the Weimar party system in three essential respects. First, the DDP, DVP, and DNVP all sustained heavy losses, ranging in the case of the DDP from 27.3 percent of what it had received in the May 1929 Saxon *Landtag* elections to 38.2 and 42.0 percent in the case of the DVP and DNVP respectively. Second, the fact that the Business Party, the Saxon Landvolk, and the People's Justice Party suffered losses of 9.6, 14.2, and 30.2 percent respectively indicated that the appeal of special-interest parties had indeed peaked and that they were experiencing increasing difficulty holding on to the support they had attracted in the second half of the 1920s. Nor, by the same token, was either the People's National Reich Association or the Christian-Social People's Service (Christlich-sozialer Volksdienst) able to establish itself as a viable force in Saxon political life, polling only 1.5 and 2.2 percent of the popular vote respectively. Third, the results of the 1930 elections confirmed what the elections the previous year had already suggested as a likely outcome of the current political crisis: the emergence of the Nazi Party as a major force in both state and national politics. The NSDAP nearly tripled the number of votes it had received a year earlier. It increased its percentage of the popular vote from 5.0 percent in May 1929 to 14.4 percent in June 1930, and it emerged from the elections as the second-largest party in the Saxon *Landtag* with a complement of fourteen seats in parliament.[63]

In the Reichstag elections that became necessary with the dissolution

60. Mahraun, "Wir und die Volkspartei," *Der Jungdeutsche,* 20 June 1930, no. 141.

61. On the DVP's vulnerability in the 1930 Saxon elections, see Dieckmann's comments before the DVP central executive committee, 4 July 1930, in the unpublished records of the German People's Party, BA Koblenz, Bestand R 45 II/46/235–47.

62. For example, see Kurt Pastenaci, "Sammlungsparolen," *Der Jungdeutsche,* 29 May 1930, no. 124; and Albrecht, "Wahlgeplänkel in Sachsen," ibid., 5 June 1930, no. 129.

63. *Wirtschaft und Statistik* 10 (1930): 694–95.

of the Reichstag on 18 July 1930, none of these developments augured well for the more established bourgeois parties in Saxony or elsewhere. Indeed, the situation within the Saxon DNVP seemed more confused than ever following a second secession from the DNVP Reichstag delegation in which four of the party's six Saxon deputies, including longtime party loyalists Albrecht Philipp and Walther Rademacher, took part.[64] This was followed by a wave of resignations from the DNVP at the state and local level[65] as Hugenberg's Pan-German allies moved quickly to take over control of the Saxon party organization and to turn it into a subservient instrument of Hugenberg's political will.[66] As what remained of the DNVP's Saxon state organization lined up behind the party's national leadership and condemned the secessionists as traitors to the party and nation,[67] the Saxon Rural League began to explore the possibility of an alliance with the Christian-National Peasants and Farmers' Party.[68] This led to an agreement whereby the Saxon Rural League ran its own slate of candidates under the name Saxon Landvolk as part of a national ticket known as the German Landvolk (Deutsches Landvolk), which carried the RLB's political imprimatur.[69] Philipp and those former Nationalists whom the CNBLP refused to accept as candidates because they were not farmers were left with no alternative but to retire from active political life[70] or to try their luck with the newly founded Conservative People's Party (Konservative Volkspartei, or KVP), which Westarp and his colleagues were trying to get up and running in time for the upcoming Reichstag elections.[71] In the meantime, the DDP party leadership had apparently been so impressed by the VNR's performance in the Saxon *Landtag* elections that it decided to join Mahraun and the leaders of the VNR in founding an entirely new political party, the German State Party (Deutsche Staatspartei). The goal of the Staatspartei was to fuse the German middle into a solid phalanx capable of defending the state against

---

64. See Philipp to the DNVP, Landesverband Westsachsen, 22 July 1930, SächsHStA Dresden, NL Philipp, 24, as well as the reports in the *Leipziger Neueste Nachrichten*, 23 July 1930, no. 204, and the *Dresdner Nachrichten*, 23 July 1930, no. 341.

65. Report of a meeting of the DNVP Dresden district organization, 28 July 1930, in the *Neue Preußische (Kreuz-)Zeitung*, 29 July 1930, no. 212.

66. For further details, see the letter to Hugenberg, 23 July 1930, BA Berlin-Lichterfelde, ADV, 216/158–62; and Beutel to Claß, 9 Sept. 1930, ibid., 194–95.

67. *Dresdner Anzeiger*, 29 July 1930, no. 351.

68. Philipp to Schiele, 24 July 1930, SächsHStA Dresden, NL Philipp, 24.

69. *Sächsische Bauern-Zeitung* 37, no. 36 (7 Sept. 1930): 381–83.

70. On Philipp's personal dilemma, see his letters to Heyde, 8 Aug. 1930, and Schiele, 24 Aug. 1930, both in SächsHStA Dresden, NL Philipp, 24.

71. For further information, see Maltzahn to Westarp, 26 July 1930; and Rademacher to Treviranus, 8 Aug. 1930, both in NL Westarp, as well as the report on a meeting of the KVP's Leipzig party organization, 31 July 1930, in the *Kölnische Zeitung*, 1 Aug. 1930, no. 416.

the radicalism on both the Left and the Right.[72] The net effect of all this activity, however, was only to underscore the deep-seated confusion that existed within the ranks of Germany's middle-class voters and to render them all the more vulnerable to Nazi penetration.

To anyone who had closely followed developments in Saxony, the NSDAP's striking victory in the Reichstag elections of 14 September 1930 could have come as no surprise. The outcome of the 1930 elections indicated that the dissolution of the Saxon party system had continued unabated since the *Landtag* elections three months earlier. It also demonstrated that the unequivocal beneficiary of the unremitting fragmentation of Saxony's nonsocialist parties was the NSDAP, whose share of the Saxon electorate jumped from 14.4 to 18.4 percent from June to September 1930. Much of this increase came at the expense of the DVP, which saw its share of the Saxon electorate fall from 8.7 percent to 6.4 percent between June and September 1930, and the WP, which failed to match the 10.6 percent of the popular vote it had received in the Saxon *Landtag* elections three months earlier, even though it remained the largest of Saxony's nonsocialist parties with 7.4 percent of the Saxon electorate. In the meantime, the fact that the DNVP's share of the Saxon vote fell marginally from 4.8 percent in June to 4.5 percent in September meant that the vast majority of Hugenberg's opponents had already abandoned the party before the onset of the campaign. Still, none of the three splinter parties that had broken off from the DNVP— the Saxon Landvolk, the Christian-Social People's Service, or the Conservative People's Party—was able to establish itself as a viable political factor with only 4.0, 2.6, and 0.95 percent of the Saxon vote respectively. Only the German State Party, whose 4.3 percent of the popular vote in the three Saxon electoral districts exceeded both what the DDP had received in the most recent state elections and the 3.8 percent of the popular vote the party received throughout the Reich as a whole, was able to avoid the fate of the other nonsocialist parties. This, however, did not signal a revival of Germany's bourgeois Left but was an anomalous event best attributed to the extraordinary strength of the VNR's organization in Dresden.[73]

V. Conclusions

The dramatic electoral breakthrough of National Socialism in 1929–30 in both Saxony and the Reich as a whole was a direct consequence of the

---

72. Jones, *German Liberalism*, 366–77.
73. *Wirtschaft und Statistik* 10 (1930): 768. Cf. the table in Jürgen Falter, Thomas Lindenberg, and Siegfried Schumann, *Wahlen und Abstimmungen in der Weimarer Republik: Materialien zum Wahlverhalten, 1919–1933* (Munich, 1986), 72.

fragmentation and dissolution of the bourgeois party system of the Weimar Republic. That this process was well under way long before the full impact of the world economic crisis was felt is apparent from developments in Saxony. There, the absence of the Catholic Center Party and a legacy of class antagonism combined with stagnant economic development through the second half of the 1920s to render the Saxon party system particularly vulnerable to the forces of dissolution that were at work in German political culture. The early success of middle-class splinter parties like the Business Party and the People's Justice Party revealed just how much more advanced the dissolution of the bourgeois party system was in Saxony than in other parts of the country. The electoral collapse of the right-wing German National People's Party after its sensational triumph in the December 1924 Reichstag elections stemmed in no small measure from the increasing appeal of special-interest parties. Yet the breakdown of the DNVP's Saxon organization was greatly accelerated by Hugenberg's policies as party chairman and by the lack of resonance these policies found among the Saxon middle classes. In the meantime, Germany's two liberal parties — the DDP and DVP — found themselves torn by internal conflicts. Those conflicts left them immobilized during a period of deepening economic crisis, and they effectively eliminated them as alternatives to the Nazi Party as a home for Saxony's increasingly disaffected middle-class voters.

The Development of Nazism in the Landscape of Socialism and Nationalism: The Case of Saxony, 1918–1933

Claus-Christian W. Szejnmann

I. Introduction

Whereas several generations of historians have produced an enormous quantity of regional and local studies about Nazism in western Germany,[1] we know comparatively little about the phenomenon in central and eastern Germany, including Saxony.[2] Developments in Saxony, however, are crucial for our understanding of Nazism in Germany.[3] Saxony was the Nazi *Gau* with by far the highest population, the most members of the Nazi Party, and one of the largest number of party branches. Indeed, it was one of the earliest strongholds of the Nazi movement. Thus Saxony was crucial for the rise of the Nazi Party on the national level from the late 1920s. Furthermore, Saxony's background as the

---

1. See especially Cornelia Rauh-Kühne, *Katholisches Milieu und Kleinstadtgesellschaft: Ettlingen, 1918–1939* (Sigmaringen, 1991); Peter Fritzsche, *Rehearsals for Fascism: Populism and Political Mobilization in Weimar Germany* (Oxford, 1990); Rudy Koshar, *Social Life, Local Politics, and Nazism: Marburg, 1880–1935* (Chapel Hill, NC, 1986); William S. Allen, *The Nazi Seizure of Power,* 2d ed. (London, 1984); and Jeremy Noakes, *The Nazi Party in Lower Saxony, 1921–1933* (London, 1971).

2. See Claus-Christian W. Szejnmann, "Review Article: The Missing Pieces Are 'Coming Home': Nazism in Central Germany," *German History* 15 (1997): 395–410. Meanwhile, however, see Benjamin Lapp, *Revolution from the Right: Politics, Class, and the Rise of Nazism in Saxony, 1919–1933* (Atlantic Highlands, NJ, 1997).

3. For more detail see Claus-Christian W. Szejnmann, *Nazism in Central Germany: The Brownshirts in 'Red' Saxony* (New York, 1999). The book includes a social profile of the Saxon NSDAP membership before 1933 (by Detlef Mühlberger) and a social profile of Saxon NSDAP voters (by Dirk Hänisch).

most industrialized and urbanized region in Germany and the cradle of Germany's working-class movement makes the development of the brownshirts in the state a particularly interesting case study. Nearly all regional studies of Nazism, however, have focused on agricultural or semi-industrialized rural areas and emphasized Nazism's middle-class constituency. The only comprehensive study about the heavily industrialized Ruhr region in western Germany is in many respects out of date.[4]

The premise of this survey is that if one wants to understand the origins, development, success, and limitations of Nazism, one has to combine an analysis of the Nazi movement and the society in which it operated. Although the conclusions presented here have to be seen in the specific context of Saxon circumstances and have to be compared with other regions in Germany, Saxony itself was also heavily influenced by developments elsewhere. Most importantly, the course of Saxon history was intrinsically linked to the Reich and — more generally — to the processes of modernization that affected societies throughout Europe.

II. The *Sonderweg* and Interwar Saxon Society

Since the 1960s, the most influential explanation of Nazism has been the theory of a German *Sonderweg,* which sees the primary origins of Nazism somewhere in the nineteenth century.[5] In Saxony too, long-term causes play a fundamental role for anyone trying to come to grips with the local Nazi movement. Politically, Saxony entered the twentieth century with a sharp polarization between a progressive working-class movement and an elite and bourgeoisie who opposed a democratic political system. Recent research has shown that powerful sectors of the Saxon bourgeoisie started to embark on a slow process of political modernization at the turn of the century.[6] It seems clear, however, that these efforts amounted to little and came too late — being interrupted by the outbreak of war in 1914 — to provide a solid foundation for a democratic system in the postwar period. While the majority of the labor movement embraced the new Republican environment, a large part of the bourgeoisie had enormous problems in adapting to it. Moreover, both had completely different visions of what kind of society they wanted to create within the new political framework. Whereas labor aimed at the welfare of the masses and their integration into the system, many members of

4. Wilfried Böhnke, *Die NSDAP im Ruhrgebiet, 1920–1933* (Bonn, 1974).

5. For a guide to the *Sonderweg* debate, see Robert G. Moeller, "The Kaiserreich Recast? Continuity and Change in Modern German Historiography," *Journal of Social History* 17 (1984): 655–83.

6. See Simone Lässig and Karl Heinrich Pohl, eds., *Sachsen im Kaiserreich: Politik, Wirtschaft und Gesellschaft im Umbruch* (Weimar, 1997).

the bourgeoisie fought this approach vehemently. They pursued policies that clung to traditional values and were marked by a fear of social leveling.

Saxon society was further burdened by a deep-rooted structural problem: an economy that had largely failed to modernize its traditional industries (particularly textiles) following early industrialization. During the Weimar Republic, Saxony's export-oriented industries suffered because of increasing competition and restrictions on trade. As in the rest of Germany, its economic development was also hampered by the dire consequences of the defeat in the war. Consequently, Saxony tended to be hit earlier, harder, and longer by economic downturns than most other regions in the Republic.

The persistence of authoritarian mentalities and the legacies of political confrontation proved to be a major obstacle to the acceptance of democratic principles. That blockage made political cooperation between the Left and Right — a prerequisite for the successful functioning of the Weimar Republic — extremely difficult. Together with long-standing economic problems, this difficulty helps explain why more and more Saxons eventually turned away from the Republican system from the late 1920s onward, and why a growing number were attracted by the alternative vision of a National Socialist revival in a Third Reich. It would be wrong, however, to construct from this a determinist explanation of German misdevelopment along the lines of the *Sonderweg* theory, because this would neglect equally important medium-term and short-term causes and would fail to take the Nazis' own contribution seriously.

Several historians have regarded the enormous crisis that German society faced after the First World War to be the primary cause for Nazism.[7] Indeed, the trauma of the "national humiliation" of November 1918 stood at the heart of the wider *völkisch* movement and its opposition to the Republic. Combined with the shock of the 1917 Bolshevik Revolution in Russia, many of these sentiments and anxieties were shared by broad strata of Saxon society. Additionally, the years after the war were marked by economic difficulties, social unrest, and political polarization. The Social Democrats' "left-Republican project" between 1922 and 1923 — exemplified by progressive reforms in the fields of education, church-state relations, the municipal code, the protection of consumer interests, and attempts to democratize the civil service and the judiciary[8] — was regarded as too radical. Such reforms were deemed to

---

7. See, for example, Geoff Eley, "What Produces Fascism: Pre-industrial Traditions or a Crisis of the Capitalist State?" in idem, *From Unification to Nazism: Reinterpreting the German Past* (reprint, London, 1992), 254–82, here 275.

8. See Karsten Rudolph, *Die sächsische Sozialdemokratie vom Kaiserreich zur Republik (1871–1923)* (Weimar, 1995).

exceed the "limits of acceptability" in the eyes of the majority of the bourgeoisie and the traditional elites.[9] Many of the bourgeoisie's views, by contrast, were seen as reactionary by organized labor. The manner in which Social Democratic–Communist rule was illegally and brutally smashed by the Reich in October 1923 — urged on and applauded by large sectors of the Saxon bourgeoisie — left little hope for political compromise or stability in Saxony. Furthermore, it became clear that the Saxon bourgeoisie was prepared to undermine the democratic framework itself, in order to defend or reconquer positions of power.

Hence the postwar period revived and deepened traditional battle lines in the new democratic environment. It also allowed extremists such as the Nazis to start linking up with more "respectable" and moderate segments within nationalist circles. For example, they found common ground in their opposition to the secularization of education. They jointly opposed a school curriculum that, instead of emphasizing nationalist and Christian beliefs, tried to foster democratic values and a toleration of other customs and beliefs. They also condemned or disrupted theater performances with a socialist or antinationalist message.

Throughout the Weimar period, however, neither nationalists nor socialists were able to govern Saxony with a coherent program over a sustained period of time. Neither side was united enough, nor able to increase a fragile advantage in the *Landtag,* to fashion a dominant position over the longer term. Eventually the Nazis convinced a large part of the Saxon population that they had found a new solution to their troubles, one that replaced divisiveness with unity, uncertainty with boldness: this was the National Socialist *Volksgemeinschaft* (national community).

III.   Beginnings of Nazi Organization in Saxony

The beginning of the Nazi movement in Saxony was similar to that in other parts of Germany. The first Nazi followers were radical antisemites and extreme nationalists who became activated by their disappointment with the outcome of the war and their rejection of the newly created Republic. Most Nazis were members of other *völkisch* groups or paramilitary formations. They joined the NSDAP due to its radicalism or because these other groups disintegrated over the years. Given that Saxony had been an extremely fertile ground for antisemites during Wilhelmine Germany, it was not surprising that the Nazi movement quickly emerged in the region. A few devoted activists who had come

---

9. See Donald Tracey, "Reform in the Early Weimar Republic: The Thuringian Example," *Journal of Modern History* 44, no. 2 (1972): 195–212, here 211–12; and Lapp, *Revolution from the Right,* 71.

into contact with the Nazis in Munich set up local party branches. Fritz Tittmann founded the first NSDAP branch in Saxony in Zwickau on 11 October 1921; this represented the fourth Nazi Party branch outside Bavaria. From Zwickau the movement spread to other districts of Saxony, particularly the southwest.

When Walther Rathenau, the Jewish German foreign minister, was assassinated by right-wing fanatics in June 1922, the NSDAP was prohibited in almost every state in Germany. In Saxony all Nazi meetings and parades were banned at the end of the year, after the local police had blamed increasing Nazi activities for the "uneasy political atmosphere."[10] When the Nazis continued to meet, a complete ban of the NSDAP followed in March 1923. As in other parts of Germany, however, the Saxon Nazis were extremely flexible in continuing their club activities underground, making it difficult for the police to intervene. Officials were also frequently lenient toward Nazi offenders. Nevertheless, one should not play down the impact of police surveillance and the reality of house searches and imprisonment. The Nazis also faced persistent pressure from the left-wing workers' movement — particularly the "proletarian hundreds" (*Proletarische Hundertschaften*) — who searched suspects for weapons and disrupted Nazi meetings. All this strengthened the Nazis' hatred of the Republican system and increased the internal cohesion of their Saxon wing.

In 1923 the Nazi movement in Saxony was still extremely small and only loosely organized. This was a common feature of the movement outside Bavaria. There were only ten NSDAP party branches and sixteen bases scattered across western Saxony, with a total of only several hundred members.[11] Followers tended to meet once a week in pubs. They came in contact with people with similar nationalist sentiments at nationalist celebrations and commemorations. These occasions included "German Days" (*Deutsche Tage*), the consecration and cultivation of war memorials, reunion celebrations of war veterans, celebrations of the foundation of the German Empire on 18 January, and gymnastic displays. These nationalist circles — which included an extremely broad section of bourgeois and upper-class society — also propagated the stab-in-the-back legend, and they were united in their opposition to Republican symbols and celebrations: for example, the commemoration of the November 1918 Revolution or the Republican black, red, and gold flag. As in other parts of Germany, Saxon Nazism was still mainly an urban

---

10. Bundesarchiv, Zwischenarchiv Dahlwitz-Hoppegarten (hereafter BA DH), Z/A VI 2029, Dresden, 9 Dec. 1922. Quoted from Szejnmann, *Nazism in Central Germany*, 27.

11. See BA DH, Z/C 17411, Zwickau, 23 Mar. 1923.

phenomenon in these early years. Although members came from all social classes, including workers, middle-class men were proportionally overrepresented.

Nazi activists in Saxony and other states were only loosely integrated into plans for the attempted coup in Munich. Its sudden failure prevented their active participation. When Hitler was imprisoned between late 1923 and late 1924 and the Nazis were banned throughout Germany, the NSDAP organization in Saxony disintegrated. However, some hard-core Saxon activists stayed together and joined the Völkisch Socialist Bloc (Völkisch-sozialer Block) and the National Socialist Freedom Movement (Nationalsozialistische Freiheitsbewegung) during the May and November 1924 Reichstag elections respectively. In contrast to many other areas of Germany, the Nazis dominated these alliances. The *völkisch* alliances in Saxony did not do particularly well in either election; but they achieved some striking results in the Vogtland, the southwestern corner of the state.[12] A significant event was the appointment of Martin Mutschmann as state leader (*Landesleiter*) of the *völkisch* alliance in Saxony in 1924. Mutschmann was a textile manufacturer from Plauen and a loyal follower of Hitler. From Plauen, the largest town of the Vogtland, the power-hungry Mutschmann rebuilt the Saxon NSDAP after Hitler's release from Landsberg prison. His increasing hold over the local movement prevented his *Gau* from being divided into smaller *Gaue* — as happened in several other cases.[13]

The period 1925–28 witnessed the slow transformation of the NSDAP into a more efficient and centralized organization geared toward seizing power through electoral means. The Nazis also demonstrated the ability to attract a hard core of devoted activists. Both developments enabled the Nazis to exploit the economic crisis that hit Germany in the late 1920s. The Nazis, and in particular the storm troopers, made up for their lack of numbers with activism and outpaced all bourgeois parties in terms of propaganda activities. Ancillary organizations were created to target all groups in society. Of national significance was that Kurt Gruber built up the Nazi youth organization in Plauen and became the first leader of the Hitler Youth in 1926. Wilhelm Tempel founded the National Socialist Student Association in Leipzig in the same year. The Nazis also introduced a weekly *Gau*

---

12. Thus in May 1924 the Völkisch Socialist Bloc gained 19 percent of the vote in the town of Plauen, and 17.6 percent in the administrative district (*Amtshauptmannschaft*) of Oelsnitz.

13. For example, the Ruhr *Gau* was divided into three *Gaue* in October 1928. See Albrecht Tyrell, *Führer befiehl . . . Selbstzeugnisse aus der 'Kampfzeit' der NSDAP* (reprint, Leipzig, 1991), 373–76.

newspaper.[14] Nevertheless, in late 1928 the Saxon NSDAP, similar to the rest of Germany, was still an extremely small political force that often resembled a chaotic movement. The NSDAP gained only 2.7 percent of the vote in the 1928 Reichstag elections in Saxony (the national average was 2.6 percent). However, although Saxon society had entered a comparatively tranquil period in the years 1925–28, dark clouds loomed. The overthrow of the working-class government in Dresden in 1923 had engraved divisions and hatred onto Saxon society. Furthermore, the consequences of hyperinflation and continuous economic strain had started the impoverishment and slow radicalization of a growing number of citizens. That radicalization in turn sparked a political fragmentation of the middle classes that became evident earlier, and developed more dramatically, in Saxony than in any other German state.[15]

It is striking that the Saxon Nazis were able to make substantial headway in some areas but continued to be hardly present in others until the early 1930s. Social, cultural, and economic conditions locally determined whether devoted leaders were more or less likely to emerge, and whether or not they would be able to build up a stable network of followers. In the Vogtland and the Erzgebirge, which later became two of the greatest Nazi strongholds in Germany, the Nazis were a natural successor to the Pan-German League (Alldeutscher Verband) and the antisemitic parties. Both groups had flourished in these districts before the First World War, due to social and ethnic tensions caused by immigration of cheap Czech labor from across the border.[16] Other contributing factors included Saxony's role as a transit station for emigrants from the east, and popular disillusionment with the inability of the traditional parties to respond to economic crisis. These were also environments where political upheaval after the war had created strong tensions and where a large number of people were affected by long-term economic decline. Substantial parts of the widespread textile and cottage industry literally faced being wiped out. The proximity to Bavaria also fostered contacts between Nazis across the border. For the extreme Right, Bavaria became a "safe haven" from restrictive laws and harassment in Saxony until the end of 1923.

---

14. *Der Nationale Sozialist für Sachsen* and its successor, the *Sächsischer Beobachter,* were published by the Straßers' Kampfverlag in Berlin. After the expulsion of Otto Straßer from the NSDAP, the Saxon Nazis founded their own daily newspaper, *Der Freiheitskampf,* in August 1930.

15. See the contribution by Larry Eugene Jones in this volume; and Lapp, *Revolution from the Right.*

16. For this, see Roger Chickering, *We Men Who Feel Most German: A Cultural Study of the Pan-German League, 1886–1914* (London, 1984); and Richard S. Levy, *The Downfall of the Anti-Semitic Political Parties in Imperial Germany* (London, 1975).

The eastern part of Saxony, which was furthest away from the Vogtland and Bavaria, was an area where the Nazis made little headway until the early 1930s. Local Nazis complained about a lack of support from their party and the difficulty of organizing propaganda in the numerous small villages. Moreover, the Nazis' nationalist and racist views were not popular among the 28,000 Sorbs (a Slav ethnic group) who lived in the area. Although a few Nazis started to become active in northwestern and central Saxony in late 1922, particularly in Leipzig and Dresden, here too the Nazis did not find favorable conditions for growth or local influence until the late 1920s. They were often hampered by personal rivalries. They also faced fierce competition from other *völkisch* parties and opposition from a particularly strong working-class movement.

IV.   Nazi Gains after 1929 and the Socialist and Nationalist Milieus

One can identify three important factors that fueled the dramatic rise of Nazism in the region from 1929 onward: the effects of the slump and the helpless reaction of the traditional parties and organizations; the disintegration of traditional social structure; and the Nazis' specific skills in exploiting the crisis. Although it is widely accepted that the economic depression and the collapse of the Weimar Republic stood in close relation to each other, it is surprising how little attention most local and regional studies of Nazism have paid to the exact linkages between the slump and growing support for the NSDAP.[17] Saxony was hit harder by the economic crisis than any other region in Germany. The number of bankruptcies per capita in Saxony was far above the Reich average between 1926 and 1932, and in mid-1929 Saxony's unemployment rate suddenly shot up far above those of other states. Nevertheless, it is extremely difficult to prove a clear relationship between the severity of the economic crisis and the strength of Nazism at the micro level of villages, towns, and cities. It is more fruitful to view the slump as a catalyst that opened up tremendous opportunities for Nazism. The Nazis profited disproportionately from a widespread feeling of anxiety due to the daily experience of misery, insecurity, social disturbances, pressures of change, and fragmentation. Their radical vision was able to gain popular support because the whole system seemed to collapse.

Recent evidence suggests that the NSDAP managed to attract voters and members from all groups in society, including a substantial stratum of workers.[18] The influential theory that Nazism was predominantly

---

17. See, for example, Böhnke, *Ruhrgebiet.*

18. See Conan J. Fischer, ed., *The Rise of National Socialism and the Working Classes in Weimar Germany* (Oxford, 1996).

a middle-class phenomenon[19] neglects the existence and motivation of the wider Nazi constituency. The recently rediscovered concept of milieu offers a wider conceptual framework than class analysis and allows for new insights into two crucial questions. Why did so many Germans, who were divided by so many other things, unite to support Nazism? And with special relevance to our discussion: Why were the brownshirts successful in working-class Saxony?

M. Rainer Lepsius explained the remarkable stability of the German party system from the beginning of the German Empire to the late 1920s by drawing attention to the deep roots parties had struck in various social structures, which he called milieus.[20] According to his argument, after about 1928 various milieus in German society "slowly disintegrated" due to "progressive industrialization, increasing mobility, and social differentiation." This disintegration in turn contributed to the collapse of the traditional party system. The Nazis were the main beneficiary of this development.

Many of Lepsius's observations hold true for Saxony. Nevertheless, whereas Lepsius identified four different milieus (conservative, liberal, Social Democratic, and Catholic), the liberal and Catholic milieus were hardly developed in Saxony. This meant that there was a particular polarization between the socialist and the nationalist milieus in the region. Some parts of the socialist milieu started to disintegrate because they were increasingly unable to perform their primary function: providing satisfactory living and workplace conditions for the masses in a modernizing environment. The Nazis skillfully contrasted former promises by the labor movement with the deteriorating conditions for workers in the Republic. The Nazis blamed this situation on the Social Democrats for not having carried out a proper revolution after the war and for selling out Germany with the Treaty of Versailles. One Saxon Nazi asked provokingly in parliament: "What, then, is the worker supposed to defend? Should the German worker even bother to defend his misery and desperation?"[21] The apparent distance between the potentially emancipatory Republican project and "the lived reality of modernity"[22] made

19. See especially Theodor Geiger, "Panik im Mittelstand," *Die Arbeit* 7 (1930): 643–52; and Seymour M. Lipset, " 'Fascism'—Left, Right, and Center," in *Political Man: The Social Bases of Politics,* ed. idem (New York, 1960), 127–79.

20. See M. Rainer Lepsius, "Parteiensystem und Sozialstruktur: Zum Problem der Demokratisierung der deutschen Gesellschaft," in *Die deutschen Parteien vor 1918,* ed. Gerhard A. Ritter (Cologne, 1973), 56–80. This survey uses the term *milieu* to describe a strong centralization of a specific culture in the form of mentalities and ways of life that were linked to political orientation.

21. *Verhandlungen des Sächsischen Landtages,* 5. Wahlperiode, 18. Sitzung, 700, 11 Dec. 1930. Quoted from Szejnmann, *Nazism in Central Germany,* 243.

22. See Helen Graham and Jo Labanyi, eds., *Spanish Cultural Studies: An Introduction: The Struggle for Modernity* (Oxford, 1996), 15.

many Saxons eventually turn to Nazism. The Nazis were increasingly regarded as a major voice of protest against anxiety, misery, and political failure. Moreover, Nazism seemed to provide a promising alternative to the existing system.

Whereas the unfolding crisis provided the vital background for radicalization, the question as to whether particular Saxons would actually join the Nazi bandwagon depended largely on social and cultural circumstances. The majority of Saxon workers were not tempted by Nazism. Northwestern and central Saxony became the great bastion of the German labor movement before the Nazi seizure of power. The deep-rooted socialist traditions in the region explain why local working-class voters were largely immune to Nazism until 1930 — longer than in the rest of the Reich. The local strength of the socialist milieu determined whether the Nazis failed or succeeded in attracting a substantial number of workers as members and voters. The less widespread, deep-rooted, and active the Social Democratic Party and its organizational network was, the less able it was to ward off and respond to the enormous challenges posed by the Nazis and the economic crisis.[23] The SPD — leaving aside the more obvious case of the German Communist Party (Kommunistische Partei Deutschlands, or KPD) — also failed to make significant inroads into the bourgeois constituency and turn itself into a people's party. Although the Social Democrats were committed to the Republic, they clung to an unrealistic socialist rhetoric: they were reluctant to make compromises with other groups, and they frequently cut themselves off from the rest of Saxon society. Moreover, the revolutionary strategy of the Communists split the workers' milieu and weakened its potential to respond to Nazism. While the majority of workers who belonged to the socialist milieu stayed loyal to the Republic, a growing minority demanded nothing less than a socialist revolution.

Whereas the SPD's claim that it could deliver a better world was undermined by the economic slump, the nationalists were poised to benefit from the crisis. Saxon nationalists had a long history of criticizing or opposing the Weimar "system." However, the many compromises all nationalist parties made with the Republican system during the 1920s,

---

23. The Social Democrats possessed by far the largest party organization in the state and were by far the largest group in the Saxon *Landtag*. We have "measured" the "strength" of the socialist milieu by comparing local SPD organizations according to various criteria. These criteria included the loyalty and commitment of followers to the party during the slump; the cultivation of socialist traditions; and the existence and size of socialist ancillary organizations. The socialist milieu was further strengthened by solid working-class neighborhoods, unionization, and a degree of cooperation between SPD and KPD. See Szejnmann, *Nazism in Central Germany*, chap. 3. Also see Franz Walter, "Sachsen — Ein Stammland der Sozialdemokratie," *Politische Vierteljahresschrift* 32, no. 2 (1991): 207–31.

together with their failure to respond to increasing desperation in their traditional constituencies, cost their political representatives dearly. As elsewhere in Germany, the majority of the Saxon middle classes eventually turned their back on the "stuffy and elitist politics of patronage and personality."[24] Either they turned to Nazism directly, or they affiliated themselves with it via special interest groups.

The slump radicalized most bourgeois clubs, whether they were oriented toward professional interests or leisure pursuits. A growing number of their members, especially younger ones, left these clubs or struggled to keep up with their membership dues. This led to a decline in club activities, leaving many clubs with heavy burdens of debt. An increasing number of club members expressed the view that an authoritarian, nationalist state was the only solution to the crisis, and began to sympathize with Nazism. More and more newspapers of the influential bourgeois press were openly supporting the NSDAP. Many local industrialists and employers finally lost their patience with a Republic that they regarded as an economic liability.[25] This development was fostered by the irresponsible strategy of the bourgeois parties, which defended political majorities against the Left by exaggerating the (unrealistic) threat of a "Soviet Saxony." The use of an increasingly aggressive language to pull together the fragmented *Bürgertum* heightened tensions and polarized society further. Anti-Marxist rhetorical excesses also drew more people toward Nazism as the most determined enemy of the Left. All these developments played into the hands of the Nazis. Although the Saxon NSDAP by the end of the Weimar Republic managed to attract members and voters from all social classes (including a substantial number of workers), the middle classes continued to be overrepresented, as they were on the national level. The Nazis' fresh image and determined appearance, coupled with their espousal of familiar values — nationalism, authoritarianism, and anti-Marxism — made them not only respectable in the eyes of many, but also the legitimate leaders of the nationalist milieu in Saxony.

Divisions between the nationalist milieu and the socialist milieu constituted one of the most fundamental experiences of Saxon society. Often such divisions were more apparent than real, however, and they normally served a specific political agenda. Most importantly, the nationalists claimed to represent a clear-cut choice between a bourgeois-nationalist government and a bolshevist regime. The SPD, however,

---

24. See Koshar, *Marburg*, 230.
25. See Claus-Christian W. Szejnmann, "Sächsische Unternehmer und die Weimarer Demokratie: Zur Rolle der sächsischen Unternehmer in der Zeit der Weltwirtschaftskrise und des Aufstiegs des Nationalsozialismus," in *Unternehmer in Sachsen: Aufstieg—Krise—Untergang—Neubeginn*, ed. Ulrich Heß et al. (Leipzig, 1998), 165–79.

firmly backed the Republic. Only the comparatively small Communist Party stood for a socialization of society. Furthermore, far from forming a united anti-Marxist bloc, the bourgeois parties and organizations were bitterly divided. In other words: distinguishing between the socialist milieu and nationalist milieu should not suggest any clear-cut or static division between them, or any homogeneity within either one. On the contrary, these milieus were dynamic phenomena that could grow, shrink, disintegrate, shift, and even overlap with one another. Indeed, the Nazis' skill was to combine nationalist and socialist values by promising to establish social justice in a strong nationalist state. To them, and to their supporters, this was not a contradiction of terms, but the only way social justice and solidarity between Germans could be realized.

In 1929 the Nazis achieved many local and regional breakthroughs that prepared the way for their "takeoff" nationally in 1930. The increasing momentum of the Saxon Nazi movement was also evident in the growth of party membership, in the number of party branches, and in expanding propaganda activities. Nazi gains in Saxony's *Landtag* elections of May 1929 and the acquisition of five seats suddenly gave them the key position in Saxony's parliament between the SPD's and KPD's forty-five seats and the bourgeois parties' forty-six seats. Subsequently, NSDAP headquarters in Munich focused considerable attention on Saxony for more than a year. A Saxon government was only formed after the Nazis, contrary to their previous antiparliamentary agitation, indicated that they would tolerate a "Marxist-free" government under Wilhelm Bünger of the German People's Party (Deutsche Volkspartei).[26]

V. The End of Parliamentary Democracy in Saxony

The developments in Saxony from June 1929 onward were an important watershed for the NSDAP. They exposed the dilemma of those party members — in particular Otto Straßer and his *Kampfverlag* in Berlin — who followed a radical revolutionary strategy of uncompromising disruption and who regarded "red" Saxony as belonging to their sphere of influence. To Hitler, tactical cooperation with the bourgeois government in Saxony opened up the chance for the Nazis to gain the ministry of the interior and hence was a crucial step toward power in Berlin. This strategy also appeased the Nazis' bourgeois voters. In that sense, developments in Saxony from June 1929 onward laid the foundation for Wilhelm Frick's participation in the government in Thuringia in early 1930.

---

26. Hitler, who had participated in the election campaign with the Nazi elite, masterminded the negotiations with Bünger. He considered raising the demand that Wilhelm Frick be appointed minister of the interior. This, however, was not a viable proposition.

But the same developments led to the expulsion of Otto Straßer and his followers when they bitterly opposed negotiations for a NSDAP coalition government with the bourgeoisie after the Saxon *Landtag* elections in June 1930.

The Nazis' toleration of Bünger's cabinet in mid-1929 reflected their cynical political tactics: they could drop their support whenever it suited them. Eventually, when Bünger advocated ratification of the Young Plan, the Nazis forced his resignation: their motion of no confidence was supported by a *Landtag* majority in February 1930. The fall of Bünger's government led to a state of political limbo. Eventually the Nazis supported a motion by the SPD and KPD to dissolve the *Landtag*. New elections were scheduled for 22 June 1930.

In those elections, the Nazis achieved their greatest electoral breakthrough in an important German state. They became by far the largest non-Marxist party in Saxony, with 14.4 percent of the vote. They benefited mainly from the dramatic decline of the traditional bourgeois parties and by the successful mobilization of former nonvoters. Another factor contributing to their strong showing was that their national headquarters, with Goebbels as newly appointed chief of propaganda, had concentrated its efforts on the campaign in Saxony. However, the Nazi strategy to create a central German bloc of National Socialist domination together with neighboring Thuringia did not come to fruition. Although most bourgeois parties supported the Nazis' bid to obtain the post of the minister of the interior for Gregor Straßer in a new coalition cabinet,[27] the proposal failed due to the resistance of the German Democratic Party (Deutsche Demokratische Partei) and the People's National Reich Association (Volksnationale Reichsvereinigung). As no agreement for a new government was reached, the "cabinet of civil servants" under Walther Schieck, which had come into existence in May 1930, continued to govern Saxony until its dissolution by the Nazis in March 1933.

Earlier and more openly than in other German states, genuine parliamentary democracy came to an end in Saxony in mid-1930. Like their party colleagues in the Reichstag, the Saxon Social Democrats grasped the nettle and tolerated Schieck's right-wing bourgeois government in order to keep the Nazis from gaining power. The Nazis had every right to feel frustrated. On the one hand, the NSDAP was growing at a breathtaking rate: it became by far the largest party in Saxony with 41.2 percent of the vote in the Reichstag elections in July 1932. The party also possessed

---

27. Hitler publicized comparatively moderate demands in the *Völkischer Beobachter* and participated personally in the coalition negotiations in Dresden. See *Völkischer Beobachter,* no. 149, 25 June 1930.

an enormous network of ancillary organizations. On the other hand, as at the Reich level, the Saxon Nazis continued to be excluded from power. Like their comrades elsewhere in Germany, they were facing decline and serious internal problems at the end of 1932.

The dismal outlook changed only when Hitler was appointed chancellor in January 1933. Subsequently the Nazis mobilized all their energies for the Reichstag elections on 5 March. During that campaign, Saxony seemed more radicalized and polarized than ever. Whereas the NSDAP's share of the vote in Saxony rose to 45 percent, thanks mainly to its strength in the southwest, Saxony was also still the great bastion of Marxism in Germany. The SPD and KPD together gained 42.7 percent of the vote, compared to only 30.6 percent in the whole Republic. Nowhere in Germany had support for the middle-class parties collapsed more dramatically than in Saxony. They gained a mere 12.3 percent of the vote there, whereas their national average was still 25.5 percent.

As in the rest of the Reich, the Nazis exploited the momentum created by the March election and seized power with great speed. Manfred von Killinger, a prominent Saxon Nazi leader and high-ranking storm trooper, became prime minister. Martin Mutschmann headed the NSDAP organization as Reich governor (*Reichstatthalter*) of Saxony.[28] Meanwhile, the SA and SS unleashed a wave of violence against the Nazis' foremost enemies, Marxists and Jews. The socialist milieu was smashed or disintegrated, except for a hard core of socialist activists. More than one-sixth of all concentration camps in the Reich were on Saxon soil in 1933. The number of people affected by the Nazi seizure of power widened gradually. The traditional nationalist milieu — its organizations, celebrations, and newspapers — was Nazified. Step by step, the Nazis stamped their racial ideology onto society. Saxony's 23,000 Jews were subject to increasing isolation, dehumanization, and eventual deportation to the extermination camps in the east. The Slav Sorbs were "Germanized," and Gustav Boeters's experiments with euthanasia and sterilization in the area of Zwickau during the Weimar Republic were followed by the killing of the mentally ill and sick in local "sanatoriums" during the Second World War.

VI. Conclusions

The Nazis themselves had contributed heavily to their rise and success in Saxony. Unfortunately, most historians have played down the Nazis' popular appeal, stressing aspects of manipulation and opportunism or

---

28. Mutschmann took over the sole leadership in Saxony after his rival Killinger fell victim to the SA purge in June 1934.

focusing on the failure and disintegration of their opponents.[29] Recently, Geoff Eley rightly called on historians to examine "the connotative principles . . . that allowed the Nazis to capture the popular imagination so powerfully before and after 1933."[30] The tendency to look at Nazism with the benefit of hindsight, constantly equating it with barbaric mass murder and extermination, has limited our understanding of the Nazis' appeal, especially before 1933. Nazism has often been described in simple terms: either as something alien to German society (i.e., it was uniquely radical, violent, racist, antisemitic, etc.), or — paradoxically — as reflecting the evil nature of German society itself. Variations on the latter view range from the "moderate" *Sonderweg* theory that many Germans shared authoritarian and antidemocratic beliefs, to the thesis that a bloodthirsty and "eliminationist" antisemitism was entrenched in German society.[31]

Nazism in Saxony was a complex phenomenon. It was a new, radical, and dynamic movement. But it also possessed features that appeared "normal" to many contemporaries. The Nazis' most crucial contribution to their own success was that they managed to hijack and monopolize the concept of the *Volksgemeinschaft.* This concept had already attracted those who had attempted to reconcile national and social integration from 1900 onward.[32] The experience of the First World War seemed to confirm that national solidarity was the "prerequisite to social liberation," for only such solidarity was deemed by members of Saxony's *Bürgertum* to guarantee the security and prosperity of individuals and the whole nation. After 1918 this consensus between the political parties disintegrated. The Nazis became the only political force that continued to focus on the nation as a whole and did not follow the other parties' retreat to particular constituencies. As Saxon society became increasingly fragmented and polarized, the promised *Volksgemeinschaft* appeared able to replace traditional divisions with harmony and unity.

---

29. For example, Helge Matthiesen's and Oded Heilbronner's sole emphasis on the "vacuum" the Nazis were able to fill in the town of Gotha and the Black Forest region seems to neglect the Nazis' own contribution to this development. See Helge Matthiesen, *Bürgertum und Nationalsozialismus in Thüringen: Das bügerliche Gotha von 1918 bis 1930* (Jena, 1994), 218–19; and Oded Heilbronner, "Der verlassene Stammtisch: Vom Verfall der bürgerlichen Infrastruktur und dem Aufstieg der NSDAP am Beispiel der Region Schwarzwald," *Geschichte und Gesellschaft* 19, no. 2 (1993): 178–201.

30. Geoff Eley, "Is There a History of the *Kaiserreich?*" in *Society, Culture, and the State in Germany, 1870–1930,* ed. idem (Ann Arbor, MI, 1996), 1–42, here 30.

31. See Daniel Goldhagen, *Hitler's Willing Executioners: Ordinary Germans and the Holocaust* (London, 1996).

32. For this see Gunther Mai, "National Socialist Factory Cell Organisation and the German Labour Front: National Socialist Labour Policy and Organisations," in *The Rise of National Socialism,* ed. Fischer, 117–36, here 124.

Hardly any expert in the field has maintained that there was a clearly defined Nazi program. However, it is crucial to see support for Nazism not only as a "negative" choice — a protest against a system that did not work,[33] or the result of irrational behavior[34] — but also as an active decision to give the Nazis a chance to put into practice their solution to the problems faced by society. The recent argument by the sociologist William Brustein that economic reasons were the "dominant motivation" for Germans to join the Nazi Party seems too extreme.[35] The evidence from Saxony nevertheless suggests that materialistic motivations did play an important role in driving many Germans toward Nazism. During the slump, all traditional parties focused on short-term strategies in order to patch up the most severe problems. They were clearly fighting a losing battle because of their financial limitations and their adherence to an orthodox economic approach that focused on balancing the budget. The Saxon Nazis supported many of these measures to ease some of the most immediate burdens: for instance, the particular misery in the region bordering Czechoslovakia. Yet the Nazis also labeled these policies as being a limited and shortsighted response. In their view, only radical reforms and large-scale programs financed by budget deficits (e.g., work programs) would pull Germany out of depression and ensure long-term growth and stability.

The Saxon Nazis also clearly aligned themselves against what they identified as the larger causes of Germany's misery. They offered sweeping reforms that allegedly would benefit nearly all Germans (though not the Jews and other racially "unfit" groups). In their view, the western powers had exploited Germany and prevented its revival since the country's defeat in the First World War. Only a united German *Volk* could free itself from this dilemma. By ridding Germany of the burdens of the First World War, the Nazis also promised to wipe out international capitalism. As Saxony was dominated by small- and medium-scale business, the Saxon middle and working classes felt particularly threatened by unrestricted large-scale capitalism and were desperate for some kind of protection.

Lastly, the Nazis' dynamic mass mobilization played a vital role in their electoral success in Saxony. The NSDAP was the first political party within the nationalist milieu to possess propaganda machinery that

---

33. Recently it has become fashionable to describe Nazism as a "people's party of protest." See, inter alia, Jürgen W. Falter, *Hitlers Wähler* (Munich, 1991), 371.

34. See, for example, George L. Mosse, *The Nationalization of the Masses: Political Symbolism and Mass Movements in Germany from the Napoleonic Wars through the Third Reich* (New York, 1975).

35. William Brustein, *The Logic of Evil: The Social Origins of the Nazi Party, 1925–1933* (London, 1996).

was broad-based and active year-round. That machinery carried the Nazi message to all citizens and challenged the Left for control of the streets. The skillful mixture of broad themes and specific appeals, combined with a reputation for dynamic youthfulness and unbending determination, helps explain why the Nazis were so successful in mobilizing former nonvoters and attracting voters from other parties. In places where Nazi propaganda dominated public life, where nationalist sentiments existed, and where they encountered the least opposition from their political opponents, the NSDAP's electoral performance was most successful. The Nazis, however, found it difficult to overcome deep-rooted Saxon traditions that proved resistant to their message.

Although Saxony's democratic system crumbled at the end of Weimar, it did not fall. The Nazis failed to take over the state government as they had done in Anhalt, Oldenburg, Mecklenburg-Schwerin, neighboring Thuringia, and Prussia. Their "seizure of power" was mainly the result of events that took place outside Saxony. Nevertheless, more and more Saxons supported, or at least endorsed, the Nazis' authoritarian solution to the crisis. The Nazis' championing of familiar nationalist and socialist values goes a long way in explaining this affinity. In the end, Hitler's followers were guaranteed a comparatively smooth seizure of power and stable rule — even in "red" Saxony.

Contributors

THOMAS ADAM received his D.Phil. from the University of Leipzig in 1998. He is currently a Feodor Lynen Research Fellow of the Alexander von Humboldt Foundation at the University of Toronto. His publications include *Leipzig—Wiege der deutschen Sozialdemokratie* (with M. Rudloff and J. Schlimper; Berlin, 1996); *Die sächsischen Wohnungsbaugenossenschaften in der DDR* (Leipzig, 1997); *Die Anfänge industriellen Bauens in Sachsen* (Leipzig, 1998); and *Arbeitermilieu und Arbeiterbewegung in Leipzig 1871–1933* (Cologne, Weimer, Vienna, 1999). He is currently writing a comparative cultural study of philanthropic foundations in German and North American cities during the nineteenth century.

CELIA APPLEGATE received her Ph.D. from Stanford University in 1987. She is Associate Professor of History at the University of Rochester. She has published *A Nation of Provincials: The German Idea of Heimat* (Berkeley, CA, 1990). Her essays include "Democracy or Reaction? The Political Implications of Localist Ideas in Wilhelmine and Weimar Germany," in *Elections, Mass Politics, and Social Change in Modern Germany*, ed. L. E. Jones and J. Retallack (New York, 1992); and "A Europe of Regions: Reflections on the Historiography of Sub-National Places in Modern Times," *American Historical Review* 104 (1999). She is currently writing a book on music and German nationalism in the nineteenth century.

PÁLL BJÖRNSSON received his Ph.D. from the University of Rochester in 1999 with a dissertation entitled "Making the New Man: Liberal Politics and Associational Life in Leipzig, 1845–1871." He is a postdoctoral fellow at the Center for Research in Humanities at the University of Iceland. His current research interests include the history of liberalism, gender, and national identities in nineteenth-century central and northern Europe.

BRETT FAIRBAIRN received his D.Phil. from the University of Oxford in 1987. Since then he has held a joint appointment at the University of

Saskatchewan in the History Department and at the Centre for the Study of Co-operatives. His publications include *Building a Dream: The Co-operative Retailing System in Western Canada, 1928–1988* (Saskatoon, 1989); *Dignity and Growth: Citizen Participation in Social Change* (ed. with H. Baker and J. Draper; Calgary, 1991); and *Democracy in the Undemocratic State: The German Reichstag Elections of 1898 and 1903* (Toronto, 1997). He is currently completing a book-length study of co-operative movements and German political culture from 1850 to the present.

CHRISTIAN JANSEN received his D.Phil. from the University of Heidelberg in 1989 and his Habil. from the Ruhr University Bochum in 1997. He is currently Adjunct Professor of Modern History at the University of Bochum. His major publications include *Einheit, Macht und Freiheit: Die Paulskirchenlinke und die deutsche Politik in der nachrevolutionären Epoche* (Düsseldorf, 2000); and *Professoren und Politik: Politisches Denken und Handeln der Heidelberger Hochschullehrer, 1914–1935* (Göttingen, 1992). He has also edited (with L. Niethammer and B. Weisbrod) *Von der Aufgabe der Freiheit: Gesellschaft und Politik im 19. und 20. Jahrhundert* (Berlin, 1995). As well as researching issues of nationalism and political legitimation in Germany, Italy, Switzerland, and Austria (1848–1945), he is completing a scholarly edition of liberal politicians' correspondence in the German Confederation (1849–71).

LARRY EUGENE JONES received his Ph.D. from the University of Wisconsin–Madison in 1970. He is Professor of History at Canisius College in Buffalo, New York. He is the author of *German Liberalism and the Dissolution of the Weimar Party System, 1918–1933* (Chapel Hill, NC, 1988) and co-editor of three anthologies on nineteenth- and twentieth-century German history, including *In Search of a Liberal Germany: Studies in the History of German Liberalism from 1789 to the Present* (with K. H. Jarausch; New York, 1990); and *Between Reform, Reaction, and Resistance: Studies in the History of German Conservatism from 1789 to 1945* (with J. Retallack; Providence, RI, 1993). He is currently completing a study of the German Right during the Weimar Republic and the role of Germany's conservative elites in the establishment of the Third Reich.

MARVEN KRUG received his Ph.D. from the University of Toronto in 1995. His dissertation, which was entitled "Civil Liberties in Imperial Germany," won the John Bullen Prize awarded by the Canadian Historical Association. Since 1998 he has been German Editor for the Internet bookseller Amazon.com.

THOMAS KÜHNE received his D.Phil. from the University of Tübingen in 1992. He is currently a research fellow of the Deutsche Forschungsgemeinschaft at the University of Bielefeld. His major publications include *Dreiklassenwahlrecht und Wahlkultur in Preußen, 1867–1914* (Düsseldorf, 1994); and *Handbuch der Wahlen zum Preußischen Abgeordnetenhaus, 1867–1918* (Düsseldorf, 1994). He is the editor of *Männergeschichte—Geschlechtergeschichte: Männlichkeit im Wandel der Moderne* (Frankfurt a. M., 1996) and the author of "Zwischen Männerbund und Volksgemeinschaft: Hitlers Soldaten und der Mythos der Kamaradshaft," *Archiv für Sozialgeschichte* 38 (1998). He is completing a cultural history of German soldiers and the myth of comradeship in the Second World War.

BENJAMIN LAPP received his Ph.D. from the University of California, Berkeley, in 1991 and holds an appointment as Associate Professor of History at Montclair State University, Montclair, New Jersey. He recently published *Revolution from the Right: Politics, Class, and the Rise of Nazism in Saxony, 1919–1933* (Atlantic Highlands, NJ, 1997). His essays include "A 'National' Socialism: The Old Socialist Party of Saxony, 1926–1932," *Journal of Contemporary History* 30 (1995); and "Der Aufstieg des Nationalsozialismus in Sachsen," in *Dresden unterm Hakenkreuz,* ed. R. Pommerin (Cologne, 1998). He is currently working on a history of Saxony under the Nazi dictatorship and a study of German-Jewish exiles.

SIMONE LÄSSIG received her D.Phil. from the Pädagogische Hochschule (now the Technical University) Dresden in 1990. She is Assistant Professor at the TU Dresden. Her publications include *Wahlrechtskampf und Wahlrechtsreform in Sachsen (1895–1909)* (Weimar, 1996); *Sachsen im Kaiserreich: Politik, Wirtschaft und Gesellschaft im Umbruch* (ed. with K. H. Pohl; Weimar, 1997); and *Landesgeschichte in Sachsen: Tradition und Innovation* (ed. with R. Aurig and S. Herzog; Bielefeld, 1997). Her essays have lately focused on the history of German Jews in the nineteenth and twentieth centuries, including "Juden und Mäzenatentum in Deutschland: Religiöses Ethos, kompensierendes Minderheitsverhalten oder genuine Bürgerlichkeit?" *Zeitschrift für Geschichtswissenschaft* 46 (1998). Her other research interests include enlightened absolutism in the German states and pre-1914 parliamentarism.

THOMAS MERGEL received his D.Phil. from the University of Bielefeld in 1992. He is Assistant Professor of Modern History and the Theory of History at the Ruhr University Bochum. He is the author of *Zwischen Klasse und Konfession: Katholisches Bürgertum im Rheinland, 1794–*

1914 (Göttingen, 1994). He has edited (with T. Welskopp) *Geschichte zwischen Kultur und Gesellschaft: Beiträge zur Theoriedebatte* (Munich, 1997); and (with C. Jansen) *Die Revolutionen von 1848/49: Erfahrung — Verarbeitung—Deutung* (Göttingen, 1998). His current historical research interests include religion, the middle classes, historiography, and political culture. He recently finished his Habilitation thesis, "Parlamentarische Kultur im Reichstag der Weimarer Republic. Politische Kommunication, symbolische Politik und Öffentlichkeit 1919–1933."

ANDREAS NEEMANN received his D.Phil. from the University of Tübingen in 1999. In 1997–98 he was a Research Fellow at the Institut für Sächsische Geschichte und Volkskunde e.V. in Dresden. His dissertation, entitled "Landtag und Politik in der Reaktionszeit: Sachsen, 1849/ 50 bis 1866," will soon be published. He has also published "Kontinuitäten und Brüche aus einzelstaatlicher Perspektive: Politische Milieus in Sachsen, 1848 bis 1850," in *Die Revolutionen von 1848/49,* ed. T. Mergel and C. Jansen (Göttingen, 1998).

CHRISTOPH NONN received his D.Phil. in 1993 from the University of Trier. He is Assistant Professor of History at the University of Cologne. His publications include *Verbraucherprotest und Parteiensystem im wilhelminischen Deutschland* (Düsseldorf, 1996). His recently published articles include "Putting Radicalism to the Test: German Social Democracy and the 1905 Suffrage Demonstrations in Dresden," *International Review of Social History* 41 (1996); and "Zwischenfall in Konitz: Antisemitismus und Nationalismus im preußischen Osten um 1900," *Historische Zeitschrift* 266 (1998). He is currently working on a study of antisemitic ritual murder rumors in modern Germany. A book entitled *Entindustrialisierung und Politik: Die Ruhrbergbaukrise 1958–1968* is forthcoming.

KARL HEINRICH POHL received his Ph.D. from the University of Hamburg in 1977 and his Habil. from the University of Bielefeld in 1989. He is Professor of History and Didactics at the Christian-Albrechts-University in Kiel. His publications include *Die Münchener Arbeiterbewegung: Sozialdemokratische Partei, Freie Gewerkschaften, Staat und Gesellschaft in München, 1890 bis 1914* (Munich, 1992); and *Adolf Müller: Geheimagent und Gesandter in Kaiserreich und Weimarer Republik* (Cologne, 1995). He has edited *Sachsen im Kaiserreich: Politik, Wirtschaft und Gesellschaft im Umbruch* (with S. Lässig; Weimar, 1997); and *Historiker in der DDR* (Göttingen, 1997). His current research interests include liberalism in the *Kaiserreich* and comparative regional history in the nineteenth and twentieth centuries.

JAMES RETALLACK received his D.Phil. from the University of Oxford in 1983. He is currently Professor of History and Chair of the Department of Germanic Languages and Literatures at the University of Toronto. He has published *Notables of the Right: The Conservative Party and Political Mobilization in Germany, 1876–1918* (London, 1988); and *Germany in the Age of Kaiser Wilhelm II* (Basingstoke, 1996). He has edited two volumes of essays with L. E. Jones (1992, 1993) and (with S. Lässig and K. H. Pohl) *Modernisierung und Region im wilhelminischen Deutschland* (Bielefeld, 1995; 2d ed. 1998). As well as completing the first of two studies of electoral culture and the authoritarian state in Saxony (1860–1918), he is currently writing books on the collapse of the German empire in 1918 and, with Peter Steinbach, on electoral culture and regionalism in German history (1830–1933).

KARSTEN RUDOLPH received his D.Phil. from the Ruhr University Bochum in 1993. He is Assistant Professor at the Institut für soziale Bewegungen at the Ruhr University. His publications include *Die sächsische Sozialdemokratie vom Kaiserreich zur Republik (1871–1923)* (Weimar, 1995). He has edited (with H. Grebing and H. Mommsen) *Demokratie und Emanzipation zwischen Saale und Elbe: Beiträge zur Geschichte der sozialdemokratischen Arbeiterbewegung bis 1933* (Essen, 1993); and (with C. Wickert) *Geschichte als Möglichkeit: Über die Chancen von Demokratie* (Essen, 1995). He is currently pursuing research on Ostpolitik in West German industry from 1945 to 1990 and on European political systems since 1945.

WOLFGANG SCHRÖDER received his D.Phil. from the University of Leipzig in 1963 and his Habil. from the Akademie der Wissenschaften in Berlin in 1972. He is currently a Research Associate with the Kommission für Geschichte des Parlamentarismus und der politischen Parteien in Bonn. His publications include *Klassenkämpfe und Gewerkschaftseinheit* (Berlin, 1965); *Wilhelm Liebknecht: Kleine politische Schriften* (Leipzig, 1976); *Ernestine: Vom ungewöhnlichen Leben der ersten Frau Wilhelm Liebknechts* (Leipzig, 1987); and a number of articles on Saxon politics in the 1860s and 1870s. He has also co-edited (with G. Seeber) *Bismarcks Sturz: Zur Rolle der Klassen in der Endphase des preußisch-deutschen Bonapartismus, 1884/85 bis 1890* (Berlin, 1977). He is currently completing a study of Saxon parliamentarism from 1866 to 1896.

HELMUT WALSER SMITH received his Ph.D. from Yale University in 1991 and is now Associate Professor of History at Vanderbilt University. He is the author of *German Nationalism and Religious Conflict: Culture, Ideology, Politics, 1870–1914* (Princeton, NJ, 1995). In addition to a number of articles on conflicts among Protestants, Catholics, and Jews in southwestern Germany, he is the author of "Geschichte zwischen den Fronten: Meisterwerke der neuesten Geschichtsschreibung und postmoderne Kritik," *Geschichte und Gesellschaft* 22 (1996). Currently completing a study of an alleged ritual murder case in Konitz, West Prussia, in the year 1900, he is also working on a social history of Bitterfeld from the Great Depression to the building of the Berlin Wall.

CLAUS-CHRISTIAN W. SZEJNMANN received his Ph.D. from King's College London, London University, in 1995. He is Lecturer in Modern European History at the University of Leicester. His major publications include *Vom Traum zum Alptraum. Sachsen in der Weimarer Republik* (Leipzig, 2000); *Nazism in Central Germany: The Brownshirts in 'Red' Saxony* (New York, 1999); "Sächsische Unternehmer und die Weimarer Demokratie: Zur Rolle der sächsischen Unternehmer in der Zeit der Weltwirtschaftskrise und des Aufstiegs des Nationalsozialismus," in *Unternehmer in Sachsen,* ed. U. Heß et al. (Leipzig, 1998); and "The Rise of the Nazi Party in the Working-Class Milieu of Saxony," in *The Rise of National Socialism and the Working Classes in Weimar Germany,* ed. C. Fischer (Oxford, 1996).

SIEGFRIED WEICHLEIN received his Ph.D. from the University of Freiburg i. Br. in 1992. He is Assistant Professor of History at Humboldt University Berlin. He has authored *Sozialmilieus und politische Kultur in der Weimarer Republik: Lebenswelt, Vereinskultur, Politik in Hessen* (Göttingen, 1996). His other publications include "Sachsen zwischen Landesbewußtsein und Nationsbildung, 1866–1871," in *Sachsen im Kaiserreich,* ed. S. Lässig and K. H. Pohl (Dresden, 1997); and "Nationalismus als Theorie sozialer Ordnung," in *Geschichte zwischen Kultur und Gesellschaft,* ed. T. Mergel and T. Welskopp (Munich, 1997). His current research interests include comparative studies of nationalism and nation-building in Germany, Catholicism and the social history of German confessionalism, and the New Deal.

HARTMUT ZWAHR received his D.Phil. in 1963 and his Habil. in 1974 from the University of Leipzig, where he is now Professor of Social and Economic History. His publications include *Zur Konstituierung des Proletariats als Klasse* (Berlin, 1978; Munich, 1980); *Herr und Knecht: Figurenpaare in der Geschichte* (Leipzig, 1990); *Ende einer Selbstzerstörung: Leipzig und die Revolution in der DDR,* 2d ed. (Göttingen, 1993); and *Revolutionen in Sachsen* (Weimar, 1996). His essays include "Die deutsche Arbeiterbewegung im Länder- und Territorienvergleich, 1875," *Geschichte und Gesellschaft* 13 (1987); "Die Sorben: Geschichte einer Selbstbehauptung zwischen Reformation und Erstem Weltkrieg," *Herbergen der Christenheit* 22 (1998); and "Die erste deutsche Nach-kriegsmesse, 1946: Wiederbelebung oder Wiedererweckung?" in *Leip-zigs Messen, 1497–1997,* 2 vols., ed. H. Zwahr, T. Topfstedt, and G. Bentele (Weimar, 1999). His current research interests include histo-ries of Leipzig's *Messen* and book trade, GDR society, and the Lusatian Sorbs.

Index

Social History, Popular Culture, and Politics in Germany
Geoff Eley, Series Editor